# Close Relationships

*This book is dedicated
to our grandson.*

# Close
# Relationships
## A Sourcebook

Clyde Hendrick
Susan S. Hendrick
Editors

Sage Publications, Inc.
*International Educational and Professional Publisher*
Thousand Oaks ▪ London ▪ New Delhi

*For information:*

Sage Publications, Inc.
2455 Teller Road
Thousand Oaks, California 91320
E-mail: order@sagepub.com

Sage Publications Ltd.
6 Bonhill Street
London EC2A 4PU
United Kingdom

Sage Publications India Pvt. Ltd.
M-32 Market
Greater Kailash I
New Delhi 110 048 India

Printed in the United States of America

*Library of Congress Cataloging-in-Publication Data*

Main entry under title:

Close relationships: A sourcebook / edited by Clyde Hendrick and Susan
S. Hendrick.
   p. cm.
Includes bibliographical references and index.
   ISBN 0-7619-1605-9 (cloth: alk. paper)
  1. Interpersonal relations. 2. Friendship. 3. Love. 4.
Interpersonal conflict. I. Hendrick, Clyde. II. Hendrick, Susan, 1944—
III. Title.
   HM1106 .C55 2000
   302—dc21                               99-050427

00  01  02  03  10  9  8  7  6  5  4  3  2  1

| | |
|---|---|
| *Acquiring Editor:* | Jim Brace-Thompson |
| *Editorial Assistant:* | Anna Howland |
| *Production Editor:* | Diana E. Axelsen |
| *Editorial Assistant:* | Cindy Bear |
| *Indexers:* | Jeanne Busemeyer/Teri Greenberg |
| *Cover Designer:* | Candice Harman |

# Contents

## Part III: RELATIONSHIP PROCESSES

# Part IV: RELATIONSHIP THREATS

# Foreword: Back to the Future and Forward to the Past

*Ellen Berscheid*

---

Once upon a time, a long time ago in a foreign land, a philosopher by the name of Auguste Comte (1798-1857) looked in his crystal ball to determine what he could see of the future of science. What he saw took him many volumes and the remainder of his lifetime to describe, partly because he continually elaborated, revised, and added to his original vision (e.g., *Cours de philosophie positive* [Comte, 1830-1842/1953]). Comte prophesied that the existing bodies of knowledge of his time would dynamically evolve, expand, and metamorphose according to "a great fundamental law." The father of "positivism" wrote, "The law is this: that each of our leading conceptions—each branch of our knowledge—passes successively through three different theoretical conditions: the theological, or fictitious; the meta-physical, or abstract; and the scientific, or positive" (quoted in Lenzer, 1975, pp. lii-liv). Today, Comte's positivist philosophy of science, or at least contemporary understandings of it, dominate all the sciences; it is exemplified by "hard" Science with a capital "S". As a consequence, the tenets of positivism are the standards by which the progress of all the sciences, including relationship science, are judged (Berscheid, 1986).

Comte identified six major branches of knowledge: mathematics, astronomy, physics, chemistry, physiology, and social physics. The last, social physics, did not exist at the time when Comte was peering into his crystal ball. But because he both foresaw and hoped that such a science would develop, he gave it a name in anticipation of its birth. In fact, he gave it several names over the course of his writings. He later named social physics "sociology" (a word he coined); still later, he called this science "la positive morale"; and by the end of his life, he was calling it "the study of humanity," according to Pickering (1993, p. 687), his most recent intellectual biographer. Whatever its name, this true final science, Comte said, would address itself to the "positive study of all the fundamental laws pertaining to social phenomena" (p. 615). Like all the abstract sciences, Comte forecast that this final science would progress through the first two stages, ultimately arriving at its zenith of refinement, the third stage. This third, last, and positive stage of science, he said, would be marked by the subordination of imagination and argumentation to the observation of "facts." Facts, he declared, would become the ultimate scientific criterion of true knowledge.

Comte initially believed that the six branches of knowledge would form a pyramid. The base of the pyramid would be mathematics, with the other branches of knowledge building on mathematics and then also on each other in an orderly and sequential pattern. Thus, the development of physics would depend on the development of astronomy, chemistry would depend on physics, physiology would depend on chemistry, and sociology would depend on physiology. Sociology (or the science of humanity), which would build on all the other sciences, would become "the queen of the sciences" (Pickering, 1993, p. 708). During the final years of his life, Comte tried to describe this pot of gold that lies at the end of science's rainbow of progression, but he died before completing *Le Système de morale positive, or Traite de l'education universelle*. Nevertheless, it is clear that the "le systeme de morale positive" Comte partially described bears little resemblance to the science that today bears the name "sociology": "Comte's sociology was a mixture of history, moral philosophy, political economy, political theory, anthropology, aesthetics, religion, international relations, philosophy of science, biology, and the inorganic sciences" (p. 708).

Toward the end of his life, Comte awarded sociology even more regency over all the other sciences than he had initially. Although Comte believed that it was necessary for sociologists to first examine the conditions of humanity's existence (society's physical environment, studied by the inorganic sciences), after sociology had been fully established, "The 'ascending order' of growing complexity and specialization, which were the criteria he had used to classify the sciences, would switch to a 'descending order'. . . . [sociology] would become the first and most general science with control over all the others" (Pickering, 1993, p. 681). Thus, Comte prophesied that, in the end, all the other sciences would become parts of the final unified science of humanity.

One's mind turns to Comte and his crystal ball on the eve of publication of this newest sourcebook for scholars actively participating in the development of a science of relationships for many reasons. Lesser among them, but perhaps worthy of mention nonetheless, is the fact that poor Comte himself could have used a science of relationships. Virtually all who have examined his personal life have reached much the same conclusion as Butler (1951), who commented, "A case history of this Frenchman would make him anything but an attractive person" (p. 405). Descending from brilliance into madness from time to time, Comte seems to have lurched from one disastrous relationship to the next (see, e.g., Pickering, 1993). His relationships with his family were strained, to say the least; he detested his sister and continually feuded with other members of his family over the numerous slights he believed he suffered at their hands. He contracted a marriage that turned sour almost immediately, perhaps portended by his signing the wedding certificate "Brutus Bonaparte Comte" (Butler, 1951, p. 404). The marriage was marked by violent arguments over money and sex and effectively ended when his wife left him some years later. His vicious attacks on the ideas of his close friend and mentor, Saint-Simon (e.g., "drivel," Comte proclaimed publicly), finally led to the end of that relationship and to the beginning of an enduring enmity between the two.

Comte did no better in his professional life. His coworkers at the Ecole Polytechnique, where he tutored in mathematics to earn his living, heartily disliked him. In one of his papers, he deliberately attacked the authorities of the school, the same authorities responsible for renewing his position there each year. Human nature being what it is, when Comte next came up for renewal, they fired him. Impoverished, he appealed to the British philosopher, John Stuart Mill, who had been much impressed by Comte's visions and who was to become one of positivism's most influential advocates. Mill arranged for three of Comte's compatriots to provide him with financial aid, but when they withdrew their support a year later, instead of being grateful for their help over a rough spot, Comte was outraged. During the final years of his life, Comte met a married woman whose husband was serving a life sentence in jail, became extremely fond of her, and suffered what some have described as a "mental aberration" when she died. The aberration appears to be that Comte refused to let death end their relationship; he visited the woman's tomb at least once each week and made it a personal policy to think of her three times each day.

But one thinks of Comte as one reads this relationship sourcebook for reasons other than what relationship science (not to mention a Dale Carnegie course) could have done for Comte personally. Foremost among these reasons is that relationship science, even in its current nascent state, approaches Comte's vision of the final science of humanity. Others, of course, have made similar claims on behalf of other scientific disciplines. Allport (1954), for example, entered a claim for psychology in the first edition of *Handbook of Social Psychology*. In his chapter on the history of social psychology, he contended that Comte's true final science "parallels our present conception of modern psychology (especially social psychology)" (p. 7).

Allport's argument, however, is riddled with weaknesses, and he clearly was aware of

at least one of them: If Comte believed that psychology was to be the true final science, then he could have said so, for psychology existed at the time Comte (1830-1842/1953) was writing *Cours de philosophie positive*. Allport (1954) attempted to explain why Comte failed to anoint psychology as the true final science by speculating that the psychology of Comte's day was "too rationalistic, too introspective, and too 'metaphysical' for his taste" (p. 7). Thus, Allport mused that Comte might have feared that if he formally named psychology as the capstone of the abstract sciences, he would retard the development of that glorious final science he hoped would evolve.

The problem with Allport's reasoning is that far from eschewing psychology as too metaphysical, Comte actively embraced the psychology of his day. He especially embraced psychology as it was reflected in the popular phrenology movement that swept France during the 19th century (where the size of one's head was believed to be an excellent indicant of one's intellectual powers and where specific faculties of the brain could be estimated by examining bumps and valleys on the cranium). Comte particularly admired Gall, who specified that the instincts were located in the back of the brain, the social sentiments in the middle, and the intellectual faculties in the front (e.g., a high forehead housed more intellect than a low forehead). "For Comte, Gall was important for . . . combating metaphysical theories of human nature and making physiology a positive science" (Pickering, 1993, p. 304).

Allport's claim that psychology is Comte's final science does not pass muster for another reason. Comte maintained that the science of humanity would have two "modes": the individual and society, studied by biology and sociology:

> Just as biology was divided into the study of organization (anatomy) and life (physiology), sociology would have two parts: the analysis of the conditions of existence and the study of the laws of continuous move-

ment. It would thus observe every social phenomenon according to its relationships with other, coexisting phenomena and to its connection with the past and future of human development. "Social statics" would be devoted to the first point of view, which was ultimately the study of order, while "social dynamics" would be consecrated to the second, which was essentially the analysis of progress. (Pickering, 1993, p. 617)

Social statics, Comte wrote, would have three divisions. The first division would be devoted to the study of the individual. Comte assigned this task to biology, and he elaborated that one of the specific tasks of this division was to establish the organic conditions of human "sociability." Endorsing Gall's views, Comte believed that sociability was an innately given disposition of the human (Pickering, 1993, p. 623). His views on the matter were not dissimilar to those of Baumeister and Leary (1995), and he would have endorsed their postulation of a "fundamental need to belong." Today, of course, neuroscientists and psychologists are actively establishing the organic conditions of human sociability (for reviews of some of these ongoing efforts, see Reis, Collins, & Berscheid, in press; Rosenzweig, 1996; Siegel, 1999). In other words, contemporary psychology, with its individualistic orientation and biological inclinations, perhaps best satisfies Comte's vision of the first division of social statics.

The second division of social statics was to be devoted to the study of the family, composed of at least the couple. Comte viewed the family as the primary unit of society. Contemporary sociology's subdiscipline of marriage and the family, combined with the hybrid disciplines of family social science and human development and ecology, would seem to best match Comte's template for this division. Finally, the third division of social statics was to be devoted to the study of society. Other subdomains of sociology (e.g., social networks) and other social and behavioral sciences (e.g., economics, anthropology, politi-

cal science) together would seem to fit Comte's bill of particulars for this division.

Because Comte's final science was to build on and to meld all three of these divisions, and because the multidisciplinary science of relationships is indeed building on virtually all of these, a claim that relationship science is the true final science would seem to be far more justified than a claim put forth by any one contemporary science, including psychology. In fact, if Comte were to read the chapters in this sourcebook, then one suspects that he would recognize his "true final science" from the content and sweeping range of the topics addressed as well as from the aims expressed by many of the authors.

But there is yet another reason why Comte would reject Allport's claim to the crown for psychology. That reason pertains to the methodology of psychology in general and of social psychology in particular. When writing his chapter for *Handbook of Social Psychology* nearly half a century ago, Allport (1954) undoubtedly was aware that this young field of study was viewed with jaundiced eyes by most psychologists, especially by the experimentalists who ruled psychology at the time and who exemplified positivist zealotry. Allport's aspirations for social psychology, especially for its acceptance as a legitimate subfield of psychology, were at least as passionate as Comte's aspirations for the development of a science of humanity. Thus, Allport no doubt realized that to gain acceptance, it would be necessary for social psychology to hew closely to the positivist line— as indeed it has, in no little part due to Allport's influence. As a consequence, and as detailed by Barone (1999), Allport gave a somewhat bowdlerized rendering of the history and features of social psychology. Depicting social psychology through a positivist lens, Allport highlighted both quantification and the experimental method as characteristic of the field. Barone argued that this is why Allport dubbed Tripplett's experiment on social facilitation as the "first" study in social psychology. (Ironically, Barone contended, a reanalysis of Triplett's data shows no evidence whatsoever of "social facilitation.") Barone argued persuasively that one effect of Allport's influential rendering was to banish from social psychology the study of dyadic social interaction, the essence of the study of social relationships. Social interaction was banished, Barone contended, because Allport recognized that the study of dyadic interaction was not as amenable to quantification and experimentation as were other social phenomena (e.g., reaction to "social stimuli").

Ironically, Allport's characterization of psychological method as experimental and quantitative, although accurate, constitutes another problem for his claim that psychology in general, and social psychology in particular, was what Comte had in mind as the final science. As Pickering (1993) observed, "Comte would not recognize the mutilated version of positivism that exists today" (p. 687). But it is that "mutilated version" of positivism, including the emphasis on quantification and experimentation, that psychology reflects so well, not the positivism that Comte believed would characterize all of the individual sciences in their last stage of refinement and, most especially, would characterize his true final science of humanity.

Comte's positivism differs from the "mutilated" positivist manifesto that is widely and rigidly endorsed by contemporary science in a number of important respects. First, Comte limited positive knowledge to the discovery of descriptive, not causal, laws: "These laws would express the relationships of succession and resemblance among phenomena. They would explain how, not why, phenomena existed. They also would allow science to perform its main function—that of making predictions about the future" (Pickering, 1993, p. 694). Thus, Comte emphasized actuarial, not causal, prediction.

Second, whereas positivism sometimes is defined, even in dictionaries, as a philosophical doctrine that decrees that sense perceptions are the only admissible basis of human knowledge and thought, Comte denounced the pursuit of sensory observations as pure empiricism:

> Although observed facts were crucial to the establishment and verification of scientific laws, the accumulation of discrete facts struck him as unsystematic, even anarchical. He believed that empiricists neglected general laws and consequently failed to provide useful or real knowledge. . . . In opposition to eighteenth-century sensationalism, he was, moreover, convinced that observation itself required more than experiencing sense impressions; facts could not be observed without the guidance of an a priori theory. (Pickering, 1993, pp. 694-695)

Thus, Comte anticipated the findings of contemporary cognitive psychology. He asserted that facts not only could not be perceived but also could not be retained without the guidance of theory; scientists, he asserted, were not passive mechanical observers. That many facts cannot be observed without the guidance of a theory he believed to be especially true for the study of humanity because its observers would be embedded within society. As a consequence, they would find it difficult to notice the ordinary. "Yet, the familiar social phenomena were the most important of all facts" (Pickering, 1993, p. 695). Only theory, which required imagination, creativity, and subjectivity, could help the observer to stand back from society and facilitate the observation of the facts of social life.

As the preceding suggests, Comte believed that the final science of humanity would be a deductive, rather than an inductive, science. He maintained that no aspect of social life could be studied in isolation. Thus, Comte took a "systems" view of social phenomena: "No aspect of society could be analyzed apart from the whole; the entire social organism had to be studied first, like a living organism in biology" (Pickering, 1993, p. 617). As an advocate of the systems approach, Comte was strongly opposed to reductionism. Ironically, reductionism is an important component of the distorted positivist manifesto. It also is a feature of contemporary psychology that many believe is hindering psychology's progress. For example, in her keynote address to the American Psychological Society ("Battle Cry," 1993), Gibson argued, "Something went wrong with this youthful field about halfway into the century"; namely, there was a halt in psychology's advance toward dealing "with the whole creature functioning adaptively in a dynamic exchange with the world of events and places and people" (pp. 12-13). Reductionism, Gibson claimed, is importantly responsible for the failure and should be assigned to the "rubbish heap."

Third, as noted previously, positivism is strongly identified with the quantification of phenomena. For example, Lenzer (1975), an influential translator of portions of Comte's writings, states,

> The triumph of the positive spirit consists in the reduction of quality to quantity in all realms of existence—in the realm of society and man as well as in the realm of nature—and the further reduction of quantity of ever larger and more abstract formulations of the relations that obtain between abstract quantities. (p. xxi)

To the contrary, Pickering (1993) writes, Comte was

> adamantly opposed to . . . the reduction of questions of quality to those of quantity. He berated those who contended that mathematics offered the only certain knowledge. He warned of the abuse of the calculus of probability—statistics—in physics, chemistry, biology, and sociology. The complexity, diversity, and variability of biological and especially social phenomena precluded their ever being expressed in mathematical equations. (p. 698)

Part of the confusion no doubt stems from Comte's initial view of mathematics as the foundation for all the sciences and his later views. In his later writings, he railed against the mathematicians and demoted mathematics from its preeminent place as the model of deductive science (replacing it with sociology).

What difference does all this make? Comte, after all, is just another "dead, white European male." The difference it makes is that a distorted and perverted version of positivism now reigns in all the sciences, including the social and behavioral sciences from which relationship science has emerged. Thus, relationship science faces the danger that, to gain acceptance as a "legitimate" field of inquiry, it will increasingly adopt the twisted version of positivism that currently pervades science. That danger is increased by the many consequences of the fact that there are, to date, no "Departments of Relationship Science" (Berscheid, 1996). Each relationship scholar has another place of employment, usually in his or her discipline of origin and degree, and that discipline, one can be sure, subscribes to distorted positivist dogma—to a philosophy of science and to methodologies that, ironically, the father of positivism would view as ill suited to the subject matter of relationship science.

Part I of this sourcebook, "Relationship Methods," illustrates both the irony and the tension suffered by relationship scholars. The first chapter in this part, by Deborah Kashy and Maurice Levesque, is a crisp, clearly written, and up-to-date treatment of "Quantitative Methods in Close Relationship Research." One expects to see such a chapter. Comte's views of more than a century ago have been so widely embraced in nearly all branches of knowledge that, at the millennium, quantitative method is believed to be de rigueur for any endeavor that aspires to achieve the status of the other sciences (Berscheid, 1986). In fact, Comte's contention that mathematics is the foundation of all sciences has so thoroughly saturated the pursuit of knowledge that if the phenomena observed cannot be quantified in some way, then the usual conclusion is "Whatever those observations may amount to, it isn't science." Comte might be pleased to see the progress being made in coping with the special statistical problems presented by dyadic research. Then again, he might not be. At the very least, he would be startled.

Most people would predict that what would startle Comte would be the next chapter in this part of the sourcebook: "Qualitative Research," by Katherine Allen and Alexis Walker. Those who have absorbed the distorted positivist manifesto might even predict that Comte would gnash his teeth on learning of the recent reemergence of what might be termed a "metaphysical" approach to relationships. It certainly is true that Comte's first disciples would have been displeased. Comte's initial view that mathematics was the most essential block in the foundation of science was controversial at the time, to say the least, and his disciples were in the minority. Those who embraced his views, including James (who imported the experimental method and the emphasis on quantification to American psychology), often hewed to the Comtian line with the fervor and rigidity that any minority that hopes to influence the majority must (Moscovici, Lage, & Naffrechoux, 1969). Even James, however, could see that his colleagues' intolerance sometimes was risible, as is illustrated by James's 1876 review of a new monthly French journal, *Revue Philosophique de la France et de l'Etranger,* edited by Theodule Ribot. After welcoming the new publication, James writes,

> The programme of [Ribot's] review is Catholic enough. Kantians and inheritors of Cousin may contribute to its columns on the same terms as Comtists and experimentalists—individual responsibility namely, and the obligation of saying something novel. Even from metaphysicians, *"facts* will be required." This temper compares pleasantly with that of certain persons in England and with us, who are as great friends of evolution and of physiological methods as M. Ribot, but whose own evolution upwards from theological beginnings seems to have stopped short at the stage of inarticulate joy over their emancipation, and for whom ev-

> ery piece of writing is good whose pages are speckled over with words like "body," "ganglion cell," "brute ancestor," [and] "visceral emotion," whilst the sight of a term like "soul," "design," or "free will" in a book affect them with a sort of foaming at the mouth. (cited in Burkhardt & Bowers, 1987, pp. 319-320, emphasis in original)

It might be noted parenthetically that relationship scientists need only consider the favored status of neuroscience, at least in psychology and among federal funding agencies, and the claims of the psychoevolutionists to feel *plus ça change, plus c'est la meme chose.*

Would Comte himself have joined his disciples in "foaming at the mouth" at the inclusion of a chapter on qualitative methods? Would he, as well, view the increasing popularity of qualitative methods and their presentation in this sourcebook as a step backward for relationship science? A good guess is that, unlike his disciples then and now, Comte himself would not have been surprised to see such a chapter in a sourcebook devoted to relationships. It has escaped popular notice that, throughout his writings, Comte warned against the premature application of mathematics in the sciences dealing with more complex phenomena: "The most difficult sciences must remain, for an indefinite time, in that preliminary state that prepares for the others the time when they too may become capable of mathematical treatment" (quoted in Lenzer, 1975, p. li).

Thus, Comte would have applauded the editors' decision to include a chapter on qualitative methods. Moreover, he would have been especially pleased with Allen and Walker's treatment of the subject, for they highlight the fact that many qualitative researchers take the position that "research . . . should incorporate an ameliorative or interventionist effort as part of the production of knowledge" (p. 24). Thus, qualitative researchers often undertake their studies in an effort to change society, not simply to describe society's present condition. As a consequence, qualitative researchers often undertake their research with a strong "point of view" and with a political aim. Another neglected fact in contemporary understandings of positivism is that the most consistent theme throughout Comte's writings was not his insistence on quantification; instead, it was his belief that the aim of the pursuit of knowledge is not knowledge for the sake of knowledge but rather knowledge to improve society and the human condition.

One cannot leave the chapter on qualitative methods without making one more observation. Allen and Walker surveyed the contents of three relationship journals and found "little use of qualitative methods," concluding "the positivist perspective continues to be overwhelmingly dominant" (p. 25). Quantification undoubtedly will continue its regency. The problem this presents for relationship scholars is that, as noted previously, they must satisfy their colleagues and employers who revere mutilated positivism (so much so that it has pervaded even the humanities, which threaten to become lesser branches of the social and behavioral sciences; for example, scholars in English literature and history who count, aggregate, and statistically analyze are highly rewarded by their employers (to the detriment and disgust of their more traditional peers).

Our temptation to highlight both quantification and instrumentation in the study of relationships is heightened not only by our disciplinary colleagues and employers but also by our eagerness to gain public acceptance of relationship science. Quantification, and especially the use of instrumentation, is the public's idea of what "real" science is. An illustrative case in point is a recent *Newsweek* article titled "The Science of a Good Marriage" (Kantrowitz & Wingert, 1999), which featured the work of Gottman and his colleagues. Gottman, of course, has been in the vanguard of developing and applying quantitative methods to phenomena that not so long ago were believed to be resistant to such treatment, and his successes in quantifying many important relationship behaviors and subjecting them to statistical analysis are widely admired among

relationship scholars. The magazine illustrated the article with a photo of a woman and a man seated facing each other, each hooked up to more wires and instruments than would be two astronauts on their way to Mars. Such illustrations no doubt enhance our scientific reputation with the public, even though they are not representative of relationship research methodology—nor are they ever likely to be.

Part II of the handbook, "Relationship Forms," begins with a chapter by Robert Milardo and Heather Helms-Erikson on "Network Overlap and Third-Party Influence in Close Relationships." Here, one can clearly see an instantiation of a problem foreseen by Comte and experienced by many relationship scholars. Whereas relationship science is dependent on the foundation of knowledge provided by the other disciplines with which it interfaces, not only have most of those disciplines not yet reached maturity, but each is severely potholed with investigative domains still in their infancy. When the needed building block is weak, the relationship scholar, before moving ahead to pursue the relationship problem of interest, must turn back to shore up the foundation. That is precisely what Milardo and Helms-Erikson do in this chapter. They attempt to clarify definitional and conceptual confusions that trouble the social network field. In so doing, they reveal to those of us who have been puzzled by the neglect of the social environment by relationship scholars (e.g., Berscheid, 1999; Karney & Bradbury, 1995) that one reason for the neglect might be conceptual ambiguities in the underlying discipline.

The remaining chapters in Part II represent a potpourri of relationship types, many of which represent typical relationship progressions throughout the life span (although the human's earliest relationships, with caretakers, is represented in Part III, "Relationship Processes," in a chapter titled "Attachment and Close Relationships" by Judith Feeney, Patricia Noller, and Nigel Roberts). From a chapter on "Children's Friendships," by Amanda Rose and Steven Asher, Part II proceeds to "Adolescent Relationships: The Art of Fugue" by W. Andrew Collins and Brett Laursen. The latter title is especially descriptive, for Collins and Laursen attempt to trace the appearance, disappearance, and transmogrified reappearance of themes that mark the adolescent's relationship world, a task so difficult that many readers will leave the chapter thankful that researchers other than themselves have undertaken it. Beverley Fehr's chapter on "The Life Cycle of Friendship" and Rosemary Blieszner's discussion of "Close Relationships in Old Age" follow and further underscore, at least for this reader, the importance of social network and other environmental approaches to questions about stability and change in an individual's close relationships. Before reaching old age, however, most people marry and some divorce and marry again. These relationships receive treatment from Janice Steil in a chapter titled "Contemporary Marriage: Still an Unequal Partnership," from Mark Fine in "Divorce and Single Parenting," and from Lawrence Ganong and Marilyn Coleman in "Remarried Families."

Steil's article particularly arouses thoughts of Comte. Steil empirically documents the unfairness of spousal division of household labor and treats the question of why so many wives appear to be subjectively content with their objectively inequitable circumstances. Why do women not rebel? In the course of attempting to answer this question, Steil takes a rather judgmental (the present situation is wrong and injurious to women) and interventionist (what women can do about it) stance. Comte would have cheered Steil's treatment of this subject, and oddly enough, his followers—Mill and James—would have joined him. In 1869, Mill published a little-known book titled *The Subjection of Women* (Mill, 1869/1969), which James reviewed for the *North American Review* along with a book published the same year on the same subject by Bushnell (1869) titled *Women's Suffrage: The Reform Against Nature* (with the title accurately reflecting Bushnell's position on the subject). James's review left no doubt where

his sympathies lay. With satire, ridicule, and sarcasm, James, the Comtist, dismembered Bushnell's argument. For example,

> The portraits he [Bushnell] untiringly draws, of women as they will appear after twenty-five years' enjoyment of the ballot, are almost too harrowing to quote. Lilies that fester smell far worse than weeds, and accordingly, whereas the "thunder" that clothes man's neck (our author never wearies of this "thunder" attribute of masculinity) looks rather well upon *him,* women's "look will be sharp, the voice will be wiry and shrill, the action will be angular and abrupt, wiliness, self-asserting boldness, eagerness for place and power" will ravage her once fair form. As for her moral state, "a strange facility of debasement and moral abandonment" which characterizes her will make her corruptions much worse than ours. Terrible hints are given of the naughtiness to which women will resort in order to procure votes and the demoralization which will take place in country districts, where the voters, male and female, "will be piled in huge wagons to be carried to the polls and will sometimes, on their return, encounter a storm that drives them into wayside taverns and other like places for the night; where"— but enough; the curious reader may find the rest of the passage on page 149. (cited in Burkhardt & Bowers, 1987, p. 249)

Mill, James's fellow Comtian, comes off much better, even though James was not entirely convinced of the wisdom of Mill's call for a new type of relationship between husbands and wives, a type of relationship based on "Mr. Mill's fervid passion for absolute equality, 'justice,' and personal independence as the *summum bonum* for everyone" (Burkhardt & Bowers, p. 255).

James concluded his review with the statement, "There can be little doubt that this small volume [by Mill] will be what the Germans call 'epoch-making,' and that it will hereafter be quoted as a landmark signalizing one distinct step in the progress of the total evolution" (cited in Burkhardt & Bowers, 1987,

p. 256). James's powers of clairvoyance failed him the day he wrote that passage, for what is remarkable, not to mention disheartening, about Steil's description of women's circumstances within marriage today and Mill's description of women's circumstances within marriage well over a century ago is their similarity. Adding to the eerie resemblance is Steil's treatment of the subject, which is uncannily similar to that of Comte's first and most influential advocates. (It should be noted that a fine chapter by Julia Wood on "Gender and Personal Relationships" in Part III of the sourcebook, "Relationship Processes," helps flesh out many of the implications that current gender differences have for relationships and, at least indirectly, perhaps helps to explain women's lack of progress in the economic world and within their own households.)

The "Relationship Forms" section also includes a chapter by Stanley Gaines, Jr., and James Liu on "Multicultural/Multiracial Relationships" and one by Letitia Anne Peplau and Leah Spalding on "The Close Relationships of Lesbians, Gay Men, and Bisexuals." These are but a few of the forms of relationships that could be included in a relationship encyclopedia when one considers the multiplicity of partner characteristics and settings that could serve to identify a relationship "form." Whether there will emerge a unified body of relationship knowledge applicable to all relationships remains a central question for relationship science (Berscheid, 1994). These two chapters have in common, however, the fact that the relationship forms they address are of current societal concern and, therefore, are of widespread interest, as are the chapters in the final part of the sourcebook, "Relationship Threats." Comte foresaw that the concerns of society would stimulate the progress and concerns of his science of humanity, and chapters such as these confirm his prediction.

Part III of the sourcebook, "Relationship Processes," includes chapters on many of the processes in which relationship scholars have long been interested—conflict, treated by Daniel Canary and Susan Messman; social support, addressed by Michael Cunningham and Anita Barbee (a tidy and informative chapter on a messy and confusing research area); intimacy, by Karen Prager (who describes her unique approach to this construct, providing a useful and not incompatible addition to Reis and Shaver's [1988] theory of intimacy); relationship maintenance, by Kathryn Dindia; a new view of emotion, by Laura Guerrero and Peter Andersen; communication, by Brant Burleson, Sandra Metts, and Michael Kirch; romantic love, by editors Susan and Clyde Hendrick (who accomplish a thorough and evenhanded review of the love literature in a very small space); and sexuality, by Susan Sprecher and Pamela Regan (the editors obviously determined that the absence of any mention of sexuality in relationships was not going to embarrass this sourcebook).

These chapters in the "Relationship Processes" section appear to be somewhat divergent in purpose. Some chapter authors, such as Susan and Clyde Hendrick, took as their aim a survey of an area to which they have contributed, soft-pedaling their own contributions so as to represent other viewpoints. Other chapter authors took the tack of primarily expressing their own works and views. Both aims are reasonable, but scanning the tremendous diversity of the topical areas covered in this sourcebook (and these are by no means exhaustive, as the Hendricks would be the first to say), one sees a need for an "annual review of relationships" similar to the *Annual Review of Psychology*. Such a review would have the purpose of detailing developments in a particular relationship topical area during the past several years. Original contributions, both theoretical and empirical, could continue to be disseminated by "advances" volumes and by the empirical journals.

As noted previously, Part IV of the sourcebook is devoted to "Relationship Threats." Since Rook's (1984) seminal article on the dark side of close relationships, attention to the threats that relationships sometimes present to individuals' well-being has grown dramatically (see, e.g., Spitzberg & Cupach, 1998). This, then, is a timely section. It includes chapters on "Extradyadic Relationships and Jealousy," by Bram Buunk and Pieternel Dijkstra; "Physical and Sexual Aggression in Relationships," by F. Scott Christopher and Sally Lloyd (a topic of growing public interest and concern); and "Depression in Close Relationships," by Steven Beach and Heather O'Mahen. Part IV concludes with a chapter on "Loss and Bereavement in Close Romantic Relationships," by John Harvey and Andrea Hansen. Perhaps it is this final chapter that Comte, in the torture of his bereavement, would have turned to first. He firmly expected that the knowledge provided by his final science of humanity would be practical and useful to the individual as well as to society. What is perhaps remarkable about relationship science, at least as it has progressed so far, is the extent to which relationship scholars have been attentive and responsive to societal concerns while attempting, at the same time, to develop a unified and cohesive science in which an understanding of process is awarded as much importance as are structure and outcomes.

In sum, one suspects that after reading this sourcebook, Comte would smile and kiss his crystal ball. That reaction, however, is more likely from those viewing relationship science from afar than from those of us in the trenches attempting to chisel Comte's scientific capstone out of the hardest rock of natural phenomena that scientists have yet dared to approach. Our problems are legion, and many of them stem from our dependence on the other sciences that comprise our foundation, as Comte forecast and as Kelley (1983) discussed more recently. In addition to the problems that arise from the fact that none of these sciences has yet fully matured and the needed information is not yet available, there is the even more nettlesome problem that to build relationship science on the foundation these sciences provide, relationship scholars must familiarize themselves with vast warehouses of scientific knowledge. Obtaining and assimilating such a wide array of knowledge is a daunting task, one that is not facilitated by our specialized training and one that requires an extraordinary amount of effortful, time-consuming, and continuing self-education.

Simply tracking developments in one's own discipline and divining their implications for relationship science is no easy task. To take just two examples from psychology, recent developments in neuroscience have potent implications for relationship science (e.g., the influence of early relationships on infant brain development [Siegel, 1999]), and the impending transition of cognitive psychology from associationist models of cognition to the connectionist perspective (e.g., as reflected in parallel distributed processing models [Smith, 1996]) represents an important opportunity for relationship scholars. In the study of the human mind, this transition appears to be akin to physics shifting from Newtonian mechanics to Einstein's special theory. Like Newtonian mechanics, associationist models, on which virtually all of our current understanding of cognitive structure (e.g., relationship schemas) and process (e.g., automatic processing vs. controlled processing) is based, will continue to "work" for the range of phenomena with which they have been so successful. But to advance, cognitive science, as well as relationship science (for which the puzzles of relationship cognition are central [Berscheid, 1994; Reis & Downey, 1999]), will need to build on these new models that appear to better account for critical data and to provide a more powerful searchlight with which to plumb the mysteries of the human mind than do associationist models. To take advantage of this development, however, relationship scholars need to keep abreast of developments in cognitive science—no quickly accomplished task.

Thus, each relationship scholar must cope with the explosion of knowledge in his or her own discipline, even if the scholar despairs of following developments in all of the other disciplines essential to the advancement of relationship science. Sometimes, in the depths of despond, one cannot help but wonder whether perhaps the task is impossible, whether this final super-science can be constructed only by those possessing super-brains able to absorb, synthesize, and then intelligently transfer an extraordinary range and volume of knowledge. Some do conclude that, indeed, it is hopeless; they give up trying to keep so many incoming developments in so many disciplines on their radar screens and retreat into their own necks of the woods and specialized interests. Others scurry back to the mainstream of their disciplines of origin, where the problems are defined; the methodological paradigms are established; the way is clear (if crowded); and the living, if not easy, is at least less demanding. Most of us try to maintain our good intentions and high aspirations; we order more filing cabinets to house even more quickly scanned and unread papers, and we install more bookcases to house all those "must read" books we will get around to during the next academic break, or surely next summer, or at least in our next reincarnations.

In any rapidly developing science, especially one that covers as much territory as does relationship science, the sheer volume of knowledge that must be absorbed is a formidable deterrent to the field's advancement (not to mention each relationship scholar's peace of mind). For relationship science to develop quickly and soundly, it is vital that some persons abandon their own scholarly pursuits from time to time and volunteer for sentry duty on the borders of relationship science. There, they not only must survey changes in the relationship domain itself but also must monitor developments in our supporting disciplines with the purpose of educating the rest of us about these developments, usually by enlisting the tutorial services of those who possess the necessary expertise. Editors of sourcebooks such as this one serve as the field's sentries. In an inchoate new science, their role is crucial. They decide what the rest of us need to know and who is best qualified to teach us. The responsibilities assumed by the contributors they select also are heavier than usual because many in their audiences are innocents, unable to separate one of Comte's facts from metaphysical fiction. One has only to glance at the topical range of the chapters in the present sourcebook to be re-

minded that each of us is uncomfortably dependent on these authors, that our usual powers of critical reading, so essential and readily available in our own areas of expertise, often are suspended for many topics encompassed by that ever-expanding territory known as relationship science.

Thus, we owe a great deal to the present editors of this sourcebook, Clyde and Susan Hendrick, just as we have owed previous editors of sourcebooks and handbooks (e.g., Duck, 1988) our gratitude and respect for assuming this responsibility for advancing the field. Without their considerable but sometimes unappreciated efforts, as well as the efforts of their contributors, most of us would deserve even more than we do the "learned ignoramus" appellation to which all scientists in this age of specialization are subject, a label that is especially deadly for relationship scholars and for the progress of relationship science.

## ▶ REFERENCES

Allport, G. (1954). The historical background of modern social psychology. In G. Lindzey (Ed.), *Handbook of social psychology, Vol. 1: Theory and method* (pp. 3-56). Reading, MA: Addison-Wesley.

Barone, D. F. P. (1999). *The problem of interaction in experimental social psychology: An historical inquiry.* Unpublished manuscript, Illinois State University, Normal.

Battle cry for a unified discipline: Gibson delivers spellbinding keynote address. (1993, July/August). *APS Observer,* pp. 12-13.

Baumeister, R. F., & Leary, M. R. (1995). The need to belong: Desire for interpersonal attachment as a fundamental human motivation. *Psychological Bulletin, 115,* 243-267.

Berscheid, E. (1986). Mea culpas and lamentations: Sir Francis, Sir Isaac, and "the slow progress of soft psychology." In S. Duck & R. Gilmour (Eds.), *The emerging field of personal relationships* (pp. 135-166). Hillsdale, NJ: Lawrence Erlbaum.

Berscheid, E. (1994). Interpersonal relationships. *Annual Review of Psychology, 45,* 79-129.

Berscheid, E. (1996, August). *From Madison to Banff: Relationship science 15 years later.* Invited address presented at the meeting of the International Society for the Study of Personal Relationships, Banff, Alberta.

Berscheid, E. (1999). The greening of relationship science. *American Psychologist, 54,* 260-266.

Burkhardt, F., & Bowers, F. (Eds.). (1987). *The works of William James: Essays, comments, and reviews.* Cambridge, MA: Harvard University Press.

Bushnell, H. (1869). *Women's suffrage: The reform against nature.* New York: Scribner.

Butler, J. D. (1951). *Four philosophies: And their practice in education and religion.* New York: Harper.

Comte, A. (1953). *The positive philosophy of Auguste Comte* (2 vols., H. Martineau, Trans.). London: Trubner. (Original work published 1830-1842 as *Cours de philosophie positive* [6 vols.])

Duck, S. (Ed.). (1988). *Handbook of personal relationships: Theory, research, and interventions.* Chichester, UK: Wiley.

Kantrowitz, B., & Wingert, P. (1999, April 19). The science of a good marriage. *Newsweek,* pp. 52-57.

Karney, B. R., & Bradbury, T. N. (1995). The longitudinal course of marital quality and stability: A review of theory, method, and research. *Psychological Bulletin, 118,* 3-34.

Kelley, H. H. (1983). Epilogue: An essential science. In H. H. Kelley, E. Berscheid, A. Christensen, J. H. Harvey, T. L. Huston, G. Levinger, E. McClintock, L. A. Peplau, & D. R. Peterson, *Close relationships* (pp. 486-503). New York: Freeman.

Lenzer, G. (Ed.). (1975). *Auguste Comte and positivism: The essential writings.* Chicago: University of Chicago Press.

Mill, J. S. (1969). *The subjection of women.* New York: Appleton. (Original work published 1869)

Moscovici, S., Lage, S., & Naffrechoux, M. (1969). Influence of a consistent minority on the response of a majority in a color perception task. *Sociometry, 32,* 365-380.

Pickering, M. (1993). *Auguste Comte: An intellectual biography* (Vol. 1). Cambridge, UK: Cambridge University Press.

Reis, H. T., Collins, W. A., & Berscheid, E. (in press). Relationships as the context for behavior. *Psychological Bulletin.*

Reis, H. T., & Downey, G. (1999). Social cognition in relationships: Building essential bridges between two literatures. *Social Cognition, 17,* 97-117.

Reis, H. T., & Shaver, P. (1988). Intimacy as an interpersonal process. In S. Duck (Ed.), *Handbook of personal relationships: Theory, research, and interventions* (pp. 367-389). Chichester, UK: Wiley.

Rook, K. S. (1984). The negative side of social interaction: Impact on psychological well-being. *Journal of Personality and Social Psychology, 46,* 1097-1108.

Rosenzweig, M. R. (1996). Aspects of the search for neural mechanisms of memory. *Annual Review of Psychology, 47,* 1-32.

Siegel, D. J. (1999). *The developing mind: Toward a neurobiology of interpersonal experience.* New York: Guilford.

Smith, E. R. (1996). What do connectionism and social psychology offer each other? *Journal of Personality and Social Psychology, 70,* 893-912.

Spitzberg, B. H., & Cupach, W. R. (1998). *The dark side of close relationships.* Mahwah, NJ: Lawrence Erlbaum.

# Preface

Close personal relationships are the very essence of human existence. Nearly as fundamental to survival as air and water are the links between persons—parent with child, lover with lover, friend with friend. More and more scholars are conducting research on this essential topic, and it is out of a collective sense of the fundamental importance of relationships and relationships research that this volume emerged. The authors whose work is included are excellent scholars who represent the variety of disciplines and topics within this relatively new area of close personal relationships.

Close relationships come in various shapes, sizes, and forms. Relationships experience a variety of interpersonal processes, undergo a number of crises and threats, and can be examined in several different ways. In recognition of this complexity in the relationships domain, we have organized the 26 chapters in this Sourcebook into four major thematic areas—Relationship Methods, Relationship Forms, Relationship Processes, and Relationship Threats—along with a Foreword.

These chapters provide a panoramic view of close relationships research as it enters a new century, and they offer highlights from current literature, original research, practical applications of existing knowledge, and projections of what avenues of research might be most productive during the years ahead. In Part I, quantitative and qualitative methods provide important lenses through which scholars can examine relationships, and both topics are presented in an interesting and accessible fashion by Kashy and Levesque (quantitative research) and Allen and Walker (qualitative research).

Part II on relationship forms includes many of the stages, types, and roles that characterize intimate relationships. In a developmental fashion, chapters address social networks (Milardo and Helms-Erikson), children's friendships (Rose and Asher), adolescent relationships (Collins and Laursen), adult friendships (Fehr), and friendships in later life (Blieszner). Chapters on multicultural and multiracial relationships (Gaines and Liu) and on gay, lesbian, and bisexual relationships (Peplau and Spalding) introduce relationship forms that are not new but are newly considered, discussed, and accepted. Finally, the alignments and realignments of traditional family structure are considered in terms of contemporary marriage (Steil), divorce and single parenting (Fine), and remarried families (Ganong and Coleman).

Many processes occur within the crucible of close relationships. Part III, on relationship processes, considers several such processes. A discussion of emotion (Guerrero and Andersen) opens this part and is followed by attachment (Feeney, Noller, and Roberts), romantic love (S. Hendrick and C. Hendrick), and sexuality (Sprecher and Regan). Intimacy is strongly linked to communication, so a chapter on intimacy (Prager) serves as a bridge to a chapter on communication (Burleson, Metts, and Kirch), followed by conflict (Canary and Messman), social support (Cunningham and Barbee), and relational maintenance (Dindia). The important topic of gender (Wood) concludes Part III.

Although close relationship researchers have done much to depathologize relationships even as they explicate relationships, the shadow side of human nature exists and is ex-plored in Part IV, on relationship threats. Here we find chapters on infidelity and jealousy (Buunk and Dijkstra), physical and sexual aggression (Christopher and Lloyd), depression (Beach and O'Mahen-Gray), and loss and bereavement (Harvey and Hansen).

Taken together, these chapters provide a wonderful commentary on the state of close relationships research, and we thank all the authors involved for giving their time, patience, and best scholarship. We also thank all the scholars whose pioneering work resulted in the interdisciplinary field of close relationships and those scholars whose work is referenced in this volume. We especially thank Ellen Berscheid for gracing this volume with the Foreword.

Thanks also go to Terry Hendrix, the friend and former Sage Publications editor without whose persistence this book would not have developed, and Jim Brace-Thompson, the Sage editor who helped bring the book into its final form. The whole staff at Sage, a publisher with whom we have worked fruitfully for many years, also deserves our deep appreciation.

Finally, we thank each other. The labors of this book would have been much more onerous without our shared editorial efforts. To the extent that these efforts have been successful, it has been the result of the editors' ongoing close personal relationship.

# Part I

---

# RELATIONSHIP
# METHODS

# Contents

# Quantitative Methods in Close Relationships Research

*Deborah A. Kashy*
*Maurice J. Levesque*

Data analysis in the field of close relationships presents unique and important challenges to researchers. The vast majority of available statistical techniques assume that the data we collect are independent from individual to individual, but such independence rarely exists in relationships research. In relationships, individuals are interdependent rather than independent. It is not uncommon for relationship researchers to avoid the independence problem by collecting data from only one person involved in a relationship or to use hypothetical scenarios. For these methods, researchers do not need to be concerned with issues of nonindependence. However, because interdependence is perhaps the defining feature of close relationships (Kelley et al., 1983; Kelley & Thibaut, 1978), avoiding interdependent data restricts researchers from seeking answers to many important questions about close relationships.

Researchers are becoming increasingly aware of this problem, and recent relationships research more often acknowledges the importance of interdependence by collecting data from both members of dyadic relationships (e.g., Bradbury, 1998).

## ► Introduction to Nonindependence

The fact that data derived from individuals who are engaged in close relationships are not independent has important implications for how the data should be analyzed and the questions researchers can ask of those data. There are two major issues involved in the analysis of nonindependent data. The first issue is that of bias in hypothesis testing. Speaking somewhat generally, if a statistical technique that assumes independence (e.g., analysis of variance [ANOVA], regression) is used with nonindependent data, then the alpha level associated with the inferential statistics generated will not accurately reflect the true probability of making a Type I error. As Kenny and his colleagues (Kenny, 1995; Kenny, Kashy, & Bolger, 1998) have shown, in some instances the statistical tests will be overly liberal (too many false positives), and in other instances the tests will be overly conservative (too many false negatives).

The second issue concerns the types of questions that we, as relationship researchers, can address. In particular, one of the most important advantages of gathering nonindependent data (data from both/all partners involved in a relationship) is that researchers can examine not only how a person's characteristics affect his or her own behavior but also how that person's characteristics affect his or her *partner's* behavior. These interdependent effects often are implied by theories regarding close relationships. For example, although perceptions of equity in relationships can be conceptualized purely in terms of one person's inputs and outcomes, it seems appropriate with respect to the theory to consider how perceptions of equity are influenced by a partner's inputs and outcomes.

Consider the following examples of relationship theory-based research that reveal the recent movement toward questions of interdependence. First, does the level of attachment-related anxiety exhibited by one partner influence the other's behavior? Attachment research has demonstrated that individuals are influenced by their partners' styles as well as by their own (Carnelley, Pietromonaco, & Jaffe, 1996; Simpson, 1990). Theories of adult attachment also articulate the role of partner behavior in activating attachment-relevant schemata (Berman, Marcus, & Berman, 1994). Second, does a person's criticism lead his or her partner to be defensive and withdraw? Gottman's (1979, 1994b) work on marital conflict has long been devoted to identifying patterns of interdependent interaction during conflict. Identifying the cycle of dysfunctional conflict has been possible only because

researchers have collected data from both partners to allow for analyses that recognize the nonindependence of married persons' behavior. Finally, treating the data from couples as nonindependent allows for the analysis of data addressing long-standing issues related to couple similarity (Kenny & Acitelli, 1994) and for the examination of new questions regarding the influence of positive illusions on well-being and relationship satisfaction (Murray, Holmes, & Griffin, 1996). These are just a few examples of the questions now being examined by relationship researchers. Clearly, interdependence between related individuals should not simply be considered a statistical annoyance. Rather, it should be embraced as an opportunity to ask old questions in new ways, to ask new questions, and to test theoretical propositions that are explicitly about interdependence.

### An Illustration of the Pitfalls of Ignoring Interdependence

To highlight a few of the problems that can arise from ignoring interdependence, consider a hypothetical study designed to examine the use of criticism in distressed and nondistressed heterosexual dating couples. In this study, both members of the dating couple are recruited, and each couple is classified as distressed or nondistressed. The amount of criticism each person uses is assessed by self-report.

Because data are collected from both members of the couple, this study avoids one common but problematic method of coping with interdependence: collecting information from only one member of a relationship. However, even when data are collected from both persons, the researcher might be tempted to analyze the data from males and females separately to avoid the analytic complications presented by interdependence. Although these approaches do not violate the statistical assumption of independence, the researcher who employs these tactics sacrifices considerable information by not taking full advantage of techniques for analyzing nonindependent data. In this case, the researcher who fails to consider the interdependence of the dating partners misses an opportunity to examine how the use of criticism by one person affects the partner's use of criticism and whether the strength of that association depends on the status of the relationship.

Even by collecting information from both partners and realizing the nonindependence of the male and female responses, the researcher might adopt yet another problematic approach. Specifically, he or she might collapse across dyad members by computing the average criticism score for each dyad. Again, the researcher loses valuable information with such an approach, and in some instances, the resulting statistics might be misleading. For example, Gonzalez and Griffin (1997) discussed how the correlations between averaged variables that result from this approach can be quite different from those obtained using each individual's scores.

Imagine now that the researcher collects data from both members of the couple but is unaware of or ignores the nonindependence. Furthermore, as one might expect, criticism is strongly reciprocal, so there is a positive correlation between men's and women's use of criticism. Because the interdependence is not considered, the researcher chooses to analyze the data treating person, not couple, as the unit of analysis (i.e., the sample size in these analyses is based on the number of individuals, not on the number of couples) and uses between-subjects data analytic techniques. The researcher first tests whether there are sex differences in the use of criticism. Although the means suggest that men use criticism more frequently than do women, the statistical test fails to obtain significance and the researcher concludes that men and women do not differ in the frequency of criticism. The researcher then tests whether there are differences in the use of criticism as a function of whether the individual is a member of a distressed or nondistressed couple. This test finds a statistically significant difference suggesting greater criticism in distressed couples.

Nonindependence compromises the validity of both of these statistical tests. The sex difference analysis is problematic because sex is an independent variable that varies within a couple (each couple has a man and a woman), and ignoring nonindependence actually increases the likelihood of a Type II error (failure to reject a false null hypothesis) (Kenny, 1995). Contrary to the researcher's conclusions, it might be that the sex difference really is statistically reliable. On the other hand, because distress is an independent variable that varies between couples (i.e., some couples are distressed and others are not), the test of distress is an overly liberal test. That is, this test is more likely to reflect a Type I error than the *p* value derived from the analysis suggests. Thus, by ignoring the nonindependence, the researcher risks missing a significant sex difference and might conclude that distressed couples use more criticism than do nondistressed couples when there is no such statistically significant difference. As Kenny and his colleagues (Kenny, 1995; Kenny et al., 1998) illustrate, the error depends on the nature of the nonindependence (i.e., positive or negative correlation between partners on the dependent measure) and on the nature of independent variable. Although the errors that result from employing inappropriate analyses will not always be so dramatic, researchers who ignore interdependence risk such errors unnecessarily because, as we show, statistical techniques are readily available for analyzing interdependent data.

### What This Chapter Does and Does Not Do

In this chapter, we focus our attention on data analytic techniques that are appropriate for studying friendship dyads, heterosexual and homosexual romantic couples, marital dyads, and families. Because the majority of research in close relationships tends to consider two-person relationships, most of the analyses we describe are for dyadic data. Kashy and Kenny (2000) expanded a number of these analyses to groups with more than two members. We provide an overview of one approach to the analysis of friendship networks that also can be applied (with some modifications) to family data. Our presentation is generally descriptive, so we do not present exact formulas. Instead, we provide citations throughout the chapter to sources that detail the computations for the various tests we describe.

Although not covered in this chapter, one of the newest methodological and data analytic advances in the study of close relationships is multilevel modeling (also known as hierarchical linear modeling). This approach can be applied to the analysis of designs involving repeated measures and data in which there are two or more levels of analysis (e.g., individuals nested within groups). Multilevel modeling is particularly important for the analysis of research that uses the social interaction diary methodology. For example, one recent use of this analysis strategy examined the influence of attachment style on perceptions of a variety of relationships over time (Pietromonaco & Barrett, 1997). Details regarding the methodology and analysis of hierarchical linear models can be found in Bryk and Raudenbush (1992), Gable and Reis (1999), and Kenny et al. (1998).

## ▶ Quantitative Methods for Dyadic Research

To begin a discussion of dyadic data analysis, one first must be aware that the appropriate analysis depends on a number of factors. All of the methods we illustrate assume that the dependent or outcome measures are interval or ratio data. The analysis of designs with nominal or ordinal dependent measures often requires other techniques that are detailed in a number of sources (Bakeman 1991; Bakeman & Quera, 1995; Gottman & Roy, 1990; Kashy & Snyder, 1995; Wickens 1993). In dyadic designs, analysis strategy choice is deter-

mined both by characteristics of the dyad and by characteristics of the independent variables.

### *Distinguishability of Dyad Members*

One important question in dyadic research and data analysis is whether the two dyad members can be distinguished from one another by some variable. In heterosexual dating relationships, dyad members are distinguishable because of their gender; each couple has one man and one woman. Similarly, in non-twin sibling dyads, the two siblings can be distinguished by birth order. However, there are many instances in which there is no such natural distinction. Same-sex friendship pairs, homosexual romantic partners, and twins all are examples of what we call *indistinguishable dyads*. The distinguishability issue is critical in a discussion of quantitative methods for relationship data because the data analytic techniques appropriate for distinguishable dyads might not be appropriate for indistinguishable dyads.

### *Types of Independent Variables*

There are three types of independent or predictor variables in dyadic research, and the appropriate data analytic approach depends on the type of variable being studied. *Within-dyads* independent variables are those that vary across the two dyad members but do not vary, on average, from dyad to dyad. In heterosexual dating couples, gender is a categorical within-dyads variable because each couple has both a man and a woman, but the "average" gender score (averaging over the two dyad members) is constant across couples. A continuous within-dyads predictor variable might be the proportion of child care tasks completed by married couples who have children. Again, the proportion differs between members of a dyad, but across all dyads the proportions sum to 100%. Note that whenever there is a categorical within-dyads predictor variable, the dyad members are distinguishable with respect to that variable.

*Between-dyads* independent variables are those that vary from dyad to dyad, but within a dyad both members have the same score. A manipulated between-dyads variable might be stress level in a study in which some couples are placed in stressful situations and others are not. A common between-dyads variable in marital conflict research is the categorization of couples as distressed or nondistressed. A continuous between-dyads variable might be the length of acquaintance for friendship dyads.

The final type of independent variable is a *mixed* variable. Mixed independent variables vary both within and between dyads. In a study of the effects of attachment avoidance on dyadic conflict, avoidance would be a continuous mixed predictor because dyad members will tend to differ on avoidance, and the average level of avoidance will be high in some couples and low in others. Gender would be a categorical mixed variable in a study that included both heterosexual and homosexual dating couples. Although mixed variables present a number of data analytic challenges, they also present some of the best opportunities to study the interdependence between individuals who are involved in close relationships.

### Hypothetical Research Example

To assist us in our presentation, consider an example based loosely on Simpson, Rholes, and Phillips's (1996) study of the effects of attachment, stress, and gender on problem solving in dating couples. In their study, the attachment orientations of both members of heterosexual dating couples were assessed, and couples then were assigned to discuss either a major or minor relationship problem. Following the videotaped dyadic interactions, participants indicated their perceptions of their partners and of their relationships. The videotapes were coded for, among other things, signs of stress and anxiety. In this study, gender is a within-dyads predictor variable, the importance of the relationship problem is a between-dyads predictor variable, and anxious/ambivalent and avoidant attachment orientations are two mixed predictor variables. Behavioral manifestations of stress and anxiety are outcome measures.

Although we retain the basics of Simpson et al. (1996), we need to make some modifications to the design that will enable us to illustrate all of the designs, models, and analysis issues we will discuss. Consider the following variation of the Simpson et al. study. Researchers are interested in the factors that might predict the tendency for married individuals to engage in destructive conflict resolution behaviors. They predict that gender, avoidant attachment style, length of relationship, and each individual's assessment of relationship equity all influence both the tendency to use criticism during discussions of relationship problems and general relationship satisfaction. In addition, they predict that the severity of the problem discussed will affect the use of criticism and postdiscussion relationship satisfaction. The researchers recruit a sample of married couples and categorize one person in the dyad as more distressed and the other as less distressed based on perceptions of equity in the relationship (i.e., the person who believes the relationship is least equitable is labeled *more distressed*). Each person also completes a measure of attachment-related avoidance and reports the length of the relationship. Couples then are randomly assigned to discuss a major or minor relationship problem. Following the interaction, each person rates his or her satisfaction with the relationship. The conversations are videotaped, and observers count the number of criticisms made by each person. Thus, this study includes the following types of variables: (a) one categorical between-dyads variable (severity of the problem discussed), (b) one continuous between-dyads variable (length of relationship), (c) two categorical within-dyads variables (gender and more distressed vs. less distressed), (d) one continuous mixed variable (avoidant attachment orientation), and (e) two dependent variables (number of criticisms and relationship satisfaction). Next, we consider the questions one might ask based on this study and illustrate the analysis approaches appropriate to answering those questions.

### Setting Up the Data

Before beginning a discussion of how to analyze dyadic data, it is important to consider how the data should be organized. There are two basic approaches to analyzing dyadic data. The first treats individual as the unit of analysis (the effective *N* is the number of individuals in the study), and the second treats dyad as the unit of analysis (the effective *N* is the number of dyads). Although we argue that dyad almost always should be treated as the unit because of nonindependence, researchers might want to leave their options open, especially if there is little evidence of nonindependence in the data. The most flexible organizational scheme is to enter the data as if individual were the unit of analysis, so that each record reflects the scores from only one dyad member, but then to have related individuals on adjacent records. With such an approach, the input statement can be used to create either an individual-as-unit data set or a dyad-as-unit data set. It is very important to include in the data set a couple identification number that is the same for both dyad members. For example, we would enter the data from our marital study so that, for each couple, the couple identification number and then the husband's scores are on the first record and the couple identification number and then the wife's scores are on the second record. The input statement could be written either for each record individually (this would be for analyses with individual as the unit of analysis) or for each pair of records (this would be for analyses that treat dyad as the unit of analysis).

### Exploring the Data

It certainly is important to test hypotheses and predictions in relationships research, but it also is important for researchers to "get to know" their data at a more general level. All too often, researchers immediately begin hypothesis testing without first examining the basic nature of the data that they have so laboriously collected. Before researchers undertake complex data analytic procedures such as structural equation modeling, ANOVA, or hierarchical linear modeling, they should routinely examine a series of basic descriptive statistics. Means and standard deviations should be computed for all variables. If the dyads are nondistinguishable, then these descriptive statistics can be computed across the entire sample. If there is a distinguishing variable (a categorical within-dyads independent variable), then the descriptive statistics can be computed separately for each level of the distinguishing variable and tests for mean differences (discussed later) should be conducted. Large differences in variability across a within-dyads variable (e.g., if the amount of criticism on the part of husbands is more variable than that on the part of wives) also should be noted because such differences might be theoretically important and could lead to restriction of range or heterogeneity of variance problems in subsequent analyses. A test of differential variance across a within-dyads variable for nonindependent data was presented in Kashy and Snyder (1995).

In addition to computing means and standard deviations, correlations should be computed across the dyad members for each variable (using Pearson correlations for distinguishable dyads and intraclass correlations for nondistinguishable dyads) as well as across variables for each dyad member (generally using Pearson correlations). In our example, it would be important to consider whether levels of criticism on the part of husbands and wives are correlated, indicating perhaps that when husbands are more critical, wives also are very critical. In addition, it would be important to examine whether criticism and satisfaction are related for husbands and wives. For example, it might be that for husbands there is little relationship between these two measures, whereas for wives the relationship is strongly negative. In the remainder of this section, we briefly describe methods for assessing and testing (a) the degree of interdependence between dyad members' outcome scores and (b) whether the correlational structure among the variables measured differs across the two dyad members.

*Measuring interdependence.* When dyad members are distinguishable, the level of nonindependence between dyad members on an outcome measure can be assessed using the standard Pearson correlation coefficient. Note that the assessment of nonindependence is conducted on the dependent variables, not the independent variables. For example, if the number of criticisms on the part of husbands and wives is being studied, then the wives' number of criticisms could be treated as the $x$ variable and the husbands' number of criticisms could be treated as the $y$ variable, and $x$ and $y$ could be correlated. Not only does this correlation indicate whether the data are nonindependent (as we already have noted), it also provides an important piece of descriptive information concerning the nature of criticism. If the correlation is statistically significant—and we concur with others' recommendations that this test should be very liberal (an alpha level of .20 often is suggested such as in Myers [1979])—then the data are not independent and dyad should be treated as the unit of analysis in all subsequent analyses. If the correlation is small and nonsignificant, then individuals can be treated as the unit of analysis. However, Kenny et al. (1998) showed that treating dyad rather than individual as the unit of analysis, even when there is little evidence of nonindependence, has very small costs in power. Therefore, we generally recommend that dyadic close relationship data be analyzed treating dyad as the unit of analysis.

Measures of nonindependence when dyad members are not distinguishable tend to be less familiar to most researchers. When dyad members are indistinguishable (e.g., a sample including only gay male couples), assignment of one person's score as $x$ and the other person's score as $y$ is totally arbitrary. Researchers sometimes use random assignment (one person is randomly assigned to $x$ and the other to $y$ for each dyad) to circumvent this problem, and they then use the Pearson correlation coefficient to measure interdependence. This strategy is problematic, however, because the solution for the correlation is not unique. That is, any other random assignment would result in a different value for the obtained correlation.

In the indistinguishable case, the *intraclass correlation* provides an estimate of nonindependence. For dyadic data, the intraclass correlation ranges from −1 to +1 and can be interpreted in the same way as the Pearson correlation. There are several ways in which to compute the intraclass correlation that were presented by Gonzalez and Griffin (1997) and Kenny (1988).

*Differences in correlations across members of distinguishable dyads.* Another of the basic descriptive questions that should routinely be addressed in relationships research is whether there are differences in the basic relationships among the variables studied for the two dyad members. For example, one might examine whether the relationship between relationship satisfaction and length of relationship is the same for husbands and wives. This question concerns the relationships between an individual-level variable that has different scores for each dyad member (satisfaction) and a dyad-level variable for which both individuals have the same score (length of relationship). If the husband's satisfaction is Variable 1, the wife's satisfaction is Variable 2, and length of relationship is Variable 3, then we are testing whether $r_{13} = r_{23}$. Because these two Pearson correlations are not independent (they come from related individuals and have a variable in common), the Williams

(1959) modification of the Hotelling test should be used. The formulas for this test, as well as an example, were presented in detail in Kashy and Snyder (1995).

One also can test whether the correlation between two individual-level variables differs across the dyad members. In our example study, we could compute the Pearson correlation between criticism and satisfaction separately for husbands and wives. Then we could test whether the relationship between these two variables differs for men and women. The two correlations are nonindependent because they come from related individuals, and it is likely that husbands' satisfaction and wives' satisfaction are related. Consequently, the difference between correlations should be tested using the Steiger (1980) modification of the Pearson-Filon test, which was presented in Kashy and Snyder (1995, Appendix A).

The analyses just presented are important first steps in the analysis of dyadic data. They provide researchers with a basic "feel" for their data and likely address some basic research questions. However, most relationships research concerns the effects of independent variables on outcome measures. For example, knowing that the wife's use of criticism is not independent of the husband's use of criticism is very important, but we are likely to be testing other hypotheses about the factors that predict the use of criticism. Thus, we now consider how to test the effects of within-dyad, between-dyad, and mixed independent variables.

### Testing the Average Effects of Within-Dyads Independent Variables (distinguishable dyads only)

If there is only one categorical within-dyads independent variable, then testing the effect of that variable while taking into account nonindependence is straightforward: A correlated groups $t$ test can be used. In such a test, the sample size ($N$) is the number of dyads. As an example, consider the question of whether there are sex differences on our measure of criticism. A difference score could be computed by taking the wife's score on criticism and subtracting from it her husband's score on criticism. The differences are averaged across dyads, and the average is tested to see whether it differs significantly from zero. If the within-dyads independent variable is continuous (e.g., proportion of child care), then the analyses are somewhat more complicated. Kashy and Kenny (2000) provided a detailed discussion of various options.

If there are two categorical within-dyads independent variables, then there is an interesting twist to the analysis. Consider the two categorical within-dyads independent variables in our example: gender and more distressed partner versus less distressed partner. One important question might be whether there are differences in the amount of criticism depending on the gender of the distressed partner. For example, it might be that criticism is particularly high when the wife is distressed. In this case, the analysis actually becomes a mixed model ANOVA that treats dyad as the unit of analysis. One of the independent variables is treated as a within-dyads factor (analogous to a within-subjects factor), and the other is transformed into a between-dyads factor. In the example, gender could remain a within-dyads variable, but distress would be transformed into a between-dyads variable that divides the couples into two groups: one containing couples in which the wives are the more distressed partners, and the other containing couples in which the husbands are the more distressed partners. This approach would yield a main effect for gender that tests whether husbands or wives are more critical in general. It would yield a second main effect that tests whether couples in which the wives are the more distressed partners are more critical than couples in which the husbands are the more distressed partners. Finally, such an analysis would yield an interaction that tests whether individuals are more critical when they are the more distressed spouses or when their partners are the more distressed spouses. It is very important to note that the effects tested in this design become confounded if there is unequal *n* for the two within-dyads classification variables, rendering interpretation of significant effects impossible. Thus, it is critical in our example that the number of couples in which the husbands are more distressed equals the number of couples in which the wives are more distressed.

### Testing the Effects of Between-Dyads Independent Variables

Consider first the case of nondistinguishable dyads. Say, for example, that a researcher is interested in examining differences in empathic accuracy in interactions between same-sex friends versus same-sex strangers (Stinson & Ickes, 1992). In this example, level of friendship (friends vs. strangers) is a categorical between-dyads independent variable. To test the effects of this variable, one could first average the empathic accuracy scores across the two members of each dyad and then conduct an independent groups *t* test (or, if the between-dyads variable has more than two levels, an ANOVA) on the dyad means.

An equivalent strategy is to treat the design as a nested ANOVA (Kashy & Kenny, 2000). In this approach, individuals are nested within dyads, and dyads are nested within levels of the independent variable. This ANOVA results in three sources of variance: variance due to the independent variable (*A*), variance due to dyads within the independent variable (*D/A*), and variance due to individuals within dyads (*S/D/A*). To test the effect of the independent variable (assuming that the data within dyads are nonindependent), the variance due to the independent variable, *A*, would be divided by the variance due to dyads within the independent variable, *D/A*.

There might be instances in which the between-dyads independent variable is continuous, as it would be if it were length of acquaintance in homosexual dating couples. In this case, a regression approach can be used such that the average score on the outcome measure (averaging across the two dyad members) would serve as the criterion score in a regression in which the between-dyads independent variable is the predictor.

If, in addition to the between-dyads independent variable, there is a within-dyads variable (i.e., the dyads are distinguishable), then a mixed model ANOVA could be conducted treating dyad as the unit of analysis. In our example, say that we simply wanted to test whether the effects of the severity of the problem discussed interacts with gender in our married couples. It might be that when a very difficult problem is discussed, the husband is more critical than the wife, but when a relatively easy problem is discussed, the wife is more critical than the husband. The ANOVA would treat the husband's and wife's criticism scores as levels of a within-dyads factor (gender), and severity of the problem would be treated as a between-dyads factor.

### Testing the Effects of Mixed Independent Variables

Mixed independent variables present a data analytic challenge for researchers and rarely have been analyzed in ways that exploit their full potential. In our example, a key predictor variable, avoidant attachment orientation, is mixed. One of the most common strategies for analyzing mixed predictor variables in dyadic research with distinguishable dyads such as dating or marital couples is to run separate regressions for men and women (e.g., Simpson, Rholes, & Nelligan, 1992). In these regressions, the mixed variable (avoidant attachment in the example) is used to predict the outcome (criticism). There are two major problems with such an approach. One problem is that there is no direct way in which to test whether the effects found for men differ from those found for women. The second problem is perhaps more critical: Interdependence is ignored. Separate regressions do not take into account that there might be relationships between (a) the man's score on the mixed variable and the woman's score on the mixed variable, (b) the man's outcome score

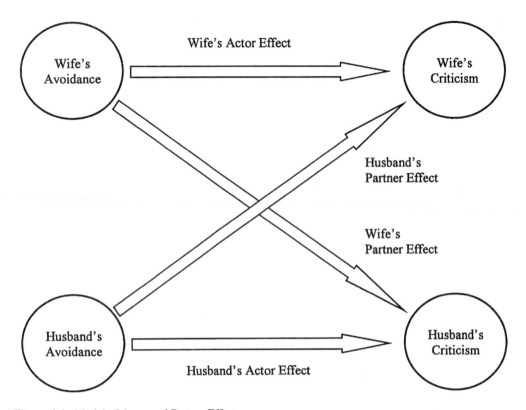

**Figure 1.1.** Model of Actor and Partner Effects

and the woman's outcome score, (c) the man's score on the mixed variable and the woman's outcome score, and (d) the woman's score on the mixed variable and the man's outcome score. In the next two subsections, we briefly describe two approaches that specifically model the types of interdependence that can occur with mixed predictor variables.

*Actor-partner interdependence model.* The actor-partner interdependence model (APIM) (Kashy & Kenny, 2000; Kenny & Cook, 1999) focuses on an important implication of nonindependence in dyadic research: One person's score on a variable can influence not only that person's score on an outcome variable but also that person's partner's score on the outcome variable. Consider again our hypothetical marital study and the mixed predictor variable, avoidant attachment style. As shown in Figure 1.1, a wife's avoidant attachment style can influence her own level of crit-

icism such that more avoidant women are more critical. It also might be that a wife's avoidant attachment style influences her husband's level of criticism such that husbands with more avoidant wives are more critical. The effect of a wife's avoidance on her own criticism is called an *actor effect,* and the effect of her avoidance on her husband's criticism is called a *partner effect* (Kenny, 1996). That is, an actor effect occurs when a person's score on a predictor variable affects that person's score on an outcome variable, whereas a partner effect occurs when a person's score on a predictor variable affects his or her partner's score on an outcome variable.

The analysis implied by the APIM is very flexible. Actor and partner effects can be estimated whenever the independent variable is mixed, regardless of whether the mixed variable is categorical or continuous. The analysis also can incorporate independent variables that are not mixed (i.e., those that are within or between dyads), but separation of actor and partner effects can occur only with mixed predictor variables. The analysis also allows for interactions among predictor variables, and any interactions with mixed variables (e.g., the interaction between gender and avoidance) can be broken into actor and partner effects. Thus, one can examine whether the effect of a husband's avoidance on his wife's criticism (the partner effect for men) differs from the effect of a wife's avoidance on her husband's criticism (the partner effect for women). Finally, this model can be used in dyadic research both when dyad members are distinguishable (e.g., married couples) and when dyad members are nondistinguishable (e.g., same-sex friends).

There are several ways in which to estimate the APIM (Kenny & Cook, 1999). One analysis strategy, referred to as the *pooled regressions* technique (Kashy & Kenny, 2000; Kashy & Snyder, 1995; Kenny, 1996), can be used for both distinguishable and nondistinguishable dyads. In this approach, two regressions are computed, and the coefficients generated by them are pooled together to derive and test the size of the actor and partner effects. A second approach uses structural equation modeling to estimate the actor and partner effects. The structural equation approach is better suited for distinguishable couples than for nondistinguishable couples. Murray et al. (1996) used this analysis technique, and although their model is more complex than our example, their study provided a good illustration of how to interpret structural equation results. Kenny and Cook (1999) described a third approach to estimating the APIM using multilevel modeling techniques.

*Levels of analysis approach.* The essence of the levels of analysis approach is that questions can be asked both at the level of the individual (e.g., "Are more avoidant individuals more critical?") *and* at the level of the dyad (e.g., "Are couples in which both members are more avoidant more critical?"). Although it might not be evident at first glance, it is possible that the relationships between two

variables at these two levels of analysis might be opposite in sign. Consider, for example, the relationship between commitment and trust in dating couples. At the dyad level, it might be that couples who are more committed, on average, also are more trusting. At the individual level, the more committed individual might be less trusting because he or she realizes that his or her partner is less committed and, therefore, more likely to end the relationship. Gonzalez and Griffin (1997, 1999) presented a fairly extended discussion of one method that can be used to estimate the levels of analysis model. Kenny and La Voie (1985) discussed a different method that can be generalized beyond dyads to groups of any size.

## ► Quantitative Methods for Multiple Partner Designs: Friendship Groups and Families

Thus far, we have discussed designs in which each individual is a member of one and only one dyad. However, many interesting questions may be asked about relationships that involve membership in multiple dyads. Families represent the most obvious multiple partner design in relationships research because within a family, a person probably is involved in separate (but likely related) dyadic relationships with each other family member. Friendship relationships also can be conceptualized as multiple dyad networks. Specifically, one can obtain data from a small group in which each person is a friend with each other person in the group. The critical difference between these two types of multiple dyad designs is the distinguishability of the group members. In families, each individual can be distinguished by his or her role in the family (e.g., mother, father), whereas in friendship networks, individuals are essentially nondistinguishable.

In the present discussion, we first describe the standard social relations model (SRM) (Kenny, 1994; Kenny & La Voie, 1984), which can be used to examine data from friendship networks (and other groups of nondistinguishable individuals). We then build on our discussion of the SRM to introduce its application to family research designs. As before, our presentation is descriptive in nature, and the reader is referred to other sources for a more technical discussion.

### The SRM With Friendship Networks and Other Nondistinguishable Groups

*The round-robin data structure.* Although there are a number of possible multiple partner data structures (Kenny, 1990), we focus on round-robin designs that occur most commonly. In a round-robin design, each person within a group interacts with or rates every other person in that group. Interactions can occur one-on-one or as a group, but the data generated must be specific to each dyadic combination. Consider a study of liking and self-disclosure among friends in which one group of friends consists of four individuals: Jesse (*J*), Chris (*C*), Pat (*P*), and Erin (*E*). In this study, every pair of friends within the group interacts, and the amount of self-disclosure is coded for each individual. Thus, for our example group, six interactions occur (*J* with *C, J* with *P, J* with *E, C* with *P, C* with *E,* and *P* with *E*), generating 12 self-disclosure scores (*J* to *C, C* to *J; J* to *P, P* to *J;* etc.). In addition to the behavioral measure of self-disclosure, individuals in the group also rate how much they like one another.

*SRM components.* The SRM proposes that any dyadic score (e.g., Jesse's disclosure to Chris) can be broken into four major components: the group mean, the actor effect, the partner effect, and the relationship effect. Consider the degree to which Jesse self-discloses to Chris. The mean simply refers to the average level of a variable in a particular group. In the example, the mean is the level of self-disclosure averaged across all interactions among members of the group. The actor effect assesses the degree to which a person's behavior is consistent across all of his or her interaction partners (e.g., Jesse discloses a great deal to everyone in the friendship group). The partner effect measures the degree to which a person tends to elicit similar behavior from all others (e.g., all of the friends tend to disclose quite a bit to Chris). Both actor and partner effects are individual-level effects. The relationship effect is inherently dyadic in that it refers to both Jesse and Chris and measures the degree to which self-disclosure is a function of the unique relationship between two people. Jesse's relationship effect with Chris would be the degree to which Jesse discloses an especially large amount to Chris, that is, more than Jesse typically discloses to other friends and more than other friends typically disclose to Chris.

A similar decomposition can be done for how much Jesse reports liking Chris. Jesse might like everyone in the friendship group a great deal, so Jesse might have a strong positive actor effect. However, Chris might not be all that well liked, so Chris might have a negative partner effect. Jesse's relationship effect with Chris measures the unique degree to which Jesse likes Chris after taking into account Jesse's actor effect and Chris's partner effect. In summary, every member of the group will have an actor effect and a partner effect for each measure, and every dyad within the group will have two relationship effects (e.g., *J* with *C, C* with *J*) for each measure.

*Questions that can be addressed.* SRM components can be used to examine a number of questions relevant to the study of friendship. First, one can examine the degree to which liking and disclosure among friends are inherently individual- or dyadic-level phenomena by contrasting the amount of variance due to the individual-level components (actor and partner) with the amount of variance due to the relationship component. Say, for example, that 25% of the variance in self-disclosure is due to actor effects, 15% is due to partner effects, and 60% is due to relationship effects. This would indicate that although there are some individuals who are "disclosers" and some individuals who consistently elicit disclosure, levels of self-disclosure among groups of close friends are primarily a function of the unique relationship between two individuals.

We should note that relationship variance is confounded with error variance unless steps are taken to estimate error. One possibility would be to use multiple indicators (or measures) of the construct being examined. The other method for estimating error, which is preferred for behavioral assessments, requires that each dyad interact on multiple occasions. For example, Chris would interact twice with each friend, and the amount of disclosure would be recorded for each interaction. Consistencies across the multiple indicators or multiple occasions would be attributed to relationship effects, and inconsistencies would provide an estimate of error variance. Kenny, Mohr, and Levesque (1999) provided a more detailed discussion of the question of separating relationship from error for interactions involving behavioral measures.

Another set of questions concerns the degree of reciprocity that occurs between friends. At the individual level, one can examine whether persons who disclose to all of their friends are generally recipients of disclosure. This correlation often is referred to as *generalized reciprocity* and involves correlating a person's actor effect with his or her partner effect. One can examine *dyadic reciprocity* by correlating the two relationship components from a dyad. Dyadic reciprocity for self-disclosure examines whether a person who discloses at an especially high level to a particular friend is disclosed to at an especially high level by that friend.

Thus, using the SRM, one can examine the degree to which friendships are unique or a reflection of individual differences that are consistent across relationships. In addition to questions of variance and reciprocity, the estimates of actor and partner effects can be correlated with personality variables. For example, if each member of the friendship group in our example completed an attachment orientation measure, then it would be possible to assess whether individuals who are more

avoidant in their attachment styles are less likely to self-disclose to all of their friends. A similar analysis in which attachment orientation scores are correlated with partner effects could determine whether secure individuals tend to be disclosed to by all others. Finally, components for different variables can be correlated: Are individuals who tend to disclose a great deal across partners (actor effect for disclosure) liked by all other group members (partner effect for liking)? Thus, many of the standard questions in friendship research can be addressed with multiple partner designs. Analyzing the type of data we describe can be accomplished with SOREMO, a data analysis program (Kenny, 1999) designed for use with round-robin data structures in which individuals are indistinguishable. There are a number of examples of the use of the SRM with acquainted individuals that provide detailed discussions of SRM methods and analysis including variants of the standard round-robin design (Dindia, Fitzpatrick, & Kenny, 1997; Kenny, 1994; Kenny & Kashy, 1994; Miller & Kenny, 1986).

### The SRM With Families

Data from families present a range of difficult data analytic issues. Such data are nearly certain to be nonindependent, and the interdependence might be quite complex. For example, there might be intragenerational similarities such that data from parents are especially similar and data from siblings are quite similar. For some variables, there might be interdependence as a function of the persons' genders (e.g., mothers' and daughters' data might be especially similar). The extension of the SRM for families allows researchers to explicitly model several patterns of interdependence within families, and it has great potential to increase our understanding of intrafamily processes (Cook, Kenny, & Goldstein, 1991; Kashy & Kenny, 1990).

*Family data structure.* To illustrate the SRM with families, consider the following example.

A researcher is interested in how families discuss significant conflicts and how those discussions relate to the family members' satisfaction with their familial relationships. Families of four, each consisting of a mother (*M*), a father (*F*), a son (*S*), and a daughter (*D*), are asked to discuss a difficult family problem, and the videotaped discussions are coded for statements that represent supportive affirmations.

Recall that social relations analysis requires round-robin data. Thus, the researcher must count the number of times the mother affirms her son (*MS*), the son affirms his mother (*SM*), the mother affirms her daughter (*MD*), the daughter affirms her mother (*DM*), the mother affirms the father (*MF*), and so on. In four-person families, this will yield 12 counts (*MF, FM, MS, SM, MD, DM, FS, SF, FD, DF, SD,* and *DS*). To collect this type of data, the family discussion can be structured in one of two ways. One possibility is to have the entire family discuss the issue. This might make it difficult to code behaviors as directed at particular persons. That is, for any given statement of affirmation, it might be difficult to determine whether it was directed at the mother, at the daughter, or perhaps at everyone. The other possibility is to have each family member interact one-on-one with each other family member. This approach simplifies the coding of behavior and might be a better reflection of dyadic relationships. When the variable under study can be measured by having the family members rate one another (e.g., individuals could rate how attached they are to each member of their family), this issue is not relevant because each family member can simply be asked to rate each other family member separately.

*SRM components with families.* As was the case with interchangeable groups, the SRM analysis with families partitions the variance in scores (either number of affirmations or rating of relationship quality) into four important components: mean, actor, partner, and relationship. However, in the case of family data, there are distinct actor and partner effects for each role, and the relationship effects refer to specific combinations of roles. That is, there is an actor effect for the mother role that estimates the degree to which a mother is affirming of all other family members, and separate actor effects also are estimated for fathers, sons, and daughters. Similarly, each role has a partner effect. For example, a negative father partner effect might indicate that a father rarely is affirmed by his family members. The relationship effects measure the unique interaction between two roles: Is a mother especially affirming of her son, more affirming than she typically is of other family members, and more affirming than other family members typically are of the son? Finally, the mean refers to the average level of response across all members of a family. It might be the case that some families are highly supportive and affirming, whereas others are not.

As was the case with interchangeable groups, in the SRM with families, one of the steps in the analysis is to compute the variance in the actor, partner, and relationship effects. The variance in the mother actor effects measures the degree to which some mothers tend to be affirming, whereas others are not. There might be little actor variance for mothers if they all are affirming (perhaps there is something implicit in the role that demands that mothers be affirming). If there is a great deal of actor variance for fathers, then some fathers are highly affirming, whereas others are not; that is, fathers' affirmation might be more of an individual difference. Similarly, high levels of partner variance for the son role might indicate that in some families sons frequently are affirmed, whereas in others they are not. Relationship variance is computed for each pair of roles. Thus, high relationship variance for sons with daughters might indicate that in some families sons frequently affirm their sisters, whereas in others they rarely affirm their sisters.

The family means, actor effects, and partner effects also can be correlated with various measures. Family means can be correlated with any family-level measures. For example, if measures of general family functioning are available, then they can be correlated with the mean affirmation scores to determine whether families in which there is more affirmation are better functioning. The actor and partner effects can be correlated with individual-level measures that are obtained for each role. For example, if mothers complete measures indicating the amount of time they spend engaging in family activities, then these measures can be correlated with mothers' actor and partner effects. The correlation with actor effects measures whether mothers who spend more time in family activities tend to be more affirming. The correlation with partner effects measures whether mothers who spend more time in family activities tend to be affirmed more frequently.

Generalized reciprocity can be estimated for each role by correlating the actor and partner effects for that role. For example, are fathers who frequently affirm the other family members also affirmed by them? Dyadic reciprocity also can be estimated for each combination of roles: If a mother is especially affirming of the father, then is the father especially affirming of her? Thus, with an SRM analysis, researchers can separate what appear to be individual tendencies and unique dyadic effects, so it is possible to determine whether relational behavior is largely consistent across relationships or more unique to each relationship.

Although a detailed discussion of the ways in which the SRM with families is implemented is beyond the scope of this chapter, we would like to note that there now are two ways in which such an analysis can be performed. The first method uses confirmatory factor analysis (CFA) and was detailed in Kashy and Kenny (1990). In this approach, the 12 scores (*MF, FM, MS, SM, MD, DM, FS, SF, FD, DF, SD,* and *DS*) serve as indicators of eight latent factors. The 3 scores that involve the mother as an actor (*MF, MS,* and *MD*) are treated as indicators of the mother actor factor. Similarly, the 3 scores that involve the father as an actor (*FM, FS,* and *FD*) are treated as indicators of the father actor factor. The son and daughter actor factors are similarly constructed. The mother partner factor is indicated by the 3 scores in which the mother is a partner (*FM,*

*SM,* and *DM*), and the other three partner factors are created in a similar fashion. The relationship effects are the unique effects or the variance that is unexplained by the individual-level factors. Structural equation modeling programs such as LISREL and EQS can be used to estimate the SRM for families using this approach.

The second approach is a very recent development and uses multilevel modeling techniques (Snidjers & Kenny, 1999). This new approach offers several important advantages over CFA, perhaps the most important being its ability to handle missing data. The CFA approach requires that each family in the sample has the same structure (in our example, every family must have a mother, a father, a son, and a daughter). The multilevel approach allows for families of varying structures to be included in the analysis.

► **Conclusion**

The field of close relationships research clearly is a growing enterprise, and researchers from a variety of academic backgrounds including psychology, family studies, communication, sociology, anthropology, and human ecology now are making important contributions to this area. As in any field, however, the progress of theory in relationships research is intimately tied with the progress of research methodology. That is, the tools that we have to answer questions can limit the types of questions that are asked or even considered. Because interdependence is the fundamental component of relationships, it is vital that relationship researchers become methodological and data analytic experts in models of nonindependent data. Over the past decade, the number of tools available for studying nonindependent data has grown tremendously, and we hope that researchers not only will learn and exploit those that have already been developed but also will turn their attention toward developing new methods and techniques.

# Contents

# Qualitative Research

*Katherine R. Allen*
*Alexis J. Walker*

There is a burgeoning interest in qualitative research and a greater appreciation for its potential contributions to the understanding of close relationships. For the same reasons that qualitative methodologies are well suited to research on families (Daly, 1992), qualitative approaches are perfectly situated to expand our knowledge of the forms of, processes in, and meanings of close relationships. According to Daly (1992), (a) families are private; (b) they manifest a collective consciousness not freely accessible to individuals outside of their borders; (c) their relationships are meant to be permanent; (d) they have shared histories; (e) the involvement of their members is intense; and (f) they reflect a mingling of individual attitudes, characteristics, and experiences. Close relationships also share these distinctive characteristics. These attributes, which present challenges to quantitative methodologies, are highly amenable to qualitative exploration.

## ▶ Defining Qualitative Research Methods

We begin with a primer on distinguishing characteristics of qualitative research, drawn from Bogdan and Biklen's (1998) and Taylor and Bogdan's (1984) summaries of the nature of this mode of inquiry. First, qualitative research is naturalistic. It tends to occur in settings where people's lives unfold such as schools, homes, neighborhoods, and public institutions. Furthermore, it is sensitive to the context in which individual behavior and social action take place. Second, qualitative research is descriptive, expressed most often in words (e.g., transcripts, narratives), pictures (e.g., photographs, videotapes), and personal or public documents (e.g., diaries, letters, autobiographies, court records) rather than numbers. Third, qualitative research is concerned with process, with how people negotiate meaning, and with how concepts or ideas come to be accepted as common sense in a particular cultural context. The concern with process makes it an ideal technique for the investigation of close relationship processes such as relational maintenance and conflict. Fourth, qualitative research is concerned with participants' own perspectives and how participants make sense of their lives. Meaning is the sine qua non of qualitative research. Finally, qualitative research is inductive. Starting at the level of observation in the so-called real world, theoretical abstractions are generated upward from empirical evidence. This quality does not deny the importance of theory, although some have interpreted the classic text by Glaser and Strauss (1967) in this way. Rather than theory being ignored, theory is relevant at all stages of the research process. The focus on hypothesis testing has been replaced, instead, by a focus on hypothesis generation. What is going on in the social setting under investigation comes into greater focus by using theory (e.g., generalizations grounded in the data) to offer tentative explanations of what is being described. Indeed, a qualitative approach is marked by the collaboration of theory and data (Daly, 1997; Emerson, Fretz, & Shaw, 1995; Gilgun, 1992).

Qualitative research includes an array of procedures that are not limited to this methodological domain but, nevertheless, are distinguished from quantitative methods because of the circumscribed focus on numbers. As Ambert, Adler, Adler, and Detzner (1995) suggested, these procedures include

> (a) oral words, whether in conversations, sentences, or monologues; (b) written words in journals, letters, autobiographies, scripts, texts, books, official reports, and historical documents; (c) the recorded field notes of observers or participants of meetings, ceremonies, rituals, and family life; (d) life histories and narrative stories in either the oral or the written form; (e) visual observations (whether live videotaped or in pictures) or other modes of self-expression such as facial expressions, body language, physical presentation of self, [and] modes of dressing. (p. 881)

### Understanding People in Social Contexts

All research studies, regardless of methodology, share certain qualities. By definition, research is implicitly or explicitly theoretical, organized around a set of ideas. All research is systematic, following procedures that others may attempt to replicate. All research is subject to biases, and investigators try to figure out ways in which to minimize or use biases effectively. All research involves one or more methods or ways of gathering evidence including observing behaviors, surveying or interviewing respondents, and examining historical documents (Fonow & Cook, 1991; Harding, 1987). Whether qualitative, quantitative, or a combination of both, researchers select from a shared repertoire of methods to generate new knowledge and/or insights about existing knowledge.

It is researchers themselves who differ in terms of their allegiances to particular ideas and ways of knowing. Researchers might share from a pool of methods, but they can differ greatly in the underlying epistemologies that shape their studies. An epistemology is a theory of knowledge and refers to the assumptions about the nature of reality that influence beliefs about what can be known and how a researcher comes to know it (Harding, 1987). Qualitative researchers, more so than quantitative researchers, pursue the discovery of new meanings rather than the testing of existing theories (Taylor & Bogdan, 1984). They also make use of the situation at hand (Fonow & Cook, 1991), inventing new strategies or piecing together meanings that arise in the research setting. As such, a qualitative researcher is a *bricoleur,* that is, a "jack of all trades or a kind of professional do-it-yourself person" (Lévi-Strauss, cited in Denzin & Lincoln, 1994, p. 2).

This inventiveness is reflective of the holistic approach to knowledge that is part of a general qualitative epistemology associated with seeing the world from the perspective of informants. Rather than separating self from subject, qualitative researchers nurture a self-conscious awareness of the inseparability of theory, data, self, and intervention in daily life (Allen, 2000). The research process is acknowledged as another site of contested relationships in which power dynamics come into play (Thompson & Walker, 1995). Research, as part of "the academic mode of production" (Stanley, 1990, p. 4), has a political dimension. By politicizing research processes and outcomes, qualitative researchers attempt to be explicitly deliberate, that is, excruciatingly self-conscious (Stacey, 1988) in how they practice their craft. Indeed, reflecting on the process of producing knowledge is an important scholarly activity (Klein & Jurich, 1993).

### An Ecological Approach to Creating Knowledge and Intervening in People's Lives

Increasingly, qualitative researchers seek to create knowledge that makes a difference in the world and that enhances, rather than exploits or detracts from, the quality of life for the people under study. Qualitative researchers, whether they are feminists (Lather, 1991; Stacey, 1990), grounded theorists (Gilgun, 1995), critical empiricists (Agger, 1998), ethnomethodologists (Gubrium & Holstein, 1993; Jaffe & Miller, 1994), interpretivists (Daly, 1997; Denzin, 1989), life course historians (Allen, 1989), narrative inquirists (Bochner, Ellis, & Tillmann-Healy, 1997; Thompson, 1996), or poststructuralists (Richardson, 1997), are less likely than quantitative researchers to pursue knowledge for knowledge's sake. They are less likely to treat scientific investigation as an objective procedure in which knowledge about the world can be discovered. Qualitative researchers take an ecological approach in linking theory and data (Emerson et al., 1995), and they are explicit, or should be explicit, about the undergirding of their philosophical and theoretical commitments to the project they are investigating. Recognizing the complexity of meanings and practices associated with qualitative research, Denzin and Lincoln (1994) provided a generic sense of what distinguishes this domain of inquiry: "Qualitative researchers study things in their natural settings, attempting to make sense of, or interpret, phenomena in terms of the meanings people bring to them" (p. 2).

One of the defining features of qualitative research is the researcher's relationship with participants or informants. Qualitative researchers typically, although not exclusively, study humans and their social relations. This quality is especially apparent in the close relationship literature, although essential features of this quality have yet to be explored and implemented to create an enriched knowledge of close relationships. To get at meanings, qualitative researchers must get close to and be involved with the people they study. The interactive involvement between participant and observer blurs the boundaries that most scholars have been trained to desire. Therefore, they experience such closeness as biased or uncomfortable (Krieger, 1991). Most researchers have been trained to be detached observers, outside the messy fray of the politics and passions of real life. With the postmodern turn in science, our positivist heritage has become decentered, and the emphasis has shifted from objectivism to an appreciation of the constructed nature of ideas and meanings (Bochner et al., 1997; Osmond, 1987; Thomas & Wilcox, 1987).

### Reflexivity and the Self-Conscious Researcher

The past two decades have witnessed an explosion of interest in using reflexive practice to deal with the obfuscation of the rigidly distinct social worlds of subject and object in the realm of research. In a provocative first-person account of the connection of social science and the self, Krieger (1991) demonstrated through her own connections to research, teaching, and personal life that "our outer depictions reflect the nature of our inner lives" (p. 132). Exposing her emotions, thoughts, and practices about the contested areas of her life as a teacher, researcher, woman, and even "failed academic," Krieger (1996) continued this reflexive practice in a subsequent work in which she subjected her own internal processes and relationships to empirical scrutiny. She acknowledged that the intimacy of her writing is challenging to readers because, besides the use of self-disclosure, she is deprivileging objective knowing.

Carrying the metaphor of the personal to the discipline of sociology, Game and Metcalfe (1996) described incorporating the formerly forbidden acknowledgment of passion for one's work to invigorate and thereby renew sociology as a way of understanding the private and the public realm of social life. Indeed, feminist writers have demonstrated that the androcentric bias of presumed intellectual neutrality, taken as a given, is in fact a tremendous bias and an impediment to seeing that which has not been formerly apparent. Building on Polanyi's (1958) notion of "tacit knowledge," DuBois (1983) described a critical and a feminist approach in which the knower cannot be separated from the known:

> When we take away the lenses of androcentrism and patriarchy, what we have left is our own eyes, ourselves, and each other. We are the instruments of observation and understanding; we are the names, the interpreters of our lives. To try to work without this instrument and this language is to do nothing other than what most of science has tried to do: pretend to leave the self and the valuing process out of science-making and thus perpetrate the image of science as the objective observer of fixed reality, the neutral seeker after an external and objectifiable truth. (p. 112)

Qualitative research is like an archaeological expedition, giving permission to see that which has been "hidden, inaccessible, suppressed, distorted, misunderstood, ignored" (DuBois, 1983, p. 109). For example, social scientists who have occupied oppressed locations in their private lives have generated new theoretical perspectives on the basis of their unique standpoint as members of a disadvantaged minority. Collins (1986) demonstrated that the experiences of African American women in particular have been distorted by

others observing "them" through a discriminating lens that reinforces their status as "other." Standing anywhere outside "the mythical norm, [which] is usually defined as white, thin, male, young, heterosexual, christian, and financially secure" (Lorde, 1984, p. 116), is to be outside legitimate sources of power. Yet, black women may refuse to accept the negative images imposed on them and instead adopt an empowered standpoint of conscious recognition of their achievements despite systematic oppression. Their self-definition can correct the biases imposed by those with a vested interest in discriminating against them (Collins, 1990). Much of the recasting of history setting the record straight about black women's experiences in this country has come about through personal narratives and research that reconceptualizes black women's experiences as subjects, not objects. Qualitative methods, therefore, are uniquely suited for first learning to see "what is there, not what we've been taught is there" (DuBois, 1983, p. 109).

### Participatory Ethnography

Of all the methods associated with a qualitative paradigm, ethnography in particular allows the researcher to enter another's social world and to come to see that world through participants' perspectives. Rather than studying people per se, the ethnographer learns about a culture from individual actors in that particular society. As Spradley (1979) defined it, *culture* refers to "the acquired knowledge that people use to interpret experience and generate social behavior" (p. 5). Rather than imposing concepts from the researcher's own culture onto the culture of those studied, ethnography is about coming to understand the insider's view.

Historically, ethnographies were characterized by degrees of participant-observer involvement (Emerson et al., 1995). At one end of the spectrum were passive observer roles and at the other end were active participant roles (Gold, 1958). Increasingly, researchers are engaging in complete participation roles to overlap more authentically with the lives of those they study (Emerson et al., 1995). Much of this shift in ethnographic practice is due to the postmodern critique of classic structural anthropology (Atkinson, 1990; Clifford & Marcus, 1986; Marcus & Fischer, 1986). Feminist researchers in particular practice an emancipatory style of doing research in which the work is *for* women, not on or about them (Smith, 1987; Stacey, 1990). Like critical empiricists in sociology (Agger, 1998) and multicultural education (Kincheloe & McLaren, 1994; McLaren, 1997) as well as action researchers in community service settings (Small, 1995), a liberatory agenda (Freire, 1970) increasingly enters the research matrix. As Reason (1994) argued:

> There is an emerging worldview, more holistic, pluralist, and egalitarian, that is essentially participative . . . [and] sees human beings as co-creating their reality through participation: through their experience, their imagination and intuition, and their thinking and their action. (p. 324)

## ▶ Qualitative Research Methods for a Postmodern World: Research on Sexual Relationships as Exemplar

Theorists and researchers are increasingly alert to the theoretical and methodological crises occurring in the postmodern world. This postpositivist turn toward interpretive and poststructuralist ways of knowing and conducting research has generated attention and excitement about what qualitative methods have to offer traditionally trained researchers (Bochner et al., 1997; Denzin & Lincoln, 1994; Lather, 1991; Thomas & Wilcox, 1987). To illustrate the crisis of representation occurring in the relationship field today, we have chosen as an example the dilemmas facing those who study sexual relationships. As but one domain of close relationships, transformations in the study of sexuality and sexual relationships mirror studies of close relationships in general. The

assumptions on which ideas about sexual relationships are based have come under tremendous scrutiny, requiring scholars to be creative and adaptive in the methods they choose to gather evidence and create knowledge. Given the very real risks prevalent in sexual relationships today, from the HIV/AIDS epidemic, to the consequences of unplanned pregnancy, to women's increasing recognition to their right of sexual agency and fulfillment (Schwartz & Rutter, 1998), a new paradigm and new research methods are needed to generate accurate knowledge about sexuality with practical utility for people's lives.

### *Shaking the Sexological Paradigm*

The foundations of knowledge about sexual relationships, characterized as the sexological paradigm, have come under scrutiny during the past several decades (Gagnon & Parker, 1995). Initially, a modern sexological paradigm emerged that combined medical and social science to investigate the biological and psychological aspects of sexuality. Although sociological dimensions were presumed, theories of sexual scripts and the stratifications associated with race, class, gender, and sexual orientation remained dormant until the end of the 20th century. The modern sexological paradigm, evident in works as diverse as Kinsey and colleagues (Kinsey, Pomeroy, & Martin, 1948; Kinsey, Pomeroy, Martin, & Gebhard, 1953) and Masters and Johnson (1966), took hold. Its basic assumptions included that sex was a natural force, the sex drive was instinctive and existed prior to social order, sex differences between men and women were fundamental, male and heterosexist images of sexuality naturally should dominate, science could produce an unbiased description of sexuality capable of helping the human race progress if properly understood, and positivist sexual knowledge was transcultural and transhistorical, where "the underlying nature of sexuality remains the same in all times and places" (Gagnon & Parker, 1995, p. 8). By the 1960s, the sexological paradigm was under attack from scientists and social activists, who challenged its accuracy and implicit political agenda. As part of the widespread critique of modernism with its progressive assumptions, all aspects of sexology were questioned, from the sexism and heterosexism that led to a universalist conception of the sexual to the privileging of scientific inquiry as the surest way in which to know "truth."

The postmodern turn brought a relational focus, in contrast to the prevalent emphasis on sex as biological or individualist. Sexual scripting "became a specific way to analyze cultural, interpersonal, and mental aspects of sexuality" (Gagnon & Parker, 1995, p. 8). Feminist studies and gay and lesbian studies also offered important critiques of both social science and sexological research, replacing the positivist view with a vision of social reality that is fragmentary, partial, and uncertain (Flax, 1987) as well as interactive. The pervasive inequality of women worldwide and the global HIV/AIDS epidemic have shaken the positivist framework within which many relationship scholars frame their questions and data.

## A Constructivist Paradigm

Gagnon and Parker (1995) described a constructionist approach as an alternative to the positivist framework in which most sexuality research has been conducted. A constructionist approach has several dimensions. First, research and theory about sexual relationships must incorporate an understanding of the relations of power and social inequality in which sexual behavior takes place. The way in which women are held accountable for men's sexual behavior, for example, is a manifestation of patriarchal society (Baber & Allen, 1992). By recognizing the gender inequities in heterosexual relationships, issues such as sexual satisfaction (Lawrance & Byers, 1995) and sexual attitude similarity (Cupach & Metts, 1995) come under a different type of scrutiny from what is allowed in a positivist approach. Second, the interactive nature of sexual meanings between social actors must

be considered. The various dimensions and transformations of sexuality do not occur in a vacuum; they are enlivened through social interactions between people who cannot be reduced to a fixed identity (e.g., white male, bisexual female). Third, traditional definitions of key concepts such as homosexuality, heterosexuality, masculinity, femininity, prostitution, and cohabitation no longer can be defined in such universalizing terms, as if there is one core definition for each. Rather, a constructivist view suggests that all knowledge is local and partial. For example, in defining sexual orientation, multiple dimensions must be accounted for to demonstrate that sexual orientation can be fluid and changeable over the life course (Klein, 1990). Fourth, rather than taking a distanced observer stance, a constructivist perspective privileges insider (informant) perspectives rather than the a priori theories generated by intellectuals. Finally, researchers must acknowledge that life-threatening problems are occurring—and always have occurred—in sexual relationships, problems such as HIV/AIDS risk, unwanted pregnancies, sexual violence, and the social engineering of sex. Research, therefore, should incorporate an ameliorative or interventionist effort as part of the production of knowledge (Gagnon & Parker, 1995).

In the current context of a technological revolution and the metaphoric shrinking of the world into a postmodern clash of cultures, it is imperative to use methods that can uncover behaviors and ideologies occurring in historically specific (e.g., local) cultures. Instead of the search for sweeping generalizations about human behavior and social relationships, a more cautious, partial, and contingent stance is necessary (Lindenbaum, 1995). Furthermore, the unit of analysis must shift to the relational level (Thompson & Walker, 1982). The postmodern turn in social science brings with it a renewed need for humility in the research process, with its concomitant acceptance of the partiality of our ability to know the "facts of life" (Lindenbaum, 1995, p. 275). Borrowing from critical theorists (Agger, 1998), we also should study what is not said and try to understand what lies beneath the visible and audible surface.

In a postmodern world, certain research methods are more suitable than others for generating these partial perspectives that are open to multiple realities. Ethnography, for example, offers greater promise than a priori quantifiable surveys to understand meanings that are not self-evident. Surveys continue to be better options than qualitative approaches if used to gather demographic data about master statuses of race, class, gender, sexual orientation, and so on (Laumann & Gagnon, 1995). Complex phenomena, such as the social relations of sexuality or forms of close relationships in which sexist, racist, and heterosexist ideology tend to distort people's recognition of their own lived reality, require in-depth methods that emphasize participant meanings to grasp new insights about previously mystified experiences.

## ► Qualitative Methods in the Close Relationship Field

To assess the use of qualitative methods in the study of close relationships, we examined recent issues of three leading journals in this interdisciplinary field over the past 5 years (1994-1998), starting with the first volume of *Personal Relationships*. We also examined the *Journal of Social and Personal Relationships* and the *Journal of Personality and Social Psychology*. We searched for the prevalence of publication of qualitative articles, types of qualitative methods, topical areas addressed, and types of data analysis techniques. We saw little use of qualitative methods in the leading empirical journals in the close relationship field. Apparently, the poststructural revolution has yet to have a major influence. The positivist perspective continues to be overwhelmingly dominant. Most scholars publishing in these journals have adopted a quantitative paradigm, even when using narrative, videotaped, or self-report data. Much of this literature reflects the data reduction strategy of converting par-

ticipants' words to numbers and then testing hypotheses. With a few exceptions, we noticed an absence of qualitative research in general, particularly of the type that uses ethnographic or feminist approaches. We now review some of this literature, first addressing the unique application of quantitative approaches to qualitative data and then examining in-depth investigations that were inherently more qualitative.

### *A Quantitative Approach to Qualitative Data*

An important strength in the existing literature is the concerted effort to combine qualitative and quantitative methodologies. In a journal with a decidedly quantitative and psychological focus, the *Journal of Personality and Social Psychology,* we observed the extent to which researchers took the language of participants and translated it into numbers for theoretically driven quantitative analysis. For example, Malle and Knobe (1997) transcribed notes written by undergraduates attempting to understand their "wonderings" about a bodily state, a feeling, a behavior, or an experience. Four of these wonderings were selected by participants and described more extensively in a questionnaire. Among other things, students described the circumstances in which their wonderings occurred and the content of those wonderings. For theoretical reasons, the authors coded these wonderings for perspective (actor vs. observer), for private versus communicative explanations, and for types of behavior (focused on all possible combinations of intentionality and observability). The authors determined that students wondered more about their own unintentional, unobservable behaviors than about the behaviors of others they interpreted as intentional and observable. This study enabled the researchers to identify actor and observer asymmetry in the behaviors that people choose to explain.

Other psychological research relies on videotaped interactions. This approach has the advantage of preserving the richness of interaction on film for repeated viewing by the researcher. Typically, however, researchers code specific aspects of interaction, counting them and perhaps rating the interaction quality (De Garmo & Forgatch, 1997b). These rates of behavioral frequency and quality then are subjected to statistical analysis.

One unique effort, described by Folkman (1997), involved four research teams applying distinct theoretical approaches to bereavement following the loss of a partner to AIDS. Folkman's team interviewed the respondents, who described the events and circumstances of the partner's death, their feelings and thoughts, the things that helped them cope, and the things that made the death more difficult. Paper-and-pencil measures were administered, and the interviews were transcribed. Each research team formulated hypotheses, coded the transcribed data, and then related its measures of coping to the paper-and-pencil assessments administered approximately one year after the death.

Nolen-Hoeksema, McBride, and Larson (1997) coded the transcripts for negative ruminative thinking, self-reflective thoughts, and references to social network problems. Pennebaker, Mayne, and Francis (1997) coded the degree to which bereaved partners used emotional language and produced a coherent narrative about the death. Stein, Folkman, Trabasso, and Richards (1997) categorized episodes in the narratives according to time (past, present, or future) and then identified the category of each appraisal (i.e., an initiating event, a belief, an emotion, a goal, a plan, or an outcome). These categories were either positive (reflected a beneficial quality or influence) or negative (reflected a negative quality or influence). Finally, Weiss and Richards (1997) constructed a Bereavement Response Scale following the sequence of events of caretaking, partner's death, rituals of departure, and dealing with grief. Separate positive and negative scores were generated for variables within each stage.

These studies were unique in that each used the same participants dealing with the same precipitating event and employed the same method of data collection. Thus, differences in results could be seen as reflecting unique theoretical approaches and their application within traditional quantitative approaches. Ironically, the data were comprised of individual narratives around the loss of a partner. As was true of a number of psychological studies within the close relationship field, the data were coded and analyzed quantitatively. Notably, in providing an overview of these four studies, Folkman (1997) identified as a limitation the use of narratives given as spontaneous responses to open-ended questions. The four studies in this special collection illustrate the potential that exists in social psychology for a truly qualitative approach. Although some might see them as qualitative, from the point of view of the qualitative research tradition, they are quantitative studies. Narrative data were changed or arranged in categories that were numerically described. These numbers then were correlated with well-being or mood measures. The highlighting of narrative data as a limitation and the use of exclusively quantitative strategies to address qualitative data point to the potential conflict across disciplines within the close relationship field regarding the definition of qualitative research.

That people wonder about their own feelings, experiences, and behaviors, as well as about those of the individuals with whom they interact, would be of interest to many in the close relationship field. We have seen a quantitative approach to these wonderings, focused on their structure and attributes. Qualitative researchers would focus on their context, how people think about and experience their wonderings, how they think their subsequent actions and interactions are influenced by these wonderings, and the specific content and meaning of their wonderings.

It is unlikely that quantitative and qualitative researchers would develop procedures that would produce identical types of data. In the end, however, both confront volumes of information yet approach the process of data reduction in unique ways. Quantitative researchers develop ways in which to categorize and count information, spell these processes and procedures out in detail, and subject the resulting counts and categories to quantitative analysis. Qualitative researchers sift through the data repeatedly and ever more systematically, moving between the data and theory in an increasingly refined way that ultimately produces a conclusion or an understanding. Consistent with a scientific approach, both subject their procedures and conclusions to the scientific scrutiny of peer review and the requirement that the research process and its findings must withstand the tests of replicability and time.

On the one hand, quantitative researchers who begin with narrative data might find it difficult, if not impossible, to imagine that a scientist could analyze such data, building to a distinct and sharp focus without the assistance of precise and pre-articulated rules, interrater reliability, and ultimately the application of statistical techniques. On the other hand, qualitative researchers might despair at the degree to which information must be abstracted from its individual, social, and cultural contexts to meet the requirements of statistical analyses.

## Using Qualitative Methods and Qualitative Analyses

We did find a number of authentic qualitative studies in the close relationship literature. Several articles used key features of qualitative research including interpretive theory, small in-depth samples, and qualitative analytic methods. Braithwaite and Baxter (1995), for example, reported on a study that "adds to the relatively small corpus of dialectically centered research on relational rituals" (p. 179), in which 25 informants from 16 married couples described their marital vow renewal experiences. Using interview data and a dialectical theoretical perspective, the authors identified three themes in their informants' discourse about their renewal vows (private-public, stability-change, and conventionality-uniqueness), thereby advancing an important conceptualization about how couples experience contradictory relationship themes. This conceptualization has received little attention to date. Braithwaite and Baxter (1995) argued,

"Relationships are maintained to the extent that the parties successfully manage over time the dynamic interplay of opposing tendencies . . . [and] a couple never resolves contradictions into some idealized state of homeostasis or transcendence" (pp. 180-181). In addition to the theoretical contribution of this work, another benefit is the focus on a relatively unexamined aspect of everyday life. Clearly, the nature of qualitative methods allows doors to open for unexplored or distorted aspects of relational dynamics.

In a second example, Masheter (1997) derived a sample of three case studies from a larger project on friendship between divorced spouses. She documented some of the details of marital relationship histories and postdivorce relations of formerly married partners with children. Using a modified analytic induction technique similar to grounded theory, Masheter selected particularly rich cases from two larger samples totaling 497 individual interviews in which 9 couples had been interviewed multiple times. Then, using a detailed episode analysis, interviewees were asked to interpret each episode, line by line. Masheter used a narrative analysis technique to identify and cluster themes in the three case studies. This analysis supported previously published findings including the importance of postdivorce networks, friendship, and former partner cooperation. It also demonstrated that postdivorce friendship, thought by previous researchers to be unrealistic, was possible whenever couples confirm personal growth for selves and each other.

A third distinct contribution was provided by Floyd (1996a), who interviewed 80 pairs of brothers, asking them to describe a situation or an event during which they felt especially close to each other. Phenomenological analyses were applied to the narratives, from which five themes were drawn. Only some of the themes had been identified in prior research. Furthermore, some themes evident from quantitative research did not emerge from the analysis of these narratives. Floyd's review of the related literature highlighted its emphasis on comparing closeness *across* rather than *within* relationship forms. This emphasis precludes exploration and understanding of within-gender, within-relationship closeness. One cannot presume that quantitative measures of relationship closeness developed and validated within this cross-relationship paradigm would provide a thorough or even an adequate assessment of closeness between brothers. Floyd argued that the findings call into question the ecological validity of closeness measures. These three examples show the use and potential significance of a new paradigm in conjunction with qualitative methods in the close relationship field.

Close relationship scholars are well schooled in the quantitative tradition and have found new ways in which to get at greater meaning by adding qualitative methods to existing research designs. We believe that the time is ripe for a new appreciation of the value of qualitative methods applied from within a poststructuralist paradigm. Important new knowledge is created when qualitative methods stand alone and are not used simply as an additive to quantitative methods. Next, we make cases for uncovering deeper meaning by starting with a qualitative approach.

## ▶ Expanding Our Collective Worldview: A Case for Qualitative Research

In this section, we demonstrate ways in which to use a qualitative approach to research. We organize this discussion around central benefits of qualitative research and draw from our own work and that of scholars whose work we know to illustrate the value of a qualitative approach for the study of close relationships.

### *Asking Deeper Questions in Qualitative Research*

By using a depth method such as qualitative research, it is possible to ask deeper questions than one can pose in a quantitative study. Rather than *yes, no,* or *how much,* in qualitative research, with the emphasis on meaning and exposing underlying processes and struc-

tures in social relations, complex questions can be employed to capture ambiguities. Allen, Blieszner, Roberto, Farnsworth, and Wilcox (1999) recently investigated how older parents perceive that their relationships with adult children are affected by family structural diversity experienced in the two generations. Noting that the contemporary discourse about families adheres to a nostalgic belief in structural homogeneity and relational harmony with little basis in reality (Coontz, 1992), they interviewed 45 older adults about their family relationships including intergenerational, lateral, and chosen kin (e.g., those whom they felt were like family but with whom they had no legal ties). Participants described in great detail the diversity they themselves had experienced including premarital pregnancy, adoption, cohabitation, multiple marriages, and providing care for grandchildren. One surprising thing about these data was the way in which participants described dynamic transformations in their family histories yet still normalized their experiences. For the most part, participants relied on messages about family decline from the popular discourse as the benchmark to compare their own experiences. This qualitative approach revealed the distinction between the reality of people's relationship structures and the ideology they used to account for how they presumably differed from a mythical norm.

### *The Researcher Is the Instrument*

Qualitative researchers are active participants in the research process and the major instrument in interview studies. Their presence is necessary to establish rapport, to foster the flow of conversation between participant and researcher, to observe details in social settings, and to write field notes about what they are observing.

Qualitative researchers bring an acknowledged theoretical and emotional sensitivity to empirical observation, interviews, and fieldwork (Kleinman & Copp, 1993). Projects are shaped by the theoretical commitments in which a researcher has been trained, by the conventions of one's discipline, and by the agenda or motivations one has as a researcher and as a citizen (Thompson, 1992). Action researchers in education, for example, might be motivated to demonstrate the harmful effects of racism on the learning environment and on the potential friendships that can be experienced by black and white students (hooks, 1994). Researchers working with impoverished groups might want to ensure that not only policymakers but also the participants themselves will benefit from their endeavor and become empowered through the research process (Small, 1995). Feminists might be motivated to do research that can improve the material conditions of the women whose lives they study (Fonow & Cook, 1991).

In a project in which we collaborated (Allen, Demo, Walker, & Acock, 1996), the first author (Allen) conducted loosely structured in-depth interviews with parents and siblings of lesbian women and gay men in her local community. She used her insider's location in multiple contexts to gain access to a sample of these adults and their families. These locations included an academic position, a private identity as a lesbian mother, an adult daughter of heterosexually married parents, and a sister of a gay brother. Allen's multiple identities and social locations—her insider's perspective—helped her to establish rapport and conduct interviews with people in the broader community. They also gave her entrée through a local chapter of a national support organization for families and friends of lesbians and gay men.

As the interviews were conducted, Allen shared the transcripts with the second author (Walker) and other members of their research team. She wrote detailed process notes about her experiences as an interviewer after each interview. Process notes are a written reflection on the experience of conducting an interview. They are a descriptive account of the researcher's experience in the field, providing a narrative of the setting and the interview process as well as emerging hunches or flashes of insight that are closely connected to that experience. They include tentative pieces of analysis, methodological difficulties or successes,

and personal emotional experiences (Lofland & Lofland, 1995, p. 88). Their consistent and regular construction following each interview enables the researcher to keep up with the volume of data and to preserve insights that emerge in the context of data collection (Kaufman, 1994).

Allen also wrote theoretical memos, which are "written records of analysis related to the formulation of theory" (Strauss & Corbin, 1990, p. 197). Their function is to help the researcher to build an understanding of the relationship, the process, or the context under study (Glaser & Strauss, 1967). She shared the texts she produced with members of the research team, who in turn responded to the texts and transcripts with their own experiences, hunches, insights, and theoretical observations. Together, the team members shaped the data analysis by posing questions that ran the gamut of insider-outsider perspectives on the process of interviewing members of a community in which other team members did not live.

As the primary instrument in the study, Allen kept a running account of her feelings, observations, and insights that emerged during the process. After conducting six in-depth interviews and writing up the process notes for each one, she prepared a memo in which she reflected on the first interviews and tried to make new meanings out of the fieldwork. A portion of the memo, excerpted as follows, reveals the awareness of the insider-outsider perspective that was facilitated by a qualitative approach:

> This study is revealing to me how much lies beneath the surface in families. Appearances reveal little; the truth waits just below. In families with a story to tell, truths don't take long to seep out. One scratch and the surface breaks. The dynamics of reflexivity work in my favor as I interview these parents. It matters that I told them I am gay; it helps the respondents and me by allowing us to know each other as real people and allowing our projections and reflections to push us toward the kind of familiarity necessary to get the interview into deeper areas. . . . I've also noticed that these older

parents are experiencing periods of emotional estrangement from particular children. It is not always the gay child who is on the outs. Parents tell stories of their prodigal son or daughter, but nearly all of them eventually make their way back in. My hunch is [that] the worst thing parents deal with is a child's drug or alcohol addiction. Having a gay child, at least to parents who have sought community support, is less an issue than the problems of their other kids. Having a child who is out of control with drugs or alcohol can be a cruel trauma. These parents seem helpless at not being able to pull their own kid out of despair. We need to explore this in our research. Are they saying that there are worse things than having a gay child? Or, does this hunch merely reflect the benefits of talking to someone empathic about what [he or she is] going through? Talking is important—to release feelings, sort out knowledge, validate oneself and one's child. Of course, these parents have come far in accepting their child. Next, we need to interview parents who are not far along on that journey. Is talking beneficial under those circumstances as well?

Theoretical memos such as this help the researcher to sharpen his or her focus; help the researcher to pay attention to his or her own influence on the content of the interview; alert the researcher to issues, concerns, and meanings that he or she had not anticipated; help the researcher to identify questions that should be asked in subsequent interviews with the same or new participants; and suggest further avenues for exploration. They help the thoughtful researcher to attend to the project's various perspectives and voices—the investigator's, the informant's (Kaufman, 1994), and the context.

### *Making Subjectivity Explicit and Useful in the Research Process*

A distinguishing feature of qualitative research is that there are many opportunities for the researcher to participate explicitly in the process of creating knowledge. This type of research allows the researcher to be transparent to self and participants and to use existing theories in explicit ways. Rather than a distanced stance, in which the researcher avoids self-consciousness in the field or other research context, having an open and theorized approach to subjectivity enhances the quality and usefulness of the work.

Emerson et al. (1995) described three key steps to using one's own subjective experience in the beginning steps of a research study. As ethnographers, their purpose is to teach students how to enter a field and not become mired in their own first impressions. Ways to be sensitive to subjectivity and yet privilege the views of the people one is investigating include (a) being open to and taking note of initial impressions by using the senses to guide what one notices, (b) observing and recording key events and incidents including one's own reactions to events and feelings, and (c) moving beyond initial reactions to an "open sensitivity to what those in the setting experience and react to as significant" (p. 28). The purpose of acknowledging oneself in the research matrix is not to privilege one's own point of view but rather to use personal reactions in a setting as a way in which to appreciate the insider's view of the people one is studying.

### ► Conclusion

Qualitative research is positioned to make unique contributions to the understanding of close relationships in ways that reflect their unique nature and forms, their distinctive processes, the individual's role in their creation and interpretation, and the contemporary sociohistorical context. These contributions also have the potential to improve the quality of people's interpersonal lives. So many dimensions of close relationships have yet to be examined in this rich and compelling way. As we bring qualitative methodologies to bear on the field, we enhance exponentially knowledge and understanding of our most private, complex, and meaningful social connections.

# Part II

---

# RELATIONSHIP FORMS

# Contents

# Network Overlap and Third-Party Influence in Close Relationships

*Robert M. Milardo*
*Heather Helms-Erikson*

In this chapter, we explore how social network theory can be a productive means of accounting for significant social experiences, with an emphasis on conditions or outcomes that characterize primary partners (e.g., spouses) and their relationships. Social networks, or an individual's array of close associates including friends and kin relations, serve as a social context in which relationships develop. Network theory, which emphasizes the importance of social context, serves to broaden the scope of inquiry from a singular interest in what occurs between primary partners to that which occurs between partners and their closest associates as these friends and kinfolk actively influence one another. Although social context can be defined in a variety of ways, each with different emphases (Adams & Allan, 1998a), network theory provides a framework and set of concepts that are expressed in terms of the actual relationships

linking individuals, relationships that define the content and structure of local communities. In focusing on primary partnerships (i.e., marriage and marriage-like relationships) and the influence of social networks, we exclude some important and well-developed areas that are tangential to our purpose including children's networks and the bidirectional effects of parents' and children's social affiliations (Cochran, Larner, Riley, Gunnarsson, & Henderson, 1990), the effects of social support and social interference on individual or relational well-being (Pierce, Lakey, Sarason, & Sarason, 1997), and the links between divorce and network relations (Feld & Carter, 1998; Milardo, 1987).

The chapter is divided into two sections. In the first section, we focus on the concept of network overlap (i.e., the degree to which primary partners share network members) and maintain joint and separate network associates including friends or kin. We emphasize the theoretical and empirical work on network overlap where we believe future work on the link between network structure and relationship outcomes should be directed. Following the review of network overlap and some closely allied measures of network structure, we examine recent work on third-party influence on marital relationships. Here, we address how relations with specific third parties influence partners or their relationships.

Throughout the chapter, we use the term *associate* as a generic reference to all types of network members including kin, friends, co-workers, and so on, although typically the networks that form the basis for most research are largely comprised of immediate kin (i.e., parents and siblings) and close friendships (Milardo, 1992). We use the abbreviations *P* (for person) and *O* (for other) to refer to partners in a close relationship such as a marriage or other forms of committed, long-standing relationships. Such abbreviations are preferable to terms such as *spouse, marriage,* and *family* that can be useful but are limiting theoretically in that they call attention to legal definitions of close relationships rather than fundamental social psychological processes that define their character (Scanzoni, Polonko, Teachman, & Thompson, 1989; Weiss, 1998). In addition, our theory should apply equally well to the substantial numbers of young cohabiting couples (Bumpass & Sweet, 1989), the rapidly increasing participation of the elderly in cohabiting relationships (Chevan, 1996), and relationships in which partners are unable to marry as in the case of gay or lesbian couples.

## ▶ Network Overlap and Related Measures of Interconnectedness

Interest in spouses' joint networks has a long academic ancestry, having appeared in the early work of Ackerman (1963), Babchuk and Bates (1963), Bott (1971), Burgess and Cottrell (1939), Goode (1956), and Zimmerman and Broderick (1956). Much of this early work attempted to link network overlap, or some measure of the number of joint and separate associates, to marital outcomes, with varying results. Babchuk and Bates (1963) reported the first clear descriptive data on couples' joint and separate associates. They reported an often-cited finding that the joint associates of spouses originate in the personal networks of husbands. Husbands dominate in the selection of friends, or so it was argued. Our reanalysis of their original data (available from the authors) found no significant gender difference in the origin of joint friendships, although in a more recent inquiry of dating couples, men again are found to more frequently be the source of the joint friendships (Bendtschneider & Duck, 1993). Babchuk and Bates (1963) also reported relatively low numbers of shared friendships, which has become a fairly stable finding in more recent research among dating couples (Kim & Stiff, 1991) and spouses (Stein, Bush, Ross, & Ward, 1992) in which the number of shared friendships averages one or two.

Ackerman (1963) made several theoretical advances regarding the possible significance of mutual associations when he hypothesized that divorce rates would be low when marriages are embedded in a network of joint affiliations and high when spouses maintain separate affiliations. Some support for the hypothesis is found based on tests with data on 62 societies from the Human Relations Area Files. Zimmerman and Broderick (1956) similarly argued that couples who maintain common interests and common social connections would have more stable marriages. Essentially, they found evidence for homogamy; that is, spouses who maintain friends similar to themselves are less likely to experience divorce. Taken together, this early work essentially argued that when spouses share associations, they are likely to be affected by the same norms and values, and to the extent that network members know one another, they can coordinate influence. Simply put, joint affiliations were viewed as an index of marital interdependence or satisfaction (Burgess & Cottrell, 1939), and the theme continues to be represented in a leading contemporary measure of marital quality, the Dyadic Adjustment Scale (Spanier, 1976).

Despite this early interest, relatively little theoretical development or empirical work has appeared until recently, and basic questions regarding the conceptualization and measurement of overlap remain as well as questions regarding the causal connection of overlap to marital outcomes. We consider each of these issues in what follows.

### Defining Network Overlap, Boundary Density, and Cross-Network Contact

Overlap typically is used to describe the proportion of network members shared by two partners in a close relationship (Milardo, 1986; Parks, 1997; Surra & Milardo, 1991). For example, spouses who share many of the same network members have relatively overlapping networks and presumably some separate associations (e.g., personal friends) that are not shared between the spouses. Two basic measures of overlap can be calculated. As an individual measure, overlap is calculated as the proportion of shared network members (e.g., jointly held friends) relative to the total number of members composing the individual's network. It may be calculated as

$$O_p = JA_p / (SA_p + JA_p) \times 100 \quad (3.1a)$$

$$O_o = JA_o / (SA_o + JA_o) \times 100, \quad (3.1b)$$

where $O_p$ and $O_o$ represent proportional measures of overlap for $P$ and $O$, respectively; $JA$ represents the number of joint associates; and $SA$ represents the number of separate associates.

As a dyadic measure, overlap is computed as the proportion of shared network members relative to the total number of unique individuals included in either partner's network. It may be calculated as

$$O_{p/o} = JA_{p/o} / (SA_p + SA_o \quad (3.2)$$
$$+ JA_{p/o}) \times 100.$$

The two measures can be quite different and differentially related to relationship outcomes. For example, Kim and Stiff (1991) reported dyadic overlap of about 10% among a small sample of undergraduate dating couples. These individuals each listed 5.8 significant others on average (including the joint associate). By comparing the networks of couples, we find that they have one member in common; dyadic overlap is approximately 10% (or 1/10.6). When we look at an individual measure of overlap based on $P$'s knowledge of the people in $O$'s network (or, conversely, the network members' knowledge of $P$), the degree of overlap appears much higher (about 73%). Of the 5.8 persons listed by each respondent on average, 4.2 (73%) said that they knew the respondent's partner, although most of these members were not considered joint friends (i.e., significant others) by both partners.

Fairly low indexes of dyadic level overlap are typical when the networks are largely comprised of non-kin, and non-kin seem to typify the networks of young, white, and middle class dating couples (e.g., 78% non-kin in Kim & Stiff, 1991). Peers might dominate the networks of young white dating couples, but they are not so characteristic of young Latino and African American dating partners (Bryant, 1996), nor are they typically characteristic of married couples (Stein et al., 1992). In these types of couples, kin often predominate, comprising approximately 50% or more of the networks of close associates (Milardo, 1992; Moore, 1990), and kinship sectors are far more likely to overlap relative to friendship sectors (Stein et al., 1992; Veiel, Crisand, Stroszeck-Somschor, & Herrle, 1991). Cohabiting lesbian couples are somewhat unique in that they share more friends but not more kin than heterosexual couples (Julien, Chartrand, & Begin, 1999; Ulin & Milardo, 1992). Perhaps this is important because it might indicate that they are creating a local environment that is composed of supportive friends in the face of a broader environment that lacks institutional or cultural support. At the same time, by excluding kin, they essentially are reflecting the closeting from selective kin and the corresponding fracturing of their networks into those who know of and approve of their relationships and those who do not know and might disapprove of their relationships (Ulin & Milardo, 1992).

Another somewhat related concept, boundary density (BD), occasionally is confused with network overlap. Niemeijer (1973) first proposed the concept of BD as the number of cross-links between members of two networks. When all the members of one partner's network know all the members of the other partner's network, we conclude that the two networks are fully cross-linked and BD is 100%. The networks we compare could be separate groupings of individuals (P's network and O's network), or they could be segments of the same network (e.g., P's kin and P's friends). BD is formally defined as the number of actual cross-links relative to the total number of possible links joining two memberships. It may be computed as

$$BD = (100 \times CL_{1,2}) / (N_1 \times N_2) \quad (3.3)$$

where $CL_{1,2}$ is the number of cross-links between the members of the two networks being compared and $N_1$ and $N_2$ refer to the total sizes of the networks (or network sectors) being compared (Niemeijer, 1973). In addition, it may be interpreted as the probability that any two people selected at random from different networks (or network sectors) will be linked to one another.

The measure of BD has to do with the interrelations among network members rather than the relationship between a network member and a target person such as a spouse. It is a structural feature that characterizes the relations of network members with one another (excluding P or O), in contrast to overlap that concerns the linkage of network members with P or O. BD is similar to Parks's (1997)

slightly more refined concept of "cross-network density" or the "extent to which members of each partner's network know and communicate with members of the other partner's network" (p. 358). Cross-network density defines the necessary (cross-)links between network members in terms of knowledge and communication with other network members. Parks was unclear about its computation, although presumably it would be calculated as BD in Equation 3.3.

BD and network overlap are unique concepts and should not be confused, as has occurred on occasion. We can imagine a situation in which all friends of spouses are shared but none of them know each other. In this case, overlap of the friendship sector is 100%, but BD is 0. Or, we can imagine a situation in which all network members of P and O know one another (BD = 100%), but P and O consider their respective networks separate and they do not share associations (overlap = 0%).

The theoretical implications of BD for families or other forms of close relationships are undeveloped but are apt to be quite distinct from overlap in terms of the causal conditions that fashion these features or their consequences. It is possible that the degree of BD could be related to the strength and effectiveness of a network's attempts to influence P or O (e.g., to leave a violent marriage). For example, when kinship and friendship sectors are more highly integrated (i.e., kin and friends know one another), they are able to coordinate attempts to influence a target individual or couple.

Parks (1997) identified another related measure of structure, "cross-network contact," referring to the degree to which "each partner knows and communicates with members of the other's network" (p. 357). Cross-network contact has been operationalized as the number or proportion of people from O's network that P has met and the amount of contact with them. It is positively correlated with measures of partners' closeness and commitment (Eggert & Parks, 1987; Parks, Stan, & Eggert, 1983). We suspect that these types of measures will be very highly correlated with overlap because, in the case of networks defined in terms of actual interaction (i.e., so-called interactive networks), overlap and cross-network contact are nearly equivalent to the individual measures of overlap defined in Equation 3.1a. In the case of networks defined in terms of significant others, or people who are important to *P,* there might be some distinctions between overlapping members and members who are known to *P* but not considered significant others by *P* or listed in *P*'s network. Stein et al. (1992) reported just such a case in which a woman depended on her husband to learn of his family: "I get the scoop from him [husband] on what his brother's kids are doing, even though I don't talk to his brother much" (p. 378). In another case, a wife reported, "He [husband] tells me what goes on with his relatives from work [in the family business], so I know what's happening when his parents call" (p. 378). Both of these cases illustrate situations in which a wife knew members of her husband's network (i.e., cross-network ties) but presumably did not consider them essential members of her own network.

### Network Overlap and Relationship Outcomes

As couples become increasingly interdependent throughout their personal lives, they are hypothesized to develop increasingly interdependent social lives (Milardo, 1986). To a certain extent, this simple hypothesis is supported. In a longitudinal study of dating, Milardo (1982) had partners keep daily records of their interactions with others. As dating relationships deepened, partners reported increases in the absolute numbers of mutual associates as well as the proportions of mutual associates. These findings have been replicated in other studies, although typically with cross-sectional data (Eggert & Parks, 1987; Kim & Stiff, 1991; Parks et al., 1983). The development of an overlapping network parallels increasing pair commitment. Structural interdependence parallels relationship inter

dependence. In moving beyond this essentially descriptive work on relationship development, we derive two basic propositions linking overlap and relationship outcomes. In one position, the effects of overlap are thought to be relatively direct and are a consequence of the placement of network members relative to one another as well as their status as jointly held associates. We refer to these forms of influence as structural effects. In another position, the effects of overlap are examined at a relational level or through the direct interaction of partners with individual third parties, some of whom are regarded as overlapping or mutual associates and some of whom are regarded as separately held associates. We consider each set of propositions, the processes they imply, and the potentially confounding factors in testing them.

*Structural effects on relationship outcomes.* Networks can affect relationships by virtue of the structure or pattern of ties among network members. Overlapping associates are thought to be important because they have a vested interest in each partner and in their relationship (Johnson & Milardo, 1984; Milardo, 1982). In this way, overlapping associates should be more highly motivated to influence pair members and pair processes relative to separately held associates. To the extent that overlapping associates know one another, they are able to coordinate influence whether that influence takes the form of instrumental support (e.g., a loan of money, explicit directions); emotional support (e.g., positive regard); recreational opportunity (e.g., a surprise anniversary party); an instance of norm regulation, sanction, or negative support; or some combination of these. These arguments call on two simultaneous features of a network: the degree of overlapping membership and the density of that membership.

Earlier, we defined the density of two networks (or two sectors of one network) as the probability that any two people drawn at random from the networks are connected, and we referred to this feature as boundary density *(BD).* To our knowledge, only one study has investigated the interconnections of *BD* with relationship or individual outcomes. Cotton (1995), in a sample of 78 couples with young children, reported that for wives, marital satisfaction was lower when the overlapping network of close friends was dense (i.e., high *BD*), a very curious finding and one not replicated for husbands in her sample. Kim and Stiff (1991) used a hybrid version of *BD* defined as the proportion of cross-links between mutual friends. It was highly correlated with dyadic overlap ($r = .65$), and taken together, overlap and the cross-linkage measure were predictive of relationship closeness between romantic partners. Others have used the term *BD* while defining it as network stability (Wilcox, 1981), or simple overlap (Hansen, Fallon, & Novotny, 1991; Kazak & Marvin, 1984).

The link between overlap and marital or primary partnership outcomes is largely supported in the literature. Cotton and her colleagues (Cotton, 1995; Cotton, Antill, & Cunningham, 1993) report that wives and husbands experience greater marital satisfaction when they share mutual friends and extended family, with about 20% of the variance in satisfaction explained. These effects might not be symmetrical with regard to gender in that husbands' knowledge of wives' associates is important for both wives' and husbands' marital satisfaction, but wives' knowledge of husbands' associates does not predict satisfaction (Cotton, 1995). Husbands' degree of overlap with their wives' networks explains about 40% to 50% of spouses' marital satisfaction. Overlap also seems to distinguish distressed and nondistressed couples, although the effect size is modest (less than 20%) (Hansen et al., 1991). Among lesbian couples, individual indexes of overlap were modest predictors of relationship closeness and stability (explained variances less than 20%) (Ulin & Milardo, 1992), although both gay and lesbian couples believe common associations with an accepting family and friends to be an important element in the maintenance of their primary partnerships.

There is some suggestion in this literature that the precise definition and enumeration of personal networks can have an effect on the predictive capability of any structural feature. Generally, procedures that limit the number of network members identified also limit the variance in structural measures. For example, Cotton et al. (1993) limited the networks identified by respondents to a maximum of 6 individuals, whereas Cotton (1995) used an upper limit of 20 network members and, not inconsequentially, reported far stronger relationships between network features and relationship outcomes.

Structural effects, or in fact any gross articulation of overlap, include an ambiguous element in that the overlap is confounded with network composition and pair interdependence. Without controlling for network composition, we cannot judge whether overlap is associated directly or indirectly with an outcome measure or whether such a correlation is purely spurious and the result of some other factor such as the proportion of kin in the network. Immediate kin, and especially parents and parents-in-law, typically are included in networks of significant others (Burger & Milardo, 1995; Wellman & Wellman, 1992), and they typically are viewed as mutual associations (Stein et al., 1992). Consequently, it is not surprising to find that when separate measures of overlap among friends versus kin are reported, kin overlap is far more substantial (Stein et al., 1992; Veiel et al., 1991).

In all the work completed thus far, there is the problem of causal priority. It is quite possible that couples who are close develop joint associations because they are close. Rather than being a cause, overlap might be a consequence of pair interdependencies. Bryant and Conger (1999), in a longitudinal study of long-term marriages, examined the connection of marital success—defined in terms of satisfaction, stability, and commitment—with several network features. "Affective overlap," or the degree to which spouses like each other's closest friends, was an insignificant predictor of later measures of marital success, contrary to the authors' predictions. They did, however, find evidence for the reverse. Marital success predicted later affective overlap for both husbands and wives. This finding suggests that essential relationship qualities, such as satisfaction and commitment, can influence beliefs about network members.

*Relational or third-party effects.* Overlapping associations are thought to build on the couple's joint enterprise and common experience, events that increase the basis for pair interdependence. Implicated here are pair identity issues in which mutual friends come to view the couple as a unit and, through mutual affiliation and joint leisure partners, increase their own sense of common identity (Surra & Milardo, 1991). Interactions with mutual associates also can result in direct benefits for how partners view one another. Larson and Bradney (1988), using a diary method of recording momentary mood states (the Experience Sampling Technique), demonstrated that spouses report the highest positive feelings toward their partners when in the company of mutual friends. These friends had the effect of transforming the attention of spouses from the mundane, constant, and ordinary business of family life to the more playful, unpredictable, and unique qualities of the partners.

Here, the effect of overlap is thought to operate through the direct relationships with third parties who are viewed as mutual or shared associates, either friends or kin. These direct effects include both provisions and preventive functions. Provisions include companionship, instrumental support, and emotional support. Preventive functions include encouraging joint investments (i.e., Johnson, Caughlin, & Huston's, 1999, structural commitments), discouraging separate and separating activities and investments, and reducing the possibility of separate and competing alliances (Klein & Milardo, 1993).

Julien and Markman (1991) presented an alternative position in which the link between overlap and marital adjustment was thought to be mediated by companionship or the degree to which spouses socialize separately or together with third parties. In their work, for both husbands and wives, overlap (individual

measures) was positively associated with marital adjustment. By contrast, having frequent leisure activities with network members apart from spouses was negatively correlated with marital adjustment. Of course, the causal direction could go either way with either process preceding the other. Nonetheless, whether the links between overlap and adjustment were mediated by indexes of "lone companionship" is unclear and would require an additional test of the effects, controlling for the mediating variable, on the link between overlap and adjustment. We suspect that when spouses maintain overlapping networks and share leisure activity, maintaining separate associations can have very positive effects on primary relationship outcomes, which is at least in part what we argue in the next section. The negative effect of lone companionship may occur only under conditions in which spouses maintain few shared associates, and this defines a moderating effect rather than a mediating effect.

► **Third-Party Effects on Close Relationships**

Thus far, we have addressed links between social networks and partnerships by exploring how couples' primary relationships are embedded in a larger social structure of relationships with other personal associates. In this section, we refocus our inquiry to a more microsystemic examination of the connections among specific social network members, partners (e.g., spouses), and primary partnerships (e.g., marriage). Here, we pay particular attention to how partners' relationships with close associates can affect their primary partnerships. For example, how does a wife's relationship with a friend affect her relationship with her husband? To address this and similar questions, we begin by discussing Marks's (1986) "three corners" conceptualization of marriage, a theoretical framework that provides a useful way in which to think about the connections among partners, third parties, and primary partnerships. Next, using principles from Marks to frame the literature, we review the small body of research that exists on third-party effects on marriage and introduce new works in progress.

### Marks's Theory of Triangles

Marks (1986), informed by the family therapy concept of "triangulation" in relationships (Bowen, 1978), presented a dynamic model regarding how married individuals balance their relationships with spouses and outside interests. This model provides a useful framework for conceptualizing third-party effects on primary partnerships in proposing that married individuals are in a constant process of balancing the demands of "three corners" of a triangle. In this model, each corner represents a domain of activity, with the three primary corners representing the inner self, the primary partnership, and important "outside" interests (e.g., work, recreation, other relationships). Marks argued that spouses' involvement in their third corners, which could be relationships with close associates, is closely related to marital dynamics:

> Insofar as people have an ongoing emotional investment in any such interest, it will enter into their emotional dynamics with their primary partners, who must then compete with it if they wish more time and attention given to the twosome, or at the very least they must in some way coordinate with it. . . . When tensions mount in a twosome, one or both partners will seek to relieve the discomfort by intensifying their interaction with their third corners. . . . Depending on the circumstances, the spouses' convergence of triangling moves may calm down a relationship to a level of cool complacency, or bring new energy into it, or heat it to the boiling point, or drive the couple far apart and then determine whether they feel sorry or glad about the situation. (p. 5)

Marks's analysis illustrates the complexity involved in balancing relations between primary partners and close associates, and it underscores the dynamic nature of relationships.

Several principles from Marks's (1986) three corners conceptualization of relationships can be applied to our consideration of third-party effects on primary partnerships. First, Marks's work emphasized the importance of considering the links between (a) the third party and the self and (b) the third party and the primary partnership (comprised of the self and the partner), all the while alluding to the potential negative and positive implications of third-party effects. Implicit in this conceptualization of relationships is the understanding that what goes on between a spouse and a third party has implications for the primary partnership. The reverse also is true. The relationship processes that spouses engage in, or fail to engage in, have implications for what they do with, or need from, their respective close associates. Marks suggested that to fully understand how relations with third parties can affect a primary partnership, it is important to consider the *process of relating,* not only in the partner's relationship with an associate but also within the primary partnership. As Marks pointed out, each dyad is characterized by interactions and relationship processes, and what occurs (or does not occur) in one relationship might affect what transpires in the other. Finally, Marks contended that each dimension of the three corners is dynamic. That is, individuals, primary partnerships, and relationships with third parties change over time, and a change in one of these three corners is likely to elicit change in another corner.

What currently is known about how the three corners of the self, primary partnership, and close associate interact is sketchy. With the exception of what can be gleaned from a handful of descriptively rich qualitative studies that, for the most part, use relatively small samples of heterosexual married individuals (Cohen, 1992; Gullestad, 1984; O'Connor,

1992; Oliker, 1989; Rubin, 1985), we know very little about the impact of relationships with third parties on marriage. The lack of research on partnered adults' close relationships with third parties can be accounted for in part by the steadfast application of the mid-century model of the "companionate marriage" in which spouses are seen as each other's best and only necessary friends. Arguing this point, Cancian (1987) contended that both American society and American researchers traditionally have held a narrow view of couples' relationships. She argued that the heterosexual couple is emphasized as the major close relationship for adults, to the exclusion of other important close relationships. Although recent studies suggest that some couples might come close to resembling such companionate unions (Risman & Johnson-Sumerford, 1998; Schwartz, 1994), it is doubtful that most adults experience their close relationships in this manner or that, even if they do, they are unaffected by their associations with third parties, whether they are close or mere acquaintances. This myopic view of adult relationships seems to have persisted, however, despite such pivotal works as Weiss's (1973) study, *Loneliness,* in which he discovered that even when people were happily married and connected to kin, they remained lonely and depressed if they did not have friends in their lives. In short, humans are inherently social and socially dynamic. They begin and end relationships, and they are influenced by their social constructions.

### Close Associates and the Self

Several studies provide insights into the connections between spouses' relations with third parties (i.e., the self and third corner) and suggest that close associates are sources of companionship (Connidis & Davies, 1990; Larson & Bradney, 1988; Rubin, 1985; Wellman & Wellman, 1992), instrumental support (Roberto & Scott, 1984-1985; Wellman & Wellman, 1992), and emotional support (Harrison, 1998; O'Connor, 1992; Oliker, 1989; Rubin, 1985). Qualitative studies (Harrison, 1998; O'Connor, 1992; Oliker, 1989; Rubin, 1985), however, point to gender differences in husbands' and wives' relationship experiences with close associates, suggesting that husbands are more likely to experience their relationships with third parties as sources of companionship and that wives are more likely to experience them as sources of emotional support. For example, Rubin's (1985) findings, based on in-depth interviews with 300 professional middle-class and working-class men and women between 25 and 55 years of age, resonate with gender differences in husbands' and wives' friendship experiences. (Rubin's vague description of her sample makes it impossible to ascertain how many of her 300 participants were married.) Most of the married men in Rubin's study reported having "augmenting relationships" with friends (defined as non-kin close associates). That is, married men tended to turn to their wives for emotional support and intimacy, and they viewed relationships outside the marriage as opportunities for conversation and companionship rather than for emotional outlet and expression. (Married men under 40 years of age were more likely to have close friendships after marriage. But even among this group, only 20% stated that their friends were sources of emotional support and intimacy.) By contrast, Rubin found that the married women in her study turned to their friends (often rather than their husbands) as sources of emotional support and intimacy. It could be suggested, then, that although both wives and husbands value emotional support and intimacy, they may achieve it in different ways and with different people (Blieszner, 1994b; Wright, 1988).

In addition to gender differences in spouses' relationship experiences with third parties, there is some evidence that the characteristics of spouses' relationships with close associates vary systematically based on the types of associates (e.g., friend, sibling) (Burger & Milardo, 1995; Wellman &

Wortley, 1989). For example, Wellman and Wortley (1989) found that parents provide a greater degree of support in a wider range of domains than do other types of kin or friends. For companionship, however, friends were found to be more supportive to spouses than were kin. In short, all network members are not created equal and should not be treated as such in research designs examining the connections among partners, close associates, and primary partnerships.

Some of the most intriguing findings related to the connections between close associates and spouses come from exploratory qualitative studies that delve into the processes occurring in spouses' relationships with their close associates outside the marriage. These findings point to spouses' (particularly wives') acquisition of two different types of emotional support: marital support and individual identity support. For example, through in-depth interviews with 17 working-class and middle-class married women and 3 divorced women who varied in age (20-59 years) and ethnicity, Oliker (1989) observed that married women sought out friends (i.e., defined as those they felt close to who were not spouses, parents, or children) rather than spouses for validation, understanding, and advice concerning their roles as wives and mothers. In addition, these wives engaged in high levels of disclosure about their marriages with their friends (a process Oliker labeled "marriage work"). These same women were certain that their husbands did not engage in marriage work with their friends.

The other striking finding related to the emotional support that wives received from their friends was the importance of identity-enhancing experiences with friends. In four very different samples (Harrison, 1998; O'Connor, 1992; Oliker, 1989; Rubin, 1985), wives reported turning to their close friends to talk about their beliefs, thoughts, and plans for or dreams of autonomy. ("Friends" is defined differently in each of these studies, and analyses do not take into account whether wives' close friends were kin or non-kin.) Harrison (1998) noted, "With friends, they [wives] believed they could 'be authentic,' find and create new identities, and present a number of alternative aspects of self" (p. 103). One of the strongest patterns to emerge from Oliker's (1989) research was the finding that married women avoided discussing issues related to autonomy and identity with their husbands, citing their husbands' control or tendency to want to change their minds as reasons, and instead turned to their friends. Taken together, these findings provide a glimpse of the processes that occur in husbands' and wives' close relationships outside of marriage and offer a springboard for exploring the connections between the primary partnership and close associates.

## Close Associates and the Primary Partnership

Whereas the findings regarding the role of relationships with close associates for spouses are far from comprehensive, even less is known about third-party effects on the marital relationship. Harrison (1998), Oliker (1989), and Rubin (1985) suggested that for married women, close friendships with female friends often make the marriage possible. Rubin (1985) proposed that, rather than being a strain on the marriage, married women's friendships are an important source of support for the marriage: "Woman after woman told of the ways in which friends fill the gaps the marriage relationship leaves, allowing the wife to appreciate those things the husband can give rather than to focus on those he can't" (p. 141). It appears that, at least for some women, relationships with close associates outside the marriage might facilitate the acceptance of the limits within the marriage.

Husbands, by contrast, might experience their own and their wives' friendships quite differently. For example, findings from one of the few published studies addressing third-party effects on marital quality show that, for husbands, frequency of contact with non-kin friends was not related to marital quality (Burger & Milardo, 1995). What did seem to matter for husbands' marital quality was their wives' frequency of contact with friends. Husbands with wives who had higher frequencies of contact with friends reported higher levels of marital negativity and ambivalence regarding their marriages and lower levels of love for their spouses. In addition, Burger and Milardo (1995) found that contact with kin was connected to marital quality for husbands and wives in different ways. For husbands, involvement with kin had a positive effect on marital quality, whereas for wives, the effect was negative. Husbands with greater contact with kin, particularly with fathers, reported greater love for their wives. By contrast, wives' greater contact with kin was linked to lower love for their husbands, greater marital negativity, and ambivalence regarding their marriages. Given Burger and Milardo's design and measures, causal direction cannot be determined, and little can be said about the *processes* occurring in spouses' relationships with kin and non-kin that might have contributed to their results. Their findings do, however, point to the complexity of spouses' multiple close relations and offer support for Marks's (1986) premise that what occurs in relationships between the self and third parties is closely linked to what occurs in the primary partnership. The findings further suggest that the type of close associate and the spouse's gender might be an important component in understanding third-party effects on marriage.

The few studies that have addressed the connections between close associates and primary partnerships have introduced questions and hypotheses worthy of more rigorous study. Building on these works, Helms-Erikson (1999a) conducted a study that examined the marital implications of husbands' and wives' relationships with close associates. Participants were drawn from a short-term longitudinal study on adolescent development and included 194 dual-earner married couples in the midst of raising at least two adolescent children. During in-home interviews, husbands and wives first were asked whether each had someone outside the immediate fam-

ily (i.e., spouse and children) whom they considered a good friend or to whom they felt close. To allow for the examination of how spouses' relationships with close associates might vary based on the type of relation, respondents who did have close associates (94% for wives, 75% for husbands) then were asked whether or not their close associates were kin and, if so, the nature of the kin relationship. Hoping to tap the complexities of the spouse-marriage-close associate connection, the researcher then asked spouses to work separately on a series of parallel measures for the friendships and marriage on various dimensions of relationship quality, marriage work, and identity-enhancing experiences. This use of parallel measures completed by both members of the marital dyad on both their marriage and friendships allows a more comprehensive look at the processes co-occurring in marriage and friendship as well as their potential links with both friendship and marital quality than has been possible previously.

Analyses conducted with 142 couples in which both husbands and wives had close associates revealed significant gender differences in husbands' and wives' relationship experiences with friends (Helms-Erikson, 1999b). A series of paired *t* tests showed mean differences in the degree to which husbands and wives talked to their friends about marital concerns in the areas of marital communication, support for work and parenting roles, the division of household labor and child care, decision making, family finances, relations with in-laws, and leisure. In every dimension except family finances, wives reported engaging their friends in marriage work more so than did husbands, whereas husbands talked more to their close associates about financial concerns than did wives. In addition, results from a series of paired *t* tests exploring gender differences in intellectually stimulating, self-affirming, and autonomy-granting experiences with friends suggest that wives, more so than husbands, experienced their relationships with close associates as identity enhancing. It should be noted, however, that the mean differences between husbands and wives, although statistically significant, were not as large as earlier qualitative researchers had proposed based on studies sampling wives only (Harrison, 1998; O'Connor, 1992; Oliker, 1989). This outcome suggests that whereas wives tend to experience their relations with close associates as sources of marital and identity support more than do husbands, husbands receive these types of support to a lesser extent from their relations with third parties. The next step in this work is to examine husbands' and wives' parallel marital experiences and the linkage to qualities of relationships with third parties.

## ▶ Conclusion

In this chapter, we have examined the potential influence of third parties on primary partnerships, first, by examining the collective or structural influence of partners' joint and separate associates and, second, by examining the specific personal relations of partners with close friends and kin. In essence, our framework provides a way to examine the social context of relationship development. Structural features (e.g., overlap, boundary density) are thought to represent key contextual features that influence primary relationship conditions (e.g., stability, commitment, satisfaction). These structural features describe the pattern of relationships between network members, and it is this patterning that is hypothesized to be uniquely influential.

Research in this area is sparse but is generally encouraging and supportive of theoretical expectations. As partners develop new primary relationships, they concurrently develop networks of shared affiliations while continuing to maintain and develop some separate affiliations. Among established couples, this overlapping of their networks is positively linked to marital stability, quality, and adjustment.

Although this initial work is promising, there are several areas in which future research is needed. Previous research often has been limited by inconsistent conceptual definitions of structure, and we hope that has been partially remedied here. Nonetheless, there remains considerable work in operationalizing these concepts. Both dyadic and individual indexes of network overlap are possible, although how these separate measures are apt to be related differentially to relationship outcomes awaits future inquiry. Then, too, simple correlations of network features (e.g., overlap, boundary density) and relationship outcomes (e.g., marital satisfaction) are ambiguous. Embedded here are the usual problems associated with inferring causality and the confounding of network features that are apt to be correlated (e.g., network overlap, network composition). For example, overlap is likely to be greater when networks are largely comprised of kin, and consequently any effect of overlap might be due to the presence of kin rather than the balance of shared affiliations. Fortunately, teasing out some of the unique effects of overlap or boundary density is a rather simple matter awaiting future research, whereas the matter of causal sequencing is a bit more difficult.

The potential for rapid advancement in our knowledge of the effects of third parties on relationship outcomes, our second focus of inquiry, also is apparent. With the groundwork laid by several rich qualitative studies, new work by Helms-Erikson promises to shed light on the ways in which the three corners of spouse, close associate, and marriage interact. By adopting a dyadic approach, one in which both partners' relationship with each other and their relationships with close associates are considered, Helms-Erikson's work promises to provide a more comprehensive understanding of the connections among the self, primary partnership, and close associates than has been explored previously. This work, however, is limited in that it explores the impact of relationships with third parties on primary partnerships for married partners only. It is unclear whether gay, lesbian, and cohabiting partners experience their relationships with close associates in ways similar to husbands and wives.

In addition to the absence of literature addressing third-party effects in more diverse partnerships, no research to date has addressed the dynamic nature of partners' relations with third parties and how they might interact with changing marriages over time. As Marks (1986) emphasized in his theorizing about the three corners of the self, marriage, and third parties, it is likely that the role third parties play and the impact they have on the self and the primary partnership vary as couples move from earlier to later stages of their relationships. It might be that connections with third parties are particularly important for or detrimental to relationship stability and quality at different points in a couple's history. Understanding how the three corners of the self, close associates, and primary partner interact over time could be a valuable tool that in turn could be used to alert couples to potentially adaptive and destructive *patterns* in ways of relating to one another and close associates over time.

The literature that does exist on the links among the self, primary partnership, and close associates speaks to the importance of attending to several factors. First, gender differences in not only partners' experiences with close associates but also the gendered nature of the impact of close associates on primary partnerships cannot be ignored (Burger & Milardo, 1995; Helms-Erikson, 1999b; Rubin, 1985). In addition, it is important for researchers to address specifically what types of social network connections (e.g., close friends, various types of kin, co-workers) are theoretically significant and of interest when studying the third-party effects on marriage (Milardo & Allan, 1997). Rather than treating all social relationships as equally influential on the marital dyad, recent research suggests that not all relationships with social network members have the same impact on primary partnerships (Burger & Milardo, 1995; Milardo & Wellman, 1992) and, therefore, attention should be given to the specific types of close associates

under investigation. At present, close friends, adult siblings, parents, and parents-in-law appear to be the most demonstrably influential, but there certainly are important ways in which intermediate friends, acquaintances, and distant kin provide important services, support, and (occasionally) interference. Finally, the possible costs of involvement with close associates for primary partnerships is a factor that should be considered when examining third-party effects on primary partnerships (Blieszner, 1994b; Blieszner & Adams, 1992; LaGaipa, 1990; Pagel, Erdley, & Becker, 1987).

Although the areas of structural influence and third-party influence are new and emerging, they suggest rich avenues for understanding fundamental relationship processes with potentially important applications for those working directly with families. Family practitioners, like researchers, are beginning to recognize the importance of the connections between third parties and primary partners, as evidenced in a recent special feature edition of *The Family Therapy Networker* (Simon, 1995). In this issue, dedicated to the role of friendship in individuals' lives over the life course, Sandmaier (1995) charged family therapists to give more attention to the importance of extrafamilial influences by creatively integrating partners' friends into the process of marital and family therapy. The literature that we reviewed offers additional guidelines for practitioners. For example, recent work suggests that husbands' involvement with kin is linked to healthy marriages, that shared associations of both partners are linked to stable and satisfying relationships, and that personal confidants are important sources of marriage work. Each of these domains of inquiry might have a direct bearing on the design of relationship enrichment programs and clinical work with partners and their families. The strength of partners' ties to one another might have much to do with the social context that they and their associates create.

# Contents

# Children's Friendships

*Amanda J. Rose*
*Steven R. Asher*

Adults often underestimate the importance of friendships in children's lives. For example, children's friendships, especially young children's friendships, might be thought of as unstable and transient and, therefore, not to be taken very seriously. Although it is true that friendships become more stable as children grow older (Berndt & Hoyle, 1985) and also show increased cooperativeness, loyalty, and intimacy with age (for a review, see Newcomb & Bagwell, 1995), it also is true that even young children's friendships have significance and can be quite enduring. Indeed, as researchers have focused increasing attention on friendship in childhood (for reviews of research on children's friendships, see Asher & Gottman, 1981; Berndt & Ladd, 1989; Bukowski, Newcomb, & Hartup, 1996; Gottman & Parker, 1986; Rubin, Bukowski, & Parker, 1998), they have come to appreciate the developmental significance of friendship.

The study of children's friendships has accelerated rapidly during recent years, and our hope in writing this chapter is to highlight some of the important aspects of our current knowledge in this area. Our focus for this chapter is on friendships—that is, children's close dyadic relationships—rather than on whether children are generally accepted or rejected by the peer group. Although it is true that children who lack friends also tend to be poorly accepted by the peer group, participation in friendship and peer acceptance have been found to be distinct constructs (for discussions of the distinction between friendship and acceptance, see Asher, Parker, & Walker, 1996; Bukowski & Hoza, 1989; Parker & Asher, 1993a, 1993b). Therefore, in writing this chapter, we drew primarily on literature dealing specifically with friendship rather than with peer acceptance (for reviews of research on peer acceptance/rejection, see Asher & Coie, 1990; Rubin et al., 1998). In reviewing the children's friendships literature, we examine the relationship benefits that children derive from their friendships, the social and emotional risks for children who have difficulties in their friendships, age and gender differences in children's friendships, and the social skills that children might need to be successful in their friendships.

## ▶ Benefits of Friendship

Friends serve important functions in children's lives (Asher & Parker, 1989; Bukowski et al., 1996; Sullivan, 1953). For example, friends meet many of the social and emotional needs of children and adolescents such as providing companionship, information on the social norms of the peer group, and a sounding board for thoughts and feelings (Buhrmester, 1996). Of the large number of benefits that children receive from having friendships and having friendships of high quality, we discuss six that have received considerable attention in theory and research (for a detailed review, see Asher & Parker, 1989).

First, friends provide children with *self-validation and ego support.* Sullivan (1953) proposed that having positive peer relationships fosters a sense of belonging and positive self-worth. In fact, children with friends have more positive self-esteem than do their friendless peers (Vandell & Hembree, 1994). One reason might be that friends are generally complimentary and supportive, and they provide an accepting environment that is reassuring about personal worth. Consider the following conversation between Naomi (4 years, 6 months) and her best friend, Eric (3 years, 6 months), recorded by Gottman and Parkhurst (1980) as part of their extensive observational study of young children's conversations with their friends (Gottman, 1983; Gottman & Parkhurst, 1980). In this conversation, nested in pretend play, Naomi reassures Eric that he is not a "dumb-dumb." Naomi and Eric's exchange illustrates how friendship can be a context for obtaining validation and support, even among young children:

**Naomi:** No, it's time for our birthday. We better clean up quickly.

**Eric:** Well, I'd rather play with my skeleton. Hold on there everyone. Snappers. I am the skeleton. . . . I'm the skeleton. Ooh, hee. . . . Hugh, ha, ha. You're hiding.

**Naomi:** Hey, in the top drawer, there's the . . .

**Eric:** I am the skeleton, whoa.

**Naomi:** There's the feet (clattering).

**Eric:** [Screams] A skeleton. Everyone, a skeleton.

**Naomi:** I'm your friend. The dinosaur.

**Eric:** Oh, hi dinosaur. You know, no one likes me.

**Naomi:** But I like you. I'm your friend.

**Eric:** But none of my other friends like me. They don't like my new suit. They don't like my skeleton suit. It's really just me. They think I'm a dumb-dumb.

**Naomi:** I know what. He's a good skeleton.

**Eric:** I am not a dumb-dumb, and that's so.

**Naomi:** I'm not calling you a dumb-dumb. I'm calling you a friendly skeleton. (Gottman & Parkhurst, 1980, p. 245)

Second, friends provide *emotional security* by being comforting companions in new or stressful situations. Freud and Dann (1951) provided a dramatic example in their report on six German Jewish children who were orphaned during World War II within their first year of life. These children were reared in a concentration camp together until about 3 years of age, when the war ended and they were taken to live together in a type of foster home in England. These children often were indifferent or aggressive toward the adults who took care of them, but they were very loyal to each other. They insisted on being together constantly and could not be happy unless the others were happy as well. Other examples of children using friends as a "secure base" come from studies in which toddlers and preschoolers were given the opportunity to explore a novel room (Ispa, 1981; Schwarz, 1972). Children explored the novel room more extensively in the presence of a peer than when alone. These findings were stronger when the peer was a friend or a familiar child than when the peer was not familiar.

Third, friendships are a context for *self-disclosure* (Berndt & Hanna, 1995). Talking with friends about salient personal issues might be important for emotional development in that it can promote self-understanding in children and adolescents (Sullivan, 1953). Children talk in an open and caring manner with friends about a variety of issues, some of which they do not want to discuss with adults. Children also self-disclose more to friends than to other children their age (for a review, see Newcomb & Bagwell, 1995). It is not surprising, then, that reciprocal friends know more about each other than do children in nonreciprocated friendships (Ladd & Emerson, 1984) and that reciprocal friends who spend a lot of time together are particularly knowledgeable about their friends' personality and preferences (Diaz & Berndt, 1982).

Children themselves certainly are aware of the place that self-disclosure has in their friendships. Consider, for example, comments made by third- through fifth-grade children who had participated in a study of children's friendships (Parker & Asher, 1993b). These comments were in response to being asked, at the conclusion of the study, whether there was anything else they would like to indicate about their friendships:

He is my very best friend because he tells me things and I tell him things.

Yesterday, me and Diana talked about how our parents got a divorce and how the world is going to end.

Jessica has problems at home and with her religion and when something happens she always comes to me and talks about it. We've been through a lot together.

Me and Tiff share our deepest darkest secrets and we talk about boys, when we grow up, and shopping. (p. 270)

Fourth, friends serve as sources of *help and guidance*. Children frequently report that giving and receiving guidance and assistance is a central part of their friendships (e.g., Furman & Bierman, 1984; Reisman & Shorr, 1978; Sharabany, Gershoni, & Hoffman, 1981). In addition, in both self-report and observational studies of children and early adolescents, higher levels of help and support have been documented in the relationships of friends than in the relationships of classmates who are only acquaintances (Berndt, 1985; Berndt & Perry, 1986). The help and guidance that friends provide can come in the form of instrumental help (e.g., rebuilding a block tower that fell over, helping with homework, giving rides to friends who do not have access to cars during adolescence) and in the form of emotional help and guidance (e.g., offering advice on how to get along with parents, teachers, and other peers) (for examples, see Fine, 1981). Moreover, friends provide guidance and assistance generously and when it is needed rather than keeping a strict count of the level of guidance and assistance they have received versus the level they have given.

Fifth, friends are *reliable allies* (Asher & Parker, 1989; Furman & Robbins, 1985). This benefit of friendship means that children have others to "stick up" for them, to be dependable and trustworthy allies, to not betray confidences, and to not do other things in the larger group that would cause them harm. Having reliable alliances with friends helps children to feel less vulnerable to the social stressors of life in groups. For example, as will be discussed later, friends can serve as a buffer for children in terms of protecting them from maltreatment from certain classmates (Hodges, Boivin, Vitaro, & Bukowski, 1999; Hodges, Malone, & Perry, 1997; Ladd, Kochenderfer, & Coleman, 1997).

Sixth, and perhaps most significant, friends provide *companionship and stimulation*. Children have the capacity to be willing, interesting, and enjoyable playmates for their friends, and children who are poor companions are unlikely to be desirable friends. LaGaipa (1981) argued that researchers should not focus on the "deeper" aspects of friendship (e.g., intimacy, emotional support) to the extent that they overlook the importance of friendships as sources of fun. In fact, LaGaipa noted:

> I suspect that fuller observations of the behavior of friendships in their natural setting would quickly reveal the "lighter" side of friendship. There is more to friendship than manifestations of prosocial behavior. . . . We would conjecture that it is difficult to maintain a friendship that is devoid of fun and laughter. (pp. 182-183)

Indeed, it is difficult to imagine a friendship between children in which companionship is not an important aspect.

## ▶ Friendship and Social-Emotional Adjustment

Given the important functions that friendships serve in children's lives, it is not surprising that children with friendship difficulties are at risk for a variety of social and emotional adjustment problems. Friendship difficulties have been operationalized in a variety of ways (for reviews, see Hartup, 1996; Hartup & Stevens, 1997; Parker & Asher, 1993a; Parker, Saxon, Asher, & Kovacs, 1999). These include being friendless, having poor-quality friendships, being friends with children who have negative or deviant characteristics, and having short-lived and unstable friendships. In the following subsections, we summarize research indicating that children with friendship difficulties are more likely than other children to feel lonely, to be victimized by peers, to have problems adjusting to school, and to engage in deviant behaviors.

### Loneliness

There is a growing research literature on the connections between children's friendship adjustment and their feelings of loneliness (for a review, see Parker et al., 1999). During the middle childhood years, children who do not have best friends are more lonely than their friended peers. This pattern has been found in school and in camp settings (Parker & Asher, 1993b; Parker & Seal, 1996; Renshaw & Brown, 1993). In these studies, children were considered to have friends if the children they reported to be friends also selected them as friends. A significant finding of these studies was that the relation between having friends and feeling less lonely generally held for children at all levels of peer acceptance (Parker & Asher, 1993b; Renshaw & Brown, 1993). Even children who were among the best-liked children in their classrooms (as measured by a rating-scale sociometric measure) were more lonely if they did not have friends than if they did have friends, and having even one friend helped children who were generally disliked by their classmates. These findings suggest that friends provide emotional benefits that are distinct from the benefits that children receive from being generally well liked by their classmates. It makes sense that having close relationships with peers who are companions, confidants, and reliable allies would contribute to children's emotional well-being in ways that are different from the contributions of being generally well accepted by the group.

Not all friendships are equal, however, in terms of their buffering effects on children's feelings of loneliness. In a study of third-through fifth-grade children (Parker & Asher, 1993b), the quality of children's friendships also was found to be related to loneliness among children who had reciprocal best friendships. Each child in this study rated his or her best friendships on six different friendship qualities: intimate exchange, validation and caring, help and guidance, companionship and recreation, conflict resolution, and conflict and betrayal. Each of these qualities was found to be related to how lonely the children were. Children who perceived that their friendships involved high levels of intimacy, validation, helping, companionship, and positive conflict resolution were less lonely than other children, and children who had particularly conflictual friendships were more lonely than other children.

Studies of children's friendships usually take a "snapshot" approach in that they assess the friendships only at one time point. This approach is limited because children's participation in friendship is dynamic. Over time, children lose some friends and gain others, and it is reasonable to expect that friendship formation, maintenance, and dissolution would influence children's emotional adjustment. Two longitudinal studies of children's friendships have found this to be the case (Parker & Seal, 1996; Renshaw & Brown, 1993). Parker and Seal (1996) tracked children's friendships at summer camp over time. An interesting pattern emerged in this study in terms of how friendship formation (i.e., *making* friends) and friendship durability (i.e., *keeping* friends) were related to loneliness. For children high on friendship durability, forming new friendships was related to their being less lonely. For children low on friendship durability, however, friendship formation was not related to loneliness. This result means that making new friends was related to feeling less lonely for children who also were keeping their old friends but not for children who were simply replacing the friends they had lost with new friends. These findings speak to the complexity of the relationship between friendship and loneliness. Further research is needed to fully understand the overlapping and distinct influences that having friends, the quality of friendships, and the stability of friendships have on children's feelings of loneliness. Additional research should address the role that the identity of children's friends plays in understanding loneliness in childhood.

### Victimization

Although most children are teased or picked on occasionally during childhood, a minority of children are consistently victimized by their peers (Kochenderfer & Ladd, 1996; Perry, Kusel, & Perry, 1988). The victimization takes the form of both verbal and physical maltreatment. Children with certain behavioral profiles are especially likely to be victimized by their peers. One such group is children who are anxious, are withdrawn, and cry easily (Olweus, 1978; Schwartz, Dodge, & Coie, 1993). These children are seen by peers as "easy targets," and because they give into demands and do not fight back, they do not discourage future victimization. A second group of victimized children does not display these submissive behaviors but instead is argumentative and ineffectually aggressive (Olweus, 1978). These children appear to provoke other children but are then unable to protect themselves from victimization.

It is reasonable to expect that having friends serves as a protective factor against victimization for children because friends support and protect one another, and studies have found that children with friends are less likely than children without friends to be victimized (Hodges et al., 1997, 1999; Ladd et al., 1997). Research by Hodges and colleagues provides particularly strong evidence for the idea that positive friendship adjustment serves as a protective factor against victimization. In one study, Hodges et al. (1997) examined whether children who were physically weak or who had behavioral profiles that were typically linked to victimization would be less likely to be victimized if they had friends. They found that having friends did decrease the likelihood that children who were weak or had "internalizing" (e.g., withdrawn) or "externalizing" (e.g., aggressive, argumentative, disruptive) behavioral profiles were victimized by peers. Moreover, friends who were not victims themselves, who were physically strong, and who did not exhibit internalizing or externalizing behavioral profiles were especially effective buffers against peer victimization. A second study in which children were followed over the course of 1 year revealed that some friendships are better buffers against victimization than are others (Hodges et al., 1999). In this study, children who had internalizing behavioral profiles at the first time point were less likely to be victimized 1 year later if they had friends at the first time point whom they perceived would support them if they were having difficulties with peers than if they had friends whom they perceived would not support them.

*School Adjustment*

There are several reasons why friendships should be important for children's success at school. Friends can help with difficult class projects or homework assignments. They can tell about assignments and activities missed due to absence, and they can provide encouragement to keep trying if troubles at school arise. Friends also play a role by making school an enjoyable environment. Children look forward to playing with their friends at recess, talking to their friends during breaks, and working collaboratively with their friends on projects.

Empirical evidence supports the idea that children who have friendship difficulties are at risk for poorer school adjustment (for reviews, see Berndt & Keefe, 1996; Birch & Ladd, 1996; Ladd & Kochenderfer, 1996). Ladd and his colleagues have shown that peer relationships are important even for young children's adjustment to kindergarten. In an initial study, children adjusted to kindergarten better if they had familiar peers in their class (Ladd & Price, 1987), and in a later study, children benefited especially from having one or more of their pre-kindergarten friends in their kindergarten class (Ladd, 1990). Children with friends in class, especially children who maintained those friendships, were more likely than children without friends to develop positive perceptions of school (Ladd, 1990). Furthermore, children with good-quality friendships were at a particular advantage for school adjustment (Ladd, Kochenderfer, & Coleman, 1996). For example, children who had friendships at the beginning of kindergarten that involved high levels of aid and assistance were more likely than other children to like school more as the year progressed. By contrast, for boys, having friendships that were particularly conflictual was related to liking school less and wanting to avoid school more as the year progressed.

Relations between good friendship adjustment and good school adjustment also are found in the later years of middle childhood and adolescence (Berndt & Keefe, 1995; Vandell & Hembree, 1994; Wentzel & Caldwell, 1997). Berndt and Keefe (1995) examined both the quality of the friendships and the identity or characteristics of the friends. Seventh- and eighth-grade students were followed from fall to spring, and the researchers examined how friendship relations in the fall related to involvement in school as well as school disruptiveness in the spring. Adolescents whose friendships involved high levels of positive qualities (e.g., intimate self-disclosure) in the fall became more involved in school as the year progressed, whereas adolescents whose friendships involved high levels of negative features (e.g., conflict, rivalry) became more disruptive. Interestingly, the detrimental effects of having friendships with negative features were strongest for adolescents whose friendships also had positive features. In addition, adolescents whose friends were involved in school in the fall became more involved by the spring, and adolescents whose friends were more disruptive in the fall became more disruptive by the spring. These findings point to both the potential positive and negative effects of friendships on school adjustment.

*Deviant Behavior*

The potentially negative influences that friends can have on children also have been acknowledged in the study of deviant behavior. For example, parents and teachers worry about children falling in with the "wrong crowd" and engaging in harmful or illegal activities as a result of peer pressure. In fact, research indicates that friends sometimes can be detrimental influences on children and adolescents by encouraging them to engage in deviant behavior; children whose friends engage in deviant behavior are more at risk for engaging in this type of behavior than are children whose friends have a more prosocial behavioral style.

Scholars interested in the influence that children have on their friends frequently refer to the research showing that friends are generally found to be similar to one another in terms of both positive and negative behavioral characteristics (for reviews, see Hartup & Stevens, 1997; Newcomb & Bagwell, 1995). The assumption is that friends exert a mutual influence on each other, resulting in greater similarity over time. For example, aggressive children frequently are found to be friends with other aggressive children (Cairns, Cairns, Neckerman, Gest, & Gariepy, 1988), and observations of aggressive children's conversations suggest that they encourage one another's deviant behavior (Dishion, Spracklen, Andrews, & Patterson, 1996).

Further evidence that children are influenced by their friends comes from studies showing that the characteristics of children's friends at one time point are predictive of the children's own behavior at a later time point in ways that involve the children and their friends becoming more similar to one another. This approach has been used to demonstrate that friends with deviant identities have a negative influence on children and adolescents (e.g., Fisher & Bauman, 1988; Kupersmidt, Burchinal, & Patterson, 1995; Vitaro, Tremblay, Kerr, Pagani, & Bukowski, 1997). For example, Kupersmidt et al. (1995) followed third- through seventh-grade students over a 4-year period, tracking changes in their aggressiveness and delinquency. Children who had aggressive friends toward the beginning of the 4-year period were more likely than other children to become more aggressive and to engage in more delinquent behavior themselves by the end of the 4-year period. Studies such as this support the idea that friends can be harmful influences on children, and they also validate parents' and teachers' concerns about the identities of children's friends.

## ► Age Differences in Friendships

Most studies of age differences in friendships have relied on children's self-reports (Bigelow & LaGaipa, 1975; Buhrmester & Furman, 1987; Furman & Bierman, 1984; Reisman & Shorr, 1978; Sharabany et al., 1981). One major finding across these studies is that older children report higher levels of self-disclosure, or sharing personal thoughts and feelings, in their friendships. Self-disclosure has been found to be an especially important aspect of friendship during adolescence. By contrast, young children's friendships are focused largely on companionship, and children in middle childhood frequently report that being loyal and being helpful are important aspects of their friendships.

Fewer studies have examined age differences in friendships by directly observing children's and adolescents' behavior with friends. Those studies that have been conducted (e.g., Denton & Zarbantany, 1996; Gottman & Mettetal, 1986; Rotenberg & Sliz, 1988), however, do tend to confirm the findings from friendship research based on children's self-reports. For example, Gottman and Mettetal (1986) studied the conversations of young friends (6-7 years of age), friends in middle childhood (11-12 years of age), and adolescent friends (16-17 years of age). Compared to the older children and adolescents, young friends talked more about activities. Older children and adolescents engaged in more gossip and personal self-disclosure than did young children, and these processes were particularly pronounced in adolescence.

Although older children's friendships do appear to involve higher levels of self-disclosure than younger children's friendships, the prevalence of intimate self-disclosure in the friendships of young children probably is underestimated. One reason is that early research on children's friendships often relied on methods that required a certain amount of verbal (and sometimes written) fluency. In one highly cited study of children's friendship expectations (Bigelow & LaGaipa, 1975), children in the first through eighth grades were asked to write essays about what they expected from their best friends that was different from what they expected from other relationships. The positive benefits of friendship in the lives of the younger children probably were underestimated in this study because of the more limited vocabularies and writing skills of younger children.

The level of self-disclosure in the friendships of young children also might be underestimated because the way in which self-disclosure is expressed in young children's friendships is not always obvious at first glance. As an example, young children have been found to use fantasy play to work through fears and insecurities (Gottman & Parkhurst, 1980). Consider the conversation between Naomi and Eric presented earlier. Eric was a child with many insecurities. The pretend play episode with the skeleton provided a context for Eric to express his worries that others think he is a "dumb-dumb" and for Naomi to reassure him that he is not. On the surface, this exchange clearly is different from that of adolescent friends who might have sat down and had a serious discussion regarding their worries about others' perceptions of them. However, it is clear that the exchange between Naomi and Eric did involve intimate self-disclosure, albeit in a different form from that typically seen in older children and adolescents. Although it is reasonable to conclude that intimate self-disclosure is more common in the friendships of older children and adolescents than in the friendships of young children, we need to closely observe the friendships of young children so as not to miss self-disclosure when it does occur.

Much of the research on age differences has focused on mean differences in the behavior displayed, reported, or expected at different ages. Another perspective on development is whether there also are age differences in the types of goals children pursue in their friendships. Several authors (Buhrmester, 1996; Parker & Gottman, 1989; Sullivan, 1953) have proposed that the overarching goals for interaction with friends change with age. Parker and Gottman (1989) argued that, for young children, an overarching goal of interaction with friends is to sustain play. For young friends, coordinating their interaction in a way that maximizes enjoyment and minimizes conflict is a challenging task. Intense and exciting play with friends can promote the development of emotion regulation skills in that children need to avoid becoming excited or upset to an extent that interferes with play. With age, the conversations of friends become increasingly important (Buhrmester, 1996; Parker & Gottman, 1989; Sullivan, 1953). An overarching goal of interaction with friends during middle childhood is fitting in with the peer group (Sullivan, 1953). Parker and Gottman (1989) suggested that friends engage in a great deal of negative gossip about their peers during middle childhood to help them determine what is and what is not acceptable behavior for their peer group. In adolescence, an overarching goal is the development of a personal identity (Erikson, 1968); the deep conversations that adolescent friends have about their beliefs, aspirations, and personal styles are thought to facilitate identity development (Buhrmester, 1996; Parker & Gottman, 1989; Sullivan, 1953).

## ► Gender Differences in Friendships

One of the most striking findings regarding the role of gender in friendships is the degree to which children limit their friendship choices to same-sex peers (for reviews of research on sex segregation, see Hartup, 1983; Leaper, 1994; Maccoby, 1990). Preference for same-sex peers has been documented as early as preschool (Howes, 1988; LaFreniere, Strayer, & Gauthier, 1984; Maccoby & Jacklin, 1987), and same-sex preference increases when children make the transition to elementary school (Maccoby & Jacklin, 1987). As with younger children, elementary school girls and boys are found to interact more frequently with same-sex peers than with cross-sex peers (Singleton & Asher, 1977; Thorne, 1986). In fact, in one study of more than 700 third- and fourth-grade students (Kovacs, Parker, & Hoffman, 1996), 1,331 reciprocal best friendships were identified, and only 63 of these were cross-sex friendships.

Given that children almost always are interacting with same-sex peers and that cross-sex interaction is limited, it is not surprising that different interaction styles arise in the friendships of girls and boys. One major difference is that girls' friendships have a strong focus on dyadic interaction, whereas boys' friendships are more likely to be situated in a larger social network. Support for this generalization comes both from observational studies and from surveying children about their social networks. Observational studies show that girls spend more one-on-one time with friends than do boys, whereas boys spend more time interacting in larger peer groups than do girls (Benenson, Apostoleris, & Parnass, 1997; Omark, Omark, & Edelman, 1975; Thorne, 1986). In addition, studies of social networks demonstrate that boys' social networks are more dense than girls' social networks (Benenson, 1994; Parker & Seal, 1996), meaning that more of boys' friends also are friends with one another. The gender difference in girls' greater tendency to focus on dyadic relationships versus boys' tendency to conduct their friendships in the context of a larger peer group appears to emerge between about 4 and 6 years of age, as assessed in both observational research (Benenson et al., 1997) and research on social networks (Benenson, 1994).

In addition, gender differences are found in the activities in which boys and girls engage with friends. Observational research on children's playtime with peers indicates that boys spend more time than girls engaged in physical activities with friends. Boys are more likely than girls to engage in rough-and-tumble play with friends (DiPietro, 1981; Ladd, 1983; Moller, Hymel, & Rubin, 1992) and to play sports and games with their friends (Lever, 1978). By contrast, girls are more likely than boys to spend their time with friends engaged in conversation (Ladd, 1983; Moller et al., 1992; Omark et al., 1975).

Studies of children's friendships also suggest that girls' friendships involve higher levels of validation, intimacy, support, and positive conflict resolution than do boys' friendships. In a study of the quality of children's best friendships (Parker & Asher, 1993b), girls reported that their friendships were higher on the dimensions of validation

and caring, intimate exchange, help and guidance, and conflict resolution as compared to boys. In addition, in one of our recent studies, we examined children's responses to vignettes representing conflict situations with a friend (Rose & Asher, 1999a) and found that girls were more likely than boys to report that they would accommodate and compromise, whereas boys were more likely than girls to report that they would assert their own self-interest and behave in a hostile manner such as with verbal aggression. In a second study, we examined children's responses to hypothetical social support situations with a friend (Rose & Asher, 1999b) and found that girls were more likely than boys to report that they would offer social support to a friend with a problem by sympathizing and expressing caring, whereas boys were more likely than girls to report that they would avoid the friend with the problem or blame the friend for having the problem. Interestingly, although this research indicates that girls' friendships are more supportive than boys' friendships and that girls' friendships involve higher levels of validation, intimacy, and positive conflict resolution, boys reported as much satisfaction with their friendships as did girls (Parker & Asher, 1993b). This outcome suggests that there might be aspects of friendship at which boys are particularly skilled, and identifying boys' friendship strengths is an important direction for future research (Crick & Rose, in press; Rose & Asher, 1999a).

These studies document that there are mean differences in the friendship behaviors of girls and boys. A separate question is whether friendship behaviors function in the same way for girls and boys in terms of meeting girls' and boys' social and emotional needs and fostering girls' and boys' social and emotional adjustment. One way in which to address this question is to examine whether specific types of friendship behaviors are related similarly for girls and boys to positive social and emotional outcomes or whether some aspects of friendship are more important for the adjustment of one gender than the other. A reasonable hypothesis might be that certain behaviors (e.g., self-disclosure) are more important to children of one gender than the other and, therefore, are not only more prevalent in the friendships of children of that gender but also more predictive of positive social and emotional adjustment for children of that gender.

To date, our knowledge is limited regarding whether certain friendship behaviors, such as self-disclosure, are actually more important for the social and emotional adjustment of one gender than the other. The few published studies addressing this question indicate that even friendship behaviors for which there are gender differences are of comparable importance for girls' and boys' adjustment. For example, although girls tend to report higher levels of certain positive friendship qualities than do boys (e.g., intimate exchange, validation and support), friendship qualities such as these have been found to be related as strongly for boys as for girls to depression (Oldenburg & Kerns, 1997), to loneliness (Parker & Asher, 1993b), and to self-esteem (Keefe & Berndt, 1996). However, several unpublished studies (Parker, Houlihan, & Casas, 1997; Rose & Asher, 1999b; Saxon & Asher, 1999) suggest that the relations between behavior within a friendship and adjustment do differ by gender. More research is needed to clarify whether particular types of behavior within a friendship function differently for girls and for boys in terms of fostering social and emotional adjustment.

## ▶ Recent Social Skills for Friendship Success: Theory, Research, and Applications

There is considerable research on social skills with peers in childhood, but it is almost entirely focused on the social skills children need to be generally well liked or well accepted by the peer group (for reviews, see Asher & Coie, 1990; Newcomb, Bukowski, & Pattee, 1993). It seems plausible that the social skills children need to be successful in their friendships are somewhat distinct from the skills children need to be generally well liked, yet very little is known about the social skills required for friendship adjustment (Rubin et al., 1998). Recently, Asher et al. (1996) proposed a "social tasks" framework for conceptualizing competence at friendship and suggested 10 different social tasks that children might need to handle well to make friends and have friendships of good quality. These tasks include, for example, being an enjoyable and resourceful companion, expressing caring and concern, being a reliable partner, helping a friend who is in need, managing disagreement, and being able to forgive. A guiding principle of the social tasks framework is that it is important to assess social competence in response to specific social situations or social tasks because individuals might be more skilled at handling some social tasks than others (Dodge, McClaskey, & Feldman, 1985; McFall, 1982).

Rose and Asher (1999a) recently examined how children's responses to the social task of managing conflicts of interest in a friendship were related to their success in friendship. Fourth- and fifth-grade children were presented with 30 hypothetical situations representing normative and fairly benign conflicts that arise in friendships such as having a disagreement with a friend over which movie to see. In response to these situations, we assessed children's goals (i.e., what they would be trying to accomplish) and their strategies (i.e., what they would do). We found that children's goals and strategies were related to how many best friends children had and to the quality of children's best friendships. For example, children who reported strategies of compromise or accommodation were rated by their best friends as less conflictual than other children were rated. Of all the goals and strategies, having revenge goals (i.e., trying to get back at a friend) was the strongest predictor of poor friendship adjustment. We found that about 6% of children consistently endorsed the revenge goal in response to these relatively mild conflicts, and the endorsement of the revenge goal was associated with having fewer friends and having friendships of poor quality.

These findings suggest that a social tasks perspective on friendship will be useful for guiding future research on the competencies children need to be successful in their friendships. Hopefully, this type of research also will provide a strong foundation for developing intervention programs for children with friendship difficulties. Previous research has indicated that children who are trained in social skills can become generally better liked by their peer group (for reviews, see Asher et al., 1996; Coie & Koeppl, 1990). However, as Asher et al. (1996) noted, even studies showing gains in peer acceptance have not shown that children make comparable gains in friendship. One possibility suggested by Furman and Robbins (1985) is that children need to be taught social skills that are relevant specifically for success in close peer relationships if children are to become more successful in their friendships. Asher et al.'s (1996) discussion of friendship tasks could provide a framework for future intervention efforts.

In addition to determining the social skills that should be taught in a friendship intervention program, researchers conducting friendship interventions would need to choose the format for implementing the program. Many social skills programs follow a focal child model in which children are taught social skills individually by an adult coach. In some studies (e.g., Ladd, 1981; Oden & Asher, 1977), children are then given the opportunity to practice these skills in a game-playing context with a peer. A different approach to friendship intervention involves a dyadic processes model. Selman and Schultz (1990) developed "peer pairing therapy" in which two children with social and emotional difficulties interact while receiving feedback from an adult coach regarding their social behavior. Although formal evaluations of this model are needed (Selman & Schultz, 1990), one reason why this is a potentially powerful model is that, at the same time as the children are learning social skills, they have the opportunity to form a specific friendship and to derive the benefits of that relationship.

Classroom-based friendship intervention programs also could be developed. Over the past few decades, a wide variety of programs have been created to teach children social skills, social problem-solving strategies, and emotional competencies (for a review, see Weissberg & Greenberg, 1998). For example, classroom-based conflict resolution programs have been implemented that resulted in children learning more effective conflict management strategies (e.g., Johnson, Johnson, Dudley, Mitchell, & Frederickson, 1997; for a review, see Johnson & Johnson, 1996). Given that children who manage conflicts of interest effectively are more successful in their friendships than are other children (Rose & Asher, 1999a), research should examine whether classroom-based conflict resolution programs such as these also result in gains in friendship adjustment for the students.

Certain instructional practices also might be beneficial for friendship adjustment. Children who engage in collaborative learning in school, for example, become more accepted by their classmates over the course of the school year than do children in traditional classrooms (Putnam, Markovchick, Johnson, & Johnson, 1996), but little research exists on the effects of cooperative learning methods on friendship formation per se. Perhaps "buddy system" techniques, in which compatible children are assigned to work together on cooperative tasks, would be particularly effective for fostering friendships.

One potential role for friendship intervention research is hypothesis testing. Well-controlled intervention research can be used to learn about the types of social skills that children need to make and maintain good friendships. For example, if teaching children how to manage conflicts of interests in their friendships resulted in improvement in the quality and maintenance of their friendships, then the findings would provide experimental support for the hypothesis that handling conflicts of interest is an important social task for friendship success. Conducting friendship intervention research, then, would not only contribute to our ability to help children but also add to our knowledge about the social skills required for children to have positive close relationships with peers.

# Contents

# Adolescent Relationships:
# The Art of Fugue

*W. Andrew Collins*
*Brett Laursen*

A fugue is a musical composition characterized by distinct melodic themes that are elaborated successively and interwoven to create a single well-defined structure. We propose that the development of close relationships during adolescence and young adulthood follows an analogous pattern. Affiliations with friends, romantic partners, siblings, and parents unfold along varied and somewhat discrete trajectories for most of the second decade of life and then coalesce during the early 20s into integrated interpersonal structures.

This chapter builds on two influential ideas about the development of relationships. The

AUTHORS' NOTE: Preparation of this chapter was supported by the Rodney S. Wallace Professorship for the Advancement of Teaching and Learning, University of Minnesota, to W. Andrew Collins and a grant from the National Institute of Child Health and Human Development (R29HD33006) to Brett Laursen.

first is Hartup's (1979) depiction of the emergence of unique social worlds during childhood. In his view, family and peer relationships are "two social worlds" that develop increasingly independent of one another, although common themes are advanced at important intersections. The second is the principle that "whenever development occurs it proceeds from a state of relative globality and lack of differentiation to a state of increasing differentiation, articulation, and hierarchic integration" (Werner, 1957, p. 126; see also Hinde & Stevenson-Hinde, 1987). We contend that close relationships initially are global and undifferentiated. The first distinctions involve family members; different patterns of interaction are established with mothers, fathers, and siblings that promote the acquisition of a diverse set of skills and abilities. The peer social world emerges from this context. Most early friendships are formed with playmates under the supervision of family members. Over time, however, different principles govern social interactions in peer relationships from those in families, and different social skills are honed and emphasized within these different dyads. During childhood, authority and obligation prevail as themes in family relationships, whereas interdependence and shared power typify friendships.

Our thesis is that differentiation and articulation continue across adolescence but that young adulthood marks a gradual hierarchic integration in the form and function of close relationship processes. Just as distinct musical themes are integrated in the resolution of a fugue, the social worlds of friends and family merge into a unified social structure that incorporates important features of both relationship systems and that manifests communal properties.

The four sections of this chapter examine this thesis. The first section outlines alternative theoretical perspectives on these developmental changes and their significance. In the second section, particular attention is given to the implications of the characteristic expansion and diversification of affiliations during adolescence. The third section outlines the primary changes in relationships with parents and peers including dating and romantic partners. The section emphasizes the fugue-like patterns of development within each relationship and the interplay among them. The fourth and final section proposes that the characteristics and functions of parent-child and peer relationships are integrated in the marital and parent-child relationships of adulthood.

## ► Theoretical Accounts of Adolescent Relationships and Relationship Change

Theoretical views of adolescent relationships have the common goal of explaining the differentiation of relationships during the second decade of life. Theorists have given particular attention to apparent increases in

distance from parents and increased closeness to peers during the second decade of life (Collins & Repinski, 1994). These views vary, however, in how they account for these complex phenomena and in their implications for the eventual integration of disparate relationships during young adulthood.

One group of theories, *endogenous change perspectives,* emphasizes biological and motivational pressures toward developmental changes in relationships. Psychoanalytic perspectives (Blos, 1979; Erikson, 1950; A. Freud, 1969; S. Freud, 1923/1949), for example, attribute perturbed parent-child relations and increasing orientation toward peers to psychic pressure for individuation from parents and a shift to interpersonal objects appropriate to adult roles. Similarly, evolutionary theorists view changing relationships as fostering autonomy and facilitating the formation of nonfamilial sexual relationships (Steinberg, 1988). Endogenous change views depict the integration of relationships in young adulthood in terms of increases in the relative dominance of peer and, especially, romantic relationships at the expense of continued intimacy between parents and offspring.

A second group of theories gives greater weight to exogenous factors in changing adolescent relationships. *Social psychological perspectives* attribute changes in relationships to pressures associated with age-graded expectations, tasks, and settings, often in combination with maturational changes (Hartup, 1979; Hill, 1988; Silverberg & Steinberg, 1990; Simmons, Burgeson, & Reef, 1988; Youniss, 1980). Thus, differences between parent-adolescent and peer relationships reflect differing salient contexts and shared activities. This view carries at least two possible implications for relationships during adolescence and for their eventual integration in young adulthood. One possibility is that, during adolescence, the proliferation of contexts and life tasks and the apparently differing demands of families and peers might heighten ambient anxiety and tensions. These negative emotions then might be expressed in conflictual or diminished interactions within the relatively safe confines of familial relationships but not in the more potentially fragile social environment of friendships. Gradually, emotional perturbations might subside or adolescents might manage emotions more constructively, allowing for improved relationships with parents and peers. A related possibility is that age-graded expectations give relatively greater emphasis to the importance of success in peer relationships. Consequently, adolescents might neglect or even devalue the importance of maintaining positive relationships with family members while investing heavily in harmonious relations with other adolescents. In adulthood, familial expectations might become more finely attuned to the demands of lives beyond the family. For example, Gans (1957) documented young adults' understanding of those times and situations in which one must respect familial obligations and those in which participation is voluntary.

Finally, two formulations emphasize functional similarities even as relationships change over time. Compared to the endogenous and exogenous change perspectives, these formulations give relatively greater emphasis to the importance of the history of relationship experiences with which an individual enters adolescence. *Attachment perspectives* hold that specific interactions vary as a function of changing developmental challenges from one age period to the next but still are guided by cognitive representations formed during early life that are essentially stable (Ainsworth, 1989; Allen & Land, 1999; Collins & Sroufe, in press; Sroufe, Egeland, & Carlson, 1999). For example, aloof and seemingly shy adolescents both elicit and actively respond to different types of overtures from peers compared to those to which more outgoing, relaxed, and sociable individuals respond (Sroufe et al., 1999). At the same time, the relationship histories of interaction partners play a role. Outgoing, relaxed, and sociable individuals are most likely to manifest these personal characteristics when interacting with others who show similar characteristics or those who appear vulnerable and needy, whereas usually positive and sociable adolescents often appear

more tense and conflict prone when interacting with aloof, unresponsive, and/or domineering partners (Collins & Sroufe, in press).

*Interdependence perspectives* also emphasize the joint patterns in which the actions, cognitions, and emotions of each member of the dyad are significant to the other's reactions. Interdependence, defined in terms of the frequency, diversity, strength, and duration of interactions, reflects the degree of closeness between two persons (Kelley et al., 1983). Thus, changes in relationships, such as those during adolescence, constitute altered patterns of interdependence. Interdependencies continue within familial relationships but in different forms from those in earlier life, whereas interdependencies increase within friendships and romantic relationships. Parents and offspring both adjust expectancies in the service of optimal interdependence (Collins, 1995, 1997). Close peers must develop skills for maintaining interdependence on the basis of shared interests, commitments, and intimacy, even when contact is relatively infrequent (Parker & Gottman, 1989). Mismatches between expectancies might precipitate conflicts, which in turn might stimulate adjustments of expectancies that both restore harmony and foster developmental adaptations in the dyad (Collins, 1995). Accounts of interdependence and attachment attempt to explain how the qualities of relationships prior to adolescence are linked to an individual's experiences with others in later life periods.

In contrast to the endogenous change and social psychological views, attachment and interdependence perspectives imply that the degree of eventual integration of parent-child and peer relationships varies across individuals and relationships. For example, histories of positive supportive relationships with parents and successful relationships with peers portend strong communal relationships with both parents and peers, including romantic partners, in young adulthood. By contrast, unreliable relationships with parents and peers may be associated with less cohesive patterns of familial and extrafamilial patterns in adulthood (Collins & Sroufe, in press).

## ▶ Relationships During Adolescence and Their Significance

Relationships during adolescence illustrate both the impact of individuals on dyads and the significance of relationships to individuals. This section addresses the functions of relationships in individual development.

### Adolescents and Their Relationship Partners

Relationships during adolescence are more extensive and diverse than relationships during childhood. Adolescents generally manifest both greater autonomy and mobility than do children. Although familial relationships remain salient, an increasing proportion of time is devoted to interactions with persons outside of the family. Not surprisingly, adolescents' casual friendships are more numerous and diverse than those of children, perhaps because of the differing opportunities available in school and at work. Romantic relationships also emerge and become increasingly common during adolescence (Brown, in press; Csikszentmihalyi & Larson, 1984).

As relationship partners, adolescents undergo extensive and rapid maturation and equally dramatic changes in sociocultural expectations for relating to others. These changes mark the shift from childhood to adolescence and also underlie additional transitions during the adolescent years. Typically, 11-year-olds, 15-year-olds, and 18-year-olds are categorized as adolescents, but individuals of these ages differ in physical and cognitive characteristics, and they encounter contrasting age-related expectations regarding their personal behavior and the type and extent of their relationships (Collins, 1997; Furman & Wehner, 1994).

### Close Relationships and Individual Development

Socialization and acculturation take place within close relationships, both with respect to proximal (e.g., neighborhood, ethnic communities) or distal (e.g., societal, cultural) contexts (Brewer & Caporael, 1990; Cooper, 1994). Close relationships are primary settings for the acquisition of skills ranging from social competencies, to motor performance (e.g., athletics, dancing), to cognitive abilities (Hartup & Laursen, 1992). For example, characteristics of problem solving in parent-adolescent dyads are correlated with measures of individual development such as ego development and identity exploration (Allen, Hauser, Bell, & O'Connor, 1994; Grotevant & Cooper, 1985). Moreover, variation in the quality (e.g., supportiveness, intimacy) of adolescent friendships is correlated with multiple outcomes for individuals (Hartup, 1993; Savin-Williams & Berndt, 1990). Thus, social development during and beyond adolescence requires continued experience in close relationships, but adolescents and their relationship partners must continually adapt to the rapid changes of adolescence.

Social networks expand rapidly during adolescence, and close relationships and their functions become both more diverse and more differentiated. For example, 11- and 13-year-olds distinguish reliably among family, peer, and teacher relationships as sources of instrumental help, intimacy, companionship, nurturance, and conflict (Furman & Buhrmester, 1992). Perceptions of primary social support shift from relationships with parents during middle childhood, to same-sex friends during early and middle adolescence, and then to same-sex friends and romantic partners during college-age years (Furman & Buhrmester, 1992). Perceptions of intimacy also show different patterns in relation to age, with close friends gradually being perceived as providing greater intimacy than parents (Hunter & Youniss, 1982). The particular friends with whom adolescents are intimate also change with age. In one cross-sectional comparison, both females and males reported greater intimacy with same-sex friends than with members of the opposite sex, although the gap was smaller for 14- to 16-year-olds than for 10- to 12-year-olds (Sharabany, Gershoni, & Hoffman, 1981). By their middle

20s, many young adults report fewer, but more stable, choices of individuals with whom they experience intimate relationships (Reis, Yi-Cheng, Bennett, & Nezlek, 1993). Age-related patterns of intimacy with peers might reflect an increase in the number and relative salience of romantic relationships during late adolescence and young adulthood (Furman & Wehner, 1994; Laursen & Williams, 1997).

Research findings show that relationships become increasingly interrelated over time. Despite the stereotype of incompatible or contradictory influences of parents and friends, parent-child relationships set the stage for both the selection of friends and the management of these relationships (Parke & Buriel, 1998). Links between qualities of friendships and romantic relationships, as well as between familial and romantic relationships, are equally impressive (Collins, Hennighausen, Schmit, & Sroufe, 1997; Feldman, Gowen, & Fisher, 1998). At the same time, relationships with parents, friends, and romantic partners serve overlapping but distinctive functions. Typical exchanges within each of these types of dyads differ accordingly. Compared to childhood relationships, the lesser distance and greater intimacy in adolescents' peer relationships may both satisfy affiliative needs and contribute to socialization for relations among equals. Intimacy with parents may provide nurturance and support but might be less important than friendships for socialization to roles and expectations during late adolescence and young adulthood (Collins, 1997; Laursen & Bukowski, 1997).

## ▶ The Nature and Course of Relationships During Adolescence

Relationships, whether transitory or long term, exhibit both continuity and change over time. In this section, we summarize findings from research on parent-adolescent and adolescent-adolescent dyads. We describe both the distinctive characteristics of these relationships during the second decade of life and the most common changes in them. We also consider some implications of adolescent relationships that may inform research on relationships and their development in other periods of life.

### *Parent-Adolescent Relationships*

Although parents and adolescents spend less time together and also behave differently with each other compared to parents and younger children, neither the importance of these relationships nor their functional significance diminishes. Most scholars today describe this process as a *transformation* in which the properties and conditions of relationships change without subverting the bond between parent and child (Collins, 1995).

*Continuities in emotional bonds and potential influence.* Contrary to popular stereotypes, considerable continuity is evident in parent-child relationships over time. Surveys in European and North American samples repeatedly have revealed that parents and adolescents alike perceive their relationships as warm and pleasant (Grotevant, 1998). Indeed, adolescents' attitudes toward parents become increasingly more positive over the course of adolescence (Feldman & Quatman, 1988; Fuligni, 1998). Of the 20% or so of families that encounter serious difficulties during this period, most have had histories of problems (Offer, Ostrov, & Howard, 1981; Rutter, Graham, Chadwick, & Yule, 1976).

Adolescents typically perceive relationships with parents as providing unique resources not provided by peers or other adults. For example, adolescents perceive their parents as a primary source of information on topics for which prior experience is relevant (Youniss & Smollar, 1985). Early to mid-adolescents typically first turn to parents under conditions of extreme stress, and even young adults often look to parents for emotional support when experiencing difficulties (Allen & Land, 1999; Fraley & Davis, 1997). Thus, emotional bonds between parents and children survive the changes of adolescence, and parents continue to serve as resources during and beyond the second decade of life.

*Changes in forms of interactions and affective expression.* Continuities in parent-adolescent relationships coexist with significant changes in the amount, content, and perceived meanings of interactions; the expressions of positive and negative affect; and the interpersonal perceptions of the interactants (Grotevant, 1998; Holmbeck, Paikoff, & Brooks-Gunn, 1995). Parents and adolescents interact less frequently than during earlier life periods (Csikszentmihalyi & Larson, 1984; Larson & Richards, 1991). This decline occurs both during early adolescence (generally 12-14 years of age) and middle adolescence (roughly 15-18 years of age) (Montemayor & Brownlee, 1987). Compared to preadolescents, adolescents report lower feelings of acceptance by parents and less satisfaction with family life and decision making (Hill, 1988; Steinberg, 1988). Both parents and adolescents report less frequent expressions of positive emotions and feelings of closeness as well as more frequent expression of negative emotions. Parents' reports of well-being and life satisfaction decline when they perceive their children to be "detaching" from them (Silverberg & Steinberg, 1990).

These general patterns often are qualified by the gender of the child or the parent (or both). Although relationships with both parents involve expressions of positive and negative emotions, some research shows that mothers and adolescents express more toward one another than do fathers and adolescents (Cowan, Drinkard, & McGavin, 1984; Papini, Datan, & McCluskey-Fawcett, 1988). Adolescents are more likely to report feeling close to their mothers than to their fathers (Atkinson & Bell, 1986; Paulson, Hill, & Holmbeck, 1991; Pipp, Shaver, Jennings, Lamborn, & Fischer, 1985). They also perceive that their mothers have a more accepting attitude toward them than do their fathers (Collins, 1995). Thus, for many adolescents, relationships with mothers provide more pleasure and affection, as well

as more conflict, than do relationships with fathers (Larson & Richards, 1991). Fathers who are highly involved with adolescents, however, tend to show more acceptance toward their sons and daughters than do less involved fathers, and their relationships with adolescents are more like typical mother-adolescent relationships (Almeida & Galambos, 1991).

To these findings from self-report studies, observational studies of parent-adolescent interactions have added information about dyadic patterns of assertiveness and disagreement. In collaborative problem-solving tasks in the laboratory, both parents and adolescents frequently display assertiveness in expressing opinions and arguing for their viewpoints (Allen et al., 1994; Steinberg, 1981). These patterns may explain the stereotype that high levels of conflict mark parent-adolescent relationships. Closer inspection, however, reveals the matter to be more complicated, as we show in the next subsection.

### Conflict in Parent-Adolescent Relationships

Both formal theories and popular impressions of adolescent development either implicitly or explicitly emphasize the significance of parent-adolescent disagreements. Conflict is expected to be more frequent and intense in these dyads than in relationships with friends, romantic partners, or other peers and adults (Laursen & Collins, 1994). Psychoanalytic views (Blos, 1979; A. Freud, 1969; S. Freud, 1923/1949) depicted these widely expected difficulties as inevitable byproducts of pubertal maturation that facilitated separation from parents as adolescents move toward adult roles. Contemporary views interpret parent-adolescent conflict as transitory perturbations that foster age-appropriate interactions between parents and their adult children (Collins, 1995; Smetana, 1989).

Recent reappraisals of the evidence on parent-adolescent conflict have refined common understanding of conflict and its significance.

One refinement is that conflict, like many other aspects of close relationships, is not an inevitable feature of adolescents' dyadic behavior but rather occurs as a function of relationship characteristics and contexts that constrain dyadic behavior (Laursen & Collins, 1994). Closed-field settings, such as those in the obligatory relationships between parents and adolescents, elevate rates of conflict and reduce the likelihood of fully equal resolutions. Pressures toward equitable solutions are less because of the barriers (e.g., kinship, social convention, financial dependency) against leaving the field. Open-field conflicts, which are more typical of voluntary relationships with peers or romantic partners, require equitable solutions to keep the relationships intact. Consequently, conflicts are likely to occur less frequently and to be resolved in mutually satisfactory ways. This social relational view provides an alternative to earlier formulations in which conflict was viewed as an inevitable and functional concomitant of close relationships in families.

A related refinement is a more differentiated view of conflicts between parents and adolescents. Most theoretical formulations have posited that conflicts increase generally as a function of the transition into adolescence. In a meta-analysis, Laursen, Coy, and Collins (1998) examined results from two categories of studies: those comparing different age groups of adolescents and those comparing groups formed on the basis of similarity in pubertal status. The results revealed that the intensity of affect associated with conflict increases somewhat between early and middle adolescence, but this change is accompanied by large decreases in the frequency of conflict across all adolescent age groups. Pubertal status was associated with a slight positive linear increase in conflict affect but was unrelated to the frequency of conflict. Thus, increased conflict does not characterize parent-adolescent relationships generally. Conflict might seem more prevalent because of the greater affective intensity of conflict episodes during the early adolescent years. One implication of this more differentiated view is that the general pattern of increasing complexity and sophistication of resolution strategies might reflect the lower frequency and relatively stable levels of affective intensity during middle to late adolescence.

Individual adolescents clearly vary in the likelihood of conflicts, however, and these individual differences are related to the timing of puberty. For example, levels of certain pubertal hormones appear to be correlated with individual differences in the intensity of conflicts (Inoff-Germain et al., 1988). Conflicts over family rules during early adolescence, for example, have been found to be especially likely in families with early-maturing offspring, both male and female (Hill, 1988). Other findings indicate that the association between pubertal timing and conflicts might differ for males and females (Steinberg, 1988).

A third refinement is that conflicts are neither inimical to closeness nor inevitably harmful to either the relationship or the partners in it. Whether conflicts are functional or dysfunctional in adolescent development depends, in part, on the characteristics of the relationships in which they occur. Constructive engagement and communication in response to conflicts may foster positive developmental changes. Parent-adolescent relationships in which parents are responsive to the adolescents' expressions of discrepant opinions are associated with an enhanced sense of identity among the adolescents as well as relatively advanced social perception skills (Grotevant & Cooper, 1985). In longitudinal research, a parental discussion style that involves supportive but challenging discussions of issues is linked to relatively advanced moral reasoning and psychosocial maturity (Allen et al., 1994; Walker & Taylor, 1991). Effectively managed conflicts also foster interpersonal adaptations to the physical, social, and cognitive changes of adolescence (Collins, 1995; Holmbeck et al., 1995). These findings strengthen the conclusion that relationship properties mediate the significance of conflict for individuals.

To summarize, the common picture of parent-adolescent relationships as discordant and disruptive has given way to a metaphor of transformation. Rather than fragmenting, these dyads are commonly characterized by continuity of emotional bonds coexisting with modifications of interactions and affective expressions that are appropriate to developmental changes in the adolescent partner (Collins, 1995). Conflicts are omnipresent, as in all close relationships, but potentially contribute positively to well-functioning relationships (Grotevant & Cooper, 1985). Parent-adolescent relationships illustrate, perhaps more clearly than any other type of dyad, the way in which accommodations to the changing characteristics of partners helps to stimulate the dynamic adaptation of obligatory relationships.

### Close Relationships
### With Peers

Adolescent relationships with peers differ from those with family members in terms of the distribution of power between participants and the permanence of the affiliations (Laursen & Bukowski, 1997). Peer relationships are voluntary and transient; participants freely initiate and dissolve interconnections. Continuing an affiliation hinges on mutually satisfactory outcomes (Murstein, 1970). Neither party can impose the terms of social interaction on the other (Piaget, 1932/1965). Yet, within these parameters, adolescents' peer relationships vary in important ways. By definition, friends and romantic partners are closer than acquaintances. Moreover, romantic relationships frequently are cross-sex affiliations, whereas friendships rarely are. Peer groups are firmly anchored on same-sex interconnections, but nearly all adolescents have acquaintances both of the same sex and the opposite sex. Lacking ties fostered by commitment and interdependence, acquaintances have no interpersonal investments in relationships. Thus, these affiliations lack the communal properties of friendships and romantic relationships.

*Expansion of social networks.* Dramatic shifts in the social world occur during adoles-

cence, and these shifts extend through young adulthood. The peer network expands dramatically as individuals become more autonomous from parents. 5th graders spend twice as much time with parents than with friends, but the reverse is true of 12th graders (Csikszentmihalyi & Larson, 1984; Larson & Richards, 1991). These changes are accompanied by alterations in the composition of the peer group. Networks initially organized in neighborhoods with close parent supervision evolve into groups of school classmates that, at best, claim perfunctory teacher supervision (Brown, 1990). From early to mid-adolescence, same-sex cliques comprised of a small number of friends or companions who hang around together give way to larger opposite-sex crowds consisting of a loose collection of cliques that are similar in reputations and salience (e.g., nerds, greasers, jocks). These settings provide opportunities for initiating cross-sex relationships (Connolly & Goldberg, in press). Late adolescents balance their time with romantic partners with continued participation in same-sex cliques, gradually decreasing time in mixed-sex groups. By young adulthood, time with romantic partners increases further at the expense of involvement with friends and crowds (Reis et al., 1993; Richards, Crowe, Larson, & Swarr, 1998). Thus, the peer group facilitates the transition from intimate relationships with parents to intimate relationships with friends and romantic partners.

*Friendships.* Relationships with peers also change qualitatively during adolescence (Rubin, Bukowski, & Parker, 1998). With social cognitive advances, adolescents adopt a more sophisticated view of close peer relationships; improved perspective-taking abilities bolster cognitive and affective ties between participants (Selman, 1980). Companionship and sharing are necessary but no longer sufficient conditions for closeness; adolescents, especially females, also expect commitment and intimacy (Youniss & Smollar, 1985). Changes in perceptions of relationships coincide with an improved appreciation of the rules of social exchange. As parental constraints on interactions with peers are gradually removed, adolescents experience the full range of rewards and costs associated with interdependence (Laursen, 1996). Differentiation among peer relationships inevitably results. As individuals develop, specific roles are assumed and defined by particular friends and romantic partners.

Friendships are the most prominent feature of peer society. Few adolescents admit to not having friends; most have extensive daily contacts with friends (Hartup, 1993). Friendships are perceived as the most important source of support during adolescence, and intimacy, mutuality, and self-disclosure with friends peak during the period (Furman & Buhrmester, 1992; Parker & Gottman, 1989). The developmental significance of friends also appears to be greater during adolescence than during other life periods. Experiences with friends shape and moderate social adaptation and academic competence (Berndt, 1996; Cairns & Cairns, 1994). Same-sex friends during adolescence, as the first intimate voluntary relationships, can provide critical interpersonal experiences that establish a template for all subsequent close peer affiliations (Sullivan, 1953). Developmentally speaking, close friendships eventually can undercut their own long-term significance, for successful adolescent friendships enable young adults to turn their full attention to romantic relationships and pair bonding.

*Romantic relationships.* Romantic relationships begin as an informal extension of the peer group. For contemporary adolescents, unsupervised mixed-sex groups have rendered obsolete the dating patterns of their parents. Today, observers (and participants) might have difficulty in distinguishing between opposite-sex friends and romantic partners (Connolly & Goldberg, in press).

Still, some things remain constant across generations. The high-status members of a social crowd are the first to initiate heterosexual contact. These nascent romances inevitably involve participants who lack intimate experi-

ence with the opposite sex (Maccoby, 1998). Socialized in same-sex cliques, males and females bring vastly different expectations and interpersonal styles to romantic relationships. By mid-adolescence, most individuals have been involved in at least one romantic relationship, and by late adolescence, most are participating in ongoing romantic relationships (Brown, in press). The social worlds of those involved in romantic relationships differ from the social worlds of those who are not, as romantic partners quickly become dominant in the relationship hierarchy (Laursen & Williams, 1997). Although romantic interconnections initially are predicated on principles of social exchange, commitment drives participants to transform this voluntary relationship into one that is more obligatory and permanent (Laursen & Jensen-Campbell, in press). Eventually, most young adults marry and reproduce, further transforming the relationship and marginalizing remaining friendships. This effectively ends the peer group's dominance of relationship experiences.

## ► The Art of Fugue: Merging Parent and Peer Relationships

This progression from primary relationships with parents, to expanded social networks and the development of friendships, to commitment to romantic partners illustrates how distinct themes emerge in relationships during childhood and adolescence. At the outset of adolescence, peer relationships are fairly global and undifferentiated. Children discriminate between friends and nonfriends, but convenience and propinquity have as much to do with these distinctions as do loyalty and intimacy. Relationship differentiation has its impetus in increasing autonomy and individuation during adolescence. A new appreciation of social exchange and shared power alter the form and function of peer relationships. Interconnections previously reserved for parents are gradually assumed and enlarged on by peers. Experience and cognitive maturity create new relationship categories and expectations. Hence, subtly nuanced distinctions between peer dyads arise, as close friends are distinguished from other friends and members of the crowd. Just as parents provide a secure base for children's first forays into the peer social world, close peers increase the confidence needed to initiate contact with potential romantic partners. Indeed, romantic relationships spring from an interpersonal framework created by friends. Eventually, males and females establish a new form of peer relationship by altering friendship exchanges to incorporate the unique attributes of romantic interconnections. Thus, peer groups beget close friendships, which in turn beget romantic relationships (Furman & Wehner, 1994; Laursen & Bukowski, 1997).

Research with young adults documents this integration of parent and peer relationships. Although the functions of relationships with parents and peers appear to be relatively distinct during adolescence, young adults' relationships with parents, friends, and romantic partners alike appear to serve the functions typified by parent-child relationships during early life (Ainsworth, 1989). In one sample of college students, friends and romantic partners most often were selected as persons with whom young adults most like to spend time (proximity seeking) and with whom they most want to be when feeling down (safe haven function). At the same time, parents were almost equally likely to be nominated as persons from whom young adults would seek advice and as the persons young adults "could always count on" (secure base function). Although the findings are cross-sectional, the authors speculated that young adults still are completing a transfer of attachment functions from parents to friends and romantic partners (Fraley & Davis, 1997).

Coexisting with these normative transformations within and between relationships are important signs of convergence in varying individual relationship systems. Significant correlations exist between friendship styles during middle and late adolescence and romantic relationship styles (Furman & Wehner, 1994). During late adolescence, displaying safe haven

and secure base behaviors with best friends is positively associated with displaying these behaviors with dating partners. Data on representations of relationships show that working models of friendships and romantic relationships also are correlated (Treboux, Crowell, Owens, & Pan, 1994). Perhaps the growing salience of romantic relationships in young adulthood makes the common relationship properties across types of relationships more apparent than before.

It is equally likely, however, that the greater integration of young adults' relationships reflects, in more similar ways from one dyad to another, their similarity to earlier relationships with parents and peers. Retrospective accounts of childhood relationships with parents are associated with young adults' current romantic attachment styles (Carnelley & Janoff-Bulman, 1992; Collins & Read, 1990; Feeney & Noller, 1990). More compelling evidence comes from longitudinal studies. In the Stony Brook Relationship Project (Waters, Merrick, Albersheim, Treboux, & Crowell, in press), significant correlations were found between secure-insecure attachment measured in the Strange Situation at 1 year of age and the Adult Attachment Interview administered 20 years later. Moreover, the latter scores were related significantly to scores of attachment security in the participants' current romantic relationships (Owens et al., 1995). Thus, young adults' perceptions of security-insecurity in their relationships with parents were correlated with ratings of security-insecurity displayed toward parents 20 years earlier and also to their perceptions of security in their relationships with completely different partners in their romantic relationships. This degree of coherence depends, of course, on considerable stability in a person's life. These researchers and others (e.g., Weinfield, in press) have found that links between earlier and later relationships are lessened by stressful and disruptive life experiences, especially those having to do with close relationships (e.g., death of a parent, other prolonged separation from a parent, instability in caregiving).

Peer relations during middle childhood and friendship during adolescence also are associated with later qualities of romantic relationships. In the Minnesota Longitudinal Study of Parents and Children, low competence with peers in middle childhood (6-12 years of age) was correlated with low levels of mutual caring, enjoyment of each other, and emotional investment in romantic relationships at 19 years of age (Hennighausen & Collins, 1998). This association holds even after quality of friendships at 16 years of age is controlled statistically. Moreover, non-normative behavior with peers at 10 to 11 years of age is associated with earlier initiation of sexual intercourse, less regular practice of contraception, and a larger number of partners by 19 years of age. Much evidence currently points to links among different types of relationships across childhood and adolescence.

## ► Conclusions and Applications

The coherence of links across time between romantic relationships and earlier relationships with either parents or peers is similar to the fugue-like merging of parent and peer relationships into a system governed by communal principles. Both patterns are consistent with developmental principles of differentiation and integration. To be sure, the picture of complementarity and change in relationships that we have described is based partly on cross-sectional comparisons and awaits confirmation by longitudinal studies. Judging from the extant findings, future studies should encompass both parent-adolescent and peer relationships and should assess a broad range of relationship properties. Especially needed are research designs that are sensitive to both similarities and differences between types of relationships and changes in these across time. In the search to document this pattern in adolescent relationships, researchers might gain significant new knowledge of how relationships during every life period change as individuals develop across time.

The potential significance of knowing more about relationships and relationship change during adolescence is abundantly apparent in the widespread efforts to intervene in relationships during adolescence. Generally, the dual premises of this work are that the qualities of adolescent relationships are related to functioning both during adolescence and during later life (Grotevant, 1998) and improving relationships can enhance individual development. Some relationship-based interventions have been strikingly effective. The most common examples are efforts to reduce high levels of conflict in some families of adolescents by improving communication and problem-solving skills and by enhancing perceptual accuracy among family members (Forgatch & De Garmo, 1997; Robin & Foster, 1989). One instance of positive developmental benefits comes from research with families in which chronic stressors (e.g., chronic illness of adolescents) constrain normative transitions toward greater autonomy. For example, in families of adolescents with insulin-dependent diabetes mellitus (IDDM), parents often monitor their children's actions and activities more closely and grant independence less readily than do parents of teenagers with no health-compromising conditions. The IDDM families also experience higher levels of parent-child conflict during middle and late adolescence than do comparison group families (Susman-Stillman, Hyson, Williams, & Collins, 1997). Programs to improve family problem-solving skills and reduce stress have been effective both in reducing conflict in these families and in enhancing adolescents' adherence to treatment regimens (Wysocki, White, Bubb, Harris, & Greco, 1995). Similarly, improving negotiation and problem-solving skills of adolescents with histories of dysfunctional relationships with peers enhances both their peer relationships and their individual adjustment and school functioning (Asher, Parker, & Walker, 1996; Dryfoos, 1990; Selman, 1980). Greater understanding of familial and close peer relationships and their interrelations might provide an even more extensive and differentiated basis for preventing the unfortunate sequelae of poorly functioning relationships during adolescence.

# Contents

# The Life Cycle of Friendship

*Beverley Fehr*

Friendships weave in and out of people's lives. Although their significance often is overlooked, friendships are an important source of meaning, happiness, enjoyment, and love. This chapter charts the life cycle of friendships, including their formation, closeness, preservation, and maintenance. Friendship deterioration, dissolution, and restoration are also discussed. The focus is on adult friendships, predominantly same-sex friendships. Gender differences are noted in cases where women's and men's friendship experiences diverge. Finally, many of the topics discussed in this chapter are given more extensive coverage in Fehr (1996).

## ▶ Friendship Formation

For a friendship to develop, environmental, individual, situational, and dyadic factors must converge.

### Environmental Factors

Day-to-day contact is conducive to the formation of friendships. Five decades ago, a landmark study revealed that friendships are likely to develop when individuals come into contact with one another through residential proximity. Festinger, Schachter, and Back (1950) asked residents of a married students' housing complex to name the three people in the complex with whom they socialized most. The person who lived next door was named most frequently, followed by the person who lived two doors down, and so on. These findings have been replicated in a number of residential settings including dormitories, condominium complexes, and naval bases.

The workplace is another avenue through which potential friends are brought into contact with one another. A large-scale survey of nearly 1,000 men found that the workplace was the most common source of friendships (26% of respondents' friendships), followed by the neighborhood (23%) (Fischer et al., 1977). The role of the workplace in the formation of women's friendships is less clear. For women who have family responsibilities, the demands of combining paid work with domestic work might prohibit the cultivation of friendships in the workplace (Allan, 1989). For women who are not employed outside the home, the neighborhood can play the same role in friendship formation as the workplace does for men (Jerrome, 1984).

Finally, other friends and relatives are an important source of new friendships (Parks & Eggert, 1991). Thus, the seeds of friendship are sown when people are in physical proximity, although recent developments in computer-mediated communication (e.g., e-mail) are enabling people to form friendships in the absence of face-to-face contact (Lea & Spears, 1995).

### Individual Factors

Although contact might be a necessary condition for the formation of friendships, it is not sufficient. For a friendship to develop, the potential friends must exhibit qualities such as physical attractiveness, social skills, and responsiveness. Physical attractiveness is weighed more heavily in attraction to romantic partners than to friends (Sprecher, 1998a). Nevertheless, looks do play a role in the formation of same- and other-sex friendships (Aboud & Mendelson, 1996) because people tend to assume similarity (e.g., in terms of personality or attitudes) between themselves and attractive people (Patzer, 1985).

Social skills also are important. In Riggio's (1986) research, socially skilled university students reported a greater number of acquaintances and close friends than did less skilled students. In a follow-up laboratory study involving actual interactions, the most socially skilled students also were liked best. Social skills are a particularly valuable asset during the early stages of friendship formation (Buhrmester, Furman, Wittenberg, & Reis, 1988).

Finally, it is well documented that individuals who behave in responsive ways (e.g.,

showing interest or concern) are liked more by their interaction partners and form closer friendships than do unresponsive individuals (Berg & Archer, 1980; Godfrey, Jones, & Lord, 1986; Guerrero, 1997). In short, people tend to cultivate friendships with those who are physically attractive, socially skilled, and responsive.

### Situational Factors

Situational factors affecting the formation of friendships include the probability of future interaction, the frequency of interactions, and how available each person is for a new relationship. With regard to the first factor, there is evidence that people respond more positively to others when they anticipate ongoing interactions rather than a single isolated encounter (Darley & Berscheid, 1967). They tend to emphasize the positive and downplay the negative so that future interactions will be pleasant and enjoyable.

Research on the mere exposure effect (Zajonc, 1968; see also Bornstein, 1989) shows that people actually report more positive feelings the more frequently they interact with others. However, even if two people are enjoying frequent pleasant contact, a friendship will not develop unless each person has sufficient time, energy, and other resources to devote to a new relationship. Middle-aged women interviewed by Gouldner and Strong (1987; see also Allan, 1989) were keenly aware of the practical limitations on the number of friendships that they could develop. A respondent's "friendship budget" depended on the number of new friendships she felt could be sustained given existing friendships and the demands of family and employment. Thus, the situations in which people find themselves can either hinder or facilitate the development of friendships.

### Dyadic Factors

Research on the role of dyadic factors in friendship formation has identified similarity, reciprocity of liking, and intimate self-disclosure as important variables. With regard to similarity, Byrne (1971) developed a laboratory paradigm in which participants were led to believe that a stranger (either real or hypothetical) held attitudes that were either similar or dissimilar to their own. Eventually, the focus shifted to the study of actual relationships. This research shows that people form friendships with those who are similar to them in terms of demographic characteristics such as age, gender, education level, income, race, ethnicity, marital status, and religiosity (Blieszner & Adams, 1992; Crandall, Schiffenhauer, & Harvey, 1997; for a review, see Fehr, 1996). Friends also tend to be similar in terms of academic interests, achievements, attitudes (Kandel, 1978a), and values (Curry & Kenny, 1974).

By contrast, there is little evidence that friends are more similar than nonfriends in terms of personality (Curry & Kenny, 1974; Werebe, 1987). However, research on personal construct similarity shows that people who view the world in a similar way are more likely to become friends (Duck, 1973b; Neimeyer & Neimeyer, 1983). Finally, people also are attracted to, and form friendships with, those who hold similar leisure or activity preferences (Fink & Wild, 1995; Sprecher, 1998a; Werner & Parmelee, 1979). In fact, in some studies, these effects have been stronger than similarity effects in the domains of attitudes (Kandel, 1978a; Werner & Parmelee, 1979) and political views (Davis, 1981).

The most commonly accepted explanations for similarity effects are that interactions with similar others serve to validate people's views and confirm that they are correct in their thinking and that it is more rewarding and enjoyable to interact with similar others than with dissimilar others (Berscheid & Walster, 1978). The rewards-of-interaction interpretation recently has received increased attention from Burleson (1994; see also Burleson, Samter, & Lucchetti, 1992), whose research shows that friends are more similar than nonfriends in terms of communication and social skills.

We also tend to like people who like us (Backman & Secord, 1959). Interestingly, if a person expects to be liked by another person, then he or she might actually behave in ways that confirm that expectation. In a study by Curtis and Miller (1986), participants who believed that they were liked by their interaction partners showed fewer distancing behaviors, were more pleasant, and engaged in more intimate self-disclosure than did those who believed that they were disliked. These behaviors served to produce liking in their interaction partners.

According to social penetration theory (Altman & Taylor, 1973), as relationships develop toward greater intimacy, self-disclosure will increase in breadth (the number of topics discussed) and depth (more personal and intimate disclosure). The greatest attraction occurs when someone begins with relatively nonpersonal disclosure and progresses to more intimate disclosure later in the interaction (Archer & Burleson, 1980). During the early stages of a relationship, it also is important that disclosures are reciprocated to establish a sense of trust (Berg & Archer, 1980). Although most of the research on the role of self-disclosure in relationship development is based on interactions between strangers in a laboratory setting, these studies mirror the real-life process of friendship formation. For example, when Miell and Duck (1986) asked respondents to describe the process of developing a friendship, the patterns of self-disclosure that were reported were consistent with those identified in laboratory studies (e.g., starting with relatively nonpersonal topics and then progressing to more intimate disclosure if the friendship seemed promising, reciprocating the other person's disclosures).

The central thesis of this section has been that friendship development occurs when there is a convergence of environmental, individual, situational, and dyadic factors. Studies of friendship formation typically focus on only one of these factors. However, these factors were examined in conjunction in Hays's (1984, 1985) longitudinal research on friendship development among 1st-year university students. He found that an environmental factor, residential proximity, was correlated positively with friendship development. An individual factor, shyness, showed a weak and negative relation. The situational factor of availability (e.g., changes in students' schedules that increased the convenience of getting together) was positively associated with friendship development. At the dyadic level, students rated the intimacy of their friendships in four areas: companionship (e.g., sharing activities), consideration (e.g., providing help and support), communication (e.g., self-disclosure), and affection. The greater the number of areas in which intimacy had been achieved, the closer the friendship. Thus, the formation of a friendship is a complex process in which a number of factors, both internal and external to the relationship, must converge.

## ▶ Achieving Closeness

To discover how friends become close, researchers generally have compared acquaintanceships with close and intimate friendships in terms of self-disclosure, similarity, interaction differences, fun and relaxation, and so on. This research provides insight into the process by which a relationship develops from an acquaintanceship into a close friendship.

### *Self-Disclosure*

As would be expected based on social penetration theory, friends disclose more intimate and personal information than do acquaintances (Hays, 1984, 1985; Hornstein & Truesdell, 1988; see also Dolgin & Minowa, 1997). Planalp and colleagues (Planalp, 1993; Planalp & Benson, 1992) found that people could identify whether tape-recorded conversations were between friends or between acquaintances with 80% accuracy by relying on the nature of self-disclosure between the interactants. Friends displayed greater knowledge of one another's lives as well as greater

mutual knowledge of other people, places, and events. They also exchanged more intimate, emotional, and detailed information (i.e., greater depth of disclosure) and self-disclosed on a greater number of topics (i.e., greater breadth). By contrast, acquaintances tended to exchange more superficial (frequently demographic) information.

Thus, intimate and personal self-disclosure continues to increase as a friendship becomes close. Rubin and Shenker (1978) suggested that the relation between intimate self-disclosure and closeness of friendships is a reciprocal one; people are more likely to reveal intimate information to close, as opposed to less close, friends, and these intimate disclosures can produce even greater closeness.

### *Similarity*

Superficial similarity (e.g., demographic characteristics) may be used as a criterion for selecting (or rejecting) friends, but as a friendship becomes close, the partners must be similar in deeper and more meaningful ways (Aboud & Mendelson, 1996; Crandall et al., 1997; Johnson, 1989). Duck and his colleagues (Duck, 1973a; Duck & Craig, 1978; Lea & Duck, 1982; see also Neimeyer & Neimeyer, 1983) proposed that at the beginning of a friendship, similarity in terms of superficial observable personality dimensions would be the strongest predictor of attraction. A few months later, similarity in values, especially important values (Lea, 1994), should emerge as the most important predictor, followed by similarity in personal constructs (i.e., how an individual construes the world). Research generally has supported these predictions.

In conclusion, friendships are formed on the basis of various types of similarity including similarity in rather superficial domains. A friendship will become close only if the partners are similar in more meaningful ways including similarities in important values and personal constructs. It should be noted that people not only form friendships because they are similar to one another but also become more similar as the friendships develop (Aboud & Mendelson, 1996; Kandel, 1978b). This increase in similarity may serve to further cement the relationship.

### Interaction Differences

Most of the research in which the interactions of acquaintances and friends have been compared has been conducted with children. For example, studies of prosocial behavior typically involve giving children opportunities to share snacks, toys, or crayons with acquaintances or friends (for a review, see Fehr, 1996). These studies show that prosocial behavior generally is greater in interactions with friends than with acquaintances. A recent study suggests that this conclusion also might generalize to adults. Halpern (1997) constructed scenarios involving various economic transactions between friends and strangers. She found that participants were more likely to benefit friends (e.g., request a lower price when selling, offer a higher price when buying). Participants also demanded higher prices when selling friends' commodities.

Finally, observational research shows that people are more fully engaged in interactions with friends than with acquaintances and show more positive communicative behaviors such as smiling, making eye contact, talking, and laughing (Planalp & Benson, 1992). These behaviors might account for the finding that friends frequently outperform acquaintances on problem-solving and memory tasks (Anderson & Ronnberg, 1997; Newcomb & Brady, 1982).

### Fun and Relaxation

Although researchers have documented the activities in which people engage with friends (see the next section on maintaining friendships), they rarely ask whether people are having fun with their friends. However, the amount of fun and relaxation experienced

might be an important indication of whether a relationship has progressed from an acquaintanceship to a friendship. When Planalp and Benson (1992) asked participants to describe the bases on which they discriminated between friends' and acquaintances' conversations, two unexpected dimensions emerged: The interactions of friends were more relaxed, friendly, and casual than those of acquaintances, and friends used more informal language that included joking and teasing. Similarly, a salient feature of the interactions of middle-aged and older women in a friendship group observed by Jerrome (1984) was the amount of joking and laughing. These women valued the opportunities for fun that were afforded by belonging to the group. Finally, based on interview data, Swain (1989) concluded that for men, the degree of comfort and relaxation experienced serves as a barometer of the closeness of same-sex friendships. These findings are reinforced by research showing that fun and relaxation are strong predictors of intimacy (Hays & Oxley, 1986) and satisfaction (Jones, 1991) in both women's and men's friendships.

## ► Maintaining Friendships

According to Duck (1994; see also Canary & Stafford, 1994), there are two paths to relationship maintenance: explicit strategic maintenance and implicit maintenance, described as "the breezy allowance of the relationship to continue by means of the routine everyday interactions and conversations that make the relationship what it is" (p. 46).

### Implicit Maintenance Strategies

For decades, friendship scholars have documented how time with friends is spent. This research shows that the activities that are performed (particularly with same-sex friends) and the conversation topics that are discussed depend on the friends' gender. Overall, there is evidence that men prefer engaging in activities (e.g., participating in sports) with friends, whereas women prefer talking (Parker & de Vries, 1993; for a review, see Fehr, 1996). For example, when Caldwell and Peplau (1982) asked undergraduates their preference between these options, more than three times as many women as men chose "just talking" with a same-sex friend; nearly twice as many men as women chose engaging in an activity. (Even when women engage in activities with friends, talk remains a central focus [Johnson & Aries, 1983].) Although this gender difference is well established in the literature, its magnitude has been questioned recently. There are arguments both that women are more activity oriented and that men are more talk oriented than has been thought (Walker, 1994; Wright & Scanlon, 1991). Duck and Wright (1993) have suggested that gender differences still might exist, however, in the topics discussed with friends.

Indeed, there is evidence that women and men discuss rather different topics with friends. Women tend to talk about personal and relationship matters, whereas men tend to talk about nonpersonal matters (e.g., sports, vehicles, work, computers) (for a review, see Fehr, 1996). In Caldwell and Peplau's (1982) study, participants were asked to list three topics that were commonly discussed with their best (same-sex) friends. Personal topics such as feelings and problems were mentioned twice as often by women than by men, whereas men's conversations centered on sports, work, and vehicles. Findings such as these have been obtained in more recent research as well. For example, when Martin (1997) asked participants to classify transcribed conversations between same-sex friends according to gender, they reported that men's conversations were identifiable by the topics they discussed—women, sports, fighting, being trapped in relationships, and bars or drinking. Women's conversations focused on relationships, men, clothing, problems with roommates, and needs/feelings. In several other studies, however, evidence of gender similarities in the content and structure of

conversations with friends has been as strong as, if not stronger than, evidence of differences (Dolgin & Minowa, 1997; Freed & Greenwood, 1996; Leaper & Holliday, 1995). Conclusions about gender differences in conversation topics also must be tempered in light of research showing that these differences are most pronounced in same-sex interactions (Fehr, 1996) and in interactions with good, as opposed to casual, friends (Clark, 1998).

Regardless of the form that activities and conversations might take for each gender, these are the types of interactions that serve to maintain and sustain friendships for both women and men. Harré (1977), for example, discussed friendship maintenance in terms of shared mundane activities (e.g., socializing over food and drink, giving rides). In Duck's (1994) view, everyday talk is the essence of relationship maintenance because the mere occurrence of talk, regardless of its content, signifies to the partners that the relationship exists and is important. Thus, friendships are maintained through the types of activities and conversations in which people naturally engage with friends, even though these interactions were not motivated by the explicit goal of relationship maintenance.

### Explicit Maintenance Strategies

The explicit strategies that people use to maintain relationships vary, depending on the nature of the relationship and the stage of its development (Canary & Stafford, 1994). Canary, Stafford, Hause, and Wallace (1993) asked participants to list the strategies (and provide behavioral examples) that they used to maintain romantic, friendship, and familial relationships. The most frequent strategy, labeled *openness,* was exemplified by the behavior of self-disclosure. The second most frequent strategy, *assurance,* involved communicating that the relationship was important. The most common behavioral manifestation of this strategy was supportiveness. The strategy of spending time together as a way of maintaining relationships (labeled *joint activi-*

*ties*) was listed next, followed by *positivity* (trying to make interactions pleasant), *cards/ letters/calls,* and *avoidance* (of relationship issues or the partner). Generally, these strategies were more likely to be used in romantic or familial relationships than in friendships.

Researchers who have focused exclusively on friendships have tended to compare the strategies used to maintain different types of friendships. For example, Matthews (1986) differentiated friendships on the basis of commitment. Her interviews with elderly women and men revealed that highly committed friendships were characterized by active maintenance including taking long trips to visit one another, letter writing, and telephone calls. By contrast, friendships that were low in commitment were maintained on a circumstantial basis (e.g., residential proximity, involvement in formal groups or clubs). If circumstances changed, then few efforts were made to continue these relationships.

Rose (1985) asked undergraduate and graduate students (single and married) to describe how they maintained same- and other-sex close friendships. The strategies of acceptance, effort, time, communication, and common interests were listed more frequently for same-sex than for other-sex friendships, whereas "no maintenance" and affection were listed more frequently for other-sex friendships. Maintenance strategies also differed depending on the participants' gender and life stage (e.g., marital status, student status). For example, unmarried participants were more likely than married participants to list spending time together as a strategy for maintaining same-sex friendships. Women were more likely than men to respond with "no maintenance" when asked about other-sex friendships.

Finally, Rose and Serafica (1986) compared the strategies used to maintain casual, close, and best same-sex friendships. Responses to the question "How do two people stay friends?" were categorized as either proximity, affection, interaction, or self-maintaining. Casual friendships were perceived as requiring more proximity and less affection than

were close or best friendships. Close and best friends did not differ on any of the maintenance categories: "Both required little proximity, some affection, and considerable interaction to maintain" (p. 280).

In summary, the literatures on the implicit and explicit maintenance of friendships point to a number of strategies that facilitate the continuation of friendships. Of these, three seem particularly important: self-disclosure, supportiveness, and spending time together. Self-disclosure, as the behavioral manifestation of openness, was the most frequently mentioned explicit maintenance strategy in Canary et al.'s (1993) study (see also Rose, 1985). Self-disclosure in the form of everyday talk also was considered a primary implicit maintenance strategy. Thus, it appears that relationship maintenance is a byproduct of self-disclosure as it naturally occurs in friendships. However, there also is evidence that people, especially women (Afifi, Guerrero, & Egland, 1994; Honeycutt & Patterson, 1997), consciously use self-disclosure as a means of maintaining and improving their friendships.

Friendships also are maintained through the provision of social support. This was the second most frequent maintenance strategy reported in Canary et al.'s (1993) research. The importance of supportiveness has surfaced in other research as well (Afifi et al., 1994; Argyle & Henderson, 1984; Honeycutt & Patterson, 1997; Walker, 1995). Like self-disclosure, social support also can be conceptualized as an implicit maintenance strategy. According to Burleson and Samter (1994), close friends are the primary source of social support for most young adults, and this has implications for the maintenance of friendships: "To maintain a close friendship, partners are thus obligated to provide comfort, help solve problems . . . celebrate victories, offer encouragement . . . and so on" (p. 74). Those authors suggest that deliberate maintenance rarely is the motivation for the provision of support. Rather, there is a tacit understanding that providing support is simply "what friends do."

Finally, research on the everyday activities and conversations of friends suggests that one of the least obvious avenues to friendship maintenance might be one of the most crucial, that is, simply spending time together. This point was underscored in the subsection on explicit maintenance, where strategies such as interaction, joint activities, spending time together, and cards/letters/calls were commonly mentioned (see also Afifi et al., 1994; Honeycutt & Patterson, 1997). As Duck (1994) argued, seemingly mundane interactions communicate that the relationship exists and is important enough that the partners have taken the time to be together.

In conclusion, friendships can be sustained in myriad ways. However, based on the literatures on implicit and explicit maintenance, it appears that friendships are most likely to thrive when friends spend time together, engage in self-disclosure, and provide support to one another.

## ▶ Deterioration and Dissolution

Friendships that are not maintained tend to deteriorate and dissolve. However, even friendships that are actively maintained might encounter difficulties that lead to the deterioration, and possible termination, of the relationships.

### Conflict and Anger in Friendships

As a friendship develops and becomes more intimate, people report not only increased benefits but also increased anger and conflict (Hays, 1985; Hays & Oxley, 1986). Although many causes of anger and conflict have been identified in marital and romantic relationships (e.g., rebuff or rejection, being mocked, cumulative annoyances, personal criticism, betrayal of trust) (Fehr, Baldwin, Collins, Patterson, & Benditt, 1999), only one of these, betrayal of trust, has received significant attention in the friendship literature

(Jones & Burdette, 1994; Shackelford & Buss, 1996). Betrayal by a friend is not a rare event; only spouses/romantic partners (and for men, co-workers) exceed friends as perpetrators and targets of betrayal (Jones & Burdette, 1994; Shackelford & Buss, 1996). In a study by Davis and Todd (1985), more than one third of the participants reported having experienced violations or betrayals in their best and closest friendships, and 37% admitted to having committed betrayals. According to Shackelford and Buss (1996), the strongest feelings of betrayal in same-sex friendships are elicited by a friend's sexual or emotional involvement with one's romantic partner, followed by a friend's failure to come to one's defense when criticized by others. Women also feel betrayed when a close same-sex friend fails to engage in intimate self-disclosure. Other research has identified breaches of confidence as a significant betrayal event in friendships (e.g., Wiseman, 1986).

The effects of betrayals on friendships are uniformly negative. In Davis and Todd's (1985) study, participants who had been betrayed rated their friendships as lower in viability (e.g., trust, respect, acceptance) and success than did participants who had not been betrayed. Those who had perpetrated betrayals rated their friendships as lower in intimacy, support, stability, and success. The literature on dealing with conflict and anger in friendships suggests a reason why betrayals have such negative effects. This research shows that when friends encounter difficulties, the most common response is passive avoidance as opposed to explicit constructive discussions of problematic issues (see Fehr, 1996, although there are exceptions to this finding [Samp & Solomon, 1998]). For example, Sillars (1980a, 1980b) found that integrative strategies (explicit constructive discussions) were least likely to be used by friends in conflict situations, even though they were most likely to produce satisfactory resolutions. Moreover, the use of integrative tactics was negatively correlated with both the frequency and duration of conflicts. Thus, it appears that when friends experience anger and conflict, the most likely response is one that is least likely to lead to a positive outcome.

### Dissolution of Friendships

The four categories of variables that must converge for a friendship to develop (environmental, individual, situational, and dyadic) also are implicated in the dissolution of friendships. Research on each of these factors is discussed, followed by research on the strategies that people use to terminate friendships.

*Environmental factors.* Frequent contact is necessary for a friendship to develop. Conversely, the loss of proximity is associated with friendship termination. Loss of proximity occurs when people move away, attend different schools, change jobs, retire, or even move within the same city (Blieszner & Adams, 1998; Matthews, 1986; Rose & Serafica, 1986). In Rose's (1984) study of college students (17-22 years of age), more than half of the participants (57.4%) had experienced the dissolution of close friendships during the previous 5 years, usually during the transition to college. (If Rose's sample had not consisted primarily of local residents, then the loss of friendships might have been even greater given claims that the majority of friendships do not survive changes such as geographic mobility [Allan, 1989].)

Thus, environmental factors such as reduced proximity contribute to the termination of friendships. It is possible that technological developments such as e-mail will mitigate these effects. So far, however, the benefits of these developments for friendship maintenance have not been demonstrated empirically.

*Individual factors.* For a friendship to develop, each person must find the other person's qualities attractive. Unfortunately, negative characteristics such as possessiveness and being demanding, moody, or boring might become apparent only after the relationship is established (Wiseman, 1986). In LaGaipa's (1987) program of research, a fre-

quent reason given for the dissolution of a friendship was the discovery of character flaws that undermined admiration for the friend (see also Blieszner & Adams, 1998; Matthews, 1986). Thus, as Duck (1982) observed, "New, surprising, and significantly negatively charged information about the other can hasten the relationship's death" (p. 7).

*Situational factors.* The situational factors that play a role in friendship formation also play a role in the dissolution of friendships. For example, friendships might dissolve when the availability of one or both partners is reduced, either by the types of environmental factors discussed earlier (e.g., moving away) or by changes in other life circumstances. In a study of friendships among middle-aged adults, Rawlins (1994) observed,

> The interviews were riddled with accounts of how vulnerable friendships were to altered circumstances . . . shifting schedules, changing jobs, moving away, developing new interests. It felt like valued friendships were continually slipping away from these adults, in most cases due to events that transcended the friendships. (p. 287)

Availability also is undermined when new friendships are formed as people discover that they lack the resources (e.g., time, energy) to maintain a roster of old and new friendships (Wilmot & Stevens, 1994). Romantic relationships pose an even greater threat to friendships. Simply put, the greater the involvement with a romantic partner, the lesser the involvement with friends. Johnson and Leslie (1982), for example, found that the number of friends decreased from an average of 4.13 for occasional daters to 1.06 for married respondents. Moreover, romantic involvement was associated with a reduction in the quality and quantity of interactions with the few friends who were retained. Women's same-sex friendships are especially likely to be sacrificed on the altar of romantic involvement given that couple-based socializing tends to occur primarily with the male partner's friends (Rose & Serafica, 1986).

In conclusion, it appears that any event that leads to decreased interactions between friends is likely to put the relationship in peril. This is not surprising given evidence presented earlier that frequent interactions are crucial for both the formation and maintenance of friendships.

*Dyadic factors.* One of the best predictors of friendship formation and maintenance is similarity. It follows that if friends become dissimilar, then their relationship might be threatened. Indeed, when asked why friendships had ended, people frequently report that they no longer had anything in common with their friends, often because they followed different life paths (Matthews, 1986; Rawlins, 1994; Wiseman, 1986). An example is the loss of friendships with other homemakers experienced by women who embark on university studies in midlife (Levy, 1981). Longitudinal studies of friendship dissolution also point to the deleterious effects of loss of similarity, particularly in meaningful domains (Duck & Allison, 1978; Kandel, 1978b).

Reciprocity of liking was another factor identified as important in the formation of friendships. Conversely, decreased liking is associated with the dissolution of friendships (Rose, 1984; Rose & Serafica, 1986). As discussed earlier, decreased liking can occur when friends reveal undesirable traits.

Finally, the unraveling of friendships also is reflected in patterns of self-disclosure. According to research by Baxter (1979, 1982), personal and intimate self-disclosure that is associated with friendship development and maintenance is avoided when a friendship is deteriorating. For example, in a scenario study, participants indicated less willingness to disclose, particularly on high intimacy and openness topics, when a desire for disengagement rather than maintenance of the friendship, was depicted (Baxter, 1979). In a subsequent diary study, disengaging friendships

were characterized by less effective and less personal communication than were growing friendships (Baxter & Wilmot, 1986).

To summarize, in the same way that environmental, individual, situational, and dyadic factors must coalesce to form a friendship, friendships are likely to dissolve when all four of these factors conspire against them. The importance of this constellation of factors is highlighted in research by Rose (1984). When she asked college students to describe the decline of a closest same-sex friendship, nearly half (47%) mentioned an environmental factor, namely physical separation (e.g., moving to another city, attending different schools). The situational factor of reduced availability also was evident, as 18% of the participants reported that old friends had been replaced by new friends and 12% attributed dissolution to one or both friends' romantic involvement. An individual-level factor (mentioned by 22% of the respondents), labeled *dislike,* included a variety of attitudes and behaviors that undermined liking for the friend (e.g., betrayal, criticism, religious differences). Rose and Serafica (1986) subsequently conducted a more finely grained analysis by soliciting dissolution accounts for different types of friendship (casual, close, and best). Participants' responses were categorized as either less proximity (e.g., friend moved), less affection (e.g., decrease in liking, commitment, or acceptance), less interaction (e.g., decrease in quantity or quality of time spent together), and interference (e.g., romantic involvement). Interestingly, different causes were identified for the dissolution of the different types of friendships. For example, casual friendships were more likely to end because of reduced proximity, whereas close and best friendships were more likely to end because of interference or decreased interaction. These findings raise the intriguing possibility that environmental, individual, situational, and dyadic factors might have differential impacts on friendship dissolution, depending on the stage of the relationship.

*Termination strategies.* Earlier, research was presented suggesting that friends are most likely to respond to conflict and anger with passive avoidance. Passivity also appears to be the modus operandi when people attempt to terminate friendships; the strategy of withdrawal/avoidance is among the most frequently reported in this literature (Baxter, 1979, 1982). In one study, 72% of the strategies that participants had used to end friendships were classified as indirect (Baxter, 1979). Passivity is also reflected in the tendency to use phrases such as "drifting apart" and "fading away" to describe the dissolution of friendships (Rawlins, 1994). Indeed, friendships generally end in this way, in contrast to the formal explicit breaking up process that characterizes romantic relationships.

## ▶ Restoring Friendships

Friendship has been described as the most fragile relationship (Wiseman, 1986). Unlike institutionalized relationships such as marriage, when a friendship deteriorates, mechanisms to assist in reconciliation and repair generally are not available. Instead, people are left to their own devices. Recently, Wilmot and his colleagues (Wilmot, 1994; Wilmot & Shellen, 1990) have begun to document the ways in which people attempt to restore broken friendships. Wilmot and Stevens (1994) asked respondents to describe the decline of a relationship (friendship, romantic, marital, or familial) and the turning points that resulted in its rejuvenation. For friendships, the most common event (reported by 33% of participants) was a change in the behavior of one or both partners including giving the other more "space," spending more time together, being more independent, and talking more. (Rejuvenation behaviors generally were related to the perceived cause of decline. For example, the behavior of giving more space was a response to the relation-

ship difficulty of one partner feeling "smothered.") The second rejuvenation event (31%) was labeled *have big relationship talk*. These talks served the explicit function of restoring the relationship and entailed apologies, arguments, setting ground rules, and the like. The third rejuvenation event (19%) involved gestures of reconciliation, followed by reassessment of the importance of the relationship (8%) and accepting or forgiving the partner (8%). Finally, a mere 2% of respondents reported that they had restored a relationship by seeking third-party help (e.g., seeing a counselor, talking to other social network members).

The relatively low rates with which these rejuvenation events were endorsed for friendships suggest that when this type of relationship deteriorates, people might not take active steps to restore it. Consistent with this conjecture, Rose (1984) reported that a number of her participants expressed regret that they had allowed friendships to deteriorate past the point where they could be salvaged. As already discussed, this passivity is a theme that also emerges in the literatures on conflict in friendships and dissolution strategies. Although the passive approach to conflict management has deleterious effects on friendships, ironically, this same approach to termination can have positive effects on the restoration of friendships. Rawlins (1994) reported that the middle-aged respondents in his sample used terms such as "drifting apart" as a means of leaving the door open to possible resumption of their relationships in the future. Similarly, some of Matthews' (1986) elderly respondents regarded "faded" friendships as relationships that could be revived. Reconciliation was perceived as much more difficult if the relationship had explicitly been terminated. Such perceptions might well be accurate. In a study by Davis and Todd (1985), friendships that had drifted apart were rated as higher in intimacy, enjoyment, viability, and the like than those that had been terminated due to violations (see also Adams & Blieszner, 1998).

In conclusion, the passive approach that people generally take to the termination of friendships can have the positive effect of leaving open the possibility of reconciliation. However, the research on rejuvenation strategies suggests that friends are relatively unlikely to engage in explicit restoration attempts. Thus, it is not clear whether people act on opportunities for friendship restoration or merely take comfort in the possibility of restoration. Perhaps most important, the literature on dealing with conflict and anger suggests that if friends would engage in more open and constructive discussion of conflict issues as they arise, then they would be much less likely to need a repertoire of rejuvenation strategies.

## ▶ Conclusions and Applications

The research discussed in this chapter was conducted with the purpose of illuminating the processes by which people develop, maintain, lose, and restore friendships. Valuable practical lessons can be extracted from these findings for people who wish to enrich their friendship lives. For those who are lacking in friendships, the literature suggests that an important first step is to seek out environments that bring them into contact with potential friends, particularly environments in which interactions with others are frequent and pleasant. Within this pool of candidates, friendships should be pursued with those who appear to have room in their lives for new friends and who are similar to themselves (e.g., in terms of demographic characteristics, attitudes, and/or leisure preferences). It also is important to cultivate the types of qualities that are desired in friends. These qualities generally revolve around social competencies (e.g., social skills, responsiveness) that can be

improved through therapeutic intervention (Adams & Blieszner, 1993). Finally, during interactions with potential friends, self-disclosures should be reciprocated and progress gradually from nonintimate to intimate topics.

Research on friendship also is relevant for people seeking to increase the closeness or intimacy of their friendships. In choosing which friendships to intensify, the literature suggests that an important consideration is similarity in meaningful domains (e.g., important values, personal construct similarity). During interactions, recommendations for achieving closeness include increasing intimate self-disclosure, engaging in prosocial behavior (particularly social support), and (perhaps less obvious) simply having fun together. These also are the types of behavior that serve to maintain friendships once they have become close.

Finally, it should be noted that friendships are not exempt from anger and conflict. In such situations, people generally react with passive avoidance. However, it has been demonstrated that explicit constructive discussion of difficult issues is most likely to result in a satisfactory outcome. Constructive discussions also are recommended for people wishing to restore lapsed friendships (along with strategies such as communicating a willingness to change problematic behaviors). Such strategies might have greater success if aimed at friendships that have faded away rather than friendships that were explicitly terminated.

In conclusion, this chapter has shown that friendships are an important source of meaning, love, happiness, enjoyment, and excitement in people's lives. The effort required to form, maintain, and restore these relationships seems a small price to pay in light of these benefits.

# Contents

# Close Relationships in Old Age

*Rosemary Blieszner*

As is true for people throughout life, those in old age rely on close relationships for their psychological well-being and even their physical health (Adams & Blieszner, 1995). Interactions with significant others buffer the effects of stressful events and situations, offer emotional sustenance and affirmation of one's identity, yield needed assistance, help structure time in meaningful ways, and provide continuity in important roles. At the same time, close relationships prompt developmental change in the participants, and the relationships themselves change over time. Close relationships entail not only benefits but also challenges and problems for those involved.

This chapter includes discussions of three key topics pertaining to late-life close relationships. One focus is on the variety and diversity of these relationships in old age. How

do such ties compare to those during the earlier years of life? How do personal characteristics and types of relationships affect the nature of social interaction during the later years? A second topic addresses the interactive dynamics of close relationships. What are the most important functions of these associations, and how do participants enact them? In what ways do close relationships contribute both to well-being and to distress in old age? The third topic details implications of current literature for theory development, future research agendas, and practice. What conceptual frameworks exist to aid in filling gaps in knowledge about old age relationships? How can current information about close relationships be used to improve the quality of life for elder citizens? These topics illustrate the depth and breadth of information available about significant others during the later years while at the same time pointing toward applications and additional research agendas.

AUTHOR'S NOTE: I thank Katherine R. Allen, Lisa M. Artale, and Karen A. Roberto for their assistance.

## ▶ Variety and Diversity of Close Relationships in Old Age

### Comparison of Close Relationships Across the Life Span

Myths about old people and aging processes abound. Many people seem to believe that the final part of life is lived in alien territory, fraught with intractable problems and disabilities. In fact, current cohorts of elders are healthier than ever, possessing many personal and social resources that allow them to engage in a full range of close relationships and associated activities. At the same time, age-related changes that affect health or lifestyle are likely to have an impact on close relationships as well. In what ways are old adults' close relationships like those of everyone else? In what ways are they different?

Most old people, even those who never married or never had children, are members of families and have frequent contact with at least some of their relatives. Most have and interact regularly with friends as well (Allen, 1989; Antonucci & Akiyama, 1995; Litwin, 1997; Phillipson, 1997). Satisfactory relations with kin depend on feelings of attachment and interdependence throughout life (Koski & Shaver, 1997; Silverstein & Bengtson, 1997). Help and gifts are passed both up and down the generational lines (Cheal, 1983; Gallagher, 1994; Lee & Aytac, 1998). Old people value the same facets of romantic relationships as do young people, namely emotional security, respect, communication, help and play behaviors, sexual intimacy, and love (Reedy, Birren, & Schaie, 1981). Likewise, similar characteristics of friends are appealing across ages including shared values and interests, trustworthiness, displays of affection, and expressions of support (Blieszner & Adams, 1992).

At the same time as these relational continuities tend to endure throughout life, it is important to note that certain age-related events, transitions, and changes in health can affect the nature of social interaction during the later years. For example, assuming significant child-rearing responsibilities for grandchildren can limit the time and energy available for friends (Baydar & Brooks-Gunn, 1998), the timing of retirement can affect the marital relationship (Szinovacz & Ekerdt, 1995), and adjusting to vision loss can require new ways of interacting with family and friends (Reinhardt, 1996). Many older adults become widowed, experience reduced mobility, move to new localities to seek desirable amenities or live closer to family, or suffer from a form of dementia. These conditions can have a significant impact on existing relationships and on the possibility of establishing new ones. In addition, old people are more likely than those in any other age group to lose a number of family members and friends to death (Moss & Moss, 1995).

Just as individuals and their circumstances change over time, relationships themselves are not static. They have beginnings, middles, and ends that are influenced by the personal developmental and social structural characteristics of those involved as well as by their patterns of everyday activities and the interactions that take place between and among the participants (Adams & Blieszner, 1994; Blieszner & Adams, 1992). Family relationships are very long term, spanning decades and encompassing strong ties among three or more generations of members (Bengtson, Rosenthal, & Burton, 1996), and many old people value highly their long-term friendships (Shea, Thompson, & Blieszner, 1988). Often, close relationships provide numerous forms of meaningful and helpful support (Felton & Berry, 1992; Murrell, Norris, & Chipley, 1992). But just because close relationships are long-standing and positive does not mean that they are immune to conflict, betrayal, and other problematic features with which participants must contend (Adams & Blieszner, 1998; Blieszner & Adams, 1998; Fingerman, 1998; Hansson, Jones, & Fletcher, 1990). Moreover, interactions occurring earlier in life can have implications for relationships later in life (Bedford, 1992; Parrott & Bengtson, 1999; Whitbeck, Hoyt, & Huck, 1994).

In summary, the close relationships of society's elders share many features in common with those of other adults, yet special circumstances associated with old age have unique effects on these associations. Some close relationships are very long-lasting, yet they change over time and are characterized by both positive and negative aspects. The following subsections contain more detailed examinations of the effects of both personal characteristics and relationship type on interactions with kin and friends.

### Influence of Personal Characteristics on Close Relationships

As indicated previously, age can affect close relationships to the extent that greater longevity signals health problems that limit social interaction or require changes in relational dynamics. One of the most common expressions of this age effect is caregiving by spouses and adult children. Extreme frailty, stroke, and dementia are examples of conditions that prompt partners and offspring to assume forms of instrumental and emotional support that can be trying for both providers and recipients (Clark & Stephens, 1996; Hinrichsen & Niederehe, 1994; Johnson & Barer, 1997). Although some research on caregiving has identified positive outcomes such as greater appreciation for the role of the care recipient in the family, most of the studies have focused on stress, burden, and negative implications for emotional closeness (Walker, Pratt, & Eddy, 1995).

Besides age group membership, other social structural characteristics that affect close relationships include gender, racial/ethnic heritage, socioeconomic class, and marital status (C. Johnson, 1995; Lopata, 1995; Roschelle, 1997). Experiences of friendship and kinship differ between men and women, blacks and whites, the rich and the poor, and those who are married and those who are not, based on divergent socialization patterns and dissimilar opportunities and constraints that affect relationships (Blieszner & Adams,

1992; Calasanti, 1993; Hatch & Bulcroft, 1992). These influences usually do not operate by themselves; rather, they intersect with each other.

In addition, close relationships are influenced by the partners' personalities, social cognitions, relationship skills, and coping strategies (Hansson & Carpenter, 1994). Traits such as extraversion and agreeableness describe propensities to affiliate with others, positive attributions enable a person to view others as attractive, skills such as assertiveness and appropriate self-disclosure promote relational development, and strategies such as seeking social support in times of stress serve to foster adjustment to difficulties. Absence or ineffective use of these personal characteristics and abilities can lead to unhappiness and loneliness (Hansson & Carpenter, 1994).

The connection between personal characteristics and close relationships is bidirectional. That is, just as individuals affect interactions, so too do relationships affect the parties involved. The deleterious effects of caregiving on the care provider's physical and mental health, mentioned previously, is one example. Others come from research by Korbin, Anetzberger, and Austin (1995), who addressed the intergenerational transmission of family violence; Paul (1997), who analyzed the effects on well-being of multiple dimensions of relationships across three age cohorts; and Ryff, Schmutte, and Lee (1996), who demonstrated how parents' assessments of their adult children's success in life affected parental well-being. Taken together, these and other studies clearly indicate that being involved in close relationships can affect one's development and well-being.

### Influence of Relationship Type on Interactions

Not only do the characteristics of relational partners affect their interactions, the type of relationship in which they are involved also has an impact. Many elders enjoy a wide range of relationships including those with family members, friends, and more casual acquaintances. Relational partners, especially siblings and friends, often are members of the elders' generation, but many elders also interact with significant others who are of older and younger generations. Some types of relationships are fairly common, whereas others are atypical. The extent to which elders have followed and continue to follow normative expectations about the types of relationships in which they are involved influences their well-being, at least to some extent.

*The effect of consanguinity.* Family members and friends serve both common and different functions in the lives of older adults. Both types of relationships can provide social support (Antonucci & Akiyama, 1995) and opportunities for meaningful leisure and other pursuits (Mancini & Sandifer, 1995). However, feelings of attachment and deep emotional security usually occur within family relationships, whereas friends typically provide companionship of a nonobligatory nature (Weiss, 1998). In fact, the voluntary nature of friendship, as compared to the sometimes obligatory nature of family interactions, is one explanation given for the finding that friends contribute more to psychological well-being in old age than do family members (Antonucci & Akiyama, 1995).

*The effect of generation.* Intragenerational relationships, such as between siblings and friends who are fairly close to one's age, offer the promise of shared understandings about current life experiences, common interpretations of past events, and role models for socialization to new aspects of life. These interactions can affirm one's sense of self and ease transitions to new stages of life. By contrast, intergenerational relationships, such as with children, grandchildren, and younger friends, provide elders with the means of expressing generativity and transmitting family and cultural lore. In these relationships, elders can try new styles of interaction (e.g., relating to grandchildren in a more relaxed way than to one's own children when they were young)

and can learn about new elements of culture (e.g., when the younger family members help their elders to become computer literate).

*The effect of degree of closeness.* Relationships and their outcomes also are likely to vary according to the degree of relatedness among family members or the extent of emotional closeness with friend network members. Typically, people see their closest relatives and friends more often than they see others, share more in common with them, and derive more satisfaction from interactions with them. By contrast, relationships with cousins, nieces, and nephews typically involve less contact and are less close, particularly if these extended kin live at a distance. Likewise, although most people have cordial relationships with those defined as "neighbor" or "acquaintance" instead of "friend," the relationships generally involve much less self-disclosure, little affection, and fewer shared activities.

*The effect of prevalence.* Normative relationships enable participants to fit in easily with the mainstream society, fostering comfortable social transactions. Examples include traditional marriage and the ensuing relationships with in-laws, traditional parenthood, interactions with siblings, and friendships with similar others. Non-normative relationships, in terms of prevalence and societal regard, can add interest and challenge to the process of aging or can be quite troublesome. Examples to consider are relationships within blended, step-, and foster families; multiway relationships that result from the linking of disparate families through adoption (whether open or closed records are involved); relationships with family-like individuals such as nannies for grandchildren and sitters for elders; incestuous or otherwise abusive relationships; and parent-child relationships when one party is incarcerated (Kaiser, 1996).

Changes in cultural values and family structure over time (e.g., with divorce) and differences among cultural subgroups, however, lead to a blurring of the classification of relationships into normative and non-normative types. For example, people ascribe kinlike status to supportive friends (Stack, 1974) and create "opportune" families (C. Johnson, 1995), emphasizing preferences and needs more than blood ties. They also convert one type of relationship to another to solve social problems, as in the case of an older adult who refers to a son's ex-wife as her "friend" to be able to maintain the relationship with her grandchildren's mother (Johnson, 1988). In these cases, family relationships become viewed less as obligatory and more as voluntary.

## ► Relationship Processes in Old Age

Throughout life, close relationships with family and friends have physical and psychological implications. Positive relationships contribute to happiness, a sense of belonging and purpose, and overall well-being, whereas negative ones are likely to yield opposite outcomes (Hansson & Carpenter, 1994). Relationships have these effects through interactional processes related to thoughts, feelings, and behaviors that occur in their enactment (Adams & Blieszner, 1994; Blieszner & Adams, 1992). Social support, manifested as instrumental, informational, and emotional succor, is one of the most important relational processes, perhaps particularly in old age.

### *Contributions to Aging Well: Social Support and Caregiving*

In gerontology, the concept of "aging well" connotes an active stance toward life on the part of old people who make decisions about their own outcomes. Not only are elders in good mental and physical health viewed as aging well, but so too are those who cope effectively with adverse health or social conditions such as widowhood or the deaths of friends (T. Johnson, 1995). In the context of

close relationships, aging well implies that elders take responsibility for their relationships with friends and relatives rather than merely hoping or assuming that their needs to give and receive support will be met. That is, they possess what Hansson and Carpenter (1994) called "relational competence." Being able to acquire needed and wanted social support contributes to aging well because elders who can do so will be able to contend appropriately with any stresses or impairments that arise. Being able to find outlets for one's own altruism also contributes to aging well because it provides elders with a continued sense of personal control, meaning, and purpose in life (Krause, Herzog, & Baker, 1992).

Family members and friends tend to provide different forms of support to those who are old. Elders usually prefer to receive help with personal care, everyday chores, and other ongoing needs from close family members, whereas friends (as age peers) are likely to focus on emotional sustenance. But these roles for assistance and caregiving are not mutually exclusive. Friends also provide instrumental and informational support when, for example, they run errands for each other or discuss new policies that affect themselves. Ties with close kin, such as spouses and siblings, certainly yield emotional support and psychological well-being (Adams & Blieszner, 1995). For example, aged parents who believe that their children would give assistance if the need arose have better psychological well-being than do those who are less certain about what their offspring's response would be (Blieszner & Hamon, 1992).

If advanced old age leads to great physical frailty or diminished cognitive functioning but institutional residence is not required or desired, then relatives step in to provide the needed care. Sometimes, they do so in conjunction with some combination of friends, neighbors, and professionals. Despite personal costs to caregivers in terms of increased number of daily tasks and complexity of schedule, elevated stress and expenses, and reduced time for other pursuits, family members (typically spouses and adult daughters) give the needed aid or coordinate its provision by others. According to research by Piercy (1998), caregivers not only pay heed to physical needs of infirm relatives, but they also attend to many aspects of the elder's environment, personal autonomy, and inclusion in ongoing family affairs. At the same time, they recognize the need to balance caregiving with responsibilities to other family members and take steps to do so, which helps to prevent them from burning out in caregiving.

From the point of view of elderly care receivers in these situations, the more help they report giving to their family members, the more in control of their own circumstances they feel and the happier they are (Pruchno, Burant, & Peters, 1997). Even those who are very dependent on others for personal care and instrumental assistance can reciprocate with affection, companionship, and advice. The care recipients in Piercy's (1998) study who required limited help recognized the need of their family members to attend to their own relational concerns and refrained from making too many requests. Thus, family ties that endure in the face of caregiving hardships can continue to contribute to the well-being of care recipients both because their own needs are being met and because they are returning a measure of support to their helpers.

### Negative Aspects of Relationships

Not all close relationships are always amiable. Problems with family and friends can range from mild incompatibilities to serious abuse and can co-reside with beneficial dimensions. Luescher and Pillemer (1998) pointed out that close relationships are complex and cannot be relegated exclusively to either positive or negative categories. They developed a theory of intergenerational ambivalence to demonstrate the paradoxes embedded in, for example, aging parent–adult child relationships. Members of both generations appreciate help and support but also strive to avoid dependence on each other. In the case of extensive help to a frail parent, both the parent and the helping child might

experience conflict between the norm of reciprocity (both parties should help each other so that they receive equal benefits in the relationship) and the norm of solidarity (close kin should help each other without regard for their own benefit). As the frailty increases, achieving balance between these norms can be increasingly difficult, leading to relational ambivalence and reduced well-being. Looking more generally at family and friend relationships, increasing impairment often comes with low social support and depression, although the causal direction between low support and depression is unclear (Newsom & Schulz, 1996).

Of course, the majority of adults over 65 years of age enjoy fairly good health and participate in a wide range of relationships with family and friends. For these people, ongoing interactions can involve disturbances for reasons such as the history of previous interactions (e.g., perceptions of parental unfairness during childhood [Bedford, 1992]), discrepancies in developmental stage (e.g., mothers and daughters having different relational needs [Fingerman, 1996]), transitions that must be negotiated (e.g., timing of retirement [Szinovacz, 1996]), long-term strain (e.g., caring for an adult child with mental retardation [Seltzer, Krauss, Choi, & Hong, 1996]), and betrayals that emerge (e.g., broken promises or revelation of confidential matters [Hansson et al., 1990]). The more serious forms of problems can cause damaging rifts in relationships, interfere with psychological well-being, and even jeopardize physical well-being (in the case of violence). In fact, in the context of multiple life events, the effect of negative interactions on negative affect is stronger than the effect of positive interactions on positive affect (Ingersoll-Dayton, Morgan, & Antonucci, 1997).

But not all negative aspects of relationships have negative effects. A history of past conflict in the parent-child relationship does not necessarily interfere with demonstrations of support and affection by adult children when parents are old, accentuating the strength of norms of familial obligation (Parrott & Bengtson, 1999). Marital complaints do not seem to differ between couples who have and have not negotiated the retirement transition, emphasizing the possibility that so-called negative events, such as loss of the work role, are not necessarily negative and do not necessarily harm close relationships (Ekerdt & Vinick, 1991). Childhood troubles with siblings do not always interfere with adult sibling relationships or personal well-being, showing the power of cognitive reappraisal of negative experiences (Bedford, 1998). Older adults seem content to retain friendships despite problems such as infrequent interactions, hurt feelings, or discovery of a friend's undesirable characteristics (Blieszner & Adams, 1998), demonstrating tolerance, adaptability, and resilience (Day, 1991; Johnson & Barer, 1997; Ramsey & Blieszner, 1999).

The overall picture that emerges from these varied approaches to research on close relationships during the later years of life is complex. Multiple facets of social contexts and personal attributes affect patterns of relating with kin and friends. Close relationships can enhance psychological well-being and the chances of aging well, but they also can detract from positive outcomes. Nevertheless, in many instances, older adults manage any relational difficulties fairly adequately, enabling the affiliations with close relatives and friends to endure over the long term.

Many researchers end their reports with lists of future studies to be done in the ongoing search for deeper understanding of close relationships and their effects on partners' lives. Following their recommendations requires use of appropriate theory and research methods. Moreover, if investigations are completed properly, then the practical implications of the results can be identified and applied to improve the quality of life in old age. These are the topics of the following section.

## ► Implications for Theory, Research, and Practice

Scholars interested in theoretical guidelines for studies of older adults' close relationships can choose from numerous gerontological, psychological, and sociological theories of human interaction (Bengtson & Schaie, 1999; Boss, Doherty, LaRossa, Schumm, & Steinmetz, 1993; Fehr, 1996). They also can rely on conceptual frameworks that have been developed specifically for examination of relationships at the end of life. These latter theories take into account the intersecting influences of physical, social, and psychological development across the whole of life more directly than do general theories. In fact, many of them emerged from life span and life course perspectives on development and old age (Baltes, Lindenberger, & Staudinger, 1997; Elder, 1997).

### *Theoretical Frameworks in Old Age Relationship Research*

*Relational competence.* Noting the significant role that close relationships play in adjustment to age-related transitions, Hansson and Carpenter (1994) set about analyzing, both conceptually and empirically, factors that contribute to the successful fulfillment of relational needs. Their definition of relational competence involves "those characteristics of the individual that facilitate the acquisition, development, and maintenance of mutually satisfying relationships" (p. 75). They focus on interpersonal skills that enable individuals to initiate and control relationships and cope effectively with stress as well as those that serve to enhance relationships such as investing in relationships and being sensitive to partners' needs. Hansson and Carpenter developed a Relational Competence Scale and tested it with a variety of research samples on several topics related to successful coping and aging. They also specified the applied implications of the theory for interventions with those who have relational competence deficits. For example, these authors pointed out that social skills or prosocial attitudes might warrant rejuvenation in the face of needing to replace relationships lost through changes such as retirement and relocation.

*Socioemotional selectivity.* According to Carstensen's theory (Carstensen, 1992; Carstensen, Isaacowitz, & Charles, 1999), throughout adulthood, individuals engage in an adaptive strategy to reduce the number of social network members with whom they interact, particularly the more peripheral relationships, yet they increase the emotional closeness to those deemed most significant in their lives. In studies of various cultural groups, regardless of background, adults demonstrated increasingly competent emotional regulation across the life span (Gross et al., 1997). However, examination of the membership in the circle of emotionally close relationships demonstrated that the extent to which both family members and friends are included depends not so much on personality variables as on whether the elder has any nuclear family members or not (Lang, Staudinger, & Carstensen, 1998). Family members tend to be the primary focus of emotional energy if they are available. In contrast to previous assumptions about old age relationships, this theory addresses social network change in terms of successful adaptation, not merely loss.

*Family solidarity.* Bengtson and colleagues have developed and refined a theory related to the behaviors that foster and maintain a sense of cohesion after offspring reach adulthood and establish their own families. This sense of cohesion, or intergenerational solidarity, is indexed by six essential components: association or contact, affection or emotional closeness, consensus or agreement, function or instrumental support and resource sharing, familism or normative obligations, and opportunity structures for family interaction. Empirical tests of interrelationships among these elements of solidarity have provided confirmation of the theory (Bengtson & Roberts, 1991) and demonstrate its utility for examining the nature and quality of relationships between parents and adult children (Parrott & Bengtson, 1999; Whitbeck et al., 1994) and between grandparents and grandchildren (Silverstein & Long, 1998). This

theory also has guided research on the effects of family relationships on the well-being of older adults (Lawrence, Bennett, & Markides, 1992; Starrels, Ingersoll-Dayton, & Neal, 1995).

*Convoy of relationships.* Moving from a focus on family relationships to the broader social network, Antonucci and colleagues developed the notion of a convoy, or a collection of social supporters, that surrounds people throughout life yet changes over time (see references in Antonucci & Akiyama, 1995). Members of the convoy include family, friends, and others whom the person knows. Convoy members might become closer or less close over time and could have either beneficial or deleterious impacts on the focal person. This framework is linked conceptually to socioemotional selectivity theory (Lansford, Sherman, & Antonucci, 1998). It has been used to study a variety of family and friend relationships as well as the implications of interactions with convoy members for health and psychological well-being (Antonucci & Akiyama, 1995; Shea et al., 1988).

*Patterns of friendship.* The multidimensional conceptual framework for friendship research articulated by Adams and Blieszner (1994; see also Blieszner & Adams, 1992) aims at integrating both social structural and developmental influences on social behavior. The framework posits that the social structural and psychological aspects of personal characteristics operate together to shape behavioral motifs that, in turn, influence both dyadic or network structure and developmental phases of the relationship. Dyadic or network structure and phases affect one another thorough processes of interaction involving cognitive, emotional, and behavioral aspects. This framework, which also could be applied to other relationships besides friendship, has received conceptual and empirical confirmation by the developers (Adams & Blieszner, 1998; Blieszner, 1995; Blieszner & Adams, 1998) as well as by Dugan and Kivett (1998) and

Prager (1995). These works illustrate the strengths of a multidimensional, multilevel approach to the analysis of interactive dynamics and the impact of relationships on well-being.

### Methodological Issues and New Directions in Research on Late-Life Close Relationships

Two very basic conceptual issues that also have implications for research methods are the definition of the relationship under study and whose definition of the relationship prevails (e.g., researcher's or respondent's). As discussed by Bedford and Blieszner (1997), many traditional definitions of *family* tend to exclude the family ties of old people and fail to acknowledge the contributions of elders to family life. Based on actual research findings, these authors offered a more realistic definition of family: "A family is a set of relationships determined by biology, adoption, marriage, and, in some societies, social designation and existing even in the absence of contact or affective involvement and, in some cases, even after the death of certain members" (p. 526). Conceptually, this definition is more inclusive of the variety and complexity of family relationships observed among old people (and others) than are definitions based on nuclear family or household membership. A methodological implication of such a definition is that it is not possible to identify family members via external observation. Rather, individuals must specify the members of their own families.

In contrast to family-related research, the study of friendship has been hampered not so much by an inappropriate definition of the term *friend* that excludes the experiences of old people as by no consensus on a definitional approach at all. In an analysis of conceptual and measurement issues in friendship research, Adams (1989) assessed the respective problems involved when investigators either predefine the term, perhaps restricting the categories of affiliation artificially, or leave

establishment of its parameters to respondents, making comparison of results across people and studies difficult. No easy solution is available. Adams's (1989) point is to caution investigators to make theoretical decisions about their definitional approach and to acknowledge the trade-offs related to one strategy or another. For example, if investigators ask respondents to report on one type of friendship (e.g., best friend), then they should not attempt to generalize the results to all types of friendships.

A persistent critique of family studies and friendship research, in gerontology as well as in other fields, has centered on the tendency to study individuals and individual-level variables but then extrapolate the results to dyads, families, and networks. In place of this approximation of family-level analysis, many researchers advocate examination of multiple family members or relational partners as the most valid means of understanding relational dynamics (Anderson, Earle, & Longino, 1997). Examples of recent research incorporating dyadic- and family-level data include research on marital support and coping (Anderson et al., 1997; Pakenham, 1998), mother-daughter relationships (Fingerman, 1996, 1998; Walker, Pratt, & Oppy, 1992), sibling ties (Connidis, 1992), relationships across three generations within families (Bengtson & Roberts, 1991; Tomlin & Passman, 1991), and caregiving to older family members (Piercy, 1998; Yates, Tennstedt, & Chang, 1999). Of course, including more than one relational partner in the research is no guarantee of a clear understanding of the phenomenon under scrutiny, as aptly illustrated by Matthews, Adamek, and Dunkle (1993). Employing five common quantitative and qualitative data analysis techniques with sample data on family caregiving, they demonstrated how the chosen analytic strategy produces varying results, leading to divergent interpretations of the data. Thus, researchers are cautioned not only to select study participants carefully but also to recognize the effects of the analytic approach on the nature of the data and their explication.

Additional methodological limitations in the literature that should be remedied in the future include the tendency to assume that all close relationships are positive and neglect study of the full range of interactive processes within them, the use of nonrepresentative samples, the disregard of the need for longitudinal designs to detect the influence of aging on relationships and identify changes in relationships over time, and the limited study of close relationships among old minority group members (Adams & Blieszner, 1995). Many existing studies have restricted the focus to family dyads while ignoring the larger family system or have neglected to incorporate the effects of the broader social environment when analyzing friendship (for an example of research on caregiving at the family level, see Piercy, 1998; for a discussion of the effects of context of friendships, see Adams & Allan, 1998b).

Intensive study of close relationships during late life is a relatively newer enterprise than similar research at other stages of the life course. Hence, recommendations for needed expansion of the knowledge base can be found for every category of family and friend relationship. The authors of each chapter in the *Handbook of Aging and the Family,* edited by Blieszner and Bedford (1995), included suggestions for additional research on related family gerontology topics, providing a wealth of thoughtful ideas. Similar identification of needed studies in the adult friendship arena have appeared in recent volumes devoted to that topic, including Blieszner and Adams (1992), O'Connor (1992), and Rawlins (1992). Furthermore, Phillipson (1997) pointed out that the way in which aging is socially constructed changes all the time, requiring ongoing attention to the implications for close relationships of new lifestyle choices, new approaches to growing old (especially among women), new perspectives on the aging of minority group members, and the like. Besides exploring uncovered dimensions of social affiliations, it is important to address the practical uses of such information in the lives of old people.

## Practical Implications of Research on Old Age Relationships

Applying research results to improvement of the human condition has been identified as the logical final step in the research act comprising description, explanation, and optimization of human aging (Baltes et al., 1997). However, not all gerontology researchers specify the practical implications of their results. Those investigating health aspects of aging, for example, might be more likely to consider the ways in which their findings could improve daily life than would those pursuing understanding of close relationships. Yet, research on close relationships has many possibilities for enhancing well-being (Adams & Blieszner, 1995). Moreover, social interventions go on constantly, whether we recognize them as such or not. For example, government programs and policies related to old age income and health care have direct impacts on family relationships such as when they encourage elders to rely on family instead of seeking assistance from formal service providers (Meyer & Bellas, 1995; Wacker, 1995). Likewise, social workers who encourage lonely old people to join senior centers in hopes of making new friendships, as well as activity directors at retirement facilities, are actually engaging in friendship intervention. For the greatest positive impacts and least harm, such interventions should be grounded intentionally in theory and research rather than being promulgated haphazardly (Adams & Blieszner, 1993).

The late-life family relationship that has received the most attention in terms of applied perspectives is marriage. Researchers and practitioners have investigated changes in marital satisfaction over the course of matrimony and have made recommendations for preserving and enhancing it (Clements, Cordova, Markman, & Laurenceau, 1997; Miller, Hemesath, & Nelson, 1997). Suggested strategies focus on maximizing positive elements of romantic relationships, using effective communication techniques, and managing conflict appropriately. Of course, these relationship methods apply across all ages and all types of relationships. Older individuals and couples might be better at using them than are less experienced persons, or perhaps their relational needs change over time. In any case, evidence shows that older couples report more enjoyable activities and less conflict in their relationships than do younger couples (Miller et al., 1997). But if difficulties prevail, then family therapy techniques can be applied successfully with elderly couples (Getzel, 1982; Hansson & Carpenter, 1994).

Other late-life family relationships, such as parent-child, sibling, and in-law affiliations, are known to entail conflict, but less attention has been given to specifying interventions geared toward their unique circumstances. Based on the results of research about relational difficulties (Bedford, 1992, 1998; Fingerman, 1996, 1998), however, it should be possible to develop programs aimed at preventing problems and improving troubled interactions (Hansson & Carpenter, 1994). Research on learning in old age suggests that elderly people certainly are capable of acquiring new interactional techniques (Baltes et al., 1997). Yet, mental health practitioners often are poorly trained for the task of working with older clients, and they are influenced by ageist biases prevalent in society at large (Butler, Lewis, & Sunderland, 1998). Thus, they might be reluctant even to attempt to apply the results of family research to aiding seniors with interpersonal difficulties.

Mental health practitioners appear to be even less apt to view friendship difficulties as needing intervention in old age than to recognize family difficulties. Yet, just as in the case of family relationships, research on late-life friendship already has uncovered a range of problems that could be addressed to the benefit of elderly friends (Adams & Blieszner, 1993, 1998; Blieszner & Adams, 1998; Hansson et al., 1990; Rook, 1989). The focus that has been taken in terms of interventions related indirectly to friendship is on strategies for preventing or reducing loneliness (Andersson, 1998; Rook, 1984). Typical approaches to combating loneliness address elders' thought processes that might be self-defeating in terms of establishing new relationships or elevating acquaintances to friend status as well as social skills that might be ineffective or unattractive.

Despite the need for more attention to interventions for close alliances at present, the growing number and increasing sophistication of studies on various close relationships in old age offers hope for success in the future. So does more attention to geriatric psychiatry in medical schools as well as clinical geropsychology and social work in clinical training programs (Butler et al., 1998). Given increased longevity, future cohorts of elders will have more opportunities than ever for relating to family members and engaging in friendships. If the support functions of close relationships remain in operation as they are now—and evidence to the contrary does not seem to be emerging—then the potential for close and meaningful relationships that contribute to aging well is strong indeed.

# Contents

# Multicultural/Multiracial Relationships

*Stanley O. Gaines, Jr.*
*James H. Liu*

Within mainstream social psychology, the literatures on interpersonal relations and intergroup relations have gained prominence, as is evident from the inclusion of separate chapters devoted to the two topics in the fourth edition of the *Handbook of Social Psychology* (Berscheid & Reis, 1998; Brewer & Brown, 1998). However, relatively few conceptual or empirical articles or chapters simultaneously address interpersonal *and* intergroup relations (Gaines, Chalfin, Kim, & Taing, 1998). In the present chapter, we examine multicultural/multiracial relationships as points of intersection between interpersonal and intergroup relations. We begin by presenting a historical overview of multicultural/multiracial rela-

tionships. Then, we address contemporary conceptual and empirical perspectives on multicultural/multiracial relationships. Finally, we describe practical applications of the study of multicultural/multiracial relationships.

## ▶ A Historical Overview of Multicultural/Multiracial Relationships

Throughout human history, individuals from differing tribes and nations have come into contact. Sometimes, intercultural/interracial contact has been manifested in making war; sometimes, intercultural and interracial contact has been manifested in making love. Taking a cue from Sigmund Freud, some social scientists (e.g., Goldwert, 1980, 1982;

AUTHORS' NOTE: The authors are indebted to Clyde Hendrick and Susan Hendrick for their constructive comments on previous versions of this chapter.

Liebman, 1976) have depicted the history of intercultural/interracial contact as a drama (a) involving the aggressive instinct at the intergroup level and (b) involving the sexual instinct at the interpersonal level. Both the aggressive instinct and the sexual instinct tend to be regarded by personality psychologists as "lower" (i.e., biologically based or animalistic) needs (Ewen, 1993). Perhaps it should not be surprising that social scientists' depiction of multicultural/multiracial relationships frequently has been negative.

When individuals from differing cultural/racial groups come into contact, one common outcome is cultural/racial hybridity. The concept of hybridity often is expressed in negative terms in the biological and social sciences. However, even if we limit ourselves to the intergroup level of analysis, some of the greatest flowerings of culture in human history have been products of hybridity. For example, China's greatest period (i.e., the Tang dynasty, 618-906) was produced by trade with India and the Middle East. Similarly, Western nations have gained a great deal from contact with Asia, Africa, and the New World during the past several hundred years, although it is not clear whether the reverse is true (DuBois, 1965/1990). Interestingly, although stability in social structure appears to depend on maintaining endogamy, new and vigorous *change* in social structure seems to depend on exogamy. Such change is at once frightening, exhilarating, and challenging for all concerned.

At the interpersonal level, the offspring of multicultural/multiracial unions have the opportunity to negotiate their own identities in adulthood. During recent years, for example, a growing number of biracial individuals have petitioned the U.S. Census Bureau to reformat its census forms for the year 2000 so that individuals can identify themselves as belonging to more than one racial group (Root, 1992, 1996). Such a possibility acknowledges that "race" always has been a social construction to a far greater degree than many, if not most, Americans historically have been willing to admit (Jones, 1997). We discuss the construction of identities further in subsequent sections of this chapter.

## ► Contemporary Conceptual Perspectives on Multicultural/Multiracial Relationships

Within the social sciences, post-World War II era theories of the occurrence of intercultural/interracial relationships frequently have reflected a sociological, rather than a psychological, orientation (Blea, 1992; Wilkinson, 1993). Sociological accounts often cite socioeconomic factors such as income and education when explaining why individuals date and marry across cultural/racial lines. For example, white women who marry men of color are presumed to do so because they stand to benefit from their husbands' superior socioeconomic status, whereas men of color who marry white women are presumed to do so because they stand to benefit from their wives' superior racial status. Notwithstanding the potential utility of socioeconomic constructs, such accounts tend to ignore the importance of *socioemotional* factors such as love and esteem in mate selection (for an exception, see Staples & Boulin Johnson, 1993). In the present chapter, we bring a decidedly psychological orientation to bear on the study of multicultural/multiracial relationships. Accordingly, we emphasize socioemotional influences in an attempt to complement much of the extant literature on socioeconomic influences on exogamous mate selection.

### *Accommodation and Relational Identities in Multicultural/Multiracial Relationships*

According to *interdependence theory* (Thibaut & Kelley, 1959), the behavioral choices that enable individuals to fulfill person-level goals do not necessarily enable individuals to fulfill relationship-level goals and vice versa. One of the best-known behavioral illustrations of interdependence theory is *accommodation* (Rusbult, Verette, Whitney, Slovik, & Lipkus, 1991), that is, individuals refraining from responding to relationship partners' anger or criticism with anger or criticism of their own (which would allow individuals to vent their frustration) and instead responding in a manner so as to defuse the partners' anger or criticism (which would allow individuals to maintain their relationships). Accommodation appears to be related in part to individuals' *relational identities,* that is, self-conceptions derived from the relationships in which individuals are partners (Aron & Aron, 1997; Rusbult & Buunk, 1993). Perhaps most important for the present chapter, an interdependence analysis would lead one to expect that individuals' relational identities and accommodative behaviors promote long-term maintenance of personal relationships, whether monocultural/monoracial or multicultural/multiracial in nature.

According to *attribution theory* (Heider, 1958), both xenophilia (i.e., attraction toward that which is unfamiliar) and xenophobia (i.e., repulsion toward that which is unfamiliar) can be understood as rational cognitive processes. However, at both the interpersonal and intergroup levels, attributional biases tend to promote xenophobia rather than xenophilia. At the interpersonal level, individuals are susceptible to *self-serving biases* that result in taking credit for successes and avoiding blame for failures (e.g., by shifting responsibility to other individuals). Similarly, at the intergroup level, members of particular groups are susceptible to *group-serving biases* that result in taking credit for successes and avoiding blame for failures (e.g., by shifting responsibility to members of other groups) (Fiske & Taylor, 1991). To the extent that individuals fail to incorporate relationship partners into their self-conceptions (Aron & Aron, 1986), individuals will tend to attribute partners' anger or criticism to their partners' own shortcomings, a tendency that can be ignited by self-serving biases and fueled even further by group-serving biases. Thus, an attributional analysis suggests that, in the absence of well-developed relational identities, the relationships that individuals enter, especially relationships that are multicultural/multiracial in nature, might be vulnerable to breakup.

During the years following Thibaut and Kelley's (1959) initial explication of interde-

pendence theory, Kelley has distinguished between given and effective outcome matrices of relationships (Kelley, 1979; Kelley & Thibaut, 1978). The *given outcome matrix* represents the set of psychological rewards and costs that individuals are likely to experience based on their personality traits, such as dominance versus submissiveness or nurturance versus hostility (Carson, 1969), after undergoing particular sequences of behavioral interactions with their relationship partners. The *effective outcome matrix,* which might or might not correspond to the given outcome matrix, is the set of psychological rewards and costs that individuals actually experience after undergoing particular sequences of behavioral interactions with their relationship partners. The concept of relational identities might aid social scientists in explaining how the given outcome matrix is *transformed* into an effective outcome matrix. For example, when two individuals with strong relational identities enter into a relationship, they may agree to maximize joint outcomes, regardless of whether one partner's dominant tendencies otherwise would lead him or her to prefer maximizing personal outcomes (Berscheid, 1985). In this manner, the dyad becomes something more than the sum of its parts, and knowledge of the inclusion of the other in the self (Aron & Aron, 1986) potentially can account for more behavioral variance across couples than can knowledge of the self per se.

### Interpersonal Resource Exchange and Romanticism in Multicultural/ Multiracial Relationships

So far, we have focused on interdependence theory (Thibaut & Kelley, 1959) in examining relationship processes among multicultural/multiracial couples. However, interdependence theory is part of a larger class of *reinforcement approaches* to studying interpersonal relations (Berscheid, 1985). Another reinforcement approach that shows promise in explaining relationship processes among multicultural/multiracial couples is *social exchange theory* (Homans, 1961), which emphasizes the reciprocity or give-and-take of behavioral interactions. For example, Gaines and Liu (1997) hypothesized that not only does *interpersonal resource exchange* (i.e., the reciprocity of affection and of respect as interpersonal resources) (Foa & Foa, 1974) help to maintain satisfying personal relationships, but *romanticism* (i.e., an orientation toward the welfare of one's romantic relationship) is positively related to individuals' giving of interpersonal resources to their partners.

Like accommodation, interpersonal resource exchange is a pro-relationship behavioral process, and like relational identity, romanticism is a pro-relationship aspect of personality. However, the concepts in question are not necessarily interchangeable. For example, interpersonal resource exchange emphasizes individuals' mutual enactment of rewarding behaviors, whereas accommodation emphasizes individuals' enactment of rewarding behaviors *after their partners have enacted costly behaviors.* Moreover, romanticism is a cultural value orientation that is transmitted by society to the individual, whereas relational identity is an aspect of identity that the individual constructs for himself or herself, often in interaction with a romantic partner. We will return to the concepts of interpersonal resource exchange and romanticism in our review of empirical research on multicultural/multiracial relationships.

### Personal and Social Identities in Multicultural/Multiracial Relationships

Relational identities also are distinct from personal identities and group identities. The latter two types of identities are addressed by *social identity theory* (Tajfel & Turner, 1979), whereby *personal identities* are defined as self-conceptions derived from individuals' unique attributes and *group identities* are defined as self-conceptions derived from the societally defined groups in which individuals are members. According to social identity theory, personal and group identities not only contribute to individuals' overall self-concept

("This is who I am") but also are reflected in individuals' overall self-esteem ("I am a good/bad person"). A central assumption underlying social identity theory is the premise that individuals' self-esteem is bolstered by extolling the virtues of individuals' in-groups *at the expense of out-groups* (Brewer, 1979; Liu & Allen, 1997; Liu, Ikeda, & Wilson, 1998). Therefore, the group-serving biases (and, for that matter, the self-serving biases) identified by attribution theory are viewed as functional within social identity theory.

Given the relative instability of multicultural/multiracial relationships, whose divorce rates are well above the overall divorce rate in the United States (Gaines & Ickes, 1997), one might be tempted to conclude that multicultural/multiracial relationships are inherently difficult to maintain. However, multicultural/multiracial relationships do not occur in a social psychological vacuum; relationship outsiders (e.g., strangers, acquaintances, perhaps even friends and family), not to mention history and custom, often place enormous pressure on multicultural/multiracial couples to break up. Moreover, many multicultural/multiracial relationships beat the odds and survive over time.

### Accounting for Multicultural/Multiracial Relationship Processes

Current formulations of social identity theory define social identities primarily, if not exclusively, as group identities whereby group membership is *ascribed* (i.e., chosen by society and applied to individuals). However, at least in so-called Western societies such as the United States, individuals' membership in certain groups (e.g., two-person groups such as relationship pairs of dyads) is *achieved* (i.e., chosen by individuals rather than by society) (Allport, 1954/1979). If the group membership itself is achieved, then perhaps the aspect of identity derived from that group membership (e.g., relational identity) is actively constructed by individuals. Just as *attachment theory* (Bowlby, 1969) currently allows individuals to be classified according

**TABLE 8.1**  Typology of Working Models of Self and Other

| | | Working Model of Self | |
|---|---|---|---|
| | | Positive | Negative |
| Working Model of Other | Positive | Secure | Preoccupied (Anxious-Ambivalent) |
| | Negative | Dismissing-Avoidant | Fearful-Avoidant |

SOURCE: Adapted from Bartholomew and Horowitz (1991). The authors express their gratitude to Kim Bartholomew for granting permission to adapt this table from the earlier work.

**TABLE 8.2**  Typology of Working Models of In-Group and Out-Group

| | | Working Model of Self | |
|---|---|---|---|
| | | Negative | Positive |
| Working Model of Out-Group | Positive | Assimilated/Assimilationist | Integrative/Accommodative |
| | Negative | Marginalized/Alienated | Separated/Segregationist |

SOURCE: Adapted from Berry, Poortinga, Segall, & Dasen (1992). The authors express their gratitude to John Berry for granting permission to adapt this table from the earlier work.

to working models of (individual) self and (individual) other (Bartholomew & Horowitz, 1991), so too may social identity theory allow individuals to be classified according to working models of in-group and out-group (Berry, Poortinga, Segall, & Dasen, 1992). As Table 8.1 illustrates, at the interpersonal level, individuals' positive versus negative working models of self and other yield a four-category typology. Individuals who possess positive working models of self *and* other are labeled as *secure,* individuals who possess a positive model of self and a negative model of other are labeled as *dismissing-avoidant,* individuals who possess a negative working model of self and a positive working model of other are labeled as *preoccupied* (or *anxious-ambivalent*) (Hazan & Shaver, 1987), and individuals who possess negative working models of self *and* other are labeled as *fearful-avoidant.*

As Table 8.2 illustrates, at the intergroup level, individuals' positive versus negative working models of in-group and out-group likewise yield a four-category typology. Note that the terms used by Berry et al. (1992) refer primarily to members of ethnic *minority* groups and do not necessarily reflect the social psychological experiences of members of ethnic *majority* groups; hence, our terminology is derived from, but is not identical to,

that of Berry et al. Individuals who possess positive working models of in-group *and* out-group are labeled as *integrative/accommodative,* individuals who possess a positive working model of in-group and a negative working model of out-group are labeled as *separated/segregationist,* individuals who possess a negative working model of in-group and a positive working model of out-group are labeled as *assimilated/assimilationist,* and individuals who possess negative working models of in-group *and* out-group are labeled as *marginalized/alienated.* Such a typology of "intergroup attachment styles" (akin to the typology of "interpersonal attachment styles" in Table 8.1) implies that although "separated" individuals indeed can succumb to group-serving biases, many (if not most) individuals are *not* necessarily susceptible to such attributional biases.

▶ **Contemporary Empirical Research on Multicultural/ Multiracial Relationships**

Just as contemporary conceptual perspectives on multicultural/multiracial relationships have been influenced strongly by sociological theory, so too has contemporary empirical research on multicultural/multiracial relationships been influenced strongly by sociological methodology. For example, qualitative accounts of 40 black-white married couples by Porterfield (1978) and of 21 black-white married couples by Rosenblatt, Karis, and Powell (1995) provide detailed information on relatively small numbers of interracial couples. In the present chapter, we focus on quantitative research that yields comparatively less information per couple but that also is based on a relatively large number of interracial couples. As was the case in the previous section, we view the psychologically oriented quantitative research reviewed in the present chapter as complementing much of the sociologically oriented qualitative research commonly employed in studies of multicultural/multiracial relationships.

### *Responses to Accommodative Dilemmas and Attachment Style*

Two recent studies (Gaines, Reis, et al., 1997; Scharfe & Bartholomew, 1995) examined responses to accommodative dilemmas as predicted by individuals' attachment style within the context of heterosexual, and primarily intracultural/intraracial, romantic relationships. Scharfe and Bartholomew (1995) used four continuous measures of attachment according to the four-category typology proposed by Bartholomew and Horowitz (1991), whereas Gaines, Reis, et al. (1997) used categorical and continuous measures of attachment according to the three-category typology proposed by Hazan and Shaver (1987), in which no distinction between dismissing-avoidant and fearful-avoidant types was made (i.e., the avoidant category came closer to describing what Bartholomew and Horowitz, 1991, later termed fearful-avoidant). Summarizing across the two studies, both Gaines, Reis, et al. (1997) and Scharfe and Bartholomew (1995) found that secure attachment was positively associated with constructive re-

sponses to partners' anger or criticism, and insecure attachment (i.e., any form of attachment not labeled as secure) was positively associated with destructive responses to partners' anger or criticism. The positive association between constructive responses to accommodative dilemmas and secure attachment was consistent for voice (but not loyalty) responses, and the positive association between destructive responses to accommodative dilemmas and insecure attachment was consistent for both exit and neglect responses.

In a replication and extension of Gaines, Reis, et al. (1997) and Scharfe and Bartholomew (1995), Gaines, Granrose, et al. (1999) examined responses to accommodative dilemmas as influenced by attachment style in a sample of 103 heterosexual interracial couples. Among both genders, attachment style was associated with responses to partners' anger or criticism, at least when summarizing across destructive (i.e., exit and neglect) responses. That is, the secure-insecure difference was significant for destructive responses as a whole (i.e., insecure individuals engaged in significantly higher rates of destructive responses than did secure individuals), but the secure-insecure difference was *not* significant for constructive responses as a whole (i.e., secure individuals did not engage in significantly higher rates of constructive responses than did insecure individuals). The lack of significance for constructive responses as a whole was due primarily to a lack of consistent secure-insecure differences for loyalty responses, a finding that might reflect the "peculiarities of loyalty" (Drigotas, Whitney, & Rusbult, 1995) as less visible and more ambiguous than other responses to accommodative dilemmas.

Together, interdependence theory (Thibaut & Kelley, 1959) and attachment theory (Bowlby, 1969) explain much of the individual difference variance in behavior within heterosexual romantic relationships in general and within *interracial* heterosexual romantic relationships in particular. The results of Gaines, Granrose, et al. (1999) provide some of the clearest evidence to date regarding the utility of conducting large-scale, quantitative, theory-driven research on personal relationship processes among interracial couples. One of the most noteworthy aspects of Gaines, Granrose, et al.'s (1999) study was the preponderance of securely attached individuals over insecurely attached individuals among interracial couples, a preponderance that not only is taken for granted in studies of (primarily) intraracial couples (Shaver & Hazan, 1993) but also runs counter to stereotypes of individuals who date and marry across racial lines as psychologically unhealthy (Porterfield, 1978; Rosenblatt et al., 1995).

### Interpersonal Resource Exchange and Romanticism

A recent study (Gaines, 1996) examined patterns of interpersonal resource exchange and interpersonal traits in heterosexual, and primarily intraracial, romantic relationships. Across separate samples of dating couples and engaged/married couples, women and men exchanged *affection* (i.e., love or emotional acceptance of another person) and *respect* (i.e., esteem or social acceptance of another person) (Foa & Foa, 1974) at significant levels. Beyond the influence of partners' giving of interpersonal resources on individuals' giving of interpersonal resources, individuals' own levels of *nurturance* (i.e., communion or a tendency to engage in affiliative behavior toward others in general) (Wiggins, 1991) was positively associated with individuals' giving of interpersonal resources. Although the construct of nurturance (an interpersonally oriented personality trait) bears some similarity to the construct of romanticism (an interpersonally oriented cultural value), Gaines (1996) did not measure romanticism per se.

In a partial replication and extension of Gaines (1996), Gaines, Rios, et al. (1999) examined interpersonal resource exchange and romanticism in a sample of 91 heterosexual interracial couples. The sample, limited to couples among whom one partner was an Anglo and the other partner was a person of color, represented a subset of the sample from the aforementioned study by Gaines, Granrose, et al. (1999). Results indicated that women and men in interracial relationships exchanged affection and respect at significant levels. Furthermore, a "romantic" model of interpersonal resource exchange (including romanticism as a predictor of individuals' giving of interpersonal resources) explained significant behavioral variance beyond that of a "universal" model of interpersonal resource exchange (excluding romanticism as a predictor of individuals' giving of interpersonal resources). The romantic model of interpersonal resource exchange explained behavioral variance across interracial couples consisting of (a) Anglos paired with African Americans and (b) Anglos paired with persons of color other than African Americans (i.e., Hispanics, Asian Americans, or Native Americans) equally well.

The results of Gaines, Rios, et al. (1999) bode well for future applications of social exchange theory (Homans, 1961) and social identity theory (Tajfel & Turner, 1979) to the study of interracial relationships. However, it is not clear whether the romantic model of interpersonal resource exchange is limited in scope to *interracial* heterosexual romantic relationships in particular or whether such a model explains behavioral variance across heterosexual romantic relationships in general. Hopefully, enterprising researchers will examine the impact of romanticism (as well as other cultural value orientations such as *individualism, collectivism,* and *familism*) (Gaines, Marelich, et al., 1997) on interpersonal resource exchange among interracial and intraracial couples alike.

### Implications for Social Identity Theory

From the standpoint of attachment theory, secure individuals enjoy higher levels of self-esteem than do their insecure counterparts (Feeney & Noller, 1996). Returning to Table 8.1, it appears that individuals who combine positive working models of self and other are especially likely to experience satisfaction with themselves and with the quality of their interpersonal relations. If an in-group can be considered an extension of self, and if an out-group can be considered an extension of other, then what predictions would one make regarding the psychological well-being of integrative/accommodative individuals from the standpoint of social identity theory?

Returning to Table 8.2, it is plausible that individuals who combine positive working models of in-group and out-group are especially likely to experience satisfaction with themselves and with the quality of their interpersonal (and intergroup) relations. That is, those individuals who are equally at home in social contexts consisting primarily of in-group members *and* in social contexts consisting primarily of out-group members might be psychologically healthier than nonintegrative/nonaccommodative (i.e., separated/segregationist, assimilated/assimilationist, or marginalized/alienated) individuals. Such a possibility is consistent with theories of black personality development (Cross, 1979; Milliones, 1980; Thomas, 1971), in which an essentially humanitarian orientation is viewed as a mark of psychological maturity. However, the related possibility that integrative/accommodative individuals are more likely than nonintegrative/nonaccommodative individuals to develop satisfying personal relationships flies in the face of traditional assumptions regarding in-group preference as a mark of psychological well-being (Penn, Gaines, & Phillips, 1993; Phillips, Penn, & Gaines, 1993).

If social scientists' conception of social identities is limited to group identities, then social scientists are unlikely to consider the possibility that integrative/accommodative individuals enjoy a social psychological advantage in personal relationships. However, if social scientists' conception of social identities is expanded to include *relational* identities, then perhaps social scientists will not immediately reject a possible integrative/accommodative relationship advantage as far-fetched. Like all relationship dyads, the multicultural/multiracial relationship dyad is an in-group

unto itself. If relationship partners view their dyad as the in-group and the rest of society as the out-group (Gaines & Ickes, 1997), then the success of multicultural/multiracial relationships might depend in part on the ease with which individuals navigate between the dyad and their respective families and between the dyad and their respective cultural/ethnic groups (Porterfield, 1978; Rosenblatt et al., 1995).

## ▶ Practical Applications of Theory and Research on Multicultural/ Multiracial Relationships

So far, we have considered multicultural/multiracial relationships from the standpoint of basic theory and research. However, perhaps the most vexing questions concerning multicultural/multiracial relationships have to do with societal attitudes toward intermarriage (Allport, 1954/1979; National Research Council, 1989). Prior to the modern civil rights movement, one tactic that white opponents of integration used to great effect was to ask white civil rights advocates, "But would you want your daughter to marry one?" Even as we enter a new millennium, linguistic, geographic, religious, and racial in-group/out-group biases continue to divide individuals in the United States and around the world (Jones, 1997). In this final section of the chapter, we address societal attitudes toward sex and marriage across cultural/racial lines as manifested in interpersonal communication (which is likely to be central to relational identities) and in mass communication (which is likely to be central to group identities).

### Interpersonal Communication

One of the most controversial issues in the literature on multicultural/multiracial relationships is the degree to which the quality of person-to-person communication is limited when two individuals are members of different cultural/racial groups. At first glance, when one considers the relatively high divorce rate for interracial couples in the United States, one might be tempted to conclude that interracial marriages tend to end in divorce *because* women and men in those relationships inevitably experience difficulty with each other (Kochman, 1981). However, the divorce rate for African American male-female couples also exceeds the national average (Hatchett, 1991), yet little (if any) of the literature on black male-female relationships would suggest that those relationships are doomed to fail because of communication problems. Also, interracial marriages are more likely to be second or later marriages for one or both partners than are intraracial marriages (Ho, 1990); in turn, second and later marriages tend to be relatively unstable, due to a variety of external factors (e.g., presence of adolescent children from partners' previous marriages) (Cherlin, 1989). In and of itself, relationship stability among multicultural/ multiracial couples does not necessarily reflect unique communication difficulties.

By the same token, even among those multicultural/multiracial relationships that remain stable over time, partners might find it necessary to consider the impact of societal stereotypes on the quality of their interactions with relationship outsiders (Gaines & Ickes, 1997; Liu, Campbell, & Condie, 1995) and on their interactions with each other. Some relationship outsiders will attack multicultural/ multiracial couples, both verbally and physically, in ways that might seem unfathomable to individuals who belong to the same cultural/ racial group as their romantic partners (Porterfield, 1978; Rosenblatt et al., 1995). Communication acts by relationship outsiders might include piercing stares and epithets (Hernton, 1965/1988). The virulence accompanying such xenophobic acts of communication from relationship outsiders are especially likely to catch white Anglo-Saxon Protestant partners in multicultural/ multiracial relationships by surprise because those partners typically have not had the same firsthand exposure to xenophobia in the past as have their culturally/

racially stigmatized partners (Porterfield, 1978; Rosenblatt et al., 1995; see also Goffman, 1963).

Ironically, even partners in multicultural/ multiracial relationships sometimes must guard against communicating prejudice to each other (e.g., trivializing each other's religious practices) (Gaines et al., 1998). Unlike interactions with relationship outsiders, which often are momentary and do not even allow relationship insiders time to respond to communication acts such as stares and epithets, relationship insiders must communicate with each other on a long-term intimate basis. To the extent that partners in multicultural/ multiracial relationships harbor residual xenophobic thoughts or feelings of their own (e.g., as a result of family upbringing), they might find it useful to enter into individual therapy (to acknowledge their xenophobic tendencies) as well as couple therapy (to express the difficulty that they experience in reducing, if not eliminating, xenophobic behavior). It is important to work with mental health professionals who not only have expertise in facilitating relationship processes such as attachment and exchange (Jacobson & Margolin, 1979; Sperling & Lyons, 1994) but also are comfortable and knowledgeable in dealing with multicultural/multiracial couples (Crohn, 1995; Ho, 1990). This is not to suggest that multicultural/multiracial couples as a whole are dysfunctional. Rather, some multicultural/multiracial couples might find that therapy enables them to build on the personal and interpersonal skills that they already possess.

But what about the children? As recently as the 1980s, a common theme pervading the literature on multicultural/multiracial offspring was that the children are likely to develop into social psychological misfits, partly because their parents are deviant and partly because the children themselves suffer from identity confusion. However, by the 1990s, a growing body of empirical research suggested that the children tend to be just as functional personally and interpersonally as their monocultural/monoracial peers (Root, 1992, 1996). So long as parents encourage children to accept the various aspects of their personal and group identities and prepare children to anticipate and respond constructively to potential slings and arrows of society, the children are likely to develop healthy self-conceptions. For those children who do experience anxiety as a result of negative interactions with xenophobic peers or authority figures, experts on multicultural/multiracial family counseling (Crohn, 1995; Ho, 1990) indicate that therapy can be applied successfully to both parent-offspring and husband-wife relationship processes.

### Mass Communication

In the United States, attitudes toward intermarriage (i.e., marriage between two individuals who differ in culture/race) (Gordon, 1964) historically have not been very favorable. Even after World War II, during which the United States established itself as a superpower in battling the twin specters of racism and anti-Semitism, prevailing attitudes toward persons of color and toward Jewish persons in the United States were ambivalent at best and hostile at worst (Allport, 1954/1979). Moreover, even after the civil rights movement, during which the U.S. Supreme Court struck down all remaining state anti-"miscegenation" (i.e., "race-mixing") laws as unconstitutional, black-white intermarriage rates in the United States continued to hover near the bottom among all Western nations (Pettigrew, 1988). Throughout the history of the United States, and particularly since the advent of motion pictures and television, the mass media have influenced and been influenced by popular stereotypes regarding dating, marriage, and sexuality involving persons from different cultural/racial groups (Gaines & Liu, 1997).

Perhaps the most ubiquitous symbol of sexuality in the United States is the fertile white female, especially in the form of the "blonde bombshell." Faye Wray, Marilyn Monroe, and Madonna are just a few examples of the seemingly endless parade of sex symbols promoted by American mass media.

Although the overt message conveyed by mass media is that these sex symbols are to be desired by heterosexual men in general, the covert message is that if these women are to be possessed by anyone, then *white* heterosexual men should be the possessors (Hernton, 1965/1988). In the post-women's rights era, not all blonde bombshells have been entirely passive in accepting their media roles. For example, Madonna's not-infrequent escapades with men of color in fantasy (e.g., the black priest in Madonna's *Like a Prayer* video) and in fact (e.g., basketball player Dennis Rodman) openly subvert the covert message of white male sexual exclusivity. Nevertheless, even Madonna, who is a natural brunette, generally has conformed to the overt message that "blondes have more fun" (hooks, 1992).

Prior to the civil rights era, Hollywood tended to portray the sheer threat of miscegenation as cause for alarm, at least when the threat involved white women. For example, *The Birth of a Nation,* widely revered as a classic in American cinema, romanticizes the Ku Klux Klan as would-be saviors of a southern white woman attempting to escape the clutches of a rapacious black man (Guerrero, 1993). One notable exception to this anti-miscegenation theme in pre-civil rights era Hollywood was the depiction of Anglo male-Asian female romance in the movies. For example, in *The World of Suzie Wong,* the protagonist leaves her tyrannical Asian male partner for a better life with a virtuous white man who wins her heart (Marchetti, 1993). This apparent paradox can be explained readily when one recognizes that in both *The Birth of a Nation* and *The World of Suzie Wong,* white male heterosexuality is affirmed.

Even in the post-civil rights era, American mass media have placed a premium on white male heterosexuality vis-à-vis miscegenation. Pairings of Anglo men and Asian women in television programs (e.g., *Gunsmoke, How the West Was Won*) remain commonplace (Espiritu, 1997). A film such as *Guess Who's Coming to Dinner?,* in which a black male-white female romance is depicted sympathetically, remains the exception rather than the rule in Hollywood. Some observers (e.g., Russell, Wilson, & Hall, 1993) argue that multicultural/multiracial relationships will not be depicted in all their variety until increasing numbers of directors of various cultural/racial backgrounds enter the film industry. In turn, political pressure from activist organizations might be necessary for directors from diverse cultural/racial backgrounds to gain a foothold in the film industry (Guerrero, 1993; Marchetti, 1993).

## ▶ Conclusion

If the problem of the 20th century was the problem of the color line, as DuBois (1903/1969) anticipated, then perhaps the problem of the 21st century will be the problem of hybridity, during which national boundaries strain (if not buckle entirely) under the weight of an emergent "global culture." How will the actions of a particular multicultural/multiracial couple influence (and be influenced by) the global culture? As we mentioned earlier in this chapter, the relational identity created by a multicultural/multiracial couple may afford the couple's offspring with a set of opportunities to negotiate their own personal and social identities. Previous conceptualizations of social identity theory (Tajfel & Turner, 1979) have not considered the possibility of a relational identity, which is positioned somewhere between personal identity and group identity. A relational identity inherently is constructed actively by individuals to a greater extent than are group identities because it is the product of two individuals and the social environment surrounding them rather than a construct shared by many individuals who might never meet each other during their lifetimes.

In many respects, an intercultural/interracial couple represents a hybrid unit. The offspring of such a unit will have multiple options for moving between the spaces suggested by Berry et al.'s (1992) typology. For example, the offspring may choose to be integrative/

accommodative (e.g., embrace the cultural heritage of both parents), assimilated/assimilationist (e.g., embrace the heritage of the parent whose culture is dominant in a given society), separated/segregationist (e.g., embrace the heritage of the parent whose culture is oppressed in a given society), or marginalized/alienated (e.g., reject the cultural heritage of both parents). By the same token, the multicultural/multiracial couple represents more than the sum of its parts. For example, two parents may argue with each other regarding their relationship commitment or satisfaction, yet the parents may close ranks when discussing political and generational issues with their offspring. It is difficult to determine whether relational or social identities are predominant in such interpersonal situations.

Regarding applications in the area of interpersonal communication, the mental health professional should avoid the pitfalls of ensuring that multicultural/multiracial couples are no different from other couples *and* assuming that multicultural/multiracial couples are completely different from other couples. On the one hand, the experience of *primary emotions* such as fear, anger, and joy tend to be universal; thus, partners in multicultural/multiracial relationships might encounter little difficulty in interpreting certain emotional content of each other's verbal and nonverbal communication. On the other hand, the experience of *secondary emotions* such as pride, guilt, and shame tend to vary across cultures (Markus & Kitayama, 1991); thus, partners in multicultural/multiracial relationships might experience considerable difficulty in interpreting certain emotional content of each other's verbal and nonverbal communication (Porter & Samovar, 1998). Particularly in cases where the mental health professional is not a member of the same ethnic group as either of the partners (e.g., an Anglo female psychotherapist working with a Latino male-African American female couple), the mental health professional might unwittingly exacerbate communication problems by misreading both partners' expressions of secondary emotions.

Regarding applications in the area of mass communication, the Hollywood director should avoid the all too common tendency to depict interracial couples and their progeny as dysfunctional. One of the most enduring images in American films and television programs throughout the second half of the 20th century has been the "tragic mulatto," an image that embodies a host of lingering fears in the United States concerning miscegenation (Ono, 1998). Given its persistence, such an image cannot be dismissed as accidental. Accordingly, the tragic mulatto image is unlikely to disappear without a conscious effort on the part of the director.

Finally, the personal relationship researcher should examine the ways in which multicultural/multiracial couples use both interpersonal communication and mass communication to build social networks. For example, anecdotal evidence suggests that many individuals in multicultural/multiracial relationships form local support groups and Internet chat rooms to exchange information regarding desirable locales in which they can feel relatively safe (Gaines & Ickes, 1997). Systematic research is needed to determine the extent to which multicultural/multiracial couples in general are sustained by actual and virtual communities.

In closing, we pose a series of questions for readers to ponder with regard to multicultural/multiracial relationship processes in theory, research, and practice. First, in what ways do multicultural/multiracial couples reflect or resist the stereotypes, social representations, and power relations of the societies in which they live? Second, how can disclosure, as well as the socioemotional bonds formed by disclosure (not to mention sexuality), help multicultural/multiracial couples to withstand the schisms present in society? Third, what are the varieties of relational hybridity that can emerge from multicultural/multiracial relationships, and do these relationship identities function primarily at the levels of personal identities, group identities, or somewhere in between? These are just a few of the questions that, we hope, future basic and applied work on multicultural/multiracial relationships will begin to answer during the next millennium.

# Contents

# The Close Relationships of Lesbians, Gay Men, and Bisexuals

*Letitia Anne Peplau*
*Leah R. Spalding*

During recent years, relationship researchers have slowly widened the scope of their inquiry to include the close relationships of lesbians and gay men. Nonetheless, empirical research on same-sex relationships still is in its infancy. In a review of publications from 1980 to 1993, Allen and Demo (1995) found that only 3 of 312 articles in the *Journal of Social and Personal Relationships* focused on some aspect of sexual orientation, as did only 2 of 1,209 articles in the *Journal of Marriage and the Family*. The past decade has seen a small but noticeable increase in research on same-sex relationships. In this chapter, we systematically review the available scientific literature on the relationships of lesbians, gay men, and bisexuals.

Studies of the intimate relationships of lesbians, gay men, and bisexuals suffer from unique problems not faced in studies of heterosexuals. Many homosexual and bisexual individuals are not fully open about their sexual orientation and, therefore, might be reluctant to volunteer for scientific research projects. Furthermore, lacking information from marriage records and census data, researchers studying same-sex couples are limited in their ability to obtain representative samples or to estimate population characteristics. With few exceptions, the research reported in this chapter is based on convenience samples of younger white adults who currently self-identify as gay or lesbian and are in relationships with same-sex partners. Researchers often provide relatively little information about how they recruited participants or how recruitment strate-

AUTHORS' NOTE: We gratefully acknowledge the support provided to Letitia Anne Peplau by a University of California, Los Angeles faculty research grant and to Leah Spalding by a Social Science Research Council Sexuality Research Postdoctoral Fellowship.

gies influence sample characteristics. In a review of research on gay male relationships published from 1958 to 1992, Deenen, Gijs, and van Naerssen (1995) suggested that there had been a gradual shift away from recruiting gay men in bars and toward the use of ads in gay publications, with a corresponding increase in the average age of participants and length of their relationships. Generalizations about lesbian and gay relationships must be made with caution.

We do not know the percentage of lesbians and gay men who currently are in committed relationships or the percentage who recently have experienced the loss of serious relationships through breakup or the deaths of partners. Many studies find that a majority of participants currently are in romantic relationships, with estimates ranging as high as 60% for gay men and 80% for lesbians in some samples (Bell & Weinberg, 1978; Harry, 1983; Peplau & Cochran, 1990; Peplau, Cochran, Rook, & Padesky, 1978; Raphael & Robinson, 1980). Also unavailable are estimates of the typical length of same-sex relationships or the frequency of long-lasting partnerships. Nonetheless, enduring relationships often have been described, especially in studies of older adults. In a recent study, 14% of the lesbian couples and 25% of the gay male couples had lived together for 10 or more years (Bryant & Demian, 1994). Today, some lesbians and gay men seek to formalize their relationships through commitment ceremonies. Others are striving to institutionalize same-sex relationships through laws and policies that recognize domestic partnerships or that would legalize same-sex marriages.

In considering the relationships of gay, lesbian, and bisexual people, it is important to recognize the social climate of prejudice and discrimination that sexual minority couples confront (James & Murphy, 1998). Although Americans' attitudes about civil rights for homosexuals have become more tolerant during recent years, many people continue to condemn homosexuality and same-sex relationships (Savin-Williams, 1996). In a recent study, Jones (1996) found that hotels were

significantly less likely to make a room reservation for a same-sex couple than for an opposite-sex couple. Walters and Curran (1996) reported biased service by clerks in a shopping mall; compared to heterosexual couples, same-sex couples received slower service and experienced more incidents of staring and rude treatment. We know relatively little about how such experiences affect the daily lives of gay and lesbian couples or about the strategies that same-sex couples use to cope with homophobia.

Research on gay and lesbian relationships serves three important purposes. First, empirical research provides more accurate descriptions of the relationships of lesbians and gay men. These findings often challenge negative cultural stereotypes about same-sex couples. Second, comparisons of same-sex and heterosexual couples provide insights about the way in which relationships are influenced by gender and social roles. Third, studies of gay and lesbian samples provide valuable information about the generalizability of relationship theories, most of which have been developed and tested on heterosexual samples.

In the following sections, we consider a range of relationship issues including the initiation of same-sex relationships, satisfaction, power, the division of labor, sexuality, conflict, commitment, and the ending of relationships. We briefly review the limited research available on the relationships of bisexuals and then offer some general conclusions.

## ▶ Beginning a Relationship

Research has begun to investigate how lesbians and gay men meet new relationship partners, how they initiate romantic relationships, and the qualities they seek in romantic partners. In a recent national survey of 1,266 same-sex couples, lesbians and gay men reported that they were most likely to meet potential dates through friends, at work, at bars, or at social events (Bryant & Demian, 1994). In general, opportunities to meet potential partners might be greater for those who live in urban areas with gay and lesbian communities (Laumann, Gagnon, Michael, & Michaels, 1994). In their efforts to meet new partners, lesbian and gay individuals might face unique challenges including societal pressures to conceal their sexual orientation, a small pool of potential partners, and limited ways in which to meet people. These factors might make it difficult to meet others with similar interests, and there is some evidence that gay male couples might have larger partner differences in age, education, and employment compared to lesbians and heterosexuals (Bell & Weinberg, 1978; Blumstein & Schwartz, 1983; Kurdek & Schmitt, 1987). Note, however, that a recent study of African Americans found considerable partner similarity among both gay men and lesbians (Peplau, Cochran, & Mays, 1997).

Negotiating the initiation of a new relationship can be awkward for anyone, but lesbian and gay male individuals might have to contend with some additional issues. For example, Rose, Zand, and Cini (1993) found that many lesbian relationships followed a "friendship script" whereby two women first became friends, then fell in love, and later initiated a sexual relationship. Some women reported difficulties with this pattern of relationship development such as problems in knowing whether a relationship was shifting from friendship to romance and problems gauging the friend's possible sexual interest.

When gay men and lesbians go on dates, they might rely on fairly conventional scripts that depict a typical sequence of events for a first date (Rose et al., 1993). For example, Klinkenberg and Rose (1994) coded 95 gay men's and lesbians' accounts of typical and actual first dates. They found many common events for both gay men and lesbians (e.g., discuss plans, dress, get to know date, go to a movie, eat or drink, initiate physical contact). Men's and women's dating scripts differed in some ways, with gay men more likely than lesbians to include sexual intimacy as part of a first date (e.g., made out, had sex) and lesbians more likely than gay men to emphasize

emotions associated with the date (e.g., evaluate feelings postdate). In many ways, the scripts reported by lesbians and gay men were similar to those reported by young heterosexual adults (Rose & Frieze, 1989).

What attributes do gay males and lesbians desire in potential partners? Researchers have used two methods to answer this question: analyses of personal advertisements placed in newspapers or other media and responses to confidential questionnaires. Many studies have compared the preferences of heterosexuals, lesbians, and gay men. In general, homosexuals want many of the same qualities in partners as do heterosexuals. Regardless of sexual orientation, individuals seek partners who are affectionate, dependable, and similar in interests and religious beliefs (Engel & Saracino, 1986). Gender often has a stronger influence on partner preferences than does sexual orientation (Davidson, 1991; Hatala & Prehodka, 1996; Laner, 1978). In personal ads, gay and heterosexual men are more likely to request physically attractive partners than are lesbian and heterosexual women (Bailey, Kim, Hills, & Linsenmeier, 1997; Feingold, 1990; Koestner & Wheeler, 1988). The ads of lesbian and heterosexual women describe in greater detail the personality characteristics they seek in partners as compared to the partners' physical characteristics (Deaux & Hanna, 1984; Hatala & Prehodka, 1996).

Several researchers have investigated whether gay men and lesbians prefer masculine or feminine partners, perhaps because of the stereotype that same-sex couples typically include a masculine or "butch" partner and a feminine or "femme" partner. To test this idea, researchers have coded descriptions of desired partners as "masculine" (e.g., seeks a partner who is physically strong or independent) or "feminine" (e.g., seeks a partner with long hair or who is submissive). Research generally has not supported the butch-femme stereotype. More often, gay men prefer men who are physically masculine and have traditionally masculine traits (Bailey et al., 1997; Davidson, 1991; Laner, 1978; Laner & Kamel, 1977). Research on lesbians' preferences has produced mixed results that do not clearly show strong preferences for "masculine" or "feminine" partners (Bailey et al., 1997; Gonzales & Meyers, 1993; Laner, 1978; Laner & Kamel, 1977).

Finally, the AIDS epidemic has prompted gay men to emphasize health in their personal advertisements. Compared to ads from the late 1970s, ads placed by gay males during the late 1980s were more likely to mention HIV status and to request sexual exclusivity (Davidson, 1991). One study found that HIV-negative men were more likely to mention the desired physical characteristics of partners, whereas HIV-positive men were more likely to mention their own physical health (Hatala, Baack, & Parmenter, 1998). Both HIV-positive and HIV-negative men preferred partners with similar HIV status.

## ▶ Relationship Quality

Stereotypes depict gay and lesbian relationships as unhappy. In one study, heterosexual college students described gay and lesbian relationships as less satisfying, more prone to discord, and "less in love" than heterosexual relationships (Testa, Kinder, & Ironson, 1987). By contrast, empirical research has found striking similarities in the reports of love and satisfaction among contemporary lesbian, gay, and heterosexual couples.

### *Comparing Satisfaction Among Lesbian, Gay, and Heterosexual Couples*

Several studies have compared gay male, lesbian, and heterosexual couples to investigate differences in the partners' love for each other and their satisfaction with their relationships. These studies either have matched homosexual and heterosexual couples on age, income, and other background characteristics that might bias the results or have controlled for these factors in statistical analyses. In an early study, Peplau and Cochran (1980) com-

pared matched samples of lesbians, gay men, and heterosexuals, all of whom currently were in romantic/sexual relationships. Among this sample of young adults, about 60% said that they were in love with their partners, and most of the rest said that they were "uncertain" about whether they were in love. On standardized love and liking scales, the lesbians and gay men generally reported very positive feelings for their partners and rated their current relationships as highly satisfying and close. No significant differences were found among lesbians, gay men, and heterosexuals on any measure of relationship quality. In a recent longitudinal study of married heterosexual and cohabiting homosexual couples, Kurdek (1998b) found similar results. Controlling for age, education, income, and years cohabiting, the three types of couples did not differ in relationship satisfaction at initial testing. Over the 5 years of this study, all types of couples tended to decrease in relationship satisfaction, but no differences were found among gay, lesbian, or heterosexual couples in the rate of change in satisfaction. Several studies have replicated the finding that gay men and lesbians report as much satisfaction with their relationships as do heterosexuals (Duffy & Rusbult, 1986; Kurdek & Schmitt, 1986a, 1986b, 1987; Peplau, Padesky, & Hamilton, 1982).

Unfortunately, virtually all studies of satisfaction in gay and lesbian relationships have been based on predominantly white samples. One exception is a survey of 398 African American lesbians and 325 African American gay men in committed relationships (Peplau et al., 1997). On average, participants had been in their relationships for more than 2 years. The majority (74% of women and 61% of men) indicated that they were in love with their partners. Only about 10% indicated that they were not in love, and the rest were unsure. In general, respondents reported high levels of closeness in their relationships, with mean scores approaching 6 on a 7-point scale. In this sample, the partners' race was unrelated to relationship satisfaction; interracial couples were no more or less satisfied, on average, than same-race couples.

Recently, researchers have begun to investigate other facets of the quality of same-sex relationships. Kurdek (1998b) predicted that gay and lesbian partners would differ from heterosexual partners in their experiences of intimacy and autonomy in their relationship. He reasoned, "If women are socialized to define themselves in terms of their relationships, then, relative to partners in married couples, those in lesbian couples should report greater intimacy" (p. 554). He assessed intimacy by self-reports of the partners' spending time together, engaging in joint activities, building identities as couples, and thinking in terms of "we" instead of "me." Analyses controlled for demographic variables. Lesbians reported significantly greater intimacy than did heterosexuals and gay men, although the effect size was small. Kurdek further predicted that if men are socialized to value independence, then gay couples should report greater autonomy than do heterosexuals. He assessed autonomy by self-reports of the partners' having major interests and friends outside of the relationships, maintaining a sense of being individuals, and making decisions on their own. Contrary to expectation, both lesbians and gay partners reported higher autonomy than did heterosexual partners.

### Correlates of Relationship Satisfaction Among Same-Sex Couples

Researchers have begun to identify factors that enhance or detract from satisfaction in same-sex relationships. Like their heterosexual counterparts, gay and lesbian couples appear to benefit from similarity between partners (Kurdek & Schmitt, 1987). Consistent with social exchange theory, perceived rewards and costs also are significant predictors of happiness in same-sex relationships (Duffy & Rusbult, 1986; Kurdek, 1991a, 1994c). A study of lesbian relationships found support for another exchange theory prediction, that satisfaction is higher when partners are equally involved in or committed to a relationship (Peplau et al., 1982). For lesbian couples,

greater satisfaction also has been linked to perceptions of greater equity or fairness in the relationship (Schreurs & Buunk, 1996). There also might be links between the balance of power in a relationship and partners' satisfaction. Several studies of lesbians and gay men have found that satisfaction is higher when partners believe that they share relatively equally in power and decision making (Eldridge & Gilbert, 1990; Harry, 1984; Kurdek, 1989, 1998b; Kurdek & Schmitt, 1986b; Peplau et al., 1982).

Individual differences in values also are associated with satisfaction in gay and lesbian relationships. For example, individuals vary in the degree to which they value dyadic attachment (Peplau et al., 1978). A person is high in attachment to the extent that he or she emphasizes the importance of shared activities, spending time together, long-term commitment, and sexual exclusivity in a relationship. Lesbians and gay men who strongly value dyadic attachment in a relationship report significantly higher satisfaction, closeness, and love for their partners than do individuals who score lower on attachment values (Eldridge & Gilbert, 1990; Peplau & Cochran, 1981; Peplau et al., 1978). Individuals also can differ in the degree to which they value personal autonomy, defined as wanting to have separate friends and activities apart from one's primary relationship. Some studies have found that lesbians and gay men who place strong emphasis on autonomy report significantly lower love and satisfaction than do individuals who score lower on autonomy values (Eldridge & Gilbert, 1990; Kurdek, 1989), but other studies have not (Peplau & Cochran, 1981; Peplau et al., 1978).

Personality also can affect same-sex relationships. In a recent investigation, Kurdek (1997b) assessed links between the "Big Five" personality traits and relationship quality among lesbian, gay, and heterosexual couples. Neuroticism emerged as a significant predictor for all types of couples. Compared to less neurotic individuals, highly neurotic partners rated their relationships as more costly and as diverging more from their ideal relationship standards. In another new line of work, Greenfield and Thelen (1997) showed that high scores on a measure of fear of intimacy were associated with lower relationship satisfaction among lesbians and gay men.

Recently, researchers have begun to consider how the social stigma of homosexuality might affect the relationships of lesbians and gay men. It has been suggested that the stress associated with concealing one's homosexuality can be harmful to relationship satisfaction. Three studies have provided some evidence that being known as gay to significant others such as parents, friends, and employers is associated with greater relationship satisfaction among gay men (Berger, 1990b) and lesbians (Berger, 1990b; Caron & Ulin, 1997; Murphy, 1989). By contrast, a recent analysis of a sample of 784 lesbian couples found no association between extent of disclosure of sexual orientation and relationship satisfaction (Beals & Peplau, 1999). A better understanding of this issue is needed.

## ▶ Power

Many Americans endorse power equality as an ideal for love relationships. For example, Peplau and Cochran (1980) investigated the relationship values of matched samples of young lesbians, gay men, and heterosexuals. All groups rated "having an egalitarian [equal power] relationship" as quite important. When asked what the ideal balance of power should be in their current relationships, 92% of gay men and 97% of lesbians said it should be "exactly equal." In a more recent study (Kurdek, 1995a), partners in gay and lesbian couples responded to multi-item measures assessing various facets of equality in an ideal relationship. Both lesbians and gay men rated equality as quite important, on average, although lesbians scored significantly higher on the value of equality than did gay men.

Not all couples who strive for equality achieve this ideal. In the Peplau and Cochran (1980) study, only 38% of gay men and 59%

of lesbians reported that their current relationships were "exactly equal." The percentages describing their same-sex relationships as equal in power have varied across studies. For example, equal power was reported by 60% of the gay men studied by Harry and De Vall (1978) and by 59% of the lesbians studied by Reilly and Lynch (1990).

Social exchange theory predicts that greater power accrues to the partner who has relatively greater personal resources such as education, money, and social standing. Several studies have provided empirical support for this hypothesis among gay men. Harry and colleagues found that gay men who were older and wealthier than their partners tended to have more power (Harry, 1984; Harry & De Vall, 1978). Similarly, in their large-scale study of couples, Blumstein and Schwartz (1983) concluded, "In gay male couples, income is an extremely important force in determining which partner will be dominant" (p. 59). For lesbians, research findings on personal resources and power are less clear-cut. In two studies, partner differences in income were significantly related to power (Caldwell & Peplau, 1984; Reilly & Lynch, 1990). By contrast, Blumstein and Schwartz (1983) concluded from their research, "Lesbians do not use income to establish dominance in their relationship[s]. They use it to avoid having one woman dependent on the other" (p. 60). Further research on the balance of power among lesbian couples is needed to clarify these inconsistent results.

A second prediction from social exchange theory is that when one person in a relationship is relatively more dependent or involved than the other, the dependent person will be at a power disadvantage. This has been called the "principle of least interest" because the less interested person tends to have more power. Studies of heterosexuals have demonstrated clearly that lopsided dependencies are linked to imbalances of power (Peplau & Campbell, 1989). To date, only one study has tested this hypothesis with same-sex couples. Among the young lesbians studied by Caldwell and Peplau (1984), there was a strong association between unequal involvement and unequal power, with the less involved person having more power.

A further aspect of power concerns the specific tactics that partners use to influence each other. Falbo and Peplau (1980) asked lesbians, gay men, and heterosexuals to describe how they influence their romantic partners to do what they want. These open-ended descriptions were reliably categorized into several influence strategies. The results led to two major conclusions. First, gender affected power tactics, but only among heterosexuals. Whereas heterosexual women were more likely to withdraw or express negative emotions, heterosexual men were more likely to use bargaining or reasoning. This sex difference did *not* emerge in comparisons of lesbians and gay men influencing their same-sex partners. Second, regardless of gender or sexual orientation, individuals who perceived themselves as relatively more powerful in their relationships tended to use persuasion and bargaining. By contrast, partners low in power tended to use withdrawal and negative emotions.

Another study comparing the intimate relationships of lesbians, gay men, and heterosexuals also found that an individual's use of influence tactics depended on his or her relative power in the relationship (Howard, Blumstein, & Schwartz, 1986). Regardless of sexual orientation, partners with relatively less power tended to use "weak" strategies such as supplication and manipulation. Those in positions of strength were more likely to use autocratic and bullying tactics, both "strong" strategies. Furthermore, individuals with male partners (i.e., heterosexual women and gay men) were more likely to use supplication and manipulation. Similarly, Kollock, Blumstein, and Schwartz (1985) found that signs of conversational dominance, such as interrupting a partner in the middle of a sentence, were linked to the balance of power. Although interruption sometimes has been viewed as a male behavior, it actually was used more often by the dominant person in the relationship, regardless of that person's gender or sexual ori-

entation. Taken together, the results suggest that although some influence strategies have been stereotyped as "masculine" or "feminine," they may more correctly be seen as a reflection of power rather than gender.

## ▶ The Division of Labor

How do gay and lesbian couples organize their lives together? Tripp (1975) noted, "When people who are not familiar with homosexual relationships try to picture one, they almost invariably resort to a heterosexual frame of reference, raising questions about which partner is 'the man' and which 'the woman' " (p. 152). Today, most lesbians and gay men reject traditional husband-wife or masculine-feminine roles as a model for enduring relationships (Blumstein & Schwartz, 1983; Harry, 1983, 1984; McWhirter & Mattison, 1984). Most lesbians and gay men are in dual-worker relationships, so that neither partner is the exclusive breadwinner and each partner has some measure of economic independence. The most common division of labor involves flexibility, with partners sharing domestic activities or dividing tasks according to personal preferences. When Bell and Weinberg (1978) asked lesbians and gay men which partner in their relationship does the "housework," nearly 60% of lesbians and gay men said that housework was shared equally. Asked whether one partner consistently did all the "feminine tasks" or all the "masculine tasks," about 90% of lesbians and gay men said no.

In a more recent study, Kurdek (1993) compared the allocation of household labor (e.g., cooking, shopping, cleaning) in cohabiting gay and lesbian couples and in heterosexual married couples. None of the couples had children. Replicating other research on married couples, the wives in this study typically did the bulk of the housework. By contrast, gay and lesbian couples were likely to split tasks so that each partner performed an equal number of different activities. Gay partners tended to arrive at equality by each partner specializing in certain tasks, whereas lesbian partners were more likely to share tasks. A study of lesbian couples raising young children found a similar pattern (Patterson, 1995). Both the biological and nonbiological mothers reported that household and decision-making activities were shared equally. There also was substantial sharing of child care activities, although the biological mothers were seen as doing somewhat more child care. In summary, although the equal sharing of household labor is not inevitable in same-sex couples, it is much more common than among heterosexuals.

## ▶ Sexuality

Sexuality is an important part of many romantic relationships. One research goal has been to describe the frequency of sexual activity in homosexual couples and to compare same-sex and heterosexual couples. Some researchers have reported that, on average, gay male couples have sex more often than do heterosexual couples, who in turn have sex more often than do lesbian couples (Rosenzweig & Lebow, 1992). In one study, for example, 46% of gay male couples reported having "sexual relations" at least three times a week, as compared to 35% of married or cohabiting heterosexual couples and 20% of lesbian couples (Blumstein & Schwartz, 1983). By contrast, a study of African Americans found no difference in reported frequencies of "having sex" among gay male and lesbian couples (Peplau, Cochran, & Mays, 1997).

These mixed results might be due to the unrepresentativeness of samples or to differences linked to ethnic background. It also is possible, however, that they reflect more fundamental problems about how to conceptualize and measure sexuality in relationships. McCormick (1994) observed that "most scientific and popular writers define sex as what people do with their genitals" (p. 34) and consider penile-vaginal intercourse to be the

"gold standard" for human sexuality. For example, in a recent survey of nearly 600 college undergraduates, 59% did not consider oral-genital contact to be "having sex" with a partner (Sanders & Reinisch, 1999), and 19% thought that penile-anal contact was not "having sex." These conceptions of sexuality might be poorly suited for understanding same-sex couples and, in particular, lesbian relationships. For example, lesbians who accept common cultural definitions of terms such as *having sex* and *sexual relations* might be less likely to interpret or describe their behavior with female partners as fitting these categories. Equally important, preconceptions based on heterosexual models of sexuality might lead researchers to ignore important erotic components of same-sex relationships. New approaches to understanding sexuality in same-sex relationships are needed.

Sexual monogamy versus openness is an issue for all intimate couples. In contrast to heterosexual and lesbian couples, gay male couples are distinctive in their likelihood of having nonmonogamous relationships. For example, 82% of the gay male couples who participated in Blumstein and Schwartz's (1983) study reported being nonmonogamous, compared to 28% of lesbian couples, 23% of heterosexual married couples, and 31% of heterosexual cohabiting couples. Other studies conducted during the 1970s and 1980s found similar patterns (Bell & Weinberg, 1978; Blasband & Peplau, 1985; McWhirter & Mattison, 1984; Peplau, 1991; Peplau & Cochran, 1981). There is some evidence that the AIDS epidemic has reduced the rates of nonmonogamy among gay men (Berger, 1990a; Deenen et al., 1995; Siegel & Glassman, 1989). In contrast to gay men, most lesbians characterize their relationships as monogamous. Estimates are that 70% to 80% of lesbian couples are monogamous (Blumstein & Schwartz, 1983). Most lesbians report that they prefer sexually exclusive relationships (Bell & Weinberg, 1978; Peplau & Amaro, 1982).

The impact of nonmonogamy may differ for lesbians and gay male couples. For example, Blumstein and Schwartz (1983) found that, among lesbian couples, nonmonogamy was associated with less satisfaction with sex with their partners and less commitment to the relationships, whereas among gay men, outside sex was unrelated to satisfaction or commitment to the relationships. Other studies also have documented this lack of association between sexual exclusivity and relationship satisfaction among gay male couples (Blasband & Peplau, 1985; Kurdek, 1988, 1991a; Silverstein, 1981). One reason for this difference is that gay male couples are more likely than lesbians to have agreements that outside sex is permissible (Blasband & Peplau, 1985).

▶ **Conflict and Violence**

Problems and disagreements are inevitable in close relationships. Research indicates that lesbian, gay male, and heterosexual couples are similar in how often and how intensely they report arguing (Metz, Rosser, & Strapko, 1994). Comparative studies of homosexual and heterosexual relationships suggest that similar types of conflict are likely to arise. In a study of 234 gay male, lesbian, and heterosexual couples, Kurdek (1994a) found that all three types of couples had very similar ratings of which topics they most frequently fought about, with intimacy and power issues ranked at the top and distrust ranked at the bottom. Some differences have been found between same-sex and heterosexual couples. For example, gay and lesbian couples report fighting less about money management than do heterosexual couples, perhaps because same-sex couples are less likely to merge their funds and more likely to have two incomes (Blumstein & Schwartz, 1983).

Some have suggested that same-sex couples might experience unique problems based on their shared gender role socialization (for a review, see Patterson & Schwartz, 1994). For lesbians, intimacy issues might be particularly important because women are socialized to place a strong value on closeness and inti-

macy. As one example, clinicians have described partners who become so close that personal boundaries are blurred and a healthy sense of individuality is threatened (Burch, 1986; Falco, 1991). This emphasis on closeness might be reflected in survey data showing that lesbians are more likely than gay men to report conflicts about work cutting into relationship time (Blumstein & Schwartz, 1983).

For gay men, gender role socialization can foster competition with intimate partners (Hawkins, 1992; Shannon & Woods, 1991; but see also McWhirter & Mattison, 1984). For example, although partners in heterosexual, lesbian, and gay male couples all feel successful when they earn high incomes, only gay men feel even more successful when they earn more than their partners do (Blumstein & Schwartz, 1983). Gay men are more likely than lesbians to report relationship conflicts over income differences or partners' unemployment (Blumstein & Schwartz, 1983; Harry, 1984).

How well do lesbians and gay men solve problems that arise in their relationships? In a recent study of 353 homosexual and heterosexual couples, Kurdek (1998b) found no differences in the likelihood of using positive problem-solving styles such as focusing on the problem and negotiating or compromising. Nor were differences found in the use of poor strategies such as launching personal attacks and refusing to talk to the partner (Kurdek, 1994b, 1998b). As with heterosexual couples, happy lesbian and gay male couples are more likely to use constructive problem-solving approaches than are unhappy lesbian and gay male couples (Kurdek, 1991b; Metz et al., 1994).

Recently, researchers have begun to investigate violence in same-sex relationships. Given problems of sampling and social desirability, it is impossible to accurately estimate the frequency of such violence. In recent studies, 48% of lesbian respondents and 30% to 40% of gay male respondents (Landolt & Dutton, 1997; Waldner-Haugrud, Gratch, & Magruder, 1997) reported having been victims of relationship violence. To date, most studies of same-sex violence have focused on lesbians, but violence actually may be very similar in lesbians' and gay men's relationships. For example, lesbians and gay men report experiencing similar types of abuse, with threats, slapping, pushing, and punching being the most common (Landolt & Dutton, 1997; Waldner-Haugrud et al., 1997). Risk factors for violence in gay male, lesbian, and heterosexual relationships also may be similar, and interviews with abused individuals suggest that battering occurs in a cycle of violence for all three types of relationships (Renzetti, 1992; Schilit, Lie, & Montagne, 1990).

Lesbians and gay men face unique difficulties in seeking professional help for relationship violence. Reluctance to reveal their sexual orientation might deter battered individuals from contacting the police or seeking therapy (Hammond, 1989). Many professionals and social service organizations are not trained to deal effectively with same-sex couples and might underestimate the severity of abuse when it occurs in same-sex relationships (Hammond, 1989; Harris & Cook, 1994). For example, counseling students who read similar scenarios depicting abuse in either a lesbian or a heterosexual couple thought that the abuse was more violent in the heterosexual relationship (Wise & Bowman, 1997). In sum, research suggests that gay men and lesbians may face rates of relationship violence similar to those of heterosexual couples but might experience greater difficulties in getting professional help.

## ▶ Maintaining and Ending a Relationship

How successful are lesbians and gay men in maintaining enduring intimate relationships? One of the few large-scale studies of lesbian, gay, and heterosexual couples (Blumstein & Schwartz, 1983) assessed the stability of relationships over an 18-month period. For couples who already had been together for at least 10 years, the breakup rate was quite low—less than 6%. For couples who had been together for only 2 years or less, some differences in the breakup rates were found— 22% for lesbian couples, 16% for gay male couples, 17% for heterosexual cohabiting couples, and 4% for married couples. Note that the biggest difference among these short-term couples was not between heterosexual and homosexual couples but between legally married couples and other couples, both heterosexual and homosexual, who were not married. In a recent 5-year prospective study, Kurdek (1998b) reported breakup rates of 7% for married heterosexual couples, 14% for cohabiting gay male couples, and 16% for cohabiting lesbian couples. Controlling for demographic variables, both cohabiting gay and cohabiting lesbian couples were significantly more likely than married heterosexuals to break up.

### *Relationship Commitment*

Several factors affect commitment and stability. A first factor concerns positive attraction forces that make a person want to stay with a partner, such as love and satisfaction with the relationship. As noted earlier, research shows that same-sex and male-female couples typically report comparable levels of happiness in their relationships.

Second, commitment is affected by barriers that make it difficult for a person to leave a relationship (Kurdek, 1998b). Barriers include anything that increases the psychological, emotional, or financial costs of ending a relationship. Heterosexual marriage can create many barriers such as the cost of divorce, investments in joint property, concerns about children, and the wife's financial dependence on her husband. These obstacles can encourage married couples to work toward improving declining relationships rather than ending them. By contrast, gay and lesbian couples are less likely to experience comparable barriers; they cannot marry legally, are less likely to own property jointly, are less likely to have children in common, might lack support from their families of origin, and so on.

Kurdek and Schmitt (1986b) systematically compared the attractions and barriers experienced by partners in gay, lesbian, and heterosexual cohabiting couples as well as married couples. All groups reported comparable feelings of love and satisfaction. But barriers, assessed by statements such as "Many things would prevent me from leaving my partner even if I were unhappy," did differ. Married couples reported significantly more barriers than did either gays or lesbians, and cohabiting heterosexual couples reported the fewest barriers of all. In a more recent longitudinal study, Kurdek (1998b) also found that lesbians and gay men reported fewer barriers than did heterosexuals, and he further demonstrated that barriers to leaving the relationships were a significant predictor of relationship stability over a 5-year period (see also Blumstein & Schwartz, 1983; Kurdek, 1992).

A third factor affecting the longevity of a relationship is the availability of alternatives. The lack of desirable alternatives typically represents a major obstacle to ending a relationship. Two studies have compared the perception of available alternatives among gay, lesbian, and heterosexual couples, and these studies differ in their findings. One study found that lesbians and married couples reported significantly fewer alternatives than did gay men and heterosexual cohabitors (Kurdek & Schmitt, 1986b). By contrast, a second study found no significant differences among lesbians, gay men, and heterosexuals, all of whom reported having moderately poor alternatives (Duffy & Rusbult, 1986).

In summary, research suggests that gay and lesbian couples can and do have committed enduring relationships. Heterosexual and homosexual couples, on average, report similar high levels of attraction toward their partners and satisfaction with their relationships. Where couples differ, however, is in the obstacles that make it difficult to end relationships. Here, the legal and social context of marriage creates barriers to breaking up that do not typically exist for same-sex partners or for co-

habiting heterosexuals. The relative lack of barriers might make it less likely that lesbians and gay men will be trapped in hopelessly miserable and deteriorating relationships. But weaker barriers also might allow partners to end relationships that could have improved if given more time and effort. As lesbians and gay men gain greater recognition as "domestic partners," the barriers for gay and lesbian relationships might become more similar to those for heterosexuals. The impact of such trends on the stability of same-sex relationships is an important topic for further investigation.

### Reactions to Ending a Relationship

The dissolution of an intimate relationship can be difficult and upsetting for anyone. The limited data currently available suggest that partners' reactions to the ending of same-sex and heterosexual relationships might be similar (Kurdek, 1997a). Kurdek (1991b) asked former partners from 26 gay male and lesbian couples about the specific emotional reactions and problems they encountered after the breakups of their relationships. The three most frequent emotional reactions were personal growth, loneliness, and relief from conflict (in that order). The three most frequently reported problems were the continuing relationship with the ex-partner, financial stress, and difficulties in getting involved with someone else. Anecdotal accounts suggest that because gay male and lesbian communities often are small, there might be pressure for ex-lovers to handle breakups tactfully and remain friends (Weinstock & Rothblum, 1996).

The death of a loved partner is devastating for anyone regardless of sexual orientation, but gay men and lesbians might face unique challenges. Some researchers have speculated that the stress of bereavement might be increased if the surviving partner has concealed his or her sexual orientation and/or the true nature of their relationship so that open grieving is not possible (McDonald & Steinhorn, 1990). Inheritance laws and employment policies about bereavement leave designed for married couples can add to the burdens faced by gay men and lesbians. An emerging area of research concerns the experiences of gay men who have lost friends and partners to AIDS (Goodkin, Blaney, Tuttle, & Nelson, 1996; Martin & Dean, 1993). In the only study to focus exclusively on the loss of a romantic partner, Kemeny, Weiner, Duran, and Taylor (1995) found that recent bereavement was associated with impaired immune functioning in a sample of HIV-positive gay men. Much remains to be learned about the bereavement experiences of lesbian and gay individuals.

## ▶ The Relationships of Bisexual Women and Men

What are relationships like for individuals who report romantic interest in both men and women? Research on this topic is severely limited. A further complication is that the term *bisexual* has been defined in widely differing ways (for a discussion, see Fox, 1996). Some scholars use the term to refer to a presumed innate human capacity to respond to partners of both sexes, whereas others characterize a person as bisexual if his or her lifetime history of sexual attractions or behavior includes partners of both sexes. Here, we focus on individuals who self-identify as bisexual, as we did in reviewing research on the relationships of men and women who self-identify as lesbian or gay.

Bisexuals are stereotyped as having poor intimate relationships. In a recent study by Spalding and Peplau (1997), heterosexual college students read vignettes that systematically varied the gender and sexual orientation of the partners in a dating relationship. Participants perceived the bisexuals as more likely than heterosexuals to be sexually unfaithful. Bisexuals also were seen as more likely than either heterosexuals or homosexuals to give sexually transmitted diseases to partners. Lesbians and gay men also might have negative stereotypes of bisexuals, for example, believ-

ing that bisexuals are denying their "true" sexual orientation or that bisexuals are likely to desert same-sex partners for heterosexual partners (Hutchins & Ka'ahumanu, 1991; Rust, 1992, 1995).

Currently, the main source of information about bisexuals' relationships is provided by Weinberg, Williams, and Pryor (1994). Beginning during the early 1980s, they interviewed 96 male and female bisexuals who attended social functions at a San Francisco center for bisexuals and later used a mailed questionnaire to collect additional data. These participants were predominantly white, well educated, nonreligious, and sexually adventurous. Their experiences probably do not represent "typical" bisexuals. A majority (84%) of the bisexual respondents in this San Francisco sample were in couple relationships, most commonly with partners of the other sex, and 19% were in heterosexual marriages. More than 80% indicated that their longest relationships had been with partners of the other sex. These bisexuals reported that they usually met other-sex partners through friends, work, or school. By contrast, they were more likely to meet same-sex partners through what the researchers termed the "sexual underground"—bars, bathhouses, sex parties, and the like.

Available evidence suggests wide differences among bisexuals in the patterning of their intimate relationships (Blumstein & Schwartz, 1977; Engel & Saracino, 1986; Weinberg et al., 1994). In the San Francisco study, 80% of bisexuals characterized their current relationships as sexually open; this most often meant that the people had relatively casual sexual liaisons with other partners in addition to their primary relationships. It is likely, however, that other bisexuals prefer to have monogamous relationships. A study of 19 bisexuals, 78 gay men and lesbians, and 148 heterosexuals found no differences in the extent to which respondents believed that the ideal relationship is sexually exclusive (Engel & Saracino, 1986).

Research on the relationships of bisexuals has barely begun, and there are many possible directions for future research. For example, how does the gender of a bisexual's partner affect the couple's relationship? Does the relationship of a bisexual woman differ on dimensions such as power, the division of labor, sexuality, and commitment if her partner is a woman as opposed to a man? A second research direction is to identify issues that might be unique to the relationships of bisexuals. As one illustration, research suggests that heterosexuals perceive bisexuals as particularly likely to be sexually unfaithful to their partners (Spalding & Peplau, 1997). How does this belief affect relationships between bisexual and heterosexual partners? Similarly, if lesbians and gay men endorse the stereotype that bisexuals are likely to abandon their same-sex lovers, then are jealousy and concerns about commitment problems in the same-sex relationships of bisexuals? Future research on the relationships of bisexual men and women can take many promising directions.

## ▶ Final Comments

The growing body of research on same-sex relationships leaves many questions unanswered. We know little about the experiences of lesbians, gay men, and bisexuals from ethnic minority and/or working class backgrounds. Similarly, a reliance on young adults as research participants means that we know little about the dating experiences of sexual minority adolescents or the relationship issues confronting middle-aged and older adults. The widely differing patterns of same-sex relationships found in non-Western cultures has received little attention from American researchers (Peplau, Spalding, Conley, & Veniegas, in press).

All close relationships are influenced by historical events. Several social trends affecting same-sex couples are noteworthy. First, the impact of the AIDS epidemic on the relationships of gay men, lesbians, and bisexuals is poorly understood. Second, many of today's middle-aged lesbians were strongly influenced by the modern feminist movement. By contrast, the relationship attitudes of younger adults, especially those in college, might be more strongly influenced by the development of "queer theory" and by lesbian, gay, and bisexual programs on campus. Third, the efforts of gay and lesbian civil rights activists to bring about the formal recognition of same-sex domestic partnerships are changing the legal and economic conditions of gay and lesbian couples. The impact of these changes has not been studied. Fourth, the increased visibility of same-sex couples raising children suggests that researchers will need to expand their focus beyond couples to include the families created by lesbians, gay men, and bisexuals. Finally, the prejudice and discrimination faced by lesbians and gay men has been well documented. Yet, little is known about how same-sex couples and families cope with social hostility and create supportive social networks.

Despite these limitations, several consistent themes emerge from the available research on gay and lesbian relationships (Kurdek, 1995b). Many lesbians and gay men are involved in satisfying close relationships. Contemporary same-sex couples in the United States often prize equality in their relationships and reject the model of traditional male-female marriage in favor of a model of best friendship. Comparisons of heterosexual and same-sex couples find many similarities in relationship quality and in the factors associated with satisfaction, commitment, and stability over time. Finally, efforts to apply basic relationship theories to same-sex couples have been largely successful. There is much commonality among the issues facing all close relationships, regardless of the sexual orientation of the partners.

# Contents

# Contemporary Marriage:
# Still an Unequal Partnership

*Janice M. Steil*

Over the past quarter century, the increased participation of married women in the paid labor force led to expectations, for many, of greater relationship equality. Indeed, egalitarian marriages are endorsed by increasing numbers of the population, and egalitarian relationships have been associated with a number of positive outcomes for both partners including increased intimacy, greater relationship satisfaction, and less depression, particularly for wives (for a review, see Steil, 1997). Yet, contemporary marriages remain unequal. Wives' increasing commitment to work *outside* the home has not been matched by husbands' commitment to increased work *inside* the home. *But why?* In this chapter, I attempt to give an overview of

AUTHOR'S NOTE: I thank Francine Deutsch, Justin Steil, the members of my work group, and Susan and Clyde Hendrick for their helpful comments on earlier versions of this chapter.

some of the most salient impediments to the achievement of relationship equality. Although the impediments are both structural and psychological, as well as multifaceted and complex, I focus particularly on psychological issues of gender, identity, and justice.

## ▶ Change and Resistance to Change

### Changing Demographics, Changing Attitudes

More than 90% of the population are married to heterosexual partners at some time in their lives. Age at first marriage has increased for both women and men, as has age at the birth of a woman's first child. Racial differences have increased dramatically such that blacks are significantly less likely to be married than either whites or Hispanics. Yet, the most noted change of the past quarter century has been the rapid influx of married women into the paid labor force. Just 25 years ago, nearly 60% of married women with husbands present were unemployed, with white women less likely to be employed than black women. By 1992, white women were just as likely to be employed as black women. Today, more than 60% of married women and nearly 64% of mothers with children under 6 years of age and husbands present are employed.

One of the most visible consequences of married women's increased labor force participation is the change in the number of dual-earner families. By 1996, of married couple families with children under 18 years of age, 4.4% had employed mothers and unemployed fathers, 28.2% had employed fathers and unemployed mothers, and 63.9% had both employed mothers and employed fathers (U.S. Bureau of the Census, 1998). By 1992, fewer than half (42%) of white men and only a third (33%) of black men served as their families' main breadwinners, defined as bringing in at least 70% of the family income. Currently, approximately one quarter of dual-earner wives earn more than their spouses (Krafft, 1994; Lewis, 1999).

The changing employment patterns have been paralleled by changing attitudes. During the early 1970s, half of all women and 48% of men said that the most satisfying lifestyle was a traditional marriage in which the husband worked and the wife stayed home and took care of the house and children, and more than 70% of women said that it was more important for a wife to help her husband's career than to have a career herself (Mason, Czajka, & Arber, 1976; Roper Organization, 1980). Similar attitudes continued into the 1980s, when surveys showed that 50% of Americans believed that "working mothers are bad for children" and that working mothers "weaken the family as an institution." Indeed, 70% of women and 85% of men reported that maternal employment was, in part, responsible for the breakdown of family life (Greenberger, Goldberg, Crawford, & Granger, 1988).

By 1990, however, more than half (57%) of the population said that the ideal marriage was one in which both the husband and the wife had jobs and shared in the responsibilities of child rearing and caring for the home (DeStefano & Colasanto, 1990). By 1996, 85% of married persons said that both the husband and wife should contribute to the family income, and 67% of survey respondents said that a husband whose wife is working full-time should spend just as many hours doing housework as does his wife (Chadwick & Heaton, 1999).

### Unchanging Asymmetries

Yet, despite the growing endorsement of husbands' and wives' sharing of both paid and domestic work, relationships remain asymmetrical. Husbands still are more likely to work full-time, to earn more, and to be in higher status positions compared to their wives. Indeed, even when wives hold high-status positions, the husbands' careers still are likely to be considered more important than the wives' careers (Rosenbluth, Steil, & Whitcomb, 1998; Steil & Weltman, 1991). Furthermore, wives, despite their involvement in the paid labor force, still are more likely to do a disproportionate share of the work in their homes and relationships and to report significantly less choice over their involvement in these activities compared to their husbands (Larson, Richards, & Perry-Jenkins, 1994). Employed wives continue to do nearly twice as much housework as do their husbands, including 80% of the repetitive, routine, and time-consuming tasks such as cooking, cleaning, and laundry (Chadwick & Heaton, 1999; Demo & Acock, 1993; Mederer, 1993). Wives also do from one-quarter to two-thirds more child care than do their husbands, and the caretaking gap varies dramatically by the type of task (Ishii-Kuntz & Coltrane, 1992a). Mothers and fathers are about equally involved in play time (Levant, Slattery, & Loiselle, 1987), but mothers spend up to three times as much time alone with their children and continue to shoulder more than 90% of the responsibility for planning, organizing, supervising, and scheduling activities (Baruch & Barnett, 1986; Lamb, 1987). Indeed, even "involved" fathers are likely to be involved primarily as "helpers" waiting to be told "what to do, when to do it, and how it should be done" (Coltrane, 1989, p. 480).

Wives also do much more of the emotional and interactional work that relationships require. Fishman (1983), in a detailed analysis of the conversations of white professional couples at home, effectively illustrated the gender differences in the work of relationships. An analysis of 52 hours of taped conversations showed that wives were three times more likely than husbands to ask questions as a means of initiating and maintaining interaction. Wives used minimal responses such as "yeah" and "umm" to demonstrate interest, whereas husbands more often used these same minimal responses to display a *lack* of interest. Wives tried more often to initiate conversations but were less successful due to husbands' failure to respond. Husbands tried less often but seldom failed because wives more often did the interactional work.

Studies asking men and women what is most important to them in relationships found that three of the top six items rated as most important by women and men alike related to interaction or emotion work—being committed to the relationship, being sociable and pleasant, and being attentive. Both men and women reported that women contributed far more in each of these areas than did their partners (Van Yperen & Buunk, 1990).

Gender differences in emotion work result in wives providing better emotional support for husbands than husbands provide for wives. More men than women say that they receive affirmation and support from their spouses (Van Fossen, 1981), and when asked to focus on the persons closest to them (excluding parents and siblings), wives were nearly twice as likely as husbands (22% vs. 12%) to describe relationships with same-sex best friends rather than with their husbands (Fischer & Narus, 1981). Indeed, 64% of a sample of

married heterosexual women reported being more emotionally intimate with other women, compared to only 11% who said that they were more emotionally intimate with men (Rosenbluth, 1997). The gender differences in nurturance hold true for both blacks and whites. Among married black women, 43% named family members (exclusive of spouses) as the persons "to whom they felt closest," 33.3% named female friends, and only 19.6% named their spouses (Brown & Gary, 1985).

### The Paradox of the Contented Wife

Although husbands and wives agree that women disproportionately bear the burden of these imbalances, the majority of both employed and unemployed wives report the division of labor as fair (Coltrane, 1996; Hawkins, Marshall, & Meiners, 1995; Lennon & Rosenfeld, 1994; Sanchez, 1994). When asked, "Thinking about who does what around the house, do you think that these arrangements are fair?" and "Thinking in terms of how fair these arrangements are, do you feel that you should be doing a lot less housework . . ., a lot more, or the same?", 94% of a national sample of husbands said that the arrangements were somewhat or very fair, 70% of wives said that they should be doing "about the same," and an additional 9% of wives said that they should be doing more (Berk, 1985). Subsequent studies have reported similar findings, with little or no difference in perceived fairness between full-time homemaker wives and wives who are employed (Blair & Johnson, 1992; Demo & Acock, 1993). Only when their share of the work at home *exceeds* the two-thirds average do wives begin to report the distribution as less than fair (Lennon & Rosenfeld, 1994).

Clearly, there is a gap between the actual and professed ideals of equal sharing, with wives as the underbenefited partners. Yet, women are not dissatisfied. Indeed, some researchers have argued that the primary paradox of the relationship literature has been women's relative lack of grievance. Why, they ask, are women so content? When men and women endorse relationships in which both partners participate in paid and unpaid labor, what do they mean? Are they endorsing equality? If so, then what does equality mean to them? Are their conceptions of an equal relationship different from the theoretical and operational definitions of social scientists?

## ▶ Relationship Equality

During the past two decades, social scientists of diverse orientations have begun to focus on the ways in which power is distributed and influence is exercised in intimate relationships. Some investigators have studied gender differences in influence strategy use. Others have focused on the extent to which power is equally shared. Yet, within this varied literature, the concept of equality often remains undefined. How, then, do both social scientists and married couples themselves think about and define equality in the context of an intimate relationship? And, is it really equality that couples seek?

### *The Social Scientists' Perspective*

Among those who study varying types of couple relationships, two dimensions on which relationship types differ seem primary. These are power (i.e., the extent to which the husband is more dominant than the wife) and role specialization (i.e., the extent to which responsibilities are assigned on the basis of gender). Traditional marriages are based on a form of benevolent male dominance coupled with clearly specialized roles. Thus, when women are employed, the responsibility for family work is retained by the women, who add the career role to their traditionally held family role. This contrasts with the egalitarian or role-sharing marriage, in which both spouses are employed, both are actively involved in parenting, and both share in the responsibilities and duties of the household (Gilbert, 1993; Peplau, 1983).

Some investigators have defined equal relationships as those in which each partner receives equal *outcomes* (Cate, Lloyd, & Henton, 1985). Others have put more emphasis on *process*. Benjamin (1988) described equal relationships as those in which two individuals participate in mutual exchange and mutual recognition. There is an openness to influence and emotional availability (Jordan, 1986). Both parties have and express desires, both parties are active and empowered, and the relationships are characterized by mutual respect (Benjamin, 1988).

Steil (1997) emphasized the multidimensional nature of equality and asserted that equal relationships require equal valuing— equal valuing of each partner's aspirations and abilities; equal valuing of each partner's desires, concerns, and needs; equal valuing of each partner's work; and equal valuing and equal investment in the relationship itself. Equal valuing is an attitude, and like all attitudes, it must have not only cognitive but also affective and behavioral components. Equal valuing requires a context of equal power. And, as the research reviewed here shows, equal power between men and women cannot be achieved in the context of separate gender roles.

### *Why Can't a Marriage Based on Separate Gender Roles Be Equal?*

Separate gender roles limit wives' access to universally valued resources such as income and job prestige, give different meanings to the resources that husbands and wives contribute to relationships, and prescribe differences in men's and women's sense of entitlement. Each of these undermines men's and women's ability to achieve an equal relationship.

*Access to resources.* Power, defined as the capacity to influence the behavior of others and to resist their influence on oneself (Huston, 1983), is commonly viewed as emanating from a person's access to valued resources.

Resources can be personal (e.g., love, affection) or concrete (e.g., money), but each resource varies in its range of influence. In relationships in which work is divided on the basis of gender, men are primarily responsible for the financial support of the family and are, therefore, more likely to develop concrete and universally valued resources (primarily earning power and prestige). Because women in such relationships are primarily responsible for the home, child rearing, and relationship maintenance, they develop primarily personal and relationship-specific resources. Thus, the gendered division of work precludes women's access to the more concrete, and often more highly valued, resources associated with paid employment and promotes wives' economic dependence on their husbands.

But paid employment is more than access to earning power. Across both sex and class, work outside the home can be a source of independent identity, increased self-esteem, and enhanced social contacts (for a review, see Steil, 1997). When a wife is unemployed, she loses her financial independence and has access only to relationship-specific resources. In addition, her access to alternative sources of achievement, self-esteem, and affirmation is severely limited. Together, these factors converge in ways that reduce her bargaining power and make it exceedingly difficult for her to interact with her spouse as an equal partner.

*Gendered meaning, gendered outcomes.* According to both resource and exchange theory, relationship inequality is explained by husbands' greater access to valued resources. In essence, these theories assert that husbands exchange greater financial and status resources for greater authority and less work at home (Scanzoni, 1979). Derivatively, then, wives who achieve equal access to these same valued resources should achieve equal power. Yet, studies consistently show that even wives who earn as much as or more than their husbands do not achieve relationship equality

(Rosenbluth et al., 1998; Steil & Whitcomb, 1992).

For men, the more they earn relative to their partners, the greater their say in decision making, the lower their involvement in domestic work, and the better they feel about themselves as spouses (Biernat & Wortman, 1991). This is not the case for women. Employed wives have greater say in marital decision making than do unemployed wives (for a review, see Steil, 1994), but husbands of employed women do not significantly increase their participation in domestic tasks, and women who earn significantly more than their husbands do not have equal say in financial matters (Steil & Weltman, 1991). Moreover, studies have shown that women who earn more than their husbands do not feel better about themselves as spouses, and for some, their husbands actually do less at home (Biernat & Wortman, 1991). Thus, access to broadly valued resources is associated with different outcomes for wives than for husbands.

The difference in outcomes is due to the different meanings ascribed to the paid work of husbands and wives. Despite the changing demographics, the vast majority of women and men continue to endorse the importance of the husband as provider (Haas, 1987; Perry-Jenkins & Crouter, 1990; Perry-Jenkins, Seery, & Crouter, 1992; Potuchek, 1992; Wilkie, 1993). Yet, neither partner likely is cognizant of the extent to which this endorsement grants power to a husband (Blumstein & Schwartz, 1983).

For women, endorsement of the male provider role consigns her earnings to a secondary status, and this gives different meanings to her earnings relative to those of her husbands. Perry-Jenkins et al. (1992) divided employed women into three groups: *co-providers,* who saw their income as important to their families and saw the provider role as equally shared; *ambivalent co-providers,* who admitted that the families were dependent on their incomes but were uncomfortable with the reality of shared economic responsibility; and *main-secondary providers,* who viewed their incomes as helpful but not vital to their families' well-being. Although none of the husbands shared the work of the home equally, husbands of both co-provider and ambivalent co-provider wives spent twice the time in household tasks as did other husbands, and co-provider wives experienced less depression than did any other group.

*Gender differences in the sense of entitlement.* If one way to influence the behavior of others is through control of valued resources, then another is to be the definer of what is possible and right (Fishman, 1983). Gendered differences in the sense of entitlement, defined as a set of attitudes about what a person feels he or she has a right to and can expect from others, are a significant factor in the unequal relations between women and men. Whereas entitlement attitudes initially are formed through early family interactions, they soon are affected by the internalization of cultural and group norms including those embedded in socially constructed gender roles. Among the most prominent of these gendered roles are those of provider and nurturer. Although each carries socially prescribed obligations and rights, the distribution is asymmetrical. Thus, for a man, the provider role carries the obligation to earn and provide for the family. These responsibilities, however, generally entitle him to put his career above that of his wife, free him from a number of responsibilities at home, entitle him to a position of greater influence, and allow him to perceive the time he devotes to his paid work as an expression of family caring. For most women, however, the provider role is perceived as interfering with her role as nurturer (for some exceptions, see Steil, 1997). Thus, even when she earns more than her husband, she is not entitled to view her career as primary (Steil & Weltman, 1991), she is not entitled to relieve herself of household work, and (unlike her husband) it would not be acceptable to say that her paid work kept her from her children (Thompson & Walker, 1989).

### What Does Relationship Equality Mean to Couples Themselves?

Although social scientists generally assert that equal relations cannot be achieved within the context of gendered roles, the public might be more ambivalent. Few studies have asked men and women what equality means to them, the extent to which they actually seek equality in their own relationships, and whether or not they believe equality (as they define it) is achievable when one partner does most of the housework and child care. In a study specifically designed to address these questions, Rosenbluth et al. (1998) asked a sample of men and women in dual-career marriages to think of couples they knew whose marriages they considered to be either equal or unequal and to describe why they characterized the relationships in those terms. The couples also were asked what they believed were the most important aspects of marital equality; the extent to which they endorsed marital equality as the ideal; the importance of equality in their own relationships; and whether a marriage in which both spouses work full-time, but one spouse does most of the household and child care tasks, is necessarily unequal. The study was based on a convenience sample of white, urban, highly educated professional couples. Thus, it cannot be said that they represent the spectrum of partners in dual-earner families compared to dual-career families. Yet, with these caveats, it is useful to review the findings and their implications as a basis for speculating on some of the justice, gender, and identity issues that make equality so difficult to achieve.

Contrary to investigator expectations, there were few differences in dual-career men's and women's attitudes toward equality. Indeed, both endorsed equality as "very important" in their own relationships. In fact, differences emerged only when husbands and wives responded on behalf of their spouses. Male respondents reported that their wives "strongly" believed that equal marriages are the ideal type of marriage. Female respondents stated that their husbands would be only "moderately" likely to hold that view. Similarly, when respondents were asked how important their jobs were to them, both men and women indicated that their jobs were "very important," with no differences in the importance ratings between men and women. When men responded on behalf of their wives, however, they perceived their wives' careers to be only "moderately" important to them, whereas women perceived their husbands' careers to be "extremely" important to them.

Despite men's and women's endorsement of equality as very important in their own relationships, asymmetries prevailed. Although 17% of the women earned more than their husbands, none of the wives' careers was considered primary. Indeed, despite the fact that the men and women had comparable careers, more than half (51%) of the male and female respondents considered the wives' careers to be less important than those of the husbands, and 65% of women and 43% of men reported that wives retained the primary responsibility for homemaking tasks. Compared to the findings of other studies suggesting that somewhere between 2% and 18% of couples share the work of the home equally (Ferree, 1991; Hochschild, 1989; Nyquist, Slivken, Spence, & Helmreich, 1985), 27.5% of the respondents in this sample reported that domestic work, *exclusive of child care,* was equally shared and that careers were equally valued.

One of the most interesting aspects of the study was the discrepancy in the criteria that respondents used in assessing the equality of others' relationships as compared to their own. When asked to consider the relationships of others, the dual-career respondents relied primarily on behavioral criteria. They most frequently described marriages as equal when they observed that domestic tasks and responsibilities were shared. When respondents reflected on their own relationships, however, they were more likely to cite the importance of feelings of mutual respect, supportiveness, commitment, and reciprocity over time rather than concrete behaviors such

as task division. When asked whether a marriage in which both spouses work full-time but one spouse does most of the household and child care tasks is necessarily unequal, nearly two thirds responded that such a marriage is *not* necessarily unequal. This response obviously stands in stark contradiction to the position of most social scientists, but more important, it also contradicts the criteria respondents themselves gave when thinking about the relationships of others. Thus, different criteria seemed to be salient when respondents were evaluating the relationships of others as compared to their own.

These findings raise a number of questions. Why would women and men primarily use feelings and attitudes to evaluate equality in their own marriages but use behavioral criteria to evaluate equality in the marriages of others? Why was equality so difficult to achieve for these highly educated respondents for whom equality reportedly was a valued and important goal?

### Equality in Our Own Relationships Versus Equality in the Relationships of Others

The literature suggests several reasons why women and men might use discrepant criteria to evaluate equality in their own marriages as compared to the marriages of others.

*Actor-observer bias.* One possibility is that relationship qualities such as supportiveness, respect, and reciprocity are more salient and accessible when thinking about our own relationships, whereas observable behaviors such as the performance of domestic tasks are more salient and easier to assess when thinking about the relationships of others. Similarly, we might know more of the situational factors, such as relative career demands, and the history of reciprocity in our own relationships, and these also might assume greater salience when we consider our own and our spouses' behaviors as compared to the behaviors of others (Jones & Nisbett, 1972).

*Gender and identity.* Alternatively, a number of gender theorists assert that, at least for women, the most highly valued outcomes are interpersonal (Thompson, 1991). In this context, then, domestic tasks are not simply undesirable work that the less powerful perform for the more powerful; rather, they are a way of taking care of others. Thus, wives do housework, in part, as an expression of love (Hochschild, 1989). Consistent with this perspective, "feeling appreciated" by their husbands for the work they do has been identified as the best predictor of wives' perceptions of marital fairness, regardless of their disproportionate responsibility for household tasks or the time spent on paid work outside the home (Blair & Johnson, 1992; Hawkins et al., 1995). Similarly, husbands' provision of emotional support was found to have a more significant effect on wives' perceived well-being and feelings of relationship burnout than were husbands' contributions to housework or child care (Erickson, 1993). Thus, from this perspective, a context of support and appreciation changes the meaning of domestic tasks (Blair & Johnson, 1992) as well as wives' perceptions of fairness within their marriages.

*The justice perspective.* The justice perspective suggests another explanation. Although wives might do housework as an expression of love, studies show that most do not find it enjoyable (Bird & Ross, 1993; Oakley, 1974). Wives report less positive affect associated with household tasks and child care than do husbands (Larson et al., 1994), and wives rank household tasks as the number one issue about which they and their husbands disagree most (Chadwick & Heaton, 1999).

Yet, when attempting to get their husbands to do more work at home, wives often are greeted with a repertoire of strategies (Deutsch, 1999) and justifications (Thompson, 1991) designed to resist. According to justice theory, when desired outcomes to which one feels entitled are perceived as unattainable, a frequent response is to redefine the situation to deny the injustice (Walster, Walster, & Berscheid, 1978). Despite respondents' endorsement of marital equality as ideal and very important in their own marriages, fewer than 28% were in relationships in which homemaking tasks were equally shared and careers were equally valued. From this perspective, then, the inability to achieve equality prompts respondents to shift their criteria from acts to attitudes and from facts to feelings. But why is equality so difficult to achieve?

## ▶ Explanations of Inequality

### Time Availability

The time availability argument asserts that because husbands spend so much time in outside employment, they simply do not have the same amount of time as their wives to spend on household labor. Yet, although husbands decrease their household labor when their job demands increase, studies show that they do not increase their participation in household labor in any significant way when job demands decrease (Biernat & Wortman, 1991). The reverse is true for women. Wives reduce their family time relatively little when employed, and wives who are employed the same number of hours as their husbands still perform much more family work (Pleck, 1985). Indeed, even if a husband is unemployed, he does much less housework than does a wife who puts in a 40-hour workweek (Blumstein & Schwartz, 1983). Thus, it seems that it is not husbands' time in outside employment that prevents them from full participation in the work of the home; rather, it is husbands' failure to share equally in the work of the home that limits wives' ability to fully participate in outside employment.

## Conscious Choice or Unconscious Identity?

Others view the persisting inequalities as a matter of conscious choice made out of concern for what works best for the family. Yet, the gendered allocation of domestic responsibilities and the asymmetrical valuing of careers probably are less a matter of conscious choice than another manifestation of internalized gender expectations. Findings reported in the previous section showed that husbands underestimated the importance to wives of their own careers, whereas wives overestimated the importance of husbands' careers to them. Other studies have found that wives, on average, overestimated their husbands' contribution to the family income relative to their husbands' estimates (Wilkie, Feree, & Ratcliff, 1998). Similarly, Silberstein (1992), in a study of white professional dual-career couples, found that nearly all men and women felt that it would be easier for wives' careers to be less successful than their husbands' careers than vice versa. Among the reasons wives gave for this disparity were (a) husbands' work was more important to their sense of self, (b) wives needed their husbands to be successful, and (c) wives feared that people would say that their husbands' lack of success was their fault for making their husbands help at home.

Dual-career couples, it seems, "build life structures with one foot in the past, mimicking traditional marriages of their parents' generation, and one foot in the feminist-influenced present" (Silberstein, 1992, p. 174). They hold not only "consciously altered expectations (about gender roles, work, family, and marriage) but also deeply socialized, internalized, and probably change resistant experiences, emotional needs, and entrenched patterns of behavior" (p. 13). The result of the foot in the past is that work is considered more important to men than to women, and family is considered more important to women than to men. Similarly, we expect that men's self-worth will be more closely tied to paid work than will women's and that women's self-worth will be more closely tied to motherhood than men's will be to fatherhood. According to this perspective, these entrenched identities influence the numerous large and small decisions and acts that make up everyday life, limiting conscious choice, muting partners' dissatisfaction with a gender-based division of labor, and impeding the achievement of more equally sharing relationships (Deutsch, 1999; West & Zimmerman, 1987).

## Justice Theory

According to justice theory, the motivation for change requires a perception of unfairness. But as the literature reviewed here showed, wives show little grievance over the inequalities of their lives at home. Rather, the strongest and most consistent finding is that the majority of employed and unemployed wives report that the unequal distribution of domestic work is fair. *But why?*

In a singularly systematic study of the predictors of a sense of injustice, Crosby (1982) showed that women are unlikely to perceive conditions as unfair until they see that other conditions are possible, want such conditions for themselves, and believe that they are entitled to them. The single most important of these criteria is the sense of entitlement, for the sense of entitlement not only determines what we have a right to expect from others but also is experienced as a moral imperative, the violation of which has strong affective and motivational consequences (Crosby, 1982; Lerner, 1987; Major, 1994; Steil, 1994; Weinglass & Steil, 1981).

*The sense of entitlement revisited.* Most justice researchers view the sense of entitlement as synonymous with the sense of deserving, but the two constructs are distinct. The sense of entitlement is based primarily on a conception of rights emanating from who we are (e.g., woman, man, wife, husband). The sense of deserving is based primarily on what we have earned as a result of what we have done (e.g., worked hard, received degree). Because who we are can emanate from either an ascribed (e.g., woman) or an achieved (e.g., professor) status, the constructs are not mutually exclusive. Yet, the distinction between entitlement and deserving is important. Attempts at change emanating from the sense of deserving seldom have the power to equalize differences emanating from the sense of entitlement. A high-earning wife, for example, might believe, on the basis of her financial contributions to the family, that she "deserves" more "help" at home. But eliciting help is not equivalent to an endorsement of shared responsibility. Until this high-earning wife redefines herself as a "co-provider," she will not feel entitled to the same "rights" as is her husband. Rather than fighting straightforward and direct battles over principles of shared responsibility (Deutsch, 1999), she will be negotiating for limited goals (i.e., help) on the basis of what she deserves. And, she will be negotiating from a lower status position.

Conversely, a husband might agree that his wife deserves (or perhaps "needs") some help. But until the responsibilities of "husband" are redefined to include an equal responsibility for the work of the home, and "fathering" is redefined to include a view of men as "co-nurturers," he will be operating from an entitlement, rather than a deserving, position. As a result, he will not perceive himself as equally responsible for the day-to-day care of either home or child(ren).

*Comparison others.* According to most justice theorists, both the sense of entitlement and sense of deserving are confirmed or challenged through the process of social comparison. The comparisons we make can be based on what we have achieved or felt entitled to in the past as well as our expectations and aspirations for the future. Usually, however, they are based on our comparisons to a similar other.

Gendered identities make sex of comparison other a particularly salient dimension of

similarity often resulting in a general preference for same-sex rather than cross-sex comparisons. Yet, when women compare their marital relationships to the relationships of other women, they tend to be satisfied with their marriages and believe that they are faring better than most. When they compare themselves to men, they tend to be less satisfied (Van Yperen & Buunk, 1991). Hochschild (1989) related the story of Nancy, an avowed egalitarian:

> In the past, Nancy had compared her responsibilities at home, her identity, her life to Evan's. Yet, as time went on, and Nancy found herself unable to renegotiate their relationship, she changed her comparison.
>
> Now, to avoid resentment, she seemed to compare herself more to other working mothers. By this standard, she was doing great. (p. 49)

For both women and men, the perception of inequality as unfair requires a shift in the choice of comparison other. In addition, women must give more emphasis to the sense of entitlement, whereas men must give more emphasis to the sense of deserving.

### Additional Gender and Identity Constraints

Other factors that impede the achievement of equality include the fact that relationship equality generally is perceived as something that primarily benefits women, that women disproportionately bear the burden of initiating change, and that women's role as change agent conflicts with their primary role as nurturer and relationship maintainer.

Women in unequal relationships suffer from excessive domesticity, restricted opportunities for personal achievement and public participation, and low self-esteem. Because simply being employed often reflects some element of increased power, independence, prestige, and self-esteem (Hunt & Hunt,

1987), any movement in the direction of equality often is viewed as beneficial to women.

For men, the achievement of equality most often is viewed in terms of costs—interference with their ability to meet career demands, loss of the power and privileges associated with being the sole provider, loss of the services of a nonemployed wife, increased stress, and demands to participate in family life in unfamiliar ways that conflict with masculine identity. Less attention has been paid to the *costs* of inequality for men, including both excessive work involvement and loss of their nurturing and caregiving selves (Hunt & Hunt, 1987). Finally, even less attention has been paid to the *benefits* of relationship equality for men—relief from the achievement and performance pressures associated with their sole breadwinner role; richer, more intimate, and more satisfying relationships with their wives and children, less relationship stress, and greater freedom to express and experience themselves more authentically (Hunt & Hunt, 1987; Steil & Whitcomb, 1992).

Two recent studies (Coltrane, 1996; Deutsch, 1999) involved interviewing samples of fathers who shared parenting equally. Because many of these men were fathers in dual-earner families in which the parents worked split shifts, the fathers were forced to overcome feelings of ambivalence and awkwardness and to assume the role of primary caretaker in their wives' absence. Unexpectedly, it was found that as men became more sensitive parents, their marital relations improved (Coltrane, 1996). As a result of learning how to care for their children, fathers paid more attention to emotional cues from their wives and engaged in more reciprocal communication.

Equal relationships are widely viewed as more stressful than more traditional relationships. Indeed, in a recent study, it was found that the most frequently cited disadvantage of relationship equality, by men and women alike, was the negative impact that equality can have on marital relationships by requiring daily negotiations and compromise. Yet, con-

trary to respondents' own expectations, study findings showed exactly the opposite. When the amounts of stress reported by men and women in equal, transitional, and traditional relationships were compared, it was found that those in equal relationships reported feeling stressed by the responsibilities arising from their marital relationships least often, whereas those in traditional relationships reported feeling stressed most often (Steil & Whitcomb, 1992). Whereas equal relationships require more frequent negotiation and compromise, it might be precisely the need for continued interpersonal contact and involvement that contributes to the high levels of satisfaction found among egalitarian couples. As one of the study's male respondents expressed:

> Maybe you end up having certain arguments that you might not have had, arguments about whose responsibility it is to do this, that, and the other. But I think, in a way, if you don't have those arguments, you end up having arguments about other things sooner or later. The arguments you have about responsibilities are not as vicious as the ones you have later about resentment. (pp. 15-16)

Perhaps because equality is viewed as primarily benefiting women, women disproportionately bear the burden of initiating change. Even for the sample of dual-career respondents described earlier in this chapter, among whom there were no differences in the extent to which they reported equality as important in their own relationships, 90% of wives and 55% of husbands said that the wives were more likely to raise issues of equality in their own relationships. Yet, women's role as change agent often is in conflict with their primary role as nurturer and relationship maintainer. Miller (1986) suggested that women often feel that attempts to act on their own behalf, or to take steps toward their own growth, are repudiations of femininity and will be viewed as attacks on men.

## ▶ Conclusion

The continuing inequality in the division of labor at home has come to symbolize the psychological complexity of modern marital relationships in which both women and men struggle with issues of identity and fairness. Integrating both the justice and the gender perspectives, Ferree (1990) pointed out that the family is simultaneously a communal structure that endeavors to satisfy the needs of all members and a locus of struggle through which each member strives to satisfy independent interests. Thus, it is only through understanding the cultural framework in which familial negotiations take place that we can understand both the resistance to change and the process by which change is emerging. Women struggle with their husbands to get them to do more work and also struggle with themselves over issues of restricted entitlement and traditional notions of mothering. Men struggle with their partners over issues of privilege and fairness and also struggle with themselves in redefining traditional notions of career and fathering (Deutsch, 1999).

When husbands resist wives' attempts at change, wives often defer. Wives pay a heavy price, however, including a devaluation of themselves (Hochschild, 1989). Equality requires strong women and fair men, for it is not conflict but rather the avoidance of conflict that signals a lack of mutual respect. To fight for equality means that a wife believes that her husband is fair-minded and capable of being as good a parent and partner as she is. Similarly, for men, the respect they have for their wives sustains their commitment to share the work of the home equally (Deutsch, 1999).

The stakes are enormous. More equal relationships offer men the opportunity to relinquish the mantle of total economic responsibility and family dependency, to involve themselves in parenting, and to more fully express their emotional and nurturing selves. More equal relationships offer women the opportunity to develop themselves professionally, to develop a sense of self independent of their husbands and children, and to achieve economic independence and higher self-esteem (Gilbert & Rachlin, 1987). Finally, men and women together will have the opportunity to be part of more intimate relationships based on the mutual reliance and respect that is so important to satisfying relationships and to both husbands' and wives' well-being.

# Contents

# Divorce and Single Parenting

*Mark A. Fine*

Divorce and single parenthood are both similar to and different from each other, which makes it challenging to discuss each in the confines of a single chapter. They are similar phenomena in the sense that they often lead to a parent raising children without another adult living in the household, and both are commonly experienced.

On the other hand, divorce and single parenthood differ in a number of important ways. Divorce is a relationship event, involving complex processes before, during, and after the actual legal event (Morrison & Cherlin, 1995). Single parenthood, by contrast, is not necessarily defined by a particular event but rather consists of a particular household configuration that can last for widely varying durations. Divorce necessarily is rooted in the experience of loss (e.g., of a relationship partner), whereas single parenthood, if not preceded by divorce or loss of a spouse, might not be. Finally, the racial and socioeconomic charac-teristics of divorced parents can differ substantially from those of individuals who become single parents through means other than divorce.

The sizable literatures on divorce and single parenthood seldom have been informed by a related body of literature from the field of close relationships. Accordingly, this chapter reviews selected aspects of how divorce and single parenthood are experienced, with special attention given to insights gleaned from the close relationship literature. I begin with a description of some demographic information related to divorce and single parenthood, provide an overview of children's and parents' adjustment in divorced- and single-parent families with an emphasis on the more voluminous literature on children's adjustment, discuss the process of relationship termination, review findings related to family processes that can affect children's adjustment in single-parent families, and conclude with implications for professional practice and future research. Throughout, divorce is considered primarily in the context of families with minor children.

# ► The Increasingly Normative Nature of Divorce and Single Parenting

Increases in divorce rates and in the proportion of single-parent families during the past 30 years have been dramatic, although the divorce rate has not risen during the past 20 years (Teachman, 2000). The proportion of white children living with two parents declined from nearly 90% in 1970 to less than 80% in 1994. For Hispanic children, the decline was from 80% to 65%, and for African American children, the decrease was from 60% to 33%. Because these figures represent only cross-sectional views, they underestimate the percentage of children who spend any portions of their childhoods in single-parent families (Teachman, 2000). More than 50% of children born in the United States during the 1990s (36% of white children and 80% of African American children) will spend at least some time living in single-parent families (Bianchi, 1995).

Not only have there been increases in the prevalence of single-parent families, there also have been meaningful changes in the *origins* of single parenthood. At the turn of the 20th century, most single-parent families resulted from the deaths of spouses (Amato, 2000). During the 1950s and 1960s, most single-parent families were formed following parental divorces. By contrast, during the 1990s, an increasing proportion of single-parent families were formed by parents who never had married. There also are important subgroup differences in these pathways to single-parent status. Most African American single mothers (56%) never are married, whereas most white single mothers (72%) are divorced or separated (Amato, 2000).

# ► Conceptual Approaches to Understanding Divorce and Single Parenthood

A number of conceptual approaches have informed the study of single parenthood and divorce/relationship termination. In this chapter, aspects of family systems, interdependence, and ecological perspectives are interwoven to provide a view of these literatures.

## *Family Systems Perspective*

Family systems theorists view the family as a system of interconnected individuals, with changes in one or more members having effects throughout the family system (Klein & White, 1996). In addition, family systems theories posit that it is possible to understand a family only by considering it as a unit; thus, it might be misleading to examine a particular dyad in the family in isolation from the entire family system. Finally, families as a system affect their environments and, in turn, are affected by the contexts around them.

With respect to divorce and single parenthood, the family systems perspective alerts us to the importance of considering the family as a whole and that it *might* be inappropriate to reduce our scope of inquiry to particular individuals or dyads within the family. These theorists might argue, for example, that one cannot understand how children are affected by divorce without understanding how children are affected by their parents and extrafamilial institutions (e.g., schools).

## *Interdependence Perspective*

The interdependence perspective directs our attention to how individuals weigh the costs and benefits of particular family arrangements and how their behaviors are affected by these evaluations (Sprecher, 1992).

According to this perspective, individuals generally are motivated by self-interest, are rational, and act to maximize benefits relative to costs in relationships.

With respect to divorce and relationship termination, this perspective suggests that individuals make decisions regarding whether to maintain their relationships on the basis of their assessment of costs and benefits (relative to alternative relationships in which they believe they could be involved) and that they terminate relationships when the cost-benefit ratios exceed what they consider to be acceptable levels.

With respect to single parenthood, the interdependence perspective suggests that single parents are motivated to maintain their single-parent status to the extent that they are satisfied with their current cost-benefit ratios. An implication of this approach is that, in addition to the well-documented costs associated with being a single parent, there also might be benefits. For example, parents without partners do not have to maintain romantic relationships and can make child-rearing decisions by themselves; until recent welfare reforms, they also received some financial benefits that they would not have received if they were married.

### Ecological Perspective

A primary feature of ecological theories is the premise that development, whether at the individual or family level, is contextual. According to Bronfenbrenner (1979), individual development is affected by four levels of environmental systems distinguished on the basis of their immediacy to the developing individual: microsystems (e.g., the family), mesosystems (e.g., child care settings, schools), exosystems (e.g., work settings, social networks), and macrosystems (e.g., societal values). Similarly, Bubolz and Sontag (1993) suggested that families are affected by a series of nested contextual and ecological systems.

Ecological theories provide a rationale for examining how certain types of interactions at the family level (e.g., parenting behaviors) and extrafamilial level (e.g., schools) affect children and parents. They also alert us to how social norms affect how single-parent families are perceived and treated.

## ▶ Effects of Divorce and Single Parenthood on Children and Parents

### Effects of Divorce and Single Parenthood on Children

*Intrapersonal outcomes for children.* The early literature on the effects of divorce and single parenthood on children emphasized negative outcomes. However, because much of this literature was based on reports by clinicians, these results are unlikely to generalize to the larger population. Indeed, later studies, using more representative samples, generally have shown that these negative consequences are smaller than was suggested by these early reports (Demo & Acock, 1988).

Nevertheless, as noted by Simons and Associates (1996), we need to be careful not to underemphasize the consequences of the family structure differences in child outcomes. When behaviors have low base rates (e.g., externalizing behaviors), even small effect sizes can translate into meaningful differences in risk. Simons and Associates found that children from divorced families were at least twice as likely to exhibit maladaptive behaviors as were those from first-marriage families, despite the effect sizes pertaining to these differences being fairly small. Similarly, Hetherington and Clingempeel (1992), in their 5-year study, found that, although family structure effect sizes were relatively small, there were consequential differences in the likelihood of behavior problems. Whereas 10% of the children in first-marriage families were above the clinical cutoff on the Child

Behavior Checklist (a rate comparable to that in normative samples), 25% to 30% of the children in divorced single-mother families were above the clinical cutoff level (based on mothers' reports). Thus, results such as these, which are typical of many other studies, have a double-edged message: The majority of children from single-mother families are functioning within the normal range, but they are two to three times as likely to have clinically significant levels of behavior problems.

With respect to health outcomes, Dawson (1991), based on the National Health Interview Survey on Child Health, found that children living with single mothers, compared to those living in first-marriage families, were more likely to have been treated for emotional or behavioral problems during the past year and to have elevated health vulnerability scores. Children whose parents divorced were similar to those whose mothers never married in terms of physical health and behavioral problems. An advantage of this study is that the route to single-mother status, divorce or never marrying, was considered. In a more recent analysis, Hoffman and Johnson (1998), based on the National Household Survey on Drug Abuse, found that the risk of drug use and abuse was highest among adolescents in single-father and stepmother families, even after controlling for a number of demographic variables. Adolescents in single-mother families also were at higher risk for drug use and abuse than were those living with both of their biological parents.

With respect to educational outcomes, Marsh (1990) found few family structure differences in educational outcomes during the final 2 years of high school among students in the High School and Beyond (HSB) study. However, using the same data set, Zimiles and Lee (1991) found small but significant family structure differences among high school sophomores. Whereas students from first-marriage families had higher achievement test scores and higher grade point averages than did those from single-parent families, the largest family structure difference was in dropout rates. Students from single-parent families were nearly three times as likely to drop out of school as were those from first-marriage families (7% vs. 20%). Similar findings from the National Longitudinal Survey of Youth were reported by Sandefur, McLanahan, and Wojtkiewicz (1992).

One of the critiques levied against much of this literature is that causal inferences (e.g., divorce causes adjustment problems) are inappropriately drawn from correlational research designs. To address this issue, several longitudinal studies have been conducted. Block, Block, and Gjerde (1986) found that children whose parents eventually divorced were described at young ages as having more negative personality characteristics, compared to those whose parents remained married. The authors speculated that many of the problems shown by children of divorce actually might be extensions of problems that began before divorce, perhaps fueled by conflictual marital and family interactions. Similarly, Baydar (1988), using data from the National Survey of Children, found that children whose parents divorced were described as more poorly emotionally adjusted both before and after divorce, compared to those whose parents were continuously married. Similar findings have been reported by Cherlin et al. (1991). Doherty and Needle (1991) extended these findings by showing that boys showed negative effects after, but not before, their parents separated, whereas girls showed negative reactions before their parents separated that persisted after divorce.

Not all studies have found that predivorce levels of adjustment and/or family characteristics were related to the extent of postdivorce adjustment difficulties. Forehand, Armistead, and Corinne (1997) found that adolescents whose parents would divorce within the subsequent 4 years did not differ in functioning from those whose parents would remain married. By contrast, adolescents whose parents were divorced at the beginning of the study were more poorly adjusted than those in either of the other two groups. The authors concluded that postdivorce factors were responsible for later adjustment differences among adolescents from different family structures. Similarly, Morrison and Cherlin (1995), based on the National Longitudinal Survey of Youth Child Supplement data, found that, during the first 2 years following divorce, there were negative effects of divorce on the academic achievement of boys and that these were not reduced after controlling for prior family characteristics.

Whereas the size of the differences between children in single-parent and first-marriage families on socioemotional dimensions of well-being tends to be small, differences are more dramatic in terms of their current (and future) *socioeconomic* well-being (Hetherington, Bridges, & Insabella, 1998; McLanahan & Sandefur, 1994). Children in single-parent families have less family income available to them and are more likely to be poor than are children in first-marriage families, particularly if they are living with mothers who are high school dropouts, separated or never married, and 24 years old or under (Amato, 2000). Furthermore, economic disadvantages are related to poorer socioemotional outcomes (Thomson, Hanson, & McLanahan, 1994).

*Long-term effects of parental divorce on children's intrapersonal adjustment.* Using the National Child Development Study, a longitudinal, nationally representative survey conducted in Great Britain, Chase-Lansdale, Cherlin, and Kiernan (1995) found that parental divorce had a moderate, long-term negative impact on adult adjustment, even after controlling for socioeconomic status, emotional problems as a child, and school performance before divorce. Chase-Lansdale et al. found that the probability of scoring above the clinical cutoff on the Malaise Inventory rose from 8% to 11% following parental divorce, suggesting that the relative risk increased nearly 40% but that most adults did not exhibit clinical levels of adjustment problems. Similarly, Kiernan (1992), based on the same data set, found that living with a single mother, compared to living with both biological parents, at 16 years of age was related to a greater likelihood of dropping out of school

(for men), leaving home by 18 years of age (for women), cohabiting before 21 years of age, having children before 23 years of age, having a birth outside of marriage, and conceiving outside of marriage. Interestingly, Kiernan found that these differences were present only for adults who lived in single-mother families *formed following divorce, not formed following the deaths of parents.* There were few differences between adults who grew up in first-marriage families and those who lost parents due to deaths.

In a meta-analytic review of the long-term effects of parental divorce on adult well-being, Amato and Keith (1991a) found that adults who experienced parental divorce exhibited lower levels of well-being on all dimensions analyzed, particularly psychological adjustment and the likelihood of later being in a single-parent family, than did those whose parents were continuously married. Effect sizes were stronger for whites than for African Americans and were stronger in clinical studies than in studies using community samples.

*Interpersonal outcomes for children.* Some authors have examined divorce outcomes that are more interpersonal in nature. Most of these studies have suggested that divorce has only small (if any) negative effects on relationship-related variables. With respect to friendship and romantic relationships among college-age individuals, Jones (1992) found that divorce had little effect on college students' friendship networks. By contrast, family conflict had negative effects on the size of and affective quality of friendship networks. Sinclair and Nelson (1998) found that college students from divorced families did not differ from those from first-marriage families on levels of intimacy in their relationships or on dysfunctional relationship beliefs. Sprecher, Cate, and Levin (1998) found that female college students with divorced parents, relative to those with nondivorced parents, were less likely to have a secure attachment style; were more likely to have an avoidant attachment style; were less pragmatic, manic, and agapic in their love styles; and were less idealistic in their romantic beliefs. There were few group differences for men. The significant differences found for women were primarily between those in the divorced group and those from intact *and* happy marriages, not between those in the divorced group and those from intact but unhappy marriages.

*Long-term effects of parental divorce on children's interpersonal adjustment.* With respect to long-term interpersonal outcomes, White (1994), using the National Survey of Families and Households (NSFH), found that there was less family solidarity (i.e., relationship quality, contact frequency, perceived and actual social support) between parents and adult children who previously had lived together in single-parent homes compared to those who had lived in first-marriage families. Amato and Booth (1996), using data from the National Study of Marital Stability Over the Life Course, found that later divorce was associated with parents' reports of more problems in their relationships with their children as early as 8 to 12 years before divorce. Those reporting problems with their children *and* who had low marital quality when the children were 10 years old reported less affection for their children when they were 18 years old. Divorce subsequently was related to further decrements in affection between fathers and children but not between mothers and children. In terms of systems theory, these results suggest that interactions in one subsystem, the parent-child dyad, are affected by processes in another subsystem, the marital dyad. In terms of ecological theory, the greater decrements in relationship quality between fathers and children relative to that between mothers and children may be partially explained by nonresidential fathers generally having less of a role to play in their children's lives compared to that of mothers.

In terms of the long-term effects of divorce on parent-child relationships, Cooney, Hutchinson, and Leather (1995), in a longitudinal study of young adults, found that the quality of parent-child relationships immediately following divorce was associated more strongly with situations arising after divorce and aspects of the divorce process itself than with predivorce family dynamics. Because the variables explained greater proportions of the variability in father-child relationships than in mother-child relationships, Cooney et al. concluded that fathers' relationships with their children following divorce are particularly susceptible to divorce-related stresses.

Burns and Dunlop (1998), in a longitudinal study of individuals who were adolescents at the times of their parents' divorces, examined the long-term consequences of divorce on later adult (23-27 years of age) relationships. Consistent with results from studies examining short-term relationship-related outcomes, they found no differences in the quality of adult relationships between those from divorced and nondivorced families. There were no differences in perceptions of relations with mothers between the two groups, but young adults from divorced families perceived their fathers as less caring (at all time periods) than did those from nondivorced families.

*Potential benefits to children from growing up in single-parent families.* Although not often examined in the scholarly literature, there is some evidence that there might be some benefits derived from growing up in a single-parent family. For example, Cooksey and Fondell (1996) found that single fathers were quite involved in their children's lives and were more likely to share a variety of activities with them than were fathers in first-marriage families. Whereas there is some controversy regarding the extent to which the presence and involvement of fathers is beneficial to children, there is evidence from first-marriage families that fathers' involvement has a beneficial effect on children's well-being (Harris, Furstenberg, & Marmer, 1998).

### Diversity Within Single-Parent Families

There is considerable diversity within single-parent families. For children and parents who are not living in first-marriage families, there is considerable change that occurs in the structures of their homes. Wojtkiewicz (1992), based on analyses of the NSFH data set, showed that children in "nonintact" families at 15 years of age typically had lived in a combination of intact and nonintact family types, suggesting that a "snapshot" view of family structure can lead to misleading inferences regarding family environment. In addition, Wojtkiewicz found that children whose mothers were not married when they were born differed considerably in their experience of family structure from those who lived with both parents at birth. Children in the first group spent very little time living in two-parent families, whereas those in the second group tended to spend approximately 50% of their childhoods in two-parent arrangements. In addition, because 30% of single parents cohabit with partners or live in their parents' households, Bumpass and Raley (1995) argued that single-parent families need to be defined based on who is living in the home rather than on parents' marital status.

Several studies, including some reviewed earlier, have found different outcomes for individuals from different types of single-parent families. For example, Demo and Acock (1996a), using the NSFH data set, found that 12- to 18-year-olds from never-married single-mother families had the lowest incomes, whereas those from divorced and stepparent families had the highest levels of mother-adolescent disagreement and the lowest levels of parental supervision. However, Downey, Ainsworth-Darnell, and Dufur (1998) found few differences in a variety of well-being domains between children living with single mothers and those living with single fathers as well as few meaningful differences in well-being between adults raised by single mothers and those raised by single fathers.

African American children might not be as detrimentally affected by living in single-parent families as are white children (Fine & Schwebel, 1991; Salem, Zimmerman, & Notaro, 1998). For example, Zimmerman, Salem, and Maton (1995) found only one signif-

icant family structure difference among urban African American adolescent males: more parental support reported by adolescents living in single-mother households than by adolescents living in other family structures. Salem et al. (1998) found only one significant family structure difference in psychosocial outcomes among African American adolescents: higher marijuana use among those living with their mothers and extended families. Similar findings (i.e., of higher well-being for African American children in single-parent families than for white children) have been reported by Acock and Demo (1994), Amato (2000), and McLanahan and Sandefur (1994).

Several explanations consistent with the systems, interdependence, and ecological perspectives have been posited for the lesser effects of single parenthood on African American children. For example, some have suggested that the greater prevalence of single-parent families in the African American community has led to less social stigma attached to this family form (Fine & Schwebel, 1991), which would improve the cost-benefit ratio of living in a single-parent family because of fewer negative interactions with societal institutions. Furthermore, the presence of supportive extended family can be understood in terms of African American families benefiting from helpful interactions with systems outside the nuclear families (Taylor, Chatters, Tucker, & Lewis, 1990).

### Effects of Divorce and Single Parenthood on Parents

Research on the effects of divorce and single parenthood on adults suggests that divorced parents are at greater risk for mental health problems than are parents from first-marriage families, although divorced parents experience enhanced well-being as time passes following divorce (Hetherington et al., 1998). Demo and Acock (1996b), using the NSFH, found small but statistically significant differences in maternal well-being across different family structures. In particular, divorced and continuously single mothers had the lowest levels of well-being, whereas those in first marriages had the highest levels of well-being. Based on the same data set, Amato (2000) found that single parents in general reported being moderately happy and healthy and reported relatively few symptoms of depression. Separated parents reported being less happy and more depressed than did divorced parents, perhaps because separated parents might be closer in time to the emotional turmoil than are divorced parents and because separation is an ambiguous state.

Using several samples, Kitson (1992) found that divorce was associated with heightened distress, continued attachment to the exspouse, low self-esteem, more contacts with health care professionals, economic problems, and a variety of other divorce-related stressors. She also found evidence that an adjustment process occurs over time given that, 4 years after separation, most of the divorced individuals did not differ from the married sample in psychological functioning.

## ▶ Process of Relationship Termination

Having addressed the consequences of divorce for children and parents, it is now appropriate to review the processes that lead to these outcomes. As noted earlier, the termination of marriages and other close relationships is most fruitfully viewed as a process that unfolds over time rather than as a discrete event. Duck (1992) conceptualized a series of five stages characterizing the extended process of relationship dissolution, suggesting that individuals do not progress through the stages in a linear fashion but rather go back and forth between the tasks in the various stages. In the *breakdown phase,* at least one partner identifies a problem in the relationship. In the *intrapsychic phase,* each partner who senses a problem begins to critically evaluate the relationship and begins to express his or her discontent to others. In the

*dyadic phase,* the dissatisfied partner shares his or her concern with the partner, and the spouses then begin the process of attempting to resolve their problems. If successful, then the relationship will continue. If not, then the couple enters the next stage, the *social phase.* During this period, partners attempt to convince others in their social network of the veracity of their perceptions of the relationship and its difficulties. Typically, the network partners split into factions such that some endorse one partner's view and others believe the other partner's view. In this stage, there is the beginning of the public story that will explain why the relationship is terminating. In the final stage, the *grave dressing phase,* the relationship is "put to rest" and the final story is constructed regarding the life course of the relationship.

Some empirical support for Duck's (1992) model emerged from a study by Hopper (1993), who investigated the accounts provided by divorced spouses of the courses of their relationships and their eventual termination. He found that partners tended to place themselves in one of two roles: the person who left the other or the person who was left by the other. The person identified as being the one who left the other tended to have particularly negative memories of the relationship, reported having many doubts about the viability of the relationship, and described motives of needing to do what was best for him or her by leaving the relationship. By contrast, the person identified as being left by the other tended to have positive memories of the relationship, reported very little (if any) doubt about the relationship, and described motives of wanting to maintain the relationship for the collective good of the family.

Despite this consistent pattern in reports by the two different types of partners (i.e., the left and the leaver), from retrospectively gathered information before divorce, Hopper (1993) was unable to predict which partner would adopt which role. His data suggested that both partners had a range of positive and negative experiences with the relationship, had some doubts about the relationship, and had a mix of personal and family motives as he or she decided how to effect change in and/or terminate the relationship. Apparently, for reasons not uncovered in this investigation, one partner begins the process of terminating the relationship, perhaps by expressing his or her doubts or concerns, a pattern that is consistent with Duck's (1992) dyadic phase. After this initial event, an extended process unfolds in which the partners come to adopt one of the two roles and construct an interpretation of the relationship and its termination that is intended for public presentation. This is quite consistent with the later phases in Duck's model as well as his observation that partners often have differing views and interpretations of events and meanings surrounding the termination of their relationship. This process of developing a socially constructed account of the termination of the relationship also is similar to the "face management" process described by Metts (1992) that involves partners constructing accounts and using language that places themselves in a good light.

There also has been empirical work aimed at elucidating various aspects of the process of relationship termination. For example, some researchers have studied factors that predict the extent to which partners are distressed following relationship termination. Kurdek (1997a) found that separation distress was positively related to the severity of neurotic characteristics reported when the relationship was intact, negatively related to the extent to which the separation was expected, and unrelated to relationship-related events preceding the separation (e.g., relationship quality). Fine and Sacher (1997), using a variant of the interdependence perspective, found that higher levels of distress following relationship termination among dating college students were longitudinally predicted by higher initial levels of commitment and alternative quality. Consistent with the notion that relationship termination is an extended process, Sprecher, Felmlee, Metts, Fehr, and Vanni (1998), in a sample of young adults who had experienced recent relationship terminations, found that current levels of breakup distress were less than retrospectively reported levels at the times of the breakups. In addition, distress at the times of the breakups and current distress were greater to the extent that individuals (retrospectively) reported that they were satisfied with and committed to the relationships, had been in longer lasting relationships, felt that their partners had initiated the breakups, perceived that their partners had better relationship alternatives than they did, and had a fearful attachment style. Unfortunately, the retrospective nature of the Sprecher et al. data suggests that the account-making and face management processes might already have occurred and affected participants' reports.

## ► Family Processes in Divorced- and Single-Parent Families and Their Links to Adjustment

A growing number of researchers have gone beyond simply comparing the adjustment of children and parents in different family structures by examining processes, interactions, and behaviors that occur in families and other environments that might affect the adjustment of children and parents. An examination of the environmental systems around children and parents is consistent with the ecological and systems perspectives. An ecological perspective guides us to look at the systems surrounding the children and family and how they influence development. For example, the family processes addressed in this section are part of the children's microsystem in that they usually involve direct interactions between parents and their children. A systems perspective leads us to consider how children, parents, parents' romantic and other relationships, and outside societal institutions mutually influence each other. In addition, some of the impetus for turning research attention to family processes has come from the realization that divorce must have its effects on outcomes through some day-to-day mechanism. In this section, research is reviewed on three types of family processes and one type of process from the larger social system (the school environment), addressed in descending order roughly reflecting the amount of research attention each area has received: parenting behaviors, marital conflict, family interactions, and school environments.

### Parenting Behaviors

There is a growing body of literature that supports the contention that authoritative parenting, or the simultaneous display of warmth and supervision parenting behaviors (the two key components of parenting style [Maccoby & Martin, 1983]), is conducive to positive child adjustment in a variety of family structures (Barnes & Farrell, 1992; Bronstein, Stoll, Clauson, Abrams, & Briones, 1994; Hetherington & Clingempeel, 1992; Lamborn, Mounts, Steinberg, & Dornbusch, 1991; Thomson et al., 1994). For example, Avenevoli, Sessa, and Steinberg (1999) showed that, across family structures, ethnicities, and social classes, authoritative parenting was associated with positive adolescent adjustment, whereas authoritarian, neglectful, and permissive parenting styles were associated with negative outcomes with an important exception. Authoritative parenting was somewhat less strongly related to self-esteem and academic achievement for African American adolescents than for other adolescents, and it even was associated with greater involvement in delinquent behaviors. Previous researchers also suggested that authoritative parenting might be less conducive to positive child outcomes in minority families than in white families (Steinberg, Dornbusch, & Brown, 1992).

Are there reliable differences in parenting between first-marriage and single-parent families? In a number of nationally representative and large data sets, McLanahan and Sandefur (1994) compared single parents and parents in first-marriage families on a number of parenting dimensions including the amount of time that mothers and fathers spend with their children, the quality of the interactions between parents and children, the amount of su-

pervision provided by parents to their children, and parental aspirations for their children. Not surprisingly, children from divorced families and those born to never-married parents had much less contact with their fathers than did those in first-marriage families.

In the NSFH data set, which is based on parental report, McLanahan and Sandefur (1994) found that approximately 24% of the children living with divorced mothers and 34% of those living with never-married mothers had no contact with their fathers during the past year. On some but not all dimensions, divorced and single mothers spent less time with their children than did mothers in first-marriage families. However, the differences were much smaller in magnitude than were those pertaining to time spent with fathers. Similarly, there were very few differences between different types of mothers in the quality of time spent with their children.

Single mothers, whether divorced or never married, exhibited less supervision and monitoring of their children; however, the differences, although significant, were small in magnitude (see also Thomson, McLanahan, & Curtin, 1992, who found that male and female single parents reported having less restrictive rules than those of married parents). In the HSB study, children from single-parent families reported receiving less help from parents with schoolwork and reported less parental supervision than did children from first-marriage families. However, children from single-parent families reported that they talked with their parents *more often* than did children from first-marriage families, perhaps reflecting that single parents are more likely to depend on their children as confidants than are other parents. Finally, from the HSB study and the National Longitudinal Survey of Youth, McLanahan and Sandefur (1994) found that children from single-parent families indicated that their parents had lower expectations for them to attend or graduate from college than did children from two-parent families. Again, these differences in substantive terms were small. Similarly, Avenevoli et al. (1999) found that parents of adolescents in first-marriage families were more authoritative, more authoritarian, less permissive, and less neglectful than were parents in single-parent families. These differences generalized across social classes and ethnicities.

It is important to note, however, that not all studies have found that single mothers are less engaged as parents than are parents in first-marriage families. In fact, Hetherington and Clingempeel (1992) found that divorced mothers were *more* frequently authoritative and *less* disengaged than were mothers in first-marriage and stepfather families. Furthermore, Bulcroft, Carmody, and Bulcroft (1998), using the NSFH data set, found that single parents provided *greater* supervision of their adolescent children's extrafamilial behaviors than did parents in first-marriage families.

It also is important to acknowledge possible variation in parenting behaviors among single parents. For example, McKenry, McKelvey, Leigh, and Wark (1996) found that divorced and separated fathers communicated with and visited their children more often than did remarried or never-married fathers, with the remarried and never-married fathers feeling that they had less influence over their children's lives than did divorced or separated fathers.

How involved and influential are fathers in the lives of children living in single-parent families? Coley (1998) found that fathers' warmth and control parenting behaviors were related to better academic achievement for third- and fourth-grade children, particularly for girls and African American children. In addition, supporting the importance of recognizing diversity within single-parent arrangements, divorced fathers were more influential in children's achievement than were fathers who had not married their children's mothers. Veneziano and Rohner (1998) found that African American and white children's perceived paternal acceptance and fathers' reports of their involvement were positively related to youths' self-reported psychological adjustment.

Another factor that needs to be considered when examining postdivorce parenting is whether the parents remarry or not. There is

some evidence that the remarriage of either or both parents can affect coparenting following divorce. For example, Christensen and Rettig (1995) found that remarriage was associated with less frequent coparental interaction, less perceived parenting support from the former spouse, and more negative attitudes about the other parent; for remarried men, it also was associated with less parenting satisfaction and lower levels of involvement in children's activities.

There also is the beginning of a literature on the factors that are predictive of effective parenting *following* divorce. DeGarmo and Forgatch (1997a) found that, after controlling for maternal distress and the negativity of confidants, behaviorally observed confidant support predicted more effective parenting practices. In addition, maternal distress was negatively related to the quality of parenting practices. These results suggest that social support from close relationships can contribute to the quality of parenting following divorce, a conclusion consistent with the ecological perspective.

### *Marital Conflict*

A substantial body of literature supports the claim that marital conflict has negative effects on children's adjustment, regardless of the family structure in which children reside. Amato and Keith (1991b), based on the results from an extensive meta-analysis, concluded that children in high-conflict first-marriage families not only were considerably less well adjusted than those in low-conflict first-marriage families but also were less well adjusted than children from divorced families. A recent study, based on the NSFH data set, found that parental conflict had negative effects on three dimensions of children's well-being (internalizing problems, externalizing problems, and trouble with peers) in both first-marriage and divorced families (Vandewater & Lansford, 1998).

There also has been some research showing that interparental cooperation—in some senses, the opposite of marital conflict—facilitates positive child adjustment. Camara and Resnick (1988) found that the extent to which parents cooperated around child-rearing issues during the postdivorce period, as well as how well they resolved their conflicts, predicted less aggression and fewer behavior problems among children 2 years following divorce. The amount of conflict per se was not consistently related to child outcomes. Conflict management variables were more strongly related to child adjustment than was family structure. These results illustrate that how conflict is resolved has a critically important influence on children (Cummings & Davies, 1994).

Conflict also affects the extent to which contact with the nonresidential parent facilitates child adjustment. Amato and Rezac (1994), based on a sample of children in single-parent families in the NSFH, found that there was a negative relation between contact with the nonresidential parent and boys' behavior problems when interparental conflict was low but that there was a positive relation between contact and behavior problems when conflict was high.

### Family Interactions

Typically, processes affecting children have been considered only in the context of parenting behaviors or the marital dyad. However, there has been some research that has considered processes at the larger family system level. Kurdek and Fine (1993a, 1993b) asked young adolescents to rate how much warmth, supervision, conflict, order, and interest existed in their families without specifying the family members who engaged in the various behaviors or interactions. They found that young adolescents' adjustment was positively related to the reported amounts of warmth, supervision, order, and interest and that it was negatively related to perceived levels of conflict.

There also have been a few attempts to examine nonlinear relations between family in-

teraction variables and child adjustment. Kurdek and Fine (1994) found curvilinear relations between family control and child outcomes. For psychosocial competence, the positive relation between family control and competence was stronger at progressively higher levels of family control, whereas low, but not moderate or high, levels of control were related to many self-regulation problems. In addition to showing the need to test for curvilinear effects, these findings also illustrate the importance of assessing how different types of family interactions are differentially related to particular child outcomes. In another study, Kurdek, Fine, and Sinclair (1995) found that family supervision and autonomy granting interacted in their relation to academic achievement; supervision was positively related to achievement only at low levels of autonomy granting.

### School and Other Extrafamilial Environments

In a particularly intriguing extension of the parenting style framework, Hetherington (1993) used teacher reports; hallway, classroom, and playground observations; and children's (10-15 years of age) reports to cluster school environments into four categories: authoritative, authoritarian, permissive, and chaotic/neglecting. From first grade on, authoritative parenting and an authoritative school environment (i.e., organized, predictable, clear rules and expectations, nurturant, responsive) were associated with higher levels of achievement and social competence and fewer child behavior problems, particularly for children in divorced and remarried families and children in first-marriage families with high levels of marital conflict. If both parents were considered to be authoritative, then there was no additional benefit to the child from being in an authoritative school. Thus, schools that were authoritative compensated for the negative effects of having fewer than two authoritative parents, particularly in single-mother families. Hetherington also found that a chaotic/neglecting school environment had the most adverse effects on children, particularly when there was no authoritative parent living in the home.

Teachman, Paasch, and Carver (1996) used the National Educational Longitudinal Survey to examine the effects of various indexes of "social capital" on the likelihood of dropping out of school before the 10th grade. They found that patterns of parental interaction with the child, the amount of contact parents had with the school, and the number of times the child changed schools were related to the chances of leaving school early. However, even after controlling for the effects of these social capital measures, children from divorced single-mother families and stepfamilies still were more likely to leave school early than were their peers in first-marriage families.

### Do Family Processes Mediate the Relations Between Divorce/Single Parenthood and Outcomes?

Researchers have attempted to identify a variety of types of variables that might explain (or mediate) the poorer adjustment levels of children in single-parent families. In general, these efforts have met with limited success. In most studies, small but significant differences in child adjustment across family structures remain even after taking the process variables into account.

For example, Kurdek, Fine, and Sinclair (1994) found that family structure and permissive, authoritative, and authoritarian parenting variables accounted for independent and significant portions of variability in young adolescents' grades, health, drug abstinence, self-esteem, and self-mastery, although the process variables accounted for a greater proportion. Similarly, Forehand, Neighbors, Devine, and Armistead (1994) found that current marital status and current levels of interparental conflict accounted for small, reliable, and independent sources of variation in adolescents' externalizing and internalizing

problems, social competence, and cognitive competence. Neither variable mediated the effects of the other on adolescent adjustment. Similarly, Summers, Forehand, Armistead, and Tannenbaum (1998) found that family process variables (quality of the parent-adolescent relationship, interparental conflict, and maternal depressive symptoms) did not mediate or moderate the association between divorce and young adult adjustment.

Some researchers have found that family process variables at least partially mediated family structure differences in child outcomes. For example, to varying extents depending on the particular outcome measures examined, McLanahan and Sandefur (1994) found that parental involvement, supervision, and aspirations reduced the differences between children in single-parent and first-marriage families. For example, parenting practices accounted for more than 50% of the differences in high school dropout rates and 20% of the differences in early childbearing. Similarly, Florsheim, Tolan, and Gorman-Smith (1998), in a sample of inner-city young adolescent males, found that family structure effects (boys from single-mother families were at greater risk for behavior problems than were boys in two-parent families) were partially mediated by a structured family environment, an effective disciplinary strategy that allowed for some degree of adolescent autonomy, and the positive involvement of a male family member.

### ► Applications for Professionals Working With Divorced and Single Parents

There are several implications for professionals derived specifically from the points made in this chapter. First, professionals need to be sensitive to differences between the experiences and reactions of family members in divorced families and those in never-married single-parent families. Divorced parents are more likely to be white and middle socioeconomic status, whereas never-married single parents are more likely to be from minority ethnic groups and/or to come from lower socioeconomic strata. Furthermore, professionals need to acknowledge that there are some never-married single parents, as well as divorced parents, who (based on their cost-benefit evaluations) prefer raising their children outside of marriage.

Second, because relationship termination is best conceptualized as a complex and extended process, relationship termination is not a "crisis" in the same sense that a natural disaster can be. Adjustment to the process takes place over an extended period of time, including periods before the actual legal event (i.e., divorce), and is unlikely to lead to severe emotional disturbance.

Third, as one gains information on individual family members, the family as a whole, or groups of families (as in an educational program), it is important to assess parenting practices, marital/partner relations, family interactions, and school and other extrafamilial environments in addition to family structure. More useful information for intervention planning will come from assessments of these process variables rather than mere family structure.

Fourth, in terms of targets for intervention, the literature suggests that practitioners are justified in focusing on parenting behaviors and family interactions that have been shown to relate to positive child development. During recent years, for example, there has been an increasing trend toward requiring divorcing parents to participate in parenting education programs designed to help them facilitate their children's development to this family transition (Fine et al., 1999). These programs typically are grounded in the notion that authoritative parenting and keeping children out of their parents' disputes facilitate children's coping efforts. Although the authoritative "formula" appears to apply to most family structures, practitioners need to be aware that authoritarian parenting might be indicated in some types of environments (e.g., violent neighborhoods).

Finally, based on findings from Hopper (1993), practitioners need to keep in mind that the "actual" events surrounding divorced parents' decisions to separate might be quite different from their constructed accounts. This is not to suggest that people's accounts of the events preceding the disruptions are not meaningful but rather that practitioners need to realize that these accounts might or might not be veridical with the actual events as they unfolded.

## ▶ Conclusions and Directions for Future Research

Amato (1993) argued that family structure should remain a focus of our research endeavors in the context of how it interacts with family processes to affect the emotional well-being of family members. Because family structure and family processes reliably and independently are related to adjustment, future research efforts could be fruitfully directed at how family processes can have differing effects on family members in different family structures. These efforts should carefully distinguish among types of single-parent families.

In addition, there is a need to identify how specific family processes are related to specific outcome domains. For example, some have suggested that parental supervision might have a greater effect on the development of children's externalizing behaviors than on their internalizing behaviors, whereas nurturance might be more salient for internalizing behaviors than for externalizing behaviors (Kurdek & Fine, 1994). More efforts need to be directed toward this sort of process-outcome specificity.

# Contents

# Remarried Families

*Lawrence H. Ganong*
*Marilyn Coleman*

The label *remarried families* is one of many that have been applied to the types of families we discuss in this chapter. Other labels include *reconstituted, blended, reconstructed, reorganized, reformed, recycled, combined, recombinant, step,* and *merged families.* We use *remarried family* and *stepfamily* interchangeably to refer to a family with an adult couple and at least one child from a previous relationship (Coleman, Ganong, & Fine, in press; Ganong & Coleman, 1994b). The key component of this definition is that one of the adults is a parent who has a legal or genetic tie to a child that the other adult, the stepparent, does not have. Note that this is a definition of families, not households. The stepchild may be of any age, from infancy to adulthood.

## ▶ Context of Remarried Families

About half of the marriages in the United States represent remarriages for one or both partners (Martin & Bumpass, 1989). In 1992, 15% of all children in the United States lived with mothers and stepfathers (U.S. Bureau of the Census, 1995). An estimated one third of U.S. children will spend time in stepfamilies (Seltzer, 1994). Remarriage rates are lower in other countries, but stepfamilies are common in Canada and Europe (Kiernan, 1992; Wu, 1994).

### Some Cautions Regarding Complexity

We are uneasy generalizing broadly about remarried families or step relationships because such generalizations ignore the complexity of stepfamilies. For example, if we address only the issues of where children reside and which adult is genetically (or legally) related to which child, then there are as many as 30 different structural configurations that stepfamilies may form (Ganong & Coleman, 1994b). For example, stepparents might reside with their stepchildren all of the time, they might have stepchildren who live with them part of the time, or they might be nonresidential stepparents who seldom (if ever) interact with their stepchildren. Terms such as *nonresidential stepparent* and *residential stepparent* suggest discrete types of experiences, but categorical terms fail to reflect the realities of stepchildren who split their residences between two households. Where children reside is important in understanding parent-child and stepparent-stepchild relationships because expectations for role enactment differ depending on whether parents and stepparents are in contact with the (step)children daily, rarely, or never. Sharing a residence full-time creates more opportunities to interact and to develop a close relationship than is the case if (step)parents and (step)children spend time together only a few days or weeks per year. Defining the specific relationship and distinguishing between family and household when providing sample descriptions are critical tasks if the data on stepfamilies are to be interpreted in a meaningful way.

*Remarriage* also is a term that encompasses several different types of relationships. Both partners might be in a second marriage, they might be in a higher order remarriage (e.g., a third or fourth marriage), or the marriage might be a remarriage for one partner

and the first marriage for the other. Remarriages generally have been treated as a single group, although there might be personality and behavioral differences between "serial marriers" and individuals in first remarriages (Brody, Neubaum, & Forehand, 1988).

In addition to the various remarriage configurations, the precursors to remarriage and remarried family relationships must be considered. They can have quite different consequences for family life. For example, among the most common pathways to remarriage are (a) first marriage–divorce–remarriage (in general, most remarriages follow at least one divorce); (b) first marriage–death of a spouse–remarriage (this pattern predominated until about 20 years ago and still is the most prevalent for older adults); (c) never-married parenthood–marriage to a person who is not the child's other parent (a first marriage that creates step relationships); (d) never-married parenthood–cohabitation (a nonmarriage that creates de facto step relationships); (e) first marriage–divorce–remarriage–divorce–remarriage–divorce–remarriage (serial remarriages; another variation would intersperse cohabiting relationships in the previously mentioned pattern); and (f) first marriage to someone who has children from a prior relationship that was ended due to death, divorce, or separation (in the case of never-married childbearing).

### Stepfamily Relationships in Social Context

Social contexts affect remarried families because cultural beliefs (e.g., norms, expectations, stereotypes, myths) about family life exert an influence on how people conduct themselves, evaluate their own situations, and expect to be regarded by others (Coleman & Ganong, 1997). Cultural beliefs affect the levels of social support that stepfamilies receive, which in turn affect their abilities to function effectively (Cherlin, 1978). Evidence supporting the impact of social contexts on stepfamilies has been found in many countries (Levin, 1993).

In general, there are three broad societal views of stepfamilies: the stepfamily as an *incomplete institution* (Cherlin, 1978), the stepfamily as a *deviant group* (Coleman & Ganong, 1997), and the stepfamily as a *reformed nuclear family* (Levin, 1993). These views are byproducts of an idealization of nuclear families. The ideal family is the middle-class, first-marriage nuclear family consisting of a mother and father and their children (Coontz, 1992). The cultural ideal of the private nuclear family is basically a European model that ignores cultural/historical family patterns of African Americans, Native Americans, Latinos, and other groups of families. This nuclear family model is associated with a moral natural imperative, and other family forms are considered to be immoral or (at best) less moral. The nuclear family ideology influences perceptions of how families should live, lowers motivations to develop other ways of functioning, and even reduces acceptance of other models of healthy family functioning. Parents who believe that there is only one natural, normal type of family might have difficulty in figuring out new roles and responsibilities when they experience marital transitions.

### Incomplete Institutionalization Hypothesis

Cherlin (1978) argued that the absence of norms for role performance, the dearth of established socially acceptable methods of resolving problems, and the lack of institutionalized social support for stepfamilies contribute to greater stress, inappropriate solutions to problems, and higher divorce rates for remarried families. Cherlin pointed to the absence of language to describe step relationships, the lack of support from social systems, and the paucity of legal regulations as illustrations of how remarried families are incompletely institutionalized. For example, poli-

cies and procedures for organizations that interact with families such as schools, youth groups, and health care systems often are designed implicitly for nuclear families (Crosbie-Burnett, 1994; Ganong, 1993), and this strains remarried family members and creates barriers for their participation. Similarly, the few legal responsibilities and rights of stepparents for stepchildren contribute to feelings of ambiguity and lack of control for stepparents (Ganong, Coleman, Killian, & McDaniel, 1998) and might serve as barriers to developing close stepparent-stepchild bonds (Ganong, Coleman, Fine, & Martin, 1999; Mason, 1998).

Critics have argued that Cherlin's (1978) views overstate the degree to which remarried families lack institutional support (Jacobson, 1995), and a few researchers have not found support for his contentions (Coleman, Ganong, & Cable, 1997). However, most researchers have found some support for the claim that expectations for enactment of stepparent roles are less clear than expectations for parent roles (Fine, Coleman, & Ganong, 1998; Ishii-Kuntz & Coltrane, 1992b). Perceptions of what stepparents should do are more variable than perceptions of what parents in the same situations should do, and there is little consensus regarding stepparent role performance.

The incomplete institutionalization hypothesis has been supported by clinicians, who note that stepparents and other stepfamily members often are unsure of how to relate to each other, an uncertainty shared by outsiders who interact with stepfamilies (Papernow, 1993; Visher & Visher, 1996). According to clinicians, societal models for nuclear families do not provide remarried families much help in anticipating problems and devising solutions.

### Stepfamilies as Deviant Groups

Stepfamilies and stepfamily roles (e.g., stepmother, stepchild) are social categories associated with generally negative attributes

(Coleman & Ganong, 1997). Stepfamilies are stigmatized through labels, cultural stereotypes, media images, and cultural myths (e.g., the wicked stepmother). When a social category or group is stigmatized, group members engage in impression management strategies to avoid being associated with negative connotations. For example, some stepparents refuse to be identified as stepmothers and stepfathers because the prefix *step-* triggers negative reactions (Ganong, Coleman, & Kennedy, 1990). Hiding stepfamily status can be an effective strategy to avoid unpleasant reactions from others, but it reduces the chance that others will offer help and moral support.

### Stepfamilies as Reconstituted Nuclear Families

For some people, the presence of two heterosexual adults means that a nuclear family unit has been created. In stepfamilies that attempt to reconstitute the nuclear family model, stepparents must assume parental roles, duties, and responsibilities, and boundaries must be drawn around the households so that family membership and household membership become identical. Although this model might work for some stepfamilies, difficulties arise when nonresidential parents and/or children do not want to sever contact and relationships with each other. Remarried adults who want to imitate a nuclear family often try to limit interaction between the children and the nonresidential parent as the stepparent and residential parent compete with the nonresidential parent over the children. Although it might seem easier for a stepfamily to operate as if the household and family were one and the same, the legal and moral responsibility for the financial support of the children generally remains with the parents unless the stepparent adopts the children (Mason, 1998). A common motivation to consider stepchild adoption is the desire to become as much like a nuclear family as possible (Ganong et al., 1998).

### ▶ Remarriage Relationships

#### Building a Strong Couple Relationship/Marriage

Family therapists contend that stability and satisfaction in stepfamilies are based on a strong couple bond (Papernow, 1993; Visher & Visher, 1996). Building a strong couple bond while developing relationships with new stepchildren and new extended kin, and perhaps while maintaining family ties that predate the formation of the remarried family, makes the process of couple bonding in remarriage different from that in first marriage. A man who marries a woman with children from prior relationships usually does not have the luxury of establishing familiar routines and patterns of living as a new husband/partner before he must learn how to be a stepfather to his new stepchildren. Unless the partner's children reside elsewhere all or most of the time (and sometimes even when they do), the new partner and stepchildren are a "package deal," and stepparents have to develop marital and stepparent-stepchild relationships concurrently. The tasks of building multiple new relationships can be daunting. Many remarried individuals are caught off guard by the discrepancy between what they expect to find and what they encounter in establishing remarriage relationships (Ganong & Coleman, 1994b).

Children demand and need attention from their parents, but parental time and energy spent in child rearing are time and energy not available for building a couple relationship. Moreover, the presence of children means that a remarried couple has an audience at least some of the time. Children perceive the remarriage differently from how adults perceive it, they generally see themselves as allies of their parents, and they might view the stepparent as an intruder (Visher & Visher, 1996). In addition, because the bond between a parent and child is older and generally stronger than that of the new husband-wife relationship, parents' loyalties might lie with their children more than with the new spouse. This might be a problem when there are conflicts between stepparents and stepchildren; parents can feel caught in the middle, and the couple relationship might suffer. During the early months and years of remarriage, there are ample opportunities for stepparents and stepchildren to disagree, and this is the time when the couple relationship is most fragile. Because the presence of a stepparent often represents a loss of status and power for children and might mean that parents spend less time with them, children might be invested in seeing the remarriage fail. Consequently, a remarried couple could be faced with trying to develop couple bonds in the presence of children who want to dissolve those bonds. Perhaps not surprisingly, the divorce rate for remarried couples with stepchildren is greater than that for couples without stepchildren (Booth & Edwards, 1992).

Unfortunately, research examining the process of building a satisfying remarriage relationship has been limited. In an in-depth study of nine remarried couples, Cissna, Cox, and Bochner (1990) found that one of the early goals of the couples was to establish the solidarity of their marriages in the minds of the stepchildren. They did this by telling the children that their marriages were the most important relationships to them and by spending time as couples planning how to present a unified front to the children. Whether or not this was an effective way in which to build a couple bond is not known. Obviously, more studies are needed on this important issue.

One reason why remarried individuals find the challenges daunting is because they do little to prepare themselves for remarriage and stepparenting (Ganong & Coleman, 1989). Remarried couples infrequently consult helping professionals prior to remarriage, rarely read self-help literature, and seldom seek advice from family and friends in remarried families (Ganong & Coleman, 1989). Adults planning to remarry talk about child rearing and housing, but these conversations tend to be rather abstract and superficial. Remarrying individuals quite often seem to be unaware of

the issues and challenges they will be facing. This could be offset if remarrying couples spent time getting to know each other and each other's children, but 30% of divorced people remarry within 1 year, and the mean length of time between divorce and remarriage is less than 4 years (Wilson & Clarke, 1992). People make relatively quick decisions about future partners, and remarriage or cohabitation often occur within months after meeting (Montgomery, Anderson, Hetherington, & Clingempeel, 1992).

More than half of those who legally remarry live together before marrying (Martin & Bumpass, 1989), and approximately 25% of the cohabiting couples in the United States are households in which one adult brings children from a prior relationship(s) (Bumpass, Sweet, & Cherlin, 1991). Given the pervasiveness of cohabiting as an alternative or a prelude to legal remarriage, it is surprisingly understudied (Brown & Booth, 1996). Little is known about how the decision to cohabit is made, how children are informed about their parents' intentions to cohabit, or what effects cohabiting has on the entire stepfamily system. A pattern found in one longitudinal study began with partial cohabitation (i.e., the prospective male partner spends a few nights per week in the mother's household), followed by a brief period of full-time living together prior to remarriage (Montgomery et al., 1992). Brown and Booth (1996) reported that prior marital experience and the presence of children from prior relationships were related to lower relationship quality for both cohabiting couples and married couples, findings that suggest similar dynamics between cohabiting couples and those who remarry. One of the motives for cohabiting might be to assess compatibility via daily interaction (Brown & Booth, 1996).

## Dynamics of Remarriage

Individuals who have been married and divorced generally remarry for more pragmatic reasons than was the case when they married the first time. For example, among the motivations to remarry are (a) companionship in old age, (b) wanting help in raising children, (c) financial assistance, and (d) friendship (Ganong & Coleman, 1989). The more pragmatic motivations to remarry and the complexity brought by stepchildren likely result in different marital dynamics in remarried families from those in first marriages.

There is growing evidence that decision making in remarriage tends to be equally shared between partners (Crosbie-Burnett & Giles-Sims, 1991; Pyke, 1994). This is mostly because women often seek more power in their remarriages than they had in their first marriages (Pyke, 1994; Pyke & Coltrane, 1996). The more equitable distribution of power in remarriages than in first marriages has been attributed to (a) lessons women learned from personal experiences in prior unions and as divorced single persons (Burgoyne & Morison, 1997; Coleman & Ganong, 1989; Pyke, 1994; Smith, Goslen, Boyd, & Reece, 1991); (b) the greater resources women often bring to remarriages, giving them more bargaining power (Crosbie-Burnett & Giles-Sims, 1991; Pyke & Coltrane, 1996); (c) shifts in beliefs regarding men's and women's roles in marriage (Burgoyne & Morison, 1997; Ishii-Kuntz & Coltrane, 1992b); and (d) women being reluctant to remarry, a stance that increases their bargaining power (Pyke, 1994). Men contribute to greater sharing of decision making in remarriage by conceding more during marital conflicts than they did in their first marriages (Hobart, 1991) and by seeking partners who will share the responsibilities for caring for others (Smith et al., 1991).

Sharing decision making does not necessarily mean that household tasks are shared equitably. It has been reported that remarried husbands do more housework than do husbands in first marriages (Deal, Stanley Hagan, & Anderson, 1992; Ishii-Kuntz & Coltrane, 1992), but most studies have found that remarried women still do most of the housework (Demo & Acock, 1993; Pyke & Coltrane, 1996) and that household duties are divided along traditional gender lines (see Chapter 10 by Steil, this volume).

Similarly, although there is evidence that women have more say in the financial matters in their remarriages than they had in their prior marriages (Burgoyne & Morison, 1997; Coleman & Ganong, 1989; Crosbie-Burnett & Giles-Sims, 1991), the manner in which finances are organized and managed in remarried families is so complex (Burgoyne & Morison, 1997; Jacobson, 1993) that it is difficult to determine how equitable financial decision making is. Partly because of financial commitments to support children from present and prior unions, and partly because of remarried individuals' desire to retain some degree of financial independence, remarried couples are more likely than those in first marriages to maintain at least part of their economic resources under the individual control of each partner.

### Remarriage Quality

Researchers using cross-sectional methods generally have found few differences in marital quality between individuals in first marriages and those in remarriages (Booth & Edwards, 1992; Deal et al., 1992). However, a longitudinal study found that marital satisfaction declined more rapidly for persons in stepfather households than for those in first marriages (Kurdek, 1991c). Although the presence of stepchildren is thought to lower marital quality for remarried adults (Brown & Booth, 1996), the effects of stepchildren on remarital quality and functioning are not always strong; in one study, children born to first marriages had a greater effect on lowering marriage quality than stepchildren had on lowering remarital quality (Kurdek, 1999). The effect of stepchildren on marital quality is unclear, but they do affect marital functioning.

Conflicts in remarriage generally center on issues related to children (Pasley, Koch, & Ihinger-Tallman, 1993; Visher & Visher, 1996). Stepchildren increase the likelihood of adult disagreements over discipline and rules for children (Hobart, 1991) and the distribution of resources to children from prior relationships (Pasley et al., 1993). Moreover, stepchildren might experience loyalty conflicts that lead to arguments with stepparents and disputes between adults (Visher & Visher, 1996). The presence of stepchildren increases stress associated with role ambiguity and role strain related to the stepparent roles (Whitsett & Land, 1992), and this in turn reduces the stepparent's satisfaction with the marriage. When both adults have children from prior relationships, marital quality is poorer than when only one adult is a stepparent, presumably because of the added complexity and increased opportunities for conflict that arise with children from more than one prior relationship (Hobart, 1991), although more research is needed in this area.

### *Remarriage Stability*

Remarriages might be as satisfying to partners as first marriages, but the dissolution rates are higher (Martin & Bumpass, 1989). A number of intrapersonal, interpersonal, and societal-level explanations have been proposed for the greater instability of remarriages (Ganong & Coleman, 1994b). Not all of these proposed causes have been tested by researchers, but there is some support for the notion that remarriages, relative to first marriages, contain a greater proportion of people who have personality characteristics (e.g., impulsivity) that predispose them to end their relationships more frequently and make them poorer marriage material (Booth & Edwards, 1992; Brody et al., 1988). Support also has been found for (a) the incomplete institutionalization hypothesis, (b) the hypothesis that a larger proportion of people who remarry than people in first marriages are accepting of divorce as a solution to marital problems, and (c) the argument that the small pool of partners for remarriage leads to matches between people with dissimilar interests and values (Booth & Edwards, 1992).

Some researchers contend that remarried individuals have fewer conflict resolution skills and are poorer communicators compared to partners in first marriages (Bray, Berger, Silverblatt, & Hollier, 1987). Given the greater complexity and more opportunities for conflict in remarriage, a lack of interpersonal communication skills could explain higher redivorce rates. However, conflict in remarriage has not been found to relate to marital satisfaction (Larson & Allgood, 1987), and not all studies report poorer communication between remarried partners than between first-marriage spouses (Brown, Green, & Druckman, 1990; Deal et al., 1992). Some researchers have argued that it is not the amount of conflict but rather the manner in which remarried couples attempt to resolve their disagreements that predicts redivorce (Pasley et al., 1993). Conflict is not inherently negative; some remarried women in power-sharing remarriages interviewed by Pyke (1994) reported more conflicts than did those in male-dominant remarriages because the women actively sought to be heard. In such marriages, conflict might represent active problem solving and, therefore, could increase the probability that remarriages will not end in divorce.

### *Older Remarriages*

Few studies have investigated remarriages in later life. Most of these studies are based on secondary analyses of large data sets that shed little light on the marital processes of older couples. Remarriages in later life might represent attempts to resolve some of the problems facing widows and widowers (e.g., loneliness), but the new unions also bring concerns regarding new family relationships (Gentry & Shulman, 1988; Peters & Liefbroer, 1997). Women are more affected by later life remarriages than are men, but the satisfaction of both men and women is related to communication and conflict resolution strategies (Pasley & Ihinger-Tallman, 1990).

## ▶ The Family System

Stepparent-stepchild relationships receive a lot of attention by researchers because they are thought to be important in predicting overall family happiness and individual well-being (Crosbie-Burnett, 1994; Visher & Visher, 1996). Whether or not they are the most critical relationships in stepfamilies is unclear, but these relationships, as well as parent-child relationships, are key in stepfamily dynamics.

### Challenges for Stepparents and Stepchildren

The challenges facing stepparents depend partly on gender and partly on their previous family experiences, but stepparents generally encounter two primary issues: developing new stepfamily relationships and maintaining existing family ties (Coleman & Ganong, 1995). All stepparents must deal with the development and maintenance of new stepfamily ties with partners/spouses, stepchildren, and extended kin. Stepparents who have children from prior relationships have the added challenges of renegotiating roles and restructuring existing relationships with co-parents and children (Coleman & Ganong, 1995). Moreover, stepparents who also are parents might have to assist old and new family members in adapting to the merger of two "family cultures" (Jacobson, 1995).

Stepchildren face similar tasks in maintaining and redefining relationships with parents while they develop new relationships with stepparents, extended stepkin, and (possibly) stepsiblings and half-siblings. Because this chapter is on stepfamily relationships, we focus mostly on issues related to developing new step relationships and maintaining them.

Stepparents and stepchildren have relationships together because of their respective ties to the stepparents' partners/children's parents. Consequently, their motivation to form attachments often is generated by the urge to please the partners/parents. The involuntary nature of stepparent-stepchild relationships might be stressful to some individuals, and some stepparents and stepchildren might experience the task of developing a relationship as a crisis.

*Developing stepparent-stepchild relationships.* It might seem paradoxical given the negative images of stepparents, but clinicians report that stepparents often begin relationships with stepchildren holding unrealistically high expectations (Papernow, 1993; Visher & Visher, 1996). Stepparents often believe that relationships will quickly evolve into emotionally close familial bonds, and they assume that stepchildren will love and accept them immediately.

Moreover, clinicians also report that some residential stepparents expect to emotionally, psychologically, financially, and behaviorally replace nonresidential parents in stepchildren's lives (Papernow, 1993; Visher & Visher, 1996). Stepparents might even adopt stepchildren to legally complete the metamorphosis from stepparent to parent (Ganong et al., 1998); however, stepparent adoption usually is possible only when the nonresidential parent is not involved in the children's lives and the stepparent is functioning as the parent.

Clinicians contend that stepparents who try to replace parents do so because the functions of parenthood are familiar and it is simpler to try to become stepchildren's new parents than to deal with stepfamily complexity and ambiguity (Visher & Visher, 1996). Extended family, friends, and social systems often support stepparents' efforts to replace nonresidential parents (Ganong & Coleman, 1997), but clinicians generally see this as problematic because it can exacerbate loyalty conflicts for children and increase the likelihood of hostile interactions between nonresidential parents and the remarried household adults (Visher & Visher, 1996).

Stepmothers might have a harder time than stepfathers in developing relationships with stepchildren. Stepmothers have more demanding roles than do stepfathers in general

(Nielsen, 1999), partly because expectations for men's and women's roles in families make it harder for stepmothers to coexist with mothers than for stepfathers to coexist with fathers. Stepmothers are expected to uphold the traditional female roles as primary caregiver and nurturer (Whitsett & Land, 1992), even though parental roles in stepmother households reportedly are less gendered than those in first-marriage families (Thomson, McLanahan, & Curtin, 1992). Clinicians contend that the traditional view of mothers is one of the most destructive challenges faced by stepfamilies (Carter, 1988). If children continue to have frequent contact with their nonresidential mothers, as they usually do, then the step-child-stepmother relationship often is more stressful (for a review, see Nielsen, 1999). Stepmothers might feel guilty because they feel that they are expected to love their new stepchildren. Furthermore, they might compare themselves to the idealized model for genetic mothers (Weaver & Coleman, 1998).

By contrast, more stepfathers find it relatively easy to assume a parent role (Erera-Weatherly, 1996). Some stepfathers see themselves as being fathers *and* friends (Fine et al., 1998). However, there is evidence that stepfathers are more satisfied with their families when they assume the father's role (Fine et al., 1998; Marsiglio, 1992). It is not known how satisfied stepchildren and mothers are with this. Men often are encouraged by their wives to function as substitute fathers, although mothers and stepfathers do not always agree about stepfathers' parenting responsibilities. This can be a source of conflict (Papernow, 1993).

Clinicians advise stepparents to focus on becoming friends with stepchildren before they attempt to discipline and set rules for them (Papernow, 1993; Visher & Visher, 1996). In a study we conducted, stepparent-stepchild relationships were emotionally closer when stepparents intentionally tried to develop friendships with stepchildren from the start of their relationships and continued their affinity-seeking and affinity-maintaining efforts after remarriage (Ganong et al., 1999).

Engaging one-on-one in favorite activities of the stepchildren was the most effective way for stepparents to build affinity. By contrast, stepparents who stopped trying to develop affinity with their stepchildren and those who never tried had more distant and conflictual relationships. Other studies have found that stepfathers who initially are warm and supportive have more positive relationships with stepchildren (Hetherington & Clingempeel, 1992).

Stepchildren are active participants in developing stepparent-stepchild relationships. How they treat stepparents affects the development of relationships. For example, in our study, stepchildren who recognized that their stepparents were doing things to get the stepchildren to like them generally responded with their own affinity-seeking efforts (Ganong et al., 1999). But not all stepchildren respond affirmatively to stepparents' actions. Hetherington and Clingempeel (1992) found that stepfathers made overtures to stepchildren early in their remarriages, attempted to share information, and engaged in other rapport-building activities—only to be ignored. Some stepfathers responded by withdrawing from the stepchildren. O'Connor, Hetherington, and Clingempeel (1997) found support for bidirectional influences in stepfamilies in that adolescent-to-adult behavior was as strong a predictor of adolescent adjustment as was adult-to-adolescent behavior. Given the prevalence of the view among clinicians that stepchildren have a great deal of influence on stepfamily interactions, it is surprising that there are not more studies examining bidirectional influences on relationships in stepfamilies. More research is needed that investigates stepchildren's contributions to building step relationships.

*Issues in maintaining stepparent-stepchild relationships.* A growing body of research on ongoing stepparent-stepchild relationships has examined how parenting styles differ between stepparents and parents or between stepparent households and adults in other structures (Coleman et al., in press). Several researchers have found that stepparents are more likely to be disengaged from their stepchildren than are fathers and mothers. Some stepfathers show little affect toward stepchildren, are less involved, and engage in relatively little supervision and control of stepchildren (Cooksey & Fondell, 1996; Erera-Weatherly, 1996; Hetherington & Clingempeel, 1992). Similar findings have been reported for stepmothers (Kurdek & Fine, 1993b).

The incomplete institutionalization hypothesis (Cherlin, 1978) can explain some of the distance between stepparents and stepchildren; beyond a general consensus that parents are to be more warm toward children and to more carefully monitor their behavior than are stepparents, there is little consistency in perceptions of the nature of the stepparent role (Fine & Kurdek, 1994). Even when stepfamily members generally agree about stepparents' role, stepparents are less sure about their roles than are other stepfamily members (Fine et al., 1998).

Cultural beliefs about stepparents suggest that stepparents are less interested in their stepchildren than parents are in their children (Coleman & Ganong, 1997). Therefore, stepparents might be more distant because they perceive that they are supposed to be. For example, people generally think that stepparents are less obligated to stepchildren than parents are to children and, therefore, that stepparents are expected to engage less frequently in supportive parental behaviors than are parents (Ganong & Coleman, 1999). Negative cultural beliefs also might empower stepchildren to disobey stepparents because of societal messages they interpret as giving them permission to do so.

Some stepparents might be disengaged from their stepchildren at the direction of their spouses (Weaver & Coleman, 1998). In particular, mothers might be extremely close to their children as a result of experiences when they were single and, as a consequence, might be unwilling to let their new spouses disrupt this intimacy by getting close to their children. Parents might be reluctant to share their parenting responsibilities and the control over children. There is some evidence that stepparents think that they should be more active in raising their stepchildren than other family members do (Fine et al., 1998). The key to successful stepparenting appears to be agreement between stepfathers and mothers on how adolescents should be raised (Skopin, Newman, & McKenry, 1993). This agreement might even supersede the level of stepparents' involvement with stepchildren in importance (Bronstein, Stoll, Clauson, Abrams, & Briones, 1994).

Disagreements over stepparents' involvement can cause problems in stepfamilies, and stepparents might withdraw from stepchildren as a way in which to reduce conflicts. Conflict over stepparents' involvement might be greater when stepchildren are adolescents because they might resist stepparents' efforts to exert authority more than do younger stepchildren. Even when positive stepparent-stepchild relationships are established when children are preadolescents, conflicts might arise when children get older (Hetherington, 1993). Adolescents might be primed to attribute negative motives to stepparents' behaviors that result in stepchildren feeling less positive toward stepparents and responding to stepparents in ways that create emotional distance between them (Russell & Searcy, 1997). Regardless of the reasons, parents are perceived to be more supportive of children than are stepparents, even in well-functioning stepfamilies (Brown et al., 1990). Efforts to improve communication between stepchildren and stepparents have been suggested to counter these perceptions (Henry & Lovelace, 1995).

Evolutionary scholars argue that stepparents invest less of themselves in their stepchildren because they are not genetically related (Daly & Wilson, 1996; Flinn, 1992). The parental investment model suggests that stepparents will not waste resources on children who do not carry their genes. This theory proposes that stepparents discriminate in favor of their own children, a proposition supported by some research (MacDonald & De Maris, 1996).

Finally, the stepparent role might not be very important to the identities of most stepparents (Thoits, 1992). Consequently, there might not be much satisfaction to them in fulfilling the role, so instead stepparents might focus their energies on work, marriage, or their own children more than they do on stepchildren.

It should be noted that not all researchers have found that stepparents differ from genetic parents in parenting style. In one study, stepfathers and mothers were similar to parents in nuclear families in permissiveness and in democratic decision making (Barber & Lyons, 1994); in supporting and monitoring adolescents (Salem, Zimmerman, & Notaro, 1998); in permissive, authoritarian, or authoritative parenting styles (Shucksmith, Hendry, & Glendinning, 1995); and in encouraging independence in adolescents (Bulcroft, Carmody, & Bulcroft, 1998).

*Changes in stepparent-stepchild relationships over time.* The findings regarding changes in step relationships over time are mixed. Stepfather-stepchild relationships often become more negative and less positive over time (Bray, 1992; Hetherington & Clingempeel, 1992). However, in a longitudinal study of both stepfathers and stepmothers, we found that some relationships with adolescent stepchildren became closer over time, some relationships grew more distant, and some did not change over a 5-year period (Ganong & Coleman, 1994a). More work is needed in this area.

*Nonresidential stepparents.* Less is known about nonresidential stepparents than is known about residential stepparents (Ganong & Coleman, 1994b). There are indications that nonresidential stepparents might experience even more difficulty than do residential stepparents in determining and establishing appropriate roles for themselves. Roles and relationships might be especially difficult to establish because nonresidential stepchildren are not in the households as much, and this provides fewer opportunities to develop rela-

tionships with them. In addition, nonresidential stepmothers often perform more caregiving tasks for children than do their fathers, yet stepmothers perceive that they get little or no benefit from their labors (Nielsen, 1999). Nonresidential stepmothers also experience little control over family decisions and get little support in their roles as stepmothers (Weaver & Coleman, 1999).

### The Effects on Stepchildren of Living With Stepparents

There have been many studies comparing stepchildren's well-being to that of children in other family structures (for reviews, see Coleman et al., in press). Effects of living with stepparents on stepchildren have been investigated more often than any other topics related to stepfamilies. We do not have the space to include this material here, and most of it does not investigate relationships per se, although relationship variables (e.g., remarital conflict, social capital) often are used as factors explaining children's outcomes.

In general, researchers have compared stepchildren to children in other family structures. During recent years, the focus has been on trying to explain generally persistent (although not uniform) but relatively small differences between stepchildren and children in first-marriage nuclear families on a variety of psychological, cognitive, and behavioral outcomes. Unfortunately, too often researchers have examined stepparents' effects on stepchildren by comparing stepparent household members to individuals from other types of households without considering individual characteristics, family process variables, and context variables. When family process variables and context variables are included in designs, they often are crudely conceptualized and measured. Perhaps as more close relationship researchers examine stepfamily relationships, these problems will be less prevalent.

One prevailing view is that stepparents have harmful effects on stepchildren. For example, inter- and intrahousehold conflicts have been proposed as reasons why stepchildren should fare worse in behavioral and psychological outcomes than do children living with both parents (Hanson, McLanahan, & Thomson, 1996). Stepparents also are not expected to invest as much social capital in raising stepchildren as they would in raising their own children, resulting in lower educational achievement for stepchildren than for children who live with both parents (Bogenscheider, 1997).

Other researchers have proposed that stepparents' influences are indirect. There are several variations of the theme that remarriage disrupts parents' abilities to competently raise their children because parents are investing time and energy in new partners (Coughlin & Vuchinich, 1996). Still others have hypothesized that family transitions due to parents' uncouplings and recouplings create stress that harms stepchildren because they must adjust to new relationships and the loss of old relationships (Kurdek, Fine, & Sinclair, 1995).

A few researchers have studied whether remarriage offsets any negative effects of living with one parent. There is some support for the idea that stepparents enhance monitoring of children and parents' child-rearing abilities (Bulcroft et al., 1998; Hawkins & Eggebeen, 1991).

### Parent-Child Relationships

The parent-child relationship in remarried family households is potentially an extremely important one. Parents are legally responsible for their children, and they are emotionally invested in them. Along with the stepparent, parents and children constitute the triad whose interactions serve as the bases for many stepfamily difficulties. However, despite the significance of the residential parent-child relationship, it is less often the primary focus of empirical studies than is the stepparent-stepchild relationship.

Stepfamily households most often consist of a stepfather and a mother and her children from a previous relationship. Probably for that reason, most stepfamily research has focused on residential stepfather families, the roles of stepfathers (Fine et al., 1998), and the stepfather-stepchild relationship (Ganong & Coleman, 1994b). Even though the clinical literature has indicated for nearly 20 years that women have more difficulties with their experiences and roles in stepfamilies than do men (Visher & Visher, 1996), the role of mothers have been neglected in research (Ganong & Coleman, 1994b). When researchers do include mothers in studies, they usually are comparing mothers' parenting behaviors to those of stepfathers (Santrock & Sitterle, 1987); asking them about their perceptions of their spouses as parents; or examining their parenting behavior (Hetherington & Clingempeel, 1992), their well-being, or their children's well-being (Demo & Acock, 1994). Mothers' perceptions about their roles and relationships in stepfamilies seldom have been investigated. This is unfortunate given the clinical importance placed on mothers' roles in the formation and integration of relationships within stepfamilies.

Hetherington and Clingempeel (1992) found that, initially, mother-preadolescent child relationships in stepfamilies deteriorated, but 2 years after the remarriage, mother-child relationships in stepfamilies were similar to those in nuclear families. Mothers in stepfamilies monitored children's behaviors during the 1st year of remarriage less than did mothers in nuclear families and divorced mothers, but over time, their behavior became more similar to that of nuclear family mothers. Although children in all family types showed increasingly negative behavior as they entered adolescence, they eventually behaved more positively toward their parents as the parents became less emotionally involved and granted them greater autonomy.

In a recent qualitative study of mothers in stepfamilies (Weaver & Coleman, 1998), it was concluded that the mother role was more salient to women than was the spousal role. In addition, mothers adopt a protector role with their children during courtship and after remarriage that manifests itself in several ways. For example, mothers defend their children against any perceived threat to safety or well-being, both outside and within stepfamilies. These sources of threat include stepfathers. The threats were not of a serious nature (e.g., child abuse) but rather were perceived by mothers as some sort of unfair treatment of their children by stepfathers. Mothers also play a gatekeeping role; that is, they control stepfathers' access to the stepchildren both before and after remarriage. Although this control lessens with the passing of time, it never disappears completely. Also, mothers mediate conflicts that arise between their spouses and their children. They try to maintain cordial relationships within their families by seeking to prevent conflict, by pacifying those in conflict, and/or by correcting situations after conflictual instances. Finally, mothers are interpreters within stepfamilies, explaining their children to their spouses and vice versa. They do this to educate one about the other so as to achieve a shared understanding. The various roles played by mothers in stepfamilies appear to affect the quality of family relationships. The defender role does not contribute to positive stepfamily integration. The gatekeeper role might be functional early in the formation of relationships, but it creates problems over time. The mediator role might facilitate relationship formation, but the role takes a heavy toll on mothers and creates stress and internal conflict for them. The interpreter role seems to be the most facilitative of the various roles. In general, mothers perceive the development of close relationships in stepfamilies to be their responsibility, and many of their behaviors are aimed at controlling family processes in an effort to avoid or reduce conflict. However, much more needs to be learned about the role of the biological mother in stepfamilies before conclusions can be drawn.

## ▶ Conclusions: Remarried Family Processes

An implicit assumption underlying many studies of stepfamilies and stepfamily members is that they *should* be similar to nuclear families (Clingempeel, Flesher, & Brand,

1988; Coleman & Ganong, 1990). Nuclear families are the standard by which stepfamily processes are compared, and when studies report lower cohesion and less emotional closeness in stepfamilies than in nuclear families, this often is interpreted as a problem for stepfamily functioning.

By contrast, most clinicians think that remarried families should *not* try to function as if they were the same as first-marriage nuclear families (cf. Papernow, 1993; Visher & Visher, 1996). To function like a nuclear family, stepfamilies must engage in distortions of reality that demand enormous emotional energy and are psychologically and interpersonally expensive. Functioning like a nuclear family requires that remarried family members act as if no other family relationships existed prior to remarriage and that ties between nonresidential parents and children must be severed, and this results in emotional suffering for both groups (Visher & Visher, 1996). Feelings of abandonment, anger, guilt, resentment, and loss are likely when these ties are severed. Clinicians contend that it is unrealistic to expect that all members of a stepfamily will accept the nuclear model for the family (Papernow, 1993). If everyone does not agree to function as a nuclear family, then this leads to stressful interactions with the dissenters.

We hypothesize that the nuclear family model can be effective when (a) the nonresidential parent and his or her kin have no contact with children in the remarried household; (b) the children are so young at the time of remarriage that they do not remember prior family life; and (c) all stepfamily members agree, implicitly or explicitly, to recreate the nuclear family (Ganong & Coleman, 1994b). Although these hypotheses have not been tested, there is evidence that some stable long-term stepfamilies function like nuclear families (Berger, 1995; O'Connor et al., 1997; Vuchinich, Vuchinich, & Wood, 1993). There is ample evidence that many similarities to nuclear family dynamics are related to individual and stepfamily outcomes such as stepparent-parent agreement on child rearing (Skopin et al., 1993). Several researchers have found that stepfamily processes are similar to those of nuclear families (Menaghan, Kowalski-Jones, & Mott, 1997; O'Connor et al., 1997). Moreover, outsiders have positive perceptions of stepfamilies who present themselves to others as nuclear families (Ganong et al., 1990), reducing stress and making the development of new family relationships easier.

The findings of some research support the clinical view that the structural complexity and variety of precursors to remarriage lead to patterns of adaptive functioning for remarried families that do not resemble first-marriage families (Anderson & White, 1986; Banker & Gaertner, 1996). It might be normal for stepfamilies to have closer parent-child coalitions (Anderson & White, 1986), for children to be less reactive to marital conflict (Hanson et al., 1996), for stepfamily members to see their families as composed of two combined groups (Banker & Gaertner, 1996), and for stepparent-stepchild relationships to be less close than parent-child bonds (Anderson & White, 1986). Marital relationships, although important in contributing to overall family well-being, might be less important to remarried families than is stepchildren and stepparents getting along (Brown et al., 1990; Ganong et al., 1999). Remarried individuals might rely on different coping strategies than do those in first marriages. Few researchers have examined the possibility that there are multiple pathways to effective stepfamily functioning.

Cultural views of stepfamilies (e.g., as incomplete institutions, as deviant, as reconstituted nuclear families) encourage stepfamilies to act as much like nuclear families as possible, regardless of whether this model fits (Coleman & Ganong, 1997). Despite these views, stepfamilies are configured in many ways—as reconstituted nuclear families, as integrated but distinct "cultures," as binuclear systems, or as separate genetic units (Berger, 1995; Erera-Weatherly, 1996). Remarried families are here to stay. The challenge to close relationship scholars is to increase understanding of the ways in which they develop and maintain themselves as effective family systems.

# Part III

---

# RELATIONSHIP PROCESSES

# Contents

# Emotion in Close Relationships

*Laura K. Guerrero*
*Peter A. Andersen*

Humans experience a wide range of emotions within their relationships. As Bowlby (1979) maintained, people feel emotion most intensely when they are developing, maintaining, renewing, disrupting, or terminating close relational bonds with others. Similarly, Oatley and Johnson-Laird (1987) contended that most "emotions of interest to humans occur in the course of . . . relationships with others" (p. 41). Andersen and Guerrero (1998b) extended this argument by proposing that interpersonal communication is the primary elicitor of most emotions.

In this chapter, we explore some of the emotional experiences that occur within close relationships. First, we discuss four clusters of emotion—affectionate, self-conscious, melancholic, and hostile groups of emotions—that often surface in response to interaction with others. Next, we examine the role that emotion plays as relationships are developed, maintained, and terminated.

## ▶ The Social Emotions

Emotions arise when people have a positive or negative affective reaction to an environmental stimulus, which can include the behaviors of another person. In addition to affect, emotions often are characterized by cognitive appraisal, physiological reaction, and behavioral tendencies (Frijda, 1986; Guerrero, Andersen, & Trost, 1998; Scherer, 1994). Most positive and negative emotional experiences occur within the context of close relationships (Bowlby, 1979; DeRivera, 1984; Schwartz & Shaver, 1987). This is not to say that emotions *always* occur in social contexts. Sometimes, individuals experience emotion when they are alone, but more typically, people experience emotion as a result of interacting with others (Andersen & Guerrero, 1998b).

Some emotions, however, are more social than others. We group emotions into four broad interpersonal categories: affectionate, self-conscious, melancholic, and hostile. Among the affectionate emotions, love, passion, and interpersonal warmth are highly social because they typically are directed toward a person. The self-conscious emotions, which include embarrassment, shame, guilt, and pride, are highly social because they tend to occur in public or interpersonal contexts. Among the melancholic emotions, loneliness and grief are especially social in that they usually stem from the absence of desired relational bonds. Finally, the hostile emotions, which include anger, hate, jealousy, envy, and hurt, all are highly social. These four clusters of emotions are embedded within social contexts and help shape and define the nature of close relationships.

### Affectionate Emotions

These emotions, which evolved in humans within the context of social interaction (Dillard, 1998), provided group members with important signs of interpersonal connection and security that enhanced cooperativeness and increased the group's survival advantage. The affectionate emotions also help people to form attachments and close dyadic bonds.

When people feel *love,* they have an intense desire to maintain close relationships with loved ones (Aron & Aron, 1991; Shaver, Morgan, & Wu, 1996). In fact, Taraban, Hendrick, and Hendrick (1998) claimed that love plays "a central role in the day-to-day lives of every person who has or desires a close relationship with another" (p. 332). When Schwartz and Shaver (1987) asked people to describe emotional experiences and their antecedents, they found that 100% of the people who reported experiencing love referenced relationships with other persons. Clearly, love is a social emotion that is commonly directed toward another person and is catalytic in developing and maintaining close interpersonal bonds.

*Passion* sometimes is conceptualized as part of love (Sternberg, 1987), although evi-

dence suggests that many people view passion as a distinct emotion. In Shaver, Schwartz, Kirson, and O'Connor's (1987) work on the prototypical knowledge of emotion, both passion and love made the list of top 10 emotion words. Perhaps the ultimate passionate experience is sexual arousal and orgasm; in fact, some people view passion and sex, including sexual desire, synonymously. Research has shown that most sexually active college students define *sexual desire* as a motivational state, and many students also define it as an emotional state or part of an emotional syndrome (Regan & Berscheid, 1996). Indeed, sexual desire often comprises a unique configuration of emotions including love, happiness, loneliness, jealousy, and guilt.

*Interpersonal warmth* has not appeared on the classic lists of human emotions, but considerable evidence suggests that it is a common emotional experience during interpersonal interaction (Andersen & Guerrero, 1998a). Interpersonal warmth includes pleasant, contented, and intimate feelings that occur during interactions with friends, romantic partners, colleagues, and family. Although English, unlike some other languages, does not have a single term with which to describe this emotion, words such as warmth, intimacy, closeness, attachment, validation, and bondedness all come close. Although feelings of warmth can occur in a cozy home setting while listening to music alone, these feelings typically occur in interpersonal contexts such as cuddling with loved ones and talking with friends after dinner.

*Joy* is a feeling of intense happiness that often is elicited by receiving praise from others or by being the object of love, affection, or admiration (Schwartz & Shaver, 1987). In fact, in Schwartz and Shaver's (1987) account, 40% of the people who reported experiencing joy did so within the context of relationships. Many other participants reported experiencing joy in the context of more general interactions with others. Thus, although joy might not be as highly social as the other affectionate emotions reviewed in this section, it often is elicited by interpersonal interaction.

Moreover, when individuals experience happiness, they almost always express their feelings of joy to other people (Rimé, Mesquita, Philippot, & Boca, 1991).

### Self-Conscious Emotions

The self-conscious emotions of embarrassment, shame, guilt, and pride (Fischer & Tangney, 1995) are intensely self-focused, but they also are about one's relationships with others (Barrett, 1995). The resulting behaviors that accompany these emotions are mainly interpersonally focused (Tangney, 1995), producing responses such as apologizing, making excuses, and giving justifications (Fischer & Tangney, 1995; Vangelisti & Sprague, 1998).

When people receive unwanted attention associated with a faux pas (Andersen & Guerrero, 1998b), an unfavorable presentation (Bradford & Petronio, 1998), or excessive praise (Miller & Leary, 1992), they often are embarrassed. *Embarrassment* is one of the most social and self-conscious emotions because it requires others "as interactive partners or as evaluative observers" (Miller, 1995, p. 323). People also can become embarrassed by their partners' behaviors, and sometimes people even strategically embarrass others (Bradford & Petronio, 1998), which underscores the interpersonal nature of the emotion.

When people perceive themselves to be inferior to others, have committed relational transgressions, or have lost face, they often feel *shame* (Andersen & Guerrero, 1998b; Ferguson & Stegge, 1995). According to Ferguson and Stegge (1995), shame is "a dejection-based emotion encompassing feelings of helplessness, sadness, and depression but also anger. In shame, there is a greater focus on other people's opinions of the self, accompanied by a sense of being exposed and observed" (p. 176). Shame is different from embarrassment in that it is a more global and enduring emotional state. Although shame can induce interpersonal aggression, it typically motivates avoidance (Tangney, 1995)

because people want to avoid the painful, relationally induced feelings that accompany shame.

When people feel that they have been unjustly hurt or injured or have failed to help someone, they often experience *guilt* (Vangelisti & Sprague, 1998). Several scholars have made the case that the primary function of guilt is to maintain positive interpersonal relationships (Andersen & Guerrero, 1998b; Baumeister, Stillwell, & Heatherton, 1994). The classic guilt-inducing situations are relational—infidelity, being overbenefited, stealing or failing to share resources in a relationship, interpersonal deception, and violations of trust (Andersen & Guerrero, 1998b; Metts, 1994). The primary communicative outcomes of guilt also are relational—reparations, confessions, apologies, excuses, promises, and remorseful behaviors, all of which are designed to repair important relationships (Vangelisti & Sprague, 1998).

*Pride* is one of the most social emotions (Barrett, 1995) because it typically occurs when people believe that they are responsible for socially valued outcomes or are socially valued themselves (Mascolo & Fisher, 1995). Interestingly, one's greatest accomplishments rarely are the source of pride until they are recognized and valued by relationally significant others (Andersen & Guerrero, 1998b). Although pride is a personally gratifying and uplifting emotion, too much pride can create rivalry, resentment, or envy. Kitayama, Markus, and Matsumoto (1995) labeled pride as one of the "positive disengaged emotions" that is inherently self-conscious but not necessarily relationally "other conscious" (p. 444).

### Melancholic Emotions

Melancholic emotions typically are experienced as negative affective states that are related to low levels of arousal and can be experienced with either low or high intensity (Guerrero et al., 1998). Within interpersonal relationships, these emotions usually are experienced due to relational loss (through breakup or death) or the inability to develop and maintain close relationships.

Although *sadness* usually is not considered one of the most social emotions, Schwartz and Shaver (1987) found that 90% of respondents who reported experiencing sadness referenced relationship issues as the cause of their negative affect. Sadness frequently is elicited by events such as rejection by others, separation from friends or family, death or illness of loved ones, and breakups of close or potentially close relationships (Schwartz & Shaver, 1987; Shaver et al., 1987). Feelings of grief and loneliness often accompany these events. Similarly, *depression,* which generally is more stable and intense than sadness, frequently is rooted in interpersonal interaction (see Chapter 25 by Beach and O'Mahen, this volume). Depressed people tend to have poor interpersonal relationships and lack social skills, and this keeps them isolated from others and creates a spiral with depression as both a cause and an effect of relational distress (Segrin, 1998).

According to Plutchik (1984), *grief* is a form of extreme sadness that is most commonly associated with relational loss (Andersen & Guerrero, 1998b; Horowitz, 1991). In fact, the death of a close friend or family member is the primary antecedent of extreme sadness approximately 20% of the time in European and North American cultures (Scherer & Wallbott, 1994; Scherer, Wallbott, Matsumoto, & Kudoh, 1988). Grief, however, is more than relational sadness in that it often contains or is associated with other emotions, such as anger and guilt (Stearns, 1993), as well as a preoccupation with thoughts about a loved one.

*Loneliness* is a melancholic emotion that arises from a discrepancy between one's desired and achieved levels of social contact (Segrin, 1998). Thus, not all lonely people have small social networks; some have many friends and acquaintances but do not feel close to anyone in particular. Rubenstein and Shaver (1982) discussed five main reasons for loneliness, all of which have their roots in reduced social and relational contacts: *lack of attachment* (having no close relational partner), *alienation* (feeling socially isolated, misunderstood, and/or unneeded), *lack of contact with people* (being alone all day or night), *forced isolation* (being stuck in the house or hospital), and *dislocation* (living far away from loved ones or having to travel often).

### Hostile Emotions

People's most positive and negative emotions usually occur within their relationships. Ironically, the closer people are, the more able they are to "push one another's buttons" and generate intense negative affect. The hostile emotions that are particularly social occur when people feel hurt or threatened by relational partners.

People experience *anger* due to unfortunate circumstances or bad luck, but the primary site of anger is in troubling interpersonal relationships. Schwartz and Shaver (1987) found that 91% of respondents who experienced anger reported that it occurred within relationships, with being insulted by a relational partner described as a very common anger-eliciting event. Canary, Spitzberg, and Semic (1998) listed the primary causes of anger as including identity threats posed in interpersonal relationships, interpersonal aggression, physical or verbal attacks, and relationship threats such as unfaithful or disloyal behavior. In these situations, being able to express anger calmly, rather than inhibiting anger or resorting to aggression, is an important relational skill (Guerrero, 1994).

*Hate,* one of the darkest of the social emotions, is an inherently interpersonal emotion because it usually is directed at another individual or group. One of the most common sources of hate is the belief that another person has caused one great personal harm (Fitness & Fletcher, 1993). Because relational partners often are highly interdependent, the greatest perceptions of harm are likely to occur in the context of close relationships (Berscheid, 1983). However, hate also can be an irrational emotion directed at strangers or acquaintances because they belong to particular social, national, or ethnic groups.

*Jealousy* is one of the most social emotions because it almost always takes place in the context of close relationships. White and Mullen (1989) defined jealousy as "a complex of thoughts, emotions, and actions that follows loss of or threat to self-esteem and/or the existence or quality of the romantic relationship. The perceived loss or threat is generated by the perception of a real or potential romantic attraction between one's partner and a (perhaps) imaginary rival" (p. 9). Romantic jealousy exists in a web of three relationships: one between the jealous person and her or his relational partner, one between the partner and a rival, and one between the jealous person and the rival. On balance, jealousy has more negative than positive effects on relationships (see Chapter 23 by Buunk & Dijkstra, this volume), although satisfaction can be enhanced if partners use constructive communication that is nonaccusatory and allows for the sincere expression of negative affect (Andersen, Eloy, Guerrero, & Spitzberg, 1995).

Although *envy* is related to jealousy, it is a distinctly different and unique emotion. Parrott (1991) conceptualized envy as transpiring "when a person lacks what another has and either desires it or wishes the other did not have it" (p. 4). Envy, in contrast to jealousy, occurs when a person does not possess a valued commodity, position, characteristic, or relationship that another person possesses (Guerrero & Andersen, 1998). Envy always occurs in an interpersonal context in which a person desires something that another person has. It can be doubly interpersonal if one is envious of another person's relationship.

Emotional *hurt* arises when people receive messages that lead them to feel strong negative affect or psychological injury. According to Vangelisti (1994b), a person feels hurt as a consequence of an interpersonal event, a word or deed, usually from a close individual whose opinion is valued. In fact, Vangelisti's research showed that when people were asked to describe a hurtful message, more than one

third of the participants described messages that focused on relationship issues (e.g., "Going out with you was the biggest mistake of my life"). Hurtful messages also can lead to relational dissatisfaction and uncertainty, and they often require relational repair in the form of retractions, apologies, or expressions of guilt (Vangelisti & Sprague, 1998).

### ► Emotions Across Relationship Stages and Processes

As noted earlier, Bowlby (1979) contended that it is at relational junctures, such as the development of new relationships and the end of old relationships, that the most intense emotions occur. "Close relationships provide the setting for a range and intensity of emotion unmatched by any other context" (Berscheid, 1983, p. 131). In this section, we review principles related to emotional experiences at the beginning, middle, and end of relationships.

#### *Initial Encounters*

Starting new relationships is a wonderful and awful thing. During initial encounters, people often feel bright emotions such as passion, infatuation, warmth, anticipation, and joy. However, people also might feel anxiety, uncertainty, fear, envy, embarrassment, and other dark emotions. In this subsection, we summarize some of the research on emotions in initial encounters by examining three general principles. First, initial encounters are exciting, novel, uncertain, and unpredictable. Second, shyness and social anxiety can prevent people from approaching others and developing new relationships. Finally, during beginning relational stages, people tend to manage their negative emotions more carefully to make positive impressions.

*Excitement and novelty.* New relationships are unpredictable novel situations. According to Berger (1997), unpredictable events give rise to arousal of the autonomic nervous system. This arousal then is subjectively experienced as positive or negative. Berger contended that "it is the unpredictability involved during the early stages of romantic relationships that characterizes feeling of romantic love" (p. 36). According to Berscheid (1983), when action sequences are interrupted and goals are hindered, negative emotions occur. By contrast, when such interruptions are consistent with one's goals or plans, positive emotions occur. New relationships are major interruptions in people's ongoing lives that might even impinge on other relationships. For example, people often complain that friends start spending less time with them when the friends are developing new romantic relationships.

Arousal characterizes early stages of relationships. Berscheid (1983) stressed that as relational partners become more interdependent, they have more opportunity to facilitate or enhance one another's goals, and this leads to high potential for emotion. However, Berscheid also argued that emotional responses are contingent on the unexpected nature of the partner's behaviors. Thus, as relationships develop and people get to know one another better, they are likely to correctly anticipate one another's behaviors and to experience less emotion. This theory also helps to explain why "on again/off again" relationships are characterized by extreme emotional highs and lows. Because these relationships are uncertain and unstable, partners in these roller-coaster relationships often have difficulty in anticipating one another's behaviors. Stable relationships might produce less intense emotions, and this is both a plus and a minus. Feelings of fear, anxiety, and embarrassment might decline, but so might feelings of passion and joy. Of course, relational uncertainties brought about by events such as infidelity, illness, conflict, and pleasant surprises can introduce uncertainty and corresponding strong emotions at any stage of a relationship.

Research on uncertainty reduction theory suggests that decreasing uncertainty during initial encounters leads to increased liking and attraction (Berger & Calabrese, 1975). People are uncomfortable with the high levels of uncertainty that typically characterize initial interactions. To reduce uncertainty, people exchange information, often via self-disclosure. However, self-disclosure must reveal primarily positive information if it is to facilitate relationship development. Finding out that someone is a liar, is always in a bad mood, or has values that are radically different from one's own is likely to decrease uncertainty while also decreasing liking and attraction. Thus, Sunnafrank (1986) suggested that a positive relationship exists between uncertainty reduction and liking only when people predict that future interaction will be rewarding.

*Social anxiety.* Personality has a major effect on the emotions people experience in initial encounters. Extroverts and sensation seekers are likely to focus on the positive emotions (e.g., excitement, happiness, warmth, passion) experienced during first meetings, first dances, and first dates. By contrast, shy and introverted individuals are likely to focus on the negative feelings (e.g., anxiety, embarrassment) experienced as a result of approaching others and possibly being rejected. Very shy and apprehensive individuals show a classic pattern of *self-consciousness, tension,* and *fear* when approaching new people and new social situations (Andersen, 1999; Andersen & Guerrero, 1989). These uncomfortable emotions produce the *withdrawal response,* causing shy people to hide, avoid social situations, or minimize their presence. They stand and sit farther away, engage in less eye contact, and fail to fully participate in interaction. These individuals often desire close relationships, but the intensity of the negative emotion is too great, so they withdraw. Even when interacting with romantic partners, fearful individuals are likely to manifest withdrawal behavior such as less gaze, more backward lean, and less affectionate behavior (Guerrero, 1996).

Shy people also tend to experience self-consciousness and reduced awareness (Andersen, 1999). The flood of self-conscious emotions overwhelms shy people, causing them to focus on negative emotional cues instead of the interpersonal situations. This, of course, produces a negative cycle: Anxiety leads to reduced social information, reduced information leads to incompetent interpersonal behavior, incompetent behavior produces negative partner reactions, and negative reactions in turn produce more anxiety. This intense emotional state turns cognitive resources inward, and according to Patterson (1995), "As cognitive resources are invested in concerns other than the immediate interaction, fewer resources are available to attend and process information about the partner" (p. 18). Whereas this process occurs to some degree in all of us, it overwhelms shy and communication-apprehensive individuals, making it harder for them to develop close relationships.

*The positivity bias.* During initial stages of relationships, individuals usually are on their best behavior so that they can foster positive impressions. Therefore, they tend to hide any negative emotions they feel and instead put on happy and cheerful faces (Metts & Bowers, 1994). Because people in new relationships tend to put their best faces forward, they also are likely to see their relationships in particularly positive terms. For example, Hendrick and Hendrick (1988) showed that new lovers tend to see one another with "rose-colored glasses" (p. 161). Research shows that people manage negative emotion differently depending on relational stage (Aune, Aune, & Buller, 1994; Aune, Buller, & Aune, 1996). During early stages, people inhibit expressions of negative emotion, perceiving such expressions to be relatively inappropriate. During initial interactions, people expect others to display more positive emotion than negative emotion, and people who display

higher than expected negative emotion tend to be perceived as deviant and unlikable (Sommers, 1984).

Once people develop intimate relationships, the imperative to hide negative emotions is suspended (Metts & Bowers, 1994). During initial interactions, people's behavior typically is governed by rules of social politeness. In developed relationships, however, more idiosyncratic behavior emerges. As Metts and Bowers (1994) put it, "Intimacy is, by definition, a state of openness and familiarity. It is the domain in which the prescription for positive emotion is suspended. In theory, a sign of intimacy is that individuals can feel and express negative emotion without incurring [negative] dispositional attributions" (p. 535). Of course, as we discuss next, too much negativity can lead to dissatisfaction.

### Maintaining Satisfying Relationships

Developing a close relationship often is a complex and difficult task, but maintaining a satisfying and intimate long-term relationship might be even more difficult (see Chapter 21 by Dindia, this volume). Research on relationship maintenance confirms the common-sense assumption that people are likely to stay together when their interactions are pleasant and happy rather than distressful and hostile (Canary & Stafford, 1994; Gottman, 1993; Gottman & Levenson, 1992). Researchers have yet to determine how specific patterns of emotional experience and expression are associated with relational maintenance, but research supports three principles. First, prosocial constructive behavior is related to relationship satisfaction and stability. Second, satisfied couples limit their use of behaviors leading to negative affect, especially when compared to their use of positive behaviors. Third, equitable relationships are characterized by more positive relational and emotional outcomes than are inequitable relationships.

*Prosocial constructive behaviors.* Prosocial constructive behaviors are aimed at thwarting or solving problems and eliciting positive affect. One of the most popular typologies of prosocial constructive maintenance behaviors was proposed by Stafford and Canary (1991), who asked dating and married couples what they did to keep their relationships satisfying. Five primary maintenance strategies emerged. *Positivity* involves creating pleasant interaction including giving compliments, acting cheerful and optimistic, and accommodating the partner's wishes. *Openness* comprises talking and listening to one another via self-disclosure, relationship talk, and sharing secrets. *Assurances* occur when partners show commitment to one another and give each other social support; statements such as "I love you" and "I'm here for you" exemplify this category of maintenance behavior. *Social networking* refers to accepting and spending time with one another's social circles by engaging in activities such as going to family and work functions together and spending time with mutual friends. Finally, *sharing tasks* involves performing chores relevant to the relationship such as sharing household responsibilities.

Several studies have confirmed that these five prosocial constructive behaviors are associated with positive relational outcomes such as satisfaction, liking, closeness, trust, and relational stability (Canary & Stafford, 1994). These associations all are positive, with one important exception: Too much openness can be detrimental in relationships (Baxter & Wilmot, 1985). Avoiding topics that cause conflict and avoiding topics that hurt the partner's feelings appear to be important maintenance strategies in their own right (Ayres, 1983; Dainton & Stafford, 1993). Thus, openness that leads to positive emotional experiences may be associated with relationship satisfaction and stability, whereas openness that leads to negative emotional experiences may be associated with dissatisfaction and instability. This contention, however, needs to be tested directly.

Finally, it is important to note that it takes two people to enact positive communication. In Filsinger and Thoma's (1988) study, couples in which one partner was nice only when the other partner was nice (i.e., positive reciprocity) were more likely to separate 1½, 2½, and 5 years later than were couples whose patterns were not contingent on one partner being nice (see Chapter 18 by Burleson, Metts, & Kirch, this volume). It is important for the survival of a relationship to initiate positivity when the partner is sad, angry, or unexpressive as well as when the partner is happy.

*Limiting negativity.* Even if couples engage in prosocial constructive behaviors, if they also engage in high levels of negative behaviors, then they are at risk for relational dissatisfaction and possible disengagement. Unfortunately, negative behaviors can be difficult to control, especially when people are feeling emotional distress. Rusbult, Drigotas, and Verette (1994) discussed how hard it is to break negative cycles during hostile interactions. People tend to reciprocate negative hurtful behaviors rather than accommodating the partner by responding to negative comments with positivity (see Chapter 19 by Canary & Messman, this volume).

Gottman's work on conflict is especially helpful in understanding the destructive effects that negative emotion and behaviors can have on couples (Gottman, 1993, 1994a; Gottman & Levenson, 1992). Distressed couples often engage in a sequence of four highly destructive behaviors: complaining/criticizing, contempt, defensiveness, and stonewalling. These four messages typically produce high levels of negative affect. In fact, couples become defensive and withdraw because they are flooded by intense negative emotion. Interestingly, men and women might differ in terms of the specific types of negative emotions they express during conflict situations. Levenson and Gottman (1985) found that men tend to exhibit more anger and contempt, whereas women tend to show more sadness and fear. Gottman's work shows that happy couples tend to limit their use of complaining/criticizing, contempt, defensiveness, and stonewalling. In fact, married couples should engage in at least a one-to-five ratio of negative-to-positive behaviors to maintain satisfaction (Gottman & Levenson, 1992). Happy couples also show less reciprocity of negative affect and destructive behaviors.

This is not to say that conflict always should be avoided. If managed effectively, conflict helps relational partners to solve problems and understand one another better. Research has shown that conflict increases as dating relationships become more committed, perhaps because couples are less concerned with impression management, but that conflict rises to especially high levels when couples are contemplating breakups or already have decided to break up (Lloyd & Cate, 1985). There might be an optimal level of moderate conflict in a committed relationship beyond which the relationship is threatened.

*Equity and emotion.* Equity theory has been used as a theoretical framework to explain why some couples are more satisfied with their relationships than are others. The theory also has been applied to relational maintenance (Canary & Stafford, 1992, 1993). According to this theory, people are happier and more committed to their relationships when the ratio between benefits and contributions is similar for both partners (Adams, 1965; Walster, Walster, & Berscheid, 1978). The key word here is *ratio*. Partners do *not* have to receive equal benefits (e.g., receiving the same amounts of love, care, and financial security) or make equal contributions (e.g., contributing the same amounts of effort, time, and financial resources) so long as the ratio between these benefits and contributions is similar.

In inequitable relationships, one of the individuals is overbenefited and the other is underbenefited. Overbenefited individuals receive more benefits and/or make fewer contributions than do their partners so that the ratios

between the partners are unbalanced. Underbenefited individuals, conversely, receive fewer benefits and/or make greater contributions than do their partners when the ratios between them are not balanced. When people are over- or underbenefited, they experience increases in distress as well as decreases in satisfaction and happiness (Walster, Walster, & Berscheid, 1978). Thus, keeping a relationship equitable is one key to relational maintenance. Some research even shows that couples in equitable relationships engage in more prosocial constructive behavior than do those in inequitable relationships (Canary & Stafford, 1992, 1993).

Emotion is linked to equity theory in at least two ways. First, some of the most important benefits and contributions in close relationships are on an emotional level (Walster, Walster, & Berscheid, 1978). For example, being loved, experiencing intimacy and interpersonal warmth, and feeling proud of someone all are important relational benefits. Likewise, displaying love through social support and sacrifice are key relational contributions. On the other hand, feeling unloved and rejected are relational costs that are associated with dissatisfaction and distress. Second, emotion is a predicted outcome in equity theory. When a relationship is equitable, the theory predicts that couples will experience happiness. When a relationship is inequitable, the predicted outcome is distress. Walster, Walster, and Traupmann (1978) found that individuals who perceived their dating relationships to be equitable reported being happier and more content than did those who perceived their dating relationships to be inequitable. Furthermore, individuals who were underbenefited reported feeling the most anger, whereas women who were overbenefited reported feeling the most guilt. Sprecher (1986) found similar results, except that men were more likely than women to feel angry as a result of being underbenefited and that women often experienced sadness in response to being underbenefited. Of course, underbenefited individuals usually experience more intense distress than do overbenefited individuals (Austin & Walster, 1974), and some overbenefited individuals might be quite content with their relationships. In any case, one key to sustaining satisfying relationships appears to be balancing benefits and contributions so that both partners feel that they are treated equitably. If this balancing act is not achieved, then feelings of anger, sadness, and guilt are likely to pervade the emotional fabric of relationships.

### Relational Endings

If, as Berscheid (1983) contended, emotions result from unexpected events and interruptions in goals and plans, then relational disengagement is perhaps the most emotional incident that humans experience. Long absences, relational separations, and deaths of loved ones are the most wrenching emotional experiences possible. Of course, sometimes leaving a bad relationship or watching one's child go off to college can bring relief, contentment, and even joy. Typically, however, negative emotions characterize relational disengagements. Thus, this subsection focuses on three principles. First, people typically experience a host of negative emotions after relational breakups, particularly when the breakups are unilateral. Second, people go through various emotional processes after the deaths of loved ones (see Chapter 26 by Harvey & Hansen, this volume). Third, people's relational expectations affect how much distress they will feel after relationships end.

*The emotional aftermath of breakups.* Ending relationships usually is a difficult task that involves major personal and relational redefinitions and, of course, painful, hurtful, and emotional experiences. Baxter (1982) stated, "The breaking up of a relationship is a phenomena known to most and dreaded by all. It accounts for some of our most intense and painful social experiences" (p. 223). Similarly, Duck (1988) argued, "There is very little pain on earth like the pain of a long-term personal relationship that is falling apart" (p. 102).

Negative emotions often are particularly intense when the decision to terminate the relationship is unilateral. In fact, after one-sided breakups, most people experience a host of negative emotions including anger, sadness, hurt, and grief (Kurdek, 1991b; Wilmot, Carbaugh, & Baxter, 1985). In Owen's (1993) study of relationship accounts, respondents described breakups as emotional injury, with statements such as "He left a huge hole in my heart," "My heart felt like a dartboard," and "I was torn to shreds" (pp. 270-271). Counter to the stereotype that women are more emotionally vulnerable to breakups, research has found that men experience more emotional trauma after unwanted breakups than do women (Hill, Rubin, & Peplau, 1976), although studies have found that *both* sexes experience substantial emotional distress (Wilmot et al., 1985).

Melancholic emotions commonly characterize relational loss. Whereas grief occurs following the deaths of loved ones, individuals also experience grief when long-term romantic relationships end. Grief is not only traumatic, it is largely involuntary, leaving the grieving person in a double state of distress. Sadness and grief can cause a set of passive behaviors including reduced social contact, immobilization (e.g., staying in bed all day), and excessive solitude (Guerrero & Reiter, 1998). Loneliness also is prevalent after relational loss. Research has shown that divorced and separated individuals tend to be lonelier than married individuals (Perlman & Peplau, 1981). Interestingly, however, when Perlman and Peplau (1981) compared people who never had been married to those who currently were married, there were no differences in loneliness. They concluded that loneliness was more a reaction to relational loss than a reaction to the absence of a relationship per se.

Guilt also is a common emotion associated with relational breakups. Typically, persons who are disengaging feel the most guilt. Individuals often try to let others down easily because they are concerned with their partners' feelings (Baxter, 1982). After all, the persons who are terminating the relationships cared (and in many cases still care) deeply for the partners. Sometimes, the "dumped" individuals feel guilty as well and feel that they are to blame for the breakups. Research has shown that any transgression that threatens, let alone destroys, relational bonds tends to produce guilt (Jones, Kugler, & Adams, 1995).

*The emotional aftermath of death.* Emotions such as sadness, grief, loneliness, and guilt often occur when loved ones die. In her classic book, *On Death and Dying,* Kubler-Ross (1969) advanced a largely emotion-based model of how individuals cope with death. According to this model, when people lose loved ones, they go through five predictable stages: denial, anger/blame, bargaining, depression, and acceptance.

During the first two stages, people block out and then express intense negative emotions. After a loved one suddenly dies, the initial response usually is denial, which often includes disbelief, shock, and a feeling of numbness. Emotions often are repressed during this stage. Soon, however, people experience anger and blame. Sometimes, there is a logical direction for blame such as a drunk driver, cigarette smoking, or a medical mistake. People might even blame themselves for the loss, and this can lead to intense feelings of guilt.

The third phase, bargaining, involves promises to oneself, one's social network, or one's god about being a better person, trying harder, or living a more healthy life. The bargaining stage often is precipitated by feelings of guilt. Bargaining might seem cognitively based, but it really is an emotion-based strategy designed to alleviate negative feelings (e.g., guilt) and to give people hope.

Before a person can accept the death of a loved one, sadness must be experienced. Thus, Kubler-Ross's (1969) fourth stage is depression. At this point, sadness, helplessness, grief, loneliness, and fear permeate one's life.

Lopata (1969) found that widows tended to feel many loneliness-related emotions including longing to be with their husbands again, wanting to love and be loved by others, and fearing that they would not be able to make new friends. Dealing with depression paves the way for the final stage of acceptance. The only way in which to get beyond the death of a loved one is to accept the loss and move on with life. Eventually, people's intense negative emotions subside into a realization of the inevitable and a gentle feeling of going with the loss rather than fighting against it.

*Expectations and relational loss.* Expectations are important throughout relationships. During the initial relational stages, people form expectancies to deal with uncertainty. Once relationships develop, it is important that partners meet or exceed one another's expectations if they are to experience happiness. Expectations also play a role during the disengagement process. When relationships end, unexpected and actual benefits might help to explain why people feel radically different levels of emotional distress (Berscheid, 1983). *Unexpected benefits* lead to high levels of emotion. Thus, individuals who are in unpredictable relationships that are full of growth and/or surprises feel high levels of emotional connection. *Actual benefits,* by contrast, refer to the level of benefits that occurs, regardless of whether expectations are met.

Based on unexpected and actual benefits, Berscheid (1983) predicted that people could experience four different types of relationships, each characterized by different levels of emotional distress on breakup. In *growth-oriented relationships,* individuals receive high levels of both unexpected and overall benefits. If this type of relationship ends, then people should expect to feel a great deal of distress, and their expectations should come true; that is, they will feel considerable distress. In *exciting relationships,* individuals receive high levels of unexpected benefits, but their overall level of benefits actually is fairly low. For example, on again/off again or uncommitted relationships sometimes are exciting and emotion filled, but the actual benefits received from these types of relationships often are low because they are so unstable. Berscheid predicted that when this type of relationship ends, individuals will expect to feel considerable distress, but they actually will feel little distress. The opposite occurs in *tranquil relationships,* where the amount of unexpected benefits is low, but the overall benefit level is high. Because these relationships are emotionally stable, individuals in tranquil relationships do not expect to feel much distress when they break up. However, they soon miss all of the benefits that the relationship provided, and their distress is much greater than anticipated. Finally, in *nothing relationships,* people receive few unexpected or overall benefits. Thus, as expected, their levels of distress at breakup will be low. Clearly, it is easiest to walk away from this type of relationship.

## ▶ Practical Implications and Conclusions

In this chapter, we have shown that the experience and expression of emotion is an interpersonal phenomenon across the life span of relationships. Although numerous practical implications can be gleaned from the literature on emotion that we have reviewed, seven implications seem particularly important.

First, relationships and emotions are inseparably intertwined. It is impossible to understand one without considering the other. Furthermore, it is normal to experience both positive and negative emotions in close relationships.

Second, it is natural for relationships to become less novel and exciting after an initial "honeymoon" period. Rather than focusing on the loss of the initial excitement and the imperfections of their partners, people should try to insert new excitement into their relationships by being pleasingly unpredictable at times. Unexpected positive behaviors can increase emotional connections between relational partners.

Third, chronic depression, loneliness, and social anxiety might prevent people from developing or maintaining long-term meaningful relationships. Individuals experiencing these phenomena often lack social skills. Thus, counseling focused on developing confidence and communication skills should be helpful.

Fourth, it is normal for people to leave their "best" behaviors behind and to exhibit more negative affect and conflict behaviors once relationships have developed to a comfortable level. To maintain happy relationships, people should focus on using proactive constructive behaviors, avoiding messages such as complaining/criticizing, contempt, defensiveness, and stonewalling as well as refraining from reciprocating negative affect.

Fifth, when people are experiencing high levels of anger, guilt, or sadness in their relationships, they should determine whether the cause could be related to an imbalance in equity. Partners should try to be fair to one another and to distribute tasks equitably to ensure relational happiness.

Sixth, when relationships end, due to either breakups or deaths, people should know that it is okay to feel bad or to feel a lack of emotion. People also should realize that healing is a slow process and that spending time engaged in enjoyable activities with friends can hasten the healing process.

Seventh, goals and expectations are tied into emotional experiences. When people communicate their needs, goals, and expectations to one another clearly, they are more likely to have their goals and expectations met. When relational partners experience increased negative affect, it might be time to renegotiate relational expectations. Also, if people feel more distress than they expected to feel after a relational breakup, it might be a sign that they took one another for granted and that it could be worthwhile to try to save the relationship.

As these implications suggest, expressing emotion effectively is one key to relational success. Emotions give relationships depth and spirit. They draw people to some individuals and repel people from others. Positive emotions create bonds of intimacy and closeness, whereas negative emotions tear people apart. At a more basic level, emotions and relationships both are essential to the human experience. To shut out emotion, people also must shut out communication with others. As Paul Simon and Art Garfunkel's famous song lyrics from *I Am a Rock* suggest, to feel no pain, people must act like rocks that cannot be moved, and to never cry, people must become islands by building deep and mighty fortresses. Instead, it might be better to take Alfred Tennyson's advice and live by the motto that it is "better to have loved and lost than never to have loved at all."

# Contents

# Attachment and Close Relationships

*Judith A. Feeney*
*Patricia Noller*
*Nigel Roberts*

One of the major developments in the field of close relationships has been the move toward more theoretically grounded research. In the area of adult love relationships in particular, much of the early work was largely atheoretical and tended to focus on describing various forms or styles of love. By contrast, now it is widely accepted that researchers need to formulate and test theories that explain how and why the different forms of love develop. Attachment theory is one of the major perspectives that has been applied in this area.

Recent attempts to understand adults' close relationships from an attachment perspective draw heavily on Bowlby's (1969, 1973, 1980) ethological theory of attachment. Bowlby's work integrated observational studies of mothers and their offspring, both human and primate. The resulting theoretical formulation highlighted the importance of the bond be-tween infants and their primary caregivers, suggesting that such a continuing bond is crucial for children's social and emotional development.

## ▶ Infant Attachment

Bowlby (1973) defined attachment behavior as "any form of behavior that results in a person attaining or retaining proximity to some other differentiated and preferred individual, usually conceived as stronger and/or wiser" (p. 292). He saw attachment behavior as having evolved through natural selection, offering infants a survival advantage by protecting them from danger. Specific attachment behaviors, such as crying and clinging, form an organized behavioral system. That is, they serve the common goal of keeping the attachment figure close by and creating "felt security." In the absence of threat, the attachment figure serves as a secure base from which the infant can explore the environment. On the other hand, if there are signs of danger, then the attachment figure serves as a safe haven to which the infant turns for support. Hence, the functions of attachment, and the defining features of an attachment bond, are proximity seeking (including separation protest), secure base, and safe haven. Bowlby acknowledged that a child usually becomes attached to more than one person but argued that the primary caregiver (usually the mother) is preferred as a safe haven when the child is distressed. Other attachment figures, such as the father and older siblings, are seen as secondary to that primary caregiver, forming a hierarchy of attachment figures.

The claim that attachment behavior has evolved through natural selection implies that its functions apply universally as part of the ground plan of the species. At the same time, Bowlby (1973) emphasized individual differences in attachment behavior. He argued that, throughout childhood and adolescence, individuals gradually build up expectations about the responsiveness of their attachment figures. These expectations, and the associated memories and beliefs about early interactions, are incorporated into "working models" of attachment that shape behavior in later relationships.

Individual differences in attachment behavior were highlighted by Ainsworth, who developed a laboratory technique (the Strange Situation) for assessing infant attachment styles based on infants' reactions to separations from and reunions with mothers and strangers (Ainsworth, Blehar, Waters, & Wall, 1978). Secure infants explore actively in their mothers' presence and, although upset by separation, are readily comforted on reunion; their mothers are warm and responsive. Avoidant infants appear to be detached and avoid close contact with their mothers; their mothers tend to be distant or rigid. Anxious-ambivalent infants show extreme distress on separation and show anger or ambivalence on reunion; their mothers tend to be insensitive or inconsistent.

Although researchers have debated the reliability and validity of infant attachment styles, there is evidence that these styles are relatively stable if family circumstances are stable (Main, Kaplan, & Cassidy, 1985) and that they predict later social functioning (Youngblade & Belsky, 1992). It also should be noted that attachment theory and research have vital practical applications with regard to the quality of child care including the care of hospitalized and institutionalized children.

## ▶ Attachment Relationships Beyond Childhood

Although Bowlby focused on childhood attachment, he saw the attachment system as playing a crucial role across the life span. Similarly, Ainsworth (1989) and Weiss (1986, 1991) argued that some adult relationships meet the criteria of attachment bonds. That is, adults sometimes seek closeness to relationship partners (proximity seeking) and experience distress if partners become unavailable (separation protest), they derive confidence and security from relationships (secure base), and they turn to partners for comfort during times of stress (safe haven). Weiss (1991) also noted other important similarities between childhood attachments and some adult relationships. For example, in both childhood and adulthood, individuals develop a sense of being bonded to specific partners. This bonding persists, despite episodes of negativity in relationships, and loss of such partners leads to grief and mourning.

Based on these points, Ainsworth (1989) and Weiss (1991) identified marital and other committed romantic relationships as the prime examples of adult attachments. For this reason, the present chapter focuses on romantic attachments. Before exploring this area in detail, however, we recognize that other close relationships can constitute attachments. Weiss (1991) argued that relationships between adults and their parents can show properties of attachment bonds, as can some close friendships and ongoing patient-therapist relationships. The claims for attachments with parents and friends have received some support from studies of the functions served by young adults' close relationships (Hazan, Zeifman, & Middleton, 1994; Trinke & Bartholomew, 1997).

There has been little systematic study of adult siblings as attachment figures. Yet, researchers have noted that sibling relationships can serve a number of developmental functions across the life span and that attachment bonds between adult siblings are possible (Cicirelli, 1995; Hazan & Shaver, 1994). As already noted, young children are thought to form secondary attachments to older siblings. This claim is supported by studies of the Strange Situation, in which older siblings often take an active role in comforting infants distressed by their mothers' departures (Stewart, 1983). Support for sibling attachments beyond childhood comes from recent studies of young adult samples. Feeney and Humphreys (1996) found that many respondents rated siblings as important figures in terms of providing closeness (proximity seeking), comfort (safe haven) and security (secure base), although siblings tended to be eclipsed as attachment figures by parents and romantic partners. Similarly, Trinke and Bartholomew (1997) found that, in terms of overall strength of attachment, siblings ranked behind partners, mothers, and fathers but ranked above best friends. Based on reported patterns of behavior, judges classified 58% of participants as being "attached" to at least one sibling; for 8% of participants, a sibling was the primary attachment figure. Together, these results suggest that adult sibling relationships merit further research.

▶ **Romantic Relationships as Attachments**

Despite similarities between infant attachments and romantic relationships, romantic attachment received little attention before Hazan and Shaver's (1987) seminal studies. Adult attachment had been measured previously using the Adult Attachment Interview (AAI) (George, Kaplan, & Main, 1985). The AAI is not considered in detail in this chapter because it assesses current thinking about childhood attachment rather than romantic attachment. Nevertheless, we note that there is some convergence between the AAI and measures of romantic attachment (Bartholomew & Shaver, 1998).

### *Early Studies of Romantic Attachment*

Hazan and Shaver (1987) reported two studies of romantic love using a simple three-paragraph measure designed to capture the features of the major attachment styles (secure, avoidant, and anxious-ambivalent) extrapolated from studies of infant attachment. Participants (respondents to a "Love Quiz" in a local newspaper and a sample of undergraduates) were asked to choose the paragraph that best described their feelings in close relationships and to complete questionnaires assessing aspects of childhood and adult relationships. The three groups defined by the forced-choice measure of attachment style differed predictably in their reports of early family relations, beliefs about love relationships, and love experiences. Table 14.1 provides a summary of results.

In addition to these empirical studies, Shaver and colleagues (Shaver & Hazan, 1988; Shaver, Hazan, & Bradshaw, 1988) presented a theoretical analysis of romantic love as attachment. This analysis dealt with the relationship between love and attachment, love as the integration of behavioral systems, and previous conceptualizations of love. In terms of the relationship between love and attachment, Shaver and Hazan (1988) argued for strong parallels between infant attachment and romantic love. These parallels included the dynamics of the two types of relationships (similar to Weiss's [1991] work on the role of proximity seeking, secure base, etc.) but also pointed to behavioral and emotional similarities (e.g., frequent eye contact, holding, powerful empathy).

**TABLE 14.1** Summary of Results From Hazan and Shaver's (1987) Studies

| | *Secure* | *Avoidant* | *Anxious-Ambivalent* |
|---|---|---|---|
| Major themes of self-report description | Comfort with intimacy and dependence; lack of anxiety about relationships | Discomfort with closeness; difficulty in depending on others | Desire for extreme closeness; anxieties about abandonment and lack of love |
| Attachment history | Relationships with parents and between parents described as warm | Mothers described as cold and rejecting | Fathers described as unfair |
| Working models | Easy to know; few self-doubts; others well-intentioned; love seen as lasting | Love seen as rarely lasting; love loses its intensity | Self-doubts; misunderstood; real love seen as rare; others less willing to commit |
| Love experiences | Happiness; trust; friendship | Fear of intimacy; low acceptance of partners | Preoccupation; strong sexual attraction; emotional volatility |

With regard to the integration of behavioral systems, Shaver and Hazan (1988) noted two clear differences between infant attachment and romantic love. Infant-caregiver bonds have highly asymmetrical patterns of caregiving, as the term *caregiver* implies. By contrast, romantic love usually involves reciprocal caregiving. Furthermore, unlike infant attachment, romantic love almost always has a sexual component. These points led Shaver and Hazan to describe romantic love as the integration of attachment, caregiving, and sexuality. Similarly, Bowlby (1969) argued that these three behavioral systems worked together to ensure the survival of the species. The three systems can vary in importance in different love relationships and at different points in time. The attachment system, however, is central; it is the first system to appear developmentally and, hence, influences the development of the others (Shaver et al., 1988).

Compared to previous conceptualizations of love, the attachment perspective offers important advantages (Shaver & Hazan, 1988). It is firmly grounded in theory, whereas many earlier studies of love lacked a theoretical base. The attachment perspective also is integrative in several senses: It is developmental in nature, linking romantic love with early social experiences; it explains both healthy and unhealthy forms of love; and it encompasses related concepts such as grief and loneliness.

Hazan and Shaver's early work on attachment soon was followed by reports from other researchers involving replications and extensions of their work and tests of their theoretical formulation. For example, Shaver and Hazan (1988) had proposed that previous conceptualizations of love (including theories of anxious love) could be subsumed within attachment theory. Questionnaire studies using multiple measures of romantic love largely supported this proposition (Feeney & Noller, 1990; Levy & Davis, 1988). At the same time, the studies showed a need to qualify some of Shaver and Hazan's (1988) assertions. These researchers had equated anxious love with anxious-ambivalent attachment, but measures of anxious love proved to be multidimensional, with one aspect (self-conscious anxiety in dealing with partners) characterizing both avoidant and anxious-ambivalent persons (Feeney & Noller, 1990).

An important question addressed in another early study concerned the *salience* of attachment-related issues. Feeney and Noller (1991) noted that existing studies in the area had relied primarily on questionnaire measures of attachment style. These measures (and, to a lesser extent, interview measures) are prone to experimenter demand; attachment-related issues might not figure strongly in participants' thinking about their romantic relationships unless primed by researchers' questioning. To overcome this problem, Feeney and Noller asked young adults to give open-ended accounts of their current dating relationships. Most respondents spontaneously referred to attachment-related issues such as closeness and affection, often discussing these issues at length. Furthermore, the content of the references was related to Hazan and Shaver's (1987) measure of attachment style, which respondents completed 2 weeks later. For example, contrasting attitudes toward the expression of affection are seen in these comments from avoidant and anxious-ambivalent respondents, respectively:

If you've got someone who "love you," "love you" all the time, then you don't want it much. But if you think that they're interested in someone else, then you want them. It adds excitement to the relationship.

I need heaps of comfort and physical affection. And my partner is extremely affectionate, which suits me down to the ground. I've always, always craved affection all my life, mainly through parental—bad parental relationships.

## Issues of Conceptualization and Measurement

Since Hazan and Shaver's (1987) studies of attachment style, issues concerning conceptualization and measurement have been focal. Their original measure was intuitively appealing, being based on a simple typology that drew parallels with the major infant styles. However, as Hazan and Shaver noted, the forced-choice item was severely limited as a measure of attachment style. Being a single item, it is likely to have limited reliability, especially given the complex response options.

The first revision of this measure retained the three descriptions but required partici-

pants to rate the applicability of each (Levy & Davis, 1988). This method offers important advantages over the forced-choice format. It recognizes that not all persons choosing a given description will endorse it to the same degree, nor will they reject the other descriptions completely. However, this method still is prone to poor reliability if the original descriptions are not internally consistent. For this reason, researchers developed multiple-item measures by breaking the descriptions into their separate components. Most factor analytic studies of these measures yielded two major factors: comfort with closeness and anxiety over relationships (for more details, see Feeney & Noller, 1996). Comfort with closeness is a bipolar factor that contrasts elements of the secure and avoidant descriptions (e.g., "I find it relatively easy to get close to others" vs. "I am nervous when anyone gets too close"). Anxiety over relationships reflects concerns about abandonment and reciprocation of love, similar to aspects of anxious-ambivalent attachment (e.g., "I often worry that my partner doesn't really love me").

While researchers were refining the three-group measure, Bartholomew (1990) proposed a four-group typology based on the assertion that attachment patterns reflect both a working model of self and a working model of the attachment figure (Bowlby, 1973). Each of these models can be broadly dichotomized as positive or negative. That is, the self can be seen as worthy of love and attention or as unworthy; the attachment figure (or "other") can be seen as caring and available or as uncaring (Bartholomew, 1990). Combining these dimensions gives rise to four attachment styles: secure (positive models of self and other), preoccupied (positive model of other, negative model of self; cf. anxious-ambivalent), dismissing (positive model of self, negative model of other), and fearful (negative models of self and other). Bartholomew and Horowitz (1991) developed prototype descriptions of the four styles (which could be presented either in a forced-choice format or with rating scales) together with interview schedules. Their empirical data supported the model; the two avoidant styles (dismissing and fearful) in particular were differentiated by measures such as assertiveness and interpersonal warmth.

Recent studies have clarified issues of conceptualization and measurement. Feeney, Noller, and Hanrahan (1994) developed a substantial pool of items covering the basic themes of attachment theory. Five factors emerged from the items and were used as clustering variables in a cluster analysis. The resulting four groups were largely similar to those discussed by Bartholomew (1990) but raised important issues. For example, participants in the dismissing group were moderately high in need for approval and preoccupation with relationships, suggesting that their attempts to maintain interpersonal distance might be driven by anxiety and self-doubt. Similarly, Brennan, Clark, and Shaver (1998) conducted a cluster analysis based on two higher order factors (anxiety and avoidance) derived from all available self-report items. The resulting four groups again resembled those described by Bartholomew (1990).

Using confirmatory factor analysis, Griffin and Bartholomew (1994) demonstrated substantial convergence across three methods of measuring adult attachment: self-report, peer-report, and interview. They also argued for a "prototype" approach to adult attachment. This approach regards the four types as important predictors of relationship outcomes (adding to the predictive power of the two dimensions) but recognizes that the boundaries between them are fuzzy. However, Fraley and Waller (1998), in their discussion of whether individual differences in adult attachment should be conceptualized as types (groups) or as dimensions, disagreed with this conclusion. They noted that this question cannot be resolved by considering issues of convenience, by examining the distributions of attachment-related variables, or by using cluster analysis. Rather, it requires the use of "taxometric" techniques, designed specifically to assess whether a construct is best understood in terms of latent types or dimensions. Taxometric techniques assess patterns of covaria-

tion between measured indicators of the construct. Results of these techniques suggest that differences in adult attachment are best understood in terms of dimensions (for more details, see Fraley & Waller, 1998).

In this chapter, research findings are discussed in terms of both types and dimensions, according to the measures used by researchers. Results can be integrated across measures. Comfort with closeness consistently orders the attachment groups (secure, preoccupied, dismissing, and fearful), and anxiety over relationships separates the preoccupied and fearful groups from the secure and dismissing groups (Feeney, 1995, 1999).

### Stability of
### Adult Attachment

Given the range of measures outlined heretofore, it is not surprising that researchers have debated the reliability of the different measures and the related question of how stable adult attachment patterns are over time. To some extent, the ongoing debate over these issues reflects a misconception that attachment theory requires near-perfect stability. Attachment theorists accept that attachment style can change, especially in the face of changing relationship experiences. However, they propose that working models generally solidify over time (Shaver, Collins, & Clark, 1996) and that the associated expectations tend to be self-fulfilling (e.g., expecting others to be rejecting might lead to a defensive interpersonal style, resulting in rejection). This perspective implies a certain degree of stability in measures of attachment style.

There now are reports of stability rates over periods from 1 week to 4 years (for details, see Feeney & Noller, 1996). With categorical measures (three or four groups), approximately one in four respondents changes attachment style from one occasion to the next. Ratings of attachment prototypes generally show moderate stability, as do multiple-item scales.

What do these data mean? Some researchers argue that instability stems largely from measurement error (Scharfe & Bartholomew, 1994), whereas others argue that it reflects real change (Baldwin & Fehr, 1995). "Instability as error" is supported by the high stability of multiple-item scales when they are attenuated for unreliability and by the fact that stability is largely unaffected by the time lag between testing. Furthermore, attempts to assess dimensional constructs using categories always underestimate stability (Fraley & Waller, 1998). However, the substantial rates of change, even for ratings by trained interviewers, suggest some "instability as change." In explaining such change, researchers again have taken different positions.

First, as already noted, change in attachment patterns might be especially likely when relationship experiences change. There is mixed support for this claim. Baldwin and Fehr (1995) reported no link between stability of attachment style and change in relationship status, and Scharfe and Bartholomew (1994) found only scattered relations between stability and life events. However, results in these studies might have been weakened by the crude measure of relationship change (Baldwin & Fehr, 1995) and by the use of participants in stable relationships (Scharfe & Bartholomew, 1994). Some support exists for the link between stability and relationship events such as involvement in steady and satisfying relationships (Feeney & Noller, 1992; Hammond & Fletcher, 1991) and relationship breakup (Kirkpatrick & Hazan, 1994).

A second perspective on change focuses on short-term instability rather than on major change. According to this perspective, individuals have multiple attachment orientations, derived over the course of varied relationship experiences (Baldwin & Fehr, 1995). At any given point in time, measures of attachment reflect the attachment orientation elicited by particular situational factors. This perspective can accommodate the finding that even those in stable relationships show some instability of attachment patterns. A recent study (Baldwin, Keelan, Fehr, Enns, & Koh-Rangarajoo, 1996) provides preliminary support for the proposition that different attachment orientations can be activated and that these influence the processing of relational information.

Finally, a third perspective on instability has posited change in attachment style as an individual difference variable. Davila, Burge, and Hammen (1997) suggested that vulnerability factors make some people more susceptible to attachment style change and that these people are similar to those who are consistently ("stably") insecure rather than to those who are secure. A longitudinal study of young women (Davila et al., 1997) generally supported these predictions, suggesting that adverse early experiences might be linked to more tentative views of self and other.

### Working Models of Attachment

Issues concerning stability are closely linked to questions about the nature of working models. Working models reflect the inner organization of the attachment system and cannot be observed directly. In this sense, they are similar to other cognitive structures such as scripts and schemata. However, working models of attachment differ from these structures in important ways: They are explicitly relational, they involve motivational and behavioral tendencies as well as conscious cognitions, they are heavily affect laden, and they are complex and multidimensional in structure (Shaver et al., 1996). Attachment theorists often talk about "models of self" and "models of other," but in a number of ways, these terms imply an oversimplistic view of their structures.

First, models of self and models of other cannot be understood without reference to each other (Bowlby, 1973). Although the two types of models are logically independent, they tend to be complementary. For example, a child who experiences attachment figures as very insensitive to his or her needs is likely to develop a negative model of both self and other.

Second, individuals might hold multiple, and potentially inconsistent, models of self and other. This situation applies particularly to dismissing and preoccupied persons, whose working models of self and other differ in valence (Klohnen & John, 1998). For example, preoccupied persons are seen as having a "positive model of other" and even show a tendency to idealize partners. However, this model might act as a defense against a less conscious, and more negative, model of other.

Third, the term *model of other* implies a single model of attachment figures. However, even young children can have separate models for different attachment figures, and adults' representations are likely to reflect the complex nature of their social experiences. Multiple models are thought to form a hierarchical structure (Collins & Read, 1994). Models at the top of the hierarchy are general and abstract; they apply widely but might not provide a good fit to particular situations. Conversely, models lower in the hierarchy are more specific, corresponding to particular types of relationships (e.g., love relationships) and even to particular partners. These models might not generalize widely, but they predict particular situations.

Collins and Read (1994) proposed four interrelated components of working models: memories of attachment-related experience; beliefs, attitudes, and expectations of self and others; attachment-related goals and needs; and plans and strategies for achieving these goals. Research has supported attachment-style differences in these variables (Feeney & Noller, 1996) but has relied mainly on self-reports, which cannot assess structural features or aspects outside of conscious awareness. Recent initiatives, however, offer some insight into the complexity and integration of working models (Mikulincer, 1995), and their strength and accessibility, assessed via response times (Baldwin, Fehr, Keedian, Seidel, & Thomson, 1993).

What are the functions of working models of attachment? These models are used to predict the behavior of others and to plan one's own behavior to achieve relational goals. Working models are thought to perform these functions by guiding emotional, cognitive, and behavioral responses to relational events (Collins & Read, 1994). Studies of both hypothetical and real relationships support this proposition. For example, when asked to explain specific partner behaviors in a hypothetical relationship, insecure individuals are more likely than secure individuals to focus on negative factors such as the unresponsive or rejecting nature of the partner (Collins, 1996). Feeney (1998) studied responses to a specific event (separation from partner) in real relationships. As seen in Table 14.2, reports of emotions, cognitions, and behaviors paint a consistent picture of the response patterns associated with each style.

The results just discussed highlight the link between attachment style and reactions to negative relationship events. Such findings bring us to the question of how attachment security and insecurity are manifested in stressful situations.

## ▶ Attachment, Stress, and Coping

We noted earlier that attachment figures serve as a safe haven in threatening situations. Bowlby (1969) discussed three types of situations that elicit infant attachment behavior: conditions of the individual (e.g., illness), conditions of the environment (threats in the social or physical environment), and conditions of the relationship (the attachment figure's absence or discouraging of proximity). By analogy, similar situations can activate attachment behavior in adults. For this reason, several studies have focused on adult attachment and responses to stress.

In presenting this research, we focus primarily on stressful events *within relationships* because of their central importance to rela-

**TABLE 14.2** Emotional, Cognitive, and Behavioral Responses to Separation Reported by Individuals From Different Attachment Groups

| Attachment Style | Emotional | Cognitive | Behavioral |
|---|---|---|---|
| Secure | I was lonely and I missed him heaps, but I didn't find it really stressful. | I didn't dwell on "He's away, he's away." When he entered my mind, I had nice thoughts about him, and moved on to other things. | I phoned him regularly, and wrote letters and things, and talked to my family and friends about it. |
| Preoccupied | I felt empty, hollow, pain, insecure inside. I feel physically sick without him. | I began to think I was unappreciated. I know it's very irrational, but it's very hard to reason rationally when you are in a relationship. | I picked arguments and blew small things into bigger issues during that time, just to get the extra attention I was missing out on. |
| Dismissing | I felt a bit lonely, but I also felt a sense of freedom, which I enjoyed. | I thought how I didn't miss her nagging me or hassling me. | I didn't take much interest. I only rang her twice, and then only to ask for money! |
| Fearful | I was just always incredibly angry and cold; very cold toward him. | I got very paranoid and jealous, because I was thinking about maybe her being unfaithful while we were apart. | I got drunk a lot. I got stoned a lot. I tried to wipeout so I didn't have to think about what might be happening. |

tionship researchers. However, we first briefly outline studies of conditions of the individual and the environment. We also note that responses to stress are likely to affect close relationships even when stressors are not relationship based. Hence, the studies mentioned in this section also are relevant to relationship outcomes and processes (discussed later in the chapter).

Studies of responses to conditions of the individual and the environment have examined stressors as diverse as pain and ill health (Feeney & Ryan, 1994; Mikulincer & Florian, 1998), anticipated involvement in a stressful experiment (Simpson, Rholes, & Nelligan, 1992), and missile attacks during the Gulf War (Mikulincer, Florian, & Weller, 1993). These studies have produced consistent sets of findings. In stressful situations, secure persons tend to make lower appraisals of threat and to seek support from others. Avoidant persons try to distance themselves from the situation and are reluctant to seek help and support even for physical symptoms. Anxious-ambiv-

alent persons focus on their negative feelings and report high levels of physical symptoms.

These findings fit with the claim that differences in attachment style reflect early experiences of dealing with distress or "affect regulation" (Kobak & Sceery, 1988). Secure individuals, experiencing responsive caregiving, learn to acknowledge distress and to seek support from others. Avoidant individuals learn to avoid acknowledging or expressing distress so as to minimize conflict with insensitive caregivers. Anxious-ambivalent individuals focus on distressing thoughts and feelings in attempting to maintain contact with inconsistent caregivers. The findings linking adult attachment with responses to stress also underline the importance of context. For example, avoidant persons might behave in a distant manner only under stress (Simpson et al., 1992).

Stressful events within relationships have been investigated in two ways. First, researchers have conducted retrospective studies of separation and reunion. Open-ended reports of separations from long-term dating partners have linked secure attachment to more constructive responses to separation and reunion (Feeney, 1998; again, see Table 14.2). In a study of couples in which the man had served overseas during the Gulf War, secure spouses reported low levels of postconflict distress and high marital satisfaction, particularly in comparison to preoccupied spouses (Cafferty, Davis, Medway, O'Hearn, & Chappell, 1994). Relations between secure attachment and reports of more positive affect during reunion were confined to men, possibly because of the more stressful nature of their separation experience.

Second, stressful events within relationships have been investigated in terms of relationship conflict. This topic is addressed in a later subsection on communication. At this point, we confine our discussion to two studies testing theory-based predictions about the effects of attachment style on responses to different types of conflict; conflict that appears to threaten the relationship should produce stronger effects than conflict that does not.

In one study, data from both "insiders" (participants) and "outsiders" (trained raters) linked anxious-ambivalent attachment to high levels of distress in response to conflict. Raters also rated the interactions of insecure participants as lower in quality (Simpson, Rholes, & Phillips, 1996). As predicted, these effects were stronger for couples who were asked to discuss issues of major conflict. Ambivalent individuals who discussed major issues perceived their partners more negatively after the discussions than before, even when interaction quality was controlled, suggesting that negative expectations influenced their perceptions. In the other study (Feeney, 1998), couples took part in three conflict interactions: one involving a specific issue (leisure time) and two designed to elicit attachment-related anxiety. In the latter interactions, one partner (man or woman, in counterbalanced order) was primed to reject the other. For all three interactions, secure individuals reported more positive expectations. How-

ever, secure attachment was linked to outsider ratings (of less negative affect and more constructive behavior) *only* in response to the partner's rejection. Thus, attachment differences again were stronger when conflict was more threatening. Of course, the destructive patterns that insecure individuals tend to display in such situations are likely to exacerbate the stress being experienced.

## ▶ Partners' Attachment Styles

As we already have seen, theoretical and empirical studies have linked working models of attachment with expectations of relationship partners and with responses to stressful events. These studies suggest that attachment style is likely to have important implications for relationship outcomes and processes. Before reviewing research focusing on these issues, we need to emphasize that, from the outset, Hazan and Shaver (1987) called for researchers to take account of the attachment styles of both partners in ongoing relationships. Two major issues are relevant here: whether there is "partner matching" in terms of attachment characteristics and whether relationship functioning is predicted by the attachment style of the partner (as well as by one's own attachment style).

### *Partner Matching*

Do couples pair up on the basis of attachment style? If so, then do partners tend to be similar or complementary in style? Studies of ongoing relationships suggest systematic patterns of pairing, especially in terms of the tendency for secure individuals to be paired with secure partners (Collins & Read, 1990; Feeney, 1994; Senchak & Leonard, 1992). There also is evidence that avoidant individuals tend to be paired with ambivalent partners (Collins & Read, 1990; Kirkpatrick & Davis,

1994), although one study has suggested pairing of ambivalent partners (Frazier, Byer, Fischer, Wright, & De Bord, 1996). Unfortunately, interpretation of these results is problematic. It is possible, for example, that secure individuals *choose* secure partners; that is, this pairing might be evident from the start. Alternatively, it might result from relationship dynamics; involvement with a secure partner might provide experiences that allow negative working models to be revised in the direction of greater security.

Hypothetical relationships also have been used to study partner matching. Pietromonaco and Carnelley (1994) found that all attachment groups felt most positive about relationships with secure partners and that only avoidant persons differentiated between avoidant and ambivalent partners (i.e., they felt less positive about avoidant partners). By contrast, Frazier et al.'s (1996) studies of hypothetical relationships suggest that ambivalent individuals are especially averse to avoidant partners. Again, these results are difficult to interpret. The method used in these studies is artificial in its explicit focus on partner attachment style and fails to distinguish between what people *think* they are attracted to, what they *are* attracted to, and what they *attain*. Without long-term longitudinal studies, the issue of partner matching remains unclear. This area also is marked by confusion concerning theory-based predictions. Frazier et al. (1996) argued that matching of similar styles reflects self-verification (i.e., the tendency to prefer those who verify one's beliefs). By contrast, Pietromonaco and Carnelley (1994) invoked self-verification theory to predict avoidant-ambivalent matching.

### Partner Effects

Studies of partner matching highlight the need to consider both partners' attachment styles. Systematic patterns of pairing imply that the attachment styles of self and partner are confounded and that researchers should try to disentangle the effects of each person's characteristics. At this point, we simply note that there is considerable evidence of partner effects, as mentioned throughout the following subsections. Partners' attachment styles also can interact in their effects on relationship functioning; however, research has only recently begun to explore this issue.

## ► Attachment and Relationship Outcomes

In this section, we briefly review research linking attachment style with the relationship outcome variables of quality and stability. This topic has received considerable attention, starting with the earliest studies of romantic attachment.

### Relationship Quality

Hazan and Shaver (1987) reported that secure attachment was associated with relationships of higher quality (more happy, friendly, and trusting). This general finding has been widely replicated across the range of attachment measures. Early studies focused primarily on dating relationships, with some evidence that relationship evaluations are linked more strongly to own avoidance (low comfort with closeness) for men and to own anxious-ambivalence (high anxiety over relationships) for women (Collins & Read, 1990; Simpson, 1990). These studies also reported partner attachment effects, with the most robust finding being the negative effect of women's relationship anxiety. Similarly, in a 3-year study of dating couples, Kirkpatrick and Davis (1994) found that avoidant men and anxious women rated their relationships negatively, as did men paired with anxious women.

Studies of romantic attachment soon were extended to marital relationships. Senchak and Leonard (1992) defined attachment at the couple level, reporting that couples with two secure partners had more intimate and satisfying marriages than did insecure and "mixed" couples. Such couple-level measures, however, say little about the role of each partner in dyadic functioning. Kobak and Hazan (1991) found that marital satisfaction was related to both the security and "accuracy" of working models (i.e., the agreement between one person's self-description and the spouse's description of that person).

More recent studies have extended these findings in important ways. Feeney, Noller, and Callan (1994) studied young married couples over a 9-month period. Concurrent analyses linked secure attachment (comfort with closeness, low anxiety over relationships) to marital satisfaction. Analyses over time were significant only for husbands; insecurity predicted later dissatisfaction, but dissatisfaction also predicted later insecurity (suggesting a revision of working models). Another study linked secure attachment to marital satisfaction across all stages of the marital life cycle (Feeney, 1994). This study also showed interactive effects of partners' attachment styles; in younger couples, the negative effect of wives' relationship anxiety was particularly marked when husbands were low in comfort. This finding is not surprising given that the needs of wives who are highly anxious and dependent are unlikely to be met by husbands who are uncomfortable with intimacy.

### Relationship Stability

Hazan and Shaver (1987) noted that secure individuals reported the most enduring relationships. Prospective studies of romantic attachment, however, have yielded more complex results. In a 10-week study of dating individuals, avoidant attachment at Time 1 predicted relationship breakup (Feeney & Noller, 1992). However, in a 3-year study that controlled for commitment and prior duration, the relationships of avoidant men and of anxious women were quite stable over time (Kirkpatrick & Davis, 1994); however, as already noted, these relationships were rated

negatively, showing the importance of the distinction between relationship quality and relationship stability.

Kirkpatrick and Hazan's (1994) 4-year follow-up of Hazan and Shaver's (1987) sample showed complex links between attachment and relationship outcomes. Attachment style at Time 1 was meaningfully related to later relationship status (e.g., secure persons were the most likely to be married). However, this prediction stemmed mainly from the relative stability of attachment style and was not significant when Time 2 attachment style was statistically controlled. Furthermore, although secure persons reported few relationship breakups, they were no more likely than insecure persons to be with the same partners at each time point. This result reflected the tendency of some ambivalent persons (28%) to have broken up with their partners but then reunited. Hence, the cross-sectional finding that the relationships of ambivalent persons are short-lived tells an incomplete story; rather, they tend to be "on again/off again."

### Summary of Outcome Research

Before leaving this topic, it is important to note that the link between secure attachment and relationship outcomes cannot be explained in terms of personality differences. Shaver and Brennan (1992) found that attachment measures showed only modest relations with personality variables. Furthermore, attachment measures were more predictive of relationship outcomes (relationship status, satisfaction, and commitment) than were personality measures.

### ▶ Attachment and Relationship Processes

We now review research linking romantic attachment with relationship processes (caregiving and sexuality, communication, emotional experience and expression, and violence). This research is crucial, having the potential to explain the mechanisms by which attachment characteristics influence the quality and stability of relationships.

### Caregiving and Sexuality

As noted earlier, Shaver and Hazan (1988) conceptualized romantic love as the integration of attachment, caregiving, and sexual behavior. This model of love has received some support from empirical studies.

In terms of caregiving, Kunce and Shaver (1994) developed self-report scales to assess caregiving style in romantic dyads. These scales (proximity, sensitivity, cooperation, and compulsive caregiving) differentiated attachment groups in a student sample in ways consistent with attachment theory. For example, secure and dismissing participants reported less compulsive caregiving than did preoccupied and fearful participants, and secure participants also reported high sensitivity. In a broad sample of married couples who completed these scales, secure attachment was negatively related to compulsive care and positively related to responsive care (a composite of proximity, sensitivity, and cooperation) (Feeney, 1996). Marital satisfaction was predicted by secure attachment and partner's responsive care. Similarly, in a study of dating and married couples, own security of attachment was related to more beneficial caring for partner, and satisfaction was predicted by own attachment and partner's attachment and caregiving styles (Carnelley, Pietromonaco, & Jaffe, 1996).

With regard to sexuality, in student samples, avoidant individuals report the most unrestricted sexuality (involving nonintimate casual sex) (Brennan & Shaver, 1995; Feeney, Noller, & Patty, 1993). Feeney et al. (1993) also found that anxious-ambivalent males and avoidant females were the least likely to report having sexual intercourse during a 6-week diary study. In a somewhat older sample, Hazan et al. (1994) found consistent links between sexual styles and attachment styles.

Secure persons reported more mutually initiated sex and less sex outside of their primary relationships. Avoidant persons reported more nonintimate sex. Anxious-ambivalent persons reported greater enjoyment of holding than of explicitly sexual behaviors, and anxious-ambivalent males were more sexually reticent than their female counterparts (cf. Feeney et al., 1993). A recent longitudinal study of young adults also linked attachment to a complex of attitudes and behaviors relevant to safer sex (Feeney, Kelly, Gallois, Peterson, & Terry, in press; Feeney, Peterson, Gallois, & Terry, 1998). Anxiety over relationships consistently predicted unsafe sex. However, comfort with closeness (a dimension of *security*) also showed some relations in the direction of unsafe sex, possibly stemming from lowered perceptions of risk.

To date, there has been little research investigating relations among all three components of the proposed model of love: attachment, caregiving, and sexuality. Such research currently is being undertaken, with preliminary results suggesting that the model is useful for understanding couple relationships, particularly at important transition points (Feeney, Ward, Noller, & Hohaus, 1998).

### Communication

Working models of attachment form as the result of actual communications between caregiver and child, and communication serves as the vehicle by which attachment relationships are negotiated from day to day (Kobak & Duemmler, 1994). Hence, individual differences in attachment patterns should be evident in communication with romantic partners. This assertion has been tested widely, especially with regard to self-disclosure and conflict resolution.

In studying the link between attachment and self-disclosure, researchers have used self-report, diary, and observational methods, and they have explored several aspects of disclosing behavior (Feeney, Noller, & Callan, 1994; Keelan, Dion, & Dion, 1998;

**TABLE 14.3** Summary of Research Findings Linking Attachment Style With Self-Disclosure

| Variable | Secure | Avoidant | Anxious-Ambivalent |
|---|---|---|---|
| General level of disclosure (self-report and observed) | High | Low | High |
| Flexibility of disclosure across situations | High | Low | Low |
| Topical reciprocity (to confederate) | High | Low | Low |
| Self-disclosure in marriage (diary-based reports) | High | Low (especially husbands) | High |
| Intimacy of disclosure (partner vs. stranger as target) | More to partner | No target effect | No target effect |
| Personal disclosure (partner vs. stranger as target) | More to partner | No target effect | No target effect |
| Comfort in disclosing (partner vs. stranger as target) | More to partner | No target effect | No target effect |
| Reported ability to elicit disclosure ("opener") | High | Low | High |

Mikulincer & Nachshon, 1991). The overall finding to emerge from these studies is that secure individuals tend to engage in more appropriate and flexible patterns of self-disclosure. Table 14.3 presents a summary of the findings, with a three-group model being used here to integrate results across diverse measures of attachment.

Studies of romantic attachment also have focused on conflict resolution and problem solving (Feeney, 1994; Feeney, Noller, & Callan, 1994; Kobak & Hazan, 1991; Pistole, 1989). Note that this issue was raised earlier in this chapter with regard to stressful events (Feeney, 1998; Simpson et al., 1996). Again, given the range of conflict variables and attachment measures, this research is best summarized in tabular form. Table 14.4 shows the destructive conflict behaviors that are associated with insecure attachment, especially anxious-ambivalent attachment. In conflict situations, negative working models seem to guide behavior in ways that tend to exacerbate conflict and alienate partners (the very outcome that is feared by those who are anxious about their relationships). As would be expected, responses to conflict are affected by the attachment styles of both partners. It also is

important to note that insecure attachment (relationship anxiety) predicts involvement in negative conflict patterns both longitudinally and concurrently (Feeney, Noller, & Callan, 1994).

Given these results and the interest in *how* attachment influences relationship outcomes, it is not surprising that researchers have proposed communication patterns as the underlying mechanism. In other words, the high relationship quality experienced by secure persons might reflect their more effective communication. In their longitudinal study of young married couples, Feeney, Noller, and Callan (1994) found little support for this mediational model; instead, attachment and communication exerted independent effects on marital satisfaction. However, using a broader sample of couples, Feeney (1994) found that the relation between attachment security and satisfaction was mediated by conflict patterns for wives and was partially mediated by conflict patterns for husbands. Finally, studying dating couples, Keelan et al. (1998) reported that the link between attachment and satisfaction was mediated by facilitative disclosure (a composite measure of self-disclosure and the ability to elicit disclosure from others).

**TABLE 14.4**  Summary of Research Findings Linking Attachment Style With Responses to Conflict

| Variable | Secure | Avoidant | Anxious-Ambivalent |
|---|---|---|---|
| Style of problem solving and conflict resolution | Integrating (problem solving); compromise; support and validation | Rejection; less support; less obliging (soothing) | Domination; obliging (soothing); less compromise |
| Marital conflict patterns | Mutual expression and negotiation | Lack of mutual discussion and understanding | Coercion; demand-withdraw; postconflict distress |
| Quality of daily marital interactions (diary-based reports) | High involvement, recognition, and satisfaction (especially husbands) | Low involvement, recognition, and satisfaction (especially husbands) | High levels of conflict and domination (especially wives) |
| Responses to major relationship stress | Constructive patterns of conversation; nonverbal expression of warmth | Low warmth; low supportiveness | Hostility; distress; coercion; few attempts to defuse conflict |

### Emotional Experience and Expression

As noted earlier, differences in attachment style are thought to reflect experiences of regulating emotion. Consistent with this claim, secure attachment has been related to more positive emotion and less negative emotion in terms of general experiences in dating relationships (Simpson, 1990) and problem solving in marriage (Fuller & Fincham, 1995). Emotional responses to relationship loss also differentiate attachment styles. Avoidant persons, for example, report little distress over the dissolution of dating relationships (Feeney & Noller, 1992; Simpson, 1990) but have major problems in adapting to divorce (Mikulincer & Florian, 1998).

Recent research has explored the link between attachment and emotion in greater depth. Some studies have relied on individual-level analyses, exploring the processing of emotional memories and responses to emotion-eliciting events (Mikulincer, 1998; Mikulincer & Orbach, 1995). Others have focused on more specific questions such as why dismissing persons report low distress in affect-laden situations (e.g., Do they conceal their distress, or are they genuinely unaffected?). A series of studies reported by Fraley, Davis, and Shaver (1988) have suggested that dismissing adults generally are able to block their emotional responses during stressful situations but show considerable arousal when made to focus on disturbing thoughts. Hence, it is likely that if they are highly invested in others, then separation or loss will cause substantial distress.

Research also has examined the experience and expression of specific emotions within dyads. In a study of dating couples, insecure attachment (low comfort with closeness, high relationship anxiety) was related to reports of more frequent experience of anger, sadness, and anxiety (Feeney, 1995). Insecurity also was linked to the tendency to control ("bottle up" or not express) these emotions, even when the frequency of emotional experience was partialed out. A study of married couples extended this research to positive emotions (Feeney, 1999). Again, attachment was linked to both the experience and control of emotion. For example, spouses high in relationship anxiety tended not to express love, and husbands low in comfort tended not to express love, happiness, or pride. These patterns are likely to have crucial implications for relationship maintenance. In fact, both of these studies provided evidence that emotional control might mediate the effect of husbands' comfort with closeness on relationship satis-

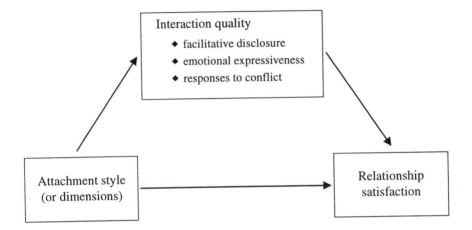

**Figure 14.1.** Effects of Attachment Characteristics on Relationship Functioning

faction (Feeney, 1999; Feeney, Noller, & Roberts, 1998).

### Violence

The association between attachment and couple violence is indirectly supported by research linking insecurity with the frequency and intensity of negative emotion and with destructive responses to conflict. This issue also has been examined directly. Holtzworth-Munroe, Stuart, and Hutchinson (1997) related attachment insecurity (defined by various measures) to reports of couple violence. Similarly, Bartholomew (1997) reported high levels of preoccupation and fearful-avoidance among men being treated for battering their female partners.

In a comprehensive study of attachment and violence in community and student samples, Roberts and Noller (1998) linked anxiety over relationships to reports of couple violence. This result parallels Bartholomew's (1997) findings. Furthermore, this association was mediated by communication patterns and could not be explained in terms of relationship satisfaction. Roberts and Noller (1998) also showed interactive effects of the violent person's anxiety over relationships and the partner's discomfort with closeness, suggesting

that violence might be precipitated by conflicts over issues of closeness and distance. Longitudinal studies are needed, however, to disentangle causal relations between attachment style and couple violence.

### Summary of Process Research

Important methodological advances have been made in studying romantic attachment including the use of partner reports (Kobak & Hazan, 1991), diary reports (Feeney, Noller, & Callan, 1994), and observations (Simpson et al., 1996). Most findings have been robust across gender, although there is evidence of the importance of men's comfort with closeness and women's anxiety over relationships. Recent tests of mediational models help to explain the effects of attachment characteristics on relationship functioning, as shown in Figure 14.1.

## ► Attachment and Parenting

Although we cannot address this issue in detail, it is fitting that we finish our review of research findings by noting that individual differences in romantic attachment have implications for parenting and, hence, for off-spring's security. Intergenerational transmission of attachment already has been supported by studies using the AAI (van IJzendoorn & Bakermans-Kranenburg, 1997).

In terms of romantic attachment, recent studies have linked attachment security to more positive attitudes to parenting. That is, among young adult samples, more secure individuals report greater desire to have children, greater confidence in their ability to relate well to young children, less endorsement of harsh disciplinary practices, and less tendency to be easily aggravated by children (Rholes, Simpson, & Blakely, 1995; Rholes, Simpson, Blakely, Lanigan, & Allen, 1997). Studies of mothers of infants and young children also have linked secure attachment to more positive appraisals of the task of being a mother, reports of more problem-focused strategies in coping with parenthood tasks, and more supportive parenting behavior in a laboratory teaching task (Mikulincer & Florian, 1998; Rholes et al., 1995).

## ▶ Practical Applications

Research into romantic attachment has important applications. At the individual level, attachment style has implications for the way in which people cope with stressful events. For example, with regard to pain and illness,

anxious-ambivalence is associated with high levels of symptom reporting and avoidance is associated with a reluctance to seek health care. These findings clearly are relevant to those seeking to understand patterns of health care use. Insecure attachment also has been linked to various types of psychopathology in college samples (Shaver & Brennan, 1992) and in a large representative sample of American adults (Mickelson, Kessler, & Shaver, 1997).

However, the major implications of attachment style are for couple and family relationships. Hence, an understanding of attachment-related issues is important for those working in marital and family therapy. Specific issues that attachment principles can address include issues of attraction and compatibility as well as relationship conflict (both the causes of conflict and responses to it). In addressing these issues, it is important to consider the combination of attachment styles represented in a dyadic relationship. Another implication of attachment theory is that even when attachment insecurity causes major relationship problems, it might be possible to revise working models and, hence, to overcome self-defeating patterns of thought and behavior. Types of therapy that are best suited to this purpose are discussed by Sperling and Lyons (1994). These therapeutic approaches might allow people to break the intergenerational chain of relationship problems.

# Contents

# Romantic Love

*Susan S. Hendrick*
*Clyde Hendrick*

The study of romantic love has become a legitimate area of scientific inquiry only during the past generation. Just because love now is studied scientifically, it does not follow that there is agreement on either the definition of love or the relations of love to other interpersonal constructs such as intimacy, trust, and commitment. Kovecses (1991) performed a linguistic analysis of love terms used in everyday life. He discovered, perhaps not surprisingly, that people use many metaphors to describe love, forming an implicit commonsense theory of love. Powerful emotional feeling is one aspect of romantic love within the commonsense theory. Yet, most emotion theories do not consider love as a "basic" emotion, an oversight castigated by Shaver, Morgan, and Wu (1996). From a different perspective, another eminent scholar observed (only partly in jest) that if she faced execution by a firing squad, unless she gave the correct definition of romantic love, she would be forced to say, "It's about 90 percent sexual desire as yet not sated" (Berscheid, 1988, p. 373). Clearly, romantic love is linked to sexual desire, greatly adding to its complexity as a topic for research (see also Chapter 16 by Sprecher & Regan, this volume).

Commonsense psychology must be respected, but in the realm of love, it cannot be the ultimate arbiter. For example, until the modern era, romantic love was not a prerequisite for marriage (Singer, 1984). Today, people increasingly view romantic love as a necessary basis for entering marriage and as a basis for staying within a marriage (Simpson, Campbell, & Berscheid, 1986). So, even commonsense can "change its mind" about the meaning of romantic love and the links of love to other variables.

If conceptions of love change historically, then it would be unreasonable to expect one tidy scientific theory of love to have become predominant in only a quarter century. Indeed, there now are many theories of love, of which we present a sampling in this chapter. In addition to theories of love, we briefly consider the link between romantic love and sexuality, some cross-cultural and life span aspects of love, and a few of the practical implications of our current knowledge of love.

## ▶ Theoretical Approaches to Romantic Love

We discuss a sample of the current popular approaches to romantic love. Because another chapter is devoted to attachment, we omit coverage of that approach. We begin with the classic theoretical distinction between passionate and compassionate love.

### *Passionate and Companionate Love*

Berscheid and Walster's (1969) tentative coverage of love in their classic book on attraction was expanded to two chapters in their second edition of *Interpersonal Attraction* (Berscheid & Walster, 1978). One chapter was devoted to romantic or passionate love, a state of intense passionate absorption of two lovers with each other in which emotion is primary and there is likely to be both anguish and ecstacy in the relationship. By contrast, the chapter on companionate love defined it simply as the affection felt for each other by two people whose lives are deeply intertwined. There is the implication that love relationships begin in the heat of passionate love, but because they are based on strong emotion that cannot endure, over time passion cools into the quiet glow of companionate love.

This theme is developed even more fully by Walster and Walster (1978), who devoted an entire book to comparing and contrasting passionate and companionate love. They noted that most passionate love affairs end in termination of the affairs. But if one is lucky, a passionate relationship can ripen into companionate love. A couple who began as passionate lovers can evolve into good friends.

"Although passionate love loses its fight against time, companionate love does not" (Walster & Walster, 1978, p. 126).

Stripped of its complexities, this approach may be dubbed the "either/or theory of love." One can be in either a state of passionate love or a state of companionate love, but not in both states at the same time. But is that really true? Is the old adage, "You can't like the one you love," an accurate description of the reality of romantic love? Perhaps one can both like and love a romantic partner—for the long term. Perhaps passion does not have to die, and perhaps companionship is important from the beginning of a romantic relationship.

More recent theorizing tends toward a "both/and" rather than an "either/or" approach to passionate and companionate love. Hatfield (1988) noted that people "are *capable* of passionate/companionate love and are likely to experience such feelings intermittently throughout their lives" (p. 193, emphasis in original). Although the two types of love still are viewed as different, the difference is "one of emphasis rather than absolute differences" (p. 207). Furthermore, most people "hope to combine the delights of passionate love with the security of companionate love in their intimate relationships—and this, of course, takes some doing" (p. 207). Hatfield viewed the successful combination of passionate and companionate love as requiring good training in intimacy skills.

Other research has found that romance and friendship often are combined. Hendrick and Hendrick (1993), using both written accounts and ratings, found that friendship-type love was the most frequently mentioned account theme. Furthermore, written accounts were consistent with the results of rating scales. In one of the studies reported, nearly half of the college students named their romantic partners as their closest friends. Both friendship and passion were important in these young adults' romantic relationships. A study by Sprecher and Regan (1998) found comparable results. Both passionate and companionate love were related to relationship satisfaction and commitment. In fact, satisfaction was linked more strongly to companionate love than to passionate love. In an interesting conceptual article, Noller (1996) explored the question of what type of love supports marriage and family. One conclusion was that "this combination of passionate and companionate love is likely to be related to the love that supports marriage and family" (p. 101).

Later in this chapter, we present evidence indicating that passion continues to play a role in long-term relationships including marriage. Both passion and friendship appear to be necessary for the maintenance of enduring romantic relationships.

### Prototype Approach to Love

What is love? A lot of ink has been spilled over this question. An agreed-on definition of love has proved elusive for both laypeople and love theorists. The prototype approach to love is one possible sensible solution to the dilemma. Prototype theory in cognitive psychology denies the value of the classical approach to defining a concept in terms of its necessary and sufficient conditions. Instead, a concept is defined in terms of its "best example" or its "best set of features," which is referred to as the prototype of the concept.

Beverly Fehr has explored the prototype approach to love very extensively (Fehr, 1988, 1993, 1994; see also Fehr & Russell, 1991). Fehr (1988) found that in a free listing of 68 features of love (and centrality ratings of those features), the prototype of love included passionate and companionate features as well as other components. However, the companionate features clearly were the most important ones. This initial work basically found that the prototype of love in general equals companionate love. These results were confirmed by Fehr and Russell (1991), who had research participants rate the prototypicality of 20 types of love. Maternal love, parental love, and friendship were the three most

prototypical examples. Romantic love was ranked fifth, but passionate love and sexual love were ranked quite low on the list. Analyses from several studies revealed that the prototypical features of love consistently found were trust, caring, honesty, friendship, and respect (Fehr, 1993).

So, what happened to "good old-fashioned lust," yearning, wanting, and the like? These features still were there in the data, but they existed as a subdued part of the prototype of love. As Fehr (1993) suggested, people do make a basic distinction between passionate and companionate love. Passionate love is specialized, whereas companionate love is more general, covering more types of love relationships.

Most prototype research has focused on love in general. Regan, Kocan, and Whitlock (1998) conducted a prototype analysis of romantic love. One group of people listed features of romantic love, and a second group rated centrality of the features. Results showed that when the focus was explicitly on romantic love, sexual attractiveness and passion were included on the list of central features. However, they were ranked well below trust, honesty, happiness, and other companionate features. The puzzle was clarified somewhat by Aron and Westbay (1996), who factored the 68 features originally used by Fehr. Aron and Westbay identified three underlying dimensions: passion, intimacy, and commitment. (These three dimensions were identified by Sternberg, 1986, as central to his theory of love, an approach considered later in the chapter.) Features on the intimacy factor were rated as significantly more central to the meaning of love than were features on the passion and commitment factors. As Aron and Westbay (1996, p. 537) noted, their results were consistent with the various results obtained by Fehr.

The results of this research tradition suggest that the most general conception of love is companionate love. This concept applies to more types of love relationships, and if one is lucky, it also applies to one's passionate love relationship. Thus, at its best, romantic love appears to be best described by this tradition as companionate love plus passion.

## Romantic Love as Self-Expansion

Aron and Aron (1986) proposed a theory, based on Eastern traditions, that assumes that all love is in some sense directed toward the self. "The idea is that the self expands toward knowing or becoming that which includes everything and everyone, the Self. The steps along the way are ones of including one person or thing, then another, then still another" (Aron & Aron, 1996, pp. 45-46).

Within this general framework, romantic love stems from two key components of the self-expansion model: basic motivation for self-expansion and the idea that a close relationship is the inclusion of the other within oneself (and, reciprocally, oneself within the other). Self-expansion motivation may be viewed as a basic drive and may include physical possessions as well as interpersonal power and influence. Falling in love provides a sense of very rapid expansion of the boundaries of self and is, therefore, a very pleasurable state of being. Including the other within the self is a facet or aspect of the particular process of self-expansion that is love. The process can be egocentric in the sense of acquiring and using the other person. However, there usually is a mutual incorporation of selves so that what is "you" becomes not just "me" but also "us."

Self-expansion may be viewed as a theory of being, a metaphysical theory about Self (with an Eastern capital S). However, as a scientific theory, it must be viewed metaphorically, a position that Aron and Aron (1996) have assumed. Viewed explicitly as a set of metaphors, this approach has great heuristic value and has generated many studies. With this approach, "The model increasingly becomes an overarching conceptual framework, much like evolutionary psychology or reward theory, encompassing a variety of relatively precise mini-theories" (p. 56).

## Romantic Love and Evolution

As Aron and Aron (1996) implied in the closing quotation in the previous subsection, evolutionary psychology has been a major development during the past decade, deriving from sociobiology and general evolutionary theory. David Buss has proposed evolutionary psychology as a new meta-theory for the psychological sciences (Buss, 1995, 1996; Buss & Kenrick, 1998). An edited volume has generalized this approach to various areas of social psychology (Simpson & Kenrick, 1997).

With respect to romantic love, the evolutionary approach is of considerable interest. We begin by noting that people often are homocentric about love, implicitly assuming that love is a distinctively human phenomenon. We are indebted to Harlow (1974) for showing that the need for love and affection exists strongly in monkeys and other primates, that such love is based on both learned and unlearned behaviors, and that learning to love during infancy typically flows in a continuous developmental line toward heterosexual relations in adulthood. Although they might not talk about love, nonhuman primates, and perhaps all mammalian species, experience a mix of emotional expressions and attachment behaviors that could be called love.

The idea that love is a trans-species phenomenon is of considerable interest to evolutionary theorists. Mellen (1981) devoted an entire book to the "evolution of love." Mellen assumed that humans evolved as hunters and gatherers, with some gender specialization also evolving because of the extreme helplessness of human infants. Survival required a high degree of infant nurturance and protection against predators. An emotional bond between breeding pairs of males and females might have enhanced offspring survival at least slightly. The link of primitive emotional bonding to differential survival rates was the beginning of the evolution of love, according to Mellen.

The evolutionary approach to love construes love as a complex set of behaviors and relations within a group, not solely a set of emotional feelings. For example, Buss (1988) defined love as a natural category of acts, represented by an evolved set of psychological mechanisms that function to perpetuate the species. If love acts are an evolutionary adaptation, then specific goal behaviors should be observed in courtship and mating. According to Buss, this sequence of goals is as follows: resource displays by males and females, relative relationship exclusivity, commitment/ marriage, sexual relations, reproduction, resource sharing, and parental investment. This sequence of "love acts" encapsulates the evolutionary task of reproduction and, hence, perpetuation of the species.

Because of initial gender specialization for childbearing, gender differences in courtship and mating might well have evolved as well. This possibility was formalized by Trivers (1972) in what is known as the differential parental investment model. Much research has been devoted to study of gender differences in reproduction strategies. Kenrick (1987) stated that such differences might be the general rule among mammals. For example, among humans, females prefer somewhat older males who show evidence of material security, whereas males prefer younger females who show evidence of fertility. Furthermore, as males age, they increasingly prefer younger females (Kenrick & Trost, 1989).

In our own research, we have found many gender differences in love and sex attitudes. Some of these differences are easily given an evolutionary interpretation. For example, Hendrick and Hendrick (1991) factor analyzed a large number of relationship scales, primarily love scales. Of the five factors that emerged, two were prominent and were named *passion* and *closeness*. These two factors bore a striking resemblance to passionate and compassionate love, described earlier in the chapter. Furthermore, both passion and closeness (i.e., emotional intimacy) could easily be viewed as serving pair-bonding functions. Passion helps to drive males and females into reproduction, and closeness provides the contact for the survival of the relationship and the offspring produced from it.

Evolutionary psychology is fascinating, and it can be fun to engage in evolutionary speculation. As a grand meta-theory, we perhaps should remain skeptical to a degree. Some specialists in evolution even argue against the general approach. For example, Lewontin (1998) argued, "We know essentially nothing about the evolution of our cognitive capabilities, and there is a strong possibility that we will never know much about it" (p. 109). Evolutionary psychology relies on the notion of "psychological mechanisms" as the proximate cause mediating between evolutionary and environmental pressures and behavior. But as Hendrick (1995) noted, a psychological mechanism is not a physical structure; it is a hypothetical construct, one that is easily disposed toward circular reasoning. Nevertheless, the future is open. As the general approach is developed during the years ahead, evolutionary psychology could become the preferred theoretical explanation for romantic love.

### Triangular Theory of Love

Robert Sternberg, one of the more important theorists of love, has proposed several relevant theories. His early work (Sternberg & Grajek, 1984) gave important support to a multidimensional approach toward love, and in additional research, Sternberg and Barnes (1985) focused on "real" versus "ideal" aspects of love relations.

Sternberg (1986) later proposed his "triangular theory of love," which posits that love is composed of three different components: intimacy, passion, and commitment. The mix of these components in varying proportions creates eight different types of love: Non-love (all three components absent), Liking (intimacy only), Infatuated Love (passion only), Empty Love (commitment only), Romantic Love (intimacy and passion), Companionate Love (intimacy and commitment), Fatuous Love (passion and commitment), and Consummate Love (all three components present).

Sternberg linked his theory to other theories and discussed how the three primary love components might change over time within a relationship and between different relationships. Although measurement of these components has been problematic (Acker & Davis, 1992; for a discussion, see Noller, 1996), the theory is elegant in both its simplicity and its comprehensiveness.

## Love Stories

More recently, Sternberg has focused on the socially constructed nature of love. Beall and Sternberg (1995) presented four perspectives on the notion of love as a universal human phenomenon (an idea we discuss more fully in the subsection on cross-cultural research on love). They presented the possibilities of (a) love as universal and defined similarly across cultures, (b) love as universal and defined differently across cultures, (c) love as nonuniversal but defined similarly across cultures, and (d) love as nonuniversal and defined differently across cultures. They found the fourth alternative most viable, and offered an extensive historical review demonstrating how love has been conceptualized and experienced differently across eras and cultures. They proposed that, to understand love during any era, one needs "information about (a) the beloved, (b) the thoughts that accompany love, (c) the feelings that accompany love, and (d) the actions, or the relations between the lover and the beloved" (pp. 433-434).

It is a natural progression from the notion of love as socially constructed to the idea of love as personally constructed within a "story." Sternberg has more recently articulated his view of love as a story (Sternberg, 1995, 1996), most completely in his book, *Love Is a Story* (Sternberg, 1998). Here, he presented more than 25 love stories such as the "garden story" (a popular story) and the "horror story" (a not surprisingly less popular story). Addressing laypersons perhaps more directly than he would relationship scholars, Sternberg sought less to persuade than to edu-cate. If people understand their own love stories (and, indeed, they typically have a hierarchy of stories with one predominating) or what might be called "guiding metaphors," then they can anticipate some of the plot twists and character manifestations likely to occur, according to Sternberg. Such anticipations give their stories (and, by implication, their lives) somewhat more predictability. Such understanding also might allow them to end destructive stories and to begin happier ones.

## Love Ways

Whereas our own work has been concerned with "styles" of love, other scholars have been occupied with the "ways" in which people communicate love to each other. Marston, Hecht, and Robers (1987) explored lovers' subjective experience of love. They sought to understand both the experiencing and communicating of love, noting that "communication is the fundamental action which both expresses and determines the subjective experience of romantic love" (p. 392). Marston et al. employed qualitative analyses of interview data to determine categories representing both communication *to* one's partner and communication *from* one's partner. The most common "communication strategies toward a partner included (a) telling the partner 'I love you'; (b) doing things for the partner; (c) being understanding and supportive; (d) touching; and (e) just being together" (Marston et al., 1987, cited in Taraban, Hendrick, & Hendrick, 1998, p. 343). "The most commonly mentioned communication strategies from the partner to the self were hearing 'I love you' from partner, touching, supportiveness, partner doing things for self, togetherness, communicating emotion, and eye contact" (p. 343).

Marston et al. (1987) then developed a typology of the experience and communication of love ("love ways"). Their typology included active love, collaborative love, committed love, intuitive love, secure love, and traditional romantic love, each with somewhat different communicational pathways (e.g., discussion of emotions in active love vs. non-verbal communicating of love in intuitive love). Although this research was interesting in a number of ways, perhaps its most significant contribution was the recognition of love as multifaceted as well as subjective and, to some degree, unique within each person's experience. In additional research, Hecht, Marston, and Larkey (1994) attempted to measure the love ways through items designed to represent the different loves (e.g., active, intuitive). Through factor analyses, they found five love factors: committed love, intuitive love, secure love, traditional romantic love, and companionate love (a combination of elements of active and collaborative love).

More recently, Marston, Hecht, Manke, McDaniel, and Reeder (1998) explored participants' subjective experiences of intimacy, passion, and commitment, the three constructs forming Sternberg's triangular theory of love (Sternberg, 1986). Detailed, semistructured, relational interviews and both qualitative and quantitative analyses of the data (from nearly 80 heterosexual romantic couples) yielded factors for both the definition and communication aspects of intimacy, passion, and commitment. The factors were largely orthogonal, but similar "ways" or "dimensions" occasionally occurred across different constructs. For example, "sex" was a factor representing a way of experiencing intimacy, whereas "sexual intimacy" was a factor representing a way of experiencing passion. However, Marston et al. (1998) concluded, "Sex as a way of experiencing intimacy, for example, may be very different from sex as a way of experiencing passion" (p. 25). Although the authors found many previously researched aspects of intimacy, passion, and commitment replicated in their own work and also provided a number of new aspects through their methodological approach, they pointed out, "The factor structures reported here are not intended to be exhaustive. There may be other important ways of intimacy, passion, and commitment that were not uncovered in the present study"

(p. 27). Such recognition of the complexity of love and the inadequacy of any single research program or paradigm to fully "capture" love is very wise.

### *Love Styles*

Another theoretical approach to love was developed by Lee (1973) and pursued empirically by Hendrick and Hendrick (e.g., 1986). This love styles approach includes six "dominant" love styles: Eros (passionate love), Ludus (game-playing love), Storge (friendship love), Pragma (practical love), Mania (possessive/dependent love), and Agape (altruistic love). A scale based on Lee's work was developed by Lasswell and Lasswell and their colleagues (Hatkoff & Lasswell, 1979; Lasswell & Lasswell, 1976), and it was revised and adapted into the original Love Attitudes Scale (LAS) (Hendrick & Hendrick, 1986), which now includes both a relationship-specific form (Hendrick & Hendrick, 1990) and a short form (Hendrick, Hendrick, & Dicke, 1998).

The love styles have been examined in the context of gender, personality, ethnicity, and so on, and some consistent findings have emerged. Gender differences have occurred in most studies (e.g., Hendrick & Hendrick, 1986), with men describing themselves as more game playing and women describing themselves as more endorsing of friendship, practicality, and possessiveness in love. Most recently, however, subtle scale differences also have led to women being somewhat more endorsing of passionate love and men being somewhat more endorsing of altruistic love, with the findings for possessive love varying (sometimes men endorsing it more, sometimes women endorsing it more). To some extent, these findings mirror cultural patterns, with both social learning theories and evolutionary psychology perspectives offering plausible explanations for such differences (Hendrick & Hendrick, 1995).

One of the most consistent themes of love style research has been the exploration of partner similarity in various types of ongoing relationships. Beginning at the "beginning," Hahn and Blass (1997) hypothesized that participants would display homogamy (choosing mates who are similar), thus preferring stimulus persons similar to themselves in love styles. In addition, they sought to discover whether there are specific love styles "consensually desired" by most people. Indeed, for the most part, persons' own love styles were correlated with their preferences for stimulus persons with the same love styles, and the most generally appealing love styles were Agape and Storge. The least appealing was Ludus. Love research also has shown similarity between actual relationship partners on Eros, Storge, Mania, and Agape (Hendrick, Hendrick, & Adler, 1988) as well as on Eros, Storge, Agape, and Ludus (Davis & Latty-Mann, 1987). Morrow, Clark, and Brock (1995) extended this line of research beyond mere similarity (although partners in this study were largely similar on the love styles) to a study of love attitudes and relationship quality. Respondents' own love styles were related to a variety of relationship characteristics (e.g., rewards, costs), as were partners' love styles (although less strongly). Greater erotic and friendship love "were associated with higher levels of rewards, satisfaction, investment and commitment, lower levels of costs, and poor alternative quality" (p. 363). Game-playing love showed the opposite pattern. These authors concluded that love styles are highly relevant to aspects of relationship quality, although additional refinement of some love styles (specifically Storge and Pragma) might be warranted.

Certain love styles also seem to lend themselves to relationship satisfaction. Eros typically is a positive predictor, and Ludus typically is a negative one (Hendrick et al., 1988). Most recently, Meeks, Hendrick, and Hendrick (1998) found that both love styles and aspects of communication were important predictors of satisfaction for dating couples. Positive love (a combination of Eros, Storge, and Agape) was a potent positive predictor, whereas game-playing love was a negative

predictor. Participants' perceptions of their partners' abilities to take perspectives and the absence of negative conflict also were predictors of satisfaction.

Ultimately, considerable evidence has accumulated to indicate that the love styles are linked with many aspects of intimate relationships, not the least of which is relational satisfaction and quality. As for the stereotype of passionate love occurring at the beginning of a relationship and evolving into companionate love over time, we counter, "Passion and friendship/companionship are not consecutive in a romantic relationship but rather are concurrent. Both play a part in relationship initiation and development as well as in relationship maintenance" (Hendrick & Hendrick, 1993, p. 465).

## ▶ Romantic Love and Sexuality

Because sexuality in relationships is discussed fully elsewhere (see Chapter 16 by Sprecher & Regan, this volume), we present only briefly some of the apparent links between sexual behavior and love. Regan (1998b) pointed out that social scientists, often coming from the interpersonal attraction paradigm, have largely viewed love as "sexless," as though love without sex is the natural state of things. More recently, however, passionate/erotic love is seen as having a sexual component. As Regan noted, "My own research also provides evidence that romantic love is a qualitatively different experience from such other varieties of interpersonal attraction as loving and liking and that sexual desire in particular is one of its essential components" (pp. 102-103).

In relating love styles to sexual styles, Frey and Hojjat (1998) employed the six love styles (Hendrick & Hendrick, 1986; Lee, 1973) and the sexual styles of "role enactment" (a drama or play script), "sexual trance" (a sensual focus script), and "partner engagement" (an intimacy script) (Mosher, 1988). Frey and Hojjat (1998) found that all of the love styles were related to the sexual style of partner engagement (Eros, Storge, Pragma, Mania, and Agape positively related and Ludus negatively related), although not one of the love styles was correlated with either sexual trance or role enactment. Thus, an intimacy-oriented sexual script was related to several love perspectives.

Our own work on love and sex has found relationships between the love styles and the sexual attitudes represented in the Sexual Attitudes Scale (Hendrick & Hendrick, 1987). These attitudes include Permissiveness (casual sexuality), Sexual Practices (responsible sexuality), Communion (idealistic sexuality), and Instrumentality (biological sexuality). Factor analyses of the love and sex scales resulted in three factors. Factor 1 included game-playing love and casual and biological sexuality (with altruistic love loading negatively) and could be characterized as casual relating. Factor 2 included erotic, altruistic, and possessive/dependent love as well as idealistic sexuality and could be characterized as intimate relating. Factor 3 included practical and friendship love, with a modest positive loading for possessive love and a modest negative loading for casual sexuality, and could be characterized as stable relating. Thus, these three factors exhibited psychometric links between love and sex attitudes.

More recently, we assessed the six love attitudes and four sexual attitudes as well as other relationship variables in a large sample of women and men (Hendrick & Hendrick, 1995). Correlational analyses were conducted separately for men and women. Of 120 correlations between sexual attitudes and both love attitudes and love/relationship questions (e.g., the importance of romantic love), 72 correlations were significant. Again we see the many links between romantic love and sexuality.

Ultimately, when considering how sex and love are linked, words might be worth a thousand psychometric pictures. In a book of text, letters, and photographs, Pickett (1995) chronicled the story of her grandparents' lives and their marriage of more than 60 years. As Pickett was compiling the book, she queried her grandmother about her sexual relationship with Keri's recently deceased grandfather:

> After his death, I asked Grandma a personal question I wasn't sure she would answer. "How old were you when you and Grandpa stopped making love?" "We never stopped making it!" she said. "We made it up to the very end. I remember our honeymoon. He wanted to spare me, but I had waited thirty-two years and I wasn't going to let him keep it." Later, I told Grandma that my mother was uncomfortable having that story made public. Grandma thought about it and said, "Well, the book would need to have some sex in it or it wouldn't be natural." (p. 5)

## ► The Social Context of Romantic Love

### *Cross-Cultural Aspects of Romantic Love*

Earlier, we presented the perspective of evolutionary psychology, which highlights love's contribution to reproductive survival value as its greatest reason for being. However, other voices speak to love's social construction within, rather than across, cultures, countries, and historical periods (Beall & Sternberg, 1995). Indeed, Dion and Dion (1996) noted that love must be understood within a cultural context. One of their meta-perspectives for examining love was that of individualism (more emphasized in Western cultures) versus collectivism (more emphasized by Asian cultures), and they argued that it is within cultural-level variables such as individualism/collectivism that romantic love can be studied most usefully.

Yet, many scholars view love as transcending time and place, although neither love's evolutionary origins nor its cultural expressions may be addressed explicitly. For example, Lindholm (1998), an anthropologist, viewed love as a human response to the "existential condition of contingency and self-consciousness" (p. 26). Such a view implies the need for a conscious self as a precursor of romantic love (for a discussion, see Hendrick & Hendrick, 1992b). However, current explorations of ancient love themes indicate that love for another might have predated documented consciousness of a self. For example, Cho and Cross (1995) drew on Chinese literature dating from 500 to 3,000 years ago to posit that phenomena such as passionate love, devoted love, obsessive love, casual love, and free mate choice were known and experienced during those eras. To explore the current existence of these love styles, the authors assessed love attitudes of Taiwanese students living in the United States using the LAS (Hendrick & Hendrick, 1990). Factor analyses revealed six different love styles but not the usual six factors. Their factors reflected Taiwanese culture such that an Eros (passionate) and Agape (altruistic) combination became "Romantic and Considerate Love," whereas an Agape and Pragma (practical) combination became "Obligatory Love." Overall, however, there were many similarities between the Taiwanese students and American samples.

In a study comparing Hong Kong, Chinese, and British respondents on both love styles and the Chinese concept of *yuan* (predestined and fated love), Goodwin and Findlay (1997) discovered that, whereas the Chinese respondents more highly endorsed yuan as well as altruistic and pragmatic love styles, the British sample also agreed relatively highly with a number of the yuan items. Thus, it is interesting to consider that, for all our attempts to discover whether Western notions of passionate love can be found in Eastern cultures, there remains a fascinating question about whether Eastern notions of fatalism as well as duty and obligation also can be found in Western concepts of love.

Doherty, Hatfield, Thompson, and Choo (1994) directly compared European Americans, Japanese Americans, and Pacific Islanders (all residing in Hawaii) on various dimensions of love and relationships. The groups did not differ in either passionate or companionate love, and attachment was similarly related to love for all of the groups. Cultural similarities also were found by Sprecher et al. (1994), who explored American, Russian, and Japanese styles of love. Although the groups exhibited some differences—Americans more endorsing of a secure attachment style, Russians more willing to consider marrying without love, and Japanese less endorsing of romantic beliefs—"the young adults from the three countries were similar in many love attitudes and experiences" (p. 363). Strong cultural similarities, as well as some differences, also were found by Lamm and Wiesmann (1997) in their systematic exploration of liking, loving, and being in love among German respondents. For example, their finding that "arousal" was identified as a key element of being "in love" was seen as supportive of Berscheid and Meyers' (1996) argument that sexual desire and arousal differentiate "love" from being "in love."

Taking a somewhat different approach, Moore (1998) underscored an essential conservatism that is one differentiating aspect between China and the West. Relying on interviews and written narrative data, Moore documented the importance of love along with the importance of propriety, seriousness, and parental approval, and the author proposed that Chinese and American youths, for example, differ not so much in motives for relating as in the relative importance of those motives (consistent with Cho & Cross, 1995, and Goodwin & Findlay, 1997). Even arranged marriage (in Sri Lanka), something seemingly discrepant from romantic love, can be implemented in ways congruent with love (deMunck, 1998).

Research by Contreras, Hendrick, and Hendrick (1996) confirmed cross-cultural similarity of love orientations. In a study of Mexican American and Anglo couples, results indicated only modest love attitude (and sexual attitude) differences among the groups. However, the Anglo American group, the bicultural group, and the Hispanic-oriented group did not differ in passionate, friendship-oriented, or altruistic love, and the groups also were similar in relationship satisfaction. Other research has shown modest cultural differences in love attitudes. Murstein, Merighi, and Vyse (1991) found that French college students were more agapic on the LAS, whereas American students reported more manic and friendship love.

Overall, much of the current close relationship literature is consistent with the conclusions of Jankowiak and Fischer (1992) in their highly cited study of the Standard Cross-Cultural Sample. They concluded, "Romantic love is a near-universal" (p. 154), a stance also assumed by Hatfield and Rapson (1996), who tentatively concluded, "Throughout the modern world, people turn out to be surprisingly similar in the way they experience passionate love" (p. 88).

In considering current love research, it becomes clear that neither a strict evolutionary interpretation nor a strict, cultural social constructivist interpretation is most helpful. Rather, as Jankowiak (1995) observed, "Romantic passion is a complex multifaceted emotional phenomenon that is a byproduct of an interplay between biology, self, and society" (p. 4).

### Romantic Love Across the Life Span

Focusing only on love in the very young ignores love in a substantial segment of humanity, yet social scientists often have posed their questions regarding love to captive audiences of college students in Western societies. An exception has been the work of Grote and Frieze (1994), who explored the love predictors of marital satisfaction in a middle-aged married sample. Their results were consistent with those for other, younger couples in that passionate love and friendship-based love were positive predictors of marital satisfaction, whereas game-playing love was a negative predictor. More recently, Grote, Frieze, and Stone (1996) employed structural modeling to examine number of children at home, length of marriage, traditionalism in division of family work, and specific love orientations as these variables related to marital satisfaction. They employed a subset of the same

middle-aged married sample and found complex relationships that differed somewhat for wives and husbands. First, for both genders, the more children at home and the longer the marriage, the greater the likelihood of a traditional gender role division of family work. For women, "Traditionalism predicted lower levels of erotic and friendship-based love . . ., which ultimately were related to lower marital satisfaction. For men, however, traditionalism was associated with strong erotic and friendship-based love, a phenomenon linked to higher marital satisfaction" (p. 211). Not surprisingly, the "status quo" in family work led to different outcomes for husbands and wives.

Once again employing largely the same subset of the middle-aged married sample, Grote and Frieze (1998) queried respondents' recall of their love for their partners at the beginning of their relationships and their perceptions of their current love. Although (perhaps not surprisingly) erotic love was perceived as currently lower than it had been at the onset of the relationships, it still was "moderately strong" (p. 104). Friendship-based love was perceived to be at the same level currently as it had been at the beginning of the relationships. Finally, husbands (only) perceived that their altruistic love was higher currently than it had been at the onset of their love relationships. In addition, husbands reported greater altruistic love than did wives at both time points. It is interesting that these husbands who reported greater altruism or "giving" in their approach to love also were largely the same husbands who, in the earlier report (Grote et al., 1996), had reported greater marital satisfaction related to greater traditional (and presumably less egalitarian/fair) family work. It might be that altruistic love does not extend to housework.

Other scholars also have explored love across the life span. Montgomery and Sorell (1997) assessed love styles and other relationship variables in four groups: (a) young, never-married college-age adults; (b) childless married participants under 30 years of age; (c) married persons (24-50 years of age) with children at home; and (d) older married persons (50-70 years of age) with no children at home. Perhaps not surprisingly, the greatest number of differences were between the married and nonmarried groups. The findings for the love styles could be considered surprising or unsurprising, depending on one's beliefs regarding love and aging. In terms of major differences, the young unmarried group members reported greater manic love and greater game-playing love than did the other group members, and the young unmarried group members were less altruistic in their love styles. The most notable findings in many ways were those of "no differences." Passionate love, the love ascribed to youth rather than to age, did not differ across the groups. And friendship-oriented love, the love ascribed to age rather than to youth, also did not differ across the groups (consistent with findings by Grote & Frieze, 1998). As Montgomery and Sorell (1997) noted, "Individuals throughout the life-stages of marriage consistently endorse the love attitudes involving passion, romance, friendship, and self-giving love" (p. 61).

Such findings are consistent with our findings and those of our colleagues. In comparing the love attitudes of young college students and those of their parents, Inman-Amos, Hendrick, and Hendrick (1994) found virtually no love attitude similarity between parents and their own adult children. When comparing the older and younger generations, however, there was *no* generational difference for passionate love, and for friendship-oriented love, there was no generational difference for sons and only a modest one for daughters.

These findings also are consistent with the Contreras et al. (1996) findings discussed earlier, which were based on a married sample ranging in age from 20 to 60 years. Passionate love was the strongest consistent predictor of relationship satisfaction for all age groups (based on gender and ethnicity). It appears that reports of passionate love's demise over the course of the life span have been greatly exaggerated. Perhaps the best concluding

commentary to a discussion of love and age is provided in a biographical "monograph" written by an author about his aged and widowed father, Clyde, who rediscovered love with an equally aged, widowed woman, Gussie:

> "You're acting like a teenager," Gussie said. "What's wrong with that?" Clyde asked. She considered the question for a moment. "Nothing," she decided. "Why should teenagers have all the fun?" he asked. "We deserve it as much as they do. More. We've earned it." They kissed and hugged and touched again. (Latham, 1997, p. 84)

## ▶ Practical Applications

We have presented a wealth of creative theories and compelling findings about love but have said little about the applications of these theories and findings to practical matters such as therapists working with troubled relationships and the experiences of "ordinary" people living out their intimate relations. Although space considerations prevent an extended discussion, we give a couple of examples here.

Suppose that a young heterosexual couple goes to premarital counseling. During one session, the counselor tells the partners about Aron and Aron's (1996) self-expansion theory and the ways in which people seek to become *more* than they currently are through their relationships with intimate romantic partners. The counselor then proposes the following exercise: "Here is some paper for each of you. List five ways in which your partner enriches you and helps you to be more of the person you want to be. . . . Now take turns telling each other what you have written on your list." Insight into each other's thoughts about love might help the partners to understand their wants and needs in this relationship.

Finally, consider a professor teaching an undergraduate relationships class who discusses several love theories and then hands out two copies of the LAS (Hendrick et al., 1998). The professor asks each student to fill out the LAS for himself or herself and then for the student's current romantic partner. Students then compare their own responses to their partners' perceived responses on the love styles. The class discusses how differences and similarities on the various love styles could potentially lead to either positive or negative relationship outcomes. During the discussion, the class realizes how a particular similarity or difference in a love style could be either positive or negative for the relationship, depending on how it was interpreted and handled.

Based on this abbreviated discussion of possible applications of love theories, it is obvious to us that there are many wonderful and potentially useful love theories available. No single theory provides "everything to everyone," yet each theory offers "something to someone." Some scholars no doubt would prefer to subsume these various approaches within one overarching meta-theory, and if we were to do so at some point in time, the overarching constructs likely would be passionate and companionate love. At least for now, however, we prefer to see a thousand flowers bloom.

# Contents

# Sexuality in a Relational Context

*Susan Sprecher*
*Pamela C. Regan*

Every day, a certain proportion of the adolescent and adult population engages in, fantasizes about, or desires to have sexual activity with relational partners. Sex with close others (e.g., spouses, committed dating partners) differs from casual sex along a number of dimensions. In particular, relational sex often has meanings and purposes that extend far beyond the physical pleasure that occurs from the joining of two bodies. For example, relational partners might engage in sexual activity to express their feelings of love, intimacy, and emotional closeness; to reaffirm their commitment to the relationship and to each other; to shift the balance of interpersonal power in the relationship; or for one partner to make restitution for nonsexual services rendered by the other. Thus, sexual activity that occurs in the context of a close relationship has important nonsexual consequences for that relationship, and nonsexual aspects of the relationship in turn have an important impact on a couple's sex life.

In this chapter, we explore sexuality in a relational context. We define *sexuality* as those interpersonal behaviors that lead to physiological arousal and the increased likelihood of orgasm for one or both partners as well as associated phenomena such as sexual desire, sexual satisfaction, and sexual attitudes. We have organized the chapter into four major sections. The first examines the role of sexuality in the attraction process, with an emphasis on sexual desirability and sexual characteristics that predict interpersonal attraction. The second section focuses on sexuality and relationship development including the role of sex during courtship and sexual attitudes and behaviors at different stages of involvement. In the third section, we discuss sex in established relationships, covering issues such as sexual frequency and variety; sexual satisfaction; and the association between sexuality and communication, exchange, and general relationship satisfaction. The final section examines the link between sex and love, with an emphasis on the most sexual type of love, namely passionate love.

## ▶ Sexuality in the Attraction Process

Before we consider the role that sex plays in developed relationships, we examine the ways in which sexuality can influence the attraction and partner selection process.

### Sexual Desirability

The characteristics that determine a person's desirability as a sex partner are not necessarily the same as those that determine his or her desirability as a long-term mate. Nonetheless, sexual desirability, or "sex appeal," is a factor that men and women often consider when evaluating potential romantic partners (Regan, Levin, Sprecher, Christopher, & Cate, 1998).

Physical attributes appear to be particularly important components of sexual desirability. For example, men and women perceive physically attractive individuals as more sexually attractive (Suman, 1990) and as sexually warmer and more responsive (Feingold, 1992) than less physically attractive others. In addition, an attractive physical appearance is considered to be the single most important desire-causing quality a person can possess (Regan & Berscheid, 1995), and both sexes emphasize physical attractiveness when evaluating others for sexual relationships (Kenrick, Groth, Trost, & Sadalla, 1993; Regan, 1998c; Regan & Berscheid, 1997).

Other aspects of physical appearance, including body size and shape, also influence sex appeal. Research indicates that obese men and women are not perceived to be as sexually attractive (or as capable of experiencing sex-

ual desire) as are normal-weight individuals (Regan, 1996). Similarly, men view the "hourglass" shape of normal-weight female figures with low waist-to-hip ratios (an index of body fat distribution) as "sexier" than the shape of women with higher waist-to-hip ratios (Singh, 1993). Conversely, women assign higher sexual desirability ratings to normal-weight men with typically masculine (as opposed to feminine) waist-to-hip ratios (Singh, 1995).

A consideration of several theoretical perspectives might explain why physical appearance is so potent a determinant of sexual desirability. For example, evolutionary theorists (e.g., Gangestad, 1993) argue that physical and genetic fitness can be of primary importance when evaluating potential sex partners. They suggest that both men and women might be expected to prefer healthy individuals who are capable of reproduction and who will pass on "good" genetic material to any resulting offspring. Insofar as physical appearance is presumed to indicate underlying genetic fitness and health (Gangestad, 1993), appearance thus becomes a particularly important aspect of sexual desirability. Social context perspectives rely on different causal mechanisms but make similar predictions. For example, social and cultural scripts (Reiss, 1986), as well as the patterns of reinforcement and punishment that people receive for their sexual behavior (Hogben & Byrne, 1998), might teach men and women that sexual desire is appropriately experienced for and directed toward individuals who are physically attractive.

### Sexual Characteristics as Predictors of Attraction

Characteristics specifically related to sexuality, including an individual's sexual history or experience and his or her sex drive, also can be important determinants of attraction. For example, people might seek as dating or marital partners those individuals with relatively little sexual experience, whereas they might prefer highly experienced partners for casual encounters. Interestingly, sexual characteristics have not received as much scrutiny as have other attributes (e.g., personality variables) in mate selection research. For example, only one study to date specifically has examined men's and women's preferences with respect to potential partners' sex drives. Regan, Levin, et al. (1998) found that women (but not men) desired that potential short-term sex partners demonstrate significantly higher levels of sexual passion and sex drive than do long-term romantic partners.

Although not as important as other factors, an individual's sexual history (e.g., past or present sexual behavior, level of sexual experience) also can influence his or her desirability as a dating and/or marriage partner. In general, research indicates that low to moderate levels of current or past sexual activity and the restriction of sexual activity to committed relationships are more likely to increase one's desirability as a partner than is a history of many sexual partners or casual sexual activity (Bettor, Hendrick, & Hendrick, 1995; Sprecher, McKinney, & Orbuch, 1991). For example, Sprecher, Regan, McKinney, Maxwell, and Wazienski (1997) found that men and women preferred sexual inexperience (i.e., chastity) more than sexual experience when considering potential dating or marriage partners. In addition, participants desired moderate sexual experience more than extensive sexual experience.

Certain sexual characteristics might be differentially important to each sex. Some researchers report, for example, that men attach greater importance to potential spouses' chastity than do women (Buss, 1989). Others, however, find no sex difference in preferences for sexual (in)experience (Hoyt & Hudson, 1981; Sprecher et al., 1997). Similarly, although both sexes view promiscuity as undesirable in dating or marital partners, women appear to judge this and related attributes (e.g., sexual availability or "easiness") more negatively than do men when considering short-term sex partners (Buss & Schmitt, 1993; Regan & Berscheid, 1997).

## ▶ Sexuality and Stages of Relationship Development

In a landmark survey study of thousands of Americans during the period 1930 to 1940, Kinsey and his colleagues found that 73% of women who were born before 1900 did not have sex until they married (Kinsey, Pomeroy, Martin, & Gephard, 1953). Today, however, the majority of women and men in the United States and in most other countries have sex prior to marriage, some only with the persons they intend to marry but many with multiple dating partners (for recent data on U.S. patterns, see Laumann, Gagnon, Michael, & Michaels, 1994). As a result, the initiation of sex no longer is confined to a single "honeymoon" period beginning the night of the marital ceremony; rather, it has become associated with particular stages of relationship development. Although there are various ways in which to conceptualize relationship development, one of the most common is as a "dating continuum" (e.g., Adams, 1986) consisting of a succession of increasingly committed stages (e.g., "casually dating," to "seriously dating," to "engagement").

Research indicates that premarital sexual permissiveness, or the expressed acceptability of sexual behavior in a premarital relationship, is associated with the relationship stage. In general, people are most accepting of sexual activity when the relationship is described as seriously dating or engaged, and they are least accepting when the relationship is described as having little or no affection or at a very early stage of development (e.g., first date) (Reiss, 1964; Sprecher, 1989). Individuals who believe that sexual activity should not occur prior to the committed/affectional stage of relationship development are said to have a relational orientation (DeLamater, 1989) or to endorse the "permissiveness with affection" sexual standard (Reiss, 1967). Individuals who view sex as acceptable very early in the relationship under conditions of pleasure and desire are referred to as having a recreational orientation and/or as endorsing the "permissiveness without affection" standard. Research indicates that men are more likely than women to adopt a recreational orientation to sexuality (Oliver & Hyde, 1993; Sprecher, 1989).

Although attitudes do not always coincide with actual behaviors, sexual activity is in fact more likely to occur at later stages of relationship development than very early in the relationship (Christopher & Cate, 1985; Peplau, Rubin, & Hill, 1977). In addition, not only do men hold more permissive attitudes about sexuality in dating relationships, but men also are more likely to engage in (or at least report) permissive behaviors including having more than one sexual relationship at a time and having casual sex (Laumann et al., 1994; Oliver & Hyde, 1993).

Many couples wait for a particular stage of relationship development to begin to have sex. In addition, sexual activity can move the couple along the dating continuum by making the partners feel closer and more committed. For example, Baxter and Bullis (1986) reported that events associated with "passion," including the first sexual encounter, were among those perceived to have the greatest positive effect on a couple's level of commitment. Similarly, Cate, Long, Angera, and Draper (1993) found that the proportion of men and women who reported that their relationship quality increased after the first intercourse experience with their current partners was significantly greater than the proportion who reported that their relationship quality decreased.

One interesting issue concerns whether the timing of sexual activity is associated with relationship outcomes. In a longitudinal study of dating couples, Peplau et al. (1977) compared those who had "early sex" to those who had "later sex." Later-sex couples reported more love (although women in these couples reported less sexual satisfaction and more sexual guilt than did women in early-sex couples). Interestingly, whether the couples had early or later sex (or no sex at all) was unrelated to whether they still were together 2 years later. More recent longitudinal research,

however, suggests that the timing of sex in a relationship does predict relationship longevity. In a longitudinal study of individuals involved in dating relationships, Simpson (1987) found that couples who were sexually active were more likely to be together 3 months later (see also Felmlee, Sprecher, & Bassin, 1990). The inconsistent results across these studies might be due to changes in societal standards about how soon in a relationship sexual activity *should* begin. In addition, there are interpretational difficulties concerning the long-term relational consequences of the timing of sexual initiation. For example, insofar as couples who begin sex later in their relationships experience more love than do couples who begin sex earlier in their relationships (Peplau et al., 1977), it is possible to conclude that postponing sexual involvement promotes relationship health and quality. It is equally likely, however, that the "type of person" who waits to have sex also is the type of person who is particularly skilled at maintaining the relationship.

## ▶ Sex in Established Relationships

Some couples might have sex only once or a few times before breaking up. The majority of dating, cohabiting, and married couples, however, have sex many times over the course of their relationships. Although partners might participate in a variety of activities together, sex is one of the most intimate behaviors in which couples engage and one that can serve as a barometer for the entire relationships (Schwartz & Rutter, 1998). This section begins with a discussion of *what* established couples do in the sexual area of their relationships, how they *feel* about these sexual aspects of their relationships, and how they *communicate* about sex. We then discuss how sex is related to other dimensions of couples' relationships including *exchange* and *general relationship satisfaction*. (For a longer review of these topics and others, see Sprecher & McKinney, 1993.)

## Sexual Frequency and Variety

According to recent national studies, young married couples have sexual intercourse two or three times a week on average but can expect the frequency to decline over the duration of their marriages (Call, Sprecher, & Schwartz, 1995; Laumann et al., 1994; Rao & DeMaris, 1995). It appears that both number of years married and the age of the partners play a role in this decline. Specifically, there are decreases in sexual frequency due to age-related factors (e.g., declines in physical abilities, increasing incidence of illness, negative attitudes about sex in the elderly) and the loss of novelty that results from having sex with the same person. There also are certain times in most marriages when sexual frequency can decline due to lack of opportunities caused by demanding jobs, parenthood, caring for elderly parents, and other factors (Greenblat, 1983). Furthermore, once sex declines even due to a temporary situation, a lower frequency can become part of the relationship schemata shared by the couple. As a result, a couple might not return to the higher frequency that was characteristic of the relationship at an earlier time. Some married couples might even cease to have sex (Donnelly, 1993).

Cohabitation has been described as a "sexier" living arrangement than marriage (Blumstein & Schwartz, 1983). Indeed, cohabiting couples report having sex more frequently than do married couples, even when other factors (e.g., age) are controlled (Blumstein & Schwartz, 1983; Call et al., 1995; Laumann et al., 1994; Rao & DeMaris, 1995). They also have sex more frequently than do dating couples (Risman, Hill, Rubin, & Peplau, 1981).

Of all couple types, male homosexual couples might have the most frequent sex, at least early in their relationships. Female homosexual couples, however, have sex less frequently than do married and cohabiting couples, although they might engage in more nongenital physical contact such as cuddling and hugging (Blumstein & Schwartz, 1983). Frequency of sex declines over time in lesbian and gay homosexual couples (Blumstein & Schwartz, 1983), just as it does in married couples.

When couples have sex, they often engage in a variety of behaviors. During earlier decades, paired sexual activities might have been limited for most couple types to brief foreplay and sexual intercourse in the missionary position. Today, however, the majority of heterosexual couples engage in a large repertoire of behaviors (including kissing, caressing, genital stimulation, and oral-genital sex), use a variety of positions for intercourse, and report being experimental in their choice of location for sex (Greeley, 1991; Laumann et al., 1994). Homosexual couples engage in many of the same sexual behaviors as do heterosexual couples but report higher frequencies of specific activities including kissing, oral-genital sex, and (for men) anal intercourse (Blumstein & Schwartz, 1983).

## Sexual Satisfaction

Most couples report that they are satisfied with the sexual aspects of their relationships (Blumstein & Schwartz, 1983; Brown & Auerback, 1981; Edwards & Booth, 1994; Greeley, 1991; Laumann et al., 1994). Satisfaction is greater for couples having more frequent sex (Blumstein & Schwartz, 1983; Greeley, 1991) and is associated with the following sexual activities: oral-genital sex (especially important to men's sexual satisfaction), orgasm (Perlman & Abramson, 1982; Pinney, Gerrard, & Denney, 1987), and (for women) having an orgasm before or at the same time as one's partner rather than after (Darling, Davidson, & Cox, 1991). Sexual satisfaction also is associated with effective communication about sex (Cupach & Comstock, 1990), sharing in sexual initiation (Blumstein & Schwartz, 1983), and sexual experimentation (Greeley, 1991). These associations between sexual activities and sexual satisfaction are likely to occur because specific pleasurable interactions lead to sexual satisfaction but also can occur, in part, because a feeling of sexual satisfaction leads to the desire for specific sexual interactions.

A number of other possible predictors of sexual satisfaction have been investigated including relationship factors (e.g., communication, intimacy), background variables (e.g., socioeconomic status), and personality characteristics (e.g., introversion-extroversion). As Lawrance and Byers (1995) noted, relationship factors are more strongly associated with sexual satisfaction than are other types of variables.

### Sexual Communication

As already noted, one factor that is closely connected to sexual satisfaction in the relationship is communication. Good overall communication between partners, as well as effective communication about sex, can contribute to the quality of the sexual relationship (Cupach & Comstock, 1990). One specific aspect of sexual communication that researchers have explored is the initiation and refusal of sexual requests. In the traditional sexual script, men are expected to initiate sexual activity, whereas women are expected to then accept or refuse these sexual requests. Many couples follow this pattern of sexual interaction (Byers & Heinlein, 1989), although women might be more comfortable with initiating sexual activity the longer they have been in their relationships (Brown & Auerback, 1981). Interestingly, men say that they would like women to initiate sex more often but not more often than they do themselves (Blumstein & Schwartz, 1983; Schwartz & Rutter, 1998). What might be most important is that couples agree about the balance of initiation in their relationships (Cupach & Metts, 1991).

Although individuals might be direct when they communicate with each other about most things, they often are indirect when they communicate about sex. For example, couples tend to use indirect strategies such as kissing, suggestive glances, playing music, consuming alcohol, and taking showers (Brown & Auerback, 1981; Byers & Heinlein, 1989). In-

direct communication might make a sexual invitation somewhat ambiguous. This, in turn, might allow the other partner, who might not be in the mood for sex, to avoid overtly rejecting the invitation and hurting the initiator. A couple's sexual initiation tactics appear to become less indirect over time as the partners become increasingly comfortable with each other (Brown & Auerback, 1981).

Refusals do occur in established relationships. Partners do not always want sex at the same time; therefore, there will be times when one partner refuses the initiation made by the other. Women more often than men refuse sex, perhaps because men are more likely to initiate (Blumstein & Schwartz, 1983; Byers & Heinlein, 1989). A rejection in a well-established relationship is likely to be direct and accompanied by an account that reduces conflict and protects the partner's feelings (e.g., "I have a headache tonight, but tomorrow night should be better") (Byers & Heinlein, 1989; Cupach & Metts, 1991).

### Sex and Exchange

Sexual activity in an intimate relationship can be the source of great pleasure and reward. However, there also can be costs associated with sexual activity including anxiety, emotional and physical pain, and embarrassment (for additional discussion, see Sprecher, 1998b).

Although the exchange elements of sex might not be explicit and salient for intimate partners, there is evidence that most people can identify the rewards and costs associated with sexual activity. For example, as part of a larger study of exchange and sexuality, Lawrance and Byers (1995) provided participants with a Rewards/Costs Checklist, which included 46 items representing either rewards or costs in the sexual relationship. Some of the items most frequently identified as rewards were feeling comfortable with the partner, having sex with the same person each time (especially important for women), how individuals feel about themselves during or after sex, and the amount of fun experienced during sexual activity. Among the items most often identified as costs were having sex when not in the mood (rated especially costly by women), having sex when the partner is not in the mood (rated especially costly by men), the (decreased) amount of sexual spontaneity, and the (decreased) frequency of sexual activity.

The ratio of sexual rewards to sexual costs in a relationship seems to be related to sexual satisfaction. Research with married, cohabiting, and dating couples reveals that sexual satisfaction is highest when sexual rewards are high, sexual costs are low, sexual rewards exceed sexual costs, the obtained rewards and costs in the relationship compare favorably to the expected rewards and costs, and one partner's sexual rewards and costs do not exceed those of the other partner (Byers, Demmons, & Lawrance, 1998; Lawrance & Byers, 1995).

The collection of sexual behaviors in which partners engage represents only one class of resources exchanged in the relationship; hence, they can be exchanged for other types of interpersonal resources. Thus, when people accommodate their partners in the sexual area of their relationships (e.g., an erotic massage, having sex when not in the mood), they might expect—and receive—reciprocation in another relational area. Furthermore, the fairer and more equitable that people perceive the sexual (and nonsexual) exchange in their relationships to be, the greater their overall level of contentment. This, in turn, might affect what they are willing to do sexually in their relationships and how they feel about it. Hatfield, Greenberger, Traupmann, and Lambert (1982) found that men and women who view their marriages as fair and equitable are more satisfied with the sex in their relationships and have sex more often compared to those who feel that their marriages are inequitable. In addition, underbenefiting inequity (i.e., receiving less overall benefit relative to one's partner) appears to be more detrimental to sexual satisfaction than is overbenefiting inequity (i.e., receiving more overall benefit relative to one's partner). An equitable relationship also is associated with marital fidelity; feeling underbenefited in a marriage predicts whether an individual will have sex with someone other than the partner, especially for women (Prins, Buunk, & Van Yperen, 1993).

### *Sex and Relationship Satisfaction and Stability*

One of the major issues that has interested close relationship researchers is why some couples maintain or increase their overall happiness, whereas other couples become dissatisfied over time and perhaps terminate their relationships. Frequent sex has been found to be associated with general relationship satisfaction (Blumstein & Schwartz, 1983; Call et al., 1995; Donnelly, 1993), although this association is weaker for lesbian couples (Blumstein & Schwartz, 1983). However, quality of sex appears to be a more important predictor of relational outcomes than is quantity of sex. Several studies reveal that sexual satisfaction is correlated with general relationship satisfaction in marriage and other committed relationships (Cupach & Comstock, 1990; Edwards & Booth, 1994; Greeley, 1991; Henderson-King & Veroff, 1994; Kurdek, 1991b; Lawrance & Byers, 1995; Oggins, Leber, & Veroff, 1993). Greeley (1991), in a national study of married individuals, reported that frequency of sex did not affect overall relationship quality once sexual satisfaction was controlled. Interestingly, neither the quality nor the quantity of sex might be as important as other nonsexual forms of intimacy in the prediction of relationship satisfaction including expressed affection (Huston & Vangelisti, 1991) and supportive communication (Sprecher, Metts, Burleson, Hatfield, & Thompson, 1995).

Sexual dissatisfaction and incompatibilities in themselves probably rarely lead to the termination of healthy, well-established relationships. To the extent that sexual dissatisfaction is symptomatic of other relational problems, however, it might be associated with conflict and termination. Blumstein and Schwartz (1983), in their large study of lesbian, gay, and heterosexual couples, reported that fighting about sex and dissatisfaction with sex—but not frequency of sex—were associated with breakups among all couple types. More recent prospective studies similarly reveal that sexual problems and/or sexual dissatisfaction predict later relationship dissolution (Edwards & Booth, 1994; Oggins et al., 1993; Veroff, Douvan, & Hatchett, 1995; White & Keith, 1990). In fact, when people are asked what led to the breakups of their marriages or close relationships, sexual incompatibility and sexual problems often are rated as at least moderately important (Cleek & Pearson, 1985; Hill, Rubin, & Peplau, 1976; Kurdek, 1991b; Sprecher, 1994).

## ▶ Sex and Love

The type of linkage that exists between sex and love has been the subject of much theoretical debate. For example, Aron and Aron (1991) divided the many theories that have touched on love or sexuality into five general categories: (a) theories of sexuality that ignore love or consider love to be one result of sexuality (e.g., classic [Freudian] psychoanalytic theory, sociobiological or evolutionary approaches), (b) theories that emphasize sexuality and consider love to be a minor feature of sexuality (e.g., attachment theory), (c) theories that consider love and sexuality to be separate (e.g., script theory, exchange theories, neo-Freudian clinical approaches), (d) theories that emphasize love and view sexuality as a minor part of love (e.g., triangular theory of love), and (e) theories that ignore sexuality or consider sexuality to be one result of love (e.g., object relations theory). As their review illustrates, there is little consensus among social scientists about the nature of the association between sexuality and love. Nonetheless, as Aron and Aron and others have noted (Hendrick & Hendrick, 1992a; Regan & Berscheid, 1999), Western European cultures seem to link sexuality and at least one type of love—passionate love—quite closely. In the following subsections, we discuss current conceptualizations of passionate love, ways in which to measure this experience, and recent empirical evidence ex-

amining the relation between passionate love and sexuality.

### Conceptualization: What Is Passionate Love?

Passionate love (also called erotic or romantic love or the state of "being in love") consists of a number of basic features. First, this type of love is an intensely emotional experience. Berscheid and Walster (1974), two of the first social scientists to speculate on the nature of "being in love," suggested that people experience passionate love when they are extremely aroused physiologically (an essential ingredient for any strong emotion) and when they believe that this arousal is caused by their partners and, therefore, is appropriately labeled *passionate love*. In addition, passionate love is assumed to be fueled by, and associated with, both positive and negative emotions. For example, Berscheid and Walster discussed the "hodgepodge of conflicting emotions" (p. 359) associated with passionate love, and more recently, Hatfield and Rapson (1990) described the "continuous interplay between elation and despair, [between] thrills and terror" (p. 128) that they believe are integral to the experience of being in love. Interestingly, however, research on beliefs about passionate love (Regan, Kocan, & Whitlock, 1998) and on correlates of passionate love in dating, cohabiting, and married couples (Sprecher & Regan, 1998) suggests that passionate love is more strongly associated with positive emotions than with negative emotions, with one important exception: Jealousy is related to feelings of passionate love; that is, not only do men and women associate jealousy with the state of being in love, but those who love passionately also tend to report feeling jealous.

Second, in contrast to more durable types of love (e.g, companionate or friendship-based love), passionate love is viewed by many theorists as an inherently unstable and short-lived phenomenon (e.g., Sternberg, 1988). Berscheid (1983), for example, concluded that passionate love has a "swift onset" but is "distressingly fragile." Some cross-sectional and longitudinal research supports this theoretical contention. Specifically, although passionate love initially might increase as a couple progresses from earlier (e.g., casual dating) to later (e.g., steady dating, engaged) courtship stages (Hatfield & Sprecher, 1986), such feelings generally appear to decline over longer periods of time in both dating and married couples (Hatfield, Traupmann, & Sprecher, 1984; Sprecher & Regan, 1998) as well as after major relational transitions (e.g., engagement to marriage, childlessness to parenthood) (Tucker & Aron, 1993).

Third, passionate love contains a strong sexual component. Lee (1988), a love theorist, concluded that passionate (or what he termed "erotic") love always begins with a strong physical attraction, and he noted that the erotic lover seeks early sexual involvement with the partner and is "eager to get to know the beloved quickly, intensely—and undressed" (p. 50). In fact, current social psychological discourse suggests that sexuality is one of the dimensions that differentiates passionate love from other varieties or types of love experience. This is not to say that other types of love are sexless; certainly, it is possible to feel sexual desire for someone who is loved companionately and to engage in sexual activities with that person. However, sexuality appears to play the strongest role in the passionate love experience.

### Measurement: How Is Passionate Love Assessed?

There are two common self-report ways in which to assess passionate love: single-item measures and multi-item scales. Single-item measures typically focus on the quantity or intensity of passionate love experienced by an individual. Although these global single-item measures are easy to use and appear relatively reliable (Sprecher & Regan, 1998), many researchers choose to use multi-item scales that have been developed specifically to measure the various theoretically important elements of passionate love. Of the various passionate

love scales that have been constructed over the years, two are particularly worthy of note: the Eros subscale of the Love Attitudes Scale developed by Hendrick and Hendrick (1986) and the Passionate Love Scale developed by Hatfield and Sprecher (1986). (For information about the Love Attitudes Scale, see Chapter 15 by Hendrick & Hendrick, this volume.) Hatfield and Sprecher (1986) drew on previous theoretical conceptualizations and measures to create the Passionate Love Scale. Items were designed to assess the cognitive, emotional, and behavioral components of the passionate love experience, and many directly or indirectly refer to sexuality (e.g., "Sometimes my body trembles with excitement at the sight of _____," "I want _____ physically, emotionally, mentally," "I sense my body responding when _____ touches me").

### Research on the Sexual Component of Passionate Love

Passionate love clearly is a highly sexualized experience. For example, research suggests that behavioral (e.g., intercourse) and physiological (e.g., sexual excitement, physiological/genital arousal) aspects of sexuality are associated with feelings of passionate love. People who are more passionately in love report experiencing higher levels of sexual excitement when thinking about their partners (Hatfield & Sprecher, 1986; Sprecher & Regan, 1998) and engaging in more frequent sexual activities with their partners (Aron & Henkemeyer, 1995) than do individuals who are less passionately in love. In addition, interviews with in-love couples reveal that sexual activity (e.g., "making love") is one of the primary ways in which they communicate their feelings of passion to each other (Marston, Hecht, Manke, McDaniel, & Reeder, 1998).

Motivational aspects of sexuality (i.e., sexual desire) also appear related to passionate love. For example, Ridge and Berscheid (1989) asked a sample of undergraduate men and women whether they believed that there was a difference between the experience of being in love with another person and that of loving another person. Fully 87% emphatically claimed that there was a difference between the two experiences. In addition, when asked to specify the nature of that difference, participants were more likely to cite sexual desire as descriptive of the passionate "in love" experience. More recently, Berscheid and Meyers (1996) asked a large sample of undergraduate men and women to list the initials of all the people they currently loved, the initials of all the people with whom they currently were in love, and the initials of all the people toward whom they currently felt sexual attraction/desire. The results indicated that 85% of the persons listed in the "in love" category also were listed in the "sexually desire" category, whereas only 2% of those listed in the "love" category (and not cross-listed in the "in love" category) were listed in the "sexually desire" category. Thus, the objects of respondents' feelings of passionate love (but not their feelings of love) also tended to be the objects of their sexual desire.

Not only do men and women experience sexual desire for the people with whom they are in love, they believe that dating partners who desire each other sexually are more likely to be passionately in love than are dating partners who do not (Regan, 1998a). In fact, a growing body of evidence indicates that sexual desire is the aspect of sexuality that is the most closely related to the passionate love experience. Regan et al. (1998) asked a sample of men and women to list, in a free response format, all of the features that they considered to be characteristic or prototypical of the state of "being in love." Of 119 spontaneously generated features, sexual desire received the second highest frequency rating (65.8%); trust was first (80.0%). In other words, when thinking of passionate love, nearly two thirds of the participants automatically thought of sexual desire. In addition, this feature was viewed as more important to the passionate love concept than were behavioral sexual events such as kissing (cited by only 10.0% of participants), touching/holding (cited by 17.5%), and sexual activity (cited by 25.0%).

Research with dating couples, although sparse, also suggests that sexual desire and passionate love share a unique connection. For example, Regan (in press) found that the self-reported amounts of sexual desire experienced by men and women for their dating partners (and not their levels of sexual activity) were significantly positively correlated with the levels of passionate love they felt for those individuals. Their feelings of desire were unrelated, however, to the amounts of companionate love and liking they experienced for their partners.

In sum, sexuality (and, in particular, sexual desire) is an important component of passionate love relationships.

## ▶ Implications and Conclusions

The majority of close relationships that individuals form throughout their lives are not sexual in nature. Rather, they consist of the intimate connections established with friends, children, parents, siblings, other relatives, and co-workers. Despite this, most adolescent and adult men and women form and maintain some types of sexual/romantic interpersonal attachments that often become their "primary" relationships and that can result in marriage or other forms of socially sanctioned long-term pairing. In this chapter, we discussed the dynamics of sex in marriage and other committed relationships, and we examined how sexuality is related to specific interpersonal phenomena including attraction, relationship development, relationship satisfaction, exchange, communication, and love.

Our emphasis was on the more positive side of relational sexuality, that is, the ways in which frequent and satisfying sexual experiences are associated with positive outcomes in nonsexual areas of relationships. However, there also exists a dark side to interpersonal sexuality. We noted that sex within close relationships can take on a number of meanings and reflect a variety of motives on the part of the individuals involved. For example, a person might use sex to express feelings of love, but he or she also might withhold, demand, or coerce sex from the partner as a way of meting out punishment and/or demonstrating interpersonal power (see Chapter 24 by Christopher & Lloyd, this volume). Furthermore, sexual involvement with individuals other than the primary partner might occur and result in negative individual and interpersonal consequences (see Chapter 23 by Buunk & Dijkstra, this volume). Potentially damaging outcomes to sexual activity can occur even within loving monogamous relationships including unwanted pregnancies, sexually transmitted diseases, and physical and emotional distress associated with sexual dysfunction or with particular sexual proclivities (e.g., transvestism, sadomasochism) that might not conform to society's or the partner's expectations.

The fact that the sexual activities and desires of relational partners are intertwined with a multitude of (positive and negative) nonsexual interpersonal phenomena has a number of practical implications. For example, although changes in sexual desire, frequency of intercourse, and satisfaction undoubtedly occur over the course of any given relationship, couples who routinely experience such fluctuations or who experience sudden and extreme alterations in the sexual aspects of their relationships might wish to seek some form of therapeutic intervention. At the same time, however, couples need to recognize that declines or changes in the sexual aspects of a love relationship do not necessarily spell interpersonal tragedy or foreshadow the end of a union. There is no "right" amount of sexual desire or activity that characterizes romantic relationships; rather, couples must judge for themselves what is "normal" with respect to sexuality. Professional intervention might be most helpful when one or both partners disagree about or are troubled by some aspect of their sexual life (e.g., mismatched levels of sexual desire, poor sexual communication, lack of sexual enjoyment).

In addition, the strong association between sexual and nonsexual relational phenomena raises some important issues for researchers and theorists in human sexuality and close relationships. First, it is clear that investigators need to devote more attention to conducting research that examines sexuality from a dyadic perspective. This involves not only collecting data from both partners but also analyzing dyadic-level variables (for examples, see Cupach & Metts, 1995; Julien, Bouchard, Gagnon, & Pomerleau, 1992).

Second, greater intellectual exchange and cooperation must occur between researchers in the fields of close relationships and human sexuality. Traditionally, these fields of study have maintained separate literatures, professional organizations, journals, and graduate training programs. As a result, until relatively recently, most research originating in the relationship field has ignored or downplayed the role of sexuality in close relationships, and most research originating in the sexuality field has focused on the individual devoid of a relational context. A rapprochement between these two areas is important if we wish to understand what couples do together sexually, how they feel about what they do, and the role that these paired sexual activities play in other domains of their relationships (and vice versa).

Third, we suggest that those social and behavioral scientists who study sexuality in the context of close relationships be more assertive in disseminating information. As noted by Schwartz (1992), "The public has an appetite for research findings—particularly on relationships. . . . And if they can't get the real thing . . ., they will rely on what's available" (p. 1). The content of articles in women's (and, increasingly, men's) magazines commonly revolves around issues of sex, love, and relationships (see, e.g., content analyses by Prusank, Duran, & De Lillo, 1993), yet the information presented often is not based on current social scientific theory or research.

In sum, the sexual attitudes and expectations that relational partners hold, the desires that they seek to fulfill, and the activities in which they engage have significant consequences, not only for themselves as individuals but also for their relationships.

# Contents

# Intimacy in Personal Relationships

*Karen J. Prager*

If intimacy is one of the most often discussed aspects of relationship functioning, then there are good reasons. It is the distinguishing mark of a person's most important and valued relationships. It is predictive of the highest levels of satisfaction, love, and trust as well as perhaps the primary reward of closeness (Prager, 1995).

Equally compelling, intimate contact is a powerful determinant of individual health and well-being. People seek intimate confidants during times of stress and find that confiding buffers them from its pathogenic effects. Self-concealment, by contrast, is associated with illness such as high blood pressure (Handkins & Munz, 1978) and depression (Larson & Chastain, 1990). Ornish (1998) had this to say of love and intimacy in his popular book, *Love and Survival:* "I am not aware of any other factor in medicine—not diet, not smoking, not exercise, not stress, not genetics, not drugs, not surgery—that has a greater impact on our quality of life, incidence of illness, and premature death from all causes" (p. 3).

Because intimate contact fosters both individual well-being and relationship satisfaction, and because it is such a highly valued aspect of personal relationships, it clearly is a process that should be better understood. My goals for this chapter are, first, to suggest a framework for organizing existing research on intimacy and, second, to use the framework to identify potential intimacy research agendas. I conclude with a brief overview of a model of intimacy-oriented couple therapy that draws on existing theory and research.

In my view, the foundations on which the intimacy research of the 21st century will rest consist of (a) theoretical and empirical work that supports a clear, specific, and valid *conception* of intimate relating (i.e., what it is, what distinguishes it from other aspects of personal relationships, how it interacts with those other aspects, and how intimate interactions over time develop into intimate relationships) and (b) reliable and valid *measures* of empirically useful conceptions of intimacy. Furthermore, intimacy scholarship should document and provide theory to explain (a) factors that influence intimacy *processes;* (b) the development of intimacy-related capacities over the *life span;* and (c) the processes by which individual, relational, and sociocultural factors affect the maintenance of intimate *relationships.* Finally, intimacy scholarship should suggest *assessment and intervention* strategies for helping people to sustain more satisfying intimate relationships. This chapter touches on each of these.

## ► Conceptualizing and Measuring Intimacy

Because of intimacy's importance and the amount of attention it has received in the literature, there have been nearly as many definitions of intimacy as there are scholars who have addressed it. Intimacy, like love, is the stuff that inspires poetry and, like love, can inspire feelings of transcendence over ordinary experience (Register & Henley, 1992). Perhaps for this reason, there is not yet a discernible consensus among scholars on what intimacy is and what researchers should be studying. Knowledge will advance more rapidly when (a) papers/articles purporting to study or measure intimacy all address the same thing and (b) one no longer can find a significant number of papers/articles measuring something like intimacy but calling it something else.

Conceptualizations of intimacy are useful to the extent that they approximate commonsense notions of what intimacy is, stimulate reliable measurement and productive research, discriminate meaningfully between intimacy and related constructs, and map the linkages among different levels of intimacy (e.g., experience, interaction, relationship). Measures of intimacy should closely reflect conceptualizations if they are to contribute to a coherent body of research about intimacy.

Because *intimacy* can refer to a host of phenomena ranging from emotions, to conversation topics, to sexuality, to relationships, I

have recommended that scholars conceptualize intimacy as a type of interaction (see also Reis & Shaver, 1988). There are advantages to thinking of intimacy as an interaction. First, intimate relationships are built on intimate interactions. Intimate relationships are, at a minimum, relationships that are characterized by frequent intimate interactions or encounters. By contrast, intimate interactions do not have to occur within intimate relationships. Some intimate interactions are opportunistic (e.g., two strangers on an airplane divulging personal information to one another) and do not serve the function of relationship development. Second, it is within intimate interactions that the emotions and personal disclosures associated with intimacy occur. Feelings of closeness or feelings of vulnerability, for example, should emerge first in interactions and then, over time, come to characterize relationships.

The conceptualization of intimacy portrayed in Figure 17.1 has emerged for me through my own research on intimacy in couple relationships (Lippert, Ghandi, Magnis, & Prager, 1998; Prager & Buhrmester, 1998) and through an exhaustive review of existing conceptualizations that I conducted a few years ago (Prager, 1995). Figure 17.1 depicts the immediate short-term effects of intimate interactions on individual experience. Furthermore, it shows that the repetition of these interactions over time can (or fail to) fulfill important individual needs as well as shape perceptions and feelings that two partners have about themselves, one another, and their relationship. It is the more abiding effects of intimate interactions that form the building blocks of intimate relationships (e.g., love, attachment, trust).

Intimate partners are interdependent in that the intimate behaviors of one (Partner A) elicit (potentially) intimate experiences in the other (Partner B). The experiences (feelings and perceptions) that Partner A's behavior elicits in Partner B prompt Partner B to behave intimately. The intimate behaviors performed by Partner B then shape the experiences of Partner A and so on. I have defined

## What is Intimacy?

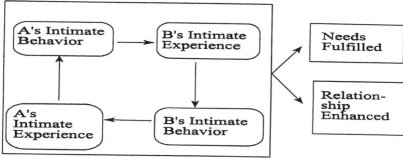

**Figure 17.1.** Intimate Interactions and Their Sequelae

intimate behaviors as the verbal or nonverbal sharing with another of that which is personal and private to the individual (e.g., verbal disclosure, active listening, physical affection, sexual contact). I suggest that intimate experience has two dimensions: (a) positive affect (e.g., feelings of pride, warmth, love, affection, gratitude, or attraction) and (b) perceptions of understanding (e.g., the perception that one is liked, accepted, understood, cared for, or loved by the other).

In an earlier review (Prager, 1995), I identified measures of intimacy that reflected the emphases of existing conceptualizations. I found that measures could reasonably be grouped according to whether they reflected primarily behavioral, affective, or more cognitive conceptions. Nevertheless, it was possible to conclude from that review that conceptualization had not fully guided measurement. Still needed are measures that (a) encompass intimacy's verbal *and* nonverbal aspects and (b) accommodate the perspectives of both partners in a relationship (for a good example of the latter, see Schaefer & Olson, 1981).

Because close linkage between conception and measurement is highly desirable, Duane Buhrmester and I recently developed a diary measure of intimacy to reflect the conception of intimacy described heretofore. This measure, the Interaction Record Form for Intimacy (IRF-I), asks research participants to rate their daily interactions on 17 items. These items load on three orthogonal factors and ac-

count for approximately 67% of the variance. The first factor, intimate behavior, consists primarily of items describing self-disclosure, whereas two additional factors reflect intimate experience. The first of the latter factors, affective tone, reflects positive pleasant feelings and an absence of quarreling and criticism. The second, listening and understanding, reflects each partner's perception that he or she listened, was listened to, and was understood. This factor structure supports the three-dimensional structure I have described here. The IRF-I showed adequate internal consistency and correlated in expected ways with other measures of intimacy (Prager & Buhrmester, 1998).

Recently, scholars have devoted more attention to the personal vulnerability elicited by intimate relating and have made efforts to incorporate this notion into definitions and measures of intimacy (e.g., Sroufe, Carlson, & Shulman, 1993). Interaction instructions developed by Linda Roberts for assessing intimacy explicitly instruct partners in couple relationships to express aspects of themselves about which they feel vulnerable (Roberts & Linney, under review). The instructions allow researchers to determine whether such expression is possible within a particular relationship as well as the types of behaviors and affective expressions such conversations elicit.

Because intimate exchanges can elicit intense emotional vulnerability, they are emotionally risky. It is the risk of vulnerability that complicates people's efforts to attain satisfying intimate relationships. These complications are discussed more fully in the section on implications for clinical practice.

## ▶ Intimacy Processes

*Intimacy processes* refer to the dynamics of interactions themselves. Several questions are of interest. First, it is important to understand what it is about an interaction that leads people to experience it as intimate. Tonya Lippert and I are currently studying the contribution that partners' global perceptions of their relationships make to their on-the-spot experiences in their interactions with one another (Lippert & Prager, under review). We have discovered that specific interaction characteristics exert substantially more influence on relationship partners' experiences of intimacy in interaction than do their global relationship perceptions. We found that the most influential (and nonoverlapping) set of interaction characteristics included self-disclosure, listening, interaction pleasantness, and expressions of needs or wants (with the latter contributing only for couples who reported histories of constructive conflict).

Second, once the key components of intimate interactions have been identified, it is important to discern their contribution to positive outcomes for individuals and relationships. Specifically, although the association between intimacy and well-being is well established, there still is much to learn about the processes by which moderating relationships among interaction components become associated with individual outcomes. Figure 17.1 suggests one possibility—that because intimacy contributes to the fulfillment of needs, it exerts positive effects on the well-being of partners (Prager & Buhrmester, 1998).

Third, once we have investigated the interrelationships among intimacy's components, we can look more closely at contextual factors that affect people's experiences of intimacy. If intimacy is conceptualized as an interaction process, then one can envision an embedded structure of contexts that affects this process. In earlier work (Prager, 1995; Prager, 1999b), I identified a multilayered model of intimacy in context that points to those contextual factors that are likely to influence the intimacy process and suggests ways in which these factors are likely to interrelate. Figure 17.2 illustrates an expanded transactional model of intimacy in which its components are affected by, and in some cases contribute to, the context within which the interaction takes place.

### Components of Intimate Interaction

When we study the interaction itself and seek to understand the immediate outcomes of that interaction, we focus on behaviors and experiences that are as close in time and place to the interaction as possible. Zeroing in on the interaction itself narrows the focus of investigation to the individual's immediate experience and its relationship to the other person's behavior. Research on interaction processes has examined nonverbal behavior, verbal behavior, or both. Both nonverbal and verbal interaction behaviors can intensify (or block) experiences of intimacy.

*Nonverbal behavior.* Nonverbal behavior contributes substantially to people's intimate experiences. The influence of nonverbal behavior probably is due to its relatively involuntary character. People's facial expressions, voice tones, postures, and gestures can reveal unspoken emotions and intentions and can override efforts at impression management. It is much more difficult to lie nonverbally than to lie with words.

*Involvement behaviors,* which convey attentiveness, interest, and active participation, directly affect experiences of intimacy in interactions. People are judged as more involved in their interactions when they sit closer to one another, maintain mutual gaze

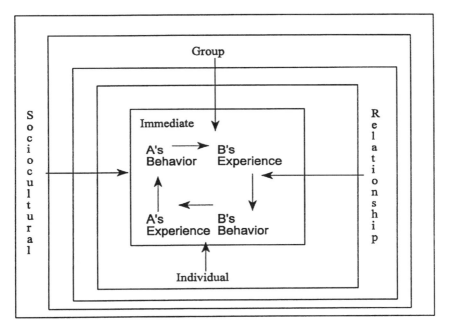

**Figure 17.2.** Intimate Interactions in Context

and open posture, lean forward, gesture, smile or otherwise demonstrate facial animation, and nod their heads while listening and talking. Each of these nonverbal behaviors has a demonstrated effect on intimate experience (for a review, see Prager, 1995).

Touch further intensifies the experience of intimacy. Wanted or invited touch on certain parts of the body, identified by Jones and Yarbrough (1985) as "vulnerable," always is experienced as intimate (e.g., on the face or torso). Sustaining a touch (e.g., arms around the shoulder or waist) can intensify the experience of intimacy generated by the touch.

*Verbal behavior.* Verbal interaction behavior has been investigated more extensively over the years than has nonverbal behavior. Self-disclosure, the revelation of personal and private information about the self, is the sine qua non of verbally intimate behavior, both from a layperson's perspective and in intimacy research. Self-disclosure can enhance positive feelings between people (Hendrick, 1981) and, early in the acquaintance process, can

create an expectation that a relationship will develop (Falk & Wagner, 1985). Self-disclosure intensifies experiences of intimacy in interactions when it addresses topics that are more personal or private; when it reveals emotions, feelings, and meanings attached to events as well as events themselves; and when it is characterized by immediacy.

Because an intimate interaction, by definition, should leave the partners feeling positively about themselves, one another, and their interaction, the behavior of the listener/responder is as important as that of the discloser. Identifying effective responsiveness and its emotional correlates, however, has proved to be challenging to personal relationship scholars.

Verbal responsiveness is important because of what it communicates. At a minimum, it must communicate that the listener is interested in and understands what is being said (Miller & Berg, 1984). In addition, it should convey acceptance, respect, and genuine caring about the speaker and what he or she is saying (Reis & Shaver, 1988). Research on verbal responsiveness indicates that it fosters intimate experience. For example, college students like new acquaintances better when they respond to personal disclosures with sympathy and a willingness to talk more about the topic (for a review, see Dindia, 1994a). Furthermore, psychotherapists' verbal responsiveness predicts progress for their clients (Barkham & Shapiro, 1986).

It is likely that all three components of intimate interaction must be present for intimacy's benefits to be experienced. My own work has explored ways in which self-disclosure's association with individual and relationship outcomes is moderated by the other two dimensions of intimate interaction. Using the IRF-I, Buhrmester and I found that self-disclosure was positively correlated with need fulfillment and relationship satisfaction (Prager & Buhrmester, 1998). Furthermore, we found that self-disclosure's effects on need fulfillment were moderated by other dimensions of intimacy in interactions. For example, women's communal needs were most likely to be met when relationship partners self-disclosed *and* demonstrated understanding. Both men's and women's communal needs were most likely to be met when negative affect in interactions was softened by partners' self-disclosures. We concluded that the effects of self-disclosure were enhanced in the presence of one of the other components of intimate interaction. We also discovered that self-disclosure served important functions even when it occurred in less intimate (e.g., negatively toned) interactions.

### Effects of Context on Intimate Experience

If we are to gain a better understanding of the processes by which, and the circumstances under which, intimate interactions foster individual well-being, then we must not limit our focus to microanalytic studies of interaction processes. Intimate interactions occur within multilayered and mutually embedded con-

texts, each of which can, alone and in concert with other contextual factors, modify the effects of intimate behavior on individual experience and, ultimately, on individual well-being. In my view, the structure depicted in Figure 17.2 offers a valuable way in which to organize existing research and to identify potential moderators of intimacy's impact.

*Immediate context.* The *immediate context* refers to situational factors close in time and space to the interaction itself. There is a demonstrable impact of situational factors on nonverbal involvement behaviors and touching.

People tend to optimize intimacy through nonverbal behaviors during interactions. If one immediate factor such as seating distance is fixed so that it is too close or too distant, for example, then people will compensate through adjustments to other involvement behaviors such as backward lean or the avoidance of mutual gaze (Argyle & Dean, 1965; Kleinke, 1986). Something as simple as seating distance, in other words, can modify the effects of gaze on people's experiences so that people who ordinarily would feel comfortable with mutual gazing find themselves avoiding it under the circumstances.

Situational factors also can moderate the experiential concomitants of being touched. Burgoon (1991) found that when college students were touched by a very attractive experimenter, they experienced the touch as conveying significantly more affection than when they were touched by a less attractive experimenter. These and other studies (for a review, see Prager, 1995) suggest that it would be misleading to make any statements about the effects of nonverbal behaviors on experiences of intimacy without taking the immediate context into account. Unfortunately, there is very little information available about the effects of situational variables on verbal intimacy.

*Individual partner context.* The *individual context* refers to stable characteristics of persons—personality traits; motivations; habitual patterns of feeling, thinking, and behaving—that affect how people interpret and respond to one another's behavior. For example, people with social anxiety are more likely to avert eye contact and lean backward during conversations and are less likely to touch others (Andersen, 1993). To the extent that individuals demonstrate habitual patterns of thinking about intimacy and of behaving in response to potentially intimate situations, the interactions they have with others will be affected in predictable ways.

Research has identified some linkages between self-disclosure and individual personality characteristics. For example, positive relationships have been found between levels of self-reported self-disclosure with a variety of partners and sensation seeking, self-esteem, an internal locus of control, and private self-consciousness (for a review, see Prager, 1995). Many of these linkages between personality and self-disclosure are modified by situational variables. An excellent example is the way in which personality characteristics interact with situational norms to predict self-disclosure. Several studies, reviewed by Prager (1995), found that people with high levels of neuroticism or low intimacy capacity were more likely than other research participants to disclose highly personal private material in inappropriate situations (e.g., with a new acquaintance). But in appropriate situations (e.g., with a close friend), these personal characteristics did not affect self-disclosure.

Research by McAdams and his colleagues indicates that there are individual differences in *intimacy motivation* that predict behavior in a variety of situations. For example, people who are high in intimacy motivation view relationships as sources of positive emotion and value talk for its own sake, particularly when it is reciprocal and noninstrumental (McAdams, 1984). College students high in intimacy motivation are more likely to self-disclose in a group setting, although they prefer dyadic interaction because of its greater potential for intimacy (McAdams & Powers, 1981). Intimacy motivation can serve as a type of readiness or inclination to evaluate social interactions according to their potential for fulfilling intimacy needs.

*Relationship context.* The extent to which intimate behaviors elicit positive emotions and perceptions of self, partner, and interaction will depend greatly on the way in which the partners define the nature of their relationship. Relationships can vary in depth (e.g., casual or new acquaintance, casual friend, close friend) and in type (e.g., friendship, romantic relationship, parent-child relationship). For example, under ordinary circumstances, sexual overtures elicit intimate experiences only in romantic relationships. Self-disclosure, on the other hand, is appropriate in relationships widely varying in depth, although the breadth and personalness that are expected will vary systematically (Miller, 1990).

Intimacy is the most salient attribute distinguishing close relationships from other personal relationships (Hayes, 1988). Indexes of intimacy that differentiate close relationships include nonverbal involvement behaviors, benefit gained from conversation, and level of emotional support. Emotional expressiveness also defines a relationship as close (for a review, see Prager, 1995).

*Sociocultural context.* The *sociocultural context* affects intimate interactions largely through situational norms that dictate appropriate nonverbal and verbal intimate behavior. It is nearly impossible to generalize about behaviors that elicit experiences of intimacy outside of their situational context because powerful sociocultural norms set emotionally salient limits on behavior in most social situations. Discernible among American college students is a norm that designates moderate self-disclosure as appropriate for people getting acquainted. People who disclose moderately in experimental getting acquainted exercises are rated by their fellow college students as better adjusted and more likable than those who disclose very little or a great deal. Furthermore, these norms are applied more strictly to men than to women; men who violate these norms are judged more harshly (Derlega & Chaikin, 1977).

### *Summary*

Research has revealed a myriad of situational, personal, relational, and sociocultural factors that shape intimate interactions. The dimensions of the interactions themselves, and the conditions under which two people interact, determine whether people experience their interactions as intimate. Personality characteristics can affect how much people are inclined to disclose and whether they are sensitive to situational cues that dictate norms for intimate expression. Relationships themselves, and the definitions that people place on them, also impose or expand the limits of acceptable intimate behavior.

## ▶ Intimate Relationships

Intimate relationships are built on frequently occurring intimate interactions and their concomitants, as the rapidly growing body of research on relationship development attests. Intimacy affects and is affected by other processes that contribute to relationship growth and commitment. Research has shown intimacy to be positively related to levels of love, trust, satisfaction, commitment, and partner understanding in close relationships (for a review, see Prager, 1995).

Because relationships provide the context within which most people expect and hope that their intimacy needs will be met, it is important to extend our investigations of intimacy beyond interactions to relationships. The best way in which to approach the study of intimate relationships is to investigate intimate interactions within those relationships and to compare relationships that are characterized by more or less frequent and rewarding intimacy. With this approach, intimacy is primarily defined as a characteristic of inter-

actions, with the discovery of its relationship-level concomitants and sequelae now a matter of empirical investigation. Scholarship then can focus on learning more about the mechanisms by which intimate interactions interact with other characteristics of relationships to produce enduring emotional and attitudinal states such as satisfaction, love, and trust (or, conversely, ambivalence and mistrust). Finally, research can augment knowledge gained from investigating the internal processes by which relationships are maintained through explorations of influential contextual factors external to relationships.

In this section, I explore processes that shape romantic relationships, close friendships, and parent-child relationships, all relationships with the potential for intimacy. Factors affecting intimate relationships, like those affecting interactions, can be organized as mutually embedded contexts, each of which exerts independent effects on individual and relationship functioning while also interacting with other factors.

### *The Individual Partner*

Most of the scholarship on intimate relationships and the forces that shape them has focused on effects of (and on) individual partners. Most likely, as Figure 17.2 illustrates, the effects of individuals and relationships on one another are *transactional* or mutually influential. A substantial body of information now is available on the transactional relationship between partners' personalities and *relationship functioning* or the satisfaction, harmony, and stability that characterizes their personal relationships. The most extensive and important segment of this literature has examined individual psychological development and its association with the characteristics of relationships with parents, peer acquaintances, friends, and romantic partners.

Although not all research on individuals in intimate relationships has taken a life span perspective, I suggest that there are many advantages to doing so. A life span perspective helps us to understand how individual vulnerabilities, needs, and preoccupations shift in concert with developing capacities and resources, on the one hand, and with a changing social milieu, on the other.

There are three interrelated approaches that have been taken to studying intimacy across the life span. The first describes the changing matrix of intimate relationships that characterizes people's social and familial networks from infancy to old age. The second describes the provisions of those relationships, particularly their impact on concurrent interpersonal and psychological functioning (and, conversely, the impact of the individuals' developing life stage-related competencies, preoccupations, and needs on those relationships). Finally, the third approach attempts to identify early-life predictors of successful intimate relating in adolescence and adulthood.

Personality theorists have argued, for several decades, that the capacity to form and maintain intimate relationships in adulthood is predicated on the fulfillment of needs and the attainment of competencies during critical earlier points in development. Object relations theorists (e.g., Klein, Winnicott) argued that preverbal and emotionally charged conceptions of oneself as a lovable worthwhile person (or as an unlovable unworthy person) are inferred from the interactions that an infant or a young child has with his or her caregivers during the early years of life. In parallel fashion, conceptions of others as more or less loving and trustworthy and of relationships as more or less fulfilling also are formed.

These highly interdependent sets of expectations of self, other, and relationship theoretically form a foundation on which more sophisticated and differentiated expectations about relationships are built as a child matures. Furthermore, these foundational expectations guide decisions about behavior in interpersonal situations that can result in self-fulfilling prophecies when others respond in kind to those behaviors. They also can guide a child's interpretations of others' behavior and the child's own subsequent emotional reactions. To the extent that later experiences confirm earlier ones, expectations (and the associated emotions and behaviors) drawn from early experiences with caregiving will generalize to other people and situations. These expectation-driven interpersonal behaviors can either help or hinder a child's efforts to get his or her interpersonal needs met at each stage of life. Bowlby (1973) called these expectations "working models." Working models purportedly furnish a map for the interpersonal world and are a major source of continuity between the experiences of youth and those of adulthood.

There is reason to believe that the changing environmental conditions and internal developmental pressures associated with successive life stages influence, and are influenced by, important personal relationships. If results of recent research are any indication, then later intimate relating is not affected only by expectations derived from experiences with the caregivers of infancy; the interpersonal competencies that children develop as a result of relating to friends in childhood and adolescence also are influential. Furthermore, the concerns and preoccupations of each stage of adulthood will introduce new opportunities and challenges that will both draw on resources acquired earlier and push adults to acquire new resources.

To identify meaningful linkages between children's learned adaptations to earlier relationship experiences and adults' efforts to form satisfying intimate relationships, researchers must be able to recognize core features shared by earlier and later competencies and the experiences that elicit them. There are several competencies with roots in childhood experiences that are apt to serve as core features, or building blocks, of adult intimacy capacity. There are theoretical (and sometimes empirical) reasons for believing that these competencies are foundational to intimacy. It is not possible here to provide a comprehensive review of the childhood interpersonal experiences and associated adaptations that share features with, and thus serve as building blocks for, later intimate relating. A few examples will suffice.

Childhood experiences and adaptations are expected to be carried forward into adulthood through working models or sets of expectations and associated behaviors about the outcomes of potentially intimate interactions. The first working model that has shown stability over time and a tendency to influence interpersonal outcomes through successive life stages is that formed in conjunction with infants' efforts to establish a sense of safety and security in the presence of their caregivers. This working model is reflected in the presence or absence of a *secure attachment* to a parent or caregiver during infancy (Ainsworth, Blehar, Waters, & Wall, 1978). Longitudinal research has shown positive associations between secure attachment histories with one or more parents or caregivers and preschool children's social outcomes (e.g., popularity with peers) (Elicker, Englund, & Sroufe, 1992). During middle childhood, children who had secure attachments to parents during infancy are better able to maintain special peer friendships and are less likely to isolate themselves from group play (Shulman, Elicker, & Sroufe, 1994). Children who had insecure (avoidant) attachments during infancy are less empathic and more likely to engage in cruel behavior toward other children (Collins, Hennighausen, Schmit, & Sroufe, 1997).

Security or insecurity of attachment is attributed to the parent-child relationship as opposed to being viewed solely as a manifestation of infant temperament. Research indicates that parents who are equally responsive to all types of affect, who make themselves available when their infants seem to need them, and who are able to remain attentive while their children play or explore happily are more likely to have securely attached infants (Main, Kaplan, & Cassidy, 1985).

Additional research has established longitudinal linkages among a secure attachment during infancy, social skills with peers during early and middle childhood, and a "capacity for vulnerability," which can signal mature adolescent intimacy capacity (Sroufe et al.,

1993). A capacity for vulnerability reflects an expectation that "others will respond to their expressions of tender feelings with sensitivity and respect" (Collins et al., 1997). Sroufe et al. (1993) asked 15½-year-olds to engage in interpersonally challenging situations with peers and used the capacity for vulnerability measure to assess adolescents' openness to emotional risks as well as lack of defensiveness and avoidance. The results of this research showed that friendship skill scores from middle childhood, themselves predicted from the infant attachment category, predicted adolescents' capacity for vulnerability, which in turn was concurrently associated with intimacy and self-disclosure in current dating relationships.

What is striking about these results is the continuity that is demonstrated from parent-child relationships, to preschool socialization skills, to middle childhood friendships, to adolescent dating relationships. This continuity supports the notion that there are developmental building blocks that contribute to an adolescent's capacity for intimacy. The findings further demonstrate that crucial competencies are gained not only during the earliest years of the parent-child relationship but also in peer relationships during later childhood.

### Relational Factors

Relational factors include the partners' definition of their relationship and the other characteristics of the relationship (e.g., levels of trust, compatibility, mutual understanding, commitment, open communication). The partners must have a reasonably well-functioning relationship to tolerate the risks of intimacy within it.

*Definition of the relationship.* Friendships, romantic relationships, and parent-child relationships all carry with them different norms for sexual expression, self-disclosure, and mutuality. These norms determine which behaviors will elicit experiences of intimacy in the partners within the context of their relationship definition. In addition, researchers have identified different types of couple relationships that are associated with different expectations for intimacy. For example, Fitzpatrick's (1988a) independent couples tolerate exceptionally high levels of intimacy, relative to other couples, as part of what appears to be an overall acceptance of intense emotional expression, both positive and negative.

*Relationship characteristics.* Two factors are likely to have a noticeable impact on couple intimacy and relationship functioning: (a) compatibility of intimacy needs and (b) effective management of conflict (Christensen & Shenk, 1991; see also Prager, 1995). Incompatibilities in people's needs and preferences for intimate contact can be a source of intense frustration and distress. When partners fail to identify ways in which to meet their respective intimacy needs, they are likely to find themselves dissatisfied with their relationship. Because partners are more likely than not to have different needs and preferences, even the most satisfied and harmonious partners eventually will confront those differences and attempt to resolve them.

The need for intimacy encompasses two interwoven needs: (a) a need for another person to fully know and understand one as one knows and understands himself or herself and (b) a need for that same person also to fully accept one as he or she is. Intimacy needs can differ from one person to the next in several ways.

Individuals vary in the strength of their needs, and these individual differences affect how they perceive and behave in different situations. Research by McAdams and his colleagues has found that people high in intimacy motivation, assessed by coding Thematic Apperception Test (TAT) responses for intimacy-related content, spent more time in intimate interaction during the assessment period and described their relationships as more satisfying (McAdams, Healy, & Krause, 1984).

My own research has revealed individual differences in how people get their intimacy

needs met. My students and I interviewed 133 couples and asked them to describe how they currently met their needs for intimacy and how their partners contributed to the fulfillment of those needs (Prager, 1999a; Sarvis & Prager, 1999). Many mentioned self-disclosure and an attentive and accepting listener, whereas others emphasized affectionate and sexual contact. Still others mentioned quiet time together. It would be relatively easy for couples to find that they favor different ways of fulfilling their intimacy needs.

Different individuals seek to fulfill different needs through intimate interactions. Whereas all intimate interactions should by definition fulfill people's needs to be understood and accepted, they also can offer other provisions—guidance and advice, opportunities for catharsis or self-clarification, and affirmations of close relationships (Derlega & Grzelak, 1979). Findings from the same group of 133 couples revealed that nearly half of our sample listed some types of intimate contact with the partner (e.g., listen, give me feedback, express pride in my accomplishments, express affection and respect) as contributing to the fulfillment of their *achievement* needs, whereas the other half of the sample just wanted to be left alone to work (Sarvis & Prager, 1999).

There are several reasons why two people with significantly different levels of intimacy motivation might find themselves in a committed marital-type relationship with one another. The intensity of sexual attraction early in the relationship and the desire to make a favorable impression on the partner might lead a person whose needs for intimacy are otherwise not high to seek out frequent intimate contact with a new romantic partner. Sometimes, it seems easier for a person who has fears about intimacy to risk highly intimate disclosures early in a relationship when the investment, and therefore the risk of hurt, is less than it will be later. Conversely, a person with high needs for intimacy might hold back his or her requests for intimate contact at first because of fears of rejection or a desire to avoid conflict. These types of behaviors, typical of new relationships, are unlikely to be sustainable once a couple has established a relationship. Therefore, it is quite possible that partners might find themselves having incompatible intimacy needs.

Dysfunctional patterns of conflict management can create a chronic climate of negative affect between the partners that overwhelms the partners' positive feelings for one another (Gottman, 1994a). This overriding negative affect appears to inhibit efforts to engage intimately with the partner, perhaps because it is too difficult, once the patterns are set, to escape the negative feelings and to experience intimacy with the partner. Research by Lindahl and Markman (1990) suggests that it is the partners' inability to handle negative affect effectively when it arises that leads to maladaptive conflict management strategies and chronic negative affect. Intimacy is exceedingly difficult to sustain in these types of distressed relationships.

### Sociocultural Factors

Sociocultural ideas shape and reflect broad political and economic patterns, and they become internalized by individuals as ideas and expectations about "the way things normally are." These ideas in turn shape people's behavior and their emotional reactions to events in their intimate relationships.

Broad sociohistorical and economic trends appear to have affected the strength of intimacy needs reported by Americans. Levinger (1994) cited several studies documenting changes in Americans' valuing of autonomy and personal control and, concomitant with these, their valuing of intimacy. Two macrolevel changes that help account for increases in intimacy needs are (a) an increasing detachment from the "web of kin relationships in traditional family systems" to a more "conjugal form" (p. 14) and (b) the spread of commerce and associated consumerism, the market orientation of which rests on a concept of the individual as a consumer who can make autonomous choices. Accompanying these changes

is an increasing preoccupation with how one conducts private relationships.

Sociocultural gender role norms also appear to have affected gender-related patterns of intimate relating. Interactions between two women tend to be higher in depth of intimacy than do interactions involving one or two male partners. Similarly, women characterize their same-sex friendships as more intimate than do men, although these gender differences in intimacy do not hold up with lesbian and gay samples (Nardi & Sherrod, 1994). Cross-sex friendships occupy an intermediate position (for a review, see Werking, 1997). Intimacy in heterosexual romantic relationships shows a somewhat predictable trajectory over time; the early and late years of marriage are high in intimacy, whereas the intermediate child-rearing years are a time of less intimacy (for a review, see Prager, 1995). Gender-stereotyped parenting roles, role overload, and a generative focus on raising children to the exclusion of individual need fulfillment all can contribute to the drop in intimacy during the middle years of marriage.

Low levels of intimacy in men's friendships reflect prevailing gender role norms that equate masculinity with self-reliance, fearlessness, and invulnerability. Men might fail to cultivate intimate friendships with one another because (a) valuing friends too highly might suggest a failure of self-reliance and (b) the vulnerability of intimate contact might threaten their feelings of masculinity to the extent that feeling masculine, for any given man, is dependent on his conformity to conventional definitions of manhood portrayed in American culture (Prager, 1995). Intimate contact with male friends also can stimulate fears of homosexual feelings.

By contrast, expectations of marriage and the changing status of women have changed concurrently, and both contribute to the likelihood that heterosexual couples will expect higher levels of intimacy in the future. Expectations of marriage have shifted so that marriage as an economic partnership has been deemphasized in favor of a view of marriage as a source of companionship, love, and intimacy. Contributing to this expectation is the gradually increasing legal and economic parity of women with men. There is evidence that intimacy is more likely when partners are relatively equal in status and influence (Canary & Emmers-Sommer, 1997). Modern conceptions of intimacy, in fact, recognize equality as a necessary condition for intimacy given that people are more genuine, open, and revealing when they have equal access to resources, self-regulation, and influence (Levinger, 1994).

## ▶ Implications for Clinical Practice

Clinicians are likely to confront intimacy problems in couples and in single adults who have difficulty in forming or maintaining intimate relationships. Intimacy problems are likely, at least in part, because intimacy opens up relationship partners to broader and more personal aspects of one another and gives them more opportunities to hurt one another. It is likely, in fact, that some betrayal of vulnerability eventually is inflicted in any intimate relationship. Intimacy processes, over time, can carry with them built-in restraints, as people inevitably experience the human limitations of their partners (Roberts & Prager, 1997).

Research evidence suggests that people do indeed have some fears of intimacy's possibly hurtful consequences. Excessive fears about intimacy's emotional risks can prevent vulnerable individuals from entering into potentially intimate relationships. In a series of studies (Descutner & Thelen, 1991; Greenfield & Thelen, 1997), Mark Thelen and his colleagues found that for gay, lesbian, and heterosexual college students, fear of intimacy was negatively related to self-disclosure, comfort with emotional closeness, and relationship satisfaction, whereas it was positively related to loneliness and trait anxiety.

Because intimacy fulfills needs, individuals who avoid intimate contact can become lonely, anxious, or depressed (Solano, 1986). The loneliness that results from lack of inti-

macy cannot be satisfied through social contact alone (Shaver & Hazan, 1985).

I call intimacy's dual potential the "intimacy dilemma" (Prager, 1999a). Intimate interaction increases the potential for both joy and sorrow in personal relationships. People experience an intimacy dilemma because they simultaneously need and fear intimate contact. Therefore, I do not recommend that clinicians concentrate solely on helping people to relate more intimately with their partners. Rather, I suggest that clinicians help people to identify their own intimacy dilemmas and address them constructively.

Relationship partners should find comfortable ways in which to *regulate intimacy*. Effective intimacy regulation seems to involve a rhythm of intimate contact alternating with more separateness in which partners' needs are fulfilled and in which conflict and recrimination are minimized.

In couples' therapy, clinicians will need to address the partners' intimacy compatibility. Because people have different needs and tastes for intimate contact, they must negotiate for what they want within their intimate relationships. People yearn to get their intimacy needs met with their partners, and couple conflicts about intimacy can be emotionally charged. So long as partners are not excessively incompatible coming into their relationships, effective problem-solving skills potentially can result in intimate interactions that are rewarding for both partners. Couples who seek therapy, however, are likely to be stuck in nonproductive cycles of conflict about intimacy. This conflict is aggravated by escalating negative affect, distorted cognitions about intimacy, and ineffective communication behavior.

Elsewhere, I have outlined a cognitive-behavioral model of intimacy-oriented couple therapy that systematically targets these three problem areas (Prager, 1999a). I draw on a couple therapy model developed by Jacobson and Christensen (1996) in which interventions simultaneously target specific behavioral change and a more cognitive and emotional change called *acceptance*. Johnson and

Greenberg (1994) defined acceptance as "a baseline attitude of consistent, genuine, noncritical interest, a tolerance" for the partner's personality.

Couples will benefit most from learning to accept (a) differences in their intimacy need strengths, (b) the different circumstances under which they prefer to get their intimacy needs met, and (c) differences in how each uses intimate interactions (i.e., what types of gratifications intimate interactions provide). These are the types of differences that often are brought into relationships and are likely to reflect personality characteristics that have grown out of early experiences with family, peer relationships, and prior romantic involvements.

Couples will benefit most from working to change (a) individual fears of intimacy that stem primarily from experiences prior to the current relationships, (b) distorted negative attributions about partners' participation (or failure to participate) in intimate contact (i.e., inappropriate personalization of partners' needs and actions), (c) lack of communication skills for engaging in intimate interactions, (d) destructive patterns of communication that shatter trust and thereby discourage intimate contact (e.g., active rejection of the other, belittlement, threats to abandon the relationship, efforts to control the partner), and (e) destructive patterns of regulating and negotiating intimacy that polarize the partners and thereby exaggerate their apparent incompatibilities.

## ► General Conclusions

Intimacy is one of the most salient and rewarding aspects of personal relationships, and intimacy brings with it benefits both to relationships and to individual well-being. Intimacy was conceptualized here as a type of interaction with three components: (a) intimate behavior, which reveals personal and private aspects of the self; (b) intimate experience or *affect,* which is positive and reflects feelings of warmth, acceptance, caring, love, pride, or appreciation; and (c) intimate experience or *perceptions,* which reflect a person's conviction that he or she has been listened to, understood, and accepted by the partner. Future research on intimacy should address intimate interaction processes, intimate relationships, or both. In the case of the former, there are two needed thrusts: (a) a focus on the interactions among intimacy's components and the emotional consequences of those interactions for individuals and their relationships and (b) a focus on the interacting contextual factors that limit or expand possibilities for intimate relating. In the case of research on intimate relationships, a life span perspective promises to offer insights into linkages between life stage-related concerns, needs, and preoccupations and the intimate relationships in an individual's network at each stage of life. In addition, research examining associations between intimacy and other aspects of relationships, including trust, commitment, compatibility, and mutual understanding, also is promising. I have especially recommended research on intimacy need compatibility in couple relationships because individual differences in intimacy needs have been documented and intimacy-related problems have shown themselves to be some of the most difficult to treat in couple therapy.

# Contents

# Communication in Close Relationships

*Brant R. Burleson*
*Sandra Metts*
*Michael W. Kirch*

The contributions of communication to relationship functioning and outcomes have attracted the attention of researchers across multiple disciplines including communication, family studies, sociology, and psychology (for reviews, see Baxter & Montgomery, 1997; Bochner, 1984; Duck & Pittman, 1994; Montgomery, 1994). This interest has yielded a literature that is remarkably large and diverse, but it lacks an organizing framework, even within specific disciplines. Thus, the major goal of this chapter is to articulate a coherent but broad theoretical framework that organizes and integrates the literature on communication in close relationships. We begin by explaining the foundations of our framework, derived from a consideration of two perspectives on communication. We then illustrate how these two perspectives generate distinct but complementary descriptions of communication in close relationships. Rather than provide a comprehensive review of literature on communication in close relationships, we develop a framework through which such a review might be conducted.

## ▶ Conceptual Approaches to Interpersonal Communication

The integrative framework developed here is informed by two prevailing approaches to interpersonal interaction: the *strategic* and the *consequential*. We are not the first to propose that communication has multiple levels or roles in relationships. For example, what we term the *strategic* approach corresponds to Duck and Pittman's (1994) notion of instrumental talk, and our *consequential* approach encompasses both their indexical and essential forms of talk.

### The Strategic Approach

The strategic approach holds that communication involves the act of producing messages intended to service goals (Dillard, 1997; Motley, 1990). Concepts at the core of this approach include *goals or intentions* (desired ends toward which communicative efforts are directed), *strategies* (generalized action schemata associated with goal attainment), *tactics* (specific communicative moves for implementing a strategy), and *plans* (step-by-step organizational sequences for ordering tactics and alternatives). Typically, goals are arranged hierarchically; some goals are situation specific (e.g., winning an argument), and some goals span contexts (e.g., protecting the face needs of one's partner).

This approach assumes that messages are purposeful and constructed with some degree of intentionality. Of course, actors are not always conscious of the goals toward which their messages are directed or conscious of the planning activity in which they engage (Motley, 1990). Moreover, this perspective does not suggest that communicators necessarily seek goals that are individually or relationally beneficial or that they have the skills necessary to meet their goals. Indeed, the strategic perspective assumes that individuals will differ in the character of the goals they pursue (e.g., prosocial vs. antisocial) as well as in their ability to achieve goals effectively (i.e., their skillfulness).

### The Consequential Approach

Communication does more than service individuals' goals. All communication in a relationship is *consequential* in that it externalizes, objectifies, and structures the relationship in which it occurs. Communication enacts the relationship; expresses images of self, other, and the relationship; creates patterns, routines, and rituals; establishes and perpetuates shared codes and other meaning systems; and reinforces communal norms and rules. In short, communication in relation-

ships creates and maintains a *relational culture* (Wood, 2000).

The consequential approach shifts the focus from individual goals and corresponding actions to the generative structuring properties of communication. That is, communication is conceptualized as a system, the properties of which not only manifest features of the persons who interact but also reformulate and constrain these features (Watzlawick, Beavin, & Jackson, 1967). Hence, analyses informed by the consequential approach focus on the transpersonal structures created through joint interaction (e.g., codes, rules, roles, rituals) and how these structures connect, constrain, and coordinate the actions of the individuals in the relationship. The consequential perspective does not necessarily suggest that actor intentions and strategies are irrelevant (but see Fisher, 1982). Rather, this perspective argues that the consequences of communication, whether intentional or unintentional, accrue over the course of time, across multiple interactions, and eventually constitute the shared codes, norms, and routines characteristic of a relational culture.

In sum, we suggest that communication can be usefully viewed as functioning both strategically (in the service of individual intentions) and consequentially (in continually constituting a dynamic relational culture). The first of these views (i.e., communication as a goal-driven enterprise) articulates well with an increasingly popular *functional approach* to the analysis of personal relationships and is the focus of the next section.

## ▶ A Strategic-Functional Approach to Communication in Close Relationships

A functional approach to interpersonal relationships (Bochner, 1984; Burleson & Samter, 1994) stresses what certain relationships typically *do* for people and, consequently, what people come to look to those relationships *for.* Furthermore, the functional perspective focuses on communication as a central means through which people both pursue and service relevant relationship functions (Burleson, 1995).

### Components of the Functional Approach

A functional approach to relationships seeks to provide an integrated treatment of the functions or provisions of different relationships, the tasks that must be accomplished if relationships are to fulfill their functions, and the communication skills needed to achieve relationship tasks. Relationships are differentially functional; people expect different relationships to do different things for them, providing them with distinct sets of material, social, emotional, and psychological goods. The peculiar combination of functions associated with a relationship helps to define how that relationship is both similar to and distinguishable from other relationships (e.g., the functions of marriage typically are distinct from those of friendship).

The functions associated with a particular type of relationship generally suggest a set of tasks around which that relationship is organized (McFall, 1982). Tasks are those actions that individuals must be able to accomplish competently if a relationship is to serve its functions. An understanding of the tasks partners must accomplish, and of the behaviors these tasks encourage or obligate partners to perform, provides the foundation for identifying skills necessary to sustain a relationship.

In general, skills represent a learned capacity to do something (Hargie, 1997). A skills analysis seeks to articulate better and worse ways of accomplishing a particular task in a particular context; the specific shape of competent behavior varies from one task to the next (Schlundt & McFall, 1985; Spitzberg & Cupach, 1989). A core assumption of our functional perspective is that the achievement of desirable relationship outcomes (e.g., continuation or intensification of the relationship, relationship satisfaction, fulfillment of relationship expectations) will vary due to individual differences in relevant communication skills.

### Tasks in Personal Relationships Serviced Through Communication Skills

There are three major classes of tasks addressed through communication in all personal relationships: instrumental tasks, relationship maintenance tasks, and interaction management tasks. *Instrumental tasks* are those that typically define the focus of an interaction and serve to distinguish one interactional episode from another (Dillard, 1997). Common instrumental tasks include gaining or resisting compliance, requesting or presenting information, and soliciting or giving support, seeking or providing amusement. Because the functions associated with particular relationships are distinct (to a greater or lesser degree), the instrumental tasks associated with each type of relationship also will be relatively distinct. Some instrumental tasks are central in particular relationships (e.g., providing support and companionship in friendships), whereas other instrumental tasks are pursued only incidentally within particular relationships and are not integrally associated with the functions characteristic of those relationships (e.g., providing information in friendships). Problematic servicing of more incidental tasks can create temporary irritations but usually will not threaten a relationship. By contrast, the fulfillment of instrumental tasks centrally associated with a relationship's major functions should substantially influence satisfaction with that relationship.

The *manner* in which instrumental tasks are communicatively addressed typically will reflect, albeit implicitly, the speaker's feelings about the relationship and how the self is viewed in regard to the other. For example, a request can convey comity or contempt, and an explanation can suggest consideration or condescension. The expression of such feelings, frequently accomplished nonverbally, has been termed the "relational" level of communication and typically is contrasted with the "report" or literal level of communication (Watzlawick et al., 1967). Research suggests that this relational level of communication is especially important in expressing feelings regarding control, trust, and intimacy (Rogers, 1989). As with the literal level of communication, messages expressed at the relational level can be conveyed more or less skillfully.

*Relationship maintenance tasks* are associated with the maintenance, management, or repair of a relationship. These tasks focus on defining the relationship, establishing its parameters, managing its tensions, and dealing with threats to its integrity and endurance. These tasks are general; that is, they are relevant to and might need to be pursued in a wide variety of relationships. For example, conflicts can arise in both public (e.g., work, civic) and personal (e.g., family, friend) relationships. The need for relationship management skills arises from routine differences between individuals, competition between partners over limited resources, natural "bumps" in the course of relationship development, and strains inherent in balancing "dialectical tensions" (Baxter & Montgomery, 1997). There are more and less skilled ways of accomplishing maintenance tasks, and differences in such skills have consequences for relationship quality, a point illustrated in a variety of literatures including those examining *relationship initiation* (Douglas, 1987); *relationship definition, intensification, and transitions* (Weber & Vangelisti, 1991); *relationship tensions such as jealousy* (see Chapter 23 by Buunk & Dijkstra, this volume); *strategic relationship maintenance* (see Chapter 21 by Dindia, this volume); *conflict management* (see Chapter 19 by Canary & Messman, this volume); *relationship transgression and repair* (Metts, 1994); and *relationship disengagement and termination* (Baxter, 1985).

*Interaction management tasks* are those associated with establishing and maintaining coherent conversation. These general tasks transcend particular interactions and include (a) producing comprehensible, informationally adequate, and pragmatically relevant messages that fit appropriately into the turn structure of conversation (Clark & Bly, 1995); (b) defining social selves and situations (McCall & Simmons, 1978); (c) maintaining face (Cupach & Metts, 1994); and (d) monitoring and managing affect (Buck, 1984). Accomplishment of these tasks forms a "background consensus" within which other tasks may be pursued. When problems arise with respect to interaction management tasks, they must be addressed so that the background consensus is restored. Thus, interactants must possess skills that enable them to repair malformed utterances (Dillon, 1997), manage social embarrassment or face threats (Cupach & Metts, 1990), and regulate affect (see Chapter 13 by Guerrero & Andersen, this volume). If these tasks are not adequately serviced, then an interactional episode might be disrupted, but the relationship usually will not be threatened unless the problem proves to be a chronic one. Individuals with serious deficits in one or more of these skills are likely to be frustrating interactional partners and, hence, might have difficulty in establishing or maintaining relationships with others.

### Communication Skills in Personal Relationships: Distinctions and Clarifications

By equipping persons to manage the various tasks associated with relationships, communication skills should contribute significantly to how well relationship functions are fulfilled and how much happiness people derive from relationships. This key hypothesis has been the focus of some, but not enough, research (Meeks, Hendrick, & Hendrick, 1998; for reviews, see Boland & Follingstad, 1987; Hargie & Tourish, 1997). Moreover, the findings of extant research are clouded by problematic conceptions of communication skills and how these skills contribute to relationship outcomes. Thus, we offer several distinctions intended to clarify the function of communication skills in personal relationships.

*Distinguishing among motivations, skills, and behaviors.* Much research examining communication in close relationships is confusing because researchers have not distinguished sharply (at both the conceptual and operational levels) among communication motivations, skills, and behaviors. In general, *communication motivation* refers to the person's intentions and goals—what the person wants to do or is trying to do, how much the person wants to do something, and the persistence with which that end is pursued (Carlson, 1990, p. 404). Motivations may be either positive or negative with respect to others; people do not always pursue positive ends toward others, even in the context of close relationships. Although some motives are more desirable or prosocial than others, this does not mean that some motives are more *skillful* than others.

*Communication skill* refers to an individual's ability to accomplish communicative goals during the course of an interaction. Communication skills constitute acquired abilities that involve the use of interpretive and expressive resources in the pursuit of certain social outcomes (Hargie, 1997; Spitzberg & Cupach, 1989). Because they represent abilities of the individual, communication skills cannot be observed directly but rather must be inferred from observed behavior. When an individual is motivated to perform at his or her maximum level of ability, observed behavior might closely correspond to the underlying level of ability. When less motivated to perform, observed behavior will be a less reliable indicator of the individual's skillfulness. Socially desirable ends can be pursued either skillfully or unskillfully, as can socially undesirable ends.

*Communication behavior* refers to the verbal and nonverbal actions that a person generates in a particular context, with such behaviors being observable by others. Observed behavior is the product of the individual's motivations or intentions, the skills the individual has available to assist in pursuing those intentions, and contextual constraints that can influence both motives and the exercise of skills. Many studies (e.g., Christensen & Shenk, 1991) have examined communication behavior as a correlate of relationship outcomes, but the results of these studies frequently are ambiguous because it often is unclear whether the observed behaviors were the product of motivations, skills, or some combination of these.

Our distinctions among communication motives, skills, and behaviors suggest that the association between communication and relationship outcomes can be quite complex. Furthermore, several factors can moderate the association between communication skills, and relationship outcomes; we examine these factors next.

*Multidimensionality of communication skills.* Skills can be differentiated along several dimensions including code (e.g., verbal vs. nonverbal), content (e.g., making assertions, asking questions), communication process (e.g., message production, message reception), and goal pursued (e.g., comforting, persuading). Thus, there is no omnibus "communication skill." This means that researchers should avoid overly general claims about the relationship between communication skills and relationship outcomes. Instead, researchers should seek to assess associations between specific, well-defined communication skills and certain outcomes in particular relationships.

*Contextual influences.* Communication skills are not exercised in some global context but rather are used in settings characterized by particular intentions, circumstances, and partners. Understanding the connection between communication skill and relational outcomes, therefore, depends on discerning how features of the context affect skill use and outcomes. For example, Burleson and Denton (1997) found that the association between husbands' perceptual accuracy (a message reception skill) and their marital satisfaction varied as a function of couples' marital distress; the association was strongly *positive* in *happy* marriages but was moderately *negative* in *distressed* marriages. In some circumstances, then, ignorance (or incompetence) might well facilitate marital bliss. Hence, researchers should adopt the working assumption that the association between communication skill and relationship outcomes is variable, and researchers should seek to explain how diverse contextual factors moderate this association.

*Whose outcomes are affected by communication skills?* The individual's exercise of communication skills can affect the individual's own outcomes, those of his or her partner, or those of some other analytic unit (e.g., the couple or their children). Some skills predict the individual's own relational outcomes; these include compliance gaining (Cody, Canary, & Smith, 1994) and self-disclosure (Tardy & Dindia, 1997), among others. But some of a person's skills should predict partner outcomes. For example, several studies have found that the support skills of one partner predict the satisfaction of the other partner (e.g., Acitelli, 1996). However, one partner's skills might not always be positively associated with the other partner's relationship satisfaction. For example, Burleson and Denton (1997) found that wives' skill levels were positively associated with their husbands' marital satisfaction only in happy marriages; in distressed marriages, some of wives' skill levels were *negatively* associated with their husbands' marital satisfaction. It appears, then, that many communication skills might be double-edged tools that can be used to either help or hurt others, depending on the motivations of the communicators. In sum, numerous factors can moderate the association between communication skill and relationship outcomes.

### Developmental Analyses of Functions and Communication Skills in Relationships

Because both relationships and the people who create them undergo marked changes over time (Blieszner, 1994a), an adequate analysis of communication in relationships needs to provide an integrated treatment of how the functions, tasks, and skills associated with particular relationships vary as both relationships and their participants develop. There are at least three ways in which relationships develop or change: over history, over time, and over the life course.

*Development over history.* Relationship possibilities, as well as the specific character of particular relationships, change over the course of historical time (Mintz & Kellogg, 1988). Consider, for example, that the relationship currently studied under the rubric of "cross-sex friendship" is, in many ways, an invention of late 20th-century Western societies (Monsour, 1997). More broadly, the form of most relationships has undergone substantial change through the centuries, even including fundamental relationships such as friendship (Lopata, 1991), marriage (Gadlin, 1977), and parent-child (Aries, 1962). Changes in the forms of these relationships imply corresponding changes in the functions that these relationships serve, the tasks that must be accomplished to achieve relationship functions, and the skills that are needed to address the mutating tasks.

*Development over time.* A second sense in which relationships "develop" is that every relationship has a history. Several researchers have charted the phases that a relationship might pass through from initial acquaintance to, for example, intimate friendship or romantic involvement (e.g., Knapp & Vangelisti, 1996). These phases of relationship development may be best viewed not as invariant sequences of events but rather as expectations associated with the conduct of a relationship at a particular point in its history (Park & Waters, 1988). Many of these expectations center on the tasks or interactions that are believed to be appropriate at particular points in relationship history.

The distinct interactions that typically occur at different points in a relationship's history often demand different types of skills

(Buhrmester, Furman, Wittenberg, & Reis, 1988; Riggio & Zimmermann, 1991). For example, early in the acquaintance process, a major task facing partners is establishing and maintaining smooth, flowing, and nonproblematic interactions (Miell & Duck, 1986). Thus, skills in initiating conversations, finding a common topic, displaying interest in the other, and so on will be particularly important determinants of satisfying interactions. If the relationship is on an "intimacy trajectory" (as in friendships and romances), then skills in self-disclosure, emotional support, and interpersonal problem solving will become important at some later point. This analysis of relationship development suggests that people may filter potential partners based on interaction skills (Shaver, Furman, & Buhrmester, 1985), with those possessing the skills needed to deal with relevant tasks "passing through" a filter and, therefore, being made available for further and more intimate interaction. In sum, personal relationships are *skilled accomplishments* (Burleson, 1995) in which different communication skills are needed to address changing demands of relationships at different points in their development.

*Development over the life course.* Whereas relationships may be said to develop over time, people's conceptions and expectations for particular relationships also develop over the course of the life cycle. Ontogenetic changes in relationship expectations influence both interactional tasks and the skills needed to accomplish those tasks. For example, considerable research shows that how people think about friends, what they do with friends, and the meanings of friendship-relevant concepts such as intimacy, loyalty, commitment, and trust change dramatically over the course of childhood, adolescence, and the adult years (Fehr, 1996, pp. 8-16). These changes hold important implications for the social skills analysis of relationship development outlined earlier. Although the general sequences of phases through which relationships pass (e.g., initial meeting, acquaintance, exploration, and commitment) might

be similar over the course of human development, the internal character of each phase might vary substantially over the life cycle. Moreover, although the general tasks addressed within each phase of a relationship might share a superficial resemblance for younger and older persons, the specific character of these tasks, and thus what constitutes relevant social skills, might exhibit developmental variations (see Chapter 4 by Rose & Asher, this volume). In sum, an adequate analysis of the social skills implicated in relationship development must itself be developmental, considering how the functions, tasks, and skills associated with a particular relationship vary according to the developmental stage of both the relationship and those involved in that relationship.

### *Summary*

The strategic-functional approach to communication in relationships focuses on how people deploy their communication skills to accomplish varied tasks associated with the functions of particular relationships. People seek to accomplish tasks in relationships to receive (or supply) the provisions of those relationships. They pursue these tasks by exercising communication skills, but because they differ in their levels of skills, they are more and less successful in accomplishing tasks and, therefore, in achieving relationship functions. The relational tasks that people seek to accomplish, and the skills needed to address these tasks, undergo continual change as societies, people, and relationships all develop.

### ▶ A Consequential-Cultural Approach to Communication in Close Relationships

Whatever the developmental status of the relationship and its partners, communication does more than accomplish tasks and fulfill relationship functions. Communication also fabricates, maintains, and modifies a dynamic, evolving relational culture. Relational cultures are "processes, structures, and practices that create, express, and sustain personal relationships and the identities of partners" (Wood, 2000, p. 77). Much like culture in the broader sense, relational cultures consist of shared meaning systems (i.e., symbolic codes); characteristic interaction routines and rituals; norms and rules that organize, sequence, and control behavior; and role structures that organize situated identities. These relational structures typically are not the intended result of partners' strategic actions but instead are outcomes or consequences of day-to-day communication within relationships. This section illustrates several features of relational culture that emerge from, are manifested in, and come to regulate communication among people in relationships. Before taking up this discussion, we offer three points of clarification that frame the existing research on relational cultures.

### Social Structure and Relational Culture

First, although any relationship culture will be unique, all relational cultures exhibit features characteristic of other relationships in their class. Relational cultures are necessarily fabricated from the cultural structures that partners bring with them from the larger society (e.g., historically situated ideas about the functions and practices of particular relationships). People enter relationships (e.g., friendships, dating, marriage, parenthood) with extensive cultural knowledge (psychologically represented as schemata, prototypes, or lay theories [Reis & Knee, 1996]). This knowledge shapes expectations about what a particular relationship should be like, what rules should operate in that relationship, and what characteristics of the relationship make it satisfying, unsuccessful, stable, and so on (Surra & Bohman, 1991). Thus, every *particular* relational culture shares some elements (or central features) in common with other relational cultures in its class.

Second, because relational partners draw from conventions in the broader language community, interactions within particular relationships will necessarily reflect a limited range of adaptations from generalized communication practices. In virtually all conversations, interactants attempt to build coherent turns, refrain from topics and speech acts that are face threatening, and accomplish some instrumental objective. What lends relational cultures their unique quality is not so much remarkable communication events as the jointly constructed variations on more or less routine and common conversational practices. For example, even the most mundane enterprise of opening a telephone conversation is adapted by intimate partners to an abbreviated but highly informative routine signaling the presence and continuity of their relationship (Hopper & Drummond, 1992).

Third, the processes by which partners jointly construct, perpetuate, and enact roles consistent with their relational culture is similar to the processes that characterize broader social cultures. Much as the "social reality" that a culture, group, or institution holds to be self-evident is "developed, transmitted, and maintained" in social interaction (Berger & Luckmann, 1966, p. 3), the "relational reality" that partners hold to be self-evident emerges from the cumulative effects of routine daily interaction (Duck, 1994). In addition, in much the same way as social reality acts back on its producers, shaping and constraining ways of thinking and behaving (Berger & Luckmann, 1966), relational cultures act back on their creators, shaping and constraining their ways of thinking and behaving. In essence, relational cultures, once created, take on the moral and practical force akin to that of a social order.

Thus, individuals create relational cultures through the routine practices of their everyday conversations, and they act in accordance with the parameters of the culture they have created (Goldsmith & Baxter, 1996). They define and reinforce the intimacy and solidarity of their relational culture by imbuing the ordinary with shared relational significance, developing shared interpretative frameworks for their own and others' behaviors and identities, and reinforcing continuity in the midst of change by creating a symbolic relational history. We have selected three lenses through which to view any particular relational culture; collectively, they capture the essence of a relational culture. These lenses are (a) jointly constructed symbolic codes that reflect the shared meanings unique to a relationship's identity, (b) interaction rituals and routines that manifest idiosyncratic adaptations of standard conversational practices, and (c) norms and rules that guide relationship conduct and practices.

### Jointly Constructed Symbolic Codes

The symbolic properties of language and interaction enable people in a relationship to construct a shared meaning system. Within this system, otherwise unremarkable objects, events, people, activities, behaviors, and partner characteristics are imbued with unique significance. In the simultaneous process of constructing and participating within this system, partners align their perceptions and channelize their behaviors. This process is perhaps most evident in the stories that people in relationships tell and in the private idioms they create.

*Stories.* People's lives are formulated and reformulated in the stories they tell (Brockmeier & Harré, 1997). More than accounts, these stories are chronologies that both reflect and affirm the values, standards, norms, and rules of the social reality in which the tellers are participants (Gergen & Gergen, 1987). Similarly, relationships are formulated and reformulated in the stories that partners jointly construct and perpetuate in their retelling (Bochner, Ellis, & Tillman-Healy, 1997). These stories give historical substance to relationships, particularly by characterizing developmental stages (e.g., how they began, how they struggled to survive or were fated to be, how they endured hardships) and critical events (e.g., first sexual encounters,

engagements, weddings, births of babies) (Veroff, Sutherland, Chadiha, & Ortega, 1993). The ability to invoke the past through stories lends relationships continuity in the midst of change.

Stories are vehicles through which individuals link themselves as relational partners and characterize their joint relational identity. That is, during early phases of development, stories provide a common language and genre of events that can be distinguished from the language and events of the individual prior to the relationship. Gergen and Gergen (1987) referred to these as "unification myths" or stories imbued with relational rhetoric and themes focusing on the struggle to reach commitment. Next are "stability narratives" or stories about how relationships have (or have not) avoided stagnation, balanced change with stability, and remained vital. Finally, the stories of those couples who endure over time manifest the elements of what Gergen and Gergen called the "romantic saga" or state of deep communion.

Such stories function to elaborate a larger system of meanings by which partners construct their relational identities and evaluate their own and partners' behaviors. Stories give substance to fundamental features of relational culture such as *values* (e.g., what is important to say or not say, possess, sacrifice for, celebrate, and endure), *beliefs* (e.g., assumptions about what a relationship is in the abstract and in the particular), and *attitudes* (e.g., opinions about right and wrong, fidelity, trust, betrayal, commitment, and correct conduct). These stories often cohere around broader controlling themes or metaphors that essentialize relationships and define partners' roles. For example, romantic relationships might be seen as the product of hard work, adventures or journeys, dangerous enterprises, or games (Sternberg, 1995). These metaphors entail various combinations of values, beliefs, attitudes, and role expectations for the persons who view their relationships from these perspectives.

To summarize, relationship stories construct relationship realities as they are believed to have occurred and as they are expected to un-fold in the future. In this sense, stories are not only lived experiences but also ways of living. As Berger and Luckmann (1966) noted about larger cultural meaning systems, and as Stern-berg (1995) noted about stories in particular, once a symbolic "truth" becomes substanti-ated in and reinforced through communica-tion practices, people tend to interpret future experiences through this lens and behave in ways that are consistent with these symbolic constructions. To the extent that these sym-bolic constructions are enlightened, optimis-tic, and charitable, relationships undoubtedly benefit from their influence. However, to the extent that these symbolic constructions are ambiguous, pessimistic, or even pernicious, relationships might lock into a relational ver-sion of the negative self-fulfilling prophecy.

*Idioms.* A second linguistic form that charac-terizes the meaning systems of relationships is personal idioms or relational symbols. These verbal and nonverbal codes are a jointly constructed lexicon that partners de-vise for concepts that are important to them. Research (Baxter, 1987; Bell & Healey, 1992) indicates that friends and romantic couples create idiomatic expressions such as nicknames, terms of affection, teasing insults, and codes that refer to sexual activities and invitations. They create labels to refer to other people, and they create terms to index spe-cific moments that hold special meaning (e.g., first dates, first fights), symbolic places where special events occurred, and special ar-tifacts (e.g., songs, movies).

Despite the variations in the content of these idiomatic expressions, they function in similar ways across relationships. At the most general level, these special codes function like the language practices of any society; they constitute a common meaning system that connects users and differentiates them from nonusers. In this regard, idioms serve the im-portant function of boundary management (Petronio, 1991). That is, because personal re-lationships are nested within overlapping so-cial networks, idioms provide for internal inti-macy and cohesiveness while being respon-sive to external contingencies. For example, terms of affection and nicknames indicate an appreciation for the special qualities of a rela-tionship and the partner. Furthermore, the fact that personal idioms cannot be understood by outsiders affords relational partners a secret code to use for communicating while in the presence of others. For example, idiomatic re-quests and routines allow partners to effi-ciently and discretely signal their preferences (e.g., to leave a party) and their assessments of the actions of other persons (e.g., a coded "put-down").

Second, idioms provide relational partners with a mechanism to manage potentially face-threatening situations in their private interac-tions, much as conventional forms of polite-ness function in social situations (Metts, 1997). For example, teasing insults are a way in which to minimize potentially damaging threats to a partner's positive face while si-multaneously addressing bothersome behav-iors or attributes. Similarly, codes to signal sexual interest provide sufficient ambiguity for couples to negotiate sexual episodes with-out feeling undue role constraints and obliga-tions that threaten negative face.

A third function that relational idioms serve is similar to that for relationship stories. Much as stories create a shared reality in terms of values, beliefs, and attitudes, rela-tional idioms create a shared symbolic code, a specialized language of sorts, that links part-ners by its very existence. Relational idioms are, in a literal sense, nonsense, much like idi-omatic expressions in the culture at large (e.g., "You're pulling my leg," "Get off my back"). But for those who understand their meanings, idioms are highly expressive. Indeed, for per-sons in close relationships, idioms communi-cate intimacy by virtue of their very existence (Hopper, Knapp, & Scott, 1981).

### Interaction Routines and Rituals

Stories and idioms frequently appear in interaction routines and rituals, which are events that occur in more or less patterned ways at fixed times and places and, especially for rituals, serve a largely symbolic purpose. These regularities provide the recurring interaction structures, both day-to-day and on special occasions, that characterize relationship cultures.

*Routines.* Interaction routines tend to develop naturally from the simple repetition of habituated daily interaction (Berger & Luckmann, 1966). For example, many couples plan their days over morning coffee and engage in "catching up" conversations at the end of their days during dinner. Friends often meet for lunch or talk on the phone to gossip, catch up, and plan activities. In general, these routines provide a degree of predictability and ongoing connection between relationship partners.

In addition to recurring occasions and topics of talk, relational cultures also manifest recurring conversational episodes that have become so routinized that they appear to be scripted. For example, couples who have been together for many years have told their relationship stories so often that they can talk in unison and/or complete each other's turns with choreographed precision (Dickson, 1995). Similarly, partners in close relationships sometimes develop scripts for play episodes that are idiosyncratic and highly synchronized (Glenn & Knapp, 1987). In successful episodes of this sort, both partners recognize the "signal" that initiates the script and smoothly enact supportive roles as performer and audience. In unsuccessful episodes, one partner fails to recognize the initiation of the script or is not able or willing to enact the appropriate role as co-performer or audience.

*Rituals.* Relationships also develop their own rituals. Some of these are variations on types of rituals that most members of the broader culture would recognize (e.g., a stylized Christmas or Passover meal, celebrating a wedding anniversary in a particular way). Other rituals, however, are not derived from cultural prototypes but rather are emergent and unique constructions of relational partners. For example, Baxter (1987) found that partners often ritualized chance occurrences because of their symbolic meanings (e.g., the continuing practice of hiding stuffed hearts that originated with a Valentine's Day trick).

Regardless of their origin, routines and rituals are an important part of a relationship's culture. They reaffirm, in much the same way as do stories, the continuity of relational connections over time (Werner, Altman, Brown, & Ginat, 1993) and across relationship transitions (e.g., early stages of parenthood) (Friese, Hooker, Kotary, & Schwagler, 1993). Of course, routines also can be dysfunctional, as in recurring patterns of complaints, accusations, and abuse. Likewise, rituals can become disassociated from their affirming symbolic meanings as in a disengaged couple's empty recognition of a wedding anniversary. The practice of recognizing the wedding anniversary often continues in the absence of genuine feeling because it has become normative behavior and might even be a way in which to follow a "rule" about hiding relationship problems from other members of the network. This brings us to the final aspect of relational culture to be discussed—norms and rules.

### Relational Norms and Rules

Norms and rules are needed to maintain, monitor, and correct the behaviors of people in relationships. They also are needed to guide relationships as they interface with other relationships in the social network. Although norms and rules both refer to patterns of behavior, we distinguish them according to their prescriptive force. Specifically, norms are typical or habitual patterns of behaviors that people come to expect in certain contexts, whereas rules are "prescriptions" for behaviors that are prohibited, obligated, or preferred in certain contexts (Shimanoff, 1980). In a sense, norms describe "what is," and rules describe "what ought to be." Violation of normative patterns can result in confusion, but violation of rules is likely to result in some form of sanction. This is evident in the research on couples' reactions to relational transgressions (Metts, 1994) and in friends' reactions to improper relational conduct (Argyle & Henderson, 1985).

The conceptual distinction drawn here between norms and rules does not mean that couples always recognize the difference. Rules often are tacit expectations for proper conduct, and so long as normative patterns are in correspondence to these expectations, couples might not realize that they actually are following relational rules. Alternatively, a rule articulated at some point in a relationship, as when a child is told never to "talk back" to his or her parents, might become normative communicative behavior even in adulthood.

Close relationships manifest a variety of communication norms in talk. For example, norms of informality are evident in the conversations of most friends. Friends regularly violate formal rules for coherent talk by interrupting and switching topics. They also freely engage in a wide range of linking behaviors such as gossip and references to shared experiences (Planalp, 1993). But in some relational cultures, norms of topic selection moderate openness; problematic topics become "taboo" and are systematically avoided (Baxter & Wilmot, 1985).

In relationships generally, interdependence means that conflict is inevitable (Baxter & Montgomery, 1997). Although there is variability across relational cultures regarding specific types of incidents and topics that prompt conflict, norms emerge within most relationship cultures that reflect more or less predictable ways of dealing with conflict (Fitzpatrick, 1988a). Some patterns reflect active and constructive negotiation of differences, whereas other patterns reflect a general tendency to avoid conflict and/or to enact episodes in ways that undermine relationship solidarity, as evidenced in repetitive exchanges of demand-withdraw patterns (Christensen & Shenk, 1991) or reciprocal negative affect (Gottman, 1994a).

These habits or typical practices are considered norms because they do not arise from prescriptions that couples have established for appropriate conduct. However, it is not surprising that relational partners also establish rules (more or less consciously) that are designed to control the potential disruptive consequences of poorly managed conflict (Honeycutt, Woods, & Fontenot, 1993). Jones and Gallois (1989) identified three such rules: consideration (e.g., not saying hurtful things), conflict resolution (e.g., being willing to say one is sorry), and positivity (e.g., being positive and supportive). Rules for managing conflict are particularly important in close relationships because they allow differences to be managed without incurring secondary damage to the identities, self-esteem, and positive face of partners (Metts, 1997).

One arena in which both norms and rules seem to operate is the complicated circumstance of network overlap. Because relationships are embedded within other network systems, they develop norms and rules for interfacing with other persons who are linked to the primary relationships. For example, a spouse might have one or two close friends with whom he or she wants to spend time. Norms emerge to accommodate these needs (e.g., bridge or poker nights, Saturday afternoon visits). Norms also emerge for the types of topics partners typically discuss in their conversations with other network members. Often, these norms develop quite naturally from shared interests and activities. At other times, however, these norms actually are the result of one or both partners following the rules for privacy regulation within a primary relationship (e.g., when family members keep certain "secrets" from the social network) (Vangelisti, 1994a).

In addition, the norms and rules of one relational culture might be inconsistent with those of the other, causing role conflict and/or negotiation of meta-rules that further define the scope conditions of more specific rules. Baxter and Widenmann's (1993) study of why partners reveal and conceal information about their dating relationships to various other network members provides a good illustration of this dilemma. Baxter and Widenmann found that couples' decisions were based on three considerations: the type of information that they contemplated revealing, the norms and rules operating in their relationships with the network members, and the norms and rules of privacy operating within their dating relationships.

In sum, norms and rules, like other aspects of a relational culture, emerge over time from recurring communication practices. Like other aspects of a relational culture, they come to govern these same communication practices. For good or ill, they are the product that acts back on the producers.

## ▶ Conclusions

Our goal in this chapter has been to sketch a framework capable of accommodating the extensive and extremely diverse body of research on communication in close relationships. We identified two broad perspectives on the nature of communication (the strategic and the consequential), and we observed that each of these fits with a respective approach to the study of personal relationships (the functional and the cultural). In concluding, we wish to underscore ways in which the strategic-functional and consequential-cultural approaches enrich each other.

Although individuals will enter into particular relationships initially by relying on widely shared conventional schemata specifying relationship functions, as they enact the emerging relationships, these individuals very likely develop unique ideas about the relationships' functions, the tasks that must be accomplished in service of those functions, and the skills needed to successfully address these tasks. These unique ideas, in turn, become powerful influences shaping individuals' expectations, not only for the particular relationships but also for all relationships of this type.

Thus, although relationship cultures are created by their members, they come to powerfully constrain the ideas and actions of their members.

Relational cultures not only influence individuals' notions about relationship functions and tasks, these cultures also affect the communication skills of their members and can do so in several distinct ways. For example, relational cultures differ in the extent to which members are expected to service certain functions and, therefore, differentially encourage (or discourage) the development of particular skill clusters. Consider that in many women's friendships, there is a strong expectation that partners will be sources of sensitive emotional support for each other, whereas many men's friendships carry few expectations for the mutual provision of sensitive emotional support. Given these different expectations, it is not surprising that seeking and providing emotional support typically occurs more frequently in women's friendships than in men's friendships and that women typically are more skilled at the provision of emotional support than are men (Kunkel & Burleson, 1998). A very different line of research indicates that parental communication in some relational cultures ("person-centered" families) encourages children's development of sophisticated social-cognitive and communication skills, whereas communication in other family cultures ("position-centered" families) tends to suppress or discourage the development of these skills (for a review, see Burleson, Delia, & Applegate, 1995). In sum, individuals shape their relational cultures through the exercise of their communication skills, but these cultures can themselves strongly influence individuals' communication skills.

The recognition that relational cultures differentially influence individual skill development suggests that these cultures can be distinguished in terms of several important theoretical dimensions. Although we cannot develop this point here, it seems clear that some relational cultures are malleable, whereas others are rigid; some are permeable, whereas others are impermeable; some are complex, whereas others are simple; and so forth. We believe that a key feature of relational cultures is that they are differentially open to change, whereas a key feature of individuals is that they are differentially skilled at effecting such change. This observation has interesting implications for therapists working with couples. It also suggests an interesting direction for future research exploring the dialectical connections between individuals and the relational cultures they fabricate through their communicative conduct.

# Contents

# Relationship Conflict

*Daniel J. Canary*
*Susan J. Messman*

Personal relationships present many opportunities for the emergence and escalation of interpersonal conflict. Conflict accompanies couple intimacy and interdependence (Braiker & Kelley, 1979), and of all social groups, families have the most conflict (Shantz & Hobart, 1989). Living with others increases the opportunity for all types of interaction, especially conflict. Conjugal partners and family members encounter frequent occasions of interpersonal boundary violations (Petronio, 1994; Vuchinich, 1984). Such violations most often lead to conflicts between romantic partners, between parents and children, and between siblings.

Yet, the frequency of conflict appears less important to relational functioning than does its management during interaction. Straus (1979) noted, "A key factor differentiating

AUTHORS' NOTE: The authors thank Bill Cupach, Brian Spitzberg, Beth Semic, and Eura Jung for their help in identifying relevant research.

what the public and many professionals regard as 'high conflict families' is not the existence of conflict *per se,* but rather, inadequate or unsatisfactory modes of managing and resolving the conflicts which are inherent in the family" (p. 85). For example, flexibility versus rigidity in conflict patterns differentiates satisfied couples from dissatisfied ones (Sillars & Wilmot, 1994) and differentiates healthy families from dysfunctional ones (Doane, 1978). In addition, satisfied romantic partners and family members demonstrate the ability to manage conflict without escalating the severity of the problem (Bochner & Eisenberg, 1987).

We assume that, like all human activities, conflict behaviors and outcomes vary widely due to a number of factors. We cannot possibly review or represent all of the research and theory connected to relationship conflict. Since our previous review of the literature (Canary, Cupach, & Messman, 1995), more than 300 research articles have been published on interpersonal conflict. In this chapter, we discuss how conflict reflects and affects relational life. More specifically, we discuss romantic couple conflict, issues unique to different family relationships, and explanations for conflict interaction. We cannot elaborate here on the many ways in which interpersonal conflict has been defined and conceptualized (for our review of that issue, see Canary et al., 1995).

## ▶ Conflict in Romantic Relationships

By *romantic relationships,* we refer to couples who are together for purposes of courtship and affection including dating, engaged, and married partners. We discuss two issues relevant to romantic couple conflict: couple types and the demand-withdraw pattern.

### Couple Types

Romantic couples differ in qualitative ways that play out in terms of interaction behavior. For example, Fitzpatrick (1988a) identified four types. *Traditionals* hold conventional attitudes with regard to sex roles, enjoy interdependence, and presume the worth of relational welfare over individual goals. *Independents* adhere to an egalitarian ideology, desire both autonomy and interdependence, and negotiate to advance their personal objectives. *Separates* uphold a conventional ideology, although they want to remain autonomous with regard to emotional connection and conflict. *Mixed* couples represent a blend of two types, with the most common being a Traditional wife and a Separate husband. Interestingly, Gottman (1994a) reported five couple types differentiated on the basis of their conflict management behaviors, three of which are "functional" and two of which are not functional. As Gottman noted, the three functional types parallel Fitzpatrick's (1988a)

types. First, *validating couples* rely on emotional connection but neutral affect in managing conflict, resembling Traditionals. Next, *volatile couples* engage each other over a wide span of large and small issues, resembling Independents. Finally, *conflict minimizers* seek to detract attention from the issue and avoid conflict, similar to Separates. The other marital types appear dysfunctional due to their use of defensiveness, withdrawal, and contempt (unlike any of Fitzpatrick's "pure" types).

Research reveals that conventionally ruled Traditionals use positive tactics, references to relationship expectations, indirect tactics regarding unimportant issues but direct confrontation regarding important issues, and sequences involving validation and "contract" sequences (e.g., husband offers information, wife agrees) (Burggraf & Sillars, 1987; Fitzpatrick, 1988b). Traditionals also reciprocate each other's disagreements. Goal-driven Independents directly discuss conflict issues, use competitive messages for large and small issues, confront partners who attempt to avoid conflict discussion, share information, and provide justifications for spouses' compliance. Fixated on autonomy, Separate partners tend to use indirect messages, avoid solving each other's problems, but confront each other when one partner complains. In brief, couple type appears to affect the manner in which couples manage conflict, although all partners tend to reciprocate behavior regardless of their couple type (Burggraf & Sillars, 1987).

### Demand-Withdraw Pattern

Many interesting forms of conflict patterns have been uncovered (for a review, see Messman & Canary, 1998). The *demand-withdraw pattern* represents an asymmetrical pattern most relevant to romantic partners (cf., Laughlin & Vangelisti, 1999). Demand-withdraw occurs when one person approaches the partner about a problem and the partner responds by attempting to avoid the issue or the person. Christensen, Heavey, and colleagues have developed a program of research on the demand-withdraw pattern (for a review, see Sagrestano, Heavey, & Christensen, 1998). Observational data reported in these studies (Christensen & Heavey, 1990; Heavey, Layne, & Christensen, 1993; Sagrestano, Christensen, & Heavey, 1998) reveal that the demand-withdraw pattern represents a dissatisfied and less powerful spouse who seeks change in the partner on a specific issue. The partner who likely benefits from the status quo avoids the other partner.

This program of research also has emphasized how sex differences might influence the demand-withdraw pattern. The findings are clear with regard to sex differences; they do exist, although they are countermanded by the person who desires change (Kluwer, de Dreu, & Buunk, 1998). In most situations, women demand and men withdraw. But sex differences are overridden by the issue of who desires change such that if a male desires change in the partner on a specific issue, then he will demand and she will withdraw. However, discontent by one person also has been associated with demands from that person's partner. For example, the wife's dissatisfaction with the husband's performance of household chores is associated with the husband demanding change in how the house is cleaned in addition to the wife demanding change from her husband (Caughlin & Vangelisti, 1999; Kluwer, Heesink, & van de Vliert, 1997). These findings indicate that the demand-withdraw pattern reflects general relational dissatisfaction in addition to how an underbenefited person might attempt to remedy his or her situation.

Kluwer et al. (1997) showed that a primary problem area for change concerns the division of household labor. Kluwer et al. examined associations among self-reports of discontentment regarding division of household labor and paid work, demand-withdraw patterns, conflict strategy type (integrative, distributive, or avoidant), constructive versus destructive outcomes of the conflicts, and traditional versus egalitarian marriage. Kluwer et al. found that both wife and husband discontentment

with household chores predicted demand-withdraw patterns, distributive conflict behaviors, and destructive outcomes (see also Chapter 10 by Steil, this volume).

## ► Family Conflicts

Conflict initially is learned through frequent interactions with family members and is further developed throughout childhood and adolescence (Dunn, 1983; Raffaelli, 1992). Several researchers have argued that childhood conflict interactions contribute to personal and social development (e.g., Shantz & Hobart, 1989). However, what is learned might or might not be positive (Alexander, 1973) and might lead to either positive or negative effects on development.

Children can experience neglect and abuse if parents manage conflict interactions incompetently (Minuchin, 1992). Conflict between parents and children also leads to adolescents' conduct disorders (Barrera, Chassin, & Rogosch, 1993), substance abuse (Montemayor, 1983), running away, and suicide attempts (Laursen & Collins, 1994). On the other hand, conflict can yield positive outcomes for families as well. For example, children can learn both effective conflict management behaviors and perspective-taking skills (Paikoff & Brooks-Gunn, 1991). Moreover, parents can develop their negotiation skills in conflicts with their children. In short, family conflicts have the potential to affect, either positively or negatively (or both), the individuals involved.

### Conflict Between Parents and Children

Parent-child relationships involve "an involuntary association, an imbalance of power and resources, and obligations for the parent to function as caregiver" (Canary et al., 1995, p. 52). Such features yield differences between parent-child conflict and conflict in other types of close relationships (see also Chapter 4 by Rose & Asher and Chapter 5 by Collins & Laursen, in this volume). For example, compared to other relationship types, parent-adolescent conflict resolutions involve more submissions, standoffs, and withdrawals (Laursen, 1993). Avoidance represents a norm of family conflict management not only when children are young but also when they are middle-aged (Fingerman, 1998; Vuchinich, 1987). Most of the research on parent-child conflict examines interactions with young children and adolescents. Relatively little research explores parent-adult child conflict.

*Conflict involving young children.* Young children learn conflict management and develop their skills through interactions with parents. Dunn and Munn (1985) indicated that children engage in conflict by the age of 18 months. By the age of 3 years, children successfully apply conflict management rules; instead of simply responding "no," children gradually learn to use justifications appropriately in conflict situations (Dunn & Munn, 1987; Dunn & Slomkowski, 1992; Eisenberg, 1992). Furthermore, between the ages of 2 and 3 years, toddlers display the ability to block mothers' control attempts by talking extensively on some other topics (Vaughn, Kopp, & Krakow, 1984).

Conflict issues between parents and young children often involve parental attempts to control the children or gain compliance. However, parents and toddlers have conflicts about a variety of issues including possessions/rights, rules of the house, manners, caretaking, destruction of objects, and independence (Dunn & Munn, 1987; Eisenberg, 1992). Shantz (1987) posited that as children get slightly older (ages 4½ to 7 years), less conflict concerning objects occurs. Instead, children attach more importance to social control issues such as others' intrusive behaviors and getting others to act in a desired manner. Often, such conflicts reflect children's attempts to gain compliance from parents rather than vice versa.

Much of the early parent-child conflict research focused on parental control and child noncompliance, although more recent research emphasizes the bidirectionality of parent-child conflict (Eisenberg, 1992; Patterson, 1982). For example, Patterson's (1982) theory of coercive control suggests that parents adapt their conflict management behaviors to children's coercive behaviors (e.g., hitting, yelling, ignoring parents) rather than vice versa. Eisenberg (1992) found that disagreements about child compliance constituted a small portion of mother-child conflict and that mothers both opposed the children more and were noncompliant to the children more than vice versa. She argued, "Children may learn more about negotiation when mothers are noncompliant than when they themselves fail to comply" (p. 25). In addition, children learn that certain utterances relegate more power or choice to the partner. Specifically, both mothers and children tended not to challenge their partners when the partners opposed requests for permission (i.e., utterances that relegate power to the partners).

*Conflict between parents and adolescents.* Although by adolescence individuals might mature in many aspects of their interaction behaviors, conflict management interactions appear to require still more maturity (Selman, 1980). For example, young children often express unmitigated hostility. Adolescents express less unmitigated hostility than do younger children; however, they do not mitigate their hostility to the extent that adults do (Vuchinich, 1984). Fletcher, Fischer, Barkley, and Smallish's (1996) findings support this contention, as mothers' conflict behaviors reflected more flexibility and positivity than did those of their teenagers.

Two main developmental changes in parent-adolescent conflict frequently appear in the literature, although some research has begun to question the occurrence of these changes. First, numerous researchers have reported a general curvilinear trend for conflict in adolescence (e.g., Selman, 1980). It appears that conflict increases beginning during early adolescence, peaks during mid-adolescence, and subsides during late adolescence

(Montemayor, 1983). Paikoff and Brooks-Gunn (1991) argued that hormonal and physiological changes during puberty play a primary role in the way in which parents and adolescents interact during conflict (see also Robin & Foster, 1989). However, Smetana (1989) did not find differences in age groups ranging from 10 to 18 years. Laursen, Coy, and Collins's (1998) meta-analysis similarly did not support the argument for a curvilinear trend; instead, they found a linear relationship in which conflict rates and total conflict (i.e., a combination of conflict rates and conflict affect) declined from early to late adolescence. In addition, Galambos and Almeida's (1992) longitudinal study revealed that conflict over domains (e.g., chores, appearance, politeness), as well as overall conflict, declined between the ages of 11 and 13 years. As one potential resolution to the controversy, Rueter and Conger (1995) theorized and found support for the contention that conflict increased in hostile and coercive families but decreased in warm and supportive families.

Second, research has supported significant effects on conflict for sex of parents and sex of children. For example, Jacob (1974) argued that adolescent boys become more assertive and forceful at the expense of their mothers but not of their fathers. Apparently, mothers tend to complement their sons' control attempts by being less dominant, whereas fathers become more dominant (Paikoff & Brooks-Gunn, 1991). Galambos and Almeida's (1992) review indicated that mothers have more conflict with adolescent children than do fathers. Nonetheless, other studies have reported no effect due to adolescent sex or parent sex (e.g., Montemayor & Brownlee, 1987). Galambos and Almeida (1992) found one effect due to parent sex, but it was opposite of the prediction of previous sex difference research. Additional research appears warranted to resolve the discrepancies regarding changes in conflict during adolescence and regarding sex differences.

Beyond examinations of developmental issues, research has focused on conflict issues between parents and adolescents. Conflict issues for adolescents have further evolved beyond those manifested during middle childhood. For example, conflict regarding personal control over one's own activities and behaviors becomes preeminent to adolescents. Key issues associated with this control include issues such as sleeping late, style of hair and dress, chores, relationships, activities, personality characteristics, bedtime and curfew, and legitimacy or correctness pertaining to points of view on given issues (Smetana, Yau, Restrepo, & Braeges, 1991). Montemayor (1983) argued that these issues most often concern routine behaviors (i.e., day-to-day activities such as chores and schoolwork) and that such issues typically occur between parents and adolescents in every generation; that is, adolescents will experience similar types of conflict later when they are adults and have adolescent children.

*Conflict between parents and adult children.* Little research has examined conflict between parents and their adult children. However, the limited research that exists indicates that conflict remains an important issue after adolescence. For example, Nelson, Hughes, Handal, Katz, and Searight (1993) found that young adults' adjustment and ego identities were negatively affected by high levels of perceived family conflict. Fingerman's (1995, 1996) research focused on an older population (i.e., elderly mothers and middle-aged daughters) and found that parent-child conflict remains significant when parents have reached old age. Fingerman (1995) indicated that mothers underestimated their daughters' negative management of and responses to their conflict. In addition, Fingerman (1996) argued that some conflicts between elderly mothers and middle-aged daughters resulted from developmental differences. For example, although both mothers and daughters reported that their relationships were important, mothers found the relationships more salient, and this led to tension between the parents and children. In addition, tension resulted from mothers and daughters having different opinions regarding the mothers' needs. These studies pique one's interest in parent-child conflict beyond adolescence.

### Conflict Between Siblings

Sibling interaction represents a major portion of children's family interactions (Bank & Kahn, 1975). Moreover, most children have siblings and experience aggressive behavior with their siblings (Dunn, 1983; Raffaelli, 1992). Sibling relationships are typified by a greater tolerance for conflict yet more anger and aggression compared to relationships with peers (Dunn & McGuire, 1992). For example, siblings typically express unmitigated hostility and oppose each other directly (vs. indirectly) in conflict (Vuchinich, 1984).

Sibling conflict has not received the level of research attention that parent-child conflict has garnered. However, studies have illustrated the nature of sibling conflict in terms of power and outcomes and have linked sibling conflict to developmental issues.

Older siblings display more power in conflict situations than do younger siblings (Shantz & Hobart, 1989). For example, Abramovitch, Corter, and Pepler (1980) observed that older siblings in the preschool age group exert control over their younger siblings by being the primary instigators of conflicts and by responding more powerfully (vs. submissively) to agonistic behaviors. Phinney (1986) observed that 5-year-olds specifically varied their conflict communication behaviors in ways that reflected their understanding that they were more powerful than younger siblings yet less powerful than older siblings. At least for preschool children, interactions with siblings seem to reflect unfair complementarity versus symmetry, where older siblings dominate younger siblings and where younger siblings submit (Dunn, 1983).

By adolescence, such power imbalances subside for siblings close in age because both have developed argument skills. Nonetheless, conflict remains an integral feature of the sibling relationship. Laursen and Collins (1994)

indicated that, after mothers, adolescents experienced the most conflict with siblings. Outcomes of sibling conflicts rarely involve compromise and most often involve either withdrawals, standoffs, submissions, or third-party interventions (Laursen & Collins, 1994). Such conflicts usually end interaction between the siblings and, if chronic and intense, can lead to deterioration of the relationships (Patterson & Bank, 1989). However, sibling relationships rarely end due to the involuntary association found in family relationships (Laursen & Collins, 1994).

### Group-Level Conflict in Families

Family conflict is not limited to dyadic interactions. Families as a group often engage in conflict situations such as at the family dinner table (Vuchinich, 1984). In addition, third-party interventions sometimes occur such as when young children's and adolescents' conflicts cannot otherwise reach resolutions (Vuchinich, 1990). A slightly different twist on group conflict occurs when conflict between parents affects children.

When children and parents experience conflicts as a group in situations such as family dinners, the conflict experience proceeds in somewhat different directions. For example, Vuchinich (1984) found that oppositions were more common between parents than between parents and children. Vuchinich, Emery, and Cassidy (1988) found that third parties affect the conflicts between family members. The final outcome of family conflicts varied based on whether or not third parties intervened, such that submission was less likely and withdrawal was more likely after third-party intervention. Moreover, avoidance strategies commonly appeared when third parties did not reciprocate conflictual turns or when conflicts ended in standoffs, which occurred 65% of the time.

Other examples of third-party intervention occur when parents attempt to mediate or resolve conflicts between siblings. Some researchers argue that parents should not intervene. Intervention might retard children's development of conflict management skills (Brody & Stoneman, 1987), and intervention typically leads to more sibling conflict and longer conflicts (Felson & Russo, 1988; Vuchinich et al., 1988). However, Ihinger (1975) argued that parental intervention can be constructive by facilitating children's learning of conflict management rules. Ross, Filyer, Lollis, Perlman, and Martin's (1994) findings supported the benefits of parental intervention and did not support parental intervention as problematic for children's conflict management. In addition, Brody, Stoneman, McCoy, and Forehand (1992) found that when parents treated siblings equally and family harmony was maintained in discussions, adolescent siblings experienced less conflict.

Conflict between parents negatively affects children's adjustment in several ways (Amato & Keith, 1991a; Lewis & Feiring, 1981). For example, Davies and Cummings (1998) found that marital discord leads to emotional insecurity for 6- to 9-year-olds, which in turn leads to adjustment problems such as withdrawal, anxiety, depression, and worry. In addition, toddlers were found to respond to adult aggression with distress (Cummings, Iannotti, & Zahn-Waxler, 1985). High levels of parental conflict also can lead to problem behaviors in children and adolescents (Robin & Foster, 1989). Moreover, parental conflict negatively affects young adults' life satisfaction and subjective well-being across cultures (Gohm, Oishi, Darlington, & Diener, 1998). However, research also shows that parents' specific use of negative conflict behaviors and physical conflict results in more detrimental effects than do high levels of conflict per se, nonphysical conflict, or divorce (Amato & Keith, 1991a; Garcia O'Hearn, Margolin, & John, 1997). Importantly, parents' positive interactions with their children mediate the effects of parental conflict on children (Fauber, Forehand, Thomas, & Wierson, 1990).

## ▶ Selected Explanations for Conflict Escalation

Although ubiquitous, conflict is not fun. Managing conflict in a constructive manner presents a challenge to the best of us. In this final section, we provide alternative points of view that help to explain why managing conflict is difficult. More precisely, we examine the communication skill deficit hypothesis, conflict management as stress management, and Gottman's models of relational dissolution.

### *Communication Skill Deficit Hypothesis*

The online management of conflict tests people's capabilities in using appropriate and effective conflict behaviors. As Sillars and Weisberg (1987) noted, "As conflicts intensify, conversations become increasingly impulsive, emotional, and improvisational. Thus, to the extent that conflicts are deepseated and volatile, it is less useful to regard communication as an instrumental act designed to resolve focused issues and more appropriate to view communication as an expressive and relational event with ambiguous goals and consequences" (p. 149). Naturally, people do not respond to conflicts only on strategic and cognitive levels. Zillmann (1990) showed how physiological reactions to escalating conflict arise when partners stoke each other's anger. Zillmann summarized reactions to conflict escalation accordingly:

Escalating conflict can be conceptualized as a sequence of provocations, each triggering an excitatory reaction that materializes quickly and that dissipates slowly. As a second sympathetic reaction occurs before the first has dissipated, the second reaction combines with the tail end of the first. As a third reaction occurs before the second and first reactions have dissipated, this third reaction combines with the tail ends of both earlier reactions. In general, the excitatory reaction to provocation late in the escalation process rides the tails of all earlier reactions. (p. 192)

The helter-skelter and emotional nature of conflict suggests that the communication skill deficit potentially applies to everyone who engages in relationship conflicts.

The communication skill deficit hypothesis holds that people in close relationships allow conflict to escalate because they lack the communicative ability to control themselves or others (Marshall, 1994). This hypothesis is also reflected in research on supportiveness and conflict, wherein people who take the perspective of the partner enact constructive conflict management strategies and thereby are more likely to succeed than are people who do not (Arriaga & Rusbult, 1998; Burleson & Samter, 1994). Evidence for the communication skill deficit hypothesis is vividly presented in research comparing abusive and nonabusive couples.

In a comparison of physically aggressive, verbally abusive, withdrawn, and nondistressed couples, Margolin, Burman, and John (1989) found that couples who had recent histories of physical aggression displayed more overt hostility (e.g., disapproval, attribution of blame, raised voices) toward one another during reenactments of recent conflicts. Interestingly, physically aggressive husbands (vs. verbally abusive and withdrawn husbands) demonstrated a lack of involvement (e.g., cold/aloof, reluctance to talk, uninvolved) and defensiveness (e.g., disagreement, reject responsibility, interrupt). Nondistressed couples (vs. abusive husbands) used more problem solving (e.g., examine barriers to solution, explain ideas) and warmth (e.g., playfulness, exhibit affection) in reenacting their conflicts. Likewise, Clearhout, Elder, and Janes (1982) found differences in the problem-solving skills of abused women and those of nonabused women. Abused women (vs. nonabused women) generated fewer and less effective problem-solving behaviors.

## Conflict as Stress Management

Research on stress and individual coping patterns to stress implicate the role that daily stress has on the communicative management of conflict. For example, Bolger and Zukerman (1995) reported that stress was powerfully linked to interpersonal conflict. Bolger and Zukerman found that high-neurotic participants reported more conflicts and a higher frequency of self-controlling and confrontational coping responses to those conflicts. For high-neurotic participants, both self-controlling and confrontational strategies were positively associated with anger and depression, and escape-avoidance tactics were positively associated with depression. For low-neurotic participants, escape-avoidance behaviors were negatively associated with depression. Bolger and Zukerman's findings suggested that highly neurotic people engage in more interpersonal conflicts, find such conflicts personally absorbing, use a wider variety of conflict coping responses, but feel that their coping responses backfire (i.e., the coping responses *increase* their own personal anger and depression).

Demand characteristics of everyday conflicts probably affect people's reactions to each other. Ohbuchi, Chiba, and Fukushima (1996) examined the effects of time pressure on Japanese students' conflict behaviors. Participants role-played being confronted by an unreasonable confederate who was either polite or rough/impolite, and participants were required to respond immediately or to wait 30 seconds. When participants had no time to consider their responses, they tended to reciprocate the confederate's behavior; however, when they waited 30 seconds, participants engaged in an appeasing manner (e.g., acknowledge the other) or a hostile manner (e.g., criticize, show anger). Ohbuchi et al. interpreted the differential effects due to time as evidence that people under stress consider mostly their own personal goals, whereas those with time consider the identity needs of the other persons and decide to reward or punish them in terms of face needs. This interpretation is supported by the research on accommodation showing that behaving constructively in response to a partner's negative behavior requires time to focus on more than the immediate pressure to respond in kind (e.g., Yovetich & Rusbult, 1994).

### Gottman's Model of Relational Decay

In an attempt to explain how couples progress toward divorce, Gottman (1994a) argued that negative conflict management behavior causes perceptual shifts that lead to unfavorable beliefs about partners. Gottman calls his theory a "cascade model," where first one observes a "decline in marital satisfaction, which leads to consideration of separation or divorce, which leads to separation, which leads to divorce" (p. 88).

According to Gottman (1994a), negative conflict behaviors lead to emotional reactions that he called *flooding* or feelings of being "surprised, overwhelmed, and disorganized by your partner's expression of negative emotions" (p. 21). Four negative behaviors are particularly corrosive and are hypothesized to occur in a general sequence: Complaining/criticizing leads to contempt, which leads to defensiveness, which leads to stonewalling (p. 415). These negative behaviors lead to an extreme experience of flooding that Gottman labeled *diffuse physiological arousal,* which is indicated by increased blood pressure, heart rate, perspiration, and other "fight versus flight" symptoms (Gottman, 1994a; Levenson & Gottman, 1985). Negative conflict messages are "absorbing" in a manner similar to the process of escalation reported by Zillmann (1990).

An individual perceives the partner's conflict messages in one of two ways: in a benign (neutral or positive) manner or in a self-defensive manner (which is a natural response to negative messages) (Gottman, 1994a). In terms of the self-defensive mode, two common reactions stem from the partner's negativity (especially complaining/criticizing, contempt, defensiveness, and stonewalling): "(a) hurt, disappointment, and perceived attack, the 'innocent victim' perception in which a person is in a stance of warding off perceived attack, or (b) hurt, disappointment, and 'righteous indignation,' in which a person is in the mode of rehearsing retaliation" (p. 412). The absorption into negativity prevents people from interacting with their partners in functional ways. Continued negativity and defensive reactions establish a "set point" that positive prosocial behaviors cannot budge. Importantly, the shift from benign to hostile attributions represents an "abrupt flip in the perception of [one's own] well-being. . . . This is the initial catastrophic change" (p. 335). Negative behaviors cause one to feel flooded and to make global and stable attributions for the partner's behavior, and this leads to distance and isolation, recasting the history of the marriage, and dissolution. Satisfied couples, on the other hand, "balance" negative behaviors with positive ones (a 5:1 ratio of positive-to-negative behaviors) and experience a sense of well-being.

## ▶ Conclusions

Recent advances in social scientific studies of relationship conflict have increased our insight into human nature. Relationship conflict research shows how toddlers learn to communicate with other people to negotiate what they want, how adolescents strive for personal control, how siblings learn from each other, and how parents display conflict behaviors that indirectly affect children's development and adjustment later in life. Importantly, this literature also reflects the development of individuals. Competitive tactics used to settle arguments over possessions and intrusion by others not only reflect toddler behavior but also occur between older but not wiser children and adults.

Pure and applied implications emerge on several levels. First, students, researchers, and practitioners alike might find it helpful to observe the dimensions of directness and cooperation when consulting the literature (van de Vliert & Euwema, 1994). These fundamental dimensions reflect decisions that social actors make in real time regarding how they react to each other. The many pragmatic lessons that might be gleaned from the conflict literature can easily be conveyed in terms of these dimensions of conflict, with most people adopting the cultural value that one should engage others in a direct and cooperative manner (Sillars & Weisberg, 1987).

Regardless of cultural value, two fundamental rules apply: "Do unto others as you would have them do unto you" and "Do not reciprocate negative affect." The reciprocation of negative affect, in particular, indicates that partners have become absorbed in the construction of a pattern that is relationally dysfunctional. Given the emotionally laden context that often accompanies conflict, partners might have great difficulty in not acting in self-defensive ways (e.g., attributing partner as cause of problems, withdrawing). In other words, during conflict people have a hard time acting in their own best strategic interests (Messman & Canary, 1998). By underscoring the prescription that one should not reciprocate negative affect, people might seek pragmatic alternatives to counterattacking one another.

Moreover, the research suggests that how people manage their conflicts answers a fundamental question regarding the quality of their personal relationships on a practical level. If people want to know the quality of their relationships, then they should look closely at how they manage conflict. Some couples appear most content to ignore issues, whereas other couples are goaded to action by such avoidance. Regardless of the variations on the theme, the management of conflict both affects and reflects how partners define their relationships. Realization of this fact might help people to become focused more on garden variety problems and less on idealized notions of relationships.

As many couple counseling and training specialists recently have discovered, troubled couples and families should learn the difference between constructive and destructive communication behaviors. In addition to learning more effective and relationally promotive behaviors, people need to understand conflict situations in general to skillfully select behaviors in actual conflict situations. For example, understanding the bidirectional nature of parent-child conflict might help some parents to gain perspective on how to interact with their children. Also, couples need to understand how certain behaviors are likely to lead to partner responses and how reciprocation of negative behaviors affects the couples both situationally and relationally.

The emotional and haphazard nature of conflict should not be underestimated. Relational parties need to appreciate each other's perspectives in conflict. For example, adult children might misconstrue elderly parents' relational needs if the children do not consider or seek the parents' points of view. Similarly, parents need to consider adolescents' particular life-stage issues and relational needs.

Conflict in close involvements takes people by surprise and unfolds in many unpredictable ways (Sillars & Weisberg, 1987). It often is emotionally taxing and makes the best of people look at their darker sides. But it also is a relational phenomenon that reflects the efforts of both partners. The pragmatic utility of the research on relationship conflict ultimately must be measured against the ability of partners to adjust to each other.

# Contents

# Social Support

*Michael R. Cunningham*
*Anita P. Barbee*

L iving through a typical day can be a challenge. Take Benjamin's Monday:

As Ashley slept late, Benjamin fixed breakfast for his wife, their son Robert, and himself and then prepared a sandwich and a snack for Robert's lunch box. He roused Ashley and asked whether she had seen his misplaced car keys. She groggily reminded him that they were on the workbench in the garage, where he had left them while working on Robert's bent bicycle wheel yesterday. Ashley dressed Robert for the school bus as Benjamin gave them both a hug and left to pick up the two other members of his car pool.

On the drive into the city, one of Benjamin's passengers mentioned that she was worrying about her father-in-law, who seemed to lose his way while driving, but her mother-in-law did not want to discuss Alzheimer's disease. The other rider mentioned that there was an Alzheimer's sup-

port group that might be able to suggest some ways in which to approach the issue.

At his desk, Benjamin was handling some routine paperwork when he was interrupted by an e-mail from a friend in another division of the company. The friend passed along a rumor that Benjamin's department might be downsized due to declining profits in the company as a whole. Benjamin experienced a cold sinking feeling in the pit of his stomach and wondered whether he could find another job before falling too far behind on his mortgage payments. His next thought was to call Ashley on her cell phone, but he decided not to ruin her day on a rumor. Benjamin pulled up his resumé on his computer screen but found it hard to concentrate on describing his recent accomplishments.

Then, a co-worker who occasionally played racquetball with him dropped in to see about a game after work. Noticing that Benjamin was pale and agitated, he jocularly asked whether anything was wrong.

Benjamin initially declined to talk about it, but the co-worker persisted, and Benjamin finally admitted his concerns about a layoff. The co-worker disclosed that he had heard that some economic projections had been made of the salary and benefits savings that would occur if Benjamin's department were eliminated and the work were outsourced to consultants. But, the friend continued, the short-term savings were not substantial enough to justify the likely productivity loss, so no change was likely in the near future. Benjamin's stomach settled down, the color returned to his cheeks, and he asked whether they could squeeze a game of racquetball into the lunch hour because he felt the need to unwind.

Benjamin's morning is similar to the experiences of millions of other people at the dawn of the 21st century. Some people might have less access to cars, cell phones, and e-mail than does Benjamin, but the problems of caring for children and aging parents, maintaining a steady income, and keeping emotions under control might be universal. The capacity of people to engage in complex cooperation, and to seek and give social support in particular, might be a defining characteristic of our species. Social support itself is defined by Cutrona (1996) as "responsiveness to another's needs and more specifically as acts that communicate caring; that validate the other's worth, feelings or actions; or that facilitate adaptive coping with problems through the provision of information, assistance or tangible resources" (p. 10).

This chapter reviews theory and research on social support, focusing on its evolutionary and childhood origins, the nature and function of social support networks, perceptions of social support, and the specific behaviors involved in seeking and providing support. Social support with friends is discussed, but particular attention is focused on social support with romantic partners, supportive interactions with medical care providers during times of illness, and social support with close associates at work. Research findings and

practical applications are discussed within each domain.

## ▶ Origins of Social Support Behaviors

### *Evolution and Social Support*

Humans live in herds or colonies, like horses and chimpanzees, rather than as solitary hunters such as tigers and mountain lions. But unlike horses, which can walk the day they are born, humans have an extremely long period of physical maturation. Prior to adulthood, humans must depend on others for food and protection. The virtue of slow development is that it affords an extended opportunity for learning skills such as language, tool use, and computer programming. The other benefit of delayed maturation is that it can encourage the development of supportive relationships.

The prototype for a supportive relationship is the nurturant behavior of a loving parent to a child. Individuals who enjoyed such relationships in their youth, and who developed a secure attachment style, expect social support to be available, are comfortable seeking it (Ognibene & Collins, 1998), and are satisfied with the support they receive (Rholes, Simpson, & Grich, 1998).

Human genetic predispositions not only afford the opportunity to learn about supportiveness by growing up slowly in a nurturant family but also support helpfulness through other mechanisms. A variety of species, from ants to Belding ground squirrels, engage in kin selection altruism, where individual organisms engage in helping to contribute to the fitness of their genetic relatives (Cunningham, 1985). Similarly, humans in collectivist societies often maintain close relations with their extended families throughout their lives, and such relatives serve as a source of help and support (Triandis, 1994).

There also were evolutionary selection pressures favoring organisms who were genetically disposed to band together with non-kin for mutual advantage (Dugatkin, 1997). Reciprocal helping behaviors among non-kin have been observed in a variety of species (Trivers, 1971) such as allogrooming by the impalas (Hart & Hart, 1992). Among humans, membership in a voluntary group can serve as a source of social identity, and this often entails normative expectations that further increase the likelihood of support among group members (Schroeder, Penner, Dovidio, & Piliavin, 1995).

Besides genetic predispositions that favor the development of helping relationships, there are more specific mechanisms that encourage social support. Infants are born with the capacity to cry (Sagi & Hoffman, 1976) and to display charming facial expressions. Expressive behaviors and a cute appearance tend to elicit caregiving behaviors from parents and unrelated adults (Langlois, Ritter, Casey, & Sawin, 1995; Malamuth, Shayne, & Pogue, 1982). Human adults retain many neonatal facial characteristics such as relatively large eyes, small noses, large heads, and hairlessness (Cunningham, Roberts, Barbee, & Druen, 1995). Compared to other mammals, both human children and human adults appear immature and underequipped to face the challenges of the world. But that helplessness might offer an adaptive advantage in stimulating social support from other people (Cunningham, 1986; Cunningham, Druen, & Barbee, 1997).

Eliciting social support requires responsive conspecifics. Such responsiveness often is motivated by feelings of empathy, an other-oriented feeling of concern and compassion resulting from witnessing another person suffer (Batson, 1991). Empathy is similar to anxiety in having state and trait components. It is experienced in response to specific situations of need but has relatively stable individual differences in threshold for elicitation and magnitude of expression. Some people are so empathic that they are moved to uncontrollable tears during every cinematic tragedy, whereas others are so detached that the sight of a dis-

membered leg does not cause an increase in their heart rate. The former type might make a more understanding friend, whereas the latter type might make a better trauma surgeon. Empathy appears to be heritable at levels that are comparable to those of other personality and emotion traits (Davis, Luce, & Kraus, 1994).

### *Evolution of Social Support Networks*

A social support network is the set of people from whom an individual can reasonably expect to receive help in time of need. The form of an individual's social network depends on the nature and form of the surrounding economy, technology, and social structure. Humans who lived in small nomadic bands traveling through the rain forests or jungles in search of game could count on their entire tribe for aid because they all were likely to be relatives or in-laws. With the development of agriculture came settled communities, greater leisure time, and the opportunity to form voluntary associations based on similar interests such as music, politics, and religion. Religious organizations, in particular, emphasized norms of mutual helpfulness to members, charity to selected nonmembers, and reappraisal of misfortune within a coherent explanatory model.

A stable source of food allowed greater longevity and population growth, and it enhanced opportunities for learning and refinement in the production of craft items ranging from pottery to plows. Technological improvements in turn aided capital accumulation, the development of industrial and trade centers, and increased specialization in work roles. But increased work specialization demanded increased geographic mobility. The second-best plow maker in a village might find better prospects by moving to the next village, which had no plow makers. Nowadays, the best data analyst in Baltimore, Maryland, might find that the best opportunity for further advancement is in Seattle, Washington, and this requires leaving family and friends behind.

## ► Analyses of Social Support Networks

As the forgoing suggests, economic support and social support were intertwined at earlier points in human social evolution but became increasingly separated in industrial and postindustrial society. Economic dislocation, urban crowding, and job stress have been linked to higher rates of infant mortality, tuberculosis, digestive diseases, and psychosis. Yet, whereas some individuals fell victim to the noxious qualities of urban life, others were relatively unaffected (Gottlieb, 1981, 1985). Casell (1974) and other pioneer investigators argued that the individual's social support network could buffer the impact of change, challenge, and loss. As Caplan (1974) noted, "The significant others help the individual mobilize his psychological resources and master his emotional burdens; they share his tasks, and they supply him with extra supplies of money, materials, tools, skills, and cognitive guidance to improve his handling of his situation" (p. 6).

Gottlieb (1985) noted that social support networks can be examined at three levels. The *macro* level focuses on an individual's involvement both with formal institutions (e.g., churches, other volunteer associations) and with informal contacts (e.g., family, friends). Mapping an individual's social support network is a challenging task, and controversies exist concerning the best measurement strategy (Bass & Stein, 1997). Research at this level has indicated that an objectively large social network increased the likelihood that support would be available during times of need (Cutrona, 1986), although that did not guarantee satisfactory support. Barrera, Sandler, and Ramsey (1981), for example, compared responses to the Arizona Social Support Interview Schedule, a network measure, to responses to the Inventory of Socially Supportive Behaviors (ISSB), a list of 40 helpful acts. Total network size correlated + .24 with the ISSB but only +.02 with satisfaction with support.

The *mezzo* level of analysis focuses on the quality of relations within a specific social aggregate such as friends. Work at this level has found, for example, that friendships that were multidimensional (i.e., the friends engaged in at least two different activities that were important to the individuals) were associated with higher self-esteem and more tangible assistance (Hirsch, 1981; Wilcox, 1981). But networks with greater density, in which one's family and friends have independent relationships with one another, were associated with greater clinical symptoms, more negative mood, lower self-esteem, less satisfying socializing, and less tangible assistance, at least in the case of women returning to college (Hirsch, 1981) and divorced women (Wilcox, 1981). Such results suggest that having access to a number of nonoverlapping social groups might aid coping and well-being.

The *micro* level of analysis focuses on the qualities of the relationship with the person to whom the individual feels most attached. Initial research at this level tended to be qualitative and documented the value of having at least one confiding relationship (Gottlieb, 1985). Recent research focuses on the microdynamics of supportive communications.

Social network analyses have yielded a wealth of valuable data, but questions can be raised about the emphasis on measures based largely on the perspective of the individual (rather than on independent assessment of each member of the network) and on formal-structural assessments of network qualities (rather than on psychological ones). If, in the sociometric tradition, each member of a sample of social support networks was assessed, then it would be possible to determine whether the number of network members with secure attachment styles, higher levels of empathy, similar cognitive styles, and/or reciprocated liking contributed to people feeling more supported and enjoying better health.

## ▶ Social Support: Perceptions and Behavior

### *Perceptions of Social Support*

As noted earlier, the social support that is objectively available to an individual and his or her satisfaction with that support are only moderately related. The objective and subjective quality of social support networks can have different antecedents. There are indications that the availability of support is linked to social skills that contribute to the development and maintenance of a broad, dense, and reliable network. By contrast, the perception of available social support and satisfaction with social support are influenced by the individual's personality such as attachment style, emotional stability, and extraversion (Sarason, Sarason, Hacker, & Basham, 1985; Von Dras & Siegler, 1997).

An individual's subjective belief that support is available generally is a better predictor of major outcomes, such as health, than are objective assessments of the person's social support network (Sarason, Sarason, & Pierce, 1994). Some investigators have suggested that an individual's generalized perception of social support is a more important predictor of positive outcomes than are the specific supportive behaviors provided by their partners (e.g., Lakey & Cassady, 1990). That suggestion is accurate at one level because perceived support represents those feelings that are left after a supportive interaction has been concluded and might have a more proximal impact on emotional adjustment, relationship satisfaction, and health than do the transactions that caused such feelings. But individuals' feelings of being cheered up (Barbee, 1990) and being supported (Cutrona & Suhr, 1994) are influenced by whether or not they receive specific supportive behaviors.

### *Social Support Behaviors*

Several typologies of social support behaviors have been offered, and each might be ap-propriate for specific goals and levels of analyses. Gottlieb (1978) empirically derived 26 categories of helping behaviors from a subset of 40 transcribed protocols. He subsequently grouped them into four general types of behaviors or influences: *emotionally sustaining behaviors, problem-solving behaviors, indirect personal influence,* and *environmental action.* Gottlieb and Wagner (1991) subsequently extended the list of support behaviors by including criticizing/undermining behaviors.

Barrera et al. (1981) extended Gottlieb's earlier work by developing the ISSB. The 40 items used in the scale were based on a broad conceptualization of social support ranging from supplying goods and services to positive regard.

Burleson (1982) offered a functional-hierarchical coding system for support interactions that included nine categories with three major levels of comforting messages. The levels of comforting messages vary in the extent to which others' feelings and perspectives are explicitly acknowledged, elaborated, and granted legitimacy. The lowest level of comforting message denies the feelings and perspectives of the distressed other, whereas the middle level implicitly recognizes the perspectives and feelings of the partner. The highest level of comforting messages provides more explicit acknowledgment and elaboration of the other's feelings and perspectives. Burleson's approach is reminiscent of scoring systems for stages of cognitive development, such as moral maturity and role-taking, in providing an assessment of the level of communication competency displayed in different comfort messages. Recently, Burleson and Goldsmith (1998) offered a theoretical interpretation of comfort messages suggesting that support that is sensitive to face concerns, encourages the distressed person to elaborate a detailed narrative that focuses on feelings and coping, and facilitates a cognitive reappraisal of events is associated with positive change.

Cutrona (1986) had participants register in diaries when stressful events occurred and when each of six behaviors occurred each day—listened to confidences, offered advice, expressed point of view, tangible assistance, expressed caring or concern, and positive feedback—reflecting the four most commonly cited social support functions (emotional sustenance, self-esteem bolstering, information/feedback, and tangible assistance). Cutrona and Suhr (1992) subsequently developed a behavioral coding system based on the categories of the Social Provision Scale. Cutrona (1986) reported that emotional support usually is well received but that people disliked receiving informational support when they felt in control of a situation.

Winstead, Derlega, Lewis, Sanchez-Hucles, and Clark's (1992) study of social support behaviors included verbal, nonverbal, and outcome measures. Individuals who interacted with opposite-sex friends, rather than with strangers, prior to giving extemporaneous speeches were less depressed and were judged to be more confident during the speeches. Individuals who discussed their feelings about public speaking felt less fear, and those who engaged in problem-solving talk felt more confident and higher in perceived social support. Eye contact during the interactions was the best predictor of coping and perceived social support.

Friends and lovers usually are inclined to be helpful, but emotional conflicts and ambivalences might be reflected in the communication of both the support seeker and the support giver in specific interactions. Barbee and Cunningham's (1995) sensitive interaction system theory (SIST) outlines how the nature of the relationship, the dimensions of the problem, and the personality and mood of both the help seeker and the help giver affect immediate and long-term outcomes. The full model is beyond the scope of this chapter (Barbee, Rowatt, & Cunningham, 1998), but we briefly describe behaviors involved in seeking and providing interactive coping.

In the SIST analysis, a distressed person's tactics for activating social support can be either direct and unambiguous about the desire for help or indirect and ambiguous about whether help is being sought (Cutrona, Suhr,

& MacFarlane, 1990). Direct support-seeking behaviors can be verbal by *asking* for help, which includes talking about the problem in a factual manner, telling the supporter about the problem, giving details of the problem, and disclosing what has been done about the problem so far.

Direct support seeking also can involve nonverbal communication (e.g., showing distress about the problem through *crying*) or can involve other direct behaviors (e.g., eye contact with furrowed brow, putting one's head on the partner's shoulder). Seekers using these acts wordlessly convey their emotional states and convey that they want some form of help to make them feel better.

Indirect support-seeking behaviors, by contrast, are more subtle and less informative. Indirect verbal strategies for activating social support are exemplified by globally *complaining* about a situation without requesting aid or by *hinting* that a problem exists. Hints and complaints can protect the seeker's self-esteem because the need for help is not made explicit, but they might not convey the nature of the problem in such a way that the supporter can provide effective solutions and so might cause the supporter to dismiss the problem. Indirect support activation behaviors also can employ nonverbal communication by subtly showing negative affect in the form of *sighing, sulking,* or *fidgeting.* Indirect nonverbal behaviors might induce a caring support giver to ask what is wrong, but they run the risk of causing the potential support giver to ignore the gestures or escape from the situation. Indeed, persistent use of indirect support activation behaviors, such as complaining and sulking, can become a social allergen or an objectively minor but emotionally major stimulus that grates on people's nerves and causes hypersensitive annoyance or disgust (Cunningham, Barbee, & Druen, 1997).

Support activation behaviors generally are intended to elicit helpful responses from the partner. A range of socially supportive behaviors is incorporated into the interactive coping typology. This typology subsumes two major theoretical dimensions of the coping process, as the Roth and Cohen (1986) dimension of either approaching or avoiding the problem or emotion is crossed with the Folkman and Lazarus (1985) dimension of focusing on the problem versus focusing on the emotion. The resulting typology (for details, see Barbee & Cunningham, 1995) includes the following: *solve* behaviors, which are problem-focused/approach behaviors designed to find an answer to the problem (e.g., giving informational and tangible support, asking questions, making suggestions); *solace* behaviors, which are emotion-focused/approach behaviors designed to elicit positive emotions and express closeness (e.g., saying the friend is a good person); *dismiss* behaviors, which are problem-focused/avoidance behaviors that minimize the significance of the problem (e.g., saying the problem is not serious); and *escape* behaviors, which are emotion-focused/avoidance behaviors that discourage the experience or display of negative emotion by the seeker of support (e.g., encouraging alcohol consumption, showing irritability). Direct support activation behaviors were more likely to produce approach behaviors than to produce avoidance behaviors (Gulley, 1994). Indirect support activation behaviors also stimulated approach behaviors, but direct activation behaviors more reliably led to approach behaviors than did indirect behaviors.

In a series of studies of the effects of helper mood on social support, people in experimentally induced positive moods were much more likely to notice friends' distress and to address it with effective supportive and problem-solving strategies than were people who were in either in neutral or negative moods (Barbee, 1991; Yankeelov, Barbee, Cunningham, & Druen, 1995). In fact, people who were sad and depressed often were so self-focused and passive that they rarely realized that their friends were in need of support. Even when they did notice, saddened supporters lacked the energy to act effectively. Negative affect in a helper due to a depressed help seeker is associated with both conflict and avoidance (Hokanson, Loewenstein, Hedeen, & Howes, 1986; Sacco & Dunn, 1990). Similarly, our re-

search found that the more supporters attributed the support seeker's problems to internal controllable causes, the more they blamed the support seeker. The greater the blame, the more supporters displayed the avoidance behaviors of dismiss and escape (Barbee, 1991).

► **Relational Issues in Social Support**

*Social Support in Romantic Relationships*

The provision of care and the provision of affection are primary expectations in dating and marriage (Cutrona, 1996). As noted earlier, such social support can aid longevity (Cunningham, Druen, et al., 1997), especially during the difficult process of childbirth (Miller & Fishkin, 1997). We asked male and female college students and their parents about the qualities desired in a partner for a long-term relationship. Consistent with the analysis of human evolution presented earlier, all groups ranked qualities that convey caring as essential (Cunningham et al., 1999). The most important mate factors included idealization (e.g., makes you feel unique and special), followed by emotional support (e.g., provides you with emotional support and help, listens to your innermost thoughts) and friendship (e.g., considerate, generous). Material values, such as physical attractiveness and wealth, were less important than care values in mate selection (cf. Buss, 1989).

In a rare prospective study, we tested the impact of helpful and unhelpful interactive coping behaviors on the stability of romantic relationships (Barbee & Yankeelov, 1992). This study examined the extent to which one member of each of 120 couples provided effective or ineffective interactive coping behaviors to the other in a laboratory situation. Both partners of each couple were called about 10 months after their participation in the study to see which couples still were together and which couples had separated. The lack of an attempt to cheer up the partner and the use of dismiss behaviors during the experimental session were significant predictors of later romantic relationship dissolution. It is likely that the inattentiveness and poor support displayed in the experimental context was representative of the interpersonal problems that led to the deterioration of the relationships.

### Gender and Social Support

Cutrona (1996) noted the interesting paradox that men were more adversely affected than women by not having romantic or marriage partners but that women were more affected than men by the quality of communication in their relationships (Gove, Hughes, & Style, 1983). One interpretation of that paradox is that women are consistently good at providing support to men, whereas men are variable in the support that they provide to women. Males have been found to offer more unhelpful dismiss and escape behaviors than do females in conflict situations (e.g., saying "Don't get so excited," "It's not that important," or "For once, put your feelings aside") (Kelley et al., 1978).

Our research on gender and social support, by contrast, suggested that gender differences in helping often depend on situational variables such as the nature of the relationship between the helper and the recipient (Barbee et al., 1993). Consistent with gender stereotypes, we found that males provided less effective forms of help to same- and opposite-sex close friends than did females. But we also found that males provided better support than did females to their romantic partners who experienced task failures. Females might have felt uncomfortable when expected to provide support to their romantic partners who did poorly (Costrich, Feinstein, Kidder, Marecek, & Pascale, 1975), perhaps causing the females to engage in dismiss and escape behaviors in that situation.

The effects of gender on social support behaviors are complex, although the genders might be more similar than different (Gold-

smith & Dun, 1997). Rather than focus on gender categories, some investigators have emphasized continuous psychological dimensions that are partially linked with gender. Expressivity includes nurturance and agreeableness and is associated with relationship success (Bailey, Hendrick, & Hendrick, 1987; Ickes, 1993). Instrumentality, which includes qualities such as task focus, confidence, and stoicism (Spence & Helmreich, 1978), also can be associated with relationship success if the partners are similar (Bailey et al., 1987). Barbee and her associates (Barbee, Cunningham, Shamblen, & Nezlek, 1999) explored the impact of expressivity and instrumentality in a diary study of social support. Males and females completed a modified version of the Rochester Interaction Record (Barbee & Felice, 1991; Reis et al., 1982) for each interaction lasting 10 minutes or longer. For all interactions involving social support, participants were asked to indicate the extent of each of four types of interactive coping behavior. Individuals high in expressivity, regardless of their own or their partners' gender, were more likely to provide solve behaviors to their interaction partners. Individuals high in expressivity and men high in instrumentality both were more likely than others to provide solace behaviors. Thus, expressive women and androgynous men might be more likely than others to provide helpful support on a day-to-day basis.

## ▶ Social Support and Health

### Health Support: Helpful and Unhelpful

We previously noted that social support has a salutory effect on health (see also Cohen & Wills, 1985; Uchino, Cacioppo, & Kielcolt-Glaser, 1996). In a study of gay men with HIV infection, for example, Hays et al. (1993) found that support from friends and lovers was correlated with less depression and anxi-

ety 1 year later. But sometimes the support offered during times of medical problems is not
helpful.

Yankeelov et al. (1995) examined the impact of medical diagnostic feedback that either threatened sex roles (a cognitive impairment that imperiled college success or a
metabolic disorder that produced weight gain)
or was irrelevant. The couple's interaction
was covertly recorded for the support activation behaviors displayed by the support seeker
and the interactive coping behaviors offered
by the help giver. Both type of support activation and type of problem affected the use of
support behaviors. Verbal activation behaviors (e.g., asking for support, complaining
about the situation) promoted approach interactive coping behaviors (e.g., solve and solace
behaviors). By contrast, nonverbal support activation behaviors (e.g., pouting, sighing) promoted helpers' use of avoidance interactive
coping behaviors (e.g., dismissing and escap-
ing behaviors). When the problem was sex
role relevant, partners seemed to take the diagnosis more seriously and provided more
helpful approach behaviors. But participants
were equally distressed by medical diagnostic
feedback that was not sex role relevant, and
their efforts to activate support were not as
successful. Thus, help seekers might undermine their chances of obtaining support by using indirect support activation strategies, and
helpers might not be maximally supportive
when they do not take the medical problem as
seriously as do their partners.

HIV is an illness that is both serious and responsive to social support. Barbee, Derlega,
Sherburne, and Grimshaw (1998) conducted a
study of the social support behaviors experienced by 42 adults who either were HIV positive (62%) or had AIDS (38%). Each participant was asked a series of questions about
instances in which people thought they were
being "supportive" but whose behavior actually was "helpful" or "not helpful" in coping
with the HIV infection. Each act was coded in
terms of the interactive coping system described earlier. Respondents generated a total

number of 435 helpful and unhelpful acts
across 256 supportive episodes. One third
(33%) of the behaviors were categorized as
solve behaviors, whereas 34% were categorized as solace behaviors, for a total of 67%
approach support behaviors. In addition, 23%
of the behaviors were categorized as escape
behaviors, whereas only 10% of the behaviors
were categorized as dismiss behaviors, for a
total of 33% avoidance behaviors.

More than half (55%) of the reported acts
were rated as helpful by the HIV patients,
with the majority of these being solve and solace behaviors. Network members differed in
their helpfulness. Fully 62% of accounts
about friends were about acts that were helpful, whereas only 38% of interactions with
family members were about helpful actions.
In addition, 30% of the unhelpful behaviors
were solve or solace behaviors, which were
seen as overprotective or intrusive (Dakof &
Taylor, 1990; Lehman, Ellard, & Wortman,
1986). The other 70% of unhelpful actions
were dismiss and escape behaviors, which often are seen as unsupportive in other contexts.

In considering unhelpful forms of support,
it is important to recall that network members
might be trying to cope with the sad prospect
of losing a loved one while simultaneously
addressing the challenge of giving effective
forms of support to the ill person. Sometimes,
network members' attempts to take over the
care of the person, or to suppress discussion
of the illness, are attempts to make *themselves*
feel more in control of the situation (Lichtman, Taylor, & Wood, 1987; Silver & Wortman, 1980). Such unhelpful support behavior
is most likely when the help giver is overwhelmed and resentful (Thompson &
Sobolew-Shubin, 1993) and receives inadequate medical advice (Coyne, Ellard, &
Smith, 1990). The support process becomes
particularly strained when the spouse of a
chronically ill patient becomes depressed
himself or herself (Dunkel-Schetter &
Bennett, 1990), a situation that might require
activation of more of the support network or
professional help.

## Medical Personnel as Sources of Social Support

The role of medical personnel in an individual's support network is quite variable. Patients generally want to feel personally connected with their physicians (Hall, Roter, & Rand, 1981), but some medical personnel believe that this is discouraged by their professional norms. In Barbee, Derlega, et al.'s (1998) study of HIV-positive individuals, however, 86% of them mentioned their health professionals when offering their accounts of supportive interactions.

Patients also might be inclined to reciprocate the care they feel they receive from their physicians and to offer them understanding, rather than hostility, when mistakes are made (Shapiro et al., 1989). Although approximately 1% of hospitalized patients suffer significant injuries due to negligence, less than 2% of those injured patients actually initiate malpractice claims (Localio et al., 1991). To understand how some physicians might foster forgiveness and others might induce litigiousness, Levinson, Roter, Mullooly, Dull, and Frankel (1997) conducted a study of the communication behaviors displayed by primary care physicians and surgeons. Patients were recruited from the physicians' waiting rooms, with 10 patient visits audiotaped for each physician. All audiotapes were coded using the Roter (1991) interaction analysis system in which each statement is coded into 1 of 38 categories involving content, process, or emotion. Variations in physician communication then were used to predict whether the physicians never had been sued for malpractice or had been sued two or more times.

Primary care physicians who never had been sued had longer visits (the average was 16.5 minutes), had a greater total number of utterances, provided more orientation to the flow of the visits (e.g., describing the steps in the examination), used more facilitation statements (e.g., asking for patient opinions, clarifying patient understanding, paraphrasing), used more humor, and laughed more. There were no significant differences between the sued and never sued groups in the medical content of the physician-patient interactions such as asking questions about a medical condition, giving information about medicine, and providing counseling, suggesting that the sued physicians were not less competent in their diagnostic approaches or medical knowledge than were those who never were sued. The findings were inconclusive for surgeons. Nonetheless, the findings suggest that physicians who engage in supportive communications with their patients might cause those patients to feel closer to their physicians and to be more supportive of the physicians if medical errors occur. Additional questions that warrant investigation are whether a physician who feels close to a patient provides better medical care and whether believing that the physician has such an attitude offers health benefits beyond those provided by the medical care itself.

## ► Exchange Relationships and Social Support at Work

Adults spend more than one third of their waking hours at their jobs. People's personal stresses are just as pressing at work as at home, and to them are added the challenges of their jobs. But the norms of the work environment generally discourage the seeking of social support there, both because it interferes with immediate productivity and because transfers, promotions, and layoffs can routinely disrupt work friendships.

The norms of employment are those of exchange relationships. In exchange relationships, people are helpful to the extent that they discharge debts by reciprocating benefits that they received in the past or expect to receive benefits in the future that are equal or equitably proportional to those that they must give (Clark & Mills, 1993). Friendship, by contrast, is a communal relationship. In a communal relationship, a person is helpful in meeting the needs of another person out of concern for that person's welfare. Thus, exchange relationships seem to be governed by norms of fairness and reciprocity, whereas communal relationships involve a norm of caring (cf. Batson, 1993).

Exchange relationships seem appropriate for giving and receiving instrumental forms of help (Wills, 1991), which are concrete acts or advice to solve specific problems. Communal relationships seem more appropriate for seeking emotional support. People who were led to desire communal relationships with new acquaintances liked the other persons more when those persons expressed sadness than when those persons did not. But people who were led to desire exchange relationships liked the other persons less when those persons expressed sadness (Clark & Taraban, 1991). In addition, people who were paired with friends (communal relationships) indicated a greater preference for talking about emotional topics than did people who were paired with strangers (exchange relationships). Finally, people in communal relationships increased their helping more when the other persons expressed sadness; such helping was not influenced by recipient sadness in exchange relationships (Clark, Ouellette, Powell, & Milberg, 1987).

People also derive more pleasure from helping those with whom they have communal relationships than with whom they have exchange relationships. When people were led to desire communal relationships, they experienced improvements in both their moods and their self-evaluations as a result of giving help to other persons. When people were led to desire exchange relationships with other persons, by contrast, there was less help offered overall and little improvement in the helpers' mood or self-evaluations as a result of providing assistance. In fact, choosing to help in an exchange relationship can cause a positive mood to deteriorate (Williamson & Clark, 1992).

The forgoing research findings raise the possibility that inducing communal relationships among employees might boost cooperation and morale in an organization. After all, employees in communal relationships should be less likely to keep track of inputs to a joint task, more likely to keep track of other employees' needs even when unable to help, more likely to help other employees (especially when the other employees are sad), and more likely to experience positive moods when they have opportunities to help fellow employees. They also should prefer not to receive immediate reciprocity for help given.

Barbee, Cunningham, Allen, and Rowatt (1999) focused on people's willingness to provide helpful and unhelpful forms of social support while in the role of supervisors who had exchange or communal relationships with problem employees. The supervisors faced employees with a combination of employee problems including nonproductivity (e.g., poor judgment and errors that affect work), unreliability (e.g., attendance problems), disaffection (e.g., apathy and alienation on the job), and acrimoniousness or unwillingness to accept leadership.

The most popular responses to employee problems in the Barbee, Cunningham, Allen, et al. (1999) study were solve behaviors (e.g., asking the employee for an explanation, sharing one's viewpoint). Males offered significantly higher levels of solve behaviors when they had communal relationships than when they had exchange relationships with the employees. Female supervisors, by contrast, offered the same high level of solve behaviors regardless of whether they had exchange or communal relationships with the subordinates.

The provision of solace behaviors followed a similar pattern. Male supervisors were more willing to build the employees' self-esteem and to offer morale-building rewards for accomplishments when they were in communal relationships than when they were in exchange relationships with the employees. Again, females offered the same high level of solace behaviors regardless of whether they were in exchange or communal relationships with the employees.

The results with solve and solace behaviors suggest that male supervisors might be induced to demonstrate more positive strategies for addressing subordinate problems if they are encouraged to develop communal relationships with their employees. But it might be premature to recommend that all male supervisors cultivate close communal relationships with their staffs. Male supervisors with communal relationships with their subordinates were more likely than males in exchange relationships, and more likely than females in either communal or exchange relationships, to engage in the avoidance behavior of dismissing the problems. These supervisors were more likely than the others to endorse potentially counterproductive actions such as minimizing the importance of the causes of the problems, making fun of the employees' situations, and covering up the problems for the employees. It is possible that males felt that their loyalty to their close friends superseded their duty to their positions, which otherwise required them to take the subordinates' problems more seriously.

Females did not try to minimize the problems of their subordinates, but they also were not as willing as males to take punitive actions. Regardless of the types of relationships that they had with the subordinates, male supervisors were significantly more willing than female supervisors to escape from an active role in handling the troubled employees. Male supervisors were more likely than female supervisors to require that the troubled subordinates handle their own problems, manifested in the form of threatening the employees, taking informal or formal disciplinary action, or firing the subordinates.

The forgoing results serve to clarify the strengths and weaknesses of both male and female supervisors. Female supervisors can adopt the style of communal relationships with their subordinates, even when they are not really close. Such supportiveness can be helpful to troubled employees, but it also can cause problems if the employees are poor fits for the organization and require discipline or termination. Male supervisors were less supportive when they were not close and were more inclined to take harsh measures. Yet, males were just as supportive as females when they were close to their subordinates, but then they were inclined to minimize their employees' deficiencies.

► **Conclusions and Future Directions**

New directions in support research can focus on the unique dynamics of seeking and giving support in specific stressful situations. Situations such as divorce, unemployment, and paraplegia; various forms of heart disease, cancer, and stroke; and different types of losses, from miscarriage, to Alzheimer's disease, to the loss of one's own youthful physical attractiveness (Cunningham, Barbee, & Druen, 1998; Harvey, 1998), each might require a subtly different blend of social support behaviors.

Another issue that requires consideration is the best means of providing support for avoidant individuals who seldom seek, and who might refuse, social support. Direct social support might not be best for everyone (Coyne & Bolger, 1990). Instead, it might be useful to encourage such individuals to explore their problems initially in a narrative format by generating written accounts. Writing might be an important step toward reducing the unproductive rumination and static thinking that tend to accompany solitary processing (Harvey, Stein, Olsen, & Roberts, 1995; Pennebaker & Harber, 1992; Spievak, 1999). The inherent requirements of writing narrative accounts might lead to positive reappraisals (Burleson & Goldsmith, 1998). Once individuals develop coherent accounts, they might be willing to seek additional social support in relatively safe settings such as in a chat room on the World Wide Web, where personal identity is not disclosed and immediate nonverbal reactions are not seen (Bass, McClendon, Brennan, & McCarthy, 1998; Dunham et al., 1998). After avoidant people have developed a sense of trust in other people's good intentions and helpfulness, they might be more willing and able to participate in face-to-face support interactions.

The long-term maintenance of social support relationships also is intriguing. Men often let their outside support relationships lapse after marriage, perhaps because their wives fill most of their needs for intimate communication (Cutrona, 1996). Yet, men might experience less stress, live longer, and be less of a burden on their spouses if they also maintained mutually supportive relationships with their same- and cross-sex friends (Barbee, Gulley, & Cunningham, 1990; Barbee, Rowatt, et al., 1998; Werking, 1997). Contact through holiday greeting cards and chats at class reunions every 5 years might not be enough of an investment to guarantee that an old friend will be supportive in the event of a divorce or layoff. Some men might need lessons from women in the art of going to lunch with a friend once every 6 months to keep in touch and to maintain the lines of supportive communication.

A second issue in the maintenance of social support relationships is that of disappointed expectations in both the help seeker and the help giver. Help seekers might feel hurt or betrayed if they do not recognize that the friends to whom they wish to confide problems might themselves be in negative moods or too preoccupied to deliver effective comfort messages (Barbee, 1990). If friends give advice that turns out to be bad advice, then the problems are multiplied. Conversely, help givers might expect to see relief and gratitude after providing hours of solace and problem-solving suggestions, and they might feel annoyed or resentful if the recipients do not cheer up (Sacco & Dunn, 1990).

Life is like a long-distance car trip, complete with detours, potholes, intermittent audio reception, strange sounds under the hood, and the eventual need to replace worn parts. But there are road maps to plan trips, gauges to monitor engine performance, and trained mechanics to fix problems. Life itself has no maps, no gauges except internal emotional reactions, and no skilled life technicians to call in when lives go awry. Instead, people have each other. And people try, as best they can, to help each other maintain a spirit of love and laughter when hitting bumps in the road and to pull each other out when they roll into ditches, as Benjamin's friend did for him.

# Contents

# Relational Maintenance

*Kathryn Dindia*

In this chapter, I define relational maintenance and then review the earliest and
most global perspectives on relational
maintenance. This is followed by a review of
the research on relational maintenance strategies and, more recently, nonstrategic behaviors that function to maintain relationships.
Finally, I briefly review three recent theoretical perspectives on relational maintenance:
Rusbult's investment model (Rusbult &
Buunk, 1993; Rusbult, Drigotas, & Verette,
1994), relational dialectics (Baxter & Montgomery, 1996), and Sigman's (1991) theoretical perspective on relational continuity and relational continuity construction units
(RCCUs).

AUTHOR'S NOTE: The author thanks the editors and
Dan Canary for their helpful feedback on an earlier version of this chapter.

## ▶ Definitions of Relational Maintenance

No single definition of *relational maintenance* exists. Relational maintenance can refer to a stage of relationship development or
to the dynamic processes involved in maintaining relationships (Canary & Stafford,
1994). What is "maintained" when a relationship is maintained can vary in at least four
ways (Dindia & Canary, 1993).

The first, and most basic, definition of relational maintenance refers to a relationship that
is continued (i.e., relational continuity)
(Dindia & Canary, 1993). This definition does
not imply anything about the maintenance of
the type, form, level, or stage of the relationship. A relationship can change, escalate, or
deescalate; so long as it does not terminate,

the relationship is maintained according to this definition.

Relational maintenance also refers to a relationship that not only is continued but is continued in a stable state (Dindia & Canary, 1993). Typically, relational stability refers to maintaining a relationship at a certain (usually advanced) level of intimacy, closeness, or other fundamental dimension of the relationship (Burgoon & Hale, 1984). Thus, relationship maintenance can refer to a period or stage in a relationship in which fundamental characteristics of a relationship are sustained at a fairly stable level, whether high or low in intimacy.

A third definition of relational maintenance refers to a relationship that is maintained in a satisfactory condition (Dindia & Canary, 1993). Although this definition can be subsumed under the preceding definition (i.e., satisfaction can be viewed as a fundamental characteristic of a relationship), this definition is and should be kept distinct. Satisfaction is unrelated to other relational dimensions; a relationship can be satisfying at any level of intimacy, familiarity, or the like. In addition, satisfaction is inherently evaluative, whereas other relational dimensions, such as intimacy and familiarity, are not inherently evaluative. Finally, relational satisfaction is the most often used conceptual and operational definition of relational maintenance.

A fourth definition of relational maintenance refers to a relationship that is kept in repair (i.e., good working condition). Relational repair is the good condition that results from continued maintenance. This definition differs slightly from the second definition where the relationship is kept at the same level (i.e., it does not escalate or de-escalate). This definition is concerned with preventing a relationship from decaying or being damaged (i.e., relational de-escalation). The term *relational repair* also is used to refer to the more specific process and strategies by which a relationship is restored to a good or sound condition after decay or damage.

Of course, all of these definitions of relationship maintenance are related. That is, when a relationship goes downhill, the level of the relationship is not maintained. Fundamental characteristics of the relationship (e.g., familiarity, attraction, connectedness) change; they decrease quantitatively, and qualitative changes also occur. The relationship moves from a higher stage to a lower stage (if one is using a stage model of relationship development). The relationship can become dissatisfying (or it became dissatisfying, and that is why it is going downhill). This process ultimately can lead to the termination of the relationship.

Accordingly, it is not surprising that definitions of relational maintenance are combined. For example, Canary and Stafford (1994) indicated that relational maintenance may be viewed as a human goal: "Most people desire long-term, stable, and satisfying relationships" (p. 4). Here, several definitions of relationship maintenance—continuity, stability, and relational satisfaction—are combined in the concept of maintenance.

Relational maintenance, as a dynamic process, refers to all the cognitive, affective, and behavioral dynamics involved in maintaining a relationship. When we speak of relational maintenance, we might be referring to a relationship that is in the process of being maintained (i.e., kept in existence, in a specified state or condition, in a satisfactory condition, or in good working condition) or to all the processes involved in maintaining the relationship (including, but not limited to, relational maintenance strategies).

None of the definitions of relational maintenance is better than any of the others. However, it is important that theorists/researchers articulate which definition of relationship maintenance they reference when using the term *relational maintenance* and whether they are using the term to refer to a relationship that is in the state or process of being maintained or to the processes involved in maintaining the relationship.

## ► Centripetal and Centrifugal Forces Affecting Relationships

The earliest and most basic and global theoretical perspectives on relational maintenance were based on the idea that there are centripetal forces that hold intimates together and centrifugal forces that pull them apart. Drawing on Lewin's (1951) concepts of driving and restraining forces, Levinger (1965) elaborated the forces that affect marital cohesiveness:

> The marriage pair is a two-person group. . . . Inducements to remain in any group include the attractiveness of the group itself and the strength of the restraints against leaving it; inducements to leave a group include the attractiveness of alternative relationships and the restraints against breaking up such existing relationships. Thus, the strength of the marital relationship would be a direct function of the attraction within and barriers around the marriage, and an inverse function of such attractions and barriers from other relationships. (p. 19)

Drawing on interdependence theory (Thibaut & Kelley, 1959), Levinger indicated that a person's attraction to a relationship is directly associated with its perceived rewards and inversely with its perceived costs. Alternative relationships are the source of their own attractions. Rewards include material, symbolic, and affectional rewards. Attractions, either to the relationship or to an alternative relationship, can vary from highly positive to highly negative (repulsions) (Levinger, 1976). Barriers against a breakup include the material, symbolic, and affectional costs of termination. Levinger (1965, 1976) reviewed the research on attractions and barriers to marriage. Attridge (1994) further elaborated and reviewed the research on the barriers to dissolution of romantic relationships.

Davis (1973) also discussed "the centripetal forces that hold intimates together and . . . the centrifugal forces that drive them apart" (p. 209). He asserted, "When the centrifugal forces become stronger than the centripetal, the intimates will break up" (p. 209).

According to Davis (1973), three factors affect the extent to which intimates are integrated. First, the external environment surrounding a relationship can act as a centripetal force holding intimates together or as a centrifugal force tearing them apart. This tendency is represented by the metaphor "going through thick and thin." The second factor is the alignment of forces holding partners together. If intimates' ties to each other are equal in strength, then such equality acts as a centripetal force, holding them together. If their ties to each other are unequal (which can occur from the onset of the relationship or over time, for a number of reasons), then such unevenness acts as a centrifugal force. The final factor that affects the degree to which intimates are integrated is the inevitable decline of the forces holding them together and the degree to which intimates are able to continually do things to "warm up their ever-cooling relationship" (p. 211).

Dialectical perspectives also posit these forces, although such forces are more than just opposite; they are dialectical in nature. Bakhtin (1981) regarded all social processes as the product of "a contradiction-ridden, tension-filled unity of two embattled tendencies" (p. 272): centripetal forces (or forces of unity) and centrifugal forces (or forces of differentiation). Baxter and Montgomery (1996), in elaborating their dialogic approach to relationships based on the work of Bakhtin, argued that centripetal-centrifugal dynamics are at the core of personal relationships. The need to connect with another is a centripetal force, and the simultaneous need to separate from the other is a centrifugal force.

## ► Relational Maintenance Strategies

Most models of relationship maintenance assume that the forces holding intimates together are less than the forces pulling them apart. Thus, partners must do things to maintain their relationship, or else it will fall apart. Indeed, Canary and Stafford (1994) listed the following as their number one proposition regarding relational maintenance: "All relationships require maintenance behaviors, or else they deteriorate" (p. 7).

Thus, partners must be proactive in maintaining their relationship; that is, they must actively engage in conscious and intentional behaviors designed to maintain their relationship. There are a number of ways in which to do so. For example, Levinger (1965) indicated that to increase the stability of a marriage, one could increase the attractiveness of the relationship, decrease the attractiveness of alternative relationships, or increase the strength of the barriers against a breakup. Focusing exclusively on barriers, Attridge (1994) argued that romantic relationships are sustained to the extent that partners desire and create barriers to dissolution. Attridge elaborated how couples can strategically create new barriers and make existing barriers stronger as a means to maintain their relationships.

Davis (1973) also discussed how centripetal and centrifugal forces could be strategically manipulated to maintain a relationship. Intimates can strategically seek out environments that they expect will hold their relationship together. According to Davis, if intimates' ties to each other are unequal, then intimates can use two techniques of reintegration:

> meta-intimate communication, in which each intimate dispassionately considers the problem in the context of the relationship and attempts to "work it out" in a way acceptable to other, and the *argument,* in which each intimate passionately considers the problem in the context of his own life and attempts to "have it out" in a way acceptable only to himself. (pp. 210-211, emphases in original)

Regarding the inevitable decline of forces holding intimates together, Davis discussed how reintegration ceremonies, such as celebrating anniversaries, can be intentionally designed to renew relationships.

### Typologies of Relational Maintenance Strategies

Based on interdependence theory (Thibaut & Kelley, 1959), Braiker and Kelley (1979) developed a measure of maintenance behaviors, defined primarily as communication behaviors engaged in by partners to reduce costs and to maximize rewards from a relationship. The behaviors included self-disclosure of feelings and relational needs, communication about the relationship and problems in the relationship, and attempts to change one's behavior to help solve problems in the relationship. This maintenance scale was derived as a result of a factor analysis in which these items where highly intercorrelated.

Since then, four typologies of relationship maintenance strategies have emerged in the literature (Ayres, 1983; Bell, Daly, & Gonzalez, 1987; Dindia & Baxter, 1987; Stafford & Canary, 1991). Ayres (1983) generated three types of strategies used to maintain stability: *avoidance strategies* (avoiding relationship change), *balance strategies* (keeping the number of favors and emotional support levels constant or balanced), and *directness strategies* (telling the other person that one would prefer the relationship to remain unchanged).

Bell et al. (1987) were interested in the relationship characteristic of affinity or liking and examined affinity maintenance strategies in marital relationships. Participants' responses were used to develop a typology that consisted of 28 strategies. Conceptual definitions and examples for each strategy can be found in Bell et al. (1987).

Dindia and Baxter (1987) built on Davis's (1973) work and defined relational maintenance to include both maintenance and repair. They developed a typology consisting of 49 categories clustered into 11 superordinate types: *changing the external environment, communication, metacommunication, avoiding metacommunication, antisocial strategies* (e.g., costs), *prosocial strategies* (e.g., rewards), *ceremonies* (e.g., celebrations, rituals), *antirituals/spontaneity, togetherness, seeking/allowing autonomy,* and *seeking outside help.* Conceptual definitions for each superordinate and subordinate category can be found in Dindia and Baxter (1987).

Finally, Stafford and Canary (1991) used the previous literature, in addition to open-ended responses from married and dating couples who indicated what they did to maintain their relationships to their satisfaction, to generate a list of relational maintenance strategies. Using a second sample and factor analysis, they derived five relational maintenance strategies: *positivity* (being positive and cheerful), *openness* (using self-disclosure and open discussion about the relationship), *assurances* (stressing commitment, showing love, and demonstrating faithfulness), *network* (spending time with common friends and affiliations), and *sharing tasks* (sharing household chores).

A number of studies have been conducted using Stafford and Canary's (1991) typology of relational maintenance strategies. Indeed, this typology dominates the literature on relational maintenance strategies for several reasons. First, it is a closed-end measure of relationship maintenance strategies, whereas Dindia and Baxter's (1987) measure is open-ended (participants are asked to list what they do to maintain a relationship, and then the researcher must code the strategies reported). Second, it is not limited to one characteristic of relationship development, whereas the Bell et al. (1987) typology is limited to affinity maintenance strategies. Third, it relies on the definition of relationship maintenance that is most studied by relationship scholars, maintaining relational satisfaction, whereas Ayres's (1983) typology refers to strategies that have to do with maintaining a relationship at a particular level of intimacy.

### Frequency of Relational Maintenance Strategies

Several studies have examined the frequency of use of various relational maintenance strategies. Canary and Stafford (1992) found that assurances were ranked highest, followed by sharing tasks, social networks, positivity, and openness. Ragsdale (1996) used a diary log to record the use of relational maintenance strategies on a daily basis over a 2-week period and found that sharing tasks was used most frequently, followed by positivity, assurances, social networks, and openness. Dainton and Stafford (1993) found sharing tasks to be the single most often mentioned relational maintenance strategy and routine maintenance behavior. According to these results, sharing tasks appears to be an underrated maintenance behavior in the scholarly literature, whereas openness appears to be an overrated maintenance behavior.

Dindia and Baxter (1987) found that married partners most frequently reported using prosocial, ceremonial, communication, and togetherness strategies. They also found that not all strategies used to maintain a relationship also were used to repair a relationship. Specifically, meta-communication occurred more frequently when the goal was repairing the relationship than when the goal was maintaining the relationship. Introducing variety, novelty, and spontaneity into the relationship occurred more frequently when the goal was maintaining the relationship than when the goal was repairing the relationship. In addition, more strategies were reported for maintenance than for repair, indicating that individuals' repertoires of strategies for maintenance are larger than their repertoires of strategies for repair.

### Variables Related to Relational Maintenance Strategies

Factors related to maintenance strategies include gender of respondent and gender of partner; type of relationship; various relational characteristics such as control mutuality, liking, and trust; relational satisfaction; and length of relationship. However, only gender, relational type, and satisfaction are considered here.

*Gender.* It has been argued that women are the "relationship specialists" (Wood, 1997b). Both men and women assume that women are more communal and relationally oriented; they assume that women, relative to men, are more responsible for maintaining relationships, do more of it, and are better at it. Several studies have tested sex differences in relationship maintenance strategies, with mixed findings.

Bell et al. (1987) studied wives' perceptions of affinity maintenance strategies and concluded that wives believed that they were more responsible for relational maintenance than were their husbands. Women reported that they were more likely to use most of the strategies than were their husbands, and they felt that they placed more importance on being the recipients of affinity maintenance strategies than did their husbands. However, only women were assessed in the study.

Dindia and Baxter (1987) assessed both wives and husbands and found no differences in husbands' and wives' reports of their own use of relational maintenance strategies. In this study, however, spouses indicated *what* strategies they used but not the *frequency* with which they used them. Thus, gender differences in frequency cannot be ruled out.

Stafford and Canary (1991) found a significant but weak gender effect for the frequency with which relationship maintenance strategies were employed. Women perceived their male partners as using more positivity, assurances, and social networks than men perceived their female partners as using, although Canary and Stafford (1992) studied partners' perceptions of their own maintenance behaviors and found the opposite; women reported using more openness, networks, and tasks than men reported using. Dainton and

Stafford (1993) found that women reported more of the following behaviors than did men: positivity, openness, talk, and antisocial behaviors. Similarly, Ragsdale (1996) employed the diary log to record the use of Canary and Stafford's (1992) relational maintenance strategies on a daily basis over a 2-week period and found that wives reported using more openness, social networks, and sharing tasks than husbands reported using. Ayres (1983) found no significant gender differences in individuals' reports of the maintenance strategies they would employ to maintain stability in a hypothetical relationship (see also Shea & Pearson, 1986).

Thus, results are inconsistent, and no clear inferences can be drawn regarding sex differences in relational maintenance strategies. Future research needs to sort out the issues of types of strategies, frequency of strategies, and whose perspective is being measured.

*Relational type.* Some researchers have suggested that individuals might use different maintenance strategies based on the type of relationship they have (romantic or friendship) or its stage (dating, seriously dating, engaged, or married).

Canary, Stafford, Hause, and Wallace (1993) studied the effect of relational type (romantic, family, or friends) on relational maintenance strategies. Positivity, openness, and assurances were used more than expected in romantic relationships but less than expected in friendships. Assurances, sharing tasks, and cards/letters/calls were used more than expected by relatives but less than expected by friends. Canary et al. interpreted these results as indicating that relational maintenance strategies are used more in romantic and family relationships than in friendships. They attributed this outcome to people being less concerned about maintaining their friendships than about maintaining their romantic and family relationships. Other research, however, has shown no strategy differences based on relationship type (Ayres, 1983; Shea & Pearson, 1986).

Based on a developmental perspective, Stafford and Canary (1991) hypothesized that maintenance strategies would differ due to stage of relationship development (dating, seriously dating, engaged, or married). They found that engaged and seriously dating individuals perceived greater partner positivity and openness than did married and dating individuals. Married, engaged, and seriously dating participants also perceived more assurances and sharing tasks then did those who were just dating. Married persons also reported the greatest perceptions of partner's use of social networks to maintain the relationship. Although most of the findings are consistent with linear models of relationship development, the finding that seriously dating and engaged couples perceived more openness and positivity than did married and dating couples supports a curvilinear model of relationship development.

*Relational satisfaction.* Relational satisfaction is the most common conceptual and operational definition of relational maintenance, and the correlation between maintenance strategies and relational satisfaction has been examined in several studies. Bell et al. (1987) studied wives' perceptions of their own and their husbands' maintenance strategies as well as wives' satisfaction with their relationships. The results indicated that wives' satisfaction with their marriages was most strongly associated with the belief that the strategies of honesty, inclusion of other, influence perceptions of closeness, listening, openness, physical affection, sensitivity, shared spirituality, and verbal affection were important to both selves and husbands. Greater perceived frequency of strategy use by both selves and husbands also was related to satisfaction.

Dindia and Baxter (1987) studied husbands' and wives' perceptions of their own maintenance strategies and relational satisfaction. Results showed that husbands' and wives' perceptions of their own maintenance strategies were unrelated to their own or their partners' relational satisfaction. However, an individual's relational satisfaction might depend more on the person's perceptions of his or her partner's maintenance strategies than on an the person's perceptions of his or her own maintenance strategies.

Stafford and Canary (1991) studied an individual's perceptions of his or her partner's maintenance strategies. Results indicated that perceptions of the partner's use of maintenance strategies were positively related to relational satisfaction. In a regression equation, perception of partner assurances was the primary predictor of relational satisfaction, whereas positivity and sharing tasks were the second and third predictors. Openness was weakly and inversely associated with relational satisfaction. Dainton, Stafford, and Canary (1994) also studied the relationship between an individual's perceptions of his or her partner's maintenance strategies and an individual's relational satisfaction. The results indicated that all five maintenance strategies (noted earlier) were positively correlated with relational satisfaction. In regression analyses, husbands' satisfaction was predicted by reports of partners' use of assurances, followed by perceptions of partner positivity, explaining more than half the variance in husbands' relational satisfaction. For wives, all five of the maintenance strategies predicted satisfaction. Specifically, wives' satisfaction was predicted by positivity, followed by sharing tasks, assurances, social networks, and openness, which predicted about half of the variance in relational satisfaction. The partial correlation for openness was negative, consistent with previous research (Stafford & Canary, 1991).

Overall, these results indicate that an individual's perception of his or her partner's relational maintenance strategies is related to an individual's relational satisfaction. However, future research needs to explore the possibility that perceptions of partner maintenance strategies affect one's satisfaction and that satisfaction affects one's own maintenance strategies.

As stated by Bell et al. (1987), "Maintenance is in the eye (attributions) of the beholder" (p. 452). Different studies have examined different perspectives on relational maintenance strategies, and as can be seen in reviewing the research on relational maintenance strategies, the results often are inconclusive. A potential moderating variable that needs to be tested in future research concerns the issue of whose perspective is measured. Studies need to include both partners' perceptions of their own and their partners' maintenance strategies. Only then can issues such as sex differences in maintenance strategies and the relationship between maintenance strategies and relational satisfaction be adequately addressed.

### Uniphasic Versus Multiphasic Relational Maintenance Strategies

Several researchers have discussed the multiphasic nature of relationship maintenance strategies. Duck (1988) claimed, "Some means for developing relationships are also means for maintaining them" (p. 100). Buley (1977) asserted, "If you know the behaviors required to strengthen a relationship, these are the same behaviors required to keep it strong" (p. 143).

Research on relationship strategies tends to be phase bound (Dindia, 1994b). That is, relationship development strategies have been studied within the boundaries of a particular stage of relationship development. For example, there are typologies of relationship initiation strategies (Baxter & Philpott, 1982), relationship escalation strategies (Tolhuizen, 1989, 1992), relationship maintenance strategies (Dindia & Baxter, 1987; Stafford & Canary, 1991), and relationship termination strategies (Baxter, 1984, 1985). I have argued that relationship development strategies are multiphasic; strategies used to initiate and escalate relationships also are used to maintain relationships, and these are the opposite of strategies to deescalate and terminate relationships. The opposite of some strategies used to initiate relationships is used to terminate relationships; for example, inclusion is used to initiate relationships, whereas exclusion is used to terminate relationships (Baxter & Philpott, 1982). Similarly, some strategies used to generate liking among nonintimates (Bell & Daly, 1984) also are used to maintain liking among intimates (Bell et al., 1987). After extensive review of the research on relationship initiation, escalation, maintenance, repair, and termination strategies, I proposed a typology of relationship development strategies that is applicable to all stages of relationship development including relationship maintenance (Dindia, 1994b).

I also conducted two studies to test the multiphasic nature of relationship strategies. In the first study (Dindia, 1991), participants reported the strategies they used to initiate, escalate, maintain, repair, and terminate relationships. Strategies were coded into 24 categories, and 10 of the categories were reported in two or more relational stages. Many of the strategies used to terminate relationships were the opposite of strategies to initiate, escalate, maintain, and repair relationships. A potential problem with the study was that participants reported on all five stages of relationship development and might have engaged in a "response set" in which they reported the same strategies across relationship stages. Thus, in a follow-up study (Dindia, 1992), participants were asked to choose relationships in which they currently were involved and, depending on the stages of their relationships, to describe the strategies they used to initiate, escalate, maintain, repair, deescalate, or terminate the relationships. The results of the study indicated 21 strategies, all of which were used in two or more relational stages. The results of this study also indicated that some of the strategies used to deescalate and terminate relationships are the opposite of strategies designed to initiate, escalate, maintain, and repair relationships.

The results of these studies provide some support for the generality and parsimony of an inclusive typology of relationship strategies rather than separate typologies of relational initiation, escalation, maintenance, and termination strategies. In other words, relationship strategies are largely multiphasic. Communication and contact are used to initiate, escalate, and maintain relationships. The opposite of communication and contact, avoidance, is used to terminate relationships. Meta-communication and indirectness are used to escalate, maintain, and terminate relationships but not to initiate relationships. Rewards, self-presentation of positive attributes, and affection are used to initiate, escalate, and maintain relationships. Their opposites—costs, self-presentation of negative attributes, and indifference—are used to terminate relationships. Similarity is used to initiate and maintain relationships, whereas dissimilarity is used to terminate relationships. Social networks are used to escalate, maintain, and terminate relationships. Two strategies appeared to be uniphasic: Spontaneity/novelty and sharing tasks/responsibilities seemed to be used exclusively to maintain relationships. On greater reflection, I suspect that one would engage in the opposite of these behaviors, such as be boring, make the relationship boring, and not share tasks/responsibilities, if one wanted to deescalate and/or terminate a relationship.

Such a multiphasic view of relationship development strategies has important theoretic implications for personal relationships in general and for relational maintenance in particular. A typology of relationship strategies that generalizes to all stages of relationship development is more parsimonious than separate typologies of relationship initiation, escalation, maintenance, deescalation, and termination strategies. In addition, a multiphasic approach to relationship maintenance is important for understanding the similarities and differences between relationship maintenance and other stages of relationship development as well as the similarities and differences between strategies designed to maintain a relationship and strategies designed to accomplish other relationship goals. Similar to the results of the research on relational maintenance and repair (Dindia & Baxter, 1987), it appears that people have finite repertoires of

strategies that they use for multiple relational goals. People do not necessarily change their relational strategies as much as they adapt them to fit their particular relational goals (e.g., initiation, maintenance, termination).

## ► Routine Relational Maintenance Behaviors

Some researchers have turned their attention to routine maintenance behaviors (Bruess & Pearson, 1995; Dainton, 1995; Dainton & Stafford, 1993; Duck, 1994). Dainton and Stafford (1993) differentiated strategic and routine maintenance behaviors by defining strategic maintenance behavior as conscious and intentional behavior enacted by partners to maintain the relationship, whereas routine maintenance behavior occurs at a lower level of consciousness and is not intentionally used to maintain the relationship. Duck (1988) argued for the need to look at routine maintenance behaviors, stating, "There are many other instances where the little things of life keep us together" (p. 99). Duck (1994) also argued, "Relational maintenance contains two elements, not one; the first is strategic planning for the continuance of the relationship; and the second is the breezy allowance of the relationship to continue by means of the everyday interactions and conversations that make the relationship what it is" (p. 46). For example, people probably do not think of asking their partners how their day went or telling their partners how their own day went as strategies to maintain their relationships. However, these acts might, nonetheless, function to maintain relationships.

Dainton and Stafford (1993) extended previous typologies of relational maintenance strategies by probing for routine maintenance behaviors used by married and dating couples. The resulting 12-category taxonomy included both strategic and routine maintenance behaviors. The researchers found that the most frequently reported maintenance behavior was sharing tasks, a category that was only infrequently mentioned in prior research. This finding led the researchers to note that sharing tasks might be a routine behavior that functions to maintain relationships, even though couples perform such sharing without the explicit purpose of maintaining their relationships.

Dainton (1995) compared couples' use of strategic and routine maintenance behaviors. Dainton developed a typology of interaction types based on a daily interaction log completed by participants. The typology consisted of six categories of interaction: instrumental, leisure, meal time, affection, conversations, and network. People rated how much thought each interaction required and how typical it was for the relationship, and these scores were combined to come up with an index of routineness. Dainton discovered that the majority of interactions in which couples engaged were routine rather than strategic. Participants rated the category of affection to be the most routine and the most important to their relationships.

Similar to routine maintenance behaviors are the rituals that function to maintain relationships. Rituals are nonstrategic or routine. Bruess and Pearson (1995) studied interpersonal rituals in marriages. They found that some rituals, such as communication rituals and daily routines and tasks (performed together), served to bond and maintain the relationships. Overall, it is clear that couples engage in both strategic and routine behaviors that function to maintain the relationships.

In reality, strategic and routine maintenance behaviors might not be dichotomous. Partners might routinely kiss each other hello and good-bye or say "I love you" without consciously and intentionally intending to maintain their relationships, and this behavior still might function to maintain the relationships. Alternatively, individuals might kiss their partners good-bye or say "I love you" as a conscious and intentional strategy to maintain their relationships. Some relational maintenance behaviors might start out as strategic but become routine (rituals) over time. Some behaviors might be strategic for some part-

ners/couples and routine for others, or they might be perceived as strategic by some partners/couples but not by others. Finally, strategic/routine might not be characteristic of maintenance behaviors in general but only characteristic of their uses on particular occasions. Hellos and good-byes might be produced routinely, but they also might be used in a strategic manner on occasion.

## ▶ Current Theoretical Perspectives on Relational Maintenance

Research on relational maintenance strategies is primarily atheoretical (but see Canary & Stafford's [1992, 1993] research on relational maintenance strategies and equity theory). However, a number of theoretical perspectives implicitly or explicitly pertain to relational maintenance (for comprehensive discussions of communication, social psychological, and dialectical approaches to relational maintenance, see Canary & Stafford, 1994; for a review and assessment of social exchange, interactional, and dialectical approaches to relational maintenance, see Canary & Zelley, in press). This section briefly addresses three theoretical perspectives that deal explicitly with the issue of relational maintenance: Rusbult's commitment theory (Rusbult & Buunk, 1993; Rusbult et al., 1994), relational dialectics (Baxter & Montgomery, 1996), and Sigman's (1991) theoretical perspective on relational continuity and RCCUs.

### *The Investment Model*

Rusbult's investment model is built on interdependence theory (Thibaut & Kelley, 1959) and explicitly addresses the issues of how and why relationships are maintained (Rusbult & Buunk, 1993; Rusbult et al., 1994). Commitment is at the heart of the investment model and refers to an individual's intentions to remain in the relationship. According to the investment model, commitment is a function of three factors: the level of satisfaction with the relationship (which is based on the ratio of rewards to costs), the perceived quality of its alternatives, and the size of investments (both intrinsic [e.g., emotions] and extrinsic [e.g., shared possessions]) in the relationship.

According to the investment model, if an individual is committed, then he or she is more likely to remain in the relationship and to engage in relational maintenance behaviors such as accommodation, derogation of alternatives, willingness to sacrifice, and perceived superiority of the relationship. Tendencies to accommodate refer to partners' responses to dissatisfaction in a relationship that differ along the active-passive and constructive-destructive dimensions. Voice (active, constructive) and loyalty (passive, constructive) constitute the relational maintenance behavior of accommodation.

There is a base of empirical support for the investment model including the hypothesis that commitment mediates maintenance behaviors (for reviews, see Rusbult & Buunk, 1993; Rusbult et al., 1994), although Canary and Zelley (in press) noted that relational maintenance behaviors also can be viewed as predictors of commitment (and, indeed, some of the longitudinal research on the model so indicates). Thus, not only do committed partners engage in relational maintenance behaviors, but relational maintenance behaviors cause further commitment.

### Relational Dialectics

According to a dialectical perspective, social systems involve contradictory and opposing forces (Baxter, 1988; Baxter & Montgomery, 1996; Montgomery, 1993). Baxter (1994) identified three dialectics of relationships: *integration-separation, stability-change,* and *expression-privacy.* Each of these dialectics is manifested in two forms: internal and external. Internal contradictions are within the relationship, and external contradictions are be-

tween the relationship and the broader social order. Other dialectical forces have been identified in the relationship literature (Altman, Vinsel, & Brown, 1981; Rawlins, 1992). Baxter and Montgomery (1996) argued that no finite set of contradictions exists in personal relationships.

Instead of viewing relationships as steady states that are maintained, a dialectical perspective views relationships as ever changing. This element of change stands in contrast to earlier models of relationship development. A dialectical model, however, suggests that relationships continually oscillate between opposite poles such as autonomy-connection and openness-closedness. Thus, maintenance, if defined as long-term stability or constancy, is incompatible with the assumptions of the dialectical perspective (Montgomery, 1993). Relational stability is impossible from a dialectical perspective. Thus, Montgomery (1993) suggested a fifth definition of relational maintenance whereby maintenance, viewed dialectically, is defined as *relational sustenance.*

A dialectical perspective views people as proactive agents who make communicative choices in how to deal with contradictions that, in turn, affect people's subsequent communicative actions. Baxter (1988) identified five dialectical coping strategies (this list is expanded to eight in Baxter & Montgomery, 1996), some of which are more effective than others in managing dialectical tensions. Cyclic alternation occurs when partners alternate between both poles of a given tension, for example, emphasizing autonomy during the week and emphasizing connection during the weekend. Segmentation involves efforts to establish separate relational domains for the fulfillment of each dialectical pole, for example, certain activities being performed separately and certain other activities being performed together. Moderation involves compromise efforts in which neither dialectical pole is fulfilled completely, for example, partners engaging in moderate levels of self-disclosure. Disqualification involves intentional ambiguity or equivocation to allow both dialectical poles to be fulfilled. Reframing involves a reconceptualization of the contradiction such that the partners no longer perceive the two dialectical poles as opposed to one another, allowing the poles to be fulfilled simultaneously.

Empirical research from a dialectical perspective has concentrated on identifying dialectical tensions and how people respond to them (Baxter, 1990; Baxter & Simon, 1993; Goldsmith, 1990; Rawlins, 1983a, 1983b). This research provides evidence that dialectical tensions are perceived as real in relationships and that partners engage in strategies (conscious and intentional) and more routine behaviors (less conscious and intentional) that function, either constructively or destructively, to respond to these tensions. The dialectical perspective provides a radically different approach to relational maintenance in comparison to social exchange perspectives.

### Relational Continuity Construction Units

Sigman (1991) noted a fundamental anomaly about social and personal relationships: Social and personal relationships are continuous despite discontinuous periods of physical and interactional co-presence. Sigman argued that couples manage the discontinuous aspects of relationships by using RCCUs, which are behaviors that relational partners engage in before, during, and after an absence that function to construct the continuity of the relationship during periods of absence.

RCCUs are divided by Sigman (1991) into three types: (a) prospective units, (b) introspective units, and (c) retrospective units. Prospective units entail behaviors that relationship partners perform before physical separation. Behaviors in this category include farewells, agenda establishments (projections of future interactions), and the use of tokens and spoors (objects left behind [e.g., a toothbrush in a lover's bathroom]).

Introspective units occur during times of relational non-co-presence. Introspective units constitute the relationship's continuity during periods of absence. Introspective units include affiliative artifacts (e.g., wedding bands, photographs of the partner) and mediated contact (e.g., greeting cards, notes, phone calls, e-mail messages).

Retrospective units occur after the period of absence has ended. Greetings and conversations that allow the partners to "catch up" on what happened to each other during the period of absence are examples of retrospective units.

Gilbertson, Dindia, and Allen (1998) studied the relationship among time spent apart, RCCUs, and relational satisfaction. The results of the study indicated that time apart was negatively related to relational satisfaction. This evidence indirectly supports the claim that periods of absence threaten the continuity of relationships. More important to the theory, female and male prospective RCCUs were positively related to female relational satisfaction, and female prospective RCCUs were positively related to male relational satisfaction when the effects of co-presence were held constant.

Considerable overlap exists between Sigman's (1991) concept of RCCUs and the relational maintenance behaviors discussed by other researchers. However, this perspective focuses exclusively on behaviors that function to maintain relational continuity (one definition of relational maintenance) during periods of physical and interaction absence. The concepts of relational continuity and RCCUs might be particularly informative to theory and research on long-distance relationships in which partners spend large amounts of time away from each other as well as to the periods of discontinuous face-to-face interaction with which all couples must deal.

## ► Importance of Theory and Research on Relational Maintenance

Regardless of which definition of relational maintenance one uses or the theoretical approach chosen, relational maintenance research is important, both theoretically and practically. If relationship maintenance is defined as everything that occurs between the initiation and termination of a relationship, then people spend more time maintaining their relationships than they do entering or exiting them (Duck, 1988). "For most people, in most relationships, this period of continuous existence *is* the relationship, as they experience it" (Duck, 1994, p. 45, emphasis in original).

The theory and research reviewed in this chapter suggests a number of potential applications for the everyday task of maintaining relationships. Among potential applications, the research suggests a number of behaviors that can be strategically employed to maintain relationships. Individuals can be taught to engage in these behaviors to maintain their relationships. The literature on strategic versus routine maintenance behaviors indicates that individuals can be taught to engage in a set of behaviors that, once they become habit, will continue to maintain their relationships. In many interpersonal communication courses, separate behaviors are taught to initiate, develop, and maintain relationships. The multiphasic view indicates that this is not necessary; a more parsimonious set of behaviors can be taught that function to initiate, develop, and maintain relationships. Finally, current theoretical perspectives on relational maintenance promise important applications. The investment model indicates relational maintenance behaviors that potentially affect and are affected by the individual's and partner's commitment level, an important variable given that experts predict that nearly half of all new marriages will end in divorce. Relational dialectics theory suggests behaviors that can be engaged in to effectively manage the contradictory and opposing forces that are inherent in all relationships. Sigman's (1991) perspective on RCCUs suggests behaviors that can be performed before, during, and after an absence to maintain a relationship when partners are apart, a perspective especially relevant to long-distance relationships and commuter couples. However, none of this information is applicable unless it penetrates interpersonal and social psychological textbooks and, even more important, the self-help literature and popular press.

People seek information to help them maintain their relationships. In particular, they turn to friends, parents, siblings, magazines, and movies as sources of relationship information and, less frequently, to self-help books (Honeycutt, 1996). However, much of this "pop psychology" is not grounded in theory and research, and it often is ideologically biased. Theory and research on relational maintenance needs to penetrate the popular press to be of help to people in their everyday tasks of maintaining relationships. Fortunately, theory and research on relational maintenance enjoy ongoing activity and status among relationship experts. Theory and research on relational maintenance should be continued and expanded into the 21st century and increasingly communicated to the general public.

# Contents

# Gender and Personal Relationships

*Julia T. Wood*

Sex differences in personal relationships have become hot topics in both popular and academic circles. John Gray dominates the popular book market with his pronouncement that women and men are from different planets. Less in the limelight and less well compensated are scholars such as Aries (1998) who assert that women and men are more alike than different. In between the extremes of Gray's claim for maximum differences between the sexes and Aries' claim for minimum ones are many scholars who offer moderate, well-reasoned judgments about the extent and types of both differences and similarities between women and men (Canary & Dindia, 1998; Duck & Wright, 1993; Gottman & Carrère, 1994).

This chapter summarizes theories and research on sex and gender in close relationships. The chapter is organized into five sections. The first section defines key concepts in the study of gender and relationships. The second section summarizes theories about the bases of gender dynamics in relationships.

The third section reviews similarities and differences between women's and men's orientations toward, and activities in, friendships. The fourth section discusses sex-related patterns in gay, lesbian, and heterosexual romantic relationships. The final section offers tentative conclusions about the extent and types of sex differences, identifies priorities for future research, and highlights the practical importance of sex and gender dynamics in human relationships.

## ▶ Definitions of Central Concepts

Although sex and gender often are used as synonyms, they actually are distinct concepts (West & Zimmerman, 1983; Wood, 1999). Sex is innate, whereas gender is socially created and learned by individuals. Being born male or female does not necessarily lead to thinking, acting, and feeling in ways that a culture defines as masculine or feminine.

Instead, biological sex usually, but not always, is transformed into culturally constructed gender as individuals interact with social structures and practices that express, uphold, and reproduce prevailing views of women and men.

## Sex

Sex is a biological quality that is determined before birth and, short of radical medical procedures, it remains stable throughout life. The usual chromosome patterns are XX for females and XY for males. (Less standard patterns are XO or XXX for females and XXY or XYY for males.) Both before and after birth, hormones govern secondary sexual characteristics such as facial hair, menstruation, and proportions of muscle and fat tissue (Jacklin, 1989).

Sex can influence tendencies toward hemispheric specialization in the human brain. Females generally are more adept at using the right brain lobe, which controls creative abilities and intuitive, holistic thinking. Males generally are more skilled in left brain functions, which govern linear thinking and abstract analytic thought (Hartledge, 1980). Females typically have more developed corpus collosa, which are the bundles of nerves connecting brain lobes. Thus, females might have an advantage in crossing from one side of the brain to the other and in using both brain hemispheres (Begley, 1995). Research linking sex and hemispheric brain specialization, however, does not prove that sex determines brain activity. It is equally possible that males and females are socialized in ways that lead to differential development of ability in the distinct lobes of the brain (Hines, 1992).

## Gender

Unlike sex, which is innate and stable, gender is learned and varies in response to cultural settings and experiences over a lifetime. Individuals acquire gender as they interact with specific others and the social world, and their understandings and performances of gender continuously evolve as they participate in different communities.

Gender consists of meanings and expectations of men and women that are created and upheld by social structures and practices. Women generally are expected to be connected to others, deferential, and emotionally expressive. Men generally are expected to be independent, assertive, and emotionally reserved. The impact of gender socialization is especially evident in patterns of caregiving. Although sex determines that women—and not men—carry fetuses, give birth, and lactate, gender accounts for the expectation that women will assume primary responsibility for caring for children and others. Studies have shown that men can be as loving, nurturing, and responsive as women (Kaye & Applegate, 1990; Risman, 1989), yet our society continues to expect women to be more involved than men in parenting. Women also are expected to care for elderly individuals, so daughters generally assume greater responsibility than do sons in caring for parents, and wives typically provide more care to in-laws than do married sons (Wood, 1994). Social expectations that women should care for others are reflected in and perpetuated by practices such as maternity leaves, which seldom are paralleled by paternity leaves.

The meaning of gender varies from culture to culture and at different times within a single culture. The rugged and physically strong exemplar of manhood that held sway in the United States during the 1700s was replaced when the industrial revolution created a paid labor force in which a man's worth was measured by what he earned (Cancian, 1987). The 1700s European American ideal of frail and decorative women was displaced by a model of women as able partners in the family livelihood during the agrarian era in the United States. When European American men were redefined as primary breadwinners in the public sphere, the Western ideal of womanhood was revised to that of homemaker (Cancian, 1987).

Gender also varies across cultures. For example, in Nepal, both sexes are expected to be nurturing, and men are as likely as women to take care of children and elderly people. In other societies, men are more emotional and concerned with appearance than are women, whereas women are more independent and emotionally restrained than are men (Mead, 1934/1968). In still other cultures, more than two genders are recognized and celebrated, and individuals sometimes change their genders (Kessler & McKenna, 1978; Olien, 1978).

Even within the United States, gender varies among social groups. Because gender is socially created, it makes sense that different social circumstances would cultivate distinct views of the sexes. For example, Gaines (1995) reported that, among African Americans and Hispanics, both sexes have strongly communal orientations. As a group, African American women are more assertive and independent and, therefore, are less inclined than European American women to smile and defer to men (Halberstadt & Saitta, 1987).

Gender intersects other social categories such as race, class, age, and sexual orientation (Collins, 1998; Spelman, 1988). For example, research indicates that lesbians tend to be more autonomous than heterosexual women (Huston & Schwartz, 1995). Because gender varies across time and social groups and in relation to other aspects of identity, women and men are not homogeneous groups.

### Sexual Orientation

Sexual orientation refers to individuals' preferences for sexual and romantic partners. Contrary to common belief, sexual orientation is not necessarily fixed permanently; rather, it appears to be somewhat fluid. As Huston and Schwartz (1996) pointed out, many individuals who currently identify themselves as lesbian or gay have had heterosexual relationships in the past and might have them again in the future. Furthermore, some individuals who once identified as gay, lesbian, or hetero-

sexual currently regard themselves as bisexual; the converse also is true.

Sexual orientation refers to more than a preference to engage in sexual activities with members of one or the other sex. It includes not only sexual preferences but also tendencies to feel and display affection and to feel romantically attracted to members of one or the other sex. Cultural views of sexual orientation are diverse and subject to change over time. For example, sexual relationships between older and younger men were the ideal in Plato's society. Today, some countries (e.g., Sweden, Denmark) accord equal legal and social rights and status to gay, lesbian, and heterosexual couples. Although that currently is not the case in the United States, the once radical disapproval of gays and lesbians has abated somewhat.

## ► Theoretical Accounts of Gendered Patterns

A number of theories attempt to describe, explain, and predict men's and women's thoughts, feelings, communication, and behaviors in close relationships. These theories fall into two broad and oppositional categories: essentialist accounts and constructionist accounts.

### Essentialist Accounts

Essentialist explanations share the fundamental premise that there is some essential innate quality (or qualities) in women and men that accounts for differences in their behaviors in relationships. The most obvious form of essentialist explanation is biological. For example, men's aggressiveness is attributed to males' testosterone levels. Sociobiologists argue that men and women engage in distinct sexual patterns in an effort to maximize the chance that their genetic lines will continue. Some scholars, particularly French feminists, claim that women's bodies and biology tie them to natural rhythms and interdependence that are not promoted by male biology. Another form of essentialist explanation accounts for sex differences as matters of divine law: God or another deity designed women to be nurturing and deferential and designed men to be instrumental and dominating.

### Constructionist Accounts

The second broad genre of explanation for sex and gender differences is constructionist theories. Common to various constructionist explanations is the basic assumption that gender is socially constructed and not innate. Constructionists believe that, aside from a few obvious differences (e.g., reproductive organs and abilities) that result from biological sex, differences between women and men are constructed and sustained through social practices that reflect the prevailing ideologies in various societies.

Constructionists argue that social structures and practices reflect and reproduce distinctly gendered identities. Institutions such as religion, the military, and schools are hierarchically organized, with men consistently, although not uniformly, occupying positions of greater power than those held by women. In concert, the structures and practices of a culture reflect and continuously recreate gendered identities and associated differences.

*Standpoint theory.* A recent and important addition to constructionist accounts is standpoint theory, which claims that the position a social group occupies in a culture shapes what members of a group know and how they know it (Harding, 1991). Standpoint theorists trace how intersections among gender, race, class, and other bases of social groupings influence group members' experiences and, thus, the identities they form and the patterns of communication they develop. Ruddick (1989) argued that women's traditional placement in domestic settings cultivates "maternal thinking," which promotes development of capacities to notice and respond to others and their needs.

Standpoint thinking provides a theoretical foundation for research on gendered speech communities. Maltz and Borker's (1982) classic study of children's play suggests that the games that girls and boys play foster distinct understandings of how, when, and why to talk. War and football, which are typical boys' games, have four defining characteristics. First, these games require a number of players, so boys learn to interact in large groups. Second, the games are structured by goals and rules, so little talk is needed to organize relationships among team members. Instead, talk is used to negotiate for power, position, and influence (e.g., who calls plays, who have key positions on the team). Third, boys' games are highly competitive not only between teams but also within teams. An individual boy's status depends on being better than other players (e.g., being the most valuable player). Finally, the bond that develops among players results from doing something together, that is, working as a team to achieve a goal.

Games more typically played by young girls tend to cultivate distinct styles and goals of interaction. First, they involve few people; usually, two or three are enough to play. Second, there are few clear-cut external goals and rules. There is no parallel in house or school for the touchdown (football) or home run (baseball). Instead, the purpose of girls' games is to interact and learn about one another. Thus, girls develop closeness primarily through talking, whereas activities are a backdrop for communication. Women generally regard communication not just as a means to instrumental goals but also as a primary goal in its own right. Third, girls' games tend to be more cooperative than competitive. Unlike soccer or war, house has no opposing team. Also, because girls' games center on relationships, they minimize competition among members of the group. Table 22.1 summarizes the rules of interaction fostered by games typically played by girls and boys.

Since Maltz and Borker's (1982) study, scholars have developed the theory that

**TABLE 22.1** Rules of Interaction Fostered by Girls' and Boys' Games

| Girls' Games | Boys' Games |
|---|---|
| Focus on building relationships with others. | Focus on accomplishing goals. Do things. |
| Include others in interaction. Avoid putting others down or outshining them. | Assert self and establish status and authority. Make yourself stand out. |
| Cooperate with and support others. Show interest in their concerns and topics, ask questions, and respond to them. | Hold others' attention. Compete to gain and hold the "talk stage." Reroute conversations, interrupt, and do not encourage others. |

males and females are socialized in distinct speech communities (Coates, 1986; Coates & Cameron, 1989; Johnson, 1989; Tannen, 1990). A speech community exists when a group of people share understandings about how to communicate (Labov, 1972). Members of a speech community have common ideas about the goals of communication, ways in which to achieve the goals, and how to interpret one another. They acquire these common views as a result of interacting with other members of their community. Although not all girls and boys are socialized into feminine and masculine speech communities, respectively, the majority are.

*Psychological theories.* Complementary to standpoint theory are two psychological theories of gendered identities: social learning theory (Bandura & Walters, 1963; Mischel, 1966), which claims that individuals learn to behave in masculine or feminine ways through observing and imitating what they see in others and by being reinforced by others, and cognitive development theories (Campbell, 1993; Piaget, 1932/1965), which assert that individuals develop an abiding identification with one gender (called gender constancy) by 3 years of age and that they actively work to become competent in meeting social expectations of their gender. These kindred theories propose that adult modeling and reinforcement teach girls to be cooperative, responsive, and caring, whereas they teach boys to be competitive, assertive, and instrumental.

*Psychoanalytic theories.* A final constructionist view is psychoanalytic or psychodynamic theory, which focuses on unconscious processes of identification and internalization that construct gender. Sigmund Freud, the father of psychoanalytic theory, contended that "anatomy is destiny." He believed that a child's genitals determine which sex he or she will identify with and that a penis is a source of envy for girls and a source of castration fear for boys.

A large number of scholars and clinicians who reject Freud's biological determinism and his reverence for the penis have developed alternative psychoanalytic theories (Chodorow, 1978, 1989). The basic principle of newer psychoanalytic accounts is that core personality is shaped by relationships during the early years of life. As the usual first primary caregivers, mothers form distinct relationships with sons and daughters. Because daughters and mothers identify with each other, girls typically develop gender identities *within relationships* and internalize their mothers as part of themselves. Because boys do not share the sex of mothers, they must establish their gender identities *apart from relationships.* Because males carve their identities relatively independent of others and females establish their identities in relation to others, the two sexes develop fundamentally different orientations to relationships. Women's documented tendencies to use communication to build connections, express empathy, and engage in personal disclosures reflect their first relationships, which featured intimacy, openness, and identification with their mothers. The lack of identification between sons and mothers, coupled with sons' need to define their identities independent of their mothers, could explain the tendencies of many adult men to strive for fairly high degrees of independence, be emotionally reserved, and rely on action other than talking to create relationships.

No one theory has emerged as clearly superior, although theories in the constructionist category have gained wider adherence than have those in the essentialist genre. Many scholars accept and work from multiple theories, usually ones in the constructionist group.

## ► Sex, Gender, and Friendship

Drawing on theories discussed in the preceding section, a great deal of research has focused on sex and gender differences in friendships. Fehr's chapter in this volume (Chapter 6) offers a thorough discussion of theories and research on friendship. Most scholars working in this area agree that both women and men value friendships and that similarities between men's and women's ways of engaging in friendship outweigh differences. Nonetheless, most scholars also think that the sexes differ to some extent and in some respects in how they enact friendships, specifically in how they communicate with friends. Yet, scholars disagree about the source and meaning of differences.

Burleson and his colleagues (Burleson, Kunkel, Samter, & Werking, 1996; Kunkel & Burleson, 1998) reported finding differences between the sexes' ways of engaging in close relationships. Echoing the thrust of research on gender differences during the 1960s and 1970s (Wood & Inman, 1993), they argued that the masculine mode of communicating reflects a skills deficit and is inferior to the feminine mode of interacting. Specifically, they argued that men tend to be less skillful than women in providing verbal comfort to others.

Not all scholars agree with Burleson and his colleagues' views of the source and meaning of observed differences between the sexes. Work conducted by Wood and Inman (1993) led them to conclude that both sexes express caring in instrumental or material ways (e.g., trading favors, doing things together) and in emotional or expressive ways (e.g., engaging in self-disclosures, talking about personal issues) but that women tend to prioritize the latter and men tend to prioritize the former. They argued that masculine and feminine modes of expressing care are different and that both are valid. Consistent with this view, Clark (1998) found sex differences in women's and men's everyday behaviors, and this led her to conclude, "Rather than characterizing sex differences as deficits, as some scholars have, perhaps we should view each sex as having developed communicative specialties" (p. 318). More research is needed to determine whether differences between men's and women's modes of engaging in friendship reflect different preferences, unequal skills, or other factors not yet identified.

### Friendships Between Women

Describing women's friendships as an evolving dialogue, Becker (1987) highlighted the communication focus that scholars repeatedly have found characterizes friendships between women. Talk between women friends tends to be personal, disclosive, and emotionally rich (Aries & Johnson, 1983; Johnson, 1996; Riessman, 1990; Rubin, 1985). Gouldner and Strong (1987) labeled women friends as "talking companions" (p. 60) because the middle-class and upper-middle-class women they interviewed said that talk was central to their friendships. Similarly, Walker (1994) found that working-class and middle-class women friends bonded through talk in which they supported each other and shared feelings. Emphasizing that the talk between women friends is not superficial, Johnson (1996) noted that women friends engage in "really talking: talk is action, not a replacement for action. Talk is primary, not secondary. Talk is sought after, not incidental" (p. 83).

Women's friendships tend to be marked not only by depth but also by breadth of scope. Typically, women friends share many aspects of their experiences, thoughts, and feelings. As a consequence, women friends generally feel that they know each other in layered and complex ways (Aries & Johnson, 1987; Johnson, 1996; Rubin, 1985).

### Friendships Between Men

Swain (1989) coined the phrase "closeness in the doing" to describe men's friendships. More than two thirds of the men studied by Swain pointed to activities other than talking when asked to describe their most meaningful times with friends. Swain's study, as well as research by others (Monsour, 1992; Sherrod, 1989; Williams, 1985), shows that playing and watching sports and doing other things together are what male friends cite most often as the basis of camaraderie and closeness. Because men typically are not socialized to engage in expressive communication, male friends are less likely to talk intimately about problems than to help each other out by suggesting diversionary activities such as going out for drinks or watching games (Cancian, 1987; Riessman, 1990).

Although men might care deeply about their male friends, they are less likely than women to express those feelings explicitly. Instead, they tend to engage in what Swain (1989) referred to as "covert intimacy," which signals intimacy indirectly and often nonverbally. Affectionate punches, backslapping, and friendly teasing are examples of displays of covert intimacy. Based on a series of studies of men's friendships, Floyd (1997b) concluded that men are not less affectionate or caring than are women but that men "simply communicate affection in different, more 'covert' ways, so as to avoid the possible ridicule that more overt expression might invite" (p. 78; see also Floyd, 1995, 1996a, 1996b, 1997a).

### Friendships Between Women and Men

Existing research indicates that each sex perceives distinct advantages to friendships with the other. Men value friendships with women because those generally provide more explicit and expressive support and more emotional closeness than do friendships with men. Many men also feel more able to discuss feelings with women than with other men (Aries & Johnson, 1987; Rubin, 1985; West, Anderson, & Duck, 1996). Women report that male friends allow them to have fun in ways that are less emotionally involving (and sometimes draining) than is typical with women friends.

One persistent issue that surfaces in research on cross-sex friendships between heterosexuals is the difficulty of closeness that does not have sexual undertones. In the film *When Harry Met Sally,* Harry says that men and women never can really be just friends because the "sex thing" inevitably gets in the way. Yet, West et al. (1996) questioned whether sexual interest and activity is necessarily a "problem" between friends. They summarized research showing that a majority of women and men enjoy sexual teasing and flirting with friends and that many people think that sexual involvement deepens friendship.

In sum, decades of research on friendships inform four general conclusions. First, both sexes value friendships and invest in them. Second, men generally are more inclined to create and express friendship instrumentally. Third, women also tend to engage in instrumental activities with friends, yet they see "real talking" as the crux of close friendship. Fourth, both sexes report that women friends are more emotionally supportive, nurturing, and responsive than are men friends.

## ▶ Sex, Gender, and Romantic Relationships

Riessman (1990) reported the results of an in-depth study of divorced people. She found that the divorced men in her study said that their marriages no longer were rewarding when their wives quit doing things such as fixing their favorite foods and meeting them at their doors when they came home. By contrast, the women in Riessman's study reported that their marriages were unsatisfying when communication no longer was strong and good. Riessman's conclusions are consistent with the instrumental and expressive preferences associated with masculine and feminine speech communities, respectively.

Heterosexual romantic relationships frequently include differences between partners. Gay and lesbian romantic relationships often, but not always, profit from intragender empathy (Brehm, 1992), which allows partners to understand and operate from consistent views of how relationships and communication operate. The influence of gender is particularly evident in seven dynamics of relationships.

### Topics of Talk

To some extent, men and women prefer different topics of talk. Women generally enjoy discussing feelings and personal issues because this is a primary way in which they develop intimacy. Masculine speech communities, however, do not emphasize personal talk, so most men are less interested in and/or skillful at it than are women. Men typically prefer to talk about politics, sports, business, and other relatively impersonal topics. Accompanying the difference in preferred topics of talk are differences in interpretations of communication. Women in heterosexual relationships might be inclined to see men's lower interest in personal talk as a rejection of intimacy, and men might not understand that talking about feelings is a primary way in which women create and express closeness. When men want to create or express closeness, they are likely to prefer a shared activity to personal talk. This is a frequent source of misunderstandings between heterosexual partners, but it is less a source of tension between gay and lesbian partners.

The doing and talking paths to closeness might underlie marital therapists' report that a recurrent problem for heterosexual couples is different views of what sex means (Bergner & Bergner, 1990). Many men view sex as a way in which to create closeness so as to talk about feelings. Reversing this sequence, women are likely to see talk as a way in which to become intimate enough to make love. Keen (1991), a scholar of men's studies, explained:

> It is not that men are only interested in sex, but that we have been so conditioned to curtail our natural needs for intimacy that only in sex do we have cultural permission to feel close to another human being. [Men] often use sexual language to express their forbidden desires for communion. (p. 78)

A second gendered dynamic surfaces in topics of talk. More than most men, women tend to enjoy sharing details of their daily lives and activities (Becker, 1987). Thus, to tell her partner about her day, a woman might itemize who was present at meetings and what is going on in their lives and might mention details about settings, food, and so forth. However, because masculine culture sees talk as a means to achieve clear results, many men regard detailed descriptions as superfluous or even boring. Men generally do not regard sharing details as sharing selves. On the other hand, men's tendency to discuss only big events and bottom lines often frustrates their heterosexual partners, who might feel that men are not sharing themselves and their lives.

### Discussing the Relationship

"Let's talk about us" probably creates more misunderstanding between women and men than does any other single phrase. Because feminine speech communities regard talk about relationships as a way in which to create closeness, many women value talking about interpersonal dynamics. From this perspective, talking about a relationship is a way in which to intensify intimacy (Acitelli, 1988; Beck, 1988; Riessman, 1990). Masculine speech communities, however, regard the primary purpose of talk as instrumental. Thus, men tend to think that talk about relationships is needed only if there are problems. "Can we talk about us?" may imply to a man that a problem exists. If no problem exists, then many men do not see the purpose of talking about relationships because most men, unlike women, do not regard talk as the bedrock of intimacy. From a feminine perspective, men's disinterest in talking about relationships might be misinterpreted as a signal that they do not care about relationships.

Same-sex romantic couples are more likely to share a preference for talking or not talking about their relationships. Gay men, like heterosexual men, are not inclined to talk at length about feelings or to discuss their relationships overtly and emotionally (Wood, 1993). Lesbian women, like their heterosexual counterparts, tend to enjoy talking explicitly and intimately about their relationships (Kirpatrick, 1989; Wood, 1993). Yet, as Huston and Schwartz (1996) pointed out, lesbians' tendency to use communication to create and enrich intimacy and to provide support might make it less than effective at solving problems, dealing with serious differences, and charting change in relationships.

### Showing Support

In some respects, women and men differ in what they consider supportive. The rules learned in masculine speech communities incline many men to use communication to do things (e.g., solve problems, give advice). Seeing their partners' frustration or unhappiness, heterosexual men are likely to help in the only way they know how, that is, by trying to fix things, often by suggesting ways in which to diminish the frustration or unhappiness. Many women, however, regard empathy and willingness to talk about problems (not solutions) as more supportive than instrumen-

tal responses. The converse also holds: When men express problems or frustrations, they might appreciate pragmatic help more than empathic responses.

Communication between lesbian partners tends to be verbally supportive and emotional, reflecting rules of interaction in feminine speech communities. Communication between gay men is less verbally supportive and may be characterized by power struggles that work against building trust and emotional intimacy (Huston & Schwartz, 1996).

### Maintaining Conversations and Relationships

Another gendered dynamic is responsibility for maintaining conversations and relationships. Conversations are kept alive by asking questions, probing others' comments, showing interest, inviting others to talk, and following up on others' comments. Without maintenance work, conversations flounder. Research indicates that women generally exceed men in maintaining communication (Beck, 1988; Fishman, 1978). They invite others to speak, ask questions about topics initiated by others, encourage elaborations, and respond to what others say. In addition, women typically use nonverbal behaviors to signal interest and involvement more than do men (Noller, 1986). As a rule, men engage less in conversational maintenance and might deter others from talking by interrupting, failing to respond to others' comments, insistently imposing their topics, or shifting to topics of their own when others have initiated topics (DeFrancisco, 1991).

The masculine assumption of independence leads many men not to feel responsible for including others in conversation. By extension, men generally are more likely than women to assume that others will speak up if they have something to say. Thus, they feel no need to invite others to talk; if others want to talk, then they will. This is at odds with the feminine inclination to work actively to involve others in conversations. Consequently, women might be hurt if men do not ask how they feel or how their days went. Conversely, men might resent being asked to talk about themselves and their activities when they have not initiated these topics.

Gendered patterns of maintenance work extend beyond specific conversations. Research consistently finds that women assume a disproportionate amount of responsibility for maintaining relationships such as keeping them on track, noticing when problems arise, addressing tensions, and setting a tone for interaction (Tavris, 1992; Thompson & Walker, 1989).

### Dealing With Conflict

Based on a series of studies she has conducted, Rusbult (1987) concluded that there are general differences between the sexes. Men (both gays and heterosexuals) are more likely than women to retreat from problems. Rusbult's research also shows that men are more likely than women to minimize problems because they do not see them as significant and/or because they do not want to engage in conflict. Gottman (1994a, 1994b) noted that some men engage in a specific type of conflict avoidance that he termed "stonewalling," which involves a rigid and resolute refusal to discuss issues in relationships.

According to Rusbult's (1987) research, women (both lesbians and heterosexuals) are more likely than men to want to talk problems through to restore emotional intimacy. Women tend to lead the way in identifying problems and sources of discontent. They also are more likely than men to initiate discussion in an effort to understand what is wrong. Rusbult also reported that women are more likely than men to show loyalty, which involves standing by a relationship even when problems are not resolved or even addressed satisfactorily.

### Equity

There is a notable gap between Americans' ideals about equity in relationships and their actual practices. A substantial majority of both women and men profess believing in equity in home responsibilities. National polls report that 75% of Americans state that wives' and husbands' jobs are equally important, and fully 90% of Americans say that women and men should share equally in parenting (Coltrane, 1996).

In practice, however, these ideals usually are not met. Wives who work outside of the home continue to do a disproportionate amount of housework and child care—as much as twice the amount that husbands do, according to some reports (Hochschild & Machung, 1989). Not only do women typically shoulder more of the burdens of homemaking and child care, but they also tend to do less satisfying chores than do men, chores that are repetitive, routine, and constrained by time deadlines and multiple simultaneous tasks (Hochschild & Machung, 1989). Compounding the inequity in responsibilities is the finding that men are more likely than women to expect and get a buffer zone or a release from responsibilities when they feel stressed or tired. Coulter and Helms-Erikson (1997) reported that husbands are more likely than wives to receive occasional reprieves from normal duties and that both husbands and wives assume that men, but not women, are entitled to this benefit. Unequal access to a buffer zone might explain why wives who work outside of the home report feeling more positive about themselves and their lives in the workplace, a pattern that is not characteristic of married men (Burley, 1991; Crosby, 1991; Hochschild, 1997).

### Violence

Another gendered dynamic that must be considered when examining romantic relationships is violence. Although violent crimes of most types have declined during the past 10 years, the incidence of male violence against women in personal relationships has remained at least constant and might be increasing (May, 1998; National Research Council, 1996). Chapter 24 by Christopher and Lloyd in this volume focuses on violence in close relationships, so detailed coverage is not needed here. I highlight only the influence of gender and sexual orientation on tendencies toward violence between intimates.

Deeply ensconced cultural assumptions of male dominance seem central to the prevalence of violence between intimates. The vast majority—up to 95%—of reported violence is inflicted by men on women (Brock-Utne, 1989; French, 1992; Kurtz, 1989; Wood, 1998b). The severity of violence also differs between the sexes. Women who abuse partners are most likely to slap, push, or shove, whereas abusive men are more likely to commit brutal and sometimes deadly assaults (Cose, 1994; Jacobson & Gottman, 1998). Furthermore, assault on intimates is linked to masculinity or hypermasculinity (Goldner, Penn, Scheinberg, & Walker, 1990). In fact, Thompson (1991) found that both women and men who have strongly masculine gender orientations tend to be more violent toward partners than do men and women who have less strong masculine and/or more strong feminine gender orientations.

There also are sex differences in reasons for committing violence against intimates. Women generally engage in violence to protect themselves or as a last resort when other modes of coping have been exhausted (Campbell, 1993). Men are more likely to use physical violence to gain control, shore up self-esteem, or diminish others (Campbell, 1993; Straus & Gelles, 1990b).

Generalizable differences between how women and men view and act in relationships can generate frustrations, misunderstandings, and tensions, especially in heterosexual relationships. Partners can reduce the likelihood that these problems will occur if they learn to appreciate the validity of different interaction styles and orientations toward relationships. Increased understanding and respect for different styles might pave the way for developing skill in both masculine and feminine interaction tendencies.

Humans are not born with understandings peculiar to a specific culture; they are born only with the ability to learn cultural values, beliefs, norms, and language. By extension, humans are capable of learning to understand and appreciate practices other than those of their native or original cultures. In Nepal, for example, Buddhist stupas and Hindu shrines typically are side by side on the streets. Although Buddhists and Hindus differ in both sacred and secular practices, they have learned to understand and respect each other's ways without giving up their own. The same type of learning frequently is seen in people who take up residence in societies different from the ones in which they originally were socialized.

A majority of both scholars and popular writers who focus on gender assume that people are capable of learning new forms of communication and the meanings they have in specific social groups. The overt message of popular authors such as Gray (1993) and Tannen (1990) is that men and women *can* learn to understand each other's communication and what it means in each other's terms. This assumption also has been made by a number of academic writers (Gottman & Carrère, 1994; Murphy & Zorn, 1996; Wood, 1997a, 1998a; Wood & Inman, 1993). Understandings of when, how, and why to communicate are not fixed at any one time and immutable thereafter. Rather, how we communicate and what culturally encoded meanings we attribute to communication presumably change over time.

## ► Conclusions

This chapter has summarized theories and research on the influence of sex and gender on personal relationships. As hinted throughout the chapter, there are practical implications of research and theories about the impact of gender on personal relationships. One important implication is the pragmatic consequence of adopting particular theoretical views of gender differences. Essentialist theories incline those who adopt them to assume that differences are both natural and inevitable. This assumption, in turn, undercuts critical reflection on one's own behavior and alternatives to it. An extreme potential effect of essentialist accounts is justification of continued inequality between women and men including rape and paternal irresponsibility. By contrast, those who adopt a constructionist theory of gender differences are more likely to assume that their own and others' behaviors can be modified in ways that foster equitable relationships.

A second important practical implication of research summarized in this chapter is sound understanding of what differences do and do not mean. For example, students and counseling clients who learn about the distinct bases and logics of masculine and feminine interaction styles are unlikely to naively assume that their partners are simply wrong if their partners feel and behave differently from how they themselves do. Insight into reasons for different feelings, behaviors, and preferences can greatly reduce misunderstandings between women and men.

A third implication of research discussed in this chapter is greater awareness of inequities that often cause tension in personal relationships. In naming specific types of inequities, researchers have made them more visible. For example, students and clients in counseling who learn about the buffer zone, psychological responsibility, and the double shift are more likely to recognize and challenge those patterns in their own relationships.

Differences between women and men, although not overwhelming in number or extent, do affect how relationships operate and the satisfaction of partners. For this reason, researchers should continue to study the impact of sex and gender on close relationships. Three priorities merit special attention in future research.

*Develop balanced views of similarities and differences.* Scholars would do well to follow the example of Canary and Dindia (1998) in titling their recent book *Sex Differences and Similarities in Communication.* Assertions that the sexes are alike and proclamations that they are different both are misleading; both present only a partial picture of interaction between women and men.

This chapter's focus on sex and gender differences in close relationships must be understood within the larger perspective of strong similarities between what the sexes want from and invest in relationships. In short, similarities between women and men outweigh differences. The sex differences that do exist are matters of degree and not dichotomy. Both sexes engage in both instrumental and expressive forms of caring, although each sex might emphasize one means of expressing care more than the other. Differences in style notwithstanding, both sexes listen, provide support, and want to transcend differences and conflicts. A key task for future researchers is to integrate findings of similarities and differences into a holistic picture of the influence of sex and gender on close relationships.

*Distinguish between sex and gender.* A second priority for future researchers is to develop and use means of distinguishing between sex and gender. Although sex often is a criterion for membership in a gender speech community, it is not necessarily or universally so. The point is that membership in a community, and not sex per se, is the most likely influence on how one learns to communicate and interpret the communication of others. Thus, some males are socialized in feminine communities, some females are socialized in masculine communities, and some members of each sex are socialized in both masculine and feminine speech communities.

The distinction between sex and gender is pervasively ignored in published research. Typically, researchers identify sex and then advance conclusions about gender differences. We cannot untangle the roles of sex and gender when the two are routinely conflated. Impressive research supports the importance of distinguishing sex from gender. For example, Risman (1989) and Ruddick (1989) found that men who were primary caregivers for children developed capacities in excess of those of men in general to attend, respond to, nurture, and comfort others. Similarly, Kaye and Applegate (1990) reported that men who cared for elderly people became more nurturing and other oriented than did men in general. Epstein (1981) reported that women developed masculine styles of thought and communication when they were involved in careers as lawyers. The longer the women worked as lawyers, the more assertive, self-confident, and competitive they became. Similarly, research on love styles (Hendrick & Hendrick, 1996) shows that "in general, the Bem classification in terms of gender role was independent of the actual sex of subjects. . . . masculinity and femininity may make as much or more difference in a person's love attitudes than is due to biological sex" (pp. 141-142). These studies suggest that communication styles reflect gender more than sex and that styles may change as individuals move into and out of particular social groups.

*Attend to intersections between gender and other aspects of identity.* A third priority for scholars is to recognize and study the interplay among aspects of personal and social identity. For example, neither sex nor gender can be understood fully in isolation. Instead, we need to explore how sex and gender intersect other basic aspects of identity and social structure such as ethnicity, sexual orientation, and class. As Harding (1991) noted, "It is

simply not true that gender relations create a set of human experiences that are more important than those created by such other inequalities as race and class" (p. 213). We need to move beyond insular analyses of sex, race, class, sexual orientation, and so forth.

To illustrate the importance of this line of inquiry, let me offer a few examples of interaction among multiple aspects of identity and social structure. Textbooks on gender routinely advance the claim that women are less assertive than men. They also regularly assert that males are the privileged members of Western society. Yet, both of these claims should be tempered by recognition of the impact of race on assertion and privilege. African American women, for example, tend to be more assertive than European American women. African American men do not routinely benefit from the so-called "male privilege" enjoyed by many European American men; African American males, in fact, often have less social status than do African American females. Economic class also figures into issues that too often have been defined strictly by sex or gender. For example, divisions of responsibility for homemaking and child care vary according to both class and gender. In the years ahead, scholars should aim to develop more layered, nuanced, and accurate understandings of how multiple aspects of identity and social structure interact in particular eras, societies, and contexts.

# Part IV

---

# RELATIONSHIP
# THREATS

# Contents

# Extradyadic Relationships and Jealousy

*Bram P. Buunk*
*Pieternel Dijkstra*

There is a wealth of historical, cross-cultural, and anecdotal evidence that the temptation to become involved in a sexual relationship outside one's marriage is a widespread phenomenon and that extradyadic sexual relationships have surfaced wherever marriages have existed. Nevertheless, as illustrated by terms such as *adultery, cheating, infidelity,* and *unfaithfulness,* extramarital sexual involvement generally is considered a serious betrayal of one's spouse. Indeed, infidelity by one's partner, and even the thought that such infidelity *might* occur, can evoke intense and aggressive jealousy among many individuals. Even more, jealousy seems to have been acknowledged as one of the most prevalent and potentially destructive experiences in love relationships. In this chapter, we focus on the tension between the apparently strong appeal of extradyadic sexual relationships and the equally strong negative response that such relationships usually evoke in one's partner. We discuss the societal context of extradyadic sexual relationships and jealousy, various theoretical perspectives on these phenomena, the factors associated with extradyadic sexual involvement, the effects of such involvement on the primary relationship, the determinants of jealousy, and therapeutic interventions for dealing with jealousy and extradyadic sex. Although our main focus is on extradyadic sex and jealousy in the context of marital relationships, we also pay attention to these phenomena in the context of other primary relationships including dating, cohabiting, and gay and lesbian relationships.

## ▶ Societal Context

### *Incidence of Extradyadic Sex*

Throughout history and in contemporary society, reports on the incidence of illegitimate children sired by men with women other than their wives testify to the consistent occurrence of extradyadic sex among males, and the fact that about 10% of children in Western societies are not sired by the legal husbands suggests that extradyadic sex is no rare phenomenon among women either. Nevertheless, there are few reliable data documenting the precise prevalence of such behavior. After reviewing 12 surveys of extramarital behavior, Thompson (1983) concluded that the probability that at least one partner in a marriage will have an extramarital relationship lies somewhere between 40% and 76%. Extradyadic sex seems to occur more often in dating and cohabiting than in marital relationships, whereas extradyadic sex seems more common in gay relationships and less common in lesbian relationships than in heterosexual relationships (Blumstein & Schwartz, 1983). Recent data indicate that there is a large cross-cultural variety in the frequency with which extradyadic sex occurs. Caraël, Cleland, Deheneffe, Ferry, and Ingham (1995) found that extramarital sex was much more prevalent in African countries than in Asian countries and that it was more prevalent among men than among women. For example, in Guinea Bissau, 38% of the men and 19% of the women had had extradyadic sex during the past year, compared to only 8% of the men and 1% of the women in Hong Kong. In the Netherlands, the comparable percentage is 5% (Van Zessen & Sandfort, 1991). It must be emphasized that these figures concern only the past year, and the lifelong incidence is likely to be considerably higher. In addition, within Western cultures there is considerable variation among various ethnic groups in the incidence of extradyadic sex. For example, more blacks than whites engage in extradyadic sex and do so more frequently (Weinberg & Williams, 1988).

extradyadic sexual relationships and with specifying the conditions under which such behavior is and is not allowed (Ford & Beach, 1951). Even today, extramarital sex is a crime according to the laws of many American states, although these laws seldom are enforced. Although attitudes in some countries became somewhat more relaxed during the "sexual revolution" of the 1970s, a majority of respondents in most Western countries consistently disapprove of extramarital relationships under all circumstances (Glenn & Weaver, 1979; Lawson & Samson, 1988). Moreover, whereas a few decades ago a negative attitude toward extradyadic sex was more prominent in the United States than in Western European countries such as Sweden, Denmark, Belgium, and the Netherlands, this gap seems to be narrowing. For example, in the Netherlands, the percentage of the adult population that considered extramarital sex to be wrong increased from only 43% in 1970 to 78% in 1997 (Sociaal en Cultureel Planbureau, 1998). Even extradyadic involvements that merely have the potential to evolve into sexual relationships (e.g., having dinner in a secluded place, dancing) are disapproved of by a majority of individuals in present society (Weis & Felton, 1987). Nevertheless, compared to marital relationships, attitudes toward infidelity are less negative in committed dating relationships and gay relationships, although this is not the case in lesbian relationships (Bailey, Gaulin, Agyei, & Gladue, 1994; Bringle, 1995; Sheppard, Nelson, & Andreoli-Mathie, 1995). Moreover, attitudes are less negative among younger individuals, the better educated and those from the upper middle class, individuals who are less religious, those living in urban areas, and those holding liberal political orientations (for a review, see Buunk & Van Driel, 1989).

### General Norms With Respect to Extradyadic Sex

Despite the occurrence of extradyadic sex all over the world, there seems to exist a universal concern with the moral regulation of

### The Double Standard

Despite the general disapproval of extradyadic sex all over the world, during all periods of history, a *double standard* has been quite common, making adultery engaged in by men much easier to forgive than adultery by women and favoring strong sanctions against female adultery. In general, a wife's adultery has been viewed as a provocation, allowing the cuckolded husband to exact revenge on the guilty parties (Daly, Wilson, & Weghorst, 1982). In a wide variety of cultures including the United States, Uganda, Canada, Sudan, and India, sexual jealousy on the part of the husband has been found to be a leading motive in homicide. In contemporary North America, where a single standard of sexual behavior has become widely accepted, recent research shows that extramarital sex engaged in by women is judged more negatively than is similar behavior engaged in by men (Mongeau, Hale, & Alles, 1994). Nevertheless, whereas male sexual jealousy also is the most important motive in nonfatal wife beating (Daly et al., 1982), research on jealousy has reported no consistent sex differences in the degree and frequency of jealousy (Bringle & Buunk, 1985; DeWeerth & Kalma, 1993), possibly as a result of the fact that many studies use measures of jealousy that assess only the general degree of jealousy, ignoring the specific circumstances under which jealousy is aroused.

## ► Theoretical Perspectives

There have been many theoretical perspectives from which jealousy and extradyadic sexual relationships have been analyzed including diverse approaches such as psychoanalysis (Jones, 1930), field theory (Lewin, 1951), script theory (Atwater, 1982), humanistic psychology (Constantine, 1976), and the self-evaluation maintenance model (Salovey & Rodin, 1986). Here, we briefly mention three theories that we think are particularly relevant for understanding the conditions under which both jealousy and extradyadic sex can occur: attachment theory, social exchange and interdependence theory, and evolutionary psychology. These theories all have a firm basis in fundamental research and, in our view, in recent years have become the best developed, most extensive, and most fruitful perspectives for studying close relationships. The three theories represent different levels of explanation. Evolutionary theory tries to explain the *ultimate* motives for engaging in extradyadic sex and behaving jealously, that is, how such behaviors might have contributed to reproductive success in our evolutionary past. Attachment theory is basically a developmental theory of *individual differences* and tries to explain why some individuals, due to their childhood histories, are more inclined to become jealous and possessive or to experience problems with building committed and sexually exclusive relationships. Social exchange and interdependence theory is aimed at explaining jealousy and extradyadic sex as related to processes of reciprocity and dependency in the *relationship*.

### *Attachment Theory*

According to attachment theory, due to differences in caregivers' responsiveness to children's needs, a majority of individuals will develop a secure attachment style, characterized by feeling comfortable with intimacy and by trusting others. However, a substantial number will develop an insecure attachment style, either avoiding intimacy and commitment or becoming overly dependent and "clinging" to their partners (see Chapter 14 by Feeney, Noller, & Roberts, this volume). Although originally proposed to explain interactions between children and parents, attachment theory has been fruitfully applied to adult intimate relationships as well (Hazan & Shaver, 1987; Miller & Fishkin, 1997). Attachment theory would predict that securely attached individuals will favor long-term committed relationships characterized by fidelity and trust, whereas individuals with an insecure attachment style will have less stable relationships and will more likely engage in extradyadic affairs. Because it is assumed that the attachment system regulates emotions and behaviors aimed at reunion with a partner, it can be hypothesized that individuals with disrupted attachment histories are more likely to interpret the behaviors of their spouses in terms of abandonment and, therefore, will have a lower threshold for adult jealousy (Sharpsteen & Kirkpatrick, 1997).

### Social Exchange and Interdependence Theory

Exchange and interdependency theory assumes that individuals form and continue relationships on the basis of reciprocity in costs and rewards in these relationships (Burgess & Huston, 1979; Thibaut & Kelley, 1959). Individuals not only will experience distress (especially in the form of frustration and anger) in situations where the others are indebted to them, but they also will be upset in situations where they are indebted to the others because of feelings of obligation, fear of being unable to repay the debts, and uncertainty about if, when, and how the debts could be repaid (Walster, Walster, & Berscheid, 1978). Therefore, relationships are more satisfying and stable when the outcomes for each partner (rewards and costs) are more or less equal. However, in the course of the relationship, partners become *dependent* on each other. They develop the ability to control and influence each other's outcomes, the outcomes of both partners become intertwined, and positive experiences of the one might vicariously become rewards for the other (e.g., "I am happy because he [she] is happy"). According to Rusbult (1983; see also Rusbult & Buunk, 1993), commitment is the subjective representation of dependency, based on high satisfaction, irretrievable investments, and low-quality alternatives. Commitment consists of a feeling of psychological attachment to the partner accompanied by the desire to maintain the relationship. One would expect that, in general, reciprocity concerns can play a role when individuals contemplate engaging in extradyadic sex and when individuals are confronted with infidelity of their partners. For example, the lower level of jealousy in gay re-

lationships, as compared to heterosexual relationships, might be due to the fact that gays (but not lesbians) engage more in extradyadic sex themselves and, therefore, consider it fair to allow their partners to do the same. Moreover, a high level of dependency and commitment will be accompanied by a stronger desire to preserve the quality and stability of one's current relationship and, therefore, by both a higher level of jealousy and a lower inclination to become involved in extradyadic sex.

### Evolutionary Psychology

This perspective is largely based on neo-Darwinist theories in evolutionary biology and assumes that present-day humans are characterized by a complex set of mental mechanisms that have evolved because such mechanisms fostered reproductive success during ancestral times. Given the importance of the pair bond for reproductive success among humans (compared to other higher primates), a universal concern with the potential threat of extradyadic sexual relationships to this bond is easy to explain. Nevertheless, for females, investing in a long-term relationship is virtually an absolute necessity to produce offspring who survive to reproduce, whereas for men, the option exists to invest minimally—only one act of sexual intercourse at the theoretical low end. As a consequence, men would have evolved a stronger tendency than women to be open to casual extradyadic sex ("short-term mating"), more or less independent of the states of their marital relationships, and men can afford to be less selective than women in choosing partners for such casual encounters (Buss, 1994; Symons, 1979). Nevertheless, evolutionary psychologists recently have suggested that extradyadic sex might have had considerable reproductive benefits for females as well. First, women might have intercourse with various men to create confusion over who are the fathers of their offspring and, thereby, elicit the investment of resources from multiple males. Second, as has been observed among birds, in choosing long-term mates, women have to make a compromise between men's genes and men's willingness to invest. That is, women married to males of low status and wealth seem to have the highest chance of engaging in extramarital sex, supposedly to increase the quality of their offspring (Baker, 1996). In general, women even seem to have developed a (usually unconscious) tendency to engage, under certain conditions, in sex with males other than their steady mates to have their eggs fertilized by the men whose sperm is most fertile and competitive. Due to this female tendency, men have faced, in the course of evolution, the risk of unknowingly investing heavily in other men's offspring without passing on their own genes. Therefore, it is easy to understand why males have developed a tendency to reduce the chances of their partners' infidelity by engaging in "mate guarding," that is, by being possessive and spending as much time with their mates as possible and by exhibiting jealousy and threatening their mates with undesirable consequences (e.g., desertion, violence) if they have been unfaithful, even when this constitutes only a single sexual act. According to this perspective, the double standard has developed as a strategy by males to reduce the reproductive costs of female adultery. But also for a female, her partner's infidelity might include other risks such as contracting a sexually transmitted disease that results in infertility, having to share her partner's resources with another woman, and losing her partner—and his resources—to another woman (Baker, 1996). Because males can copulate with females while minimizing their investments, evidence of an emotional bond might be a reliable indicator to females of the potential loss of their partners' investments (Buss, Larsen, Westen, & Semmelroth, 1992).

## ▶ Psychological Correlates of Extradyadic Sexual Involvement

Some therapists have suggested that involvement in extramarital affairs often stems from psychological problems such as the seeking of narcissistic joy, a sense of insecurity, a low frustration tolerance, a fear of commitment, and immaturity (cf. Glass & Wright, 1992; Pietropinto & Simenauer, 1977). Although such claims seem quite overstated, there is some evidence that individuals who engage in extradyadic sex often are characterized by lower levels of mental health. For example, dating infidelity is related to lower self-esteem (Sheppard, Nelson & Andreoli-Mathie, 1995); participants in sexually open marriages have been in marital therapy relatively often (Watson, 1981); women with histrionic personality disorders (i.e., characterized by helplessness and dependency, sensitivity to criticism, identity disturbances, marked mood swings, and impulsivity) are relatively more likely to enter into affairs (Apt & Hurlbert, 1994); and women low in conscientiousness, high in narcissism, and high in psychoticism seem particularly inclined to commit various acts of infidelity (Buss & Shackelford, 1997). Although little research has directly examined the association between attachment styles and extradyadic sexual involvement, Hazan and Shaver (1994) did find that anxious-ambivalently attached individuals more often engaged in one-night stands, and Miller and Fishkin (1997) found that avoidant-anxiously attached men (but not women) sought many more partners over a 30-year period than did securely attached men. Finally, Seal, Agostinelli, and Hannet (1994) found that the willingness to engage in extradyadic sex was related to sociosexuality, a concept developed by Simpson and Gangestead (1991) referring to the willingness to engage in casual, uncommitted sexual relations.

Committing adultery is related not only to personality characteristics but also to *relationship characteristics*. It is a widely held assumption among both clinicians and laypeople that adultery stems primarily from problems in the primary relationship (Glass & Wright, 1992; Taylor, 1986). Indeed, in general, dissatisfaction with the quality of marriage is, particularly among women, associated with a positive attitude toward extramarital sex, with fantasizing about it, and with actually engaging in such behavior (Edwards & Booth, 1976; Spanier & Margolis, 1983; Wiggins & Lederer, 1984). Furthermore, in line with social exchange theory, one study showed that women who feel overbenefited *and* women who feel underbenefited in their relationships have relatively strong desires to engage in extradyadic sexual relationships and have more of such relationships, whereas among men, neither the strength of extradyadic sexual desires nor the frequency of affairs is related to the degree of reciprocity in their primary relationships (Prins, Buunk, & Van Yperen, 1992). On the other hand, there is evidence that sexual deprivation in marriage is more closely related to involvement in extramarital sex among men (Buss & Shackelford, 1997; Glass and Wright, 1985). Glass and Wright (1992) identified four types of justification that might justify a sexual extramarital relationship for the respondent: *sexual variety* (e.g., sexual experimentation, sexual excitement, novelty, change), *emotional intimacy* (e.g., intellectual sharing, companionship, self-esteem, respect), *extrinsic motivation* (e.g., getting even with the spouse, career advancement), and a *love* dimension (e.g., receiving love, falling in love). Men were higher in sexual justification, and women were higher in love justification, although this result was found only for women who had been involved in such affairs. All the sex differences we discussed here are in line with evolutionary theory, which would suggest that the inclination to engage in extradyadic sex among men is more sexually motivated and that women would be more inclined to engage in extradyadic sex when their marital relationships no longer are satisfying and they are looking for new partners who could offer more support and protection. Put differently, it would be unlikely for a happily married woman to enter into an affair. Indeed, Meyering and Epling-McWerther (1986) found that, in the decision to become involved in an extradyadic affair, men were more affected by the perceived payoffs (e.g., the possibility of sexual variation) and women were more affected by the costs (e.g., the probability of strong guilt feelings and the marriage being negatively affected).

In addition, there is evidence that, as interdependence theory would predict, extradyadic sex might be particularly likely to occur in relationships characterized by low dependency and low commitment. Buunk (1980a) found that those who had been engaged in extradyadic sex and were inclined to do so in the future were lower in emotional dependency, that is, a feeling of emotional attachment to their partners accompanied by the perception that their relationships surpass what one could expect in other relationships. Johnson and Rusbult (1989) found that those with low commitment were more open to contact with attractive members of the opposite sex, whereas those high in commitment tended to derogate attractive potential partners. A study by Buunk and Bakker (1995a) showed that commitment to a steady partner was a major important determinant of the intention to engage in extradyadic sexual relationships, and in line with interdependence theory (Rusbult & Buunk, 1993), it was mainly through their effect on commitment that a lack of satisfaction, attractive alternatives, and low investments in their relationships contributed to the intention to have extradyadic sexual intentions.

In addition to the personal and relational characteristics discussed thus far, the *social context* often will play an important role in fostering extradyadic sexual involvement. For example, opposite-sex friendships can constitute a powerful opportunity for sexual affairs. Atwater (1982) found that, among many women, extramarital affairs evolved gradually in the process of developing intimate friendships. This is consistent with the finding by Wiggins and Lederer (1984) that those who had affairs with co-workers had happier marriages than did those who had affairs with others such as neighbors and strangers. Furthermore, the chances of extradyadic sexual involvement might be enhanced in a social environment with relatively favorable norms regarding extradyadic sex. For example, Buunk and Bakker (1995b) demonstrated that, in addition to positive attitudes and having been involved in extradyadic sex in the past, *descriptive norms* (i.e., the perception that relatively many of one's friends had been or would get involved in extradyadic sex) and *injunctive norms* (i.e., the perception that one's friends do not disapprove of extradyadic sex) were independent predictors of the willingness to engage in extradyadic sex.

## ► Involvement in Extradyadic Affairs

Individuals involved in extradyadic relationships often find themselves in situations where strong problems generated by these relationships conflict with the strong attraction to the extradyadic partners. Extradyadic relationships often have a very high reward potential and can at least temporarily surpass the primary relationships in terms of sexual excitement, personal growth, self-discovery, and communication. However, such positive aspects often are overshadowed by practical and emotional problems accompanied with the maintenance of a secret affair including the requirement that one has to have a private place to meet; that one has to be careful in telephoning, writing, and seeing the extramarital partner; that one has to cope with feelings of conflict, anxiety, and guilt; that one has to face the risk of jeopardizing the primary relationship; and that one has to deal with the risk of contracting a sexually transmitted disease such as AIDS (Atwater, 1982; Buunk, 1980b; Choi, Catania, & Dolcini, 1994). In line with the double standard, Spanier and Margolis (1983) found that guilt was experienced more by females (59%) than by males (34%). An additional problem faced by individuals engaged in extradyadic affairs might be the unequal involvement that can occur in these affairs, for example, when only one of the partners wants to give up his or her primary relationship and particularly when the extradyadic partner does not have a primary relationship (e.g., an affair between a

married man and a single woman) (Richardson, 1985). Remarkably, little is known about the stability of extradyadic relationships. In a study among 59 women who had had sexual affairs outside their marriages without their spouses being aware of them, Hurlbert (1992) found that affairs had lasted longer when they were characterized by a higher degree of love, when the partners had known each other longer before the affairs began, and (in the case of predominantly sexual affairs) when they had more positive attitudes toward sex.

## ► Effects of Extradyadic Sex On the Primary Relationship

Extradyadic sexual relationships often will constitute a serious threat to the primary relationships. Even when the adulterous individuals have no intent to end the primary relationships, the primary relationships might in various ways look bleak compared to the romance and sexual excitement experienced in the extradyadic relationships. Nevertheless, many of those involved in extradyadic sexual relationships claim that such relationships did not have adverse effects, or even that they had positive effects, on the primary relationships (Hunt, 1974). Of course, such claims might be rationalizations of one's adulterous behavior. In this context, it is noteworthy that individuals tend to assume that the effects of their own extradyadic affairs are relatively benign but that affairs of their partners are more harmful to their relationships. For example, in a study by Hansen (1987), about 40% of the men respondents felt that their own extradyadic relationships had hurt their primary relationships, whereas more than 70% felt that this was true of extradyadic relationships of their partners. In an interesting approach, Charny and Parnass (1995) asked practicing therapists to describe in depth specific extramarital affairs with which they were familiar. According to these therapists, in more than half of the cases, a one-time extramarital relationship had a negative impact on the marital relationship including divorce and a high level of distress. Indeed, cross-culturally, infidelity is a major cause of divorce (Betzig, 1989), and in studies of divorced couples, extramarital relationships consistently are indicated as a frequent (although seldom as *the* most frequent) reason for divorce (Burns, 1984). But it is difficult, if not impossible, to draw from this type of research firm conclusions about the consequences of extramarital relationships for the stability of marriages, especially given that we do not know how many or which couples remain together despite extramarital affairs. In general, it seems that extradyadic sexual relationships can likely lead to divorce when they stem primarily from dissatisfaction with the primary relationships (Buunk, 1987). In such cases, extradyadic relationships might just be a factor that speeds up, rather than causes, the decision to divorce. Indeed, Spanier and Margolis (1983) found that whereas nearly 40% of their sample of 205 divorcees had been involved in extramarital affairs, most respondents felt that these affairs were a consequence, rather than a cause, of their marital problems. Many of these affairs seem to begin during the first 4 years of the marriage (cf. Hunt, 1974).

## ▶ Jealousy as a Response to Actual or Imagined Extradyadic Sex of One's Partner

Most extradyadic relationships are kept secret from the primary partners, and even when these cuckolded partners get obvious clues that the other partners might be having affairs, such clues often are denied because the offended partners might not *want* to know they are being cheated on. According to the therapists studied by Charny and Parnass (1995), nearly half of the cuckolded spouses did not consciously acknowledge their spouses' extramarital behavior, although there were indications that they really knew about the affairs. Remarkably, fully 58% of

the betrayed spouses were seen as expressing explicit or tacit acceptance of their partners' affairs. On the other hand, some individuals are extremely jealous about and hypersensitive to every cue that their partners might be unfaithful, for example, changes in normal routine and sexual behavior, exaggerated displays of affection, and the reluctance to discuss a certain other person (Shackelford & Buss, 1997). Whereas it often is associated with suspiciousness about and oversensitivity to the partner's interest in others, jealousy can be seen as a multidimensional concept (Buunk, 1997; Pfeiffer & Wong, 1989), and at least three different types of jealousy can be distinguished. First, jealousy may be defined as a negative emotional response to involvement of one's partner in relationships with others. This type of jealousy is labeled *reactive* jealousy (Buunk, 1997) and also is called *emotional* or *provoked* jealousy (Hoaken, 1976; Pfeiffer & Wong, 1989). Second, jealousy may have a more inner directed nature and take the form of *anxious* jealousy (Buunk, 1997), which also is labeled as *cognitive* or *neurotic* jealousy by other authors (Guerrero, Eloy, Jorgensen, & Andersen, 1993; Mathes, Roter, & Joerger, 1981; Pfeiffer & Wong, 1989). In this type of jealousy, the individual cognitively generates images of the partner becoming actively involved with someone else, which results in more or less obsessive anxiety, upset, suspiciousness, and worrying. Third, jealousy may have the function of preventing a partner from becoming sexually unfaithful. This type of jealousy, therefore, is called *preventive* jealousy (Buunk, 1997), which also is labeled as *suspicious, behavioral,* or *unprovoked* jealousy by other authors (Bringle, 1991; Hoaken, 1976; Pfeiffer & Wong, 1989). In this type of jealousy, an individual is overly reactive to even slight indications of interest by the partner in a third person and might go to considerable lengths to prevent intimate contact of the partner with a third party.

Whereas their partners' actual or imagined infidelity will be experienced as a threat by both men and women, according to evolutionary psychology, men and women will differ in the aspects of their partners' behavior on which they focus while assessing the threat. Because men face the problem of paternity confidence, and women face the problem of securing their partners' investment of resources, male jealousy would be specifically focused on the sexual aspects of the partners' extramarital activities and female jealousy on the emotional involvement of their partners with the rivals (Symons, 1979). There is, indeed, evidence that men focus more on the sexual aspects of extradyadic affairs than do women (Buunk, 1986; Buunk & Hupka, 1987) and that women focus more on the time that their partners spend with the rivals (Francis, 1977). The most direct evidence for gender differences in the focus of jealousy comes from Buss et al. (1992), who developed a research paradigm that presented participants with dilemmas in which they had to choose between a partner's sexual unfaithfulness and a partner's emotional unfaithfulness as the most upsetting event. Buss et al. found that more men than women selected a partner's sexual infidelity as the most upsetting event, whereas more women than men reported a partner's emotional infidelity as the most upsetting event. Participants also were more physiologically upset, as measured by heart rate and electrodermal responses, in line with the predicted gender difference. The finding that men reported being distressed more by sexual infidelity and women more by emotional infidelity has since been replicated several times, for example, in the United States, the Netherlands, and Germany (Buunk, Angleitner, Oubaid, & Buss, 1996; see also Bailey et al., 1994). A number of researchers have argued that the gender difference should not be attributed to innate differences, as Buss et al. (1992) did, but rather is more properly explained by the fact that men assume that sexual infidelity of their partners usually implies emotional infidelity and that women assume that emotional infidelity of their partners usually implies sexual infidelity (Harris & Christenfeld, 1996; DeSteno & Salovey, 1996).

An additional situational factor influencing the degree of jealousy is *rival characteristics.* In line with an evolutionary-psychological perspective, it has been found that jealousy is evoked particularly by those characteristics that contribute most to the rival's value as a partner, with women reporting more jealousy than men when the rivals were physically attractive and men reporting more jealousy than women when the rivals possessed status-related characteristics (Buss, Shackelford, Choe, & Buunk, in press; Dijkstra & Buunk, 1998; Hupka & Eshett, 1988). In general, individuals become particularly jealous when the rivals are seen to possess characteristics that their partners might find important and, therefore, will derogate the rivals most on those dimensions that they perceive to be important to their partners (Schmitt, 1988). Moreover, rivals who surpass individuals on dimensions that are important to the individuals' self-esteem have been found to be the most threatening (DeSteno & Salovey, 1996). Finally, the level of acquaintance with a rival appears to play a role. For example, Pines and Aronson (1983) found that, particularly for men, the least jealousy-evoking rivals were those whom participants did not know personally, whereas the most jealousy-evoking rivals were those whom participants knew personally, in particular those of whom they were envious (see also Hupka & Eshett, 1988).

## ► Psychological Correlates of Jealousy

Jealousy has long been linked to *personality characteristics* such as insecurity and low self-esteem (Mead, 1977; Sullivan, 1953). In general, it is assumed that individuals with low self-esteem will feel more threatened when their partners are attracted to others and, therefore, will experience more jealousy. There is considerable support for this assumption, especially among women (Buunk, 1997; Hansen, 1987; Peretti & Pudowski, 1997), and variables directly related to self-esteem, such as feelings of personal inadequacy and negative self-models, also have been found to be associated with jealousy (Guerrero, 1998; Peretti & Pudowski, 1997). In addition, there is consistent evidence for a positive association of jealousy with neuroticism, with more neurotic individuals experiencing a considerably greater amount of jealousy than less neurotic individuals (Buunk, 1997; Mathes, 1991; Melamed, 1991; Tarrier, Beckett, Harwood, & Ahmed, 1989). Numerous other individual difference variables have been related to jealousy, but most of these variables have been examined in only one or two isolated studies. For example, there is evidence that individuals who are prone to jealousy are more introverted and socially anxious (Buunk, 1997; Tarrier et al., 1989), are more rigid (Buunk, 1997), have a more external locus of control (White, 1984), and think more irrationally (Lester, Deluca, Hellinghausen, & Scribner, 1985).

Attachment theory suggests that individuals with disrupted attachment histories are more likely to interpret the behavior of their spouses in terms of abandonment and, therefore, will have a lower threshold for adult jealousy. Indeed, individuals with an insecure attachment style have been found to be more jealous than individuals with a secure attachment style (Radecki-Bush, Farrell, & Bush, 1993). Buunk (1997) found that anxious-ambivalent participants were the most jealous, followed by avoidant participants, with securely attached individuals experiencing the least jealousy. That individuals with an anxious-ambivalent attachment style are particularly jealous given their overly dependent attitudes seems easy to understand, but why would an avoidant style be accompanied by jealousy? It might be that those with an avoidant style actually *are* quite dependent on their partners but feel that they are not meeting the needs of their partners by their distant attitudes and, therefore, are concerned about losing their partners. Although attachment styles are related to personality characteristics such as self-esteem, neuroticism, and social anxiety that are associated with jealousy, Buunk found that the effect of attachment style on jealousy was independent of such personality variables. In addition, there is evidence that attachment styles affect the behaviors individuals exhibit in response to suspected or actual infidelity. Individuals with an avoidant attachment style use relatively fewer relationship-maintaining behaviors such as talking about the problem and coming to an understanding, are especially likely to direct their anger and blame against the rivals, and are less likely to seek social support. Individuals with a preoccupied or anxious-ambivalent attachment style, on the other hand, are more likely to use surveillance behavior (e.g., looking through their partners' belongings), to blame themselves, and to resist expressing anger (presumably out of fear of rejection). By contrast, securely attached individuals, in response to their partners' infidelity, express anger toward the partners and, in general, adopt more productive coping strategies aimed at maintaining their relationships (Guerrero, 1998; Radecki-Bush et al., 1993; Sharpsteen & Kirkpatrick, 1997).

One of the reasons why jealousy is particularly characteristic of individuals with low self-esteem, a high level of neuroticism, and an insecure attachment style might be that such individuals become very involved in their relationships. Indeed, Radecki-Bush, Bush, and Jennings (1988) found that low self-esteem fosters dependency in relationships, and most research examining the associated *relationship characteristics* has focused in some way on the degree to which individuals feel dependent on their partners. Social exchange and interdependency theory would predict that, because someone who is more dependent has more to lose, jealousy will be more frequent and intense among those highly dependent on their relationships. In line with this prediction, jealousy has been found to be more strongly related to loving than to liking (Mathes & Severa, 1981; Pfeiffer & Wong, 1989; White, 1984), to be associated with emotional dependency (Buunk, 1995), and to be less common among those who maintained separate identities (including having their own activities that did not include their partners) (Mathes & Severa, 1981). White (1981) found that jealousy was more prevalent in individuals who felt more involved in their relationships than did their partners, for example, because they perceived that there were more opposite-sex friends available to their partners or that their partners were physically more attractive than themselves. Related to the concept of relationship involvement, jealousy has been found to decrease as individuals hold stronger beliefs in monogamy, feel more secure about their relationships, and experience more relationship satisfaction (Pines & Aronson, 1983; see also Buunk, 1991).

Although, in line with social exchange theory, Buunk (1995), Buunk and Bakker (1997), and Bringle and Boebinger (1990) found that individuals who are inclined to engage in extradyadic sexual and erotic behaviors are more likely to indicate that they will tolerate such behaviors from their partners, other studies indicate that the opposite might occur and that individuals might project their own adulterous urges onto their partners. For example, Pines and Aronson (1983) found that, in general, individuals who had had real or fantasized sexual involvement with others felt more jealous of threats of their partners' infidelity. Francis (1977) found men and women to differ; whereas jealous women were *less* likely to be involved with third parties, jealous men were *more* likely to be involved in extradyadic relationships, suggesting that men project their unfaithful urges onto their partners. Furthermore, women in particular seem to become less jealous the more extradyadic sexual affairs their husbands have had, whereas among men, jealousy seems unaffected by the number of affairs their wives have had (Buunk, 1995). From an evolutionary perspective, this result is easy to understand. For men, *any* act of intercourse with a third person is a potential threat, whereas for women, the fact that their partners have been unfaithful a number of times while maintaining their commitment might lead women, under some conditions, to adapt to their partners' infidelity.

## ► Coping With Jealousy

Eventually accepting their partners' infidelity might be the result of a process of *coping* with jealousy through which individuals reappraise the threat. Several authors (e.g., Mathes, 1991; Sharpsteen, 1991; White, 1981) have used Lazarus's model of coping (Lazarus & Folkman, 1984) to describe how individuals deal with jealous feelings. After the primary appraisal, during which the degree of threat to the relationships is assessed, during secondary appraisal, individuals evaluate the availability of coping strategies that might reduce the threat. Coping strategies are not limited to deliberate conscious attempts to modify the threat but also might consist of unconscious instinctive reactions to a jealousy event such as spontaneously expressing anger. Through such strategies, individuals might not only let off steam but also warn rivals to stay away and alert partners to be more cautious and take the individuals' feelings into account. Many ways of coping with jealousy have been identified, and several attempts have been made to summarize these by the use of factorial analysis into broader categories including avoidance of the spouse, reappraisal of the situation, and communication with the partner (Buunk, 1982; Constantine, 1976; Hansen, 1987).

Men and women seem to differ in the ways in which they cope with jealousy situations. A recurrent finding is that, in response to a jealousy-evoking event, women in particular have the tendency to think that they are "not good enough," to doubt themselves more than do men (Buunk, 1995), and to try making themselves look more attractive (Buss & Shackelford, 1997; Mullen & Martin, 1994). In addition, men more often report that they would get drunk or high when confronted with their partners' infidelity (DeWeerth & Kalma, 1993). Moreover, research consistently has shown that women are more inclined than men to endorse aggressive action against the rivals (DeWeerth & Kalma, 1993; Paul, Foss, & Galloway, 1993). This finding contradicts actual homicide statistics showing that many more men than women commit homicides out of jealousy (Daly et al., 1982). Possible explanations for this discrepancy are that women are more likely than men to admit intentions of violence toward the rivals; that women are less likely than men to convert their violent intentions into actual behavior; and that women might physically injure the rivals but, unlike some men, would not kill the rivals. But before acting aggressively in response to their partners' infidelity, to avoid such infidelity in the first place, men are more inclined to act more possessively toward their partners than are women (Paul et al., 1993; Daly et al., 1982), in particular when their partner is young (Buss & Shackelford, 1997).

## ▶ Therapeutic Interventions Aimed at Jealousy and Extradyadic Affairs

Therapists and counselors often are confronted with relationships in which infidelity is a serious issue. For example, one study showed that in 26% of marriage counseling cases, extramarital sex is considered one of the major problems (Sprenkle & Weis, 1978). If extramarital sex is one of the problems with which a couple is dealing, then the therapist usually sees each partner individually, after which joint sessions begin. During these individual sessions, the therapist sometimes is confronted with the secret infidelity of one of the partners without being able to share this information with the other partner because of confidentiality. A therapist, in general, does not like to be placed in this position and, therefore, usually asks the unfaithful partner to break off all extramarital contacts. In the joint sessions, the couple will explore the meaning of the extramarital affair to the partners' relationship—the motives for engaging in the extramarital affair, the degree of commitment to the extramarital affair, and the degree of actual or desired commitment to the marriage. When the extramarital affair is out in the open, the therapist also must deal with the victimized partner's injured self-esteem and feelings of jealousy, anger, and hurt. In so doing, both partners are asked to take responsibility for their contributions to the affair and to stop blaming each other. A partner's infidelity may be redefined, for example, by viewing the affair as an attempt to regain emotional contact with the partner, and the victimized partner then can take part of the responsibility for the lack of emotional contact in the marriage. Finally, individuals have to make a decision about the future course of their marriage, and when they agree on extramarital sex as a supplement to their marriage, therapy will focus in particular on the balance between the desire for sexual variety and the commitment to the "central" relationship (see, e.g., Elbaum, 1981; Sprenkle & Weis, 1978).

Although treatment of jealousy often occurs in the context of global relationship improvement or in the counseling after extramarital sex, jealousy of one of the partners also might be the focus of couple therapy in the absence of a partner's infidelity such as in the case of morbid or pathological jealousy. Whereas during the beginning and middle of the 20th century jealousy was primarily treated by psychoanalysts who viewed jealousy as a defense against homosexual tendencies or as a projection of one's own desire to be unfaithful, during the past two decades, therapists have mostly relied on counseling that includes behavioral and cognitive components and that emphasizes communication between the partners. Therapies that include one or more of these components are behavioral systems therapy (Margolin, 1981), cognitive therapy (Dolan & Bishay, 1996), and rational emotive behavior therapy (Ellis, 1996).

In general, both partners enter into therapy and work through the jealousy problem by the use of homework assignments. The *behavioral* component of therapy assumes that the jealous behavior is repeated because it is reinforced by the perceived loss of a partner or one's self-esteem. The aim of therapy, therefore, is to disrupt this cycle that leads to (often unreasonable) jealousy with behavioral techniques such as fixed role-playing (e.g., play for a week someone who is not unreasonably jealous), reinforcement methods (e.g., reward oneself with a pleasant activity after having refrained from jealous behavior, penalize oneself after having acted jealous), courting fearful situations (e.g., have one's partner dance with someone else and practice "reasonable" jealousy), and using timetables for expressing jealousy (e.g., talking about jealousy each day only between 9 and 10 p.m.) (Ellis, 1996; Ridley, 1996).

The *cognitive* component of therapy assumes that unreasonable jealousy is at least partly caused by irrational beliefs about a partner's infidelity and by a misinterpretation of neutral stimuli as a threat to the relationship (Dolan & Bishay, 1996). Cognitive therapy, therefore, aims to change faulty cognitive schemata that individuals hold with regard to their partners' infidelity and to become more "reasonably" jealous. Therefore, in treatment, first the individual's irrational beliefs about the partner's infidelity are identified, as are the origins of these cognitions (Bishay, Petersen, & Tarrier, 1989). Cognitive interventions include techniques such as identifying and disputing irrational beliefs (e.g., asking oneself "Why must I be totally loved?"), practicing rational coping using anti-jealousy statements (e.g., "I can be a happy person even if my partner loves others besides me"), using cognitive distraction (e.g., thinking of something else, meditating), and using positive imagery (e.g., imagining defeating all rivals) (Ellis, 1996).

Open and constructive *communication* often is difficult for individuals experiencing jealousy. For example, a study by Francis (1977) showed that, in general, individuals are reluctant to express their jealous feelings to their partners, thereby inhibiting communication and risking further escalation of jealous feelings. Communication between partners can be enhanced by techniques such as role-playing and role reversal (i.e., pretending to be one's partner), focusing on the possible "jealousy" in the nonjealous partner (to enable jealousy to be shared more equally), and reframing jealousy as a sign of love (Ridley, 1996).

# ▶ Conclusion

The temptation to engage in extradyadic sex and the tendency to respond with jealousy to such behavior by one's partner are interrelated and universal human phenomena, both of which are part of our human evolutionary heritage. Nevertheless, there is considerable variation across individuals, relationships, situations, and cultures in the likelihood that one will become involved in extradydadic sex and in the likelihood that one will exhibit various forms of jealousy. In particular, jealousy seems more likely, and extradyadic sex less likely, the more a relationship is characterized by involvement, dependency, commitment, and secure attachment. The awareness of the potential negative effects that extradyadic relationships might have on primary relationships finds expression in a virtually universal normative disapproval of extradyadic sex. Ironically, the potential fury of jealousy also causes most affairs to be covert, and this accentuates the aversive consequences following disclosure. Jealousy will, even among individuals who aim to have a sexually liberal lifestyle, reliably surface when an extradyadic sexual affair is disclosed or discovered. Although it has potentially destructive consequences, jealousy is basically a response aimed at protecting the relationship and, from an evolutionary perspective, protecting one's reproductive opportunities. Nevertheless, given the conflicts that both jealousy and extradyadic sex can create in primary relationships, these issues often come up in the context of therapy and counseling, and a number of therapeutic interventions have been developed to deal with such issues. However, given the deeply rooted motivations that underlie both jealous and adulterous tendencies, it would be unrealistic to expect that any interventions or cultural changes ever will eliminate the problems that these tendencies can generate in intimate relationships.

# Contents

# Physical and Sexual Aggression in Relationships

*F. Scott Christopher*
*Sally A. Lloyd*

Individuals enter dating and marriage with dreams of building relationships that will enrich their lives and fulfill both partners' wishes. Unfortunately, relationships do not always develop in these ways, and they can take unexpected turns. Experiencing violence represents one such unexpected turn. Empirical scrutiny of relational violence has primarily focused on two forms of aggression: physical and sexual. We review current findings in both areas, and for each we survey estimates of incident rates and offer an overview of associated individual, social, and dyadic correlates. It is our hope that this analysis will provide insights into these forms of violence.

## ▶ Physical Violence

Physical violence in intimate relationships is primarily defined in terms of physical actions and the use of force, for example, as "the use or threat of physical force or restraint carried out with the intent of causing pain or injury to another" (Sugarman & Hotaling, 1989, p. 4). Within such a definition, it is important to pay attention to qualitative differences in the frequency and severity of violence. For example, Johnson (1995) distinguished between patriarchal terrorism and common couple violence. Patriarchal terrorism flows from the patriarchal tradition granting men control over women and "involves the systematic use of not only violence, but economic subordination, threats, isolation, and other control tactics" (p. 284). Common couple violence, on the other hand, is used to denote "the dynamic . . . in which conflict 'gets out of hand,' leading usually to 'minor' forms of violence, and more rarely escalating into serious, sometimes even life-threatening, forms of violence" (p. 285).

Three sources of data have been used to estimate how often physical violence occurs in intimate relationships. First, the lowest esti-mates are seen in official crime reports pro-vided by the U.S. Department of Justice. Ac-cording to these estimates, 9% to 15% of all homicides are committed by intimates. Each year, approximately 1,300 women and 800 men are killed, and 200,000 are assaulted, by intimate partners (Barnett, Miller-Perrin, & Perrin, 1997).

Representative surveys provide a second source of data. The National Family Violence Survey estimates the yearly incidence of mari-tal violence to be 16%. Over the lifetimes of their marriages, 28% of couples report one or more acts of physical violence (Straus & Gelles, 1990a). Reports of physical violence among cohabiting couples are even higher, ranging as high as 35% (Stets & Straus, 1989). Among dating partners from 18 to 30 years of age, 30% report using physical ag-gression during the past 12 months (Stets & Henderson, 1991).

Third, for some groups, the only available estimates of violence are from nonrepresen-tative surveys. For example, between 12% and 36% of high school students report experienc-ing or enacting physical violence with dating partners (Gray & Foshee, 1997). In addition, violence in gay and lesbian relationships oc-curs at a rate approximately equal to the rates for heterosexual couples, ranging from 11% to 26% (Barnett et al., 1997).

There is controversy about comparing rates of violence between the genders. Some re-searchers read their results as indicative of equal rates of assaults perpetrated by men and women (e.g., Straus, 1993). Yet, a closer ex-amination reveals that women sustain the overwhelming majority of injuries due to men's greater size and strength and the use of more harm-inducing tactics of violence. Even when using the same behavioral action, men are far more likely to cause severe injuries than are women (Langley, Martin, & Nada-Raja, 1997). The claim of "equal violence" between the genders does not take into ac-count the function and context of violence. For men, the function often is one of control and intimidation, whereas for women, the function often is self-defense and resistance to that control (Jacobson & Gottman, 1998; Lloyd & Emery, 2000).

## ▶ Correlates of Physical Violence in Intimate Relationships

During the early stages of research on vio-lence in intimate relationships, the emphasis was on personality and sociodemographic factors that "predicted" who would be violent and who would be victimized. Over time, the emphasis shifted from individual-level vari-ables to interpersonal variables. This section covers each of these arenas, examining both individual correlates and relationship dynam-ics and then concluding with an examination of the developmental course of violence over time. We concentrate on violence in hetero-sexual relationships and violence perpetrated by men, which reflects the limitations and foci of current literature.

### *Individual Correlates*

We have organized the examination of in-dividual correlates of physical violence into seven arenas: sociodemographic factors, so-cial stress, intergenerational transmission of violence, alcohol, characteristics of women who have been battered, characteristics of male batterers, and typologies of violent men.

*Sociodemographic factors.* Both premarital and marital violence are more likely to occur among individuals 30 years of age or under (Cate, Henton, Koval, Christopher, & Lloyd, 1982; Pan, Neidig, & O'Leary, 1994). Vio-lence is more prevalent at lower income lev-els, reflecting the increased stress of living in financial uncertainty or poverty (Holtzworth-Munroe, Smutzler, & Bates, 1997; Magdol, Moffitt, Caspi, & Silva, 1998). However, there is not a consistent association between education and marital violence (Straus, 1990). Similarly, when income levels are controlled, racial differences tend to drop out, although this too is an inconsistent association (Cazenave & Straus, 1990). Holtzworth-Munroe, Smutzler, and Bates (1997) noted that the relationship between intimate violence and race might well be mediated by other variables such as network embeddedness and class.

*Social stress.* Although some researchers have found a relationship between social stress and intimate violence, Sugarman and Hotaling (1989) noted that social stress is an inconsistent risk marker. Perhaps this inconsistency arises because the relationship between social stress and violence is mediated by other factors. For example, Straus (1990) found that men under high stress are more likely to be violent toward their wives if they also experienced physical punishment as children, believe that a husband should dominate a marriage and that slapping one's wife is appropriate, feel that their marriages are not rewarding, and are socially isolated.

*Intergenerational transmission of violence.* Perhaps no other variable has been so highly touted as *the* explanation for why intimate violence occurs. Yet, several thoughtful analyses of the intergenerational transmission of violence have demonstrated that its explanatory power has limitations. First, intergenerational transmission of violence is an inconsistent risk marker for explaining women's victimization (Carden, 1994). The research on men is more consistent, demonstrating that men who witness violence are more likely to be violent toward their female partners (Simons, Lin, & Gordon, 1998). Second, although witnessing violence increases the risk for male violence, the actual transmission rate is only in the range of 30% (Kaufman & Ziegler, 1987). Third, there is evidence that hostility, stress, ineffective conflict resolution, fear of abandonment, dependency, and a distant relationship with parents act as mediators of the intergenerational link (Barnett et al., 1997; Magdol et al., 1998). Men's internal working model of rela-

tionships might play an additional critical role (Carden, 1994).

*Alcohol.* Alcohol has been reported as a factor in 20% to 80% of incidents of marital violence. Violence perpetrated by men with alcohol problems tends to be more severe and frequent (Barnett et al., 1997; Carden, 1994). Violent substance abusers tend to be more hostile, suspicious, and interpersonally inadequate than nonviolent substance abusers (Brown, Werk, Caplan, Shields, & Seraganian, 1998). Prospective studies demonstrate that early substance abuse and problem drinking are predictive of later abusive behavior toward an intimate partner (Heyman, O'Leary, & Jouriles, 1995; Leonard & Senchak, 1996; Magdol et al., 1998).

*Characteristics of women who have been battered.* The analysis of female victims of intimate violence has come a long way from the early assertions that battered wives are "masochistic." Recent work emphasizes that women who have been battered do not display a "personality profile" per se (Holtzworth-Munroe, Smutzler, & Sandin, 1997; Lloyd & Emery, 2000). Rather, most of the differences between battered and nonbattered women are consequences of the physical violence itself. For example, the reactions to being battered during courtship or marriage include lowered self-esteem and sense of well-being; heightened mistrust of men; greater social isolation, stress, depression, and withdrawal; and symptoms associated with posttraumatic stress disorder (Astin, Lawrence, & Foy, 1993; Emery & Lloyd, 1994; Holtzworth-Munroe, Smutzler, & Sandin, 1997).

Over time, an interesting transition has taken place in the social construction of the woman who is battered. Kanuha (1996) noted that she was depicted during the early days of the shelter movement as a "true victim"—a woman who could garner all our sympathies because she was socially acceptable (i.e., white, middle class), helpless, and blameless (i.e., she did not fight back). This construction resulted in an emphasis on the battered woman as an individual without agency (Mahoney, 1994). However, recent analyses of women who have been battered highlight the resistance and resiliency that these women display rather than their purported deficits (Jacobson & Gottman, 1998; Lloyd & Emery, 2000).

*Characteristics of male batterers.* Male batterers are likely to have low self-esteem, hold traditional sex role attitudes and adversarial sexual beliefs, and be more accepting of the use of violence (Carden, 1994; Holtzworth-Munroe, Bates, Smutzler, & Sandin, 1997; O'Keefe, 1997). However, many of these characteristics of the aggressive male are considered inconsistent risk markers (Holtzworth-Munroe, Bates, et al. 1997; Sugarman & Hotaling, 1989).

Some batterers display psychopathology including evidence of antisocial and borderline personality disorders. Men who are violent are likely to show symptoms of posttraumatic stress disorder (including depression, anxiety, and dissociation) as well as heightened levels of defensiveness and violation of the rights of others (Dutton, 1995a; Holtzworth-Munroe, Bates, et al., 1997; O'Leary, Malone, & Tyree, 1994).

Battering men are intensely dependent on their intimate relationships and often fear being abandoned. Yet, simultaneously, they are unable to maintain close relationships due to their anger and impulsivity. This dependency can be linked to patterns of disrupted and preoccupied attachment to their partners, traumatic or symbiotic bonding, and/or intense jealousy (Bookwala & Zdaniuk, 1998; Dutton, 1995a; Lloyd, 1999). Dutton (1995a) attributed these patterns to "deep-seated feelings of powerlessness that have their origins in the man's early development" (p. 121), specifically, to an abusive and rejecting father who uses shame and humiliation to attack the boy's sense of self.

*Typologies of violent men.* Recent investigations have emphasized the heterogeneity of men who are physically violent toward their intimate partners. Holtzworth-Munroe and Stuart (1994) identified three types of batterers. *Dysphoric-borderline* batterers engage in moderate to severe violence against their wives. These men are emotionally volatile, distressed, and dependent. They have difficulty in controlling their anger and can exhibit borderline and schizoidal personality characteristics. *Generally violent/antisocial* batterers also use moderate to severe physical abuse. These men experienced the highest levels of violence in their families of origin, are violent toward others outside their families, and might have histories of criminal behavior and substance abuse. They are the most likely to display an antisocial personality disorder. *Family-only* batterers tend to engage in less severe violence toward their wives. They are not violent outside their families, and they report the most stable and satisfactory marital relationships. Their use of violence likely results from marital stress rather than from psychopathology.

Jacobson, Gottman, and colleagues developed a typology of batterers based on measurements of heart rate reactivity. Type I batterers, or *cobras,* reduced their heart rates over the course of marital interaction, whereas Type II batterers, or *pit bulls,* increased their heart rates. Cobras are more likely to have been violent with friends, strangers, and coworkers and are more likely to have observed their fathers behaving violently toward their mothers. They are more severely violent toward their wives and are more likely to have been assessed as antisocial, drug dependent, and aggressive-sadistic. Ultimately, cobras display a sense of entitlement to get whatever they want by whatever means necessary; they will not be controlled. Pit bulls, on the other hand, are characterized by less severe violence toward their wives and are not as likely to exhibit psychopathology. Instead, dependency and emotional insecurity characterize this group of batterers. Their fear of abandonment produces jealous rages that escalate into violence (Gottman et al., 1995; Jacobson & Gottman, 1998; Jacobson, Gottman, & Shortt, 1995).

### Relational Dynamics

During the past decade, a number of studies of communication dynamics have been conducted and have contributed to a heightened understanding of the marital interactions and interpersonal patterns of violent couples (Lloyd, 1999). We have organized this work into five areas: social skill deficits, everyday interaction and conflict, behavioral coding of marital interaction, dominance and power dynamics, and marital distress.

*Social skill deficits.* Spouses in violent-distressed marriages demonstrate both general and marital processing skill deficits that contribute to problem-solving difficulties (Anglin & Holtzworth-Munroe, 1997). Violent men report fewer reactions of support and sympathy and report more reactions of feeling irritated and angry toward their wives in reaction to their wives' expressions of distress and attempts to influence. These men are less able to deescalate anger by producing anger-controlling or prosocial attributions (Ekhardt, Barbour, & Davidson, 1998; Holtzworth-Munroe & Smutzler, 1996). They also are more likely to attribute hostile intent to the actions of their wives and to display higher levels of verbal aggression, spouse-specific anger, hostility, and blaming (Holtzworth-Munroe & Hutchinson, 1993; Infante, Sabourin, Rudd, & Shannon, 1990; Lloyd & Emery, 1994; Riggs & O'Leary, 1996).

These skill deficits might be most evident in situations that are perceived as threatening. Messages that entail character attacks, curses and threats, potential public embarrassment, perceived wife rejection or abandonment, extreme jealousy, and violations of the man's need for control all appear to be prime catalysts to physical aggression (Bookwala & Zdaniuk, 1998; Holtzworth-Munroe & Hutchinson, 1993; Lloyd & Emery, 2000; Sabourin, 1995).

*Everyday interaction and conflict.* In describing their daily interaction, violent husbands in distressed marriages see themselves as "doing more and getting less." This is a result of a tendency to overemphasize their own caring gestures and to underemphasize their wives' caring gestures (Langhinrichsen-Rohling, Smutzler, & Vivian, 1994). Violent men also are very focused on their relationships and report strong motivations of love for remaining with their wives (Langhinrichsen-Rohling, Schlee, Monson, Ehrensaft, & Heyman, 1998). In addition, distressed-violent couples describe daily interactions that are volatile and enmeshed (Lloyd, 1996).

Violent and nonviolent couples provide different descriptions of naturally occurring conflicts. Ongoing conflicts, as described by violent couples, are highly ritualized and reactive. They contain patterns of reciprocity of negativity that can lead to violence (Margolin, John, & O'Brien, 1989). Lloyd (1990) noted that violent couples might have a tendency to strive for resolution to all their arguments. These couples do not appear to be able to "let the small stuff go." However, their use of ineffective conflict strategies, such as anger and verbal attack, tends to ensure that resolution of conflicts will be difficult (Lloyd, 1990).

*Behavioral coding of marital interaction.* A fruitful arena of investigation has been the observation of marital interaction. In these studies, couples' videotaped problem discussions are coded in detail for interaction patterns. Such studies have revealed that violent husbands enact higher levels of threat, blame, negativity, and negative reciprocity and also tend to engage in cycles of attack and defend (Burman, John, & Margolin, 1992; Cordova, Jacobson, Gottman, Rushe, & Cox, 1993; Leonard & Roberts, 1998). In addition, violent husbands use highly provocative forms of anger including belligerence and contempt. They are unlikely to acknowledge that there is anything wrong with their behavior, and they are more controlling (Jacobson et al., 1994). Moreover, violent couples are high in overt hostility and defensiveness. They display rigid and highly sequenced behavior patterns, in particular, exchanges of hostile and angry behavior. Nonviolent couples, on the other hand, are able to deescalate their conflicts and break out of patterns of negativity (Burman, Margolin, & John, 1993).

Using the typology of battering men as cobras (Type I) versus pit bulls (Type II), Gottman et al. (1995) noted differences in marital interaction patterns. Cobras tend to exhibit more provocative and abusive anger earlier in the discussion of a marital problem than do pit bulls. The emotional aggression of cobras tends to decrease over the course of the discussion, whereas the emotionality of pit bulls tends to increase. Gottman et al. concluded that cobras are characterized by "focused attention" aimed at controlling their wives. Cobras strive to maximize their wives' feelings of fear and to minimize their wives' expressions of anger. Pit bulls, on the other hand, respond with a loss of emotional control to their wives' attempts to gain independence. Their jealous rages are a response to a fear of abandonment (Gottman et al., 1995).

*Dominance and power dynamics.* Some of the marital interaction studies directly examine issues of dominance and power. The struggle for relational control is apparent in the interactions of violent-distressed couples, as evidenced by strong patterns of nonacceptance of partners' direct assertions and high rates of competition and nonsupport statements (Sabourin, 1995). Even in relatively satisfied marriages, physically violent husbands tend to more often assert their rights and are more domineering (Rogers, Castleton, & Lloyd, 1996). In distressed-violent couples, there are higher levels of both husband and wife demand-withdraw patterns, and this also might be indicative of a struggle for power (Babcock, Waltz, Jacobson, & Gottman, 1993).

Coan, Gottman, Babcock, and Jacobson (1997) noted a "bat-em-back tendency" in the interaction of violent men with their wives, whereby every low-level negative affect from the wives (e.g., complaint, sadness, anger)

seems to be batted back with an "in your face" quality of contempt or belligerence. In particular, the cobra batterers reciprocated their wives' behaviors with high-intensity negative affect. Coan et al. speculated that these batterers might feel compelled to reject all attempts at influence on the part of their wives.

Dominance patterns are predictive over time. In a prospective study of newlywed couples, Leonard and Senchak (1996) noted that a husband-dominated relationship, coupled with verbal aggression, is predictive of later marital aggression. Ultimately, violence might be enacted as a tactic to ensure winning arguments despite poor communication skills and as an attempt to make up for a lack of power in the marriage (Babcock et al., 1993; Lloyd & Emery, 2000).

*Marital distress.* Given the literature reviewed on the interaction patterns found in relationships with violent husbands, it is not too surprising that researchers have found a consistent and strong relationship between marital distress and husband violence (Holtzworth-Munroe, Bates, et al., 1997). However, there are several noteworthy caveats in this association. Some couples report the presence of violence in the context of high marital satisfaction, declines in marital satisfaction might be a consequence of husband violence rather than a cause, and distress might predict violence only when it interacts with other variables such as husband's alcohol use and hostility (Heyman et al., 1995; Holtzworth-Munroe, Bates, et al., 1997; Leonard & Senchak, 1996; Lloyd, 1996; O'Leary et al., 1989).

### The Developmental Course of Violence Over Time

There are several significant longitudinal studies of the developmental course of violence. In Magdol et al.'s (1998) study of prospective risk factors for intimate violence, the strongest predictors of reduced risk of intimate abuse at 21 years of age were good parent-child attachment; growing up in a high-income and two-parent household; staying in school; and the absence of delinquency, substance abuse, and conduct problems.

Studies of courtship and the 1st year of marriage indicate that for those couples who marry despite the presence of physical aggression, the chances of continued physical aggression during their marriages are quite high (Bradbury & Lawrence, 1999; O'Leary et al., 1989). A premarital relationship characterized by high levels of overt verbal hostility and passive aggression, and a newlywed relationship characterized by ineffective conflict strategies and husband's alcohol consumption, increases the probability of subsequent physical aggression (Leonard & Senchak, 1996; O'Leary et al., 1994). Severe male aggression during courtship or the newlywed phase predicts a decline in satisfaction and an increased risk for dissolution (Bradbury & Lawrence, 1999; Heyman et al., 1995).

A longitudinal study of severe battering in marriage reveals that within 2 years, a significant proportion of wives (38%) do leave their marriages (Jacobson, Gottman, Gortner, Berns, & Shortt, 1996). Predictors of divorce include emotional abuse by the husband, wife dissatisfaction, husband physiological arousal, and wife defending herself assertively. Predictors of husbands' continued use of severe violence are husband's domineeringness, negativity, belligerence, and contempt. Even among the men who decrease their use of violence, levels of emotional abuse remain high.

*Summary*

Clearly, there have been significant advancements in the study of physical violence in close relationships. The field has moved from identifying risk factors to testing complex conceptual models that emphasize power dynamics and the interplay of socialization, personality, problem-solving skills, and the emotional and interactional nature of relationships.

## ▶ Marital Rape

When compared to other literatures focused on violence in close relationships, it is striking how little is known about men who rape their wives and the factors that foster and support these acts. This lack of empirical inquiry might reflect society's struggle in deciding whether marital rape exists. The sometimes held contemporary attitude that rape cannot occur in marriage has historical and legal foundations that undoubtedly have influenced society's willingness to pursue and accept research in this area (Finkelhor & Yllö, 1985; Russell, 1982).

Our ability to report on the prevalence of marital rape is hampered by the fact that there are no national probability studies on marital rape. Two studies provide the best estimates to date. Finkelhor and Yllö (1985) used a probability sample of women from Boston. In this sample, 10% of the women experienced sex because of a spouse's or a cohabiting partner's threats or use of physical force. A similar prevalence rate, 14%, emerged from Russell's (1982) random sample of women from the San Francisco area. Some women experienced a single isolated case of spousal rape (31%) (Russell, 1982), but a large proportion of women faced repetitive incidents. Approximately one third of these victims were raped more than 20 times over the course of their relationships (Finkelhor & Yllö, 1985; Russell, 1982).

### A Typology

Prevalence rates by themselves provide an incomplete picture of marital rape. Finkelhor and Yllö (1985) developed a typology that describes these women's experiences. *Battering* rape involved husbands who beat their wives. For some wives, the beatings were a precursor to the rapes; for others, the beatings continued during the rapes. The link between the two forms of abuse is common; between 37% (Russell, 1982) and 40% (Finkelhor & Yllö, 1985) of women experiencing marital rape concurrently experienced severe physical abuse. *Force-only rape* was typified by husbands who had not previously physically abused their wives but who used just enough force to engage in sex acts that their spouses did not want. Close to 40% of marital rapes fell into this category (Finkelhor & Yllö, 1985).

The presence or absence of violence was not central to the third type because only some of the husbands in this category were physically violent. Instead, in *obsessive rapes,* husbands characteristically were sexually obsessed and willing to use force to obtain their sexual goals. Their sexual interests reflected sadistic predilections; sexual torment and mistreatment of their wives resulted in the husbands' sexual pleasure and gratification. These men typically became obsessed with forcing their wives into humiliating and degrading sexual acts.

### Their Marriages

The caveat about a limited number of studies in this area applies to what is known about marriages where husbands rape their wives. Still, there are hints in the literature about the characteristics of these marriages. For example, DeMaris (1997) examined physically abusive marriages and found that couples with nonviolent husbands averaged 6.75 sex acts a month, whereas couples with violent husbands averaged 11.08 sex acts a month. Although unable to directly measure husbands' use of sexual extortion, DeMaris used indirect measures to show that the elevated levels of sexual frequency might have been partly due to a climate of fear created by husbands. DeMaris speculated that wives living in this fearful climate more readily acquiesce to their husbands' sexual demands. Additional analy-

sis by DeMaris and Swinford (1996) supports this conjecture. Forced sex and threats of retaliation by husbands predicted wives' fears that they would be hit if they argued or did things that their husbands did not like.

Thus, fear plays a role in why wives might not resist their husbands' sexual assaults. Previous experiences with being beaten result in some wives protecting themselves during the assaults by "going limp" (Finkelhor & Yllö, 1985). Others learn that resistance is futile; their husbands will likely physically overpower them despite the wives' best efforts. Fear is not the only reason why wives do not resist. Some wives are concerned about their children becoming aware of the rapes, some "keep the peace" in their marriages by submitting to their husbands' demands, and some simply believe that they have no right to say no to their spouses' sexual demands.

### ▶ Sexual Coercion and Aggression in Dating Relationships

As is true of marital rape, scholars have yet to undertake a national probability study that would allow accurate estimates of the prevalence of the sexual coercion and aggression that occurs in dating relationships. The best estimates originate in the landmark work of Koss and her colleagues. They used a national sample of colleges that included more than 3,000 female students. Just over half (53.7%) of these young women experienced some forms of sexual victimization since they were 14 years of age (Koss, Gidycz, & Wisneiwski, 1987). Among these, 15.4% were victims of rape and 12.1% were victims of attempted rape. Another 12.1% were coerced into sexual acts by pressure, continual arguments, or by men in positions of authority. Koss and her colleagues investigated the types of relationship between the men and women in these cases (Koss, Dinero, Seibel, & Cox, 1988). In the cases involving rape, just over 50% of the time the men and women were seriously or casually dating.

Although compelling, these figures must be viewed within a particular context because additional findings by Koss and her colleagues provide certain counterpoints (Koss et al., 1987). When the more than 3,000 men in the sample reported on their sexual behavior toward women, differences emerged. Few of the men's self-reported actions identified them as either rapists (4.4%) or attempted rapists (3.3%). Similarly, fewer men reported sexually coercing women (7.2%) than women reported being victimized in this way. Undoubtedly, men's self-presentation interests resulted in an underreporting of these incidents. However, women were not always willing to label their own experiences as rape, especially in cases involving dating partners. Even when the sexually aggressive interactions fit the legal standards of rape, 73.0% of women who were casually dating and 71.2% of those who were seriously dating did not define their experiences as crimes.

Reports on the prevalence of men's experiences of unwanted sexual involvement are limited by the use of smaller nonrepresentative samples. Between 16% (Struckman-Johnson, 1988) and 22.7% (Muehlenhard & Cook, 1988) of the men in these studies engaged in unwanted coitus or sexual activity. This most often took the form of nonviolent coercion given that few men experienced force (O'Sullivan, Byers, & Finkelman, 1998; Struckman-Johnson, 1988). Comparing single men's and women's sexual victimization experiences based solely on these figures must be done cautiously. Single women experience more overall sexual coercion while dating (Christopher, Madura, & Weaver, 1998; O'Sullivan et al., 1998) and suffer more grievous and long-term consequences as a result (O'Sullivan et al., 1998; Struckman-Johnson, 1988).

### Explaining Sexual Coercion and Assault in Dating

A range of factors contribute to the occurrence of sexual coercion and assault in dating relationships. For example, social attitudes, gendered dating roles, peers, dating experiences, and individual characteristics all play a role. Koss and Cleveland (1997) proposed that these and related variables be viewed as overlapping ecologies that co-jointly contribute to incidences of single male sexual aggression.

*Social attitudes.* Burt (1980) proposed the hypothesis that our culture supports men's sexual aggression toward women by endorsing attitudes such as a belief in myths about rape. Examples of such myths include the belief that women can avoid being raped if they choose, that women ask for rape when they dress in a particular way, and that women lie about being raped. Scholarly attention to Burt's hypothesis generally shows that rape-supportive attitudes exist, but belief in these attitudes is not uniform. For example, a consistent finding across studies is that men hold more rape-supportive attitudes than do women (Lonsway & Fitzgerald, 1994). Even this finding might need to be qualified. Comparisons of men who hold traditional sex role beliefs to men who hold less traditional beliefs show that sex role traditional men are more apt to endorse men's use of sexual aggression in dating (Muehlenhard, 1988), although not all investigators reach this conclusion (e.g., Szymanski, Devlin, Chrisler, & Vyse, 1993).

*Gendered dating roles.* Role theory holds that society offers individuals scripts or roles that prescribe ways in which to think about and behave in interpersonal interactions. Individuals who are just beginning to date one another might find such prescriptions useful because people usually possess little information about their dating partners and can rely on roles to structure their interactions. Male role expectations typically include asking a woman for a date, suggesting activities for the date, being sexually knowledgeable, initiating sexual involvement, and pressing for greater sexual involvement (Poppen & Segal, 1988). Role expectations for women focus on attracting a date, keeping his attention, and being the "sexual gate-keeper"—the one who decides the sexual limits. Moreover, role prescriptions seem to dictate that it is normative for couples who are seriously dating to be highly sexually involved with one another (Cohen & Shotland, 1996).

Certain qualities of these roles can contribute to acts of sexual aggression. For example, a woman's role as sexual gatekeeper puts her at a disadvantage if she "allows" coitus to occur too early; her partner might see her as sexually "easy" or immoral. Being so pejoratively judged puts women at risk. Single men who are sexually coercive often justify their actions by describing their victims in this devalued manner (Kanin, 1985) and by focusing on the fact that the couples previously had engaged in the sexual acts in question (Kanin, 1983; Koss & Cleveland, 1997). Similarly, men's role expectation that they should try to increase sexual involvement might lead them to ignore their partners' sexual wishes if such wishes are at odds with their own.

Lloyd and Emery (2000) proposed that several themes underlie these role expectations. Male role expectations put men actively in control of the progression of their relationships. Expectations for women make women dependent on the men to move their relationships toward greater emotional and sexual intimacy. Once emotional intimacy is established, however, it falls on the women to maintain it. In addition, dating is valued more when it is romantic. Couples structure their interactions in ways that increase and enhance feelings of romance and define romantic experiences as salient points of relationship development. Couples also believe strongly in the ideal of equality, which serves to mask power and dominance issues during courtship.

When taken to an extreme, men's theme of being in control can lead them to take responsibility for their own and their partners' sexuality. They might push for greater sexual intimacy while ignoring their partners' wishes to limit sexual involvement simply because the men are in control. The theme of romanticism can lead couples to ignore or downplay such coercive acts after they occur. Couples also might redefine aggressive acts in a way that makes the acts more palatable to keep the romance alive in the relationships (Lloyd & Emery, 2000). Women's themes of dependency and relationship caretaker might prime them to look at their victimization experiences in such a light. This conceptualization might help to explain why so many women in dating relationships from Koss's sample (Koss et al., 1987) did not define their victimization experiences as rape. It also is noteworthy that when women do define their victimization experiences as rape or assault, they often blame themselves and excuse the aggressors (Lloyd & Emery, 2000).

*Peers.* Empirical investigations (Boeringer, Shehan, & Akers, 1991; Christopher, Madura, et al., 1998; Garrett-Gooding & Senter, 1987) provide insights into the peer networks of single men who sexually coerce their dates. These men build friendships with other men who value and provide status for erotic achievements. Their peers often engage in similar sexually aggressive behaviors and reinforce each other's actions. Moreover, their discussions about women create justifications for their sexual aggression (Christopher & McQuaid, 1998). From these men's perspectives, women deserve to be sexually victimized if, in their terms, they sexually tease men, dress provocatively, and/or have the reputation of being sexually promiscuous (Kanin, 1985).

Given the social support for heightened experiences of masculinity, it is not surprising that membership in all-male groups is linked to aggressive behavior. For example, comparisons of fraternity members and independents reveal that fraternity members are more apt to use coercive means to achieve sexual involvement (Petty & Dawson, 1989). Similarly, when asked about the perpetrators of their sexual abuse, female students at one college overidentified members of fraternities and sports teams as their sexual assailants (Frinter & Rubinson, 1993).

*Dating relationship experiences.* Certain settings related to dating are more likely to covary with acts of sexual coercion. For example, sexual coercion usually occurs in a private setting (Gwartney-Gibbs & Stockard, 1989) such as a parked car (Muehlenhard & Linton, 1987), an apartment, or a house (Miller & Marshall, 1987). Alcohol also often is involved in sexually aggressive incidents (Muehlenhard & Linton, 1987). It is not unusual for the perpetrator, the victim, or both to have been using alcohol prior to acts of sexual aggression (Copenhaver & Grauerholz, 1991). Alcohol's specific contribution, however, is not completely clear. Most likely, the use of alcohol by aggressive men is a strategic choice that accomplishes two goals. First, it allows them to absolve themselves of responsibility for their actions. Second, it might lower the inhibitions or cloud the judgments of their intended victims (Koss & Cleveland, 1997).

Other relational experiences that covary with men's use of sexual coercion focus more on the dyadic relationship. These include issues of power and control. Differences in power are evident in that sexually coercive men are more likely to ask their partners for dates, to drive during dates, and to pay for dates than are noncoercive men (Muehlenhard & Linton, 1987). Moreover, evidence of power assertion can be found in the finding that men's use of sexual coercion is associated with attempts to control their dating partners in other areas of their relationships (Christopher & McQuaid, 1998; Stets & Pirog-Good, 1989).

A couple's self-identified stage of dating plays a role. Sexual coercion more frequently occurs in seriously, as opposed to casually, dating relationships (Christopher, Owens, & Stecker, 1993a; Kanin, 1969). In some cases, the sexual norms typically associated with monogamous dating also might play a role. The man might see sexual intercourse as his "right" that comes with an agreement to date the woman (Koss & Cleveland, 1997). Other cases involve couples engaging in consensual, precoital sexual behaviors such as kissing and breast or genital fondling but where the women do not want to engage in intercourse (Kanin, 1969; Kanin & Parcell, 1977). Coercive men who experience this level of sexual involvement might interpret such consensual involvement as a sign of sexual willingness and conclude that their dating partners were leading them on even if that was not the women's intention (Kanin, 1969; Muehlenhard & Linton, 1987).

Dyadic conflict and men's feelings of ambivalence about the future of their relationships further typify sexually coercive men's dating relationship experiences (Christopher, Madura, et al., 1998; Christopher, Owens, & Stecker, 1993b). Conflict is linked directly to the use of sexual coercion but also operates indirectly through attempts to control one's partner (Christopher & McQuaid, 1998). Both dyadic conflict and feeling ambivalent about the relationship can contribute to men devaluing their partners. Casting their partners in such a light allows men to justify using sexual coercion (Kanin, 1969).

*Individual traits and experiences.* A number of individual traits characterize sexually coercive men. A strong consistent finding is that these men possess a constellation of attitudes that allows them to justify their behavior. For example, they believe in rape myths and view men's and women's sexual relationships as inherently adversarial (Christopher et al., 1993a, 1993b; Koss & Dinero, 1988). They accept interpersonal violence (Malamuth, 1986) and endorse the use of force in relationships, especially as a means of gaining sexual access (Garrett-Gooding & Senter, 1987; Koss & Dinero, 1988).

Hall and Hirschman (1991) theorized that sexually aggressive men possess affective disinhibitors or affective states that can result in a loss of personal control. Indirect support for their proposition comes from findings that sexually aggressive men are more impulsive than nonaggressive men (Petty & Dawson, 1989). More direct support originates in findings that these men often experience a longstanding brooding anger (Christopher et al.,

1993b), an anger possibly based on the perception that women have treated them poorly (Lisak & Roth, 1988). The fact that sexually coercive men also feel hostile toward women (Christopher et al., 1993a; Malamuth, Sockloski, Koss, & Tanaka, 1991) and are high in sexual dominance (Muehlenhard & Falcon, 1990) and authoritarianism (Walker, Rowe, & Quinsey, 1993) provides additional support for Hall and Hirschman's (1991) proposition.

Sexually coercive men's sexuality has several unique characteristics besides a predisposition to use aggression. These men are highly focused on their sexuality. They experience nearly twice as many orgasms a week as do their noncoercive counterparts (Kanin, 1983). They also are more likely to be aroused by erotica involving rape (Malamuth, 1986), have more lifetime sexual partners, and lose their virginity earlier in life relative to noncoercive men (Koss & Dinero, 1988). They might engage in more than one act of aggression, and previous acts increase the likelihood that they will act aggressively in future sexual relationships (Christopher, Madura, et al., 1998). Surprisingly, they are apt to judge their sexual lives as unsatisfactory (Kanin, 1983). Taken as a whole, a reasonable conclusion would be that these men seek high levels of sexual stimulation but are unsatisfied by their experiences. Hence, they continue to seek new and novel sources of sexual stimulation (Lalumiere, Chalmers, Quinsey, & Seto, 1996).

### Sexually Coercive Women

The corpus of knowledge about sexually coercive women is limited. What is known often parallels the findings for male sexual aggression. For example, the attitudes of sexually coercive women include an acceptance of interpersonal aggression and the belief that sexual relationships between men and women are adversarial (Burke, Stets, & Pirog-Good, 1988; Christopher et al., 1993a). Additional evidence suggests that these women possess affective disinhibitors. Sexually coercive

women feel hostile toward men and possess a brooding anger, both of which are related to their use of sexual coercion (Christopher, Madura, et al., 1998; Christopher et al., 1993b).

The relationship conditions associated with women's use of sexual coercion suggest that their relationship experiences are problematic. Both relational and sexual conflict, as well as feelings of ambivalence (Christopher, Madura, et al., 1998; Christopher et al., 1993a), predict their use of coercion. These women also are more apt to judge their sexual interactions with their partners as involving costs and generally are dissatisfied with their sexual relationships (Christopher, McQuaid, & Updegraff, 1998). These findings probably are not that surprising given that sexually coercive women feel hostile toward men, are angry, and believe that men's and women's sexual relationships are adversarial. Such a belief structure is likely to contribute to relational conflict and experiences of ambivalence.

## ▶ Conclusions and Implications

In this chapter, we have reviewed research focused on physical violence and sexual aggression in romantic relationships. The pictures painted by these findings are compelling and demonstrate a need for intervention. Interventions can range from attempting to intervene before problems develop to one-on-one counseling. Page limitations prevent us from fully exploring the different implications for intervention offered by our review. In closing, however, we want to highlight selected implications that might be useful.

The first implication focuses on the heterogeneity of aggressor offenders. As evidenced by the conceptualization of patriarchal terrorism and common couple violence (Johnson, 1995), and by the typologies of men who batter (Gottman et al., 1995) and husbands who rape (Finkelhor & Yllö, 1985), it is clear that there is no single "type" of individual who uses aggression in interpersonal relationships.

Thus, interventions must be tailored to specific populations given that no single "silver bullet" approach exists that will be effective with all groups.

Second, the literature on both physical and sexual aggression suggests that aggressive men often hold attitudes that reflect their acceptance of interpersonal coercion and force. Such attitudes likely represent cognitive-based, relational schemata that these men use to justify their violent acts. The consistency of the findings about attitudes across studies suggests that interventions should challenge aggressive men to specifically question the veracity of these attitudes and to more generally change their thinking about close relationships.

Third, our review demonstrates that issues of control and conflict management are central to acts of interpersonal aggression. One implication of this seems obvious. It suggests that instructing couples in effective conflict management skills can potentially reduce the likelihood of future aggression. A more subtle implication, however, suggests that we should be asking dating couples to evaluate the power distribution and conflict in their relationships. Dyadic partners might want to question whether their relationships should continue if the conflict is punctuated with cycles of strongly vented and negative reciprocity or if one partner is preoccupied with controlling the other's life. Our review indicates that these interaction patterns often covary with aggressive acts and should be treated as signals that aggression can become part of the fabric of one's relationship.

# Contents

# Depression in Close Relationships

*Steven R. H. Beach*
*Heather A. O'Mahen*

The close relationships of depressed persons are particularly likely to be disrupted, and depressed persons often are acutely aware of the impact of relationship difficulties on their moods. Indeed, the idea that threats to one's sense of belongingness in close relationships could result in increased negative behavior and affect (Baumeister & Leary, 1995) has a certain intuitive appeal that is not merely the creation of recent theorists. In his 17th-century classic text, *The Anatomy of Melancholia,* Burton (1621/1927) identified marital problems as a possible source of both misery and depression. Indeed, as noted by Berscheid (1983), it is hard to imagine the quality of close relationships not being related to one's level of suffering and happiness. Confirming this intuition, evidence linking relationship quality to mood,

happiness, and symptoms of depression has accumulated in several disciplines (for a review, see Beach, 1996). The marital relationship, as the paradigmatic long-term intimate relationship between equals, provides a convenient context in which to examine reciprocal effects. Likewise, symptoms of depression provide a convenient common metric to use in examining effects. Accordingly, after a very brief review of evidence of the link between disturbance in a variety of close relationships and depression, we focus more narrowly on the link between marital discord and depression. We highlight issues concerning direction of causality, specific interpersonal processes that might be of particular interest, and an intermediate-level theory that helps to organize much of the theoretical and empirical literature, specifically, Hammen's (1991) stress generation theory. Finally, we turn to goal-theory as a broader theoretical framework that might help to further integrate the literature on close relationships and depression (both clini-

AUTHORS' NOTE: This chapter was supported by a grant from the National Science Foundation (SBR-9511385) awarded to Steven Beach.

cal and nonclinical), and we suggest new directions for investigation.

## ► Relationships and Depression: Issues of Association and Causation

A strong association between depression and relationship disturbance has been noted in a number of different relationship literatures. However, the reasons provided for the association have varied. Accordingly, it is informative to briefly consider the various explanations that have been provided and the types of associations that have been noted.

### The Link Between Relationship Distress and Depression

Evidence that depressive symptoms are related to interpersonal distress has been found across a broad range of research designs and assessment strategies. For example, in a review of the marital literature, Whisman (in press) found that, across 17 cross-sectional studies, marital quality was negatively related to both depressive symptomatology and diagnostic depression. In their review of the child depression literature, Cummings and Davies (1994; see also Cummings, Dearth-Pendley, & Smith, in press) noted that the parenting behavior of depressed persons often is compromised. Depressed parents use both inconsistent and lax parenting, on the one hand, and forceful, controlling conflict strategies, on the other. In both cases, depressed parents make it less likely that conflicts with their children will end in compromise. In their recent review of the postpartum depression literature, Whiffen and Johnson (1998) suggested that both social support from close others and social provisions within the marital relationship might be important in understanding the onset of depression postpartum. Likewise, in their review of adolescent depression, Barrera and Li (1996) suggested that support from peers

and family members is strongly and negatively related to depressive symptoms. Disturbance in co-worker relationships also has been found in the relationships of individuals experiencing depression (Beach, Martin, Blum, & Roman, 1993a). Accordingly, across various stages of the life cycle, in various populations, and with regard to various close relationships, there is a strong inverse relationship between the quality of close relationships and the level of depression. These findings suggest a robust link between depression and relationship difficulties in general (see also Joiner & Coyne, 1999). However, cross-sectional associations appear to be interpreted differently in these different literatures. In some literatures, a strong cross-sectional correlation is taken as evidence of the impact of depression on close relationships (e.g., in the parenting and adolescent literatures). In other literatures, a similar cross-sectional relationship might be interpreted as evidence of the impact on depression of disruptions in close relationships (e.g., the postpartum literature). Thus, the presence of a strong cross-sectional association leaves open the question of direction of the effect between interpersonal difficulties and depression.

Can we establish the direction of causal relation between social provisions and level of dysphoria? Can we better explicate the specific causal mechanisms that give rise to the observed covariation between interpersonal disruptions and depressive symptoms? To probe these questions in more detail, we examine recent work on marital problems and depression.

### Is There a Causal Relationship Between Marital Problems and Depression?

Possible causal relationships between marital discord and depression include an effect of marital discord on depression, an effect of depression on marital discord, and a bidirectional pattern of causation. To tease apart these possibilities, a range of causal models has been investigated using structural equation modeling approaches (Beach et al., 1995; Burns, Sayers, & Moras, 1994; Fincham, Beach, Harold, & Osborne, 1997; Kurdek, 1998a).

*Beach et al. (1995).* In a national random probability sample of women working full-time ($N = 577$), Beach et al. found a significant effect of marital satisfaction on depressive symptomatology 1 year later. Women who endorsed low levels of marital satisfaction showed greater future depressive symptoms. This effect remained even after controlling for the association between marital satisfaction and depression at the initial assessment. Accordingly, the prospective effect of marital satisfaction on depression for women might be generalizable to a broad cross section of employed women. For men, controlling for initial depressive symptoms reduced the prospective effect of marital satisfaction on depression to nonsignificance.

*Burns, Sayers, and Moras (1994).* Burns et al. investigated relationship satisfaction and depression in a sample of 115 patients receiving cognitive therapy for depression. Married patients ($n = 68$) rated their marital relationships, and unmarried patients ($n = 47$) rated their closest intimate relationships. Reciprocal effects between relationship satisfaction and depression were investigated. Burns et al. found no evidence that depression exerted a causal effect on relationship satisfaction. However, they found a significant, albeit weak, effect of relationship satisfaction on depression.

*Fincham, Beach, Harold, and Osborne (1997).* Fincham et al. examined a series of complementary causal models in a sample of 150 newlywed couples. Couples were assessed at two time points separated by an 18-month interval. Replicating earlier work, marital satisfaction and depressive symptomatology were related to each other cross-sectionally. For husbands, there were significant cross-lagged effects from earlier marital satisfaction to later depressive

symptomatology and from earlier depressive symptomatology to later marital satisfaction. By contrast, marital satisfaction affected later depressive symptomatology among wives, whereas depressive symptoms did not exert a significant effect on later marital satisfaction. Accordingly, the Fincham et al. study suggests that the flow of causality from marital dissatisfaction to depression might be more pronounced when it is the wife rather than the husband who is depressed.

*Kurdek (1998a).* Kurdek examined a series of models similar to those examined by Fincham et al. (1997) using a sample of 198 newlywed couples. For both husbands and wives, marital quality and depressive symptoms were related to each other cross-sectionally, and changes in level of depressive symptoms covaried with changes in level of marital quality. In contrast to the Fincham et al. (1997) study, however, longitudinal paths generally were nonsignificant, and patterns did not differ significantly for husbands and wives.

### Summary

Together, these results replicate and extend the pivotal hypothesis of covariation between marital discord and depression. That is, marital problems both covary with current symptoms of depression and covary over time with symptoms of depression (see also Karney, in press). However, the results also highlight the difficulty in using longitudinal designs to identify the direction of causality between marital problems and depression, largely because of the difficulty of specifying in advance the correct time course for lags (Fisher, 1970).

Variability in patterns across samples also suggests that there might be bidirectional effects, that the effects might vary slightly by gender, and that the effect of marital problems on depressive symptoms might occur at shorter lags than those used to date. These considerations suggest that advances in the longitudinal investigation of the link between marital discord and depression must go hand in hand with advances in theoretical understanding of the link between these constructs.

## ▶ Depression and Problems in Close Relationships: Possible Causal Mechanisms

Longitudinal research makes salient the possible bidirectional nature of the link between marital problems and depression. In this section, we examine coercion, psychological abuse, and lack of support as potential causal agents for effects of marital processes on depression. We also consider communication, reassurance seeking, negative feedback seeking, and poor role performance as potential causal agents for the effects of depression on marital processes. We discuss the stress generation model (Hammen, 1991) as an integrative framework that might help organize many of the bidirectional effects observed between marital problems and depression (for an extension to premarital romantic relationships, see Davila, in press).

### Problem-Solving Deficits and Coercive Processes

Marital difficulties often are traced to difficulties in problem solving (Markman, Stanley, & Blumberg, 1994). At the same time, negative behavior displayed during problem-solving discussions is a robust cross-sectional correlate of marital satisfaction (Weiss & Heyman, 1997), suggesting that poor marital problem solving is a potential source of stress generation in marriage. However, Christian, O'Leary, and Vivian (1994) found that, among discordant couples, depression was associated with poorer self-reported problem-solving skills in both husbands and wives. Confirming these self-reported deficits is a literature on the communication problems of depressed persons.

Much of the research on problem-solving communication difficulties in depression has been influenced by the coercion model (Biglan, Lewin, & Hops, 1990; Hops et al., 1987). This model identifies depressive behavior (i.e., self-derogation, physical and psychological complaints, displays of depressed affect) as a functional, albeit coercive, set of behaviors that are most likely to be reinforced when there is a high level of negative verbal behavior in the home environment. It has been found that partners react to depressive behavior differently from how they react to critical or aggressive behavior, both emotionally (Biglan, Rothlind, Hops, & Sherman, 1989) and behaviorally (Hops et al., 1987). In particular, partners are much less likely to respond to depressive behavior with verbal aggression than they are to reciprocate verbal aggression (Beach, Brooks, Nelson, & Bakeman, 1993). For spouses who are fearful of angering their partners, the different pattern of partner response can render depressive behavior a highly reinforced pattern of behavior (note the similarity to Coyne's [1976] hypothesis). In addition, depressive behavior is most likely to appear in the context of potentially conflictual discussions with the partner (Hinchliffe, Hooper, & Roberts, 1978; Schmaling & Jacobson, 1990), suggesting that depressive behavior is, in part, a response to the stress of such circumstances. Thus, the coercion model might provide a framework for understanding the way in which depressive behavior supplants more adaptive coping behaviors.

### Expressed Emotion and Psychological Abuse

Depressed individuals also might be particularly responsive to various forms of criticism from close others. For example, Vaughn and Leff (1976) found that depressed people were particularly vulnerable to family tension and to hostile statements made by family members. Schless, Schwartz, Goetz, and Mendels (1974) also demonstrated that this vulnerability to marital and family-related stresses persisted in depressed persons even after recovery. Hooley, Orley, and Teasdale (1986) expanded these findings when they reported that the level of "expressed emotion" predicted relapse of depression. As they noted, expressed emotion is an index whereby implied criticism of the target individual figures prominently. Likewise, Mundt, Fiedler, Ernst, and Backenstrass (1996) found that "covert criticism" and long chains of negative marital interaction predicted relapse for a subgroup of endogenously depressed patients.

This research is supplemented by earlier observational work that reported that spouses of depressed partners seldom agreed with their partners, offered help in an ambivalent manner, and often evaluated their depressed partners negatively (Hautzinger, Linden, & Hoffman, 1982). The sum of these results suggests that depressed persons both are differentially sensitive to negative emotion and appear to have an increased frequency of conflictual interactions with their partners.

These findings hold particular meaning for women in physically abusive relationships. Women in these relationships often report that psychological abuse has more negative effects than does physical abuse (Arias, 1995; Folingstad, Rutledge, Berg, Hause, & Polek, 1990). One mediator of the effect of physical violence on depression, then, might be the level of verbal humiliation, overcontrol, and criticism expressed by the partner (i.e., psychological abuse) that often is a concomitant of physical violence (see Chapter 24 by Christopher & Lloyd, this volume).

### Loss of Support

Perceived support often is a better predictor of individual reactions to stressors than is received support. In fact, received support often is unrelated to various psychological symptoms (Barrera, 1986) and does not show stress-buffering effects (Cohen & Wills, 1985). In a provocative analysis of this problem, Lakey and Lutz (1996) noted that the interaction of support behavior with a range of individual characteristics and expectations might be important. Lakey, McCabe, Fisicario, and Drew (1996) had participants rate an array of possible support providers on general level of perceived support. Data from three samples indicated that characteristics of both the supporters and the perceivers influenced ratings of supportiveness. However, in each study, the Perceiver × Supporter interaction accounted for the greatest amount of variance in support judgments. They concluded that "supportiveness is in the eye of the beholder" (Lakey & Lutz, 1996, p. 451). Their findings suggest that the therapeutic implementation of a universal set of supportive behaviors might prove ineffectual in that different individuals could vary in their perceptions of supportive behaviors. Accordingly, it might be necessary to assess positive behaviors in an ideographic and context-sensitive manner to find greater evidence for an effect of positive partner behavior on depressive symptomatology (see Chapter 20 by Cunningham & Barbee, this volume).

### Summary

The three models discussed in this section help to concretize the types of interpersonal processes that can generate depression and the way in which depression can generate interpersonal disturbance. It is useful to note that these interpersonal processes share certain properties. In particular, coercive processes, psychological abuse, and perceived low supportiveness of the partner all reflect situations in which the partner is engaging in behavior that can damage the person's sense of competence and/or the person's sense that others are available who care about him or her. Each of the three models also suggests mechanisms that could unfold over relatively short time periods. Indeed, one might reasonably hypothesize very fast effects of psychological abuse on depression, moderately fast effects of a coercive environment, and a somewhat slower time frame for low perceived partner supportiveness to exert its effect. Accordingly, these considerations highlight the potential complexity of examining lagged effects of interpersonal processes on depression.

## ▶ Stress Generation Theory as an Integrative Framework

Hammen's (1991) stress generation theory expands on the coercion hypothesis by positing that depressed individuals can generate stress in their environments, particularly in their interpersonal environments, in a variety of ways. The increased level of stress to which depressed persons are exposed, in turn, exacerbates their depressive symptomatology. Hammen's model suggests that, in addition to the effect of marital dissatisfaction and various other stresses on later depressive symptoms, depressive symptoms should lead to a variety of marital difficulties and should increase marital stress (and perhaps dissatisfaction). The theory is supported by evidence that depressed persons often are seen as a burden (Coyne, Kahn, & Gotlib, 1987; Coyne, Kessler, et al., 1987), that spouses might be silently upset with depressed partners (Biglan et al., 1989), and that spouses might be ambivalent about the causes of their partners' impairment (Coyne & Benazon, in press). In a direct test of stress generation theory, Hammen (1991) compared unipolar depressed women to bipolar, medically ill, and control group women. She found that unipolar depressed patients experienced more stressful life events than did controls and that stressful interpersonal events were the most elevated among the unipolar depressed group.

### Stress Generation and Communication

Davila, Bradbury, Cohan, and Tochluk (1997) extended the stress generation paradigm by examining the effects of depression on behaviors emitted during a supportive interaction and the subsequent effect on the individual's depression. Elaborating previous findings that depressed persons are less effective at providing and eliciting support (Rook, Pietromonaco, & Lewis, 1994), Davila et al. (1997) found that wives with greater levels of depressive symptomatology showed more negative (but not less positive) support behaviors and expectations. In keeping with Hammen's (1991) theory, negative support behaviors mediated the effect of prior depressive symptoms on later marital stress. Marital stress, in turn, predicted more depressive symptoms.

### Stress Generation and Reassurance Seeking

Reassurance-seeking behaviors represent another potential category of stress generators in relationships. Particularly when conjoined with depression and negative feedback seeking, reassurance-seeking behavior is associated with negative reactions by close others (Joiner, Alfano, & Metalsky, 1993; Katz & Beach, 1997; Katz, Beach, & Anderson, 1996). Coyne's interactional theory of depression suggests that, in the context of depression, demands for reassurance and support from the partner can contribute to partner rejection (Coyne, 1976; Coyne, Kahn, et al., 1987). Supporting the theory, significant associations between reassurance seeking and depression have been found (Joiner et al., 1993; Joiner & Metalsky, 1995; Katz & Beach, 1997). Expanding on Coyne's theory, Joiner and Metalsky (1995) proposed that both reassurance-seeking and negative feedback-seeking can be important in accounting for the negative impact of depression on others. That is, depressed persons search both for negative feedback consistent with their self-views and for reassurance, creating confusing and increasingly intense interpersonal demands. Thus, the three-way interaction of depression, reassurance seeking, and negative feedback seeking should predict rejection by others. Extending and replicating the Joiner and Metalsky theory in the realm of romantic relationships (Joiner & Metalsky, 1995; see also

Joiner et al., 1993), Katz and Beach (1997) found that men were significantly more likely to report relationship dissatisfaction when their partners reported elevated depressive symptoms in conjunction with elevated levels of reassurance seeking and negative feedback seeking.

### Stress Generation and Poor Role Performance

Failure to perform well in various roles (e.g., work, family) also could be associated with stress generation. A study by Wells et al. (1989) provided evidence that depressed persons report more difficulties in role performance. They found that persons with significant but subclinical depressive symptoms exhibited substantially poorer performance at work and at home compared to persons with a variety of other ailments. Replicating and extending these results, a study of 495 adults by Beach, Martin, Blum, and Roman (1993b) found that role functioning was related to level of depressive symptoms. Furthermore, decreased functioning was reported both by the depressed persons and by the spouses or others close to the depressed persons. Accordingly, role performance decrements are reported by both self and others and can constitute an important source for the generation of stress in marriage and continuing vulnerability to future episodes of depression.

The decrement in role performance that stems from a depressive episode and the resulting negative reactions from close others also might lead depressed persons to reorganize their lives so that they have fewer performance demands (Coyne & Calarco, 1995). Such changes also have the potential to constrict both opportunities for social interaction and opportunities for self-enhancement. Hence, role decrements might survive the depressive episode and leave the previously depressed person with substantially impoverished social and coping resources. If this is the case, then it could contribute to a higher risk of relapse.

### Summary

The stress generation framework highlights the way in which several problematic behavior patterns might come to supplant more adaptive, problem-focused coping behavior as a result of dysphoria or a depressive episode. Depressed persons might be more likely to both expect and provide negative support behavior and also might be more likely to direct negative behavior toward partners in the context of problem solving. Because support and problem solving represent two important areas of marital functioning, difficulties in these areas could easily accumulate over time to create misunderstandings and unnecessary disagreements. Likewise, poor role performance might not immediately affect partner satisfaction or relationship quality but could exert a cumulative effect over time. As these examples suggest, in contrast to the rapid effect of marital dissatisfaction on depression, one might anticipate that a longer time course would be required to capture the impact of depression on marital satisfaction. As with the effect of marital discord on depression, however, this expectation could vary substantially depending on the particular effect examined, with the effects on poor communication or problem solving appearing before the effects on poor role performance. As these considerations suggest, there might be substantial complexity in determining the optimal lag to capture the effect of depression on marital discord or vice versa. Not only might there not be a single lag time that best captures the reciprocal influences of marital discord and depression on each other, there might not be a single lag time that best captures the effects going in a single direction.

### ▶ Individual Differences and Bidirectional Effects of Depression

There is strong potential for some type of individual difference analysis to contribute to our understanding of the bidirectional effects of depression and marital processes. Accordingly, we consider, for illustrative purposes, two robust individual difference variables that might modify the action or time course of depressogenic or stress-generating processes (Davila, in press; Joiner, in press).

### Can Individual Differences in Attachment Style Contribute to This Model?

Over the past decade, attachment theory has provided an increasingly useful framework for explaining patterns of adult interaction. In addition to predicting the quality of close relationships, attachment style also has important implications for well-being and coping (see Chapter 14 by Feeney, Noller, and Roberts, this volume).

One question raised by attachment style findings is whether avoidantly attached persons, who might enter marriage more dysphoric and with a less positive view of their partners, are at greater or lesser risk of depression in response to marital discord as compared to anxiously attached persons, who might enter marriage with an overidealized view of their partners (Feeney & Noller, 1990). Currently, it appears that avoidantly attached persons seem to be at particularly increased risk for clinical depression (Carnelley, Pietomonaco, & Jaffe, 1994), but both avoidant and preoccupied individuals appear to be at increased risk for dysphoria (Carnelley et al., 1994; Cole-Detke & Kobak, 1996; Roberts, Gotlib, & Kassel, 1996). Thus, it is those with avoidant attachment styles who seem most likely to display the stress-generating behaviors highlighted in the previous section.

The evidence on the effects of attachment style on partner interactions suggests that some individual differences might render the individual more sensitive to conflicts within the relationship (Davila, in press). In particular, a negative view of self and of the self's ability to elicit positive reactions from others (cf. Bartholomew & Horowitz, 1991), or the combination of a negative view of self and a negative view of the availability of others, might be related to stress generation by fostering negative feedback seeking, reassurance seeking, and negative support behaviors. Likewise, a negative view of self might increase vulnerability to dysphoria when faced with interpersonal stress. Accordingly, the vicious cycle described by the stress generation model might be most pronounced for persons with a negative model of self or with both a negative model of self and other.

### Are Gender Differences Important?

Because women are about twice as likely as men to experience clinical depression (Weissman, 1987), it is important to remain alert for possible gender differences in the relationship between marital discord and depression. However, existing cross-sectional data do not reveal large gender differences in the magnitude of the cross-sectional relationship between marital discord and depression (Beach, Smith, & Fincham, 1994). This lack of difference is somewhat surprising given that there are several reasons to expect gender differences in the discord depression association. For example, women are more likely to be the relationship "maintainers" and, therefore, might have a sense of increased responsibility both for their relationships and for the status of their relationships (Bar Tal & Frieze, 1977; Lerner, 1987). This sense of responsibility, coupled with women's preferential use of emotion-focused coping, might lead women to blame themselves for marital problems, consequently placing them at greater risk of depression (Nolen-Hoeksema, 1987). As a result, one might hypothesize a relatively stronger effect of marital discord on depressive symptomatology for women than for men (Fincham et al., 1997).

Conversely, the male gender role is more consistent with activity and displays of anger and retaliation (Kuebli & Fivush, 1992). Thus, men might be less likely to take responsibility for marital discord and more likely to minimize the seriousness of partner concerns. Feelings of an inability to "win" in conflict, coupled with a tendency to withdraw from negative situations, seemingly are consistent with a relatively stronger effect of depression on later marital satisfaction for men than for women. Accordingly, one might anticipate stronger stress generation effects for men. These gender differences in the "impact" of various individual difference variables, such as coping (for women) and withdrawal (for men), highlight the potential complexity of attempting to model longitudinal effects.

In view of this complexity, it is not surprising that the longitudinal data reviewed earlier do not strongly support the presence of gender differences in magnitude or direction of effects. Accordingly, hypotheses regarding gender differences should be viewed as speculative at present. It seems likely that identifying such differences, if they exist, will require attention to better specification of the lag over which effects might operate and clarification of the specific processes influenced by gender.

## ► Depression and Marriage: Conceptual Integration Through Goal Theory

The preceding overview of the literature has highlighted several key issues in our current understanding of the connection between marital discord and depression. First, there is a robust relationship between marital discord and depression. In addition, marital discord tends to change as depression changes, leading to substantial covariation over time (Karney, in press). Second, use of longitudinal data to test the link between marital discord and depression might be premature until we have specified the underlying processes that account for the linkage of these two constructs. Better specification of the underlying processes should allow us to identify the ideal lag time for assessments and so increase the likelihood that we will identify lagged ef-

fects, as well as individual difference variables that moderate these effects, if they exist. Third, there is good reason to believe that interpersonal distress can intensify or prolong depressive symptoms and that depressive symptoms create vulnerability to greater interpersonal stress. This potentially vicious cycle is captured well by Hammen's (1991) stress generation model, and this model is sufficiently general to guide both the study of effects within the marital relationship and the study of effects in a broad range of close relationships. Finally, it seems likely that some individuals are more vulnerable to one or both pathways in the stress generation model. There are many potential implications of the forgoing analysis, not the least of which is the strong potential for a general model of the relationship between depression and processes in close relationships. However, we would suggest that the potential of this emerging model can be better appreciated if we further elaborate the model from a goal theoretic perspective.

### Goal Theory as a Source of Theoretically Guided Elaboration

Goal theory provides a framework for describing and better understanding unintended negative patterns of behavior that can commonly emerge in the context of marital conflict and depression (Fincham & Beach, 1999). We begin with four premises: All behavior is goal directed (Miller, Galanter, & Pribram, 1960); goals can vary widely (Austin & Vancouver, 1996); spouses might not be aware of what a given relationship goal is; and affect will result from moving either toward or away from goals, with avoidance goals generating negative affect as discrepancies are reduced and approach goals generating positive affect as discrepancies are reduced (Carver & Scheier, in press).

These considerations suggest three distinct types of goals (Carver & Scheier, in press). *Approach* goals are prototypic positive goals associated with pressure to move toward a given state. *Avoidance* goals are associated with pressure to move away from a given state. Carver and Scheier (in press) noted, however, that avoidance goals quite commonly are connected with associated approach goals. The resulting *combination* goals have both avoidance poles that individuals move away from in any direction possible and approach poles that attract individuals as they move further from the avoidance goals. Such combination goals are presumed to be quite stable. Movement away from an avoidance goal most likely produces a different type of affect (e.g., relief) from that produced by movement toward an approach goal (e.g., elation), allowing one to distinguish their effect if one uses a two-dimensional affect system. Approach and avoidance systems are likely to be physiologically distinct, perhaps with approach goals reflecting activity in the behavioral approach system and avoidance goals reflecting activity in the behavioral inhibition system (Gray, 1987). Avoidance goals appear to have an inherent primacy, perhaps reflected in the common tendency for negative behavior to be relatively more salient than positive behavior in dyadic interaction. Accordingly, when one partner's behavior is seen as threatening, such threats should activate the goal of reducing the threat and deactivate various approach goals, at least temporarily. However, there might be individual differences related to temperament and early attachment experiences that contribute to individual differences in reactivity to perceived partner threats.

A goal framework suggests that defensive behavior should be associated with an increase in negative affect along with a decrease in positive affect, the classic signature of depression. As suggested earlier, this affective pattern should be easier to produce among those with a negative model of self and other. Couples in which both partners are vulnerable to defensive reactions should be more prone to long chains of negative interactions, should have a harder time exiting from negative interactions, and should be more prone to view partner behavior as negative and threatening. Accordingly, such couples should have a poorer prognosis than those in which only one partner is prone to defensive reactions.

### Some Specific Implications

These simple premises provide a rich set of theoretical connections among relational circumstances, personal characteristics, stress generation, and dysphoria. In particular, attachment models may be viewed as providing an index of an individual's vulnerability with regard to two sets of central or core goal states: positive self-evaluation (and the avoidance of negative self-evaluation) and relational security (and the avoidance of abandonment). Accordingly, persons with a negative view of self and other might be relatively more likely to experience partner behavior as threatening negative evaluation of the self or abandonment by the other. Because such threats capture attention and deactivate approach goals, individuals with a negative model of self and other might be chronically primed to adopt defensive goals, to experience more severe erosion of positive affect, and to experience more severe exacerbation of negative affect. Furthermore, once adopted, defensive goals should lead to negative expectations regarding partner behavior, more negative support and problem-solving behavior, and greater difficulty in engaging in normal role performance. These are the patterns described earlier as stress-generating behaviors of depressed persons.

Accordingly, a goals perspective might help to integrate an individual difference perspective with a stress generation perspective in accounting for depressive reactions. For example, one reason why attachment styles might be related to depression is that the goals tapped by attachment style are quite hard to give up. It might be particularly difficult to disengage from key attachment figures or goals related to one's identity. In addition, it is very difficult to disengage from avoidance goals. In such cases, the individual might perceive that there are few other goals of equal significance (Linville, 1987) or that giving up the goal is not an option, so the individual might cling to the goal despite the seeming inevitability of failure. In this way, goal theory proves to be a useful framework in which to explicate the means through which vulnerability factors interact with interpersonal events to produce depression and also can help models to better incorporate contextual effects such as stressful life events, personal characteristics, and the family history of the individual.

## ► Clinical Implications

Current empirical support for reciprocal effects between depression and relationship satisfaction, although far from complete, is sufficient to provide important support for the use of marital therapy in treating depression.

O'Leary and Beach (1990) investigated the effectiveness of behavioral marital therapy (BMT) in the treatment of depression. Discordant couples in which the wives were suffering from depression were randomly assigned to either BMT or cognitive therapy (CT). O'Leary and Beach found that both treatment forms effectively reduced depressive symptomatology but that only BMT improved marital satisfaction. These effects were maintained at 1-year follow-up. In an examination of pretherapy predictors of outcome in this study, Beach and O'Leary (1992) reported that individuals with pre-therapy negative cognitive styles did more poorly in BMT, whereas those with negative pre-therapy marital environments did more poorly in CT. These findings suggest that BMT might be particularly useful for couples reporting relatively high levels of marital discord. In addition, the findings suggest that, for couples reporting only modest marital difficulties, individual CT might be an appropriate intervention.

In a replication of the O'Leary and Beach (1990) study, Jacobson, Dobson, Fruzzetti, Schmaling, and Salusky (1991) found that both BMT and individual CT reduced depressive symptoms among depressed persons but that only BMT produced improvements in marital satisfaction. Jacobson et al. also included couples in which the wives were depressed but not maritally discordant. In these cases, individual CT was superior to BMT. In keeping with suggestions by O'Leary and Beach (1990), these findings suggest that the effectiveness of BMT might be limited to maritally discordant couples. However, ongoing research examining BMT for the treatment of depression in the absence of reported marital discord might yet produce evidence of positive impact (Cordova & Gee, in press). Accordingly, the applicability of marital therapy to couples who are not complaining of marital problems remains an open question.

In another study providing support for the use of conjoint therapy in the treatment of depression, Foley, Rounsaville, Weissman, Sholomaskas, and Chevron (1989) randomly assigned 18 depressed individuals to either an individual or a couple format of interpersonal therapy (Klerman, Weissman, Rounsaville, & Chevron, 1995). Foley et al.'s (1989) sample differed from the sample in O'Leary and Beach's (1990) and Jacobson et al.'s (1991) samples in that partners were more symptomatic, showing 78% lifetime histories of some forms of psychiatric disorder. In addition, whereas the two previous studies were limited to depression in wives, the Foley et al. (1989) study included husbands with depression as well. As in the previous two studies, patients in both individual and conjoint therapies showed reductions in depressive symptomatology. In addition, only those in conjoint therapy exhibited improvements in marital satisfaction.

In sum, these studies point to the utility of marital therapy in treating depression, particularly when the couple is discordant. However, it is clear that this initial round of outcome work might not fully capture the power of marital interventions for depression. As we continue to develop more powerful models of the reciprocal relationship between marital problems and depression, we are likely to find additional points of clinical intervention and to substantially enhance the effectiveness of marital interventions for depression. It seems likely that advances guided by the stress generation model and an integration of the stress generation model with an individual difference perspective will produce a variety of new suggestions for clinical technique. If this is the case, then there will be substantial development and improvement in the use of marital treatments for depression during the coming decade.

## ▶ Conclusions

This chapter has suggested that the broad theoretical framework provided by goal theory can stimulate greater interchange among the various theoretical perspectives that have been brought to bear on depression in marriage. In addition, it appears that goal theory is broad enough to bridge the distance among the many types of close relationships and their relations to depression. At the broadest level, we suggest that a goal-theoretic framework might prove useful in identifying points of connection between apparently disparate theoretical accounts and the empirical data that support them. At an intermediate level of abstraction, we suggest that stress generation theory can organize many of the bidirectional effects between marital processes and depression and might stimulate researchers to refine the questions being asked. At a specific level, we suggest that three types of problem behaviors are of particular importance in accounting for the impact of marital discord on depression: coercive processes, psychological abuse, and erosion of support. Likewise, three problem behaviors are of particular importance in accounting for the impact of depression on marital discord: communication, reassurance and negative feedback seeking, and decreased role performance. Attention to each of these levels of abstraction might prove useful in developing more comprehensive explanatory models. Better models, in turn, will help to guide better investigations of longitudinal effects and so provide better tests of causal hypotheses. Such investigations are, in turn, likely to suggest more powerful forms of intervention for depression and better ways in which to help ameliorate the negative impact of depression on close relationships.

# Contents

# Loss and Bereavement in Close Romantic Relationships

*John H. Harvey*
*Andrea M. Hansen*

If we live long enough, practically all of us will lose romantic or married partners to dissolution, divorce, or death over the course of our lives. This outcome is one of the givens of life. A philosopher, Hazrat Khan, addressed the grief inherent in love when he said, "The sorrow of the lover is continual, in the presence and absence of the beloved: in the presence for fear of the absence, and in the absence in longing for the presence. The pain in love becomes in time the life of the lover" (quoted in Welwood, 1990, p. 12).

In this chapter, we review theories and evidence concerning loss and bereavement in close romantic relationships. In so doing, we present an argument that people will function more effectively in close relationships to the extent that they are cognizant of their major losses and willing to recognize and work on them as an important developmental task (Erikson, 1963). In a second major section,

we describe evidence collected from a sample of persons over 60 years of age who were single and attempting to find partners for possible close relationships (Hansen, 1998). Many of the individuals in this group were simultaneously engaged in multiple processes of grieving, decision making, and self-presentation regarding possible new relationships. Thus, we believe that this chapter epitomizes the complex loving and grieving experience endemic to human life.

Some caveats are in order. There are many gaps in the available literature on comparison of loss and bereavement experiences. Little research has focused on the links among grief experiences for different types of losses. There is scant evidence comparing death experiences to divorce or dissolution experiences. In addition, there has been little work comparing and contrasting loss and bereavement associated with diverse types of romantic relationships including people at different ages and development points as well as heterosexual or homosexual relationships. A further gap in the literature is the general absence of work on how past losses accumulate, are associated with long-term bereavement, and affect present functioning and relationships (Harvey & Miller, 1998). There even is debate about whether and how people grieve major losses, with suggestive evidence that at least some parents do not show typical grieving patterns in association with the loss of their children to sudden infant death syndrome (Wortman & Silver, 1989). This latter debate on parental loss is not considered in our review and analysis. However, in terms of loss and bereavement among people experiencing romantic close relationships ending in death or dissolution, there is little evidence to suggest that the grieving process is not pervasive and intensive, at least for periods during most people's lives.

## ▶ Conceptual Issues on Relationship Loss

In previous work (e.g., Harvey, 1996), we have defined a major loss as a reduction in resources for which a person has an emotional investment. In the extensive literature on death and dying, bereavement has been defined as the person's multidimensional responses to loss, and grief has been defined as the emotional responses to loss (Moss & Moss, 1995). In general, these definitions also apply to close relationship dissolution.

Major losses need to be differentiated from minor ones (e.g., the loss of an insignificant personal possession) in consequence, and the former are the experiences of concern to us in this chapter. Viorst (1986) discussed the continuum of types of loss encountered by all humans in her book, *Necessary Losses*. But this continuum includes many losses that we would conceive as minor in the overall spectrum. In close relationships, death and dissolution represent major loss events. Death and

dissolution both can involve psychologically important subcomponents such as loss of physical presence, nurturing interaction, affection, intellectual stimulation, sexual union, economic health, and future mutual plans. It is these subcomponents that people report to be most daunting in implications for present activities in contemplating their relationship losses (Harvey, Barnes, Carlson, & Haig, 1995).

We view bereavement as a process associated with major losses that, at both conscious and unconscious levels, is ongoing to different degrees throughout much of our lives. Other grief theorists (e.g., Rando, 1993) also support the idea of grief as a process, although possibly viewing it as more seasonal and specifically linked to particular loss experiences. We have known for some time that grieving involves considerable work. In his classic article, "Symptomatology and Management of Acute Grief," Lindemann (1944) coined the term "grief work" as reflecting the cognitive and emotional labor involved in adapting to major loss. Lindemann spoke of tasks such as emancipation from the bondage to the deceased, readjustment to the environment in which the deceased is missing, and formation of new relationships.

We believe that terms such as *bondage* are unfortunate in the context of adjustment. We prefer an experience connoting *embracing* of these past relationships while, at the same time, the individual takes the steps leading to new identities, relationships, and practical realities. For the person experiencing considerable grief, these steps might require a great amount of time and energy. It has been suggested that people can move readily through grief associated with relationship loss within 18 to 24 months (Pennebaker, 1990). Our work in this area, however, suggests that no firm time lines can be specified. A person might be relatively well integrated into a new close relationship and yet have residual grief associated with the loss of a past relationship. In fact, in work by Harvey et al. (1995), one couple in their 60s reported that a basis for their current strong marriage was their mutual acceptance of (their frequently discussed) fond memories of their lives with their deceased spouses.

What is a good outcome associated with the bereavement process? We prefer the term *adaptation* to frequently used terms such as *healing, recovery,* and *moving on,* although we think that the latter are respectable terms in this field of work. Adaptation seems to us to embody a successful outcome given our view that, for many people, some degree of mental-emotional energy will continue to be directed toward the loss event (sometimes in the form of dreams). By adaptation, we mean that the person has confronted the loss experience and many of its personal meanings and is functioning in society. The individual probably is cognizant that the loss event continues to affect parts of his or her psychological well-being. Adaptation also means that we recognize that our major losses are a part of who we are, that they have contributed to our learning about self and the world, and that our identities and behavior will continue to reflect, in some ways, these major loss experiences.

The logic of our position on adaptation relates to the "broken hearts or broken bonds" argument articulated by Stroebe, Gergen, Gergen, and Stroebe (1992). In their analysis, Stroebe et al. noted that a common historical view of how people can best deal with a major loss is by moving beyond the loss, that is, by breaking the bond and endorsing a view that "the past is past." Moving on, they suggest, involves an avoidance of, or distraction from, thinking about the lost other. On the other hand, Stroebe et al. also pointed to the more contemporary (and what they referred to as "somewhat romantic") view of maintaining bonds to the deceased in the form of long-term grieving and "broken hearts." We are not necessarily advocating letting a broken heart continue to be broken. Rather, we are arguing that regardless of what we do to forget, avoid, distract ourselves from, or move beyond our major losses, they will continue to affect us, and a better approach to peace and effective functioning might be to entertain and consciously work with them as symbols of our deepest identities (Brantner, 1977).

A powerful recognition of continued ties is Ellis's (1995) book, *Final Negotiation,* in which she describes her 9-year love affair with Eugene Weinstein, a man who was gradually dying of emphysema and who also was 20 years older than her. This complex relationship was embedded within a landscape of other major events including loss (e.g., she lost her brother in the Air Florida flight that crashed into the Potomac River in 1982) and her becoming an academic sociologist, the same field in which Weinstein was a highly visible professional. Ellis wrote of how she and Weinstein negotiated between denial and acceptance and how they confronted situations of overwhelming loss (e.g., when she was denied the right to make medical decisions even as he was failing badly because they were unmarried). As Ellis made clear, her negotiation of this relationship continues now over a decade after Weinstein's death, as does her negotiation of their story.

Ellis's (1995) argument about the intricate unfolding of her story of love and loss applies to a great many other stories of love and loss. As relationship scholars, we have only skimmed the surface in understanding these stories and in helping real people recognize the psychological processes at work in their lives across love and loss.

### Basic Processes in Adapting to the Loss of Close Others

Obviously, there are many types of reactions to major losses in the form of relationship divorce, dissolution, and the deaths of close others. We briefly review theory and research reflecting basic reactions and major changes in the survivors after such losses.

Horowitz (1976), Janoff-Bulman (1992), and Rando (1993) all contended that loss by death of close others leads to cognitive schema changes that are similar to the idea of identity change described earlier. Despite humans' apparent tendency to be cognitively conservative (Janoff-Bulman, 1992), schema changes seem necessary when losses such as death and dissolution occur. These schema changes can evolve through a stage involving a new assumptive world about the fact that such major negative events are possible and do happen to us, obsessive wondering about "what-ifs" regarding the loss events (now referred to as "counterfactual thinking" in cognitive social psychology [Roese, 1997]), "survivor guilt," and a host of other internal and external social interaction dynamics including avoidance of close others.

Rando (1993) argued that it is essential for schema work to continue such that the grieving person reappraises the event, self, and lost other as well as the implications of this loss. She argued that it is likely that this "working through" (Horowitz, 1976) eventually will involve steps such as reviewing and remembering realistically, reviving and reexperiencing the feelings of loss, relinquishing the old assumptive world, developing a new relationship with the departed other, adopting new ways of being in the world, and forming a new identity. A pattern of bereavement indicative of "complicated mourning" is especially common during the 1st year after the death of a spouse or close romantic other. This pattern often involves depression, anger, intrusions into consciousness of images of the deceased, holding the self and the deceased responsible for the profound sense of loss the self is experiencing, and efforts to avoid thinking of the deceased loved one (Horowitz, Bonanno, & Holen, 1993; Rando, 1993).

Another fairly common type of grief associated with loss by death of spouse or close romantic other is that which focuses on the unresolved conflict existing in the relationship at the time of death (Parkes & Weiss, 1983; Raphael, 1983). This bereavement process involves not only coming to terms with the loss of the relationship but also mourning what never was realized that had been anticipated and hoped for in terms of psychological harmony in the relationship.

Whereas the forgoing ideas and evidence have derived from work on loss by death, work by Harvey, Weber, and Orbuch (1990) and Weiss (1975) suggested that somewhat similar adaptation processes might be at work in dissolution. There are obvious differences when the loss event involves death as opposed to dissolution. When death occurs, for example, the survivor cannot continue to interact with the former partner and perhaps address issues of fault, guilt, and forgiveness regarding relationship events. Nonetheless, we assume that there is considerable overlap in grief and coping reactions.

Weiss (1975) was the first scholar to articulate the value of storytelling in the form of accounts (i.e., story-like interpretations) for people in the throes of marital separation. In his research with persons in the group "Parents Without Partners," he found that people who could form accounts of the sequences of separation events, and especially of the determinants of the events, felt better about their ability to understand the events and to control their reactions to them. Without fairly full accounts, the anxiety and feelings of despair of these respondents were great, and they saw no clear way in which to achieve hope and solutions to their psychic pain.

Harvey et al. (1990) and Orbuch (1997) developed the accounts concept further in terms of its meaning and implications and applied it to a variety of loss situations including those involving dissolution, death, airline disasters, incest, and related events leading to posttraumatic stress. Their findings supported Weiss's (1975) conclusions about the value of account making in the context of major loss. Harvey et al. (1990) also found that an essential step in effective account making involves confiding parts of one's account to a caring and empathic other (Harvey, Orbuch, Chwalisz, & Garwood, 1991; Orbuch, Harvey, Davis, & Merbach, 1994).

### Comparison of Loss and Bereavement Experiences

There has been little research comparing survivors' reactions to different types of relationship loss, and in this section we review the few studies that have been done. As will be seen, one of the values of this line of inquiry is to spotlight particular reactions such as disenfranchised grief.

One line of investigation has involved comparison of groups of bereaved persons who recently have lost children, parents, or spouses. For example, Bass, Noelker, Townsend, and Deimling (1990) found that, in general, the intensity of different grief responses was greater for loss of a child than for loss of a spouse and was greater for loss of a spouse than for loss of a parent. Other writers have addressed the special significance for parents of loss of children as an "out-of-season," reverse-order death (with parents expected to die before children) and a psychologically unjust human event (e.g., Morrell, 1988).

In another study, Barnes, Harvey, Carlson, and Haig (1996) compared the grief and coping responses of persons over 65 years of age and persons in their 20s to the loss of loved ones (usually spouses for the older respondents and a combination of siblings and romantic close others for the younger respondents). The losses had occurred during the past year. Barnes et al. found that, on a variety of adaptation measures (e.g., resolution, anger, guilt), the older respondents showed more positive steps toward adaptation than did the younger respondents. Furthermore, consistent with Harvey et al.'s (1990) model of coping with severe stressors, older persons, who presumably were more experienced in dealing with loss than were younger persons, reported more account making and confiding in close others as ways of coping.

The most significant literature on comparison experiences has concerned programs of work on the lives of widows at different ages and stages after the loss of their husbands. There are more than 13 million widows over 65 years of age in the United States alone (O'Bryant & Hansson, 1995). There also are more than 1 million new widows in the 35- to 54-year age range in the United States *every year* (Levinson, 1997). Also, according to recent census data, in the age range of 65 years or over, men still die an average of 7 years earlier than women. Thus, one can easily see the

major health and policy issue looming for our understanding of widowhood and women's coping with the loss of their spouses. These statistics do not include women who lose romantic nonmarital partners including those in homosexual relationships.

Lund, Caserta, and Dimond (1989) reported that early after the loss of their spouses, older women (average age in the 60s) showed greater depression than did similarly aged men and that bereaved women and men both exhibited greater depression than similar-aged nonbereaved control groups. The preponderance of findings on age as a vulnerability factor for grieving widows suggests that younger widows (Stroebe & Stroebe, 1987) and younger families (Hansson, Fairchild, Vanzetti, & Harris, 1992) are at greater risk for negative outcomes than are older individuals and families. This pattern of evidence might reflect several dynamics including the greater anticipation of and preparation for death later in life, the greater acceptance of death later in life, and the greater feeling of injustice if death occurs relatively early in life. As Barnes et al. (1996) argued, this evidence also might be partially explained by the greater experience most older people have in telling their stories of loss and gaining solace as a consequence of their account-making and confiding activities as compared to younger people.

O'Bryant and Hansson (1995) reported that, given reasonable social support networks, both younger and older women adapt relatively well to widowhood over time. In a longitudinal study of persons over 65 years of age, McCrae and Costa (1988) found that widows did not differ from married controls at a 10-year follow-up on measures of depression and general well-being.

The concept of disenfranchised grief is particularly relevant to older persons who have lost spouses to death. Disenfranchised grief pertains to grief that is not widely recognized in society and for which there usually is a limited support system (Doka, 1989). Because it is assumed that older persons die more often than do younger persons, the grief of elderly women and men who lose spouses and romantic others might be given little due by others, especially younger persons and even family members. When older persons evidence normal responses to bereavement such as lack of energy, confusion, loneliness, and social withdrawal, these behaviors sometimes are interpreted as problems reflective of old age (Moss & Moss, 1995).

One investigation that compared grief experiences of persons who had lost spouses to death to those of persons who had lost spouses to divorce was carried out by Farnsworth, Lund, and Pett (1989). A sample of 110 widowed persons was compared to a sample of 109 divorced persons. All respondents were over 50 years of age (although divorced persons were slightly younger on average) and had been widowed or divorced within the past 2 years. Farnsworth et al. found that widowed and divorced respondents experienced similar feelings of emotional shock, helplessness and avoidance, and grief. Both samples felt relatively positive about their psychological strength and coping, and they were similar in terms of their overall life satisfaction. Divorced participants had significantly more difficulty with anger, guilt, and confusion, whereas widowed participants were significantly more depressed.

Farnsworth et al. (1989) offered several explanations for the differences between widowed and divorced persons. The divorced persons' greater anger, guilt, and confusion might have been caused by stigmatization of their experience and ongoing discussions involving blame and rebuke in their families. Farnsworth et al. also felt that the somewhat older widowed respondents might have reflected a "generation effect" in their greater depression. The widowed group might have been less socialized to express their grief, might actually have had more physical ailments associated with their circumstances, and might have had less helpful support networks than the divorced group. The reactions to loss of divorced persons who have dependent children also are strongly influenced by the effectiveness and perceived fairness of the custody arrangements (Ahrons, 1994).

Farnsworth et al.'s (1989) study shows the difficulty of comparing samples on criteria of loss that are aggregations of diverse experiences, as is true with divorce and death. At a minimum, care needs to be taken to ensure control or comparability of general physical, familial support, and socioeconomic conditions across such groups.

## ▶ The Relationship Between Loss and Love During the Golden Years

Whereas there has been extensive research on the dynamics of dating and early relationship commitment behaviors among people in their 20s through their 40s, there has been relatively little research on these activities among people in their 60s or older. This paucity of research exists despite the huge shift of the population toward this age range that is only a decade or so away (Coleman, 1997). Furthermore, the prominent relationship between the loss of former spouses or lovers to death or dissolution and the quest for new romantic relationships has been even more neglected in the aging, coping, and close relationship literatures.

In one of the key studies done to date regarding dating among people in their "golden years," Bulcroft and O'Connor (1986) investigated the romantic behavior of 45 people between 62 and 95 years of age living in or near Minneapolis, Minnesota. Their principal finding was that older persons, similar to younger persons, reported many infatuations; embraced romance and its trappings (e.g., candlelight dinners) in courting; and emphasized the value of hugging, touching, and kissing—the same behaviors strongly associated with youthful courtship.

Bulcroft and Bulcroft (1991) used data from the National Survey of Families and Households to conduct logistic regression analyses identifying significant predictors of dating for persons 60 years of age or older. The strongest predictor of propensity to date in later life was gender, with men being significantly more likely than women to engage in dating. Younger males had a higher likelihood of dating. Other factors that increased the probability of dating and had a positive effect included comparative health, driving ability, single-family residence, organizational participation, and contacts with siblings.

As reported in a book titled *Late Love*, Simpson (1994) interviewed 50 men and women who married after 55 years of age. Her respondents also reported high degrees of zest in romantic and sexual activities while they were dating prior to marriage. Some had taken care of sick and eventually dying spouses, and they indicated that the new dating period was helpful to them in renewing their vitality for intimacy.

### Juggling Grief and Romantic Yearnings

We conducted a study of the quest for romance among single people beyond 60 years of age. It was expected that people who had engaged in account making and confided in close others regarding their loss of past relationships would show persistence in the pursuit of new romantic relationships relative to persons who reported that they had engaged in little account making and confiding. Many people work for long periods to adapt to major losses such as the deaths of spouses. Successful reentry into dating and relating activities might require finding new romantic partners who are willing to work collaboratively on losses in each person's life. Thus, such relationships, like all close relationships to some degree, probably contain mutual therapeutic support as well as romance. There is likely to be a fine balance between therapeutic support and romance in such relationships. Through narrative inputs provided by respondents, we hoped to learn more about this balance.

Another perspective from which to explore the relationship between loss and love is the dialectic conception of relationships (Baxter & Montgomery, 1996). These theorists pro-

vide fascinating analysis of the extent to which every close relationship involves a "ceaseless interplay between contrary or opposing tendencies" (p. 3). In the context of the present chapter, dialectics might help us to understand how people in close relationships can be simultaneously moving closer together and separating psychologically. As implied by Baxter and Montgomery, this dialectic tendency might or might not be recognized by a couple. We suggest that, to the extent such a tendency exists, part of the dialectic tension arises from people's continued bereavement and sense of being incomplete associated with past close relationships and possibly past major losses in general. Baxter and Montgomery argued that dialectic tension is natural in its evolution in relationships and helps a couple to achieve a type of equilibrium.

Extrapolating from the dialectic logic, we would expect that people who explicitly recognize the role of past relationship losses in their lives, while working on finding or establishing new, close romantic relationships, would be more persistent in searching for such relationships. Based on both the account-making and confiding and dialectic positions, we also expected that persistence in pursuing romance would be particularly strong when people were able to engage in confiding about previous losses with their new partners.

### A Study of Seniors Seeking Romantic Relationships

This study involved administering a questionnaire that included structured and narrative items to 90 individuals (58 women and 32 men) over 60 years of age living in Arizona and Iowa. The average age of the women was 68.5 years, and the average age of the men was 69.7 years. All of these individuals had been single for at least 1 year, and all were heterosexuals. All had reasonable health such that they could be involved in the pursuit of social relationships. Of the 90 individuals, 70 were widows or widowers, 16 were divorced, and 4 had been in long-term nonmarital relationships that had ended. Fully 75% of the sample currently were involved in dating behavior (defined as going on dates at least occasionally) or had been involved in dating behavior at one time after the loss of their spouses or previous romantic partners.

### Approach to the Research

A questionnaire was created to investigate individuals' persistence in pursuing romantic relationships. It contained the following questions: Are you interested in dating and possibly finding a new spouse or romantic partner? How regularly do you date? How regularly do you want to date? Are you persisting in trying to find romantic partners? If you are, what means do you use? Respondents also were asked about their possible continuing grief regarding the loss of partners. They were explicitly asked about the extent to which they had developed story-like understandings of past losses and confided parts of their understandings to close others, whether the others were romantic possibilities, good friends, or relatives. Specific questions concerning account making and confiding were as follows: Did you develop an account or story-like understanding of the loss of your significant other? If so, did you confide parts of that understanding in persons close to you such as good friends, new romantic interests, or family?

Respondents also were asked questions regarding their hopes for close relationships in the future and the extent to which they found closeness in contacts with friends and family members. All of these questions were answered through open-ended questionnaire items. To help us better understand respondents' answers, we interviewed about 10% of the sample who had answered the questionnaire items. All others filled out and mailed in the questionnaire.

A general depression measure was administered to respondents to evaluate whether depression was related to the results. Given the possibility that respondents were continuing to grieve about past losses, some of the re-

spondents might show relatively high levels of depression. The 30-item Geriatric Depression Scale (GDS) developed by Brink et al. (1982) was used in the study. This instrument contains straightforward items such as the following: Are you basically satisfied with your life? Do you frequently feel like crying? Scores of 20 to 30 are defined as showing moderate or severe depression. The instrument was standardized using elderly samples in the same general age range as the respondents in the present study.

After respondents answered items on the questionnaire and the GDS, they were interviewed regarding their open-ended answers. They were asked to clarify responses that were brief and/or that they felt deserved emphasis as part of their experiences of searching for partners and closeness at this stage of their lives.

### Some Results

The mean depression score for the sample was 12.4, which is defined by Brink et al. (1982) as clearly falling within the normal range. Women and men did not differ. Depression also was not significantly different for widows and widowers as compared to divorced persons. Overall, we concluded that general depression was not a particular problem experienced by the sample.

Open-ended items were coded for theoretically meaningful points by two independent raters, whose reliability was 92% in scoring for points and themes in the narratives. Responses were coded concerning whether respondents were continuing or had given up in pursuit of romantic relationships. Respondents were defined as giving up if they indicated that they had dated to some degree after the loss of primary close relationships but now no longer desired to have such relationships (for whatever reasons). Also, responses were coded concerning whether respondents indicated that they had engaged in account making and confiding regarding their relationship losses. Respondents were defined as having engaged in account making and confiding if they indicated that they had worked to develop personal understandings of their losses and had confided part of those understandings to close others; they also were asked to indicate who those close others were.

It was found that 28 of 58 women fell into the "giving up" category, whereas 5 of 32 men fell into this category. All respondents who no longer were active in dating indicated that they had engaged in some degree of dating and romantic quests after the loss of their previous romantic relationships. Inactive women and men indicated that their lack of pursuit or interest was related to the loss of spouses or lovers with whom they had been in highly satisfying long-term relationships.

Partial excerpts of explanations for lack of dating persistence include the following:

> I've looked around and tried [dating] a bit, but I'm devoted to his memory. He meant everything to me.

> [I] would like to find someone, but no one can compare to her.

> I've discovered that all the good ones are taken already.

> I'd like to fall in love again, but I never want to care for an invalid husband again. It is too draining.

> I still have an appetite, and my health is good for my age, but most men my age are too frail to engage in active dating lives.

Partial excerpts of those indicating that they were very active in dating included the following:

> I take advantage of meeting every man I can. I meet them in organizations, at my temple, [and] on AOL [America Online].

> I take out a different woman every 3rd night. I'm dating and having more fun than I did when I was a teenager dating.

> I'm in a singles organization that has dances, socials, and the like. It keeps me busy a few days a week and fulfills my dating needs.

Following is a more in-depth excerpt for the "giving up" category from the narrative of a 65-year-old woman. She discussed why she no longer was dating. She also projected a theme of not expecting to date much in the future and to focus social and emotional interests on close friends and family members, especially grandchildren:

> [For the first 2 years since my husband's death,] I tried going out occasionally. I was fixed up by friends and met people in support groups. But I soon discovered how difficult it would be to find anyone who could fill my husband's shoes. He was such a wonderful person, and we had such a good relationship [for 38 years].
>
> I always compared each new person to him, [and] none came close. . . . I now have a circle of close female friends, and I dote on my grandchildren. . . . They bring me such pleasure. . . . I would like to be in love and married again, but the older I get, I doubt very much that it is possible.

In further narratives, however, many of the women in the "giving up" category noted that another reason for their lack of continued seeking of romantic partners was the relative scarcity of available men (e.g., in their age range, "interested," with the requisite qualities). Most of these women were in their late 60s or 70s.

Some of the women who were classified as having given up said that they had ceased going out with men only because men had become so scarce in their geographical areas; for example, a few had been farm wives and still lived in less metropolitan areas. The following excerpt illustrates one 73-year-old woman's quest for romance for a long time and her current feeling that it would not occur again in her life. She noted a theme that recurred for women in their mid-70s and older, that is, that the men became fewer in number and availability with each passing year:

> I did not and do not care to be in an all-women's environment. Before my husband died, we had an understanding that it would

be okay for me, or for him if I died first, to remarry. In the first few years, I tried desperately to find a new mate. I dated every man my friends suggested and any available men from church. But as I've grown older, fewer ask me out. . . . I suspect, with regret, that I shall always be single now.

By and large, neither the 5 men who were classified as having given up nor the 27 who were classified as active in dating noted availability as an issue. A few of the men and women who were classified as having given up reported grief to the point that they were haunted by memories of past close relationships. The following excerpt from a 62-year-old man is illustrative:

For the first 2 years [since my wife's death], she was constantly on my mind. I know that bothered women when I would go out on dates. I was in such a fog that I don't even remember what I did at work; it could not have been very good work. Going out socially became impossible for my partners and myself. For them, I was no fun and I could not even make small talk. For me, it was agonizing. My wife meant the world to me, and these relationships were meaningless. I've stopped dating at this time [5 years after the wife's death].

Fully 40 of 58 women in the study had narratives that were coded as having engaged in account making and confiding. This proportion compares to 14 of 32 men whose narratives showed activity in account making and confiding. Partial excerpts from narratives showing account making and confiding included the following:

I frequently go to divorced and widowed support group meetings. I'm not afraid to tell my story. I talk about my wife and how I feel being a widower [for 4 years].

I've learned over and over in life the value of close friends being there to listen and talk with you about your losses. I've got some of the best close friends in the world.

I cry, pray, talk about, and mourn the loss of my husband of 55 years just about every other day. But I know that that is good, and even the men I go out with have accepted my strong feelings not to let his memory die and often want to hear about what made my husband so special.

Partial excerpts from narratives not showing much account making and confiding included the following:

I believe grief is a private matter.

No, [I] haven't talked much and don't really have any close friends.

I think that my friends and family would get tired of my whining over why she's not with me at the best time in my life.

I don't want to think about her death. It's too distressing.

What's past is past, and I've tried to move on in my thoughts. I do cry a lot about why he had to die so young.

As noted previously, 28 of 58 women respondents had given up their romantic quests. Of the 30 who remained active in dating, 28 indicated that they had spent considerable time and energy in account making and confiding regarding their loss of past close relationships. If they commented on the effect of such thinking, feeling, and behavior in their lives, they emphasized the positive impact.

Regarding the question of confidants with whom to discuss their losses, 22 of these 28 women noted that their account making and confiding continued in the context of discussing previous partners with current romantic partners. Following is an in-depth excerpt from the narrative of a 63-year-old woman outlining this position:

[After my husband's death,] I had to help myself. . . . I worked on myself. I privately reflected long and hard about our life together. But I joined support groups [e.g., Young Energetic Widowed Singles] and met the man I intend to marry in one of them. He had lost his wife in 1989, about the same time I [had] lost my husband. We have been dating about 2 years. We have recovered from our grief and have a happy relationship. It's a real blessing. We talk often about our deceased spouses and how they would approve of our new relationship. We have shared our grief and stories, and [we] are not afraid to shed tears. . . . But we go on and appreciate each day in our new life. You have a right to have and express your memories of your former life. You have to talk, talk, talk—never stop. We are now sharing our experiences with other widows and widowers. We hope to help them in their grief and help them be successful in making their new lives.

As for the men's account making and confiding, there was less evidence that they had engaged in such activity or that it was related to their current dating. Fully 27 of 32 men were judged not to have given up in their dating pursuits. Of these 27 men, 14 noted that they had engaged in regular account making and confiding, and each also mentioned that these had been done both with close friends and with new romantic partners. All 14 also noted the positive influence of discussion of their losses with close others.

As has been noted in reviews of account making and confiding as a way of coping with loss (Orbuch, 1997), women tend to show a stronger inclination to use this approach than do men. The present evidence also suggests that women are more active account makers and confiders. Even among the 28 women who were inactive in dating, 12 indicated that they had engaged in account making and confiding. The 5 men who had given up in their dating pursuits did not indicate that they engaged in account making and confiding.

Neither past research nor the present study is conclusive in ruling out the use of account making and confiding as major ways that men cope with loss. Men might simply be more reluctant to admit that they use these means of coping with loss.

We also asked questions about future plans for closeness and relations with family and

friends. Most respondents indicated that they had, and expected to continue to have, relations with some group of friends and family members who were close and supportive. Such relations were emphasized more by persons who were classified as having given up on dating and romantic relationships. Some women said that they had no choice but to revert to close relationships with other women because so few men were in their networks.

### Dialectics and Sex Differences in Seniors' Romantic Quests

Overall, this research provides information about singles over 60 years of age and how their romantic quests are intertwined with their resolution of past losses of close relationships. The data are supportive of the extrapolations from the account-making and confiding and dialectic positions on grief and persistence in romantic pursuits.

As we have interpreted the dialectic position, it was well accommodated by the relatively high number of women and men who showed persistence. Simultaneous to their persistence, both women and men reported having introduced their feelings about the loss of previous partners for discussion with new partners. Our importing of dialectic logic to this situation was based on the assumption that it is realistic and might be helpful to recognize and address the loss-love linkages with new partners. The narrative evidence supported that assumption by showing a large number of accounts in which people suggested how their discussion of past relationships with new partners was a positive part of their current relationships.

The evidence also strongly points to the different situations encountered by females and males seeking romantic partners. Our results suggest that many females give up their quests because of the low numbers of available men and/or the females' conclusion that those men available do not compare well to their previous husbands or lovers. Men in this age range generally do not have availability as an issue. It was found, however, that a few men showed continued devotion to deceased spouses, with one showing such devotion to the point of felt "bondage" in how it impaired his persistence in seeking new romance in his life.

Women also showed a tendency to be more involved in account making and confiding regarding their losses than were men. In discussing this difference, we suggested that such a tendency had been found in previous research. But the evidence might not be conclusive if men are reluctant to admit the use of these coping activities or if they do not even recognize that they are using such activities. If the difference is real, then it resonates with a generally held belief and some evidence that women are more expressive and possibly more analytic about relationships and major loss events than are men (Harvey, 1996).

This research was an initial study of seniors' narratives of their searches for new romantic partners in the context of their coping with the loss of past partners (reported more fully in Hansen, 1998). It emphasizes the concepts of account making and confiding and the dialectics in relationships as useful in understanding the behavior of people in these situations. Aside from the practical issue of availability of men in this age range for interested women, the study also points to the issue of why some people conclude that they are so devoted to the memories of the qualities of lost others that they will not pursue new partners.

## ▶ Conclusions and Future Directions

We believe that work on loss and bereavement in close relationships is an extremely timely topic in light of the great numbers of aging baby boomers and the extension of the life course for many people. Undoubtedly, counselors and therapists will see more and more clients who present their stories of loss and pain associated with loves lost to divorce or dissolution and death. Our review, our analysis, and the study reported point to many directions for further research. Prominent among the gaps in the literature are the two following avenues of work. First, we need comparisons of different types of loss across people at different developmental stages, in different socioeconomic situations, and in different cultures. Second, we need further and more systematic examinations of the linkages between people's close relationship losses and quests for love at midlife and beyond.

How can counselors and practitioners make use of the ideas and findings discussed in this chapter? The most important message from this work to the applied worker is that many people in their senior years might be simultaneously working on the processes of grieving the loss of close others while also searching for others with whom to have romantic closeness. This "juggling of grief and romantic yearnings," as we have termed it, can be the source of major conflict and ambivalence on the part of individuals. They might find balance difficult to achieve, particularly if their current close others do not endorse their dual quests.

In these situations, counselors and practitioners can assure the individuals that both quests are natural, a part of the lives of many senior persons, and may be undertaken without guilt. As our respondents suggest, couples can continue to think and have feelings about their lost loved ones and, at the same time, work to have strong current relationships. We believe that success in this dialectic venture can be attained by people's mutual respect for diverse histories of love relationships and recognition of the continuity of these histories throughout people's lives.

Scholars and practitioners who are concerned with the whole patterns and passages of people's lives must become more sophisticated about the intricately woven threads of adults' loves and losses. These threads and their varied fabrics are only vaguely understood at present.

# References

Aboud, F. E., & Mendelson, M. J. (1996). Determinants of friendship selection and quality: Developmental perspectives. In W. M. Bukowski, A. F. Newcomb, & W. W. Hartup (Eds.), *The company they keep: Friendship in childhood and adolescence* (pp. 87-112). Cambridge, UK: Cambridge University Press.

Abramovitch, R., Corter, C., & Pepler, D. J. (1980). Observations of mixed-sex sibling dyads. *Child Development, 51,* 1268-1271.

Acitelli, L. (1988). When spouses talk to each other about their relationship. *Journal of Social and Personal Relationships, 5,* 185-199.

Acitelli, L. K. (1996). The neglected links between marital support and marital satisfaction. In G. R. Pierce, B. R. Sarason, & I. G. Sarason (Eds.), *Handbook of social support and the family* (pp. 83-104). New York: Plenum.

Acker, M., & Davis, K. E. (1992). Intimacy, passion and commitment in adult romantic relationships: A test of the triangular theory of love. *Journal of Social and Personal Relationships, 9,* 21-50.

Ackerman, C. (1963). Affiliations: Structural determination of differential divorce rates. *American Sociological Review, 69,* 13-20.

Acock, A. C., & Demo, D. H. (1994). *Family diversity and well-being.* Thousand Oaks, CA: Sage.

Adams, B. N. (1986). *The family: A sociological interpretation.* San Diego: Harcourt Brace Jovanovich.

Adams, J. S. (1965). Inequity in social exchange. In L. Berkowitz (Ed.), *Advances in experimental social psychology* (Vol. 2, pp. 267-299). New York: Academic Press.

Adams, R. G. (1989). Conceptual and methodological issues in studying friendships of older adults. In R. G. Adams & R. Blieszner (Eds.), *Older adult friendship: Structure and process* (pp. 17-41). Newbury Park, CA: Sage.

Adams, R. G., & Allan, G. (1998a). Contextualizing friendship. In R. G. Adams & G. Allan (Eds.), *Placing friendship in context* (pp. 1-17). New York: Cambridge University Press.

Adams, R. G., & Allan, G. (Eds.). (1998b). *Placing friendship in context.* Cambridge, UK: Cambridge University Press.

Adams, R. G., & Blieszner, R. (1993). Resources for friendship intervention. *Journal of Sociology and Social Welfare, 20,* 159-175.

Adams, R. G., & Blieszner, R. (1994). An integrative conceptual framework for friendship research. *Journal of Social and Personal Relationships, 11,* 163-184.

Adams, R. G., & Blieszner, R. (1995). Aging well with friends and family. *American Behavioral Scientist, 39,* 209-224.

Adams, R. G., & Blieszner, R. (1998). Structural predictors of problematic friendships in later life. *Personal Relationships, 5,* 439-447.

Afifi, W. A., Guerrero, L. K., & Egland, K. L. (1994, May). *Maintenance behaviors in same- and opposite-sex friendships: Connections to gender, relational closeness, and equity issues.* Paper presented at the International Network on Personal Relationships Conference, Iowa City, IA.

Agger, B. (1998). *Critical social theories.* Boulder, CO: Westview.

Ahrons, C. (1994). *The good divorce.* New York: HarperCollins.

Ainsworth, M. D. S. (1989). Attachments beyond infancy. *American Psychologist, 44,* 709-716.

Ainsworth, M. D. S., Blehar, M. S., Waters, E., & Wall, S. (1978). *Patterns of attachment: A psychological study of the Strange Situation.* Hillsdale, NJ: Lawrence Erlbaum.

Alexander, J. F. (1973). Defensive and supportive communication in normal and deviant families. *Journal of Consulting and Clinical Psychology, 40,* 223-231.

Allan, G. (1989). *Friendship: Developing a sociological perspective.* London: Harvester Wheatsheaf.

Allen, J. P., Hauser, S. T., Bell, K. L., & O'Connor, T. G. (1994). Longitudinal assessment of autonomy and relatedness in adolescent-family interactions as predictors of adolescent ego development and self-esteem. *Child Development, 65,* 179-194.

Allen, J. P., & Land, D. J. (1999). Attachment in adolescence. In J. Cassidy & P. R. Shaver (Eds.), *Handbook of attachment: Theory, research, and clinical applications* (pp. 319-335). New York: Guilford.

Allen, K. R., (1989). *Single women/family ties: Life histories of older women.* Newbury Park, CA: Sage.

Allen, K. R. (2000). A conscious and inclusive family studies. *Journal of Marriage and the Family, 62,* 79-92.

Allen, K. R., Blieszner, R., Roberto, K. A., Farnsworth, E. B., & Wilcox, K. L. (1999). Older adults and their children: Family patterns of structural diversity. *Family Relations, 48,* 151-157.

Allen, K. R., & Demo, D. H. (1995). The families of lesbians and gay men: A new frontier in family research. *Journal of Marriage and the Family, 57,* 111-127.

Allen, K. R., Demo, D. H., Walker, A. J., & Acock, A. C. (1996, November). *Older parents of gay and lesbian adult children.* Paper presented at the annual meeting of the National Council on Family Relations, Kansas City, MO.

Almeida, D., & Galambos, N. (1991). Examining father involvement and the quality of father-adolescent relations. *Journal of Research on Adolescence, 1,* 155-172.

Allport, G. W. (1979). *The nature of prejudice.* Reading, MA: Addison-Wesley. (Original work published 1954)

Altman, I., & Taylor, D. A. (1973). *Social penetration: The development of interpersonal relationships.* New York: Holt, Rinehart & Winston.

Altman, I., Vinsel, A., & Brown, B. H. (1981). Dialectic conceptions in social psychology: An application to social penetration and privacy regulation. In L. Berkowitz (Ed.), *Advances in experimental social psychology* (Vol. 14, pp. 107-160). San Diego: Academic Press.

Amato, P. R. (1993). Family structure, family process, and family ideology. *Journal of Marriage and the Family, 55,* 50-54.

Amato, P. R. (2000). Diversity within single-parent families. In D. H. Demo, K. A. Allen, & M. A. Fine (Eds.), *Handbook of family diversity* (pp. 149-172). New York: Oxford University Press.

Amato, P. R., & Booth, A. (1996). A prospective study of divorce and parent-child relationships. *Journal of Marriage and the Family, 58,* 356-365.

Amato, P. R., & Keith, B. (1991a). Parental divorce and adult well-being: A meta-analysis. *Journal of Marriage and the Family, 53,* 43-58.

Amato, P. R., & Keith, B. (1991b). Parental divorce and the well-being of children: A meta-analysis. *Psychological Bulletin, 110,* 26-46.

Amato, P. R., & Rezac, S. J. (1994). Contact with nonresident parents, interparental conflict, and children's behavior. *Journal of Family Issues, 15,* 191-207.

Ambert, A., Adler, P. A., Adler, P., & Detzner, D. R. (1995). Understanding and evaluating qualitative research. *Journal of Marriage and the Family, 57,* 879-893.

Andersen, P. A. (1993). Cognitive schemata in personal relationships. In S. Duck (Ed.), *Individuals in relationships* (pp. 1-29). Newbury Park, CA: Sage.

Andersen, P. A. (1999). *Nonverbal communication: Forms and functions.* Mountain View, CA: Mayfield.

Andersen, P. A., Eloy, S. V., Guerrero, L. K., & Spitzberg, B. H. (1995). Romantic jealousy and relational satisfaction: A look at the impact of jealousy experience and expression. *Communication Reports, 8,* 77-85.

Andersen, P. A., & Guerrero, L. K. (1989, February). *Avoiding communication: Verbal and nonverbal dimensions of defensiveness.* Paper presented at the annual meeting of the Western States Communication Association, Spokane, WA.

Andersen, P. A., & Guerrero, L. K. (1998a). The bright side of relational communication: Interpersonal warmth as a social emotion. In P. A. Andersen & L. K. Guerrero (Eds.), *Handbook of communication and emotion: Research, theory, applications, and contexts* (pp. 303-329). San Diego: Academic Press.

Andersen, P. A., & Guerrero, L. K. (1998b). Principles of communication and emotion in social interaction. In P. A. Andersen & L. K. Guerrero (Eds.), *Handbook of communication and emotion: Research, theory, applications, and contexts* (pp. 49-96). San Diego: Academic Press.

Anderson, J., & Ronnberg, J. (1997). Cued memory collaboration: Effects of friendship and type of retrieval cue. *European Journal of Cognitive Psychology, 9,* 273-287.

Anderson, J., & White, G. (1986). An empirical investigation of interactive and relationship patterns in functional and dysfunctional nuclear families and stepfamilies. *Family Process, 25,* 407-422.

Anderson, T. B., Earle, J. R., & Longino, C. F. (1997). The therapeutic role in late life: Husbands, wives, and couples. *International Journal of Aging and Human Development, 45,* 49-65.

Andersson, L. (1998). Loneliness research and intervention: A review of the literature. *Aging and Mental Health, 2,* 264-274.

Anglin, K., & Holtzworth-Munroe, A. (1997). Comparing the responses of maritally violent and nonviolent spouses to problematic marital and nonmarital situations: Are the skills deficits of physically aggressive husbands and wives global? *Journal of Family Psychology, 11,* 301-313.

Antonucci, T. C., & Akiyama, H. (1995). Convoys of social relations: Family and friendships within a life span context. In R. Blieszner & V. H. Bedford (Eds.), *Handbook of aging and the family* (pp. 355-371). Westport, CT: Greenwood.

Apt, C., & Hurlbert, D. F. (1994). What constitutes sexual satisfaction? Direction for future research. *Journal of Sexual and Marital Therapy, 9,* 285-289.

Archer, R. L., & Burleson, J. A. (1980). The effects of timing of self-disclosure on attraction and reciprocity. *Journal of Personality and Social Psychology, 38,* 120-130.

Argyle, M., & Dean, J. (1965). Eye contact, distance, and affiliation. *Sociometry, 28,* 289-304.

Argyle, M., & Henderson, M. (1984). The rules of friendship. *Journal of Social and Personal Relationships, 1,* 211-237.

Argyle, M., & Henderson, M. (1985). The rules of relationships. In S. Duck & D. Perlman (Eds.), *Understanding personal relationships: An interdisciplinary approach* (pp. 63-84). London: Sage.

Arias, I. (1995, October). *The impact of psychological abuse on battered women.* Paper presented at the National Violence Prevention Conference of the Centers for Disease Control and Prevention, Des Moines, IA.

Aries, E. (1998). Gender differences in interaction: A reexamination. In D. Canary & K. Dindia (Eds.), *Sex differences and similarities in communication* (pp. 65-81). Mahwah, NJ: Lawrence Erlbaum.

Aries, E., & Johnson, F. (1983). Close friendship in adulthood: Conversational content between same-sex friends. *Sex Roles, 9,* 1183-1196.

Aries, P. (1962). *Centuries of childhood: A social history of family life* (R. Baldick, Trans.). New York: Vintage Books.

Aron, A., & Aron, E. N. (1986). *Love and the expansion of self: Understanding attraction and satisfaction.* New York: Hemisphere.

Aron, A., & Aron, E. N. (1991). Love and sexuality. In K. McKinney & S. Sprecher (Eds.), *Sexuality in close relationships* (pp. 25-48). Hillsdale, NJ: Lawrence Erlbaum.

Aron, A., & Aron, E. N. (1997). Self-expansion and including other in the self. In S. Duck (Ed.), *Handbook of personal relationships* (2nd ed., pp. 251-270). Chichester, UK: Wiley.

Aron, A., & Henkemeyer, L. (1995). Marital satisfaction and passionate love. *Journal of Social and Personal Relationships, 12,* 139-146.

Aron, A., & Westbay, L. (1996). Dimensions of the prototype of love. *Journal of Personality and Social Psychology, 70,* 535-551.

Aron, E. N., & Aron, A. (1996). Love and expansion of the self: The state of the model. *Personal Relationships, 3,* 45-58.

Arriaga, X. B., & Rusbult, C. E. (1998). Standing in my partner's shoes: Partner perspective taking and reactions to accommodative dilemmas. *Personality and Social Psychology Bulletin, 24,* 927-948.

Asher, S. R., & Coie, J. D. (Eds.). (1990). *Peer rejection in childhood.* New York: Cambridge University Press.

Asher, S. R., & Gottman, J. M. (1981). *The development of children's friendships.* New York: Cambridge University Press.

Asher, S. R., & Parker, J. G. (1989). The significance of peer relationship problems in childhood. In B. H. Schneider, G. Attili, J. Nadel, & R. P. Weissberg (Eds.), *Social competence in developmental perspective* (pp. 5-23). Dordrecht, Netherlands: Kluwer Academic.

Asher, S. R., Parker, J. G., & Walker, D. L. (1996). Distinguishing friendship from acceptance: Implications for intervention and assessment. In W. M. Bukowski, A. F. Newcomb, & W. W. Hartup (Eds.), *The company they keep: Friendship in childhood and adolescence* (pp. 366-405). New York: Cambridge University Press.

Astin, M. C., Lawrence, K. J., & Foy, D. W. (1993). Posttraumatic stress disorder among battered women: Risk and resiliency factors. *Violence and Victims, 8,* 17-28.

Atkinson, B., & Bell, N. (1986, March). *Attachment and autonomy in adolescence.* Paper presented at the annual meeting of the Society for Research on Adolescence, Madison, WI.

Atkinson, P. (1990). *The ethnographic imagination.* London: Routledge.

Attridge, M. (1994). Barriers to dissolution of romantic relationships. In D. J. Canary & L. Stafford (Eds.), *Communication and relational maintenance* (pp. 141-164). San Diego: Academic Press.

Atwater, L. (1982). *The extramarital connection.* New York: Irvington.

Aune, K. S., Aune, R. K., & Buller, D. B. (1994). The experience, expression, and perceived appropriateness of emotion across levels of relationship development. *Journal of Social Psychology, 134,* 141-150.

Aune, K. S., Buller, D. B., & Aune, R. K. (1996). Display rule development in romantic relationships: Emotion management and perceived appropriateness of emotions across relationship stages. *Human Communication Research, 23,* 115-143.

Austin J. T., & Vancouver J. B. (1996). Goal constructs in psychology: Structure, process, and content. *Psychological Bulletin, 120,* 338-375.

Austin, W., & Walster, E. (1974). Reactions to confirmations and disconfirmations of expectancies of equity and inequity. *Journal of Personality and Social Psychology, 30,* 208-213.

Avenevoli, S., Sessa, F. M., & Steinberg, L. (1999). Family structure, parenting practices, and adolescent adjustment: An ecological examination. In E. M. Hetherington (Ed.), *Coping with divorce, single parenting, and remarriage* (pp. 65-90). Mahwah, NJ: Lawrence Erlbaum.

Ayres, J. (1983). Strategies to maintain relationships: Their identification and perceived usage. *Communication Quarterly, 31,* 62-67.

Babchuk, N., & Bates, A. P. (1963). The primary relations of middle-class couples: A study of male dominance. *American Sociological Review, 28,* 377-384.

Babcock, J. C., Waltz, J., Jacobson, N. S., & Gottman, J. M. (1993). Power and violence: The relation between communication patterns, power discrepancies, and domestic violence. *Journal of Consulting and Clinical Psychology, 61,* 40-50.

Baber, K. M., & Allen, K. R. (1992). *Women and families: Feminist reconstructions.* New York: Guilford.

Backman, C. W., & Secord, P. F. (1959). The effect of perceived liking on interpersonal attraction. *Human Relations, 12,* 379-383.

Bailey, J. M., Gaulin, S., Agyei, Y., & Gladue, B. A. (1994). Effects of gender and sexual orientation on evolutionary relevant aspects of human mating. *Journal of Personality and Social Psychology, 66,* 1081-1093.

Bailey, J. M., Kim, P. Y., Hills, A., & Linsenmeier, J. A. W. (1997). Butch, femme, or straight acting? Partner preferences of gay men and lesbians. *Journal of Personality and Social Psychology, 73,* 960-973.

Bailey, W. C., Hendrick, C., & Hendrick, S. S. (1987). Relation of sex and gender role to love, sexual attitudes, and self-esteem. *Sex Roles, 16,* 637-648.

Bakeman, R. (1991). Analyzing categorical data. In B. M. Montgomery & S. Duck (Eds.), *Studying interpersonal interaction* (pp. 255-274). New York: Guilford.

Bakeman, R., & Quera, V. (1995). Log-linear approaches to lag-sequential analysis when consecutive codes may and cannot repeat. *Psychological Bulletin, 118,* 272-284.

Baker, R. (1996). *Sperm wars: The science of sex.* New York: Basic Books.

Bakhtin, M. M. (1981). *The dialogic imagination: Four essays by M. M. Bakhtin* (M. Holquist, Ed.; C. Emerson & M. Holquist, Trans.). Austin: University of Texas Press.

Baldwin, M. W., & Fehr, B. (1995). On the instability of attachment style ratings. *Personal Relationships, 2,* 247-261.

Baldwin, M. W., Fehr, B., Keedian, E., Seidel, M., & Thomson, D. W. (1993). An exploration of the relational schemata underlying attachment styles: Self-report and lexical decision approaches. *Personality and Social Psychology Bulletin, 19,* 746-754.

Baldwin, M. W., Keelan, J. P. R., Fehr, B., Enns, V., & Koh-Rangarajoo, E. (1996). Social-cognitive conceptualization of attachment working models: Availability and accessibility effects. *Journal of Personality and Social Psychology, 71,* 94-109.

Baltes, P. B., Lindenberger, U., & Staudinger, U. M. (1997). Life span theory in developmental psychology. In R. M. Lerner (Ed.), *Handbook of child psychology, Vol. 1: Theoretical models of human development* (5th ed., pp. 1029-1143). New York: John Wiley.

Bandura, A., & Walters, R. (1963). *Social learning and personality development.* New York: Holt, Rinehart & Winston.

Bank, S., & Kahn, M. D. (1975). Sisterhood-brotherhood is powerful: Sibling subsystems and family therapy. *Family Process, 14,* 311-337.

Banker, B. S., & Gaertner, S. L. (1996). Achieving stepfamily harmony: An intergroup relations approach. *Journal of Family Psychology, 12,* 310-325.

Barbee, A. P. (1990). Interactive coping: The cheering up process in close relationships. In S. Duck & R. Silver (Eds.), *Personal relationships and social support* (pp. 46-65). London: Sage.

Barbee, A. P. (1991, October). *The role of emotions and cognitions in the interactive coping process.* Paper presented at the meeting of the Society of Experimental Social Psychology, Columbus, OH.

Barbee, A. P., & Cunningham, M. R. (1995). An experimental approach to social support communications: Interactive coping in close relationships. *Communication Yearbook, 18,* 381-413.

Barbee, A. P., Cunningham, M. R., Allen, A., & Rowatt, T. (1999). *Effects of supervisor race, gender, and closeness on responses to problem employees.* Unpublished manuscript, University of Louisville.

Barbee, A. P., Cunningham, M. R., Shamblen, S. R., & Nezlek, J. (1999). *Giving and receiving social support: A diary study of interactive coping.* Unpublished manuscript, University of Louisville.

Barbee, A. P., Cunningham, M. R., Winstead, B. A., Derlega, V. J., Gulley, M. R., Yankeelov, P. A., & Druen, P. B. (1993). Effects of gender role expectations on the social support process. *Journal of Social Issues, 49*(3), 175-190.

Barbee, A. P., Derlega, V. J., Sherburne, S. P., & Grimshaw, A. (1998). Helpful and unhelpful forms of social support for HIV-positive individuals. In V. J. Derlega & A. P. Barbee (Eds.), *HIV and social interaction* (pp. 83-105). Thousand Oaks, CA: Sage.

Barbee, A. P., & Felice, T. L. (1991). *Summary of data from the Louisville Diary Study.* Unpublished manuscript, University of Louisville.

Barbee, A. P., Gulley, M. R., & Cunningham, M. R. (1990). Support seeking in close relationships. *Journal of Social and Personal Relationships, 7,* 531-540.

Barbee, A. P., Rowatt, T., & Cunningham, M. R. (1998). When a friend is in need: Feelings about seeking, giving, and receiving social support. In P. A. Anderson & L. K. Guerrero (Eds.), *Handbook of communication and emotion: Research, theory, applications, and contexts* (pp. 281-301). San Diego: Academic Press.

Barbee, A. P., & Yankeelov, P. A. (1992, June). *Social support as a mechanism for relationship maintenance.* Paper presented at the meeting of the International Society of the Study of Personal Relationships, Orono, ME.

Barber, B. L., & Lyons, J. M. (1994). Family processes and adolescent adjustment in intact and remarried families. *Journal of Youth and Adolescence, 23,* 421-436.

Barkham, M., & Shapiro, D. A. (1986). Counselor verbal response modes and experienced empathy. *Journal of Counseling Psychology, 33,* 3-10.

Barnes, G. M., & Farrell, M. P. (1992). Parental support and control as predictors of adolescent drinking, delinquency, and related problem behaviors. *Journal of Marriage and the Family, 54,* 763-776.

Barnes, M. K., Harvey, J. H., Carlson, H., & Haig, J. (1996). The relativity of grief: Differential adaptation reactions of younger and older persons. *Journal of Personal & Interpersonal Loss, 1,* 375-392.

Barnett, O. W., Miller-Perrin, C. L., & Perrin, R. D. (1997). *Family violence across the life span.* Thousand Oaks, CA: Sage.

Barrera, M. (1986). Distinctions between social support concepts, measures, and models. *American Journal of Community Psychology, 14,* 413-455.

Barrera, M., Chassin, L., & Rogosch, F. (1993). Effects of social support and conflict on adolescent children of alcoholic and nonalcoholic fathers. *Journal of Personality and Social Psychology, 64,* 602-612.

Barrera, M., & Li, S. A. (1996). The relation of family support to adolescents' psychological distress and behavior problems. In G. R. Pierce, B. R. Sarason, & I. G. Sarason (Eds.), *Handbook of social support and the family* (pp. 313-343). New York: Plenum.

Barrera, M., Sandler, I. N., & Ramsey, T. B. (1981). Preliminary development of a scale of social support: Studies on college students. *Journal of Community Psychology, 9,* 435-447.

Barrett, K. C. (1995). A functionalist approach to shame and guilt. In J. P. Tangney & K. W. Fischer (Eds.), *Self-conscious emotions: The psychology of shame, guilt, embarrassment, and pride* (pp. 25-63). New York: Guilford.

Bar Tal, D., & Frieze, I. H. (1977). Achievement motivation for males and females as a determinant of attributions for success and failure. *Sex Roles, 3,* 301-314.

Bartholomew, K. (1990). Avoidance of intimacy: An attachment perspective. *Journal of Social and Personal Relationships, 7,* 147-178.

Bartholomew, K. (1997). Adult attachment processes: Individual and couple perspectives. *British Journal of Medical Psychology, 70,* 249-263.

Bartholomew, K., & Horowitz, L. M. (1991). Attachment styles among young adults: A test of a four category model. *Journal of Personality and Social Psychology, 61,* 226-244.

Bartholomew, K., & Shaver, P. R. (1998). Methods of assessing adult attachment: Do they converge? In J. A. Simpson & W. S. Rholes (Eds.), *Attachment theory and close relationships* (pp. 25-45). New York: Guilford.

Baruch, G. K., & Barnett, R. C. (1986). Consequences of fathers' participation in family work: Parents' role strain and well-being. *Journal of Personality and Social Psychology, 51,* 983-992.

Bass, D. M., McClendon, M. J., Brennan, P. F., & McCarthy, C. (1998). The buffering effect of computer support network on caregiver strain. *Journal of Aging and Health, 10,* 20-43.

Bass, D. M., Noelker, L. S., Townsend, A. L., & Deimling, G. T. (1990). Losing a relative: Perceptual differences between spouses and adult children. *Omega, 21,* 21-40.

Bass, L. A., & Stein, C. H. (1997). Comparing the structure and stability of network ties using the Social Support Questionnaire and the Social Network List. *Journal of Social and Personal Relationships, 14,* 123-132.

Batson, C. D. (1991). *The altruism question: Toward a social-psychological answer.* Hillsdale, NJ: Lawrence Erlbaum.

Batson, C. D. (1993). Communal and exchange relationships: What is the difference? *Personality and Social Psychology Bulletin, 19,* 677-683.

Baumeister, R. F., & Leary, M. R. (1995). The need to belong: Desire for interpersonal attachments as a fundamental human motivation. *Psychological Bulletin, 117,* 497-529.

Baumeister, R. F., Stillwell, A. M., & Heatherton, T. F. (1994). Guilt: An interpersonal approach. *Psychological Bulletin, 115,* 243-267.

Baxter, L. A. (1979). Self-disclosure as a relationship disengagement strategy: An exploratory investigation. *Human Communication Research, 5,* 215-222.

Baxter, L. A. (1982). Strategies for ending relationships: Two studies. *Western Journal of Speech Communication, 46,* 223-241.

Baxter, L. A. (1984). Trajectories of relationship disengagement. *Journal of Social and Personal Relationships, 1,* 29-48.

Baxter, L. A. (1985). Accomplishing relationship disengagement. In S. Duck & D. Perlman (Eds.), *Understanding personal relationships: An interdisciplinary approach* (pp. 243-265). London: Sage.

Baxter, L. A. (1987). Symbols of relationship identity in relationship cultures. *Journal of Social and Personal Relationships, 4,* 261-280.

Baxter, L. A. (1988). A dialectical perspective on communication strategies in relationship development. In S. Duck (Ed.), *Handbook of personal relationships: Theory, research, and interventions* (pp. 257-273). Chichester, UK: Wiley.

Baxter, L. A. (1990). Dialectical contradictions in relationship development. *Journal of Social and Personal Relationships, 7,* 69-88.

Baxter, L. A. (1994). A dialogic approach to relationship maintenance. In D. J. Canary & L. Stafford (Eds.), *Communication and relational maintenance* (pp. 233-254). San Diego: Academic Press.

Baxter, L. A., & Bullis, C. (1986). Turning points in developing romantic relationships. *Human Communication Research, 12,* 469-493.

Baxter, L. A., & Montgomery, B. M. (1996). *Relating: Dialogues and dialectics.* New York: Guilford.

Baxter, L. A., & Montgomery, B. M. (1997). Rethinking communication in personal relationships from a dialectical perspective. In S. Duck (Ed.), *Handbook of personal relationships: Theory, research, and interventions* (2nd ed., pp. 325-349). Chichester, UK: Wiley.

Baxter, L. A., & Philpott, J. (1982). Attribution-based strategies for initiating and terminating relationships. *Communication Quarterly, 30,* 217-224.

Baxter, L. A., & Simon, E. P. (1993). Relationship maintenance strategies and dialectical contradiction in personal relationships. *Journal of Social and Personal Relationships, 10,* 225-242.

Baxter, L. A., & Widenmann, S. (1993). Revealing and not revealing the status of romantic relationships to social networks. *Journal of Social and Personal Relationships, 10,* 321-337.

Baxter, L. A., & Wilmot, W. W. (1985). Taboo topics in close relationships. *Journal of Social and Personal Relationships, 2,* 253-269.

Baxter, L. A., & Wilmot, W. (1986). Interaction characteristics of disengaging, stable, and growing relationships. In R. Gilmour & S. W. Duck (Eds.), *The emerging field of personal relationships* (pp. 145-159). Hillsdale, NJ: Lawrence Erlbaum.

Baydar, N. (1988). Effects of parental separation and reentry into union on the emotional well-being of children. *Journal of Marriage and the Family, 50,* 967-981.

Baydar, N., & Brooks-Gunn, J. (1998). Profiles of grandmothers who help care for their grandchildren in the United States. *Family Relations, 47,* 385-393.

Beach, S. R. H. (1996). Marital therapy in the treatment of depression. In C. Mundt, M. J. Goldstein, K. Hahlweg, & P. Fiedler (Eds.), *Interpersonal factors in the origin and course of affective disorders* (pp. 341-361). London: Gaskell Academic.

Beach, S. R. H., Brooks, A. E., Nelson, G. M., & Bakeman, R. (1993, November). *The relationship between aggressive and depressive behavior revisited.* Paper presented at the annual meeting of the Association for the Advancement of Behavior Therapy, Atlanta, GA.

Beach, S. R. H., Hanwood, E. M., Horan, P. M., Katz, J., Blum, T. C., Martin, J. K., & Roman, P. M. (1995, November). *Marital effects on depression: Measuring the longitudinal relationship.* Paper presented at the annual meeting of the Association for the Advancement of Behavior Therapy, Washington, DC.

Beach, S. R. H., Martin, J. K., Blum, T. C., & Roman, P. M. (1993a). Effects of marital and co-worker relationships on negative affect: Testing the central role of marriage. *American Journal of Family Therapy, 21,* 312-322.

Beach, S. R. H., Martin, J. K., Blum, T. C., & Roman, P. M. (1993b). Subclinical depression and role fulfillment in domestic settings: Spurious relationships, imagined problems, or real effects? *Journal of Psychopathology and Behavioral Assessment, 15,* 113-128.

Beach, S. R. H., & O'Leary, K. D. (1992). Treating depression in the context of marital discord: Outcome and predictors of response for marital therapy versus cognitive therapy. *Behavior Therapy, 23,* 507-528.

Beach, S. R. H., Smith, D. A., & Fincham, F. D. (1994). Marital interventions for depression: Empirical foundation and future prospects. *Applied and Preventive Psychology, 3,* 233-250.

Beall, A. E., & Sternberg, R. J. (1995). The social construction of love. *Journal of Social and Personal Relationships, 12,* 417-438.

Beals, K., & Peplau, L. A. (1999). *The quality of lesbian relationships: Effects of disclosure and community involvement.* Unpublished manuscript, University of California, Los Angeles.

Beck, A. (1988). *Love is never enough.* New York: Harper & Row.

Becker, C. (1987). Friendships between women: A phenomenological study of best friends. *Journal of Phenomenological Psychology, 18,* 59-72.

Bedford, V. H. (1992). Memories of parental favoritism and the quality of parent-child ties in adulthood. *Journal of Gerontology: Social Sciences, 47,* S149-S155.

Bedford, V. H. (1998). Sibling relationship troubles and well-being in middle and old age. *Family Relations, 47,* 369-376.

Bedford, V. H., & Blieszner, R. (1997). Personal relationships in later life families. In S. Duck (Ed.), *Handbook of personal relationships* (2nd ed., pp. 523-539). New York: John Wiley.

Begley, S. (1995, March 27). Gray matters. *Newsweek,* pp. 48-54.

Bell, A. P., & Weinberg, M. A. (1978). *Homosexualities: A study of diversity among men and women.* New York: Simon & Schuster.

Bell, R. A., & Daly, J. A. (1984). The affinity-seeking function in communication. *Communication Monographs, 51,* 91-115.

Bell, R. A., Daly, J. A., & Gonzalez, C. (1987). Affinity-maintenance in marriage and its relationship to women's marital satisfaction. *Journal of Marriage and the Family, 49,* 445-454.

Bell, R. A., & Healey, J. G. (1992). Idiomatic communication and interpersonal solidarity in friends' relational cultures. *Human Communication Research, 18,* 307-335.

Bendtschneider, L., & Duck, S. (1993). What's yours is mine and what's mine is yours: Couple friends. In P. J. Kalbfleisch (Ed.), *Interpersonal communication: Evolving interpersonal relationships* (pp. 169-186). Hillsdale, NJ: Lawrence Erlbaum.

Benenson, J. F. (1994). Ages four to six years: Changes in the structures of play networks of girls and boys. *Merrill-Palmer Quarterly, 40,* 478-487.

Benenson, J. F., Apostoleris, N. H., & Parnass, J. (1997). Age and sex differences in dyadic and group interaction. *Developmental Psychology, 33,* 538-543.

Bengtson, V., Rosenthal, C., & Burton, L. (1996). Paradoxes of families and aging. In R. H. Binstock & L. K. George (Eds.), *Handbook of aging and the social sciences* (4th ed., pp. 263-287). San Diego: Academic Press.

Bengtson, V. L., & Roberts, R. E. L. (1991). Intergenerational solidarity in aging families: An example of formal theory construction. *Journal of Marriage and the Family, 53,* 856-870.

Bengtson, V. L., & Schaie, K. W. (Eds.). (1999). *Handbook of theories of aging.* New York: Springer.

Benjamin, J. (1988). *The bonds of love.* New York: Pantheon.

Berg, J. H., & Archer, R. L. (1980). Disclosure or concern: A second look at liking for the norm breaker. *Journal of Personality, 48,* 245-257.

Berger, C. R. (1997). *Planning strategic interaction: Attaining goals through communicative action.* Mahwah, NJ: Lawrence Erlbaum.

Berger, C. R., & Calabrese, R. J. (1975). Some explorations in initial interactions and beyond: Toward a developmental theory of interpersonal communication. *Human Communication Research, 1,* 99-112.

Berger, P., & Luckmann, T. (1966). *The social construction of reality: An essay in the sociology of knowledge.* New York: Doubleday.

Berger, R. (1995). Three types of stepfamilies. *Journal of Divorce and Remarriage, 24,* 35-50.

Berger, R. M. (1990a). Men together: Understanding the gay couple. *Journal of Homosexuality, 19*(3), 31-49.

Berger, R. M. (1990b). Passing: Impact on the quality of same-sex couple relationships. *Social Work, 35,* 328-332.

Bergner, R., & Bergner, L. (1990). Sexual misunderstanding: A descriptive formulation. *Psychotherapy, 27,* 464-467.

Berk, S. (1985). *The gender factory.* New York: Plenum.

Berman, W. H., Marcus, L., & Berman, E. R. (1994). Attachment in marital relations. In M. B. Sperling & W. H. Berman (Eds.), *Attachment in adults: Clinical and developmental perspectives* (pp. 204-231). New York: Guilford.

Berndt, T. J. (1985). Prosocial behavior between friends in middle childhood and early adolescence. *Journal of Early Adolescence, 5,* 307-317.

Berndt, T. J. (1996). Exploring the effects of friendship quality on social development. In W. M. Bukowski, A. F. Newcomb, & W. W. Hartup (Eds.), *The company they keep: Friendship in childhood and adolescence* (pp. 346-365). New York: Cambridge University Press.

Berndt, T. J., & Hanna, N. A. (1995). Intimacy and self-disclosure in friendships. In K. J. Rotenberg (Ed.), *Disclosure processes in children and adolescence* (pp. 57-77). New York: Cambridge University Press.

Berndt, T. J., & Hoyle, S. G. (1985). Stability and change in childhood and adolescent friendships. *Developmental Psychology, 21,* 1007-1015.

Berndt, T. J., & Keefe, K. (1995). Friends' influence on adolescents' adjustment to school. *Child Development, 66,* 1312-1329.

Berndt, T. J., & Keefe, K. (1996). Friends' influence on social adjustment: A motivational analysis. In J. Juvonen & K. R. Wentzel (Eds.), *Social motivation: Understanding children's school adjustment* (pp. 248-278). New York: Cambridge University Press.

Berndt, T. J., & Ladd, G. W. (Eds.). (1989). *Peer relationships in child development.* New York: John Wiley.

Berndt, T. J., & Perry, T. B. (1986). Children's perceptions of friendships as supportive relationships. *Developmental Psychology, 22,* 640-648.

Berry, J. W., Poortinga, Y. H., Segall, M. H., & Dasen, P. R. (1992). *Cross-cultural psychology: Research and applications.* Cambridge, UK: Cambridge University Press.

Berscheid, E. (1983). Emotion. In H. H. Kelly, E. Berscheid, A. Christensen, J. H. Harvey, T. L. Huston, G. Levinger, E. McClintock, L. A. Peplau, & D. R. Peterson (Eds.), *Close relationships* (pp. 110-168). San Francisco: Freeman.

Berscheid, E. (1985). Interpersonal attraction. In G. Lindzey & E. Aronson (Eds.), *Handbook of social psychology* (3rd ed., Vol. 2, pp. 413-484). New York: Random House. ˙

Berscheid, E. (1988). Some comments on love's anatomy: Or whatever happened to old-fashioned lust? In R. J. Sternberg & M. L. Barnes (Eds.), *The psychology of love* (pp. 359-374). New Haven, CT: Yale University Press.

Berscheid, E., & Meyers, S. A. (1996). A social categorical approach to a question about love. *Personal Relationships, 3,* 19-43.

Berscheid, E., & Reis, H. T. (1998). Attraction and close relationships. In D. T. Gilbert, S. T. Fiske, & G. Lindzey (Eds.), *Handbook of social psychology* (4th ed., Vol. 2, pp. 193-281). New York: McGraw-Hill.

Berscheid, E., & Walster, E. (1969). *Interpersonal attraction.* Reading, MA: Addison-Wesley.

Berscheid, E., & Walster, E. (1974). A little bit about love. In T. L. Huston (Ed.), *Foundations of interpersonal attraction* (pp. 355-381). New York: Academic Press.

Berscheid, E., & Walster, E. H. (1978). *Interpersonal attraction* (2nd ed.). Reading, MA: Addison-Wesley.

Bettor, L., Hendrick, S. S., & Hendrick, C. (1995). Gender and sexual standards in dating relationships. *Personal Relationships, 2,* 359-369.

Betzig, L. (1989). Causes of conjugal dissolution: A cross-cultural study. *Current Anthropology, 30,* 676-694.

Bianchi, S. M. (1995). The changing demographic and socioeconomic characteristics of single-parent families. *Marriage and Family Review, 20,* 71-97.

Biernat, M., & Wortman, C. B. (1991). Sharing of home responsibilities between professionally employed women and their husbands. *Journal of Personality and Social Psychology, 60,* 840-860.

Bigelow, B. J., & LaGaipa, J. L. (1975). Children's written descriptions of friendship. *Developmental Psychology, 11,* 857-858.

Biglan, A., Lewin, L., & Hops, H. (1990). A contextual approach to the problem of aversive practices in families. In G. R. Patterson (Ed.), *Depression and aggression in family interaction* (pp. 103-129). Hillsdale, NJ: Lawrence Erlbaum.

Biglan, A., Rothlind, J., Hops, H., & Sherman, L. (1989). Impact of distressed and aggressive behavior. *Journal of Abnormal Psychology, 98,* 218-228.

Birch, S. H., & Ladd, G. W. (1996). Interpersonal relationships in the school environment and children's early school adjustment: The role of teachers and peers. In J. Juvonen & K. R. Wentzel (Eds.), *Social*

*motivation: Understanding children's school adjustment* (pp. 199-225). New York: Cambridge University Press.

Bird, C., & Ross, C. (1993). Houseworkers and paid workers: Qualities of the work and effects on personal control. *Journal of Marriage and the Family, 55,* 913-925.

Bishay, N. R., Petersen, N., & Tarrier, N. (1989). An uncontrolled study of cognitive therapy for morbid jealousy. *British Journal of Psychiatry, 154,* 386-389.

Blair, S., & Johnson, M. (1992). Wives' perceptions of the fairness of the division of household labor: The intersection of housework and ideology. *Journal of Marriage and the Family, 54,* 570-581.

Blasband, D., & Peplau, L. A. (1985). Sexual exclusivity versus openness in gay male couples. *Archives of Sexual Behavior, 14,* 395-412.

Blea, I. I. (1992). *La Chicana and the intersection of race, class, and gender.* New York: Praeger.

Blieszner, R. (1994a). Close relationships over time. In A. L. Weber & J. H. Harvey (Eds.), *Perspectives on close relationships* (pp. 1-17). Boston: Allyn & Bacon.

Blieszner, R. (1994b). Feminist perspectives on friendship: Intricate tapestries. In D. L. Sollie & L. A. Leslie (Eds.), *Gender, families, and close relationships: Feminist research journeys* (pp. 120-141). Thousand Oaks, CA: Sage.

Blieszner, R. (1995). Friendship processes and well-being in the later years of life: Implications for interventions. *Journal of Geriatric Psychiatry, 28,* 165-183.

Blieszner, R., & Adams, R. G. (1992). *Adult friendship.* Newbury Park, CA: Sage.

Blieszner, R., & Adams, R. G. (1998). Problems with friends in old age. *Journal of Aging Studies, 12,* 223-238.

Blieszner, R., & Bedford, V. H. (Eds.). (1995). *Handbook of aging and the family.* Westport, CT: Greenwood.

Blieszner, R., & Hamon, R. K. (1992). Filial responsibility: Attitudes, motivators, and behaviors. In J. W. Dwyer & R. T. Coward (Eds.), *Gender, families, and elder care* (pp. 105-119). Newbury Park, CA: Sage.

Block, J. H., Block, J., & Gjerde, P. F. (1986). The personality of children prior to divorce: A prospective study. *Child Development, 57,* 827-840.

Blos, P. (1979). *The adolescent passage.* New York: International Universities Press.

Blumstein, P., & Schwartz, P. (1977). Bisexuality: Some social psychological issues. *Journal of Social Issues, 33*(2), 30-45.

Blumstein, P., & Schwartz, P. (1983). *American couples: Money, work, sex.* New York: William Morrow.

Bochner, A. P. (1984). The functions of human communication in interpersonal bonding. In C. C. Arnold & J. W. Bowers (Eds.), *Handbook of rhetorical and communication theory* (pp. 544-621). Boston: Allyn & Bacon.

Bochner, A. P., & Eisenberg, E. M. (1987). Family process: Systems perspectives. In C. R. Berger & S. H. Chaffee (Eds.), *Handbook of communication science* (pp. 540-563). Newbury Park, CA: Sage.

Bochner, A. P., Ellis, C., & Tillman-Healy, L. M. (1997). Relationships as stories. In S. Duck (Ed.), *Handbook of personal relationships: Theory, research, and interventions* (2nd ed., pp. 307-324). Chichester, UK: Wiley.

Boeringer, S. B., Shehan, C. L., & Akers, R. L. (1991). Social context and social learning in sexual coercion and aggression: Assessing the contribution of fraternity membership. *Family Relations, 40,* 58-64.

Bogdan, R. C., & Biklen, S. K. (1998). *Qualitative research in education* (3rd ed.). Boston: Allyn & Bacon.

Bogenscheider, K. (1997). Parental involvement in adolescent schooling: A proximal process with transcontextual validity. *Journal of Marriage and the Family, 59,* 718-733.

Boland, J. P., & Follingstad, D. R. (1987). The relationship between communication and marital satisfaction: A review. *Journal of Sex and Marital Therapy, 13,* 286-313.

Bolger, N., & Zukerman, A. (1995). A framework for studying personality in the stress process. *Journal of Personality and Social Psychology, 69,* 890-902.

Bookwala, J., & Zdaniuk, B. (1998). Adult attachment styles and aggressive behavior within dating relationships. *Journal of Social and Personal Relationships, 15,* 175-190.

Booth, A., & Edwards, J. N. (1992). Starting over: Why remarriages are more unstable. *Journal of Family Issues, 13,* 179-194.

Bornstein, R. F. (1989). Exposure and affect: Overview and meta-analysis of research, 1968-1987. *Psychological Bulletin, 106,* 265-289.

Boss, P. G., Doherty, W. J., LaRossa, R., Schumm, W. R., & Steinmetz, S. K. (1993). *Sourcebook of family theories and methods.* New York: Plenum.

Bott, E. (1971). *Families and social networks* (2nd ed.). New York: Free Press.

Bowen, M. (1978). *Family therapy in clinical practice.* Northvale, NJ: Jason Aronson.

Bowlby, J. (1969). *Attachment and loss, Vol. 1: Attachment.* New York: Basic Books.

Bowlby, J. (1973). *Attachment and loss, Vol. 2: Separation: Anxiety and anger.* New York: Basic Books.

Bowlby, J. (1979). *The making and breaking of affectional bonds.* London: Tavistock.

Bowlby, J. (1980). *Attachment and loss, Vol. 3: Loss: Sadness and depression.* New York: Basic Books.

Bradbury, T. N. (Ed.). (1998). *The developmental course of marital dysfunction.* New York: Cambridge University Press.

Bradbury, T. N., & Lawrence, E. (1999). Physical aggression and the longitudinal course of newlywed marriage. In X. Arriaga & S. Oskamp (Eds.), *Violence in intimate relationships* (pp. 181-202). Thousand Oaks, CA: Sage.

Bradford, L., & Petronio, S. (1998). Strategic embarrassment: The culprit of emotion. In P. A. Andersen & L. K. Guerrero (Eds.), *Handbook of communication and emotion: Research, theory, applications, and contexts* (pp. 99-118). San Diego: Academic Press.

Braiker, H. B., & Kelley, H. H. (1979). Conflict in the development of close relationships. In R. L. Burgess & T. L. Huston (Eds.), *Social exchange in developing relationships* (pp. 135-168). New York: Academic Press.

Braithwaite, D. O., & Baxter, L. A. (1995). "I do" again: The relational dialectics of renewing marriage vows. *Journal of Social and Personal Relationships, 12,* 177-198.

Brantner, J. (1977). Positive approaches to dying. *Death Education, 1,* 293-304.

Bray, J. H. (1992). Family relationships and children's adjustment in clinical and nonclinical stepfather families. *Journal of Family Psychology, 6,* 60-68.

Bray, J., Berger, S. H., Silverblatt, A. H., & Hollier, A. (1987). Family process and organization during early remarriage: A preliminary analysis. In J. P. Vincent (Ed.), *Advances in family intervention, assessment, and theory* (pp. 253-279). Greenwich, CT: JAI.

Brehm, S. (1992). *Intimate relationships* (2nd ed.). New York: McGraw-Hill.

Brennan, K. A., Clark, C. L., & Shaver, P. R. (1998). Self-report measurement of adult attachment: An integrative overview. In J. A. Simpson & W. S. Rholes (Eds.), *Attachment theory and close relationships* (pp. 46-76). New York: Guilford.

Brennan, K. A., & Shaver, P. R. (1995). Dimensions of adult attachment, affect regulation, and romantic relationship functioning. *Personality and Social Psychology Bulletin, 21,* 267-283.

Brewer, M. B. (1979). Ingroup bias in the minimal intergroup situation: A cognitive-motivational analysis. *Psychological Bulletin, 86,* 307-324.

Brewer, M. B., & Brown, R. J. (1998). Intergroup relations. In D. T. Gilbert, S. T. Fiske, & G. Lindzey (Eds.), *Handbook of social psychology* (4th ed., Vol. 2, pp. 554-594). New York: McGraw-Hill.

Brewer, M. B., & Caporael, L. R. (1990). Selfish genes versus selfish people: Sociobiology as origin myth. *Motivation and Emotion, 14,* 237-243.

Bringle, R. G. (1991). Psychosocial aspects of jealousy: A transactional model. In P. Salovey (Ed.), *The psychology of jealousy and envy* (pp. 103-132). New York: Guilford.

Bringle, R. G. (1995). Sexual jealousy in the relationships of homosexual and heterosexual men: 1980 and 1992. *Personal Relationships, 2,* 313-325.

Bringle, R. G., & Boebinger, K. L. G. (1990). Jealousy and the third person in the love triangle. *Journal of Social and Personal Relationships, 7,* 119-133.

Bringle, R. G., & Buunk, B. P. (1985). Jealousy and social behavior: A review of person, relationship, and situational determinants. In P. Shaver (Ed.), *Review of personality and social psychology* (Vol. 6, pp. 241-264). Beverly Hills, CA: Sage.

Brink, T. L., Yesavage, J. A., Lum, O., Heersema, P. H., Adey, M., & Rose, T. L. (1982). Screening tests for geriatric depression. *Clinical Gerontologist, 1,* 37-43.

Brockmeier, J., & Harré, R. (1997). Narrative: Problems and promises of an alternative paradigm. *Research on Language and Social Interaction, 30,* 263-283.

Brock-Utne, B. (1989). *Feminist perspectives on peace and peace education.* New York: Pergamon.

Brody, G. H., Neubaum, E., & Forehand, R. (1988). Serial marriage: A heuristic analysis of an emerging family form. *Psychological Bulletin, 103,* 211-222.

Brody, G. H., & Stoneman, Z. (1987). Sibling conflict: Contributions of the siblings themselves, the parent-sibling relationship, and the broader family system. *Journal of Children in Contemporary Society, 19,* 39-54.

Brody, G. H., Stoneman, Z., McCoy, J. K., & Forehand, R. (1992). Contemporaneous and longitudinal associations of sibling conflict with family relationship assessments and family discussions about sibling problems. *Child Development, 63,* 391-400.

Bronfenbrenner, U. (1979). *The ecology of human development: Experiments by nature and design.* Cambridge, MA: Harvard University Press.

Bronstein, P., Stoll, M. F., Clauson, J., Abrams, C. L., & Briones, M. (1994). Fathering after separation or divorce: Factors predicting children's adjustment. *Family Relations, 43,* 469-479.

Brown, A. C., Green, R., & Druckman, J. (1990). A comparison of stepfamilies with and without child-focused problems. *American Journal of Orthopsychiatry, 60,* 556-566.

Brown, B. B. (1990). Peer groups and peer cultures. In S. S. Feldman & G. R. Elliott (Eds.), *At the threshold: The developing adolescent* (pp. 171-196). Cambridge, MA: Harvard University Press.

Brown, B. B. (in press). "You're going with who?!" Peer group influences on adolescent romantic relationships. In W. Furman, B. B., Brown, & C. Feiring (Eds.), *Contemporary perspectives on adolescent romantic relationships.* New York: Cambridge University Press.

Brown, D. R., & Gary, L. E. (1985). Social support network differentials among married and nonmarried black females. *Psychology of Women Quarterly, 9,* 229-241.

Brown, M., & Auerback, A. (1981). Communication patterns in initiation of marital sex. *Medical Aspects of Human Sexuality, 15,* 105-117.

Brown, S. L., & Booth, A. (1996). Cohabitation versus marriage: A comparison of relationship quality. *Journal of Marriage and the Family, 58,* 668-678.

Brown, T. G., Werk, A., Caplan, T., Shields, N., & Seraganian, P. (1998). The incidence and characteristics of violent men in substance abuse treatment. *Addictive Behaviors, 23,* 573-586.

Bruess, C. J. S., & Pearson, J. C. (1995, November). *Like sands through the hourglass: Rituals in day-to-day marriage.* Paper presented at the annual meeting of the Speech Communication Association, San Antonio, TX.

Bryant, A. S., & Demian. (1994). Relationship characteristics of American gay and lesbian couples: Findings from a national survey. *Journal of Gay and Lesbian Social Services, 1,* 101-117.

Bryant, C. M. (1996). *Subcultural variations in the social network support of Latinos, African Americans, and Anglos: What is the association between the development of heterosexual relationships and the support of friends and family members?* Unpublished doctoral dissertation, University of Texas at Austin.

Bryant, C. M., & Conger, R. D. (1999). Marital success and domains of social support in long-term relationships: Does the influence of network members ever end? *Journal of Marriage and the Family, 61,* 437-450.

Bryk, A. S., & Raudenbush, S. W. (1992). *Hierarchical linear models.* Newbury Park, CA: Sage.

Bubolz, M. M., & Sontag, M. S. (1993). Human ecology theory. In P. G. Boss, W. J. Doherty, R. LaRossa, W. R. Schumm, & S. K. Steinmetz (Eds.), *Sourcebook of family theories and methods: A contextual approach* (pp. 419-448). New York: Plenum.

Buck, R. (1984). *Communication of emotion.* New York: Guilford.

Buhrmester, D. (1996). Need fulfillment, interpersonal competence, and the developmental contexts of early adolescent friendship. In W. M. Bukowski, A. F. Newcomb, & W. W. Hartup (Eds.), *The company they keep: Friendship in childhood and adolescence* (pp. 158-185). New York: Cambridge University Press.

Buhrmester, D., & Furman, F. (1987). The development of companionship and intimacy. *Child Development, 58,* 1101-1113.

Buhrmester, D., Furman, W., Wittenberg, M. T., & Reis, H. T. (1988). Five domains of interpersonal competence in peer relationships. *Journal of Personality and Social Psychology, 55,* 991-1008.

Bukowski, W. M., & Hoza, B. (1989). Popularity and friendship: Issues in theory, measurement, and outcome. In T. J. Berndt & G. W. Ladd (Eds.), *Peer relationships in child development* (pp. 15-45). New York: John Wiley.

Bukowski, W. M., Newcomb, A. F., & Hartup, W. W. (Eds.). (1996). *The company they keep: Friendship in childhood and adolescence.* New York: Cambridge University Press.

Bulcroft, K. A., & O'Connor, M. (1986). The importance of dating relationships on quality of life for older persons. *Family Relations, 35,* 397-401.

Bulcroft, R. A., & Bulcroft, K. A. (1991). The nature and functions of dating in later life. *Research on Aging, 13,* 244-260.

Bulcroft, R. A., Carmody, D. C., & Bulcroft, K. A. (1998). Family structure and patterns of independence giving to adolescents: Variations by age, race, and gender of child. *Journal of Family Issues, 19,* 404-435.

Buley, J. L. (1977). *Relationships and communication.* Dubuque, IA: Kendall/Hunt.

Bumpass, L. L., & Raley, R. K. (1995). Redefining single-parent families: Cohabitation and changing family realities. *Demography, 32,* 97-109.

Bumpass, L. L., & Sweet, J. A. (1989). National estimates of cohabitation. *Demography, 26,* 615-625.

Bumpass, L. L., Sweet, J. A., & Cherlin, A. (1991). The role of cohabitation in declining rates of marriage. *Journal of Marriage and the Family, 53,* 913-927.

Burch, B. (1986). Psychotherapy and the dynamics of merger in lesbian couples. In T. S. Stein & C. J. Cohen (Eds.), *Contemporary perspectives on psychotherapy with lesbians and gay men* (pp. 57-72). New York: Plenum.

Burger, E., & Milardo, R. M. (1995). Marital interdependence and social networks. *Journal of Social and Personal Relationships, 12,* 403-415.

Burgess, E. W., & Cottrell, L. S. (1939). *Predicting success or failure in marriage.* Englewood Cliffs, NJ: Prentice Hall.

Burgess, R. L., & Huston, T. L. (1979). *Social exchange in developing relationships.* New York: Academic Press.

Burggraf, C. S., & Sillars, A. L. (1987). A critical examination of sex differences in marital communication. *Communication Monographs, 54,* 276-294.

Burgoon, J. K. (1991). Relational message interpretations of touch, conversational distance, and posture. *Journal of Nonverbal Behavior, 15,* 233-259.

Burgoon, J. K., & Hale, J. L. (1984). The fundamental topoi of relational communication. *Communication Monographs, 51,* 19-41.

Burgoyne, C. B., & Morison, V. (1997). Money in remarriage: Keeping things simple—and separate. *Sociological Review, 45,* 363-395.

Burke, P. J., Stets, J. E., & Pirog-Good, M. A. (1988). Gender identity, self-esteem, and physical and sexual abuse in dating relationships. *Social Psychology Quarterly, 51,* 272-285.

Burleson, B., Kunkel, A., Samter, W., & Werking, K. (1996). Men's and women's evaluations of communication skills in personal relationships: When sex differences make a difference—and when they don't. *Journal of Social and Personal Relationships, 13,* 201-224.

Burleson, B. R. (1982). Social cognition, empathic motivation, and adults' comforting strategies. *Human Communication Research, 10,* 295-304.

Burleson, B. R. (1994). Friendship and similarities in social-cognitive and communication abilities: Social skill bases of interpersonal attraction in childhood. *Personal Relationships, 1,* 371-389.

Burleson, B. R. (1995). Personal relationships as a skilled accomplishment. *Journal of Social and Personal Relationships, 12,* 575-581.

Burleson, B. R., Delia, J. G., & Applegate, J. L. (1995). The socialization of person-centered communication: Parental contributions to the social-cognitive and communication skills of their children. In M. A. Fitzpatrick & A. L. Vangelisti (Eds.), *Explaining family interactions* (pp. 34-76). Thousand Oaks, CA: Sage.

Burleson, B. R., & Denton, W. H. (1997). The relationship between communication skills and marital satisfaction: Some moderating effects. *Journal of Marriage and the Family, 59,* 884-902.

Burleson, B. R., & Goldsmith, D. J. (1998). How the comforting process works: Alleviating emotional distress through conversationally induced reappraisals. In P. A. Andersen & L. K. Guerrero (Eds.), *Handbook of communication and emotion: Research, theory, applications, and contexts* (pp. 245-280). San Diego: Academic Press.

Burleson, B. R., & Samter, W. (1994). A social skills approach to relationship maintenance: How individual differences in communication skills affect the achievement of relationship functions. In D. J. Canary & L. Stafford (Ed.), *Communication and relational maintenance* (pp. 61-90). San Diego: Academic Press.

Burleson, B. R., Samter, W., & Lucchetti, A. E. (1992). Similarity in communication values as a predictor of friendship choices: Studies of friends and best friends. *Southern Communication Journal, 57,* 260-276.

Burley, K. (1991). Family-work spillover in dual-career couples: A comparison of two time perspectives. *Psychological Reports, 68,* 471-480.

Burman, B., John, R. S., & Margolin, G. (1992). Observed patterns of conflict in violent, nonviolent, and nondistressed couples. *Behavioral Assessment, 14,* 15-37.

Burman, B., Margolin, G., & John, R. S. (1993). America's angriest home videos: Behavioral contingencies observed in home reenactments of marital conflict. *Journal of Consulting and Clinical Psychology, 61,* 28-39.

Burns, A. (1984). Perceived causes of marriage breakdown and conditions of life. *Journal of Marriage and the Family, 46,* 551-562.

Burns, A., & Dunlop, R. (1998). Parental divorce, parent-child relations, and early adult relationships: A longitudinal Australian study. *Personal Relationships, 5,* 393-407.

Burns, D. D., Sayers, S. L., & Moras, K. (1994). Intimate relationships and depression: Is there a causal connection? *Journal of Consulting and Clinical Psychology, 62,* 1033-1043.

Burt, M. R. (1980). Cultural myths and supports for rape. *Journal of Personality and Social Psychology, 38,* 217-230.

Burton, R. (1927). *The anatomy of melancholia* (F. Dell & P. Jordan-Smith, Eds.). New York: Tudor. (Original work published 1621)

Buss, D. M. (1988). Love acts: The evolutionary biology of love. In R. J. Sternberg & M. L. Barnes (Eds.), *The psychology of love* (pp. 100-117). New Haven, CT: Yale University Press.

Buss, D. M. (1989). Sex differences in human mate preferences: Evolutionary hypotheses tested in 37 cultures. *Behavioral and Brain Sciences, 12,* 1-49.

Buss, D. M. (1994). *The evolution of desire: Strategies of human mating.* New York: Basic Books.

Buss, D. M. (1995). Evolutionary psychology: A new paradigm for psychological science. *Psychological Inquiry, 6,* 1-30.

Buss, D. M. (1996). The evolutionary psychology of human social strategies. In E. T. Higgins & A. W. Kruglanski (Eds.), *Social psychology: Handbook of basic principles* (pp. 3-38). New York: Guilford.

Buss, D. M., & Kenrick, D. T. (1998). Evolutionary social psychology. In D. T. Gilbert, S. T. Fiske, & G. Lindzey (Eds.), *The handbook of social psychology* (Vol. 2, 4th ed., pp. 982-1026). New York: McGraw-Hill.

Buss, D. M., Larsen, R. J., Westen, D., & Semmelroth, J. (1992). Sex differences in jealousy: Evolution, physiology, and psychology. *Psychological Science, 3,* 251-255.

Buss, D. M., & Schmitt, D. P. (1993). Sexual strategies theory: An evolutionary perspective on human mating. *Psychological Review, 100,* 204-232.

Buss, D. M., & Shackelford, T. K. (1997). Susceptibility to infidelity in the first year of marriage. *Journal of Research in Personality, 31,* 193-221.

Buss, D. M., Shackelford, T. K., Choe, J., Dijkstra, P., & Buunk, B. P. (In press). Distress about mating rivals. *Personal Relationships.*

Butler, R. N., Lewis, M. I., & Sunderland, T. (1998). *Aging and mental health: Positive psychosocial and biomedical approaches* (5th ed.). Boston: Allyn & Bacon.

Buunk, B. P. (1980a). Extramarital sex in the Netherlands: Motivations in social and marital context. *Alternative Lifestyles, 3,* 11-39.

Buunk, B. P. (1980b). Sexually open marriages: Ground rules for countering potential threats to marriage. *Alternative Lifestyles, 3,* 312-328.

Buunk, B. P. (1982). Strategies of jealousy: Styles of coping with extramarital involvement of the spouse. *Family Relations, 31,* 13-18.

Buunk, B. P. (1986). Husbands' jealousy. In R. A. Lewis & R. E. Salt (Eds.), *Men in families* (pp. 97-114). Beverly Hills, CA: Sage.

Buunk, B. P. (1987). Conditions that promote breakups as a consequence of extradyadic involvements. *Journal of Social and Clinical Psychology, 5,* 271-284.

Buunk, B. P. (1991). Jealousy in close relationships: An exchange-theoretical perspective. In P. Salovey (Ed.), *The psychology of jealousy and envy* (pp. 148-177). New York: Guilford.

Buunk, B. P. (1995). Sex, self-esteem, dependency, and extradyadic sexual experiences as related to jealousy responses. *Journal of Social and Personal Relationships, 12,* 147-153.

Buunk, B. P. (1997). Personality, birth order, and attachment styles as related to various types of jealousy. *Personality and Individual Differences, 23,* 997-1006.

Buunk, B. P., Angleitner, A., Oubaid, V., & Buss, D. M. (1996). Sex differences in jealousy in evolutionary and cultural perspective: Tests from the Netherlands, Germany, and the United States. *Psychological Science, 7,* 359-363.

Buunk, B. P., & Bakker, A. B. (1995a). Commitment to the relationship, extradyadic sex, and AIDS-preventive behavior. *Journal of Applied Social Psychology, 27,* 1241-1257.

Buunk, B. P., & Bakker, A. B. (1995b). Extradyadic sex: The role of descriptive and injunctive norms. *Journal of Sex Research, 32,* 313-318.

Buunk, B. P., & Bakker, A. B. (1997). Responses to unprotected extradyadic sex by one's partner: Testing predictions from interdependence and equity theory. *Journal of Sex Research, 34,* 387-397.

Buunk, B. P., & Hupka, R. B. (1987). Cross-cultural differences in the elicitation of sexual jealousy. *Journal of Sex Research, 23,* 12-22.

Buunk, B. P., & Van Driel, B. (1989). *Variant lifestyles and relationships.* Newbury Park, CA: Sage.

Byers, E. S., Demmons, S., & Lawrance, K. (1998). Sexual satisfaction within dating relationships: A test of the interpersonal exchange model of sexual satisfaction. *Journal of Social and Personal Relationships, 15,* 257-267.

Byers, E. S., & Heinlein, L. (1989). Predicting initiations and refusals of sexual activities in married and cohabiting heterosexual couples. *Journal of Sex Research, 26,* 210-231.

Byrne, D. (1971). *The attraction paradigm.* New York: Academic Press.

Cafferty, T. P., Davis, K. E., Medway, F. J., O'Hearn, R. E., & Chappell, K. D. (1994). Reunion dynamics among couples separated during Operation Desert Storm: An attachment theory analysis. In K. Bartholomew & D. Perlman (Eds.), *Advances in per-*

sonal relationships, Vol. 5: *Attachment processes in adulthood* (pp. 309-330). London: Jessica Kingsley.

Cairns, R., & Cairns, B. D. (1994). *Lifelines and risks: Pathways of youth in our time.* New York: Cambridge University Press.

Cairns, R. B., Cairns, B. D., Neckerman, H. J., Gest, S. D., & Gariepy, J. L. (1988). Social networks and aggressive behavior: Peer support or peer rejection? *Developmental Psychology, 24,* 815-823.

Calasanti, T. M. (Ed.). (1993). Socialist-feminist perspectives on aging [Special issue]. *Journal of Aging Studies, 7*(2).

Caldwell, M., & Peplau, L. (1982). Sex differences in same-sex friendship. *Sex Roles, 8,* 721-732.

Caldwell, M. A., & Peplau, L. A. (1984). The balance of power in lesbian relationships. *Sex Roles, 10,* 587-600.

Call, V., Sprecher, S., & Schwartz, P. (1995). The incidence and frequency of marital sex in a national sample. *Journal of Marriage and the Family, 57,* 639-650.

Camara, K. A., & Resnick, G. (1988). Interparental conflict and cooperation: Factors moderating children's post-divorce adjustment. In E. M. Hetherington & J. D. Aresteh (Eds.), *Impact of divorce, single parenting, and stepparenting on children* (pp. 169-195). Hillsdale, NJ: Lawrence Erlbaum.

Campbell, A. (1993). *Men, women, and aggression.* New York: Basic Books.

Canary, D., & Dindia, K. (Eds.). (1998) *Sex differences and similarities in communication: Critical essays and empirical investigations of sex and gender in interaction.* Mahwah, NJ: Lawrence Erlbaum.

Canary, D. J., Cupach, W. R., & Messman, S. J. (1995). *Relationship conflict: Conflict in parent-child, friendship, and romantic relationships.* Thousand Oaks, CA: Sage.

Canary, D. J., & Emmers-Sommer, T. M. (1997). *Sex and gender differences in personal relationships.* New York: Guilford.

Canary, D. J., Spitzberg, B. H., & Semic, B. A. (1998). The experience and expression of anger in interpersonal settings. In P. A. Andersen & L. K. Guerrero (Eds.), *Handbook of communication and emotion: Research, theory, applications, and contexts* (pp. 189-213). San Diego: Academic Press.

Canary, D. J., & Stafford, L. (1992). Relational maintenance strategies and equity in marriage. *Communication Monographs, 59,* 243-267.

Canary, D. J., & Stafford, L. (1993). Preservation of relational characteristics: Maintenance strategies, equity, and locus of control. In P. J. Kalbfleisch (Ed.), *Interpersonal communication: Evolving interpersonal relationships* (pp. 237-259). Hillsdale, NJ: Lawrence Erlbaum.

Canary, D. J., & Stafford, L. (1994). Maintaining relationships through strategic and routine interaction. In D. J. Canary & L. Stafford (Eds.), *Communication*

*and relational maintenance* (pp. 3-22). San Diego: Academic Press.

Canary, D. J., Stafford, L., Hause, K. S., & Wallace, L. A. (1993). An inductive analysis of relational maintenance strategies: Comparisons among lovers, relatives, friends, and others. *Communication Research Reports, 10,* 5-14.

Canary, D. J., & Zelley, E. D. (2000). Current research programs on relational maintenance behaviors. In *Communication Yearbook, 23.* Thousand Oaks, CA: Sage.

Cancian, F. M. (1987). *Love in America: Gender and self-development.* New York: Cambridge University Press.

Caplan, G. (1974). *Support systems and community mental health: Lectures on conceptual development.* New York: Behavioral Publications.

Carden, A. D. (1994). Wife abuse and the wife abuser: Review and recommendations. *The Counseling Psychologist, 22,* 539-582.

Carlson, N. R. (1990). *Psychology* (3rd ed.). Boston: Allyn & Bacon.

Caraël, M., Cleland, J., Deheneffe, J. C., Ferry, B., & Ingham, R. (1995). Sexual behavior in developing countries: Implications for HIV control. *AIDS, 9,* 1171-1175.

Carnelley, K. B., & Janoff-Bulman, R. (1992). Optimism about love relationships: General vs. specific lessons from one's personal experiences. *Journal of Social and Personal Relationships, 9,* 5-20.

Carnelley, K. B., Pietromonaco, P. R., & Jaffe, K. (1994). Depression, working models of others, and relationship functioning. *Journal of Personality and Social Psychology, 66,* 127-140.

Carnelley, K. B., Pietromonaco, P. R., & Jaffe, K. (1996). Attachment, caregiving, and relationship functioning in couples: Effects of self and partner. *Personal Relationships, 3,* 257-277.

Caron, S. L., & Ulin, J. (1997). Closeting and the quality of lesbian relationships. *Families in Society, 78,* 413-419.

Carson, R. C. (1969). *Interaction concepts of personality.* Chicago: Aldine.

Carstensen, L. L. (1992). Social and emotional patterns in adulthood: Support for socioemotional selectivity theory. *Psychology and Aging, 7,* 331-338.

Carstensen, L. L., Isaacowitz, D. M., & Charles, S. T. (1999). Taking time seriously: A theory of socioemotional selectivity. *American Psychologist, 54,* 165-181.

Carter, E. A. (1988, November). Counseling stepfamilies effectively. *Behavior Today,* pp. 1-2.

Carver, C. S., & Scheier, M. F. (in press). Theme and issues in the self-regulation of behavior. In R. Wyer, Jr. (Ed.), *Advances in social cognition,* Vol. 12: *Perspectives on behavioral self-regulation.* Mahwah, NJ: Lawrence Erlbaum.

Casell, J. (1974). Psychosocial processes and stress: Theoretic formulations. *International Journal of Health Service, 4,* 471-482.

Cate, R., Lloyd, S., & Henton, J. (1985). The effect of equity, equality, and reward level on the stability of students' premarital relationships. *Journal of Social Psychology, 125,* 715-721.

Cate, R. M., Henton, J. M., Koval., J. E., Christopher, F. S., & Lloyd, S. A. (1982). Premarital abuse: A social psychological perspective. *Journal of Family Issues, 3,* 79-90.

Cate, R. M., Long, E., Angera, J. J., & Draper, K. K. (1993). Sexual intercourse and relationship development. *Family Relations, 42,* 158-164.

Caughlin, J. P., & Vangelisti, A. L. (1999). Desire for change in one's partner as a predictor of the demand/withdraw pattern of marital communication. *Communication Monographs, 66,* 66-89.

Cazenave, N. A., & Straus, M. A. (1990). Race, class, network embeddedness, and family violence: A search for potent support systems. In M. A. Straus & R. J. Gelles (Eds.), *Physical violence in American families* (pp. 321-340). New Brunswick, NJ: Transaction Publishers.

Chadwick, B. A., & Heaton, T. B. (1999). *Statistical handbook on the American family.* Phoenix, AZ: Orynx.

Charny, I. W., & Parnass, S. (1995). The impact of extramarital relationships on the continuation of marriages. *Journal of Sex and Marital Therapy, 21,* 101-115.

Chase-Lansdale, P. L., Cherlin, A. J., & Kiernan, K. E. (1995). The long-term effects of parental divorce on the mental health of young adults: A developmental perspective. *Child Development, 66,* 1614-1634.

Cheal, D. J. (1983). Intergenerational family transfers. *Journal of Marriage and the Family, 45,* 805-813.

Cherlin, A. (1978). Remarriage as an incomplete institution. *American Journal of Sociology, 84,* 634-650.

Cherlin, A. (1989). Remarriage as an incomplete institution. In J. M. Henslin (Ed.), *Marriage and family in a changing society* (pp. 492-501). New York: Free Press.

Cherlin, A. J., Furstenberg, F. F., Chase-Lansdale, P. L., Kiernan, K. E., Robins, P. K., Morrison, D. R., & Teitler, J. O. (1991). Longitudinal studies of effects of divorce on children in Great Britain and the United States. *Science, 252,* 1386-1389.

Chevan, A. (1996). As cheaply as one: Cohabitation in the older population. *Journal of Marriage and the Family, 58,* 656-667.

Cho, W., & Cross, S. E. (1995). Taiwanese love styles and their association with self-esteem and relationship quality. *Genetic, Social, & General Psychology Monographs, 121,* 283-309.

Chodorow, N. (1978). *The reproduction of mothering: Psychoanalysis and the sociology of gender.* Berkeley: University of California Press.

Chodorow, N. (1989). *Feminism and psychoanalytic theory.* New Haven, CT: Yale University Press.

Choi, K. H., Catania, A., & Dolcini, M. M. (1994). Extramarital sex and HIV risk behavior among U.S. adults: Results from the National AIDS Behavioral Survey. *American Journal of Public Health, 84,* 2003-2007.

Christensen, A., & Heavey, C. L. (1990). Gender and social structure in the demand/withdraw pattern of marital conflict. *Journal of Personality and Social Psychology, 59,* 73-81.

Christensen, A., & Shenk, J. L. (1991). Communication, conflict, and psychological distance in nondistressed, clinic, and divorcing couples. *Journal of Consulting and Clinical Psychology, 59,* 458-463.

Christensen, D. H., & Rettig, K. D. (1995). The relationship of remarriage to post-divorce co-parenting. *Journal of Divorce and Remarriage, 24,* 73-88.

Christian, J. L., O'Leary, K. D., & Vivian, D. (1994). Depressive symptomatology in maritally discordant women and men: The role of individual and relationship variables. *Journal of Family Psychology, 8,* 32-42.

Christopher, F. S., & Cate, R. M. (1985). Premarital sexual pathways and relationship development. *Journal of Social and Personal Relationships, 2,* 271-288.

Christopher, F. S., Madura, M., & Weaver, L. (1998). Premarital sexual aggressors: A multivariate analysis of social, relational, and individual correlates. *Journal of Marriage and the Family, 60,* 56-69.

Christopher, F. S., & McQuaid, S. (1998, June). *Dating relationships and men's sexual aggression: A test of a relationship-based model.* Paper presented at the biennial meeting of the International Society for the Study of Personal Relationships, Saratoga Springs, NY.

Christopher, F. S., McQuaid, S., & Updegraff, K. (1998, November). *Relational predictors of single women's use of sexual coercion.* Paper presented at the annual meeting of the National Council on Family Relations, Milwaukee, WI.

Christopher, F. S., Owens, L. A., & Stecker, H. L. (1993a). An examination of men's and women's premarital sexual aggressiveness. *Journal of Social and Personal Relationships, 10,* 511-527.

Christopher, F. S., Owens, L. A., & Stecker, H. L. (1993b). Exploring the dark side of courtship: A test of a model of male premarital sexual aggressiveness. *Journal of Marriage and the Family, 55,* 469-479.

Cicirelli, V. G. (1995). *Sibling relationships across the life span.* New York: Plenum.

Cissna, K. N., Cox, D. E., & Bochner, A. P. (1990). The dialectic of marital and parental relationships within the stepfamily. *Communication Monographs, 57*(1), 44-61.

Clark, H. H., & Bly, B. (1995). Pragmatics and discourse. In J. L. Miller & P. D. Eimas (Eds.), *Speech, language, and communication* (pp. 371-410). San Diego: Academic Press.

Clark, M. S., & Mills, J. (1993). The difference between communal and exchange relationships: What it is and is not. *Personality and Social Psychology Bulletin, 19,* 684-691.

Clark, M. S., Ouellette, R., Powell, M. C., & Milberg, S. (1987). Interpersonal attraction in exchange and communal relationships. *Journal of Personality and Social Psychology, 53,* 93-103.

Clark, M. S., & Taraban, C. (1991). Reactions to and willingness to express emotion in communal and exchange relationships. *Journal of Experimental Social Psychology, 27,* 324-336.

Clark, R. (1998). A comparison of topics and objectives in a cross section of young men's and women's everyday conversations. In D. Canary & K. Dindia (Eds.), *Sex differences and similarities in communication: Critical essays and empirical investigations of sex and gender in interaction* (pp. 303-319). Mahwah, NJ: Lawrence Erlbaum.

Clark, S. L., & Stephens, M. A. P. (1996). Stroke patients' well-being as a function of caregiving spouses' helpful and unhelpful actions. *Personal Relationships, 3,* 171-184.

Clearhout, S., Elder, J., & Janes, C. (1982). Problem-solving skills of rural battered women. *American Journal of Community Psychology, 10,* 605-613.

Cleek, M. G., & Pearson, T. A. (1985). Perceived causes of divorce: An analysis of interrelationships. *Journal of Marriage and the Family, 47,* 179-183.

Clements, M. L., Cordova, A. D., Markman, H. J., & Laurenceau, J. (1997). The erosion of marital satisfaction over time and how to prevent it. In R. J. Sternberg & M. Hojjat (Eds.), *Satisfaction in close relationships* (pp. 335-355). New York: Guilford.

Clifford, J., & Marcus, G. E. (Eds.). (1986). *Writing culture: The poetics and the politics of ethnography.* Berkeley: University of California Press.

Clingempeel, W. G., Flesher, M., & Brand, E. (1988). Research on stepfamilies: Paradigmatic constraints and alternative proposals. In J. P. Vincent (Ed.), *Advances in family intervention: Assessment and theory* (pp. 229-251). Greenwich, CT: JAI.

Coan, J., Gottman, J. M., Babcock, J., & Jacobson, N. (1997). Battering and the male rejection of influence from women. *Aggressive Behavior, 23,* 375-388.

Coates, J. (1986). *Women, men, and language: Studies in language and linguistics.* London: Longman.

Coates, J., & Cameron, D. (1989). *Women in their speech communities: New perspectives on language and sex.* London: Longman.

Cochran, M., Larner, M., Riley, D., Gunnarsson, L., & Henderson, C. R. (1990). *Extending families: The social networks of parents and their children.* New York: Cambridge University Press.

Cody, M. J., Canary, D. J., & Smith, S. W. (1994). Compliance-gaining goals: An inductive analysis of ac-

tors' goal types, strategies, and successes. In J. A. Daly & J. M. Wiemann (Eds.), *Strategic interpersonal communication* (pp. 33-90). Hillsdale, NJ: Lawrence Erlbaum.

Cohen, L. L., & Shotland, R. L. (1996). Timing of first sexual intercourse in a relationship: Expectations, experiences, and perceptions of others. *Journal of Sex Research, 33,* 291-299.

Cohen, S., & Wills, T. A. (1985). Stress, social support, and the buffering hypothesis. *Psychological Bulletin, 98,* 319-357.

Cohen, T. F. (1992). Men's families, men's friends: A structural analysis of constraints on men's social ties. In P. M. Nardi (Ed.), *Men's friendships* (pp. 115-131). Newbury Park, CA: Sage.

Coie, J. D., & Koeppl, G. K. (1990). Adapting intervention to the problems of aggressive and disruptive rejected children. In S. R. Asher & J. D. Coie (Eds.), *Peer rejection in childhood* (pp. 309-337). New York: Cambridge University Press.

Cole-Detke, H., & Kobak, R. (1996). Attachment processes in eating disorders and depression. *Journal of Consulting and Clinical Psychology, 64,* 282-290.

Coleman, M. (1997). Review of *Handbook of Aging and the Family,* edited by R. Blieszner & V. H. Bedford. *Contemporary Psychology, 42,* 325-326.

Coleman, M., & Ganong, L. (1989). Financial management in stepfamilies. *Lifestyles: Family and Economic Issues, 10,* 217-232.

Coleman, M., & Ganong, L. (1990). Remarriage and stepfamily research in the 1980s: Increased interest in an old family form. *Journal of Marriage and the Family, 52,* 925-940.

Coleman, M., & Ganong, L. (1995). Family reconfiguring following divorce. In S. Duck & J. Wood (Eds.), *Confronting relationship challenges* (pp. 73-108). Thousand Oaks, CA: Sage.

Coleman, M., & Ganong, L. (1997). Stepfamilies from the stepfamily's perspective. *Marriage and Family Review, 26,* 107-122.

Coleman, M., Ganong, L., & Cable, S. (1997). Perceptions of stepparents: An examination of the incomplete institutionalization and social stigma hypotheses. *Journal of Divorce and Remarriage, 26,* 25-48.

Coleman, M., Ganong, L., & Fine, M. (in press). Decade review on remarriage and stepfamilies. *Journal of Marriage and the Family.*

Coley, R. L. (1998). Children's socialization experiences and functioning in single-mother households: The importance of fathers and other men. *Child Development, 69,* 219-230.

Collins, N. L. (1996). Working models of attachment: Implications for explanation, emotion, and behavior. *Journal of Personality and Social Psychology, 71,* 810-832.

Collins, N. L., & Read, S. J. (1990). Adult attachment, working models, and relationship quality in dating couples. *Journal of Personality and Social Psychology, 58,* 644-663.

Collins, N. L., & Read, S. J. (1994). Cognitive representations of attachment: The structure and function of working models. In K. Bartholomew & D. Perlman (Eds.), *Advances in personal relationships* (Vol. 5, pp. 53-90). London: Jessica Kingsley.

Collins, P. (1998). *Fighting words.* Minneapolis: University of Minnesota Press.

Collins, P. H. (1986). Learning from the outsider within: The sociological significance of black feminist thought. *Social Problems, 33*(6), 14-32.

Collins, P. H. (1990). *Black feminist thought: Knowledge, consciousness, and the politics of empowerment.* Boston: Unwin Hyman.

Collins, W. A. (1995). Relationships and development: Family adaptations to individual change. In S. Shulman (Ed.), *Close relationships and socioemotional development* (pp. 128-154). Norwood, NJ: Ablex.

Collins, W. A. (1997). Relationships and development during adolescence: Interpersonal adaptation to individual change. *Personal Relationships, 4,* 1-14.

Collins, W. A., Hennighausen, K. H., Schmit, D. T., & Sroufe, L. A. (1997). Developmental precursors of romantic relationships: A longitudinal analysis. In S. Shulman & W. A. Collins (Eds.), *Romantic relationships in adolescence: Developmental perspectives* (New Directions for Child Development, No. 78, pp. 69-84). San Francisco: Jossey-Bass.

Collins, W. A., & Repinski, D. J. (1994). Relationships during adolescence: Continuity and change in interpersonal perspective. In R. Montemayor, G. Adams, & T. Gullotta (Eds.), *Personal relationships during adolescence* (pp. 7-36). Thousand Oaks, CA: Sage.

Collins, W. A., & Sroufe, L. A. (in press). Capacity for intimate relationships: A developmental construction. In W. Furman, B. B. Brown, & C. Feiring (Eds.), *Contemporary perspectives on adolescent romantic relationships.* New York: Cambridge University Press.

Coltrane, S. (1989). Household labor and the routine production of gender. *Social Problems, 5,* 473-490.

Coltrane, S. (1996). *Family man: Fatherhood, housework, and gender equality.* New York: Oxford University Press.

Connidis, I. A. (1992). Life transitions and the adult sibling tie: A qualitative study. *Journal of Marriage and the Family, 54,* 972-982.

Connidis, I. A., & Davies, L. (1990). Confidants and companions in later life. *Journal of Gerontology: Social Sciences, 45,* 141-149.

Connolly, J., & Goldberg, A. (in press). Romantic relationships in adolescence: The role of friends and peers in their emergence and development. In W. Furman, B. B., Brown, & C. Feiring (Eds.), *Contemporary perspectives on adolescent romantic relationships.* New York: Cambridge University Press.

Constantine, L. L. (1976). Jealousy: From theory to intervention. In D. H. E. Olson (Ed.), *Treating relationships* (pp. 383-398). Lake Mills, IA: Graphic Publishing.

Contreras, R., Hendrick, S. S., & Hendrick, C. (1996). Perspectives on marital love and satisfaction in Mexican American and Anglo couples. *Journal of Counseling and Development, 74,* 408-415.

Cook, W. L., Kenny, D. A., & Goldstein, M. J. (1991). Parental affective style risk and the family system: A social relations model analysis. *Journal of Abnormal Psychology, 100,* 492-501.

Cooksey, E. C., & Fondell, M. M. (1996). Spending time with his kids: Effects of family structure on fathers' and children's lives. *Journal of Marriage and the Family, 58,* 693-707.

Cooney, T. M., Hutchinson, M. K., & Leather, D. M. (1995). Surviving the breakup? Predictors of parent-adult child relations after parental divorce. *Family Relations, 44,* 153-161.

Coontz, S. (1992). *The way we never were: American families and the nostalgia trap.* New York: Basic Books.

Cooper, C. R. (1994). Cultural perspectives on continuity and change in adolescents' relationships. In R. Montemayor, G. Adams, & T. Gullotta (Eds.), *Personal relationships during adolescence* (pp. 78-100). Thousand Oaks, CA: Sage.

Copenhaver, S., & Grauerholz, E. (1991). Sexual victimization among sorority women: Exploring the link between sexual violence and institutional practices. *Sex Roles, 24,* 31-41.

Cordova, J. V., & Gee, C. B. (in press). Couple therapy for depression with or without co-occurring relationship distress. In S. R. H. Beach (Ed.), *Marital and family processes in depression.* Washington, DC: American Psychological Association.

Cordova, J. V., Jacobson, N. S., Gottman, J. M., Rushe, R., & Cox, G. (1993). Negative reciprocity and communication in couples with a violent husband. *Journal of Abnormal Psychology, 102,* 559-564.

Cose, E. (1994, August 8). Truths about spouse abuse. *Newsweek,* p. 49.

Costrich, N., Feinstein, J., Kidder, L., Marecek, J., & Pascale, L. (1975). When stereotypes hurt: Three studies of penalties for sex-role reversals. *Journal of Experimental Social Psychology, 11,* 520-530.

Cotton, S. (1995). *Support networks and marital satisfaction.* Unpublished manuscript, Macquarie University, Sydney, Australia.

Cotton, S., Antill, J., & Cunningham, J. (1993). Network structure, network support, and the marital satisfaction of husbands and wives. *Australian Journal of Psychology, 45,* 176-181.

Coughlin, C., & Vuchinich, S. (1996). Family experience in preadolescence and the development of male delinquency. *Journal of Marriage and the Family, 58,* 491-501.

Coulter, A., & Helms-Erikson, H. (1997). Work and family from a dyadic perspective: Variations in inequality. In S. Duck (Ed.), *Handbook of personal relationships* (2nd ed., pp. 487-503). West Sussex, UK: Wiley.

Cowan, G., Drinkard, J., & McGavin, L. (1984). The effects of target, age, and gender on use of power strategies. *Journal of Personality and Social Psychology, 57,* 1391-1398.

Coyne, J. C. (1976). Depression and the response of others. *Journal of Abnormal Psychology, 85,* 186-193.

Coyne, J. C., & Benazon, N. R. (in press). Coming to terms with the nature of depression in marital research and treatment. In S. R. H. Beach (Ed.), *Marital and family processes in depression.* Washington, DC: American Psychological Association.

Coyne, J. C., & Bolger, N. (1990). Doing without social support as an explanatory concept. *Journal of Social and Clinical Psychology, 9,* 148-158.

Coyne, J. C., & Calarco, M. M. (1995). Effects of the experience of depression: Application of focus group and survey methodologies. *Psychiatry: Interpersonal and Biological Processes, 58,* 149-163.

Coyne, J. C., Ellard, J. H., & Smith, D. A. F. (1990). Social support, interdependence, and the dilemmas of helping. In B. R. Sarason, I. G. Sarason, & G. R. Pierce (Eds.), *Social support: An interactional view* (pp. 129-149). New York: John Wiley.

Coyne, J. C., Kahn, J., & Gotlib, I. H. (1987). Depression. In T. Jacob (Ed.), *Family interaction and psychopathology* (pp. 509-533). New York: Plenum.

Coyne, J. C., Kessler, R. C., Tal, M., Turnbull, J., Wortman, C. B., & Greden, J. F. (1987). Living with a depressed person. *Journal of Consulting and Clinical Psychology, 55,* 347-352.

Crandall, C. S., Schiffenhauer, K. L., & Harvey, R. (1997). Friendship pair similarity as a measure of group value. *Group Dynamics: Theory, Research, and Practice, 1,* 133-143.

Crick, N. R., & Rose, A. J. (in press). Toward a gender-balanced approach to social-emotional development: A look at relational aggression. In P. H. Miller & E. K. Scholnick (Eds.), *Toward a feminist developmental psychology.* New York: Routledge.

Crohn, J. (1995). *Mixed matches: How to create successful interracial, interethnic, and interfaith relationships.* New York: Fawcett Columbine.

Crosbie-Burnett, M. (1994). The interface between stepparent families and schools: Research, theory, policy, and practice. In K. Pasley & M. Ihinger-Tallman (Eds.), *Stepparenting: Issues in theory, research, and practice* (pp. 199-216). Westport, CT: Greenwood.

Crosbie-Burnett, M., & Giles-Sims, J. (1991). Marital power in stepfather families: A test of normative resource theory. *Journal of Family Psychology, 4,* 484-496.

Crosby, F. (1991). *Juggling: The unexpected advantages of balancing career and home for women and their families.* New York: Free Press.

Crosby, F. J. (1982). *Relative deprivation and working women.* New York: Oxford University Press.

Cross, W. E., Jr. (1979). The negro-to-black conversion experience: An empirical analysis. In A. W. Boykin, A. J. Franklin, & J. F. Yates (Eds.), *Research directions of black psychologists* (pp. 107-130). New York: Russell Sage.

Csikszentmihalyi, M., & Larson, R. (1984). *Being adolescent: Conflict and growth in the teenage years.* New York: Basic Books.

Cummings, E. M., & Davies, P. (1994). *Children and marital conflict: The impact of family dispute and resolution.* New York: Guilford.

Cummings, E. M., Dearth-Pendley, G., & Smith, D. A. (in press). Parental depression and family functioning: Towards a process-oriented model of children's adjustment. In S. R. H. Beach (Ed.), *Marital and family processes in depression.* Washington, DC: American Psychological Association.

Cummings, E. M., Iannotti, R. J., & Zahn-Waxler, C. (1985). The influence of conflict between adults on the emotion and aggression of young children. *Developmental Psychology, 21,* 495-507.

Cunningham, M. R. (1985). Levites and brother's keepers: A sociobiological perspective on prosocial behavior. *Humboldt Journal of Social Relations, 13,* 35-67.

Cunningham, M. R. (1986). Measuring the physical in physical attractiveness: Quasi-experiments on the sociobiology of female facial beauty. *Journal of Personality and Social Psychology, 50,* 925-935.

Cunningham, M. R., Barbee, A. P., & Druen, P. B. (1997). Social antigens and allergies: The development of hypersensitivity in close relationships. In R. Kowalski (Ed.), *Aversive interpersonal behaviors* (pp. 190-215). New York: Plenum.

Cunningham, M. R., Barbee, A. P., & Druen, P. B. (1998). Passion lost and found. In J. Harvey (Ed.), *Handbook of personal and interpersonal loss* (pp. 153-164). New York: John Wiley.

Cunningham, M. R., Druen, P. B., & Barbee, A. P. (1997). Angels, mentors, and friends: Trade-offs among evolutionary, social, and personality variables in the evaluation of physical attractiveness. In J. Simpson & D. Kenrick (Eds.), *Evolutionary social psychology* (pp. 109-140). Mahwah, NJ: Lawrence Erlbaum.

Cunningham, M. R., Roberts, R., Barbee, A. P., & Druen, P. B. (1995). "Their ideas of beauty are, on the whole, the same as ours": Consistency and variability in the cross-cultural perception of female physical attractiveness. *Journal of Personality and Social Psychology, 68,* 261-279.

Cunningham, M. R., Rowatt, T. J., Rowatt, W. C., Miles, S., Ault-Gauthier, L. K., Shamblin, S., Bettler, R., & Barbee, A. P. (1999). *Men and women are from earth: Life-trajectory dynamics in mate choices.* Unpublished manuscript, University of Louisville.

Cupach, W. R., & Comstock, J. (1990). Satisfaction with sexual communication in marriage: Links to sexual satisfaction and dyadic adjustment. *Journal of Social and Personal Relationships, 7,* 179-186.

Cupach, W. R., & Metts, S. (1990). Remedial processes in embarrassing predicaments. In J. A. Anderson (Ed.), *Communication yearbook 13* (pp. 323-362). Newbury Park, CA: Sage.

Cupach, W. R., & Metts, S. (1991). Sexuality and communication in close relationships. In K. McKinney & S. Sprecher (Eds.), *Sexuality in close relationships* (pp. 93-110). Hillsdale, NJ: Lawrence Erlbaum.

Cupach, W. R., & Metts, S. (1994). *Facework.* Thousand Oaks, CA: Sage.

Cupach, W. R., & Metts, S. (1995). The role of sexual attitude similarity in romantic heterosexual relationships. *Personal Relationships, 2,* 287-300.

Curry, T. J., & Kenny, D. A. (1974). The effects of perceived and actual similarity in values and personality in the process of interpersonal attraction. *Quality and Quantity, 8,* 27-44.

Curtis, R. C., & Miller, K. (1986). Believing another likes or dislikes you: Behaviors making the beliefs come true. *Journal of Personality and Social Psychology, 51,* 284-290.

Cutrona, C. E. (1986). Behavioral manifestations of social support: A microanalytic investigation. *Journal of Personality and Social Psychology, 51,* 201-208.

Cutrona, C. E. (1996). The interplay of negative and supportive behaviors in marriage. In G. R. Pierce, B. R. Sarason, & I. G. Sarason (Eds.), *Handbook of social support and the family* (pp. 173-194). New York: Plenum.

Cutrona, C. E., & Suhr, J. A. (1992). Controllability of stressful events and satisfaction with spouse support behaviors. *Communication Research, 19,* 154-174.

Cutrona, C. E., Suhr, J. A., & MacFarlane, R. (1990). Interpersonal transactions and the psychological sense of support. In S. Duck & R. Silver (Eds.), *Personal relationships and social support* (pp. 30-45). London: Sage.

Dainton, M. (1995, November). *Interaction in maintained marriages: A description of type, relative routineness, and perceived importance.* Paper presented at the annual meeting of the Speech Communication Association, San Antonio, TX.

Dainton, M., & Stafford, L. (1993). Routine maintenance behaviors: A comparison of relationship type, partner similarity, and sex differences. *Journal of Social and Personal Relationships 10,* 255-271.

Dainton, M., Stafford, L., & Canary, D. J. (1994). Maintenance strategies and physical affection as predictors of love, liking, and satisfaction in marriage. *Communication Reports, 7,* 88-98.

Dakof, G. A., & Taylor, S. E. (1990). Victim's perceptions of social support: What is helpful from whom? *Journal of Personality and Social Psychology, 58,* 80-89.

Daly, K. (1992). The fit between qualitative research and characteristics of families. In J. F. Gilgun, K. Daly, & G. Handel (Eds.), *Qualitative methods in family research* (pp. 3-11). Newbury Park, CA: Sage.

Daly, K. (1997). Re-placing theory in ethnography: A postmodern view. *Qualitative Inquiry, 3,* 343-365.

Daly, M., & Wilson, M. I. (1996). Violence against stepchildren. *Current Directions in Psychological Science, 5,* 77-80.

Daly, M., Wilson, M., & Weghorst, S. J. (1982). Male sexual jealousy. *Ethology and Sociobiology, 3,* 11-27.

Darley, J. M., & Berscheid, E. (1967). Increased liking as a result of the anticipation of personal contact. *Human Relations, 20,* 29-40.

Darling, C. A., Davidson, J. K., & Cox, R. P. (1991). Female sexual response and the timing of partner orgasm. *Journal of Sex and Marital Therapy, 17,* 3-21.

Davidson, A. G. (1991). Looking for love in the age of AIDS: The language of gay personals, 1978-1988. *Journal of Sex Research, 28,* 125-137.

Davies, P. T., & Cummings, E. M. (1998). Exploring children's emotional security as a mediator of the link between marital relations and child adjustment. *Child Development, 69,* 124-139.

Davila, J. (in press). Paths to unhappiness: The overlapping courses of depression and romantic dysfunction. In S. R. H. Beach (Ed.), *Marital and family processes in depression.* Washington, DC: American Psychological Association.

Davila, J., Bradbury, T. N., Cohan, C. L., & Tochluk, S. (1997). Marital functioning and depressive symptoms: Evidence for a stress generation model. *Journal of Personality and Social Psychology, 73,* 849-861.

Davila, J., Burge, D., & Hammen, C. (1997). Why does attachment style change? *Journal of Personality and Social Psychology, 73,* 826-838.

Davis, D. (1981). Implications for interaction versus effectance as mediators of the similarity-attraction relationship. *Journal of Experimental Social Psychology, 17,* 96-116.

Davis, K. E., & Latty-Mann, H. (1987). Love styles and relationship quality: A contribution to validation. *Journal of Social and Personal Relationships, 4,* 409-428.

Davis, K. E., & Todd, M. J. (1985). Assessing friendships: Prototypes, paradigm cases, and relationship description. In S. Duck & D. Perlman (Eds.), *Understanding personal relationships: An interdisciplinary approach* (pp. 17-38). London: Sage.

Davis, M. H., Luce, C., & Kraus, S. J. (1994). The heritability of characteristics associated with dispositional empathy. *Journal of Personality, 62,* 369-391.

Davis, M. S. (1973). *Intimate relations.* New York: Free Press.

Dawson, D. A. (1991). Family structure and children's health and well-being: Data from the 1988 National Health Interview Survey on Child Health. *Journal of Marriage and the Family, 53,* 573-584.

Day, A. T. (1991). *Remarkable survivors: Insight into successful aging among women.* Washington, DC: Urban Institute.

Deal, J., Stanley Hagan, M., & Anderson, E. (1992). The marital relationship in remarried families. *Monographs of the Society for Research in Child Development, 57*(2-3, Serial No. 227).

Deaux, K., & Hanna, R. (1984). Courtship in the personals column: The influence of gender and sexual orientation. *Sex Roles, 11,* 363-375.

Deenen, A. A., Gijs, L., & van Naerssen, L. X. (1995). Thirty-five years of research into gay relationships. *Journal of Psychology and Human Sexuality, 7*(4), 19-39.

DeFrancisco, V. (1991). The sounds of silence: How men silence women in marital relations. *Discourse and Society, 2,* 413-423.

DeGarmo, D. S., & Forgatch, M. S. (1997a). Confidant support and maternal distress: Predictors of parenting practices for divorced mothers. *Personal Relationships, 4,* 305-317.

DeGarmo, D. S., & Forgatch, M. S. (1997b). Determinants of observed confidant support for divorced mothers. *Journal of Personality and Social Psychology, 72,* 336-345.

DeLamater, J. (1989). The social control of human sexuality. In K. McKinney & S. Sprecher (Eds.), *Human sexuality: The societal and interpersonal context* (pp. 30-62). Norwood, NJ: Ablex.

DeMaris, A. (1997). Elevated sexual activity in violent marriages: Hypersexuality or sexual extortion? *Journal of Sex Research, 34,* 361-373.

DeMaris, A., & Swinford, S. (1996). Female victims of spousal violence: Factors influencing their level of fearfulness. *Family Relations, 45,* 98-106.

Demo, D. H., & Acock, A. C. (1988). The impact of divorce on children. *Journal of Marriage and the Family, 50,* 619-648.

Demo, D. H., & Acock, A. C. (1993). Family diversity and the division of domestic labor: How much have things really changed? *Family Relations, 42,* 323-331.

Demo, D. H., & Acock, A. C. (1994). *Family diversity and well-being.* Thousand Oaks, CA: Sage.

Demo, D. H., & Acock, A. C. (1996a). Family structure, family process, and adolescent well-being. *Journal of Research on Adolescence, 6,* 457-488.

Demo, D. H., & Acock, A. C. (1996b). Singlehood, marriage, and remarriage: The effects of family structure and family relationships on mothers' well-being. *Journal of Family Issues, 17,* 388-407.

deMunck, V. C. (1998). Lust, love, and arranged marriages in Sri Lanka. In V. C. de Munck (Ed.), *Romantic love and sexual behavior: Perspectives from the social sciences* (pp. 285-300). Westport, CT: Praeger.

Denton, K., & Zarbantany, L. (1996). Age differences in support processes in conversations between friends. *Child Development, 67,* 1360-1373.

Denzin, N. K. (1989). *Interpretive biography.* Newbury Park, CA: Sage.

Denzin, N. K., & Lincoln, Y. S. (1994). Introduction: Entering the field of qualitative research. In N. K. Denzin & Y. S. Lincoln (Eds.), *Handbook of qualitative research* (pp. 1-17). Thousand Oaks, CA: Sage.

DeRivera, J. (1984). The structure of emotional relationships. In P. Shaver (Ed.), *Emotions, relationships, and health* (pp. 116-145). Beverly Hills, CA: Sage.

Derlega, V. J., & Chaikin, A. L. (1977). Privacy and self-disclosure in social relationships. *Journal of Social Issues, 33,* 102-115.

Derlega, V. J., & Grzelak, J. (1979). Appropriateness of self-disclosure. In G. J. Chelune (Ed.), *Self-disclosure: Origins, patterns, and implications of openness in interpersonal relationships* (pp. 151-176). San Francisco: Jossey-Bass.

Descutner, C. J., & Thelen, M. H. (1991). Development and validation of a Fear of Intimacy Scale. *Psychological Assessment, 3,* 218-225.

DeStefano, L., & Colasanto, D. (1990). The gender gap in America: Unlike 1975, today most Americans think men have it better. *Gallup Poll News Service, 54*(37), 1-7.

DeSteno, D. A., & Salovey P. (1996). Evolutionary origins of sex differences in jealousy? Questioning the fitness of the model. *Psychological Science, 7,* 367-372.

Deutsch, F. (1999). *Halving it all: How equally shared parenting works.* Cambridge, MA: Harvard University Press.

DeWeerth, C., & Kalma, A. P. (1993). Female aggression as a response to sexual jealousy: A sex role reversal. *Aggressive Behavior, 19,* 265-279.

Diaz, R. M., & Berndt, T. J. (1982). Children's knowledge of a best friend: Fact or fantasy? *Developmental Psychology, 18,* 787-794.

Dickson, F. D. (1995). The best is yet to be: Research on long-lasting marriages. In J. T. Wood & S. Duck (Eds.), *Under-studied relationships: Off the beaten track* (pp. 22-50). Thousand Oaks, CA: Sage.

Dijkstra, P., & Buunk, B. P. (1998). Jealousy as a function of rival characteristics: An evolutionary perspective. *Personality and Social Psychology Bulletin, 24,* 1158-1166.

Dillard, J. P. (1997). Explicating the goal construct: Tools for theorists. In J. O. Greene (Ed.), *Message production: Advances in communication theory* (pp. 47-69). Mahwah, NJ: Lawrence Erlbaum.

Dillard, J. P. (1998). Foreword: The role of affect in communication, biology, and social relationships. In P. A. Andersen & L. K. Guerrero (Eds.), *Handbook of communication and emotion: Research, theory, applications, and contexts* (pp. xvii-xxxii). San Diego: Academic Press.

Dillon, J. (1997). Questioning. In O. D. Hargie (Ed.), *The handbook of communication skills* (pp. 134-158). London: Routledge.

Dindia, K. (1991, November). *Uniphasic versus multiphasic relational maintenance and change strategies.* Paper presented at the annual meeting of the Speech Communication Association, Atlanta, GA.

Dindia, K. (1992, November). *A typology of relational maintenance and change strategies.* Paper presented at the annual meeting of the Speech Communication Association, Chicago.

Dindia, K. (1994a). The intrapersonal-interpersonal dialectical process of self-disclosure. In S. Duck (Ed.), *Dynamics of relationships* (pp. 27-57). Thousand Oaks, CA: Sage.

Dindia, K. (1994b). A multiphasic view of relationship maintenance strategies. In D. J. Canary & L. Stafford (Eds.), *Communication and relational maintenance* (pp. 91-110). San Diego: Academic Press.

Dindia, K., & Baxter, L. (1987). Strategies for maintaining and repairing marital relationships. *Journal of Social and Personal Relationships, 4,* 143-158.

Dindia, K., & Canary, D. J. (1993). Definitions and theoretical perspectives on maintaining relationships. *Journal of Social and Personal Relationships, 10,* 163-173.

Dindia, K., Fitzpatrick, M. A., & Kenny, D. A. (1997). Self-disclosure in spouse and stranger interaction: A social relations analysis. *Human Communication Research, 23,* 388-412.

Dion, K. K., & Dion, K. L. (1996). Cultural perspectives on romantic love. *Personal Relationships, 3,* 5-17.

DiPietro, J. A. (1981). Rough and tumble play: A function of gender. *Developmental Psychology, 17,* 50-58.

Dishion, T. J., Spracklen, K. M., Andrews, D. W., & Patterson, G. R. (1996). Deviancy training in male adolescent friendships. *Behavior Therapy, 27,* 373-390.

Doane, J. A. (1978). Family interaction and communication deviance in disturbed and normal families: A review of research. *Family Process, 17,* 357-376.

Dodge, K. A., McClaskey, C. L., & Feldman, E. (1985). Situational approach to the assessment of social competence in children. *Journal of Consulting and Clinical Psychology, 53,* 344-353.

Doherty, R. W., Hatfield, E., Thompson, K., & Choo, P. (1994). Cultural and ethnic influences on love and attachment. *Personal Relationships, 1,* 391-398.

Doherty, W. J., & Needle, R. H. (1991). Psychological adjustment and substance use among adolescents before and after a parental divorce. *Child Development, 62,* 328-337.

Doka, K. J. (1989). Disenfranchised grief. In K. J. Doka (Ed.), *Disenfranchised grief* (pp. 3-11). Lexington, MA: Lexington Books.

Dolan, M., & Bishay, N. R. (1996). The role of the sexual behavior/attractiveness schema in morbid jealousy. *Journal of Cognitive Psychotherapy, 10,* 41-61.

Dolgin, K. G., & Minowa, N. (1997). Gender differences in self-presentation: A comparison of the roles of flatteringness and intimacy in self-disclosure to friends. *Sex Roles, 36,* 371-380.

Donnelly, D. A. (1993). Sexually inactive marriages. *Journal of Sex Research, 30,* 171-179.

Douglas, W. (1987). Affinity-testing in initial interactions. *Journal of Social and Personal Relationships, 4,* 3-15.

Downey, D. B., Ainsworth-Darnell, J. W., & Dufur, M. J. (1998). Sex of parent and children's well-being in single-parent households. *Journal of Marriage and the Family, 60,* 878-893.

Drigotas, S. M., Whitney, G. A., & Rusbult, C. E. (1995). On the peculiarities of loyalty: A diary study of responses to dissatisfaction in everyday life. *Personality and Social Psychology Bulletin, 21,* 596-609.

Dryfoos, J. G. (1990). *Adolescents at risk: Prevalence and prevention.* New York: Oxford University Press.

DuBois, B. (1983). Passionate scholarship: Notes on values, knowing, and method in feminist social science. In G. Bowles & R. D. Klein (Eds.), *Theories of women's studies* (pp. 105-116). London: Routledge.

Du Bois, W. E. B. (1969). *The souls of black folk.* New York: Signet Classics. (Original work published 1903)

Du Bois, W. E. B. (1990). *The world and Africa: An inquiry into the part which Africa has played in world history.* New York: International Publishers. (Original work published 1965)

Duck, S. (1982). A topography of relationship disengagement and dissolution. In S. Duck (Ed.), *Personal relationships, Vol. 4: Dissolving personal relationships* (pp. 1-30). San Diego: Academic Press.

Duck, S. (1988). *Relating to others.* Chicago: Dorsey.

Duck, S. W. (1992). The role of theory in the examination of relationship loss. In T. L. Orbuch (Ed.), *Close relationship losses: Theoretical approaches* (pp. 3-27). New York: Springer-Verlag.

Duck, S. (1994). Steady as (s)he goes: Relational maintenance as a shared meaning system. In D. J. Canary & L. Stafford (Eds.), *Communication and relational maintenance* (pp. 45-60). San Diego: Academic Press.

Duck, S., & Allison, D. (1978). I liked you but I can't live with you: A study of lapsed friendships. *Social Behavior and Personality, 6,* 43-47.

Duck, S., & Craig, G. (1978). Personality similarity and the development of friendship: A longitudinal study. *British Journal of Social and Clinical Psychology, 17,* 237-242.

Duck, S., & Pittman, G. (1994). Social and personal relationships. In M. L. Knapp & G. R. Miller (Eds.), *Handbook of interpersonal communication* (2nd ed., pp. 676-695). Thousand Oaks, CA: Sage.

Duck, S., & Wright, P. H. (1993). Reexamining gender differences in same-gender friendships: A close look at two kinds of data. *Sex Roles, 28,* 709-727.

Duck, S. W. (1973a). Personality similarity and friendship choice: Similarity of what, when? *Journal of Personality, 41,* 543-558.

Duck, S. W. (1973b). Similarity and perceived similarity of personal constructs as influences in friendship choice. *British Journal of Social and Clinical Psychology, 12,* 1-6.

Duffy, S. M., & Rusbult, C. E. (1986). Satisfaction and commitment in homosexual and heterosexual relationships. *Journal of Homosexuality, 12*(2), 1-24.

Dugan, E., & Kivett, V. R. (1998). Implementing the Adams and Blieszner conceptual model: Predicting interactive friendship processes of older adults. *Journal of Social and Personal Relationships, 15,* 607-622.

Dugatkin, L. A. (1997). The evolution of cooperation: Four paths to the evolution and maintenance of cooperative behavior. *Bioscience, 47,* 355-362.

Dunham, P. J., Hursham, A., Litwin, E. M., Gusella, J., Ellsworth, C., & Dodd, P. W. D. (1998). Computer mediated social support: Single young mothers as a model system. *American Journal of Community Psychology, 26,* 281-306.

Dunkel-Schetter, C., & Bennett, T. L. (1990). Differentiating the cognitive and behavioral aspects of social support. In B. R. Sarason & I. G. Sarason (Eds.), *Social support: An interactional view* (pp. 267-296). New York: John Wiley.

Dunn, J. (1983). Sibling relationships in early childhood. *Child Development, 54,* 787-811.

Dunn, J., & McGuire, S. (1992). Sibling and peer relationships in childhood. *Journal of Child Psychology and Psychiatry, 33,* 67-105.

Dunn, J., & Munn, P. (1985). Becoming a family member: Family conflict and the development of social understanding. *Child Development, 56,* 480-492.

Dunn, J., & Munn, P. (1987). Development of justification in disputes with another sibling. *Developmental Psychology, 23,* 791-798.

Dunn, J., & Slomkowski, C. (1992). Conflict and the development of social understanding. In C. U. Shantz & W. W. Hartup (Eds.), *Conflict in child and adoles-*

*cent development* (pp. 70-92). New York: Cambridge University Press.

Dutton, D. G. (1995a). *The batterer: A psychological profile.* New York: Basic Books.

Dutton, D. G. (1995b). Intimate abusiveness. *Clinical Psychology: Science and Practice, 2,* 207-224.

Edwards, J. N., & Booth, A. (1976). Sexual behavior in and out of marriage: An assessment of correlates. *Journal of Marriage and the Family, 38,* 73-81.

Edwards, J. N., & Booth, A. (1994). Sexuality, marriage, and well-being: The middle years. In A. S. Rossi (Ed.), *Sexuality across the life course* (pp. 233-259). Chicago: University of Chicago Press.

Eggert, L. L., & Parks, M. R. (1987). Communication network involvement in adolescents' friendships and romantic relationships. In M. L. McLaughlin (Ed.), *Communication yearbook* (pp. 283-322). Newbury Park, CA: Sage.

Eisenberg, A. R. (1992). Conflicts between mothers and their young children. *Merrill-Palmer Quarterly, 38,* 21-43.

Ekerdt, D. J., & Vinick, B. H. (1991). Marital complaints in husband-working and husband-retired couples. *Research on Aging, 13,* 364-382.

Ekhardt, C. I., Barbour, K. A., & Davidson, G. C. (1998). Articulated thoughts of maritally violent and nonviolent men during anger arousal. *Journal of Consulting and Clinical Psychology, 66,* 259-269.

Elbaum, P. L. (1981). The dynamics, implications, and treatment of extramarital sexual relationships for the family therapist. *Journal of Marital and Family Therapy, 7,* 489-495.

Elder, G. H. (1997). The life course and human development. In R. M. Lerner (Ed.), *Handbook of child psychology, Vol. 1: Theoretical models of human development* (5th ed., pp. 939-991). New York: John Wiley.

Eldridge, N. S., & Gilbert, L. A. (1990). Correlates of relationship satisfaction in lesbian couples. *Psychology of Women Quarterly, 14,* 43-62.

Elicker, J., Englund, M., & Sroufe, L. A. (1992). Predicting peer competence and peer relationships in childhood from early parent-child relationships. In R. Parke & G. Ladd (Eds.), *Family-peer relationships: Modes of linkage.* Hillsdale, NJ: Lawrence Erlbaum.

Ellis, A. (1996). The treatment of morbid jealousy: A rational emotive behavior therapy approach. *Journal of Cognitive Psychotherapy, 10,* 23-33.

Ellis, C. (1995). *Final negotiations: A story of love, loss, and chronic illness.* Philadelphia: Temple University Press.

Emerson, R. M., Fretz, R. I., & Shaw, L. L. (1995). *Writing ethnographic fieldnotes.* Chicago: University of Chicago Press.

Emery, B. C., & Lloyd, S. A. (1994). A feminist perspective on the study of women who use aggression in close relationships. In D. L. Sollie & L. A. Leslie

(Eds.), *Feminism and the study of family and close relationships: Conceptual, personal, and methodological issues in current research* (pp. 237-262). Thousand Oaks, CA: Sage.

Engel, J. W., & Saracino, M. (1986). Love preferences and ideals: A comparison of homosexual, bisexual, and heterosexual groups. *Contemporary Family Therapy, 8,* 241-250.

Epstein, C. (1981). *Women in law.* New York: Basic Books.

Erera-Weatherly, P. I. (1996). On becoming a stepparent: Factors associated with the adoption of alternative stepparenting styles. *Journal of Divorce and Remarriage, 25,* 155-174.

Erickson, R. (1993). Reconceptualizing family work: The effects of emotion work on perceptions of marital quality. *Journal of Marriage and the Family, 4,* 301-313.

Erikson, E. (1950). *Childhood and society.* New York: Norton.

Erikson, E. (1963). *Childhood and society* (2nd ed.). New York: Norton.

Erikson, E. H. (1968). *Identity, youth, and crisis.* New York: Norton.

Espiritu, Y. L. (1997). *Asian American women and men: Labor, laws, and love.* Thousand Oaks, CA: Sage.

Ewen, R. B. (1993). *An introduction to theories of personality* (4th ed.). Hillsdale, NJ: Lawrence Erlbaum.

Falbo, T., & Peplau, L. A. (1980). Power strategies in intimate relationships. *Journal of Personality and Social Psychology, 38,* 618-628.

Falco, K. L. (1991). *Psychotherapy with lesbian clients.* New York: Brunner/Mazel.

Falk, D. R., & Wagner, P. N. (1985). Intimacy of self-disclosure and response processes as factors affecting the development of interpersonal relationships. *Journal of Social Psychology, 125,* 557-570.

Farnsworth, J., Lund, D. A., & Pett, M. A. (1989). Management and outcomes of loss in later life: A comparison of bereavement and divorce. In D. A. Lund (Ed.), *Older bereaved spouses* (pp. 155-166). Washington, DC: Hemisphere.

Fauber, R., Forehand, R., Thomas, A. M., & Wierson, M. (1990). A mediational model of the impact of marital conflict on adolescent adjustment in intact and divorced families: The role of disrupted parenting. *Child Development, 61,* 1112-1123.

Feeney, J. A. (1994). Attachment style, communication patterns, and satisfaction across the life cycle of marriage. *Personal Relationships, 1,* 333-348.

Feeney, J. A. (1995). Adult attachment and emotional control. *Personal Relationships, 2,* 143-159.

Feeney, J. A. (1996). Attachment, caregiving, and marital satisfaction. *Personal Relationships, 4,* 401-416.

Feeney, J. A. (1998). Adult attachment and relationship-centered anxiety: Responses to physical and emotional distancing. In J. A. Simpson & W. S. Rholes

(Eds.), *Attachment theory and close relationships* (pp. 189-218). New York: Guilford.

Feeney, J. A. (1999). Adult attachment, emotional control, and marital satisfaction. *Personal Relationships, 6,* 169-185.

Feeney, J. A., & Humphreys, T. (1996, November). *Parental, sibling, and romantic relationships: Exploring the functions of attachment bonds.* Paper presented at the Fifth Australian Family Research Conference, Brisbane.

Feeney, J. A., Kelly, L., Gallois, C., Peterson, C., & Terry, D. J. (in press). Attachment style, assertive communication, and safer sex behavior. *Journal of Applied Social Psychology.*

Feeney, J. A., & Noller, P. (1990). Attachment style as a predictor of adult romantic relationships. *Journal of Personality and Social Psychology, 58,* 281-291.

Feeney, J. A., & Noller, P. (1991). Attachment style and verbal descriptions of romantic partners. *Journal of Social and Personal Relationships, 8,* 187-215.

Feeney, J. A., & Noller, P. (1992). Attachment style and romantic love: Relationship dissolution. *Australian Journal of Psychology, 44,* 69-74.

Feeney, J. A., & Noller, P. (1996). *Adult attachment.* Thousand Oaks, CA: Sage.

Feeney, J. A., Noller, P., & Callan, V. J. (1994). Attachment style, communication, and satisfaction in the early years of marriage. In K. Bartholomew & D. Perlman (Eds.), *Advances in personal relationships, Vol. 5: Attachment processes in adulthood* (pp. 269-308). London: Jessica Kingsley.

Feeney, J. A., Noller, P., & Hanrahan, M. (1994). Assessing adult attachment: Developments in the conceptualization of security and insecurity. In M. B. Sperling & W. H. Berman (Eds.), *Attachment in adults: Theory, assessment, and treatment* (pp. 128-152). New York: Guilford.

Feeney, J. A., Noller, P., & Patty, J. (1993). Adolescents' interactions with the opposite sex: Influence of attachment style and gender. *Journal of Adolescence, 16,* 169-186.

Feeney, J. A., Noller, P., & Roberts, N. (1998). Emotion, attachment, and satisfaction in close relationships. In P. A. Andersen & L. K. Guerrero (Eds.), *Handbook of communication and emotion: Research, theory, applications, and contexts* (pp. 473-505). San Diego: Academic Press.

Feeney, J. A., Peterson, C., Gallois, C., & Terry, D. J. (1998). *Attachment style as a predictor of sexual attitudes and behavior in late adolescence.* Unpublished manuscript, University of Queensland, Australia.

Feeney, J. A., & Ryan, S. M. (1994). Attachment style and affect regulation: Relationships with health behavior and family experiences of illness in a student sample. *Health Psychology, 13,* 334-345.

Feeney, J. A., Ward, C., Noller, P., & Hohaus, L. (1998, April). *Attachment, caregiving, and sexuality in the transition to parenthood.* Paper presented at the meeting of the Society of Australasian Social Psychologists, Christchurch, New Zealand.

Fehr, B. (1988). Prototype analysis of the concepts of love and commitment. *Journal of Personality and Social Psychology, 55,* 557-579.

Fehr, B. (1993). How do I love thee? Let me consult my prototype. In S. Duck (Ed.), *Individuals in relationships* (pp. 87-120). Newbury Park, CA: Sage.

Fehr, B. (1994). Prototype-based assessment of laypeople's views of love. *Personal Relationships, 1,* 309-331.

Fehr, B. (1996). *Friendship processes.* Thousand Oaks, CA: Sage.

Fehr, B., Baldwin, M., Collins, L., Patterson, S., & Benditt, R. (1999). Anger in close relationships: An interpersonal script analysis. *Personality and Social Psychology Bulletin, 25,* 299-312.

Fehr, B., & Russell, J. A. (1991). The concept of love viewed from a prototype perspective. *Journal of Personality and Social Psychology, 60,* 425-438.

Feingold, A. (1990). Gender differences in effects of physical attractiveness on romantic attraction: A comparison across five research paradigms. *Journal of Personality and Social Psychology, 59,* 981-993.

Feingold, A. (1992). Good-looking people are not what we think. *Psychological Bulletin, 111,* 304-341.

Feld, S., & Carter, W. C. (1998). Foci of activity as changing contexts for friendship. In R. G. Adams & G. Allan (Eds.), *Placing friendship in context* (pp. 136-152). New York: Cambridge University Press.

Feldman, S. S., Gowen, L. K., & Fisher, L. (1998). Family relationships and gender as predictors of romantic intimacy in young adults: A longitudinal study. *Journal of Research on Adolescence, 8,* 263-286.

Feldman, S. S., & Quatman, T. (1988). Factors influencing age expectations for adolescent autonomy: A study of early adolescents and parents. *Journal of Early Adolescence, 8,* 325-343.

Felmlee, D., Sprecher, S., & Bassin, E. (1990). The dissolution of intimate relationships: A hazard model. *Social Psychology Quarterly, 53,* 13-30.

Felson, R. B., & Russo, N. (1988). Parental punishment and sibling aggression. *Social Psychology Quarterly, 51,* 11-18.

Felton, B. J., & Berry, C. A. (1992). Do the sources of urban elderly's social support determine its psychological consequences? *Psychology and Aging, 7,* 89-97.

Ferguson, T. J., & Stegge, H. (1995). Emotional states and traits in children: The case of guilt and shame. In J. P. Tangney & K. W. Fischer (Eds.), *Self-conscious emotions: The psychology of shame, guilt, embarrassment, and pride* (pp. 174-197). New York: Guilford.

Ferree, M. M. (1990). Beyond separate spheres: Feminism and family research. *Journal of Marriage and the Family, 52,* 866-884.

Ferree, M. M. (1991). The gender division of labor in two-earner marriages. *Journal of Family Issues, 12,* 158-180.

Festinger, L., Schachter, S., & Back, K. (1950). *Social pressures in informal groups: A study of human factors in housing.* New York: Harper.

Filsinger, E. E., & Thoma, S. J. (1988). Behavioral antecedent of relational stability and adjustment: A five-year longitudinal study. *Journal of Marriage and the Family, 50,* 585-595.

Fincham, F. D., & Beach, S. R. H. (1999). Conflict in marriage: Implications for working with couples. *Annual Review of Psychology, 50,* 47-77.

Fincham, F. D., Beach, S. R. H., Harold, G. T., & Osborne, L. N. (1997). Marital satisfaction and depression: Longitudinal relationships for husbands and wives. *Psychological Science, 3,* 351-357.

Fine, G. A. (1981). Friends, impression management, and preadolescent behavior. In S. R. Asher & J. M. Gottman (Eds.), *The development of children's friendships* (pp. 29-52). New York: Cambridge University Press.

Fine, M., & Kurdek, L. (1994). A multidimensional cognitive-developmental model of stepfamily adjustment. In K. Pasley & M. Ihinger-Tallman (Eds.), *Stepparenting: Issues in theory, research, and practice* (pp. 15-32). Westport, CT: Greenwood.

Fine, M. A., Coleman, M., Gable, S., Ganong, L. H., Ispa, J., Morrison, J., & Thornburg, K. R. (1999). Research-based parenting education for divorcing parents: A university-community collaboration. In T. R. Chibocos & R. M. Lerner (Eds.), *Serving children and families through community-university partnerships: Success stories* (pp. 249-256). Norwell, MA: Kluwer.

Fine, M. A., Coleman, M., & Ganong, L. (1998). Consistency in perceptions of the stepparent role among stepparents, parents, and stepchildren. *Journal of Social and Personal Relationships, 15,* 810-828.

Fine, M. A., & Sacher, J. A. (1997). Predictors of distress following relationship termination among dating couples. *Journal of Social and Clinical Psychology, 16,* 381-388.

Fine, M. A., & Schwebel, A. I. (1991). Resiliency in black children from single-parent families. In W. A. Rhodes & W. K. Brown (Eds.), *Why some children succeed despite the odds* (pp. 23-40). New York: Praeger.

Fingerman, K. (1996). Sources of tension in the aging mother and adult daughter relationship. *Psychology and Aging, 11,* 591-606.

Fingerman, K. (1998). Tight lips? Aging mothers' and adult daughters' responses to interpersonal tensions in their relationships. *Personal Relationships, 5,* 121-138.

Fingerman, K. L. (1995). Aging mothers' and adult daughters' perceptions of conflict behaviors. *Psychology and Aging, 10,* 639-649.

Fink, B., & Wild, K. (1995). Similarities in leisure interests: Effects of selection and socialization in friendships. *Journal of Social Psychology, 135,* 471-482.

Finkelhor, D., & Yllö, K. (1985). *License to rape: Sexual abuse of wives.* New York: Holt, Rinehart & Winston.

Fischer, C. S., Jackson, R. M., Stueve, C. A., Gerson, K., Jones, L. M., & Baldassare, M. (1977). *Network and places: Social relations in the urban setting.* New York: Free Press.

Fischer, J. L., & Narus, L. R., Jr. (1981). Sex roles and intimacy in same sex and other sex relationships. *Psychology of Women Quarterly, 5,* 411-458.

Fischer, K. W., & Tangney, J. P. (1995). Self-conscious emotions and the affect revolution: Framework and overview. In J. P. Tangney & K. W. Fischer (Eds.), *Self-conscious emotions: The psychology of shame, guilt, embarrassment, and pride* (pp. 1-24). New York: Guilford.

Fisher, B. A. (1982). The pragmatic perspective on human communication: A view from systems theory. In F. E. X. Dance (Ed.), *Human communication theory* (pp. 47-69). New York: Harper & Row.

Fisher, F. M. (1970). A correspondence principle for simultaneous equation models. *Econometrica, 38,* 73-92.

Fisher, L. A., & Bauman, K. E. (1988). Influence and selection in the friend-adolescent relationship: Findings from studies of adolescent smoking and drinking. *Journal of Applied Social Psychology, 18,* 289-314.

Fishman, P. (1978). Interaction: The work women do. *Social Problems, 25,* 397-406.

Fishman, P. (1983). Interaction: The work women do. In B. Thorne, C. Kramarae, & N. Henley (Eds.), *Language, gender, and society* (pp. 89-101). Rowley, MA: Newbury House.

Fiske, S. T., & Taylor, S. E. (1991). *Social cognition* (2nd ed.). New York: McGraw-Hill.

Fitness, J., & Fletcher, G. J. O. (1993). Love, hate, anger, and jealousy in close relationships: A prototype and cognitive appraisal analysis. *Journal of Personality and Social Psychology, 65,* 942-958.

Fitzpatrick, M. A. (1988a). *Between husbands and wives: Communication in marriage.* Newbury Park, CA: Sage.

Fitzpatrick, M. A. (1988b). Negotiation, problem solving, and conflict in various types of marriages. In P. Noller & M. A. Fitzpatrick (Eds.), *Perspectives on marital interaction* (pp. 245-270). Philadelphia: Multilingual Matters.

Flax, J. (1987). Postmodernism and gender relations in feminist theory. *Signs, 12,* 621-643.

Fletcher, K. E., Fischer, M., Barkley, R. A., & Smallish, L. (1996). A sequential analysis of the mother-ado-lescent interactions of ADHD, ADHD/ODD, and normal teenagers during neutral and conflict discussions. *Journal of Abnormal Child Psychology, 24,* 271-297.

Flinn, M. (1992). Paternal care in a Caribbean village. In B. S. Hewlett (Ed.), *Father-child relations: Cultural and biosocial contexts* (pp. 57-84). New York: Aldine de Gruyter.

Florsheim, P., Tolan, P., & Gorman-Smith, D. (1998). Family relationships, parenting practices, the availability of male family members, and the behavior of inner-city boys in single-mother and two-parent families. *Child Development, 69,* 1437-1447.

Floyd, K. (1995). Gender and closeness among friends and siblings. *Journal of Psychology, 129,* 193-202.

Floyd, K. (1996a). Brotherly love I: The experience of closeness in the fraternal dyad. *Personal Relationships, 3,* 369-385.

Floyd, K. (1996b). Communicating closeness among siblings: An application of the gendered closeness perspective. *Communication Research Reports, 13,* 27-34.

Floyd, K. (1997a). Brotherly love II: A developmental perspective on liking, love, and closeness in the fraternal dyad. *Journal of Family Psychology, 11,* 196-209.

Floyd, K. (1997b). Communicating affection in dyadic relationships: An assessment of behavior and expectancies. *Communication Quarterly, 45,* 68-80.

Foa, U. G., & Foa, E. B. (1974). *Societal structures of the mind.* Springfield, IL: Charles C Thomas.

Foley, S. H., Rounsaville, B. J., Weissman, M. M., Sholomaskas, D., & Chevron, E. (1989). Individual versus conjoint interpersonal psychotherapy for depressed patients with marital disputes. *International Journal of Family Psychiatry, 10,* 29-42.

Folingstad, D. R., Rutledge, L. L., Berg, B. J., Hause, E. S., & Polek, D. S. (1990). The role of emotional abuse in physically abusive relationships. *Journal of Family Violence, 5,* 107-120.

Folkman, S. (1997). Introduction to the special section: Use of bereavement narratives to predict well-being of gay men whose partners died of AIDS—Four theoretical perspectives. *Journal of Personality and Social Psychology, 72,* 851-854.

Folkman, S., & Lazarus, R. S. (1985). If it changes, it must be a process: A study of emotion and coping during three stages of a college examination. *Journal of Personality and Social Psychology, 48,* 150-170.

Fonow, M. M., & Cook, J. A. (1991). Back to the future: A look at the second wave of feminist epistemology and methodology. In M. M. Fonow & J. A. Cook (Eds.), *Beyond methodology: Feminist scholarship as lived research* (pp. 1-15). Bloomington: Indiana University Press.

Ford, C. S., & Beach, F. A. (1951). *Patterns of sexual behavior.* New York: Harper.

Forehand, R., Armistead, L., & Corinne, D. (1997). Is adolescent adjustment following parental divorce a function of predivorce adjustment? *Journal of Abnormal Child Psychology, 25,* 157-164.

Forehand, R., Neighbors, Devine, D., & Armistead, L. (1994). Interparental conflict and parental divorce: Individual, relative, and interactive effects on adolescents across four years. *Family Relations, 43,* 387-393.

Forgatch, M. S., & De Garmo, D. S. (1997). Adult problem solving: Contributor to parenting and child outcomes in divorced families. *Social Development, 6,* 237-253.

Fox, R. C. (1996). Bisexuality in perspective: A review of theory and research. In B. A. Firestein (Ed.), *Bisexuality: The psychology and politics of an invisible minority* (pp. 3-50). Thousand Oaks, CA: Sage.

Fraley, R. C., & Davis, K. E. (1997). Attachment formation and transfer in young adults' close friendships and romantic relationships. *Personal Relationships, 4,* 131-144.

Fraley, R. C., Davis, K. E., & Shaver, P. R. (1998). Dismissing-avoidance and the defensive organization of emotion, cognition, and behavior. In J. A. Simpson & W. S. Rholes (Eds.), *Attachment theory and close relationships* (pp. 249-279). New York: Guilford.

Fraley, R. C., & Waller, N. G. (1998). Adult attachment patterns: A test of the typological model. In J. A. Simpson & W. S. Rholes (Eds.), *Attachment theory and close relationships* (pp. 77-114). New York: Guilford.

Francis, J. L. (1977). Toward the management of heterosexual jealousy. *Journal of Marriage and Family Counseling, 3,* 61-69.

Frazier, P. A., Byer, A. L., Fischer, A. R., Wright, D. M., & De Bord, K. A. (1996). Adult attachment style and partner choice: Correlational and experimental findings. *Personal Relationships, 3,* 117-136.

Freed, A. F., & Greenwood, A. (1996). Women, men, and type of talk: What makes the difference? *Language in Society, 25,* 1-26.

Freire, P. (1970). *Pedagogy of the oppressed.* New York: Herder & Herder.

French, M. (1992). *The war against women.* New York: Summit.

Freud, A. (1969). Adolescence as a developmental disturbance. In G. Caplan & S. Lebovici (Eds.), *Adolescence: Psychological perspectives* (pp. 5-10). New York: Basic Books.

Freud, A., & Dann, S. (1951). An experiment in group upbringing. In R. Eisler (Ed.), *The psychoanalytic study of the child* (pp. 127-168). New York: International Universities Press.

Freud, S. (1949). *The infantile genital organization of the libido* (Collected Papers, Vol. 2). London: Hogarth. (Original work published 1923)

Frey, K., & Hojjat, M. (1998). Are love styles related to sexual styles? *Journal of Sex Research, 35,* 265-271.

Friese, J. H., Hooker, K. A., Kotary, L., & Schwagler, J. (1993). Family rituals in the early stages of parenthood. *Journal of Marriage and the Family, 55,* 633-642.

Frijda, N. H. (1986). *The emotions.* New York: Cambridge University Press.

Frinter, M. P., & Rubinson, L. (1993). Acquaintance rape: The influence of alcohol, fraternity membership, and sports team membership. *Journal of Sex Education and Therapy, 19,* 272-284.

Fuligni, A. (1998). Authority, autonomy, and parent-adolescent conflict and cohesion: A study of adolescents from Mexican, Chinese, Filipino, and European backgrounds. *Developmental Psychology, 34,* 782-792.

Fuller, T. L., & Fincham, F. D. (1995). Attachment style in married couples: Relation to current marital functioning, stability over time, and method of assessment. *Personal Relationships, 2,* 17-34.

Furman, W., & Bierman, K. L. (1984). Children's conceptions of friendship: A multimethod study of developmental changes. *Developmental Psychology, 20,* 925-931.

Furman, W., & Buhrmester, D. (1992). Age and sex differences in perceptions of networks and personal relationships. *Child Development, 63,* 103-115.

Furman, W., & Robbins, P. (1985). What's the point? Issues in the selection of treatment objectives. In B. H. Schneider, K. H. Rubin, & J. E. Ledingham (Eds.), *Children's peer relations: Issues in assessment and intervention* (pp. 41-54). New York: Springer-Verlag.

Furman, W., & Wehner, E. A. (1994). Romantic views: Toward a theory of adolescent romantic relationships. In R. Montemayor, G. R. Adams, & T. P. Gullotta (Eds.), *Personal relationships during adolescence* (pp. 168-195). Thousand Oaks, CA: Sage.

Gable, S. L., & Reis, H. T. (1999). Now and then, them and us, this and that: Studying relationships across time, partner, context, and person. *Personal Relationships, 6,* 415-432.

Gadlin, H. (1977). Private lives and public order: A critical view of the history of intimate relations in the United States. In G. Levinger & H. Raush (Eds.), *Close relationships: Perspectives on the meaning of intimacy* (pp. 33-72). Amherst: University of Massachusetts Press.

Gagnon, J. H., & Parker, R. G. (1995). Conceiving sexuality. In R. G. Parker & J. H. Gagnon (Eds.), *Conceiving sexuality: Approaches to sex research in a postmodern world* (pp. 3-16). New York: Routledge.

Gaines, S. (1995). Relationships between members of cultural minorities. In J. T. Wood & S. Duck (Eds.), *Understanding relationship processes, Vol. 6: Understudied relationships: Off the beaten track* (pp. 51-88). Thousand Oaks, CA: Sage.

Gaines, S. O., Jr. (1996). Impact of interpersonal traits and gender-role compliance on interpersonal resource exchange among dating and married couples. *Journal of Social and Personal Relationships, 13,* 241-261.

Gaines, S. O., Jr., Chalfin, J., Kim, M., & Taing, P. (1998). Communicating prejudice in personal relationships. In M. L. Hecht (Ed.), *Communicating prejudice* (pp. 163-186). Thousand Oaks, CA: Sage.

Gaines, S. O., Jr., Granrose, C. S., Rios, D. I., Garcia, B. F., Page, M. S., Farris, K. R., & Bledsoe, K. L. (1999). Patterns of attachment and responses to accommodative dilemmas among interethnic/interracial couples. *Journal of Social and Personal Relationships, 16,* 277-287.

Gaines, S. O., Jr., & Ickes, W. (1997). Perspectives on interracial relationships. In S. Duck (Ed.), *Handbook of personal relationships* (2nd ed., pp. 197-220). Chichester, UK: Wiley.

Gaines, S. O., Jr., & Liu, J. H. (1997). Romanticism and interpersonal resource exchange among interethnic couples. In S. O. Gaines, Jr., with R. Buriel, J. H. Liu, & D. I. Rios (Eds.), *Culture, ethnicity, and personal relationship processes* (pp. 91-118). New York: Routledge.

Gaines, S. O., Jr., Marelich, W. D., Bledsoe, K. L., Steers, W. M., Henderson, M. C., Granrose, C. S., Barajas, L., Hicks, D., Lyde, M., Takahashi, Y., Yum, N., Rios, D. I., Garcia, B. F., Farris, K. R., & Page, M. S. (1997). Links between race/ethnicity and cultural values as mediated by racial/ethnic identity and moderated by gender. *Journal of Personality and Social Psychology, 72,* 1460-1476.

Gaines, S. O., Jr., Reis, H. T., Summers, S., Rusbult, C. E., Cox, C. L., Wexler, M. O., Marelich, W. D., & Kurland, G. J. (1997). Impact of attachment style on reactions to accommodative dilemmas in close relationships. *Personal Relationships, 4,* 93-113.

Gaines, S. O., Jr., Rios, D. I., Granrose, C. S., Bledsoe, K. L., Farris, K. R., Page Youn, M. S., & Garcia, B. F. (1999). Romanticism and interpersonal resource exchange among African American-Anglo and other interracial couples. *Journal of Black Psychology, 25,* 461-489.

Galambos, N. L., & Almeida, D. M. (1992). Does parent-adolescent conflict increase in early adolescence? *Journal of Marriage and the Family, 54,* 737-747.

Gallagher, S. K. (1994). Doing their share: Comparing patterns of help given by older and younger adults. *Journal of Marriage and the Family, 56,* 567-578.

Game, A., & Metcalfe, A. (1996). *Passionate sociology.* London: Sage.

Gangestad, S. W. (1993). Sexual selection and physical attractiveness: Implications for mating dynamics. *Human Nature, 4,* 205-235.

Ganong, L. (1993). Family diversity in a youth organization: Involvement of single-parent families and stepfamilies in 4-H. *Family Relations, 42,* 286-292.

Ganong, L., & Coleman, M. (1989). Preparing for remarriage: Anticipating the issues, seeking solutions. *Family Relations, 38,* 28-33.

Ganong, L., & Coleman, M. (1994a). Adolescent stepchild-stepparent relationships: Changes over time. In K. Pasley & M. Ihinger-Tallman (Eds.), *Stepparenting: Issues in theory, research, and practice* (pp. 87-106). New York: Greenwood.

Ganong, L., & Coleman, M. (1994b). *Remarried family relationships.* Thousand Oaks, CA: Sage.

Ganong, L., & Coleman, M. (1999). *New families, new responsibilities: Intergenerational obligations following divorce and remarriage.* Mahwah, NJ: Lawrence Erlbaum.

Ganong, L., Coleman, M., Fine, M., & Martin, P. (1999). Stepparents' affinity-seeking and affinity-maintaining strategies with stepchildren. *Journal of Family Issues, 20,* 299-327.

Ganong, L., Coleman, M., & Kennedy, G. (1990). The effects of using alternate labels in denoting stepparent or stepfamily status. *Journal of Social Behavior and Personality, 5,* 453-463.

Ganong, L., Coleman, M., Killian, T., & McDaniel, A. K. (1998). Attitudes toward obligations to assist an elderly parent or stepparent after later-life remarriage. *Journal of Marriage and the Family, 60,* 595-610.

Gans, H. (1957). *The urban villagers.* Glencoe, IL: Free Press.

Garcia O'Hearn, H., Margolin, G., & John, R. S. (1997). Mothers' and fathers' reports of children's reactions to naturalistic marital conflict. *Journal of the American Academy of Child and Adolescent Psychiatry, 36,* 1366-1373.

Garrett-Gooding, J., & Senter, R. (1987). Attitudes and acts of sexual aggression on a university campus. *Sociological Inquiry, 57,* 348-371.

Gentry, M., & Schulman, A. (1988). Remarriage as a coping response for widowhood. *Psychology and Aging, 3,* 191-196.

George, C., Kaplan, N., & Main, M. (1985). *An Adult Attachment Interview.* Unpublished manuscript, University of California, Berkeley.

Gergen, K. J., & Gergen, M. M. (1987). Narratives of relationship. In R. Burnett, P. McGhee, & D. D. Clarke (Eds.), *Accounting for relationships* (pp. 269-315). New York: Methuen.

Getzel, G. (1982). Helping elderly couples in crisis. *Social Casework, 63,* 515-521.

Gilbert, L. A. (1993). *Two careers, one family: The promise of gender equality.* Newbury Park, CA: Sage.

Gilbert, L. A., & Rachlin, V. (1987). Mental health and psychological functioning of dual-career families. *The Counseling Psychologist, 15,* 7-49.

Gilbertson, J., Dindia, K., & Allen, M. (1998). Relational continuity constructional units and the maintenance of relationships. *Journal of Social and Personal Relationships, 15,* 774-790.

Gilgun, J. F. (1992). Definitions, methodologies, and methods in qualitative family research. In J. F. Gilgun, K. Daly, & G. Handel (Eds.), *Qualitative methods in family research* (pp. 22-39). Newbury Park, CA: Sage.

Gilgun, J. F. (1995). We shared something special: The moral discourse of incest perpetrators. *Journal of Marriage and the Family, 57,* 265-281.

Glaser, B. G., & Strauss, A. L. (1967). *The discovery of grounded theory: Strategies for qualitative research.* New York: Aldine de Gruyter.

Glass, S. P., & Wright, T. L. (1985). Sex differences in type of extramarital involvement and marital dissatisfaction. *Sex Roles, 12,* 1101-1119.

Glass, S. P., & Wright, T. L. (1992). Justifications for extramarital relationships: The association between attitudes, behaviors, and gender. *Journal of Sex Research, 29,* 361-387.

Glenn, N. D., & Weaver, C. N. (1979). Attitudes toward premarital, extramarital, and homosexual relations in the U.S. in the 1970s. *Journal of Sex Research, 15,* 108-118.

Glenn, P. J., & Knapp, M. L. (1987). The interactive framing of play in adult conversations. *Communication Quarterly, 35,* 48-66.

Godfrey, D. K., Jones, E. E., & Lord, C. G. (1986). Self-promotion is not ingratiating. *Journal of Personality and Social Psychology, 50,* 106-115.

Goffman, E. (1963). *Stigma: Notes on the management of spoiled identity.* Englewood Cliffs, NJ: Prentice Hall.

Gohm, C. L., Oishi, S., Darlington, J., & Diener, E. (1998). Culture, parental conflict, parental marital status, and the subjective well-being of young adults. *Journal of Marriage and the Family, 60,* 319-334.

Gold, R. L. (1958). Roles in sociological field observations. *Social Forces, 36,* 217-223.

Goldner, V., Penn, P., Scheinberg, M., & Walker, G. (1990). Love and violence: Gender paradoxes in volatile attachments. *Family Process, 19,* 343-364.

Goldsmith, D. (1990). A dialectical perspective on the expression of autonomy and connection in romantic relationships. *Western Journal of Speech Communication, 54,* 537-556.

Goldsmith, D. J., & Baxter, L. A. (1996). Constituting relationships in talk: A taxonomy of speech events in social and personal relationships. *Human Communication Research, 25,* 87-114.

Goldsmith, D. J., & Dun, S. A. (1997). Sex differences and similarities in the communication of social support. *Journal of Social and Personal Relationships, 14,* 317-337.

Goldwert, M. (1980). *History as neurosis: Paternalism and machismo in Spanish America.* Lanham, MD: University Press of America.

Goldwert, M. (1982). *Psychic conflict in Spanish America: Six essays on the psychohistory of the region.* Lanham, MD: University Press of America.

Gonzales, M. H., & Meyers, S. A. (1993). "Your mother would like me": Self-presentation in the personal ads of heterosexual and homosexual men and women. *Personality and Social Psychology Bulletin, 19,* 131-142.

Gonzalez, R., & Griffin, D. (1997). On the statistics of interdependence: Treating dyadic data with respect. In S. Duck (Ed.), *Handbook of personal relationships: Theory, research, and interventions* (2nd ed., pp. 271-302). Chichester, UK: Wiley.

Gonzalez, R., & Griffin, D. (1999). The correlational analysis of dyad-level data in the distinguishable case. *Personal Relationships, 6,* 449-469.

Goode, W. J. (1956). *After divorce.* New York: Free Press.

Goodkin, K., Blaney, N. T., Tuttle, R. S., & Nelson, R. H. (1996). Bereavement and HIV infection. *International Review of Psychiatry, 8,* 201-216.

Goodwin, R., & Findlay, R. (1997). "We were just fated together" . . . Chinese love and the concept of *yuan* in England and Hong Kong. *Personal Relationships, 4,* 85-92.

Gordon, A. I. (1964). *Intermarriage.* Boston: Beacon.

Gottlieb, B. H. (1978). The development and application of a classification scheme of informal helping behaviors. *Canadian Journal of Behavioral Science, 10,* 105-115.

Gottlieb, B. H. (1981). Social networks and social support in community mental health. In B. H. Gottlieb (Ed.), *Social networks and social support* (pp. 11-43). London: Sage.

Gottlieb, B. H. (1985). Social support and the study of personal relationships. *Journal of Social and Personal Relationships, 2,* 351-375.

Gottlieb, B. H., & Wagner, F. (1991). Stress and support processes in close relationships. In J. Eckenrode (Ed.), *The social context of coping* (pp. 165-188). New York: Plenum.

Gottman, J., & Carrère, S. (1994). Why can't men and women get along? Developmental roots and marital inequities. In D. Canary & L. Stafford (Eds.), *Communication and relational maintenance* (pp. 203-229). San Diego: Academic Press.

Gottman, J. M. (1979). *Marital interaction: Experimental investigations.* New York: Academic Press.

Gottman, J. M. (1983). How children become friends. *Monographs of the Society for Research in Child Development, 78*(3, Serial No. 201).

Gottman, J. M. (1993). A theory of marital dissolution and stability. *Journal of Family Psychology, 7,* 57-75.

Gottman, J. M. (1994a). *What predicts divorce: The relationship between marital processes and marital outcomes.* Hillsdale, NJ: Lawrence Erlbaum.

Gottman, J. M. (1994b). *Why marriages succeed or fail.* New York: Simon & Schuster.

Gottman, J. M., Jacobson, N. S., Rushe, R. R., Shortt, J. W., Babcock, J., La Taillade, J. J., & Waltz, J. (1995). The relationship between heart rate reactivity, emotionally aggressive behavior, and general violence in batterers. *Journal of Family Psychology, 9,* 227-248.

Gottman, J. M., & Levenson, R. W. (1992). Marital processes predictive of later dissolution: Behavior, physiology, and health. *Journal of Personality and Social Psychology, 63,* 221-233.

Gottman, J. M., & Mettetal, G. (1986). Speculations about social and affective development: Friendship and acquaintanceship through adolescence. In J. M. Gottman & J. G. Parker (Eds.), *Conversations of friends: Speculations on affective development* (pp. 192-237). New York: Cambridge University Press.

Gottman, J. M., & Parker, J. G. (Eds.). (1986). *Conversations of friends: Speculations on affective development.* New York: Cambridge University Press.

Gottman, J. M., & Parkhurst, J. (1980). A developmental theory of friendship and acquaintanceship processes. In W. A. Collins (Ed.), *Minnesota symposia on child psychology* (Vol. 13, pp. 197-253). Hillsdale, NJ: Lawrence Erlbaum.

Gottman, J. M., & Roy, A. K. (1990). *Sequential analysis: A guide for behavioral researchers.* New York: Cambridge University Press.

Gouldner, H., & Strong, M. S. (1987). *Speaking of friendship: Middle-class women and their friends.* Westport, CT: Greenwood.

Gove, W. R., Hughes, M., & Style, C. B. (1983). Does marriage have positive effects on the psychological well-being of the individual? *Journal of Health and Social Behavior, 24,* 122-131.

Gray, H. M., & Foshee, V. (1997). Adolescent dating violence: Differences between one-sided and mutually violent profiles. *Journal of Interpersonal Violence, 12,* 126-141.

Gray, J. (1993). *Men are from Mars, women are from Venus.* New York: HarperCollins.

Gray, J. A. (1987). *The psychology of fear and stress.* Cambridge, UK: Cambridge University Press.

Greeley, A. M. (1991). *Faithful attraction: Discovering intimacy, love, and fidelity in American marriage.* New York: St. Martin's.

Greenberger, E., Goldberg, W. A., Crawford, T. J., & Granger, J. (1988). Beliefs about the consequences of marital employment for children. *Psychology of Women Quarterly, 12,* 35-59.

Greenblat, C. S. (1983). The salience of sexuality in the early years of marriage. *Journal of Marriage and the Family, 45,* 289-299.

Greenfield, S., & Thelen, M. (1997). Validation of the Fear of Intimacy Scale with a lesbian and gay male population. *Journal of Social and Personal Relationships, 14,* 707-716.

Griffin, D. W., & Bartholomew, K. (1994). The metaphysics of measurement: The case of adult attachment. In K. Bartholomew & D. Perlman (Eds.), *Advances in personal relationships, Vol. 5: Attachment processes in adulthood* (pp. 17-52). London: Jessica Kingsley.

Gross, J. J., Carstensen, L. L., Pasupathi, M., Tsai, J., Skorpen, C. G., & Hsu, A. Y. C. (1997). Emotion and aging: Experience, expression, and control. *Psychology and Aging, 12,* 590-599.

Grote, N. K., & Frieze, I. H. (1994). The measurement of friendship-based love in intimate relationships. *Personal Relationships, 1,* 275-300.

Grote, N. K., & Frieze, I. H. (1998). "Remembrance of things past": Perceptions of marital love from its beginnings to the present. *Journal of Social and Personal Relationships, 15,* 91-109.

Grote, N. K., Frieze, I. H., & Stone, C. A. (1996). Children, traditionalism in the division of family work, and marital satisfaction: "What's love got to do with it?" *Personal Relationships, 3,* 211-228.

Grotevant, H. D. (1998). Adolescent development in family contexts. In W. Damon & N. Eisenberg (Eds.), *Handbook of child psychology, Vol. 3: Social, emotional, and personality development* (pp. 1097-1150). New York: John Wiley.

Grotevant, H., & Cooper, C. (1985). Patterns of interaction in family relationships and the development of identity exploration in adolescence. *Child Development, 56,* 415-428.

Gubrium, J. F., & Holstein, J. A. (1993). Phenomenology, ethnomethodology, and family discourse. In P. G. Boss, W. J. Doherty, R. LaRossa, W. R. Schumm, & S. K. Steinmetz (Eds.), *Sourcebook of family theories and methods* (pp. 651-672). New York: Plenum.

Guerrero, E. (1993). *Framing blackness: The African American image in film.* Philadelphia: Temple University Press.

Guerrero, L. K. (1994). "I'm so mad I could scream": The effects of anger expression on relational satisfaction and communication competence. *Southern Communication Journal, 59,* 125-141.

Guerrero, L. K. (1996). Attachment-style differences in intimacy and involvement: A test of the four-category model. *Communication Monographs, 63,* 269-292.

Guerrero, L. K. (1997). Nonverbal involvement across interactions with same-sex friends, opposite-sex friends, and romantic partners: Consistency or change? *Journal of Social and Personal Relationships, 14,* 31-58.

Guerrero, L. K. (1998). Attachment-style differences in the experience and expression of romantic jealousy. *Personal Relationships, 5,* 273-291.

Guerrero, L. K., & Andersen, P. A. (1998). The dark side of jealousy and envy: Desire, delusion, desperation, and destructive communication. In B. H. Spitzberg

& W. R. Cupach (Eds.), *The dark side of close relationships* (pp. 33-70). Mahwah, NJ: Lawrence Erlbaum.

Guerrero, L. K., Andersen, P. A., & Trost, M. (1998). Communication and emotion: basic concepts and approaches. In P. A. Andersen & L. K. Guerrero (Eds.), *Handbook of communication and emotion: Research, theory, applications, and contexts* (pp. 5-24). San Diego: Academic Press.

Guerrero, L. K., Eloy, S. V., Jorgensen, P. F., & Andersen, P. (1993). Hers or his? Sex differences in the experience and communication of jealousy in close relationships. In P. J. Kalbfleish (Ed.), *Interpersonal communication: Evolving interpersonal relationships* (pp. 109-132). Hillsdale, NJ: Lawrence Erlbaum.

Guerrero, L. K., & Reiter, R. L. (1998). Expressing emotion: Sex differences in social skills and communicative responses to anger, sadness, and jealousy. In D. J. Canary & K. Dindia (Eds.), *Sex differences and similarities in communication* (pp. 321-350). Mahwah, NJ: Lawrence Erlbaum.

Gullestad, M. (1984). *Kitchen table society.* Oslo, Norway: Universities Forlaget.

Gulley, M. R. (1994). The sequential analysis of social support: Elicitation and provision behaviors. *Dissertation Abstracts International: The Sciences and Engineering, 54,* 543.

Gwartney-Gibbs, P., & Stockard, J. (1989). Courtship aggression and mixed sex peer groups. In M. A. Pirog-Good & J. E. Stets (Eds.), *Violence in dating relationships: Emerging social issues* (pp. 185-204). New York: Praeger.

Haas, L. (1987). Wives' orientation toward breadwinning. *Journal of Family Issues, 7,* 358-381.

Hahn, J., & Blass, T. (1997). Dating partner preferences: A function of similarity of love styles. *Journal of Social Behavior and Personality, 12,* 595-610.

Halberstadt, A., & Saitta, M. (1987). Gender, nonverbal behavior, and perceived dominance: A test of the theory. *Journal of Personality and Social Psychology, 53,* 257-272.

Hall, G. C. N., & Hirschman, R. (1991). Toward a theory of sexual aggression: A quadripartite model. *Journal of Consulting and Clinical Psychology, 59,* 662-669.

Hall, J. (1987). On explaining gender differences: The case of nonverbal communication. In P. Shaver & C. Hendrick (Eds.), *Sex and gender* (pp. 177-200). Newbury Park, CA: Sage.

Hall, J. A., Roter, D. L., & Rand, C. S. (1981). Communication of affect between patient and physician. *Journal of Health and Social Behavior, 22,* 18-30.

Halpern, J. J. (1997). Elements of a script for friendship in transactions. *Journal of Conflict Resolution, 41,* 835-868.

Hammen, C. L. (1991). The generation of stress in the course of unipolar depression. *Journal of Abnormal Psychology, 100,* 555-561.

Hammond J. R., & Fletcher, G. J. O. (1991). Attachment styles and relationship satisfaction in the development of close relationships. *New Zealand Journal of Psychology, 20,* 56-62.

Hammond, N. (1989). Lesbian victims of relationship violence. *Women and Therapy, 8*(1/2), 89-105.

Handkins, R. E., & Munz, D. C. (1978). Essential hypertension and self-disclosure. *Journal of Clinical Psychology, 34,* 870-875.

Hansen, A. (1998). *Narrative evidence of coping with relationship loss and the pursuit of romance in the golden years.* Unpublished honors thesis, University of Iowa.

Hansen, F., Fallon, A., & Novotny, S. (1991). The relationship between social network structure and marital satisfaction in distressed and nondistressed couples: A pilot study. *Family Therapy, 18,* 101-114.

Hansen, G. L. (1987). Extradyadic relations during courtship. *Journal of Sex Research, 23,* 382-390.

Hanson, T. L., McLanahan, S. S., & Thomson, E. (1996). Double jeopardy: Parental conflict and stepfamily outcomes for children. *Journal of Marriage and the Family, 58,* 141-154.

Hansson, R. O., & Carpenter, B. N. (1994). *Relationships in old age.* New York: Guilford.

Hansson, R. O., Fairchild, S., Vanzetti, N., & Harris, G. (1992, June). *The nature of family bereavement.* Paper presented at the Sixth International Conference on Personal Relationships, Orono, ME.

Hansson, R. O., Jones, W. H., & Fletcher, W. L. (1990). Troubled relationships in later life: Implications for support. *Journal of Social and Personal Relationships, 7,* 451-463.

Harding, S. (1987). Introduction: Is there a feminist method? In S. Harding (Ed.), *Feminism and methodology* (pp. 1-14). Bloomington: Indiana University Press.

Harding, S. (1991). *Whose science? Whose knowledge? Thinking from women's lives.* Ithaca, NY: Cornell University Press.

Hargie, O. D. (1997). Communication as a skilled performance. In O. D. Hargie (Ed.), *The handbook of communication skills* (pp. 7-28). London: Routledge.

Hargie, T. C., & Tourish, D. (1997). Relational communication. In O. D. Hargie (Ed.), *The handbook of communication skills* (pp. 358-382). London: Routledge.

Harlow, H. F. (1974). *Learning to love.* Northvale, NJ: Jason Aronson.

Harré, R. (1977). Friendship as an accomplishment: An ethnogenic approach to social relationships. In S. Duck (Ed.), *Theory and practice in interpersonal attraction* (pp. 339-354). New York: Academic Press.

Harris, C. R., & Christenfeld, N. (1996). Jealousy and rational responses to infidelity across gender and culture. *Psychological Science, 7,* 378-379.

Harris, K. M., Furstenberg, F. F., Jr., & Marmer, J. K. (1998). Paternal involvement with adolescents in intact families: The influence of fathers over the life course. *Demography, 35,* 201-216.

Harris, R. J., & Cook, C. A. (1994). Attributions about spouse abuse: It matters who the batterers and victims are. *Sex Roles, 30,* 553-565.

Harrison, K. (1998). Rich friendships, affluent friends: Middle-class practices of friendship. In R. G. Adams & G. Allan (Eds.), *Placing friendship in context* (pp. 92-116). New York: Cambridge University Press.

Harry, J. (1983). Gay male and lesbian relationships. In E. Macklin & R. Rubin (Eds.), *Contemporary families and alternative lifestyles* (pp. 216-234). Beverly Hills, CA: Sage.

Harry, J. (1984). *Gay couples.* New York: Praeger.

Harry, J., & De Vall, W. B. (1978). *The social organization of gay males.* New York: Praeger.

Hart, B. L., & Hart, L. A. (1992). Reciprocal allogrooming in impala, *Aepyceros melampus. Animal Behaviour, 44,* 1073-1083.

Hartledge, L. (1980, March). *Identifying and programming for differences.* Paper presented at the Parent and Professional Conference on Young Children With Special Needs, Cleveland, OH.

Hartup, W. W. (1979). The social worlds of childhood. *American Psychologist, 34,* 944-950.

Hartup, W. W. (1983). Peer relations. In P. H. Mussen & E. M. Hetherington (Eds.), *Handbook of child psychology, Vol. 4: Socialization, personality, and social development* (pp. 103-196). New York: John Wiley.

Hartup, W. W. (1993). Adolescents and their friends. In B. Laursen (Ed.), *Close friendships in adolescence* (New Directions for Child Development, No. 60, pp. 3-22). San Francisco: Jossey-Bass.

Hartup, W. W. (1996). The company they keep: Friendships and their developmental significance. *Child Development, 67,* 1-13.

Hartup, W. W., & Laursen, B. (1992). Conflict and context in peer relations. In C. H. Hart (Ed.), *Children on playgrounds: Research perspectives and applications* (pp. 44-84). Albany: State University of New York Press.

Hartup, W. W., & Stevens, N. (1997). Friendships and adaptation in the life course. *Psychological Bulletin, 121,* 355-370.

Harvey, J. H. (1996). *Embracing their memory: Loss and the social-psychology of story-telling.* Boston: Allyn & Bacon.

Harvey, J. H. (Ed.). (1998). *Perspectives on loss: A sourcebook.* New York: Brunner/Mazel.

Harvey, J. H., Barnes, M. K., Carlson, H. R., & Haig, J. (1995). Held captive by their memories: Managing grief in relationships. In S. Duck & J. T. Wood (Eds.), *Confronting relationship challenges* (pp. 210-233). Thousand Oaks, CA: Sage.

Harvey, J. H., & Miller, E. D. (1998). Toward a psychology of loss. *Psychological Science, 9,* 429-434.

Harvey, J. H., Orbuch, T. L., Chwalisz, K., & Garwood, G. (1991). Coping with sexual assault: The roles of account-making and confiding. *Journal of Traumatic Stress, 4,* 515-531.

Harvey, J. H., Stein, S. K., Olsen, N., & Roberts, R. J. (1995). Narratives of loss and recovery from a natural disaster. *Journal of Social Behavior and Personality, 10,* 313-330.

Harvey, J. H., Weber, A. L., & Orbuch, T. L. (1990). *Interpersonal accounts: A social psychological perspective.* Oxford, UK: Blackwell.

Hatala, M. N., Baack, D. W., & Parmenter, R. (1998). Dating with HIV: A content analysis of gay male HIV-positive and HIV-negative personal advertisements. *Journal of Social and Personal Relationships, 15,* 268-276.

Hatala, M. N., & Prehodka, J. (1996). A content analysis of gay male and lesbian personal advertisements. *Psychological Reports, 78,* 371-374.

Hatch, L. R., & Bulcroft, K. (1992). Contact with friends in later life: Disentangling the effects of gender and marital status. *Journal of Marriage and the Family, 54,* 222-232.

Hatchett, S. J. (1991). Women and men. In J. S. Jackson (Ed.), *Life in black America* (pp. 84-104). Newbury Park, CA: Sage.

Hatfield, E. (1988). Passionate and companionate love. In R. J. Sternberg & M. L. Barnes (Eds.), *The psychology of love* (pp. 191-217). New Haven, CT: Yale University Press.

Hatfield, E., Greenberger, D., Traupmann, J., & Lambert, P. (1982). Equity and sexual satisfaction in recently married couples. *Journal of Sex Research, 17,* 18-32.

Hatfield, E., & Rapson, R. L. (1990). Passionate love in intimate relationships. In B. S. Moore & A. Isen (Eds.), *Affect and social behavior* (pp. 126-152). Cambridge, UK: Cambridge University Press.

Hatfield, E., & Rapson, R. L. (1996). *Love and sex: Cross-cultural perspectives.* Boston: Allyn & Bacon.

Hatfield, E., & Sprecher, S. (1986). Measuring passionate love in intimate relationships. *Journal of Adolescence, 9,* 383-410.

Hatfield, E., Traupmann, J., & Sprecher, S. (1984). Older women's perceptions of their intimate relationships. *Journal of Social and Clinical Psychology, 2,* 108-124.

Hatkoff, T. S., & Lasswell, T. E. (1979). Male-female similarities and differences in conceptualizing love. In M. Cook & G. Wilson (Eds.), *Love and attraction: An international conference* (pp. 221-227). Oxford, UK: Pergamon.

Hautzinger, M., Linden, M., & Hoffman, N. (1982). Distressed couples with and without a depressed partner: An analysis of their verbal interaction. *Journal of Behaviour Therapy and Experimental Psychology, 13,* 307-314.

Hawkins, A. J., & Eggebeen, D. J. (1991). Are fathers fungible? Patterns of coresident adult men in maritally disrupted families and young children's well-being. *Journal of Marriage and the Family, 53,* 958-972.

Hawkins, A., Marshall, C., & Meiners, K. (1995). Exploring wives' sense of fairness about family work. *Journal of Family Issues, 16,* 693-721.

Hawkins, R. L. (1992). Therapy with male couples. In S. Dworkin & F. Gutierrez (Eds.), *Counseling gay men and lesbians* (pp. 81-94). Alexandria, VA: American Association for Counseling and Development.

Hays, R. B. (1984). The development and maintenance of friendship. *Journal of Social and Personal Relationships, 1,* 75-98.

Hays, R. B. (1985). A longitudinal study of friendship development. *Journal of Personality and Social Psychology, 48,* 909-924.

Hays, R. B. (1988). Friendship. In S. W. Duck (Ed.), *Handbook of personal relationships* (pp. 391-408). New York: John Wiley.

Hays, R. B., McKusick, L., Pollack, L., Hilliard, R., Hoff, C., & Coates, T. J. (1993). Disclosing HIV seropositivity to significant others. *AIDS, 7,* 1-7.

Hays, R. B., & Oxley, D. (1986). Social network development and functioning during a life transition. *Journal of Personality and Social Psychology, 50,* 305-313.

Hazan, C., & Shaver, P. R. (1987). Romantic love conceptualized as an attachment process. *Journal of Personality and Social Psychology, 52,* 511-524.

Hazan, C., & Shaver, P. R. (1994). Attachment as an organizational framework for research on close relationships. *Journal of Psychological Inquiry, 5,* 1-22.

Hazan, C., Zeifman, D., & Middleton, K. (1994, July). *Adult romantic attachment, affection, and sex.* Paper presented at the Seventh International Conference on Personal Relationships, Groningen, Netherlands.

Heavey, C. L., Layne, C., & Christensen, A. (1993). Gender and conflict structure in marital interaction: A replication and extension. *Journal of Consulting and Clinical Psychology, 61,* 16-27.

Hecht, M. L., Marston, P. J., & Larkey, L. K. (1994). Love ways and relationship quality. *Journal of Social and Personal Relationships, 11,* 25-43.

Heider, F. (1958). *The psychology of interpersonal relations.* Hillsdale, NJ: Lawrence Erlbaum.

Helms-Erikson, H. (1999a). *We get by with a little help from our friends?: Friendships as a social context for marriage.* Unpublished doctoral dissertation, Pennsylvania State University.

Helms-Erikson, H. (1999b, November). *Marriage and friendship: Marital quality and spouses' marriage work with close friends and each other.* Paper presented at the 61st annual conference of the National Council on Family Relations, Irvine, CA.

Henderson-King, D. H., & Veroff, J. (1994). Sexual satisfaction and marital well-being in the first years of marriage. *Journal of Social and Personal Relationships, 11,* 509-534.

Hendrick, C. (1995). Evolutionary psychology and models of explanation. *Psychological Inquiry, 6,* 47-49.

Hendrick, C., & Hendrick, S. S. (1986). A theory and method of love. *Journal of Personality and Social Psychology, 50,* 392-402.

Hendrick, C., & Hendrick, S. S. (1988). Lovers wear rose-colored glasses. *Journal of Social and Personal Relationships, 5,* 161-183.

Hendrick, C., & Hendrick, S. S. (1990). A relationship specific version of the Love Attitudes Scale. *Journal of Social Behavior and Personality, 5,* 239-254.

Hendrick, C., & Hendrick, S. S. (1991). Dimensions of love: A sociobiological interpretation. *Journal of Social and Clinical Psychology, 10,* 206-230.

Hendrick, C., & Hendrick, S. (1996). Gender and the experience of heterosexual love. In J. T. Wood (Ed.), *Gendered relationships* (pp. 131-148). Mountain View, CA: Mayfield.

Hendrick, C., Hendrick, S. S., & Dicke, A. (1998). The Love Attitudes Scale: Short form. *Journal of Social and Personal Relationships, 15,* 147-159.

Hendrick, S. S. (1981). Self-disclosure and marital satisfaction. *Journal of Personality and Social Psychology, 40,* 1150-1159.

Hendrick, S. S., & Hendrick, C. (1987). Multidimensionality of sexual attitudes. *Journal of Sex Research, 23,* 502-526.

Hendrick, S. S., & Hendrick, C. (1992a). *Liking, loving, and relating* (2nd ed.). Pacific Grove, CA: Brooks/Cole.

Hendrick, S. S., & Hendrick, C. (1992b). *Romantic love.* Newbury Park, CA: Sage.

Hendrick, S. S., & Hendrick, C. (1993). Lovers as friends. *Journal of Social and Personal Relationships, 10,* 459-466.

Hendrick, S. S., & Hendrick, C. (1995). Gender differences and similarities in sex and love. *Personal Relationships, 2,* 55-65.

Hendrick, S. S., Hendrick, C., & Adler, N. L. (1988). Romantic relationships: Love, satisfaction, and staying together. *Journal of Personality and Social Psychology, 54,* 980-988.

Hennighausen, K. H., & Collins, W. A. (1998, March). *Romantic relationships and sexuality.* Paper presented at the annual meeting of the Society for Research on Adolescence, San Diego.

Henry, C. S., & Lovelace, S. G. (1995). Family resources and adolescent family life satisfaction in remarried family households. *Journal of Family Issues, 16,* 765-786.

Hernton, C. C. (1988). *Sex and racism in America.* New York: Doubleday. (Original work published 1965)

Hetherington, E. M. (1993). An overview of the Virginia Longitudinal Study of Divorce and Remarriage with a focus on early adolescence. *Journal of Family Psychology, 7,* 39-56.

Hetherington, E. M., Bridges, M., & Insabella, G. M. (1998). What matters? What does not? Five perspectives on the association between marital transitions and children's adjustment. *American Psychologist, 53,* 167-184.

Hetherington, E. M., & Clingempeel, W. G. (1992). Coping with marital transitions: A family systems perspective. *Monographs of the Society for Research in Child Development, 57*(2-3, Serial No. 227).

Heyman, R. E., O'Leary, K. D., & Jouriles, E. N. (1995). Alcohol and aggressive personality styles: Potentiators of serious physical aggression against wives? *Journal of Family Psychology, 9,* 44-57.

Hill, C. T., Rubin, Z., & Peplau, L. A. (1976). Breakups before marriage: The end of 103 affairs. *Journal of Social Issues, 32*(1), 147-168.

Hill, J. P. (1988). Adapting to menarche: Familial control and conflict. In M. R. Gunnar & W. A. Collins (Eds.), *Development during the transition to adolescence: Minnesota symposia on child psychology* (Vol. 21, pp. 43-77). Hillsdale, NJ: Lawrence Erlbaum.

Hinchliffe, M., Hooper, D., & Roberts, F. J. (1978). *The melancholy marriage.* New York: John Wiley.

Hinde, R., & Stevenson-Hinde, J. (1987). Interpersonal relationships and child development. *Developmental Review, 7,* 1-21.

Hines, M. (1992, April 19). [Untitled report]. *Health Information Communication Network,* p. 2.

Hinrichsen, G. A., & Niederehe, G. (1994). Dementia management strategies and adjustment of family members of older patients. *The Gerontologist, 34,* 95-102.

Hirsch, B. J. (1981). Social networks and the coping process: Creating personal communities. In B. H. Gottlieb (Ed.), *Social networks and social support* (pp. 149-171). London: Sage.

Ho, M. K. (1990). *Intermarried couples in therapy.* Springfield, IL: Charles C Thomas.

Hoaken, P. C. S. (1976). Jealousy as a symptom of psychiatric disorder. *Australian and New Zealand Journal of Psychiatry, 10,* 47-51.

Hobart, C. (1991). Conflict in remarriages. *Journal of Divorce and Remarriage, 15,* 69-86.

Hochschild, A. (1989). *The second shift.* New York: Viking.

Hochschild, A. (1997). *The time bind: When work becomes home and home becomes work.* New York: Metropolitan.

Hochschild, A., with Machung, A. (1989). *The second shift: Working parents and the revolution at home.* New York: Viking/Penguin.

Hodges, E. V. E., Boivin, M., Vitaro, F., & Bukowski, W. M. (1999). The power of friendship: Protection against an escalating cycle of victimization. *Developmental Psychology, 35,* 94-101.

Hodges, E. V. E., Malone, M. J., & Perry, D. G. (1997). Individual risk and social risk as interacting determi-

nants of victimization in the peer group. *Developmental Psychology, 33,* 1032-1039.

Hoffman, J. P., & Johnson, R. A. (1998). A national portrait of family structure and adolescent drug use. *Journal of Marriage and the Family, 60,* 633-645.

Hogben, M., & Byrne, D. (1998). Using social learning theory to explain individual differences in human sexuality. *Journal of Sex Research, 35,* 58-71.

Hokanson, J. E., Loewenstein, D. A., Hedeen, C., & Howes, M. J. (1986). Dysphoric college students and roommates: A study of social behaviors over a three-month period. *Personality and Social Psychology Bulletin, 12,* 311-324.

Holmbeck, G. N., Paikoff, R. L., & Brooks-Gunn, J. (1995). Parenting adolescents. In M. H. Bornstein (Ed.), *Handbook of parenting, Vol. 1: Children and parenting* (pp. 91-118). Hillsdale, NJ: Lawrence Erlbaum.

Holtzworth-Munroe, A., Bates, L., Smutzler, N., & Sandin, E. (1997). A brief review of the research on husband violence. I: Maritally violent versus nonviolent men. *Aggression and Violent Behavior, 2,* 65-99.

Holtzworth-Munroe, A., & Hutchinson, G. (1993). Attributing negative intent to wife behavior: The attributions of maritally violent versus nonviolent men. *Journal of Abnormal Psychology, 102,* 206-211.

Holtzworth-Munroe, A., & Smutzler, N. (1996). Comparing the emotional reactions and behavioral intentions of violent and nonviolent husbands to aggressive, distressed, and other wife behaviors. *Violence and Victims, 11,* 319-340.

Holtzworth-Munroe, A., Smutzler, N., & Bates, L. (1997). A brief review of the research on husband violence. III: Sociodemographic factors, relationship factors, and differing consequences of husband and wife violence. *Aggression and Violent Behavior, 2,* 285-307.

Holtzworth-Munroe, A., Smutzler, N., & Sandin, E. (1997). A brief review of the research on husband violence. II: The psychological effects of husband violence on battered women and their children. *Aggression and Violent Behavior, 2,* 179-213.

Holtzworth-Munroe, A., & Stuart, G. L. (1994). Typologies of male batterers: Three subtypes and the differences among them. *Psychological Bulletin, 116,* 476-497.

Holtzworth-Munroe, A., Stuart, G. L., & Hutchinson, G. (1997). Violent versus nonviolent husbands: Differences in attachment patterns, dependency, and jealousy. *Journal of Family Psychology, 11,* 314-331.

Homans, G. C. (1961). *Social behavior: Its elementary forms.* New York: Harcourt, Brace, & World.

Honeycutt, J. M. (1996). How "helpful" are self-help relational books? Common sense or counterintuitive information. *Personal Relationship Issues, 3,* 1-3.

Honeycutt, J. M., & Patterson, J. (1997). Affinity strategies in relationships: The role of gender and imagined interactions in maintaining liking among college roommates. *Personal Relationships, 4,* 35-46.

Honeycutt, J. M., Woods, B. L., & Fontenot, K. (1993). The endorsement of communication conflict rules as a function of engagement, marriage, and marital ideology. *Journal of Social and Personal Relationships, 10,* 285-304.

hooks, b. (1992). *Black looks: Race and representation.* Boston: South End.

hooks, b. (1994). *Teaching to transgress: Education as the practice of freedom.* New York: Routledge.

Hooley, J. M., Orley, J., & Teasdale, J. D. (1986). Levels of expressed emotion and relapse in depressed patients. *British Journal of Psychiatry, 148,* 642-647.

Hopper, J. (1993). The rhetoric of motives in divorce. *Journal of Marriage and the Family, 55,* 801-813.

Hopper, R., & Drummond, K. (1992). Accomplishing interpersonal relationships: The telephone openings of strangers and intimates. *Western Journal of Communication, 56,* 185-199.

Hopper, R., Knapp, M. L., & Scott, L. (1981). Couples' personal idioms: Exploring intimate talk. *Journal of Communication, 31*(1), 23-33.

Hops, H., Biglan, A., Sherman, L., Arthur, J., Friedman, L., & Osteen, V. (1987). Home observation of family interactions of depressed women. *Journal of Consulting and Clinical Psychology, 55,* 341-346.

Hornstein, G. A., & Truesdell, S. E. (1988). Development of intimate conversation in close relationships. *Journal of Social and Clinical Psychology, 7,* 49-64.

Horowitz, M. J. (1976). *Stress response syndromes.* Northvale, NJ: Jason Aronson.

Horowitz, M. J. (1991). Person schemas. In M. J. Horowitz (Ed.), *Personal schemas and maladaptive interpersonal patterns* (pp. 13-31). Chicago: University of Chicago Press.

Horowitz, M. J., Bonanno, G. A., & Holen, A. (1993). Pathological grief: Diagnosis and explanation. *Psychological Medicine, 55,* 260-273.

Howard, J. A., Blumstein, P., & Schwartz, P. (1986). Sex, power, and influence tactics in intimate relationships. *Journal of Personality and Social Psychology, 51,* 102-109.

Howes, C. (1988). Same- and cross-sex friendships: Implications for interaction and social skills. *Early Childhood Research Quarterly, 3,* 21-37.

Hoyt, L. L., & Hudson, J. W. (1981). Personal characteristics important in mate preference among college students. *Social Behavior and Personality, 9,* 93-96.

Hunt, J., & Hunt, L. (1987). Male resistance to role symmetry in dual-earner households: Three alternative explanations. In N. Gerstel & H. Gross (Eds.), *Families at work* (pp. 192-203). Philadelphia: Temple University Press.

Hunt, M. (1974). *Sexual behavior in the 1970s.* Chicago: Dell.

Hunter, F. T., & Youniss, J. (1982). Changes in the functions of three relations during adolescence. *Developmental Psychology, 18,* 806-811.

Hupka, R. B., & Eshett, C. (1988). Cognitive organization of emotion: Differences between labels and descriptors of emotion in jealousy situations. *Perceptual and Motor Skills, 66,* 935-949.

Hurlbert, D. F. (1992). Factors influencing a woman's decision to end an extramarital relationship. *Journal of Sex and Marital Therapy, 18,* 104-113.

Huston, M., & Schwartz, P. (1995). The relationships of lesbians and gay men. In J. T. Wood & S. Duck (Eds.), *Understanding relationship processes, Vol. 6: Understudied relationships: Off the beaten track* (pp. 89-121). Thousand Oaks, CA: Sage.

Huston, M., & Schwartz, P. (1996). Gendered dynamics in the romantic relationships of lesbians and gay men. In J. Wood (Ed.), *Gendered relationships* (pp. 163-176). Mountain View, CA: Mayfield.

Huston, T. L. (1983). Power. In H. H. Kelley, E. Berscheid, A. Christensen, J. H. Harvey, T. L. Huston, G. Levinger, E. McClintock, L. A. Peplau, & D. R. Peterson (Eds.), *Close relationships* (pp. 169-219). New York: Freeman.

Huston, T. L., & Vangelisti, A. L. (1991). Socioemotional behavior and satisfaction in marital relationships: A longitudinal study. *Journal of Personality and Social Psychology, 61,* 721-733.

Hutchins, L., & Ka'ahumanu, L. (Eds.). (1991). *Bi any other name: Bisexual people speak out.* Boston: Alyson.

Ickes, W. (1993). Traditional gender roles: Do they make, and then break, our relationships? *Journal of Social Issues, 49*(3), 71-86.

Ihinger, M. (1975). The referee role and norms of equity: A contribution toward a theory of sibling conflict. *Journal of Marriage and the Family, 37,* 515-524.

Infante, D. C., Sabourin, T. C., Rudd, J. E., & Shannon, E. A. (1990). Verbal aggression in violent and nonviolent marital disputes. *Communication Quarterly, 38,* 361-371.

Ingersoll-Dayton, B., Morgan, D., & Antonucci, T. (1997). The effects of positive and negative social exchanges on aging adults. *Journal of Gerontology: Social Sciences, 52,* S190-S199.

Inman-Amos, J., Hendrick, S. S., & Hendrick, C. (1994). Love attitudes: Similarities between parents and between parents and children. *Family Relations, 43,* 456-461.

Inoff-Germain, G., Arnold, G. S., Nottelmann, E. D., Susman, E. J., Cutler, G. B., & Chrousos, G. P. (1988). Relations between hormone levels and observational measures of aggressive behavior of young adolescents in family interactions. *Developmental Psychology, 24,* 129-139.

Ishii-Kuntz, M., & Coltrane, S. (1992a). Predicting the sharing of household labor: Are parenting and housework distinct? *Sociological Perspectives, 4,* 629-647.

Ishii-Kuntz, M., & Coltrane, S. (1992b). Remarriage, stepparenting, and household labor. *Journal of Family Issues, 13,* 215-233.

Ispa, J. (1981). Peer support among Soviet day care toddlers. *International Journal of Behavioral Development, 4,* 255-269.

Jacklin, C. (1989). Female and male: Issues of gender. *American Psychologist, 44,* 127-133.

Jacob, T. (1974). Patterns of family conflict and dominance as a function of child age and social class. *Developmental Psychology, 10,* 1-12.

Jacobson, D. (1993). What's fair: Concepts of financial management in stepfamily households. *Journal of Divorce and Remarriage, 19,* 221-238.

Jacobson, D. (1995). Incomplete institution or culture shock: Institutional and processual models of stepfamily instability. *Journal of Divorce and Remarriage, 24,* 3-18.

Jacobson, N. S., & Christensen, A. (1996). *Integrative couple therapy: Promoting acceptance and change.* New York: Norton.

Jacobson, N. S., Dobson, K., Fruzzetti, A. E., Schmaling, K. B., & Salusky, S. (1991). Marital therapy as a treatment for depression. *Journal of Consulting and Clinical Psychology, 59,* 547-557.

Jacobson, N. S., & Gottman, J. M. (1998). *When men batter women: New insights into ending abusive relationships.* New York: Simon & Schuster.

Jacobson, N. S., Gottman, J. M., Gortner, E., Berns, S., & Shortt, J. W. (1996). Psychological factors in the longitudinal course of battering: When do the couples split up? When does the abuse decrease? *Violence and Victims, 11,* 371-392.

Jacobson, N. S., Gottman, J. M., & Shortt, J. W. (1995). The distinction between Type I and Type II batterers: Reply to Ordnuff et al. (1995), Margolin et al. (1995), and Walker (1995). *Journal of Family Psychology, 9,* 272-279.

Jacobson, N. S., Gottman, J. M., Waltz, J., Rushe, R., Babcock, J., & Holtzworth-Munroe, A. (1994). Affect, verbal content, and psychophysiology in the arguments of couples with a violent husband. *Journal of Consulting and Clinical Psychology, 62,* 982-988.

Jacobson, N. S., & Margolin, G. (1979). *Marital therapy: Strategies based on social learning and behavior exchange principles.* New York: Brunner/Mazel.

Jaffe, D. J., & Miller, E. M. (1994). Problematizing meaning. In J. F. Gubrium & A. Sankar (Eds.), *Qualitative methods in aging research* (pp. 51-64). Thousand Oaks, CA: Sage.

James, S. E., & Murphy, B. C. (1998). Gay and lesbian relationships in a changing context. In C. J. Patterson & A. R. D'Augelli (Eds.), *Lesbian, gay, and bisexual identities in families* (pp. 99-121). New York: Oxford University Press.

Jankowiak, W. R. (Ed.). (1995). *Romantic passion: A universal experience.* New York: Columbia University Press.

Jankowiak, W. R., & Fischer, E. F. (1992). A cross-cultural perspective on romantic love. *Ethnology, 31,* 149-155.

Janoff-Bulman, R. (1992). *Shattered assumptions: Towards a new psychology of trauma.* New York: Free Press.

Jerrome, D. (1984). Good company: The sociological implications of friendship. *Sociological Review, 32,* 696-715.

Johnson, C. L. (1988). *Ex familia: Grandparents, parents, and children adjust to divorce.* New Brunswick, NJ: Rutgers University Press.

Johnson, C. L. (1995). Cultural diversity in the late-life family. In R. Blieszner & V. H. Bedford (Eds.), *Handbook of aging and the family* (pp. 307-331). Westport, CT: Greenwood.

Johnson, C. L., & Barer, B. M. (1997). *Life beyond 85 years: The aura of survivorship.* New York: Springer.

Johnson, D. J., & Rusbult, C. E. (1989). Resisting temptation: Devaluation of alternative partners as a means of maintaining commitment. *Journal of Personality and Social Psychology, 57,* 967-980.

Johnson, D. W., & Johnson, R. T. (1996). Conflict resolution and peer mediation programs in elementary and secondary schools: A review of the research. *Review of Educational Research, 66,* 459-506.

Johnson, D. W., Johnson, R. T., Dudley, B., Mitchell, J., & Frederickson, J. (1997). The impact of conflict resolution training on middle school students. *Journal of Social Psychology, 137,* 11-21.

Johnson, F. (1989). Women's culture and communication: An analytical perspective. In C. Lont & S. Friedley (Eds.), *Beyond boundaries: Sex and gender diversity in communication* (pp. 301-316). Fairfax, VA: George Mason University Press.

Johnson, F. (1996). Friendships among women: Closeness in dialogue. In J. T. Wood (Ed.), *Gendered relationships* (pp. 79-94). Mountain View, CA: Mayfield.

Johnson, F. L., & Aries, E. J. (1983). The talk of women friends. *Women's Studies International Forum, 6,* 353-361.

Johnson, M. A. (1989). Variables associated with friendship in an adult population. *Journal of Social Psychology, 129,* 379-390.

Johnson, M. P. (1995). Patriarchal terrorism and common couple violence: Two forms of violence against women. *Journal of Marriage and the Family, 57,* 283-294.

Johnson, M. P., Caughlin, J. P., & Huston, T. L. (1999). The tripartite nature of marital commitment: Personal, moral, and structural reasons to stay married. *Journal of Marriage and the Family, 60,* 160-177.

Johnson, M. P., & Leslie, L. (1982). Couple involvement and network structure: A test of the dyadic withdrawal hypothesis. *Social Psychology Quarterly, 45,* 34-43.

Johnson, M. P., & Milardo, R. (1984). Network interference in pair relationships. *Journal of Marriage and the Family, 46,* 893-899.

Johnson, S. M., & Greenberg, L. S. (1994). Emotion in intimate relationships: Theory and implications for therapy. In S. M. Johnson & L. S. Greenberg (Eds.), *The heart of the matter: Perspectives on emotion in marital therapy* (pp. 3-26). New York: Brunner/Mazel.

Johnson, T. F. (1995). Aging well in contemporary society. *American Behavioral Scientist, 39,* 120-130.

Joiner, T. E., Jr. (in press). Nodes of consilience between interpersonal-psychological theories of depression. In S. R. H. Beach (Ed.), *Marital and family processes in depression.* Washington, DC: American Psychological Association.

Joiner, T. E., Jr., Alfano, M. S., & Metalsky, G. I. (1993). Caught in the crossfire: Depression, self-consistency, self-enhancement, and the response of others. *Journal of Social and Clinical Psychology, 20,* 179-193.

Joiner, T. E., Jr., & Coyne, J. C. (1999). *The interactional nature of depression.* Washington, DC: American Psychological Association.

Joiner, T. E., Jr., & Metalsky, G. I. (1995). A prospective test of an integrative interpersonal theory of depression: A naturalistic study of college roommates. *Journal of Personality and Social Psychology, 69,* 778-788.

Jones, D. A. (1996). Discrimination against same-sex couples in hotel reservation policies. *Journal of Homosexuality, 31*(1-2), 153-159.

Jones, D. C. (1991). Friendship satisfaction and gender: An examination of sex differences in contributors to friendship satisfaction. *Journal of Social and Personal Relationships, 8,* 167-185.

Jones, D. C. (1992). Parental divorce, family conflict, and friendship networks. *Journal of Social and Personal Relationships, 9,* 219-235.

Jones, E. (1930). Die Eifersucht: Vortrag, gehalten in der "Groupe d'Etudes philosophiques et scientifiques pour L'examen des tendances nouvelles" an der Soubonne in Paris. *Die Psychologische Bewegingen, 2.*

Jones, E., & Gallois, C. (1989). Spouses' impressions of rules for communication in public and private marital conflicts. *Journal of Marriage and the Family, 51,* 957-967.

Jones, E., & Nisbett, R. (1972). The actor and the observer: Divergent perceptions of causality. In E. E. Jones, D. E. Kanouse, H. H. Kelly, R. E. Nisbett, S. Valins, & B. Weiner (Eds.), *Attribution: Perceiving the causes of behavior* (pp. 79-84). Morristown, NJ: General Learning Press.

Jones, J. M. (1997). *Prejudice and racism* (2nd ed.). New York: McGraw-Hill.

Jones, S. E., & Yarbrough, E. (1985). A naturalistic study of the meanings of touch. *Communication Monographs, 52,* 19-56.

Jones, W. H., & Burdette, M. P. (1994). Betrayal in relationships. In A. L. Weber & J. H. Harvey (Eds.), *Perspectives on close relationships* (pp. 243-262). Boston: Allyn & Bacon.

Jones, W. H., Kugler, K., & Adams, P. (1995). You always hurt the one you love: Guilt and transgressions against relationship partners. In J. P. Tangney & K. W. Fischer (Eds.), *Self-conscious emotions: The psychology of shame, guilt, embarrassment, and pride* (pp. 301-321). New York: Guilford.

Jordan, J. (1986). *The meaning of mutuality.* Wellesley, MA: Wellesley College, Stone Center.

Julien, D., Bouchard, C., Gagnon, M., & Pomerleau, A. (1992). Insiders' views of marital sex: A dyadic analysis. *Journal of Sex Research, 29,* 343-360.

Julien, D., Chartrand, E., & Begin, J. (1999). Social networks, structural interdependence, and conjugal adjustment. *Journal of Marriage and the Family, 61,* 516-530.

Julien, D., & Markman, H. (1991). Social support and social networks as determinants of individual and marital outcomes. *Journal of Social and Personal Relationships, 8,* 549-568.

Kaiser, P. (1996). Relationships in the extended family and diverse family forms. In A. E. Auhagen & M. von Salisch (Eds.), *The diversity of human relationships* (pp. 142-170). New York: Cambridge University Press.

Kandel, D. B. (1978a). Homophily, selection, and socialization in adolescent friendships. *American Journal of Sociology, 84,* 427-436.

Kandel, D. B. (1978b). Similarity in real-life adolescent friendship pairs. *Journal of Personality and Social Psychology, 36,* 306-312.

Kanin, E. J. (1969). Selected dyadic aspects of male sex aggression. *Journal of Sex Research, 5,* 12-28.

Kanin, E. J. (1983). Rape as a function of relative sexual frustration. *Psychological Reports, 52,* 133-134.

Kanin, E. J. (1985). Date rapists: Differential sexual socialization and relative deprivation. *Archives of Sexual Behavior, 14,* 219-231.

Kanin, E. J., & Parcell, S. R. (1977). Sexual aggression: A second look at the offended female. *Archives of Sexual Behavior, 6,* 67-76.

Kanuha, V. (1996). Domestic violence, racism, and the battered women's movement in the United States. In J. L. Edelson & Z. C. Eisikovits (Eds.), *Future interventions with battered women and their families* (pp. 34-50). Thousand Oaks, CA: Sage.

Karney, B. R. (in press). Depressive symptoms and marital satisfaction in the early years of marriage: The implications of a growth curve analysis. In S. R. H. Beach (Ed.), *Marital and family processes in depression.* Washington, DC: American Psychological Association.

Kashy, D. A., & Kenny, D. A. (1990). Analysis of family research designs: A model of interdependence. *Communication Research, 17,* 462-483.

Kashy, D. A., & Kenny, D. A. (2000). The analysis of data from dyads and groups. In H. T. Reis & C. M. Judd (Eds.), *Handbook of research methods in social psychology.* Cambridge, UK: Cambridge University Press.

Kashy, D. A., & Snyder, D. K. (1995). Measurement and data analytic issues in couples research. *Psychological Assessment, 7,* 338-348.

Katz, J., & Beach, S. R. H. (1997). Romance in the crossfire: When do women's depressive symptoms predict partner relationship dissatisfaction? *Journal of Social and Clinical Psychology, 16,* 243-258.

Katz, J., Beach, S. R. H., & Anderson, P. (1996). Self-enhancement versus self-verification: Does spousal support always help? *Cognitive Therapy and Research, 20,* 345-360.

Kaufman, J., & Ziegler, E. (1987). Do abused children become abusive parents? *American Journal of Orthopsychiatry, 57,* 186-197.

Kaufman, S. R. (1994). In-depth interviewing. In J. F. Gubrium & A. Sankar (Eds.), *Qualitative methods in aging research* (pp. 123-136). Thousand Oaks, CA: Sage.

Kaye, L., & Applegate, J. (1990). Men as elder caregivers: A response to changing families. *American Journal of Orthopsychiatry, 60,* 86-95.

Kazak, A. E., & Marvin, R. S. (1984). Differences, difficulties, and adaptation: Stress and social networks in families with a handicapped child. *Family Relations, 33,* 67-77.

Keefe, K., & Berndt, T. J. (1996). Relations of friendship quality to self-esteem in early adolescence. *Journal of Early Adolescence, 16,* 110-129.

Keelan, J. P. R., Dion, K. K., & Dion, K. L. (1998). Attachment style and relationship satisfaction: Test of a self-disclosure explanation. *Canadian Journal of Behavioural Science, 30,* 24-35.

Keen, S. (1991). *Fire in the belly.* New York: Bantam Books.

Kelley, H. H. (1979). *Personal relationships: Their structures and processes.* Hillsdale, NJ: Lawrence Erlbaum.

Kelley, H. H., & Thibaut, J. W. (1978). *Interpersonal relations: A theory of interdependence.* New York: John Wiley.

Kelley, H. H., Berscheid, E., Christensen, A., Harvey, J. H., Huston, T. L., Levinger, G., McClintock, E., Peplau, L. A., & Peterson, D. R. (Eds.). (1983). *Close relationships.* New York: Freeman.

Kelley, H. H., Cunningham, J. D., Grisham, J. A., Lefebvre, L. M., Sink, C. R., & Yablon, G. (1978). Sex differences in comments made during conflict within close heterosexual pairs. *Sex Roles, 4,* 473-492.

Kelley, H. H., & Thibaut, J. W. (1978). *Interpersonal relations: A theory of interdependence.* New York: John Wiley.

Kemeny, M. E., Weiner, H., Duran, R., & Taylor, S. E. (1995). Immune system changes after the death of a partner in HIV-positive gay men. *Psychosomatic Medicine, 57,* 547-554.

Kenny, D. A. (1988). The analysis of data from two-person relationships. In S. Duck, D. F. Hay, S. E. Hobfoll, W. Ickes, & B. M. Montgomery (Eds.), *Handbook of personal relationships: Theory, research, and interventions* (pp. 57-77). Chichester, UK: Wiley.

Kenny, D. A. (1990). Design issues in dyadic research. In C. Hendrick & M. S. Clark (Eds.), *Review of personality and social psychology, Vol. 11: Research methods in personality and social psychology* (pp. 164-184). Newbury Park, CA: Sage.

Kenny, D. A. (1994). *Interpersonal perception: A social relations analysis.* New York: Guilford.

Kenny, D. A. (1995). The effect of nonindependence on significance testing in dyadic research. *Personal Relationships, 2,* 67-75.

Kenny, D. A. (1996). Models of nonindependence in dyadic research. *Journal of Social and Personal Relationships, 13,* 279-294.

Kenny, D. A. (1999). *SOREMO* [computer program]. Available: http://nw3.nai.net/7Edakenny/ kenny.htm

Kenny, D. A., & Acitelli, L. K. (1994). Measuring similarity in couples. *Journal of Family Psychology, 8,* 417-431.

Kenny, D. A., & Cook, W. L. (1999). Partner effects in relationship research: Conceptual issues, analytic difficulties, and illustrations. *Personal Relationships, 6,* 433-438.

Kenny, D. A., & Kashy, D. A. (1994). Enhanced co-orientation in the perception of friends: A social relations analysis. *Journal of Personality and Social Psychology, 67,* 1024-1033.

Kenny, D. A., Kashy, D. A., & Bolger, N. (1998). Data analysis in social psychology. In D. Gilbert, S. Fiske, & G. Lindzey (Eds.), *The handbook of social psychology* (Vol. 1, 4th ed., pp. 233-265). New York: McGraw-Hill.

Kenny, D. A., & La Voie, L. (1984). The social relations model. In L. Berkowitz (Ed.), *Advances in experimental social psychology* (pp. 141-182). Orlando, FL: Academic Press.

Kenny, D. A., & La Voie, L. (1985). Separating individual and group effects. *Journal of Personality and Social Psychology, 48,* 339-348.

Kenny, D. A., Mohr, C. D., & Levesque, M. J. (1999). *A social relations partitioning of variance of dyadic behavior.* Unpublished manuscript, University of Connecticut.

Kenrick, D. T. (1987). Gender, genes, and the social environment: A biosocial interactionist perspective. In

P. Shaver & C. Hendrick (Eds.), *Sex and gender* (pp. 14-43). Newbury Park, CA: Sage.

Kenrick, D. T., Groth, G. E., Trost, M. R., & Sadalla, E. K. (1993). Integrating evolutionary and social exchange perspectives on relationships: Effects of gender, self-appraisal, and involvement level on mate selection criteria. *Journal of Personality and Social Psychology, 64,* 951-969.

Kenrick, D. T., & Trost, M. R. (1989). A reproductive exchange model of heterosexual relationships: Putting proximate economics in ultimate perspective. In C. Hendrick (Ed.), *Close relationships* (pp. 92-118). Newbury Park, CA: Sage.

Kessler, S., & McKenna, W. (1978). *Gender: An ethnomethodological approach.* New York: John Wiley.

Kiernan, K. E. (1992). The impact of family disruption in childhood on transitions made in young adult life. *Population Studies, 46,* 213-224.

Kim, H. J., & Stiff, J. B. (1991). Social networks and the development of close relationships. *Human Communication Research, 18,* 70-90.

Kincheloe, J. L., & McLaren, P. L. (1994). Rethinking critical theory and qualitative research. In N. K. Denzin & Y. S. Lincoln (Eds.), *Handbook of qualitative research* (pp. 138-157). Thousand Oaks, CA: Sage.

Kinsey, A. C., Pomeroy, W. B., & Martin, C. E. (1948). *Sexual behavior in the human male.* Philadelphia: W. B. Saunders.

Kinsey, A. C., Pomeroy, W. B., Martin, C. E., & Gebhard, P. H. (1953). *Sexual behavior in the human female.* Philadelphia: W. B. Saunders.

Kirkpatrick, L. E., & Davis, K. E. (1994). Attachment style, gender, and relationship stability: A longitudinal analysis. *Journal of Personality and Social Psychology, 66,* 502-512.

Kirkpatrick, L. E., & Hazan, C. (1994). Attachment styles and close relationships: A four-year prospective study. *Personal Relationships, 1,* 123-142.

Kirpatrick, M. (1989). Middle age and the lesbian experience. *Women's Studies Quarterly, 17,* 87-96.

Kitayama, S., Markus, H. R., & Matsumoto, H. (1995). Culture, self, and emotion: A cultural perspective on "self-conscious" emotions. In J. P. Tangney & K. W. Fischer (Eds.), *Self-conscious emotions: The psychology of shame, guilt, embarrassment, and pride* (pp. 439-464). New York: Guilford.

Kitson, G. C. (1992). *Portrait of divorce: Adjustment to marital breakdown.* New York: Guilford.

Klein, D. M., & Jurich, J. A. (1993). Meta-theory and family studies. In P. G. Boss, W. J. Doherty, R. LaRossa, W. R. Schumm, & S. K. Steinmetz (Eds.), *Sourcebook of family theories and methods* (pp. 31-67). New York: Plenum.

Klein, D. M., & White, J. M. (1996). *Family theories: An introduction.* Thousand Oaks, CA: Sage.

Klein, F. (1990). The need to view sexual orientation as a multivariable dynamic process: A theoretical perspective. In D. P. McWhirter, S. A. Saunders, & J. M. Reinisch (Eds.), *Homosexuality/heterosexuality: Concepts of sexual orientation* (pp. 277-282). New York: Oxford University Press.

Klein, R., & Milardo, R. M. (1993). Third-party influence on the management of personal relationships. In S. Duck (Ed.), *Social context and relationships* (pp. 55-77). Newbury Park, CA: Sage.

Kleinke, C. L. (1986). Gaze and eye contact: A research review. *Psychological Bulletin, 100,* 78-100.

Kleinman, S., & Copp, M. A. (1993). *Emotions and fieldwork.* Newbury Park, CA: Sage.

Klerman, G. L., Weissman, M. M., Rounsaville, B., & Chevron, E. S. (1995). Interpersonal psychotherapy for depression. *Journal of Psychotherapy Practice & Research, 4,* 342-351.

Klinkenberg, D., & Rose, S. (1994). Dating scripts of gay men and lesbians. *Journal of Homosexuality, 26*(4), 23-35.

Klohnen, E. C., & John, O. P. (1998). Working models of attachment: A theory-based prototype approach. In J. A. Simpson & W. S. Rholes (Eds.), *Attachment theory and close relationships* (pp. 115-140). New York: Guilford.

Kluwer, E. S., de Dreu, C. K. W., & Buunk, B. P. (1998). Conflict in intimate vs. non-intimate relationships: When gender role stereotyping overrides biased self-other judgment. *Journal of Social and Personal Relationships, 15,* 637-650.

Kluwer, E. S., Heesink, J. A. M., & van de Vliert, E. (1997). The marital dynamics of conflict over the division of labor. *Journal of Marriage and the Family, 59,* 635-653.

Knapp, M. L., & Vangelisti, A. L. (1996). *Interpersonal communication and human relationships* (3rd ed.). Boston: Allyn & Bacon.

Kobak, R. R., & Duemmler, S. (1994). Attachment and conversation: Toward a discourse analysis of adolescent and adult security. In K. Bartholomew & D. Perlman (Eds.), *Advances in personal relationships, Vol. 5: Attachment processes in adulthood* (pp. 121-149). London: Jessica Kingsley.

Kobak, R. R., & Hazan, C. (1991). Attachment in marriage: Effects of security and accuracy of working models. *Journal of Personality and Social Psychology, 60,* 861-869.

Kobak, R. R., & Sceery, A. (1988). Attachment in late adolescence: Working models, affect regulation, and representations of self and others. *Child Development, 59,* 135-146.

Kochenderfer, B. J., & Ladd, G. W. (1996). Peer victimization: Cause or consequence of school maladjustment? *Child Development, 67,* 1305-1317.

Kochman, T. (1981). *Black and white styles in conflict.* Chicago: University of Chicago Press.

Koestner, R., & Wheeler, L. (1988). Self-presentation in personal advertisements: The influence of implicit notions of attractiveness and role expectations. *Journal of Social and Personal Relationships, 5,* 149-160.

Kollock, P., Blumstein, P., & Schwartz, P. (1985). Sex and power in interaction: Conversational privileges and duties. *American Sociological Review, 50,* 34-46.

Korbin, J. E., Anetzberger, G. J., & Austin, C. (1995). The intergenerational cycle of violence in childhood and elder abuse. *Journal of Elder Abuse and Neglect, 7,* 1-15.

Koski, L. R., & Shaver, P. R. (1997). Attachment and relationship satisfaction across the life span. In R. J. Sternberg & M. Hojjat (Eds.), *Satisfaction in close relationships* (pp. 26-55). New York: Guilford.

Koss, M. P., & Cleveland, H. H. (1997). Stepping on toes: Social roots of date rape lead to intractability and politicization. In M. D. Schwartz (Ed.), *Researching sexual violence against women: Methodological and personal perspectives* (pp. 4-21). Thousand Oaks, CA: Sage.

Koss, M. P., & Dinero, T. E. (1988). Predictors of sexual aggression among a national sample of male college students. In R. A. Prentky & V. L. Quinsey (Eds.), *Human sexual aggression: Current perspectives. Annals of the New York Academy of Sciences, 528,* 133-146.

Koss, M. P., Dinero, T. E., Seibel, C. A., & Cox, S. L. (1988). Stranger and acquaintance rape. *Psychology of Women Quarterly, 12,* 1-24.

Koss, M. P., Gidycz, C. A., & Wisniewski, N. (1987). The scope of rape: Incidence and prevalence of sexual aggression and victimization in a national sample of higher education students. *Journal of Consulting and Clinical Psychology, 55,* 162-170.

Kovacs, D. M., Parker, J. G., & Hoffman, L. W. (1996). Behavioral, affective, and social correlates of involvement in cross-sex friendship in elementary school. *Child Development, 67,* 2269-2286.

Kovecses, Z. (1991). A linguist's quest for love. *Journal of Social and Personal Relationships, 8,* 77-97.

Krafft, S. (1994). Why wives earn less than husbands. *American Demographics, 16*(1), 16-17.

Krause, N., Herzog, A. R., & Baker, E. (1992). Providing support to others and well-being in later life. *Journal of Gerontology: Psychological Sciences, 47,* P300-P311.

Krieger, S. (1991). *Social science and the self: Personal essays on an art form.* New Brunswick, NJ: Rutgers University Press.

Krieger, S. (1996). *The family silver: Essays on relationships among women.* Berkeley: University of California Press.

Kubler-Ross, E. (1969). *On death and dying.* New York: Macmillan.

Kuebli, J., & Fivush, R. (1992). Gender differences in parent-child conversations about past events. *Sex Roles, 27,* 683-698.

Kunce, L. J., & Shaver, P. R. (1994). An attachment-theoretical approach to caregiving in romantic relationships. In K. Bartholomew & D. Perlman (Eds.), *Advances in personal relationships, Vol. 5: Attachment processes in adulthood* (pp. 205-237). London: Jessica Kingsley.

Kunkel, A. W., & Burleson, B. R. (1998). Social support and the emotional lives of men and women: An assessment of the different cultures perspective. In D. J. Canary & K. Dindia (Eds.), *Sex differences and similarities in communication* (pp. 101-125). Mahwah, NJ: Lawrence Erlbaum.

Kupersmidt, J. B., Burchinal, M., & Patterson, C. J. (1995). Developmental patterns of childhood peer relations as predictors of externalizing behavior problems. *Development and Psychopathology, 7,* 825-843.

Kurdek, L. (1999). The nature and predictors of the trajectory of change in marital quality for husbands and wives over the first 10 years of marriage. *Developmental Psychology, 35,* 1283-1296.

Kurdek, L. A. (1988). Relationship quality of gay and lesbian cohabiting couples. *Journal of Homosexuality, 15*(3/4), 93-118.

Kurdek, L. A. (1989). Relationship quality in gay and lesbian cohabiting couples: A 1-year follow-up study. *Journal of Social and Personal Relationships, 6,* 39-59.

Kurdek, L. A. (1991a). Correlates of relationship satisfaction in cohabiting gay and lesbian couples. *Journal of Personality and Social Psychology, 61,* 910-922.

Kurdek, L. A. (1991b). The dissolution of gay and lesbian couples. *Journal of Social and Personal Relationships, 8,* 265-278.

Kurdek, L. A. (1991c). Marital stability and changes in marital quality in newly wed couples: A test of the contextual model. *Journal of Social and Personal Relationships, 8,* 27-48.

Kurdek, L. A. (1992). Relationship stability and relationship satisfaction in cohabiting gay and lesbian couples: A prospective longitudinal test of the contextual and interdependence models. *Journal of Social and Personal Relationships, 9,* 125-142.

Kurdek, L. A. (1993). The allocation of household labor in gay, lesbian, and heterosexual married couples. *Journal of Social Issues, 49*(3), 127-139.

Kurdek, L. A. (1994a). Areas of conflict for gay, lesbian, and heterosexual couples: What couples argue about influences relationship satisfaction. *Journal of Marriage and the Family, 56,* 923-934.

Kurdek, L. A. (1994b). Conflict resolution styles in gay, lesbian, heterosexual nonparent, and heterosexual parent couples. *Journal of Marriage and the Family, 56,* 705-722.

Kurdek, L. A. (1994c). The nature and correlates of relationship quality in gay, lesbian, and heterosexual cohabiting couples. In B. Greene & G. M. Herek (Eds.), *Lesbian and gay psychology* (Vol. 1, pp. 113-155). Thousand Oaks, CA: Sage.

Kurdek, L. A. (1995a). Developmental changes in relationship quality in gay and lesbian cohabiting couples. *Developmental Psychology, 31,* 86-94.

Kurdek, L. A. (1995b). Lesbian and gay couples. In A. R. D'Augelli & C. J. Patterson (Eds.), *Lesbian, gay, and bisexual identities over the life span* (pp. 243-261). New York: Oxford University Press.

Kurdek, L. A. (1997a). Adjustment to relationship dissolution in gay, lesbian, and heterosexual partners. *Personal Relationships, 4,* 145-161.

Kurdek, L. A. (1997b). Relation between neuroticism and dimensions of relationship commitment: Evidence from gay, lesbian, and heterosexual couples. *Journal of Family Psychology, 11,* 109-124.

Kurdek, L. A. (1998a). The nature of predictors of the trajectory of change in marital quality over the first 4 years of marriage for first-married husbands and wives. *Journal of Family Psychology, 12,* 494-510.

Kurdek, L. A. (1998b). Relationship outcomes and their predictors: Longitudinal evidence from heterosexual married, gay cohabiting, and lesbian cohabiting couples. *Journal of Marriage and the Family, 60,* 553-568.

Kurdek, L. A., & Fine, M. A. (1993a). Parent and nonparent residential family members as providers of warmth and supervision to young adolescents. *Journal of Family Psychology, 7,* 245-249.

Kurdek, L. A., & Fine, M. A. (1993b). The relation between family structure and young adolescents' appraisals of family climate and parent behaviors. *Journal of Family Issues, 14,* 279-290.

Kurdek, L. A., & Fine, M. A. (1994). Family acceptance and family control as predictors of adjustment problems in young adolescents: Linear, curvilinear, or interactive effects? *Child Development, 65,* 1137-1146.

Kurdek, L. A., Fine, M. A., & Sinclair, R. J. (1994). The relation between parenting transitions and adjustment in young adolescents: A multi-sample investigation. *Journal of Early Adolescence, 14,* 412-432.

Kurdek, L. A., Fine, M. A., & Sinclair, R. J. (1995). School adjustment in sixth graders: Parenting transitions, family climate, and peer norm effects. *Child Development, 66,* 430-445.

Kurdek, L. A., & Schmitt, J. P. (1987). Partner homogamy in married, heterosexual cohabiting, gay, and lesbian couples. *Journal of Sex Research, 23,* 212-232.

Kurdek, L. A., & Schmitt, J. P. (1986a). Early development of relationship quality in heterosexual married, heterosexual cohabiting, gay, and lesbian couples. *Developmental Psychology, 22,* 305-309.

Kurdek, L. A., & Schmitt, J. P. (1986b). Relationship quality of partners in heterosexual married, heterosexual cohabiting, and gay and lesbian relationships. *Journal of Personality and Social Psychology, 51,* 711-720.

Kurtz, D. (1989). Social science perspectives on wife abuse: Current debates and future directions. *Gender & Society, 3,* 489-505.

Labov, W. (1972). *Sociolinguistic patterns.* Philadelphia: University of Pennsylvania Press.

Ladd, G. W. (1981). Effectiveness of a social learning method for enhancing children's social interaction and peer acceptance. *Child Development, 52,* 171-178.

Ladd, G. W. (1990). Having friends, keeping friends, making friends, and being liked by peers in the classroom: Predictors of children's early school adjustment? *Child Development, 61,* 1081-1100.

Ladd, G. W. (1983). Social networks of popular, average, and rejected children in school settings. *Merrill-Palmer Quarterly, 29,* 283-307.

Ladd, G. W., & Emerson, E. S. (1984). Shared knowledge in children's friendships. *Developmental Psychology, 20,* 932-940.

Ladd, G. W., & Kochenderfer, B. J. (1996). Linkages between friendship and adjustment during early school transitions. In W. M. Bukowski, A. F. Newcomb, & W. W. Hartup (Eds.), *The company they keep: Friendship in childhood and adolescence* (pp. 322-345). New York: Cambridge University Press.

Ladd, G. W., Kochenderfer, B. J., & Coleman, C. C. (1996). Friendship quality as a predictor of young children's early school adjustment. *Child Development, 67,* 1103-1118.

Ladd, G. W., Kochenderfer, B. J., & Coleman, C. C. (1997). Classroom peer acceptance, friendship, and victimization: Distinct relational systems that contribute uniquely to children's school adjustment? *Child Development, 68,* 1181-1197.

Ladd, G. W., & Price, J. M. (1987). Predicting children's social and school adjustment following the transition from preschool to kindergarten. *Child Development, 58,* 1168-1189.

LaFreniere, P. L., Strayer, F. F., & Gauthier, R. (1984). The emergence of same-sex affiliative preferences among preschool peers: A developmental/ethological perspective. *Child Development, 55,* 1958-1965.

LaGaipa, J. J. (1981). Children's friendships. In S. Duck & R. Gilmour (Eds.), *Personal relationships, Vol. 3: Developing personal relationships* (pp. 161-185). San Diego: Academic Press.

LaGaipa, J. J. (1987). Friendship expectations. In R. Burnett, P. McGhee, & D. D. Clarke (Eds.), *Accounting for relationships: Explanation, representation, and knowledge* (pp. 134-157). London: Methuen.

LaGaipa, J. J. (1990). The negative effects of informal support systems. In S. Duck (Ed.), *Personal relationships and social support* (pp. 122-139). Newbury Park, CA: Sage.

Lakey, B., & Cassady, P. B. (1990). Cognitive processes in perceived social support. *Journal of Personality and Social Psychology, 59,* 337-343.

Lakey, B., & Lutz, C. J. (1996). Social support and preventive and therapeutic interventions. In G. R. Pierce, B. R. Sarason, & I. G. Sarason (Eds.), *Handbook of social support and the family* (pp. 435-465). New York: Plenum.

Lakey, B., McCabe, K. M., Fisicario, S. A., & Drew, J. B. (1996). Environmental and perceived determinants of support perceptions: Three generalizability studies. *Journal of Personality and Social Psychology, 70,* 1270-1280.

Lalumiere, M. L., Chalmers, L. J., Quinsey, V. L., & Seto, M. C. (1996). A test of the mate deprivation hypothesis of sexual coercion. *Ethology and Sociobiology, 17,* 299-318.

Lamb, M. E. (1987). Introduction: The emergent American father. In M. E. Lamb (Ed.), *The father's role: Cross-cultural perspectives* (pp. 3-26). Hillsdale, NJ: Lawrence Erlbaum.

Lamborn, S. D., Mounts, N. S., Steinberg, L., & Dornbusch, S. M. (1991). Patterns of competence and adjustment among adolescents from authoritative, authoritarian, indulgent, and neglectful families. *Child Development, 62,* 1049-1065.

Lamm, H., & Wiesmann, U. (1997). Subjective attributes of attraction: How people characterize their liking, their love, and their being in love. *Personal Relationships, 4,* 271-284.

Landolt, M. A., & Dutton, D. G. (1997). Power and personality: An analysis of gay male intimate abuse. *Sex Roles, 37,* 335-359.

Laner, M. R. (1978). Media mating II: "Personals" advertisements of lesbian women. *Journal of Homosexuality, 4*(1), 41-61.

Laner, M. R., & Kamel, G. W. L. (1977). Media mating I: Newspaper "personals" ads of homosexual men. *Journal of Homosexuality, 3*(2), 149-162.

Lang, F. R., Staudinger, U. M., & Carstensen, L. L. (1998). Perspectives on socioemotional selectivity in later life: How personality and social context do (and do not) make a difference. *Journal of Gerontology: Psychological Sciences, 53,* P21-P30.

Langhinrichsen-Rohling, J., Schlee, K. A., Monson, C. M., Ehrensaft, M., & Heyman, R. (1998). What's love got to do with it? Perceptions of marital positivity in H-to-W aggressive, distressed, and happy marriages. *Journal of Family Violence, 13,* 197-212.

Langhinrichsen-Rohling, J., Smutzler, N., & Vivian, D. (1994). Positivity in marriage: The role of discord and physical aggression against wives. *Journal of Marriage and the Family, 56,* 69-79.

Langley, J., Martin, J., & Nada-Raja, S. (1997). Physical assault among 21-year-olds by partners. *Journal of Interpersonal Violence, 12,* 675-684.

Langlois, J. H., Ritter, J. M., Casey, R. J., & Sawin, D. B. (1995). Infant attractiveness predicts maternal behaviors and attitudes. *Developmental Psychology, 31,* 464-472.

Lansford, J. E., Sherman, A. M., & Antonucci, T. C. (1998). Satisfaction with social networks: An examination of socioemotional selectivity theory across cohorts. *Psychology and Aging, 13,* 544-552.

Larson, D. G., & Chastain, R. L. (1990). Self-concealment: Conceptualization, measurement, and health implications. *Journal of Social and Clinical Psychology, 9,* 439-455.

Larson, J. H., & Allgood, S. M. (1987). A comparison of intimacy in first-married and remarried couples. *Journal of Family Issues, 8,* 319-331.

Larson, R., & Richards, M. H. (1991). Daily companionship in late childhood and early adolescence: Changing developmental contexts. *Child Development, 62,* 284-300.

Larson, R., Richards, M., & Perry-Jenkins, M. (1994). Divergent worlds: The daily emotional experience of mothers and fathers in the domestic and public spheres. *Journal of Personality and Social Psychology, 6,* 1034-1046.

Larson, R. W., & Bradney, N. (1988). Precious moments with family members and friends. In R. M. Milardo (Ed.), *Families and social networks* (pp. 107-126). Newbury Park, CA: Sage.

Lasswell, T. E., & Lasswell, M. E. (1976). I love you but I'm not in love with you. *Journal of Marriage and Family Counseling, 38,* 211-224.

Latham, A. (1997). *The ballad of Gussie & Clyde: A true story of true love.* New York: Villard.

Lather, P. (1991). *Getting smart: Feminist research and pedagogy with/in the postmodern.* New York: Routledge.

Laumann, E. O., & Gagnon, J. H. (1995). A sociological perspective on sexual action. In R. G. Parker & J. H. Gagnon (Eds.), *Conceiving sexuality: Approaches to sex research in a postmodern world* (pp. 183-213). New York: Routledge.

Laumann, E. O., Gagnon, J. H., Michael, R. T., & Michaels, S. (1994). *The social organization of sexuality: Sexual practices in the United States.* Chicago: University of Chicago Press.

Laursen, B. (1993). Conflict management among close friends. In B. Laursen (Ed.), *Close friendship in adolescence: New directions for child development* (pp. 39-54). San Francisco: Jossey-Bass.

Laursen, B. (1996). Closeness and conflict in adolescent peer relationships: Interdependence with friends and romantic partners. In W. M. Bukowski, A. F. Newcomb, & W. W. Hartup (Eds.), *The company they keep: Friendship in childhood and adolescence* (pp. 186-210). New York: Cambridge University Press.

Laursen, B., & Bukowski, W. M. (1997). A developmental guide to the organization of close relationships.

*International Journal of Behavioral Development, 21,* 747-770.

Laursen, B., & Collins, W. A. (1994). Interpersonal conflict during adolescence. *Psychological Bulletin, 115,* 197-209.

Laursen, B., & Jensen-Campbell, L. A. (in press). The nature and functions of social exchange in adolescent romantic relationships. In W. Furman, B. B., Brown, & C. Feiring (Eds.), *Contemporary perspectives on adolescent romantic relationships.* New York: Cambridge University Press.

Laursen, B., Coy, K. C., & Collins, W. A. (1998). Reconsidering changes in parent-child conflict across adolescence: A meta-analysis. *Child Development, 69,* 817-832.

Laursen, B., & Williams, V. (1997). Perceptions of interdependence and closeness in family and peer relationships among adolescents with and without romantic partners. In S. Shulman & W. A. Collins (Eds.), *Romantic relationships in adolescence: Developmental perspectives* (New Directions for Child Development, No. 78, pp. 3-20). San Francisco: Jossey-Bass.

Lawrance, K., & Byers, E. S. (1995). Sexual satisfaction in long-term heterosexual relationships: The interpersonal exchange model of sexual satisfaction. *Personal Relationships, 2,* 267-285.

Lawrence, R. H., Bennett, J. M., & Markides, K. S. (1992). Perceived intergenerational solidarity and psychological distress among older Mexican Americans. *Journal of Gerontology: Social Sciences, 47,* S55-S65.

Lawson, A., & Samson, C. (1988). Age, gender, and adultery. *British Journal of Sociology, 39,* 409-440.

Lazarus, R. S., & Folkman, S. (1984). *Stress. appraisal, and coping.* New York: Springer.

Lea, M. (1994). *From social attraction to relationship: Similarity, commonality, and self-referent support in friendships.* Unpublished manuscript, University of Manchester.

Lea, M., & Duck, S. (1982). A model for the role of similarity of values in friendship development. *British Journal of Social Psychology, 21,* 301-310.

Lea, M., & Spears, R. (1995). Love at first byte: Building personal relationships over computer networks. In J. T. Wood & S. Duck (Eds.), *Understudied relationships: Off the beaten track* (pp. 197-233). Thousand Oaks, CA: Sage.

Leaper, C. (1994). Exploring the consequences of gender segregation on social relationships. *New Directions for Child Development, 65,* 67-86.

Leaper, C., & Holliday, H. (1995). Gossip in same-gender and cross-gender friends' conversations. *Personal Relationships, 2,* 237-246.

Lee, J. A. (1973). *The colors of love: An exploration of the ways of loving.* Don Mills, Ontario: New Press.

Lee, J. A. (1988). Love styles. In R. J. Sternberg & M. L. Barnes (Eds.), *The psychology of love* (pp. 38-67). New Haven, CT: Yale University Press.

Lee, Y., & Aytac, I. A. (1998). Intergenerational financial support among whites, African Americans, and Latinos. *Journal of Marriage and the Family, 60,* 426-441.

Lehman, D. R., Ellard, J. H., & Wortman, C. B. (1986). Social support for the bereaved: Recipients' and providers' perspectives on what is helpful. *Journal of Consulting and Clinical Psychology, 54,* 438-446.

Lennon, M. C., & Rosenfeld, S. (1994). Relative fairness and the division of housework: The importance of options. *American Journal of Sociology, 100,* 506-531.

Leonard, K. E., & Roberts, L. J. (1998). The effects of alcohol on the marital interactions of aggressive and nonaggressive husbands and their wives. *Journal of Abnormal Psychology, 107,* 602-615.

Leonard, K. E., & Senchak, M. (1996). Prospective prediction of husband marital aggression within newlywed couples. *Journal of Abnormal Psychology, 105,* 369-380.

Lerner, H. G. (1987). Female depression: Self-sacrifice and self-betrayal in relationships. In R. Formanek & A. Guiran (Eds.), *Women and depression: A life span perspective* (pp. 200-221). New York: Springer.

Lerner, M. (1987). Integrating societal and psychological rules of entitlement: The basic task of each societal actor and fundamental problem of the social sciences. *Social Justice Research, 1,* 107-125.

Lester, D., Deluca, G., Hellinghausen, W., & Scribner, D. (1985). Jealousy and irrationality in love. *Psychological Reports, 56,* 210.

Levant, R. F., Slattery, S. C., & Loiselle, J. E. (1987). Fathers' involvement in housework and child care with school-aged daughters. *Family Relations, 36,* 152-157.

Levenson, R. W., & Gottman, J. M. (1985). Physiological and affective predictors of change in relationship satisfaction. *Journal of Personality and Social Psychology, 49,* 85-94.

Lever, J. (1978). Sex differences in the complexity of children's play and games. *American Sociological Review, 43,* 471-483.

Levin, I. (1993). Family as mapped realities. *Journal of Family Issues, 14,* 82-91.

Levinger, G. (1965). Marital cohesiveness and dissolution: An integrative review. *Journal of Marriage and the Family, 27,* 19-28.

Levinger, G. (1976). A social psychological perspective on marital dissolution. *Journal of Social Issues, 32*(1), 21-47.

Levinger, G. (1994). Figure versus ground: Micro- and macroperspectives on the social psychology of personal relationships. In R. Erber and R. Gilmour (Eds.), *Theoretical frameworks for personal rela-*

*tionships* (pp. 1-28). Hillsdale, NJ: Lawrence Erlbaum.

Levinson, D. S. (1997). Young widowhood: A life change journey. *Journal of Personal & Interpersonal Loss, 2,* 277-291.

Levinson, W., Roter, D. L., Mullooly, J. P., Dull, V. T., & Frankel, R. M. (1997). Physician-patient communication: The relationship with malpractice claims among primary care physicians and surgeons. *Journal of the American Medical Association, 277,* 553-559.

Levy, J. A. (1981). Friendship dilemmas and the intersection of social worlds: Re-entry women on the college campus. *Research in the Interweave of Social Roles: Friendship, 2,* 143-170.

Levy, M. B., & Davis, K. E. (1988). Love styles and attachment styles compared: Their relations to each other and to various relationship characteristics. *Journal of Social and Personal Relationships, 5,* 439-471.

Lewin, K. (1951). *Field theory in social science.* New York: Harper.

Lewis, D. E. (1999, March 17). Women's gains tied to jump in incomes. *The Boston Globe,* p. A1.

Lewis, M., & Feiring, C. (1981). Direct and indirect interactions in social relationships. *Advances in Infancy Research, 1,* 129-161.

Lewontin, R. C. (1998). The evolution of cognition: Questions we will never answer. In D. Scarborough & S. Sternberg (Eds.), *Methods, models, and conceptual issues: An invitation to cognitive science* (Vol. 4, pp. 107-132). Cambridge, MA: MIT Press.

Lichtman, R. R., Taylor, S. E., & Wood, J. V. (1987). Social support and marital adjustment after breast cancer. *Journal of Psychosocial Oncology, 5,* 47-74.

Liebman, S. B. (1976). *Exploring the Latin American mind.* Chicago: Nelson-Hall.

Lindahl, K. M., & Markman, H. J. (1990). Communication and negative affect regulation in the family. In E. A. Blechman (Ed.), *Emotions and the family* (pp. 99-115). Hillsdale, NJ: Lawrence Erlbaum.

Lindemann, E. (1944). Symptomatology and management of acute grief. *American Journal of Psychiatry, 101,* 141-148.

Lindenbaum, S. (1995). Culture, structure, and change: Sex research after modernity. In R. G. Parker & J. H. Gagnon (Eds.), *Conceiving sexuality: Approaches to sex research in a postmodern world* (pp. 273-278). New York: Routledge.

Lindholm, C. (1998). The future of love. In V. C. de Munck (Ed.), *Romantic love and sexual behavior: Perspectives from the social sciences* (pp. 17-32). Westport, CT: Praeger.

Linville, P. W. (1987). Self-complexity as a cognitive buffer against stress-related illness and depression. *Journal of Personality and Social Psychology, 3,* 94-120.

Lippert, T., Ghandi, S., Magnis, E., & Prager, K. J. (1998, June). *The experience of intimacy in daily life: A study of couples.* Paper presented at the annual meeting of the International Society for the Study of Personal Relationships, Saratoga Springs, NY.

Lippert, T., & Prager, K. J. (Under review). Daily experiences of intimacy: A study of couples.

Lisak, D., & Roth, S. (1988). Motivational factors in nonincarcerated sexually aggressive men. *Journal of Personality and Social Psychology, 55,* 795-802.

Litwin, D. (1997). Single older women and the family. In I. Deitch & C. W. Howell (Eds.), *Counseling the aged and their families* (pp. 25-40). Alexandria, VA: American Counseling Association.

Liu, J. H., & Allen, M. W. (1997). *The evolution of political complexity in Maori Hawke's Bay: Archaeological history and its challenge to intergroup theory in psychology.* Unpublished manuscript, Victoria University, Wellington, New Zealand.

Liu, J. H., Campbell, S. M., & Condie, H. (1995). Ethnocentrism in dating preferences for an American sample: The ingroup bias in social context. *European Journal of Social Psychology, 25,* 95-115.

Liu, J. H., Ikeda, K., & Wilson, M. S. (1998). Interpersonal environment effects on political preferences: The "middle path" for conceptualizing social structure in New Zealand and Japan. *Political Behavior, 20,* 183-212.

Lloyd, S. A. (1990). Conflict types and strategies in violent marriages. *Journal of Family Violence, 5,* 269-284.

Lloyd, S. A. (1996). Physical aggression and marital distress: The role of everyday marital interaction. In D. D. Cahn & S. A. Lloyd (Eds.), *Family violence from a communication perspective* (pp. 177-198). Thousand Oaks, CA: Sage.

Lloyd, S. A. (1999). The interpersonal and communication dynamics of wife battering. In X. Arriaga & S. Oskamp (Eds.), *Violence in intimate relationships* (pp. 91-111). Thousand Oaks, CA: Sage.

Lloyd, S. A., & Cate, R. M. (1985). The developmental course of conflict in premarital relationship dissolution. *Journal of Social and Personal Relationships, 2,* 179-194.

Lloyd, S. A., & Emery, B. C. (2000). *The dark side of courtship: Physical and sexual aggression.* Thousand Oaks, CA: Sage.

Lloyd, S. A., & Emery, B. C. (1994). Physically aggressive conflict in romantic relationships. In D. Cahn (Ed.), *Conflict in personal relationships* (pp. 27-46). Hillsdale, NJ: Lawrence Erlbaum.

Localio, A. R., Lawthers, A. G., Brennan, T. A., Laird, N. M., Herbert, L. E., Peterson, L. M., Newhouse, J. P., Weiler, P. C., & Hiatt, H. H. (1991). Relation between malpractice claims and adverse events due to negligence: Results of the Harvard Malpractice

Study III. *New England Journal of Medicine, 325,* 245-251.

Lofland, J., & Lofland, L. H. (1995). *Analyzing social settings* (3rd ed.). Belmont, CA: Wadsworth.

Lonsway, K. A., & Fitzgerald, L. F. (1994). Rape myths: In review. *Psychology of Women Quarterly, 18,* 133-164.

Lopata, H. Z. (1969). Loneliness: Forms and components. *Social Problems, 17,* 248-261.

Lopata, H. Z. (1991). Friendship: Historical and theoretical introduction. In H. Z. Lopata & D. R. Maines (Eds.), *Friendship in context* (pp. 1-22). Greenwich, CT: JAI.

Lopata, H. Z. (1995). Feminist perspectives on social gerontology. In R. Blieszner & V. H. Bedford (Eds.), *Handbook of aging and the family* (pp. 114-131). Westport, CT: Greenwood.

Lorde, A. (1984). *Sister outsider.* Freedom, CA: Crossing Press.

Luescher, K., & Pillemer, K. (1998). Intergenerational ambivalence: A new approach to the study of parent-child relations in later life. *Journal of Marriage and the Family, 60,* 413-425.

Lund, D. A., Caserta, M. S., & Dimond, M. F. (1989). Impact of spousal bereavement on the subjective well-being of older adults. In D. A. Lund (Ed.), *Older bereaved spouses* (pp. 3-15). Washington, DC: Hemisphere.

Maccoby, E., & Martin, J. (1983). Socialization in the context of the family: Parent-child interaction. In E. M. Hetherington (Ed.), *Handbook of child psychology, Vol. 4: Socialization, personality, and social development* (pp. 1-101). New York: John Wiley.

Maccoby, E. E. (1990). Gender and relationships: A developmental account. *American Psychologist, 45,* 513-520.

Maccoby, E. E. (1998). *The two sexes: Growing up apart, coming together.* Cambridge, MA: Harvard University Press.

Maccoby, E. E., & Jacklin, C. N. (1987). Gender segregation in childhood. In H. W. Reese (Ed.), *Advances in child development* (Vol. 20, pp. 239-288). San Diego: Academic Press.

MacDonald, W. L., & De Maris, A. (1996). Remarriage, stepchildren, and marital conflict: Challenges to incomplete institutionalization hypothesis. *Journal of Marriage and the Family, 57,* 387-398.

Magdol, L., Moffitt, T. E., Caspi, A., & Silva, P. A. (1998). Developmental antecedents of partner abuse: A prospective-longitudinal study. *Journal of Abnormal Psychology, 107,* 375-389.

Mahoney, M. R. (1994). Victimization or oppression? Women's lives, violence, and agency. In M. A. Fineman & R. Mykitiuk (Eds.), *The public nature of private violence* (pp. 59-92). New York: Routledge.

Main, M., Kaplan, N., & Cassidy, J. (1985). Security in infancy, childhood, and adulthood: A move to the level of representation. *Monographs of the Society for Research in Child Development, 50*(1-2, Serial No. 209).

Major, B. (1994). From social inequality to personal entitlement: The role of social comparisons, legitimacy appraisals, and group membership. In M. Zanna (Ed.), *Advances in experimental social psychology* (pp. 293-355). San Diego: Academic Press.

Malamuth, N. M. (1986). Predictors of naturalistic sexual aggression. *Journal of Personality and Social Psychology, 50,* 953-962.

Malamuth, N. M., Shayne, E., & Pogue, B. (1982). Infant cues and stopping at a crosswalk. *Personality and Social Psychology Bulletin, 4,* 334-338.

Malamuth, N. M., Sockloski, R. J., Koss, M. P., & Tanaka, J. S. (1991). Characteristics of aggressors against women: Testing a model using a national sample of college students. *Journal of Consulting and Clinical Psychology, 59,* 670-681.

Malle, B. F., & Knobe, J. (1997). Which behaviors do people explain? *Journal of Personality and Social Psychology, 72,* 288-304.

Maltz, D., & Borker, R. (1982). A cultural approach to male-female miscommunication. In J. Gumpertz (Ed.), *Language and social identity* (pp. 196-216). Cambridge, UK: Cambridge University Press.

Mancini, J. A., & Sandifer, D. M. (1995). Family dynamics and the leisure experiences of older adults: Theoretical viewpoints. In R. Blieszner & V. H. Bedford (Eds.), *Handbook of aging and the family* (pp. 132-147). Westport, CT: Greenwood.

Marchetti, G. (1993). *Romance and the "yellow peril": Race, sex, and discursive strategies in Hollywood fiction.* Berkeley: University of California Press.

Marcus, G. E., & Fischer, M. M. J. (1986). *Anthropology as cultural critique: An experimental moment in the human sciences.* Chicago: University of Chicago Press.

Margolin, G. (1981). A behavioral-systems approach to the treatment of marital jealousy. *Clinical Psychology Review, 1,* 469-487.

Margolin, G., Burman, B., & John, R. S. (1989). Home observations of married couples reenacting naturalistic conflicts. *Behavioral Assessment, 11,* 101-118.

Margolin, G., John, R. S., & O'Brien, M. (1989). Sequential affective patterns as a function of marital conflict style. *Journal of Social and Clinical Psychology, 8,* 45-61.

Markman, H., Stanley, S., & Blumberg, S. I. (1994). *Fighting for your marriage.* San Francisco: Jossey-Bass.

Markus, H., & Kitayama, S. (1991). Culture and self: Implications for cognition, emotion, and motivation. *Psychological Review, 98,* 224-253.

Marks, S. R. (1986). *Three corners: Exploring marriage and the self.* Lexington, MA: Lexington Books.

Marsh, H. W. (1990). Two-parent, stepparent, and single-parent families: Changes in achievement, attitudes, and behaviors during the last two years of high school. *Journal of Educational Psychology, 82,* 327-340.

Marshall, L. L. (1994). Physical and psychological abuse. In W. R. Cupach & B. H. Spitzberg (Eds.), *The dark side of interpersonal communication* (pp. 281-311). Hillsdale, NJ: Lawrence Erlbaum.

Marsiglio, W. (1992). Stepfathers with minor children living at home: Parenting perceptions and relationship quality. *Journal of Family Issues, 13,* 195-214.

Marston, P. J., Hecht, M. L., Manke, M. L., McDaniel, S., & Reeder, H. (1998). The subjective experience of intimacy, passion, and commitment in heterosexual love relationships. *Personal Relationships, 5,* 15-30.

Marston, P. J., Hecht, M. L., & Robers, T. (1987). "True love ways": The subjective experience and communication of romantic love. *Journal of Social and Personal Relationships, 4,* 387-407.

Martin, J. L., & Dean, L. (1993). Bereavement following death from AIDS: Unique problems, reactions, and special needs. In M. S. Stroebe, W. Stroebe, & R. O. Hansson (Eds.), *Handbook of bereavement* (pp. 317-330). Cambridge, UK: Cambridge University Press.

Martin, R. (1997). "Girls don't talk about garages!": Perceptions of conversation in same- and cross-sex friendships. *Personal Relationships, 4,* 115-130.

Martin, T. C., & Bumpass, L. L. (1989). Recent trends in marital disruption. *Demography, 26,* 37-51.

Mascolo, M. F., & Fischer, K. W. (1995). Developmental transformations in appraisals for pride, shame, and guilt. In J. P. Tangney & K. W. Fischer (Eds.), *Self-conscious emotions: The psychology of shame, guilt, embarrassment, and pride* (pp. 64-113). New York: Guilford.

Masheter, C. (1997). Former spouses who are friends: Three case studies. *Journal of Social and Personal Relationships, 14,* 207-222.

Mason, K. O., Czajka, J. L., & Arber, S. (1976). Change in U.S. women's sex-role attitudes, 1964-1974. *American Sociological Review, 41,* 573-596.

Mason, M. A. (1998). The modern American stepfamily: Problems and possibilities. In M. Mason & A. Skolnick (Eds.), *All our families: New policies for a new century* (pp. 95-116). New York: Oxford University Press.

Masters, W. H., & Johnson, V. E. (1966). *Human sexual response.* Boston: Little, Brown.

Mathes, E. W. (1991). A cognitive theory of jealousy. In P. Salovey (Ed.), *The psychology of jealousy and envy* (pp. 52-79). New York: Guilford.

Mathes, E. W., Roter, P. M., & Joerger, S. M. (1981). A convergent validity study of six jealousy scales. *Psychological Reports, 49,* 23-31.

Mathes, E. W., & Severa, N. (1981). Jealousy, romantic love, and liking: Theoretical considerations and preliminary scale development. *Psychological Reports, 49,* 23-31.

Matthews, S. (1986). *Friendships through the life course.* Beverly Hills, CA: Sage.

Matthews, S. H., Adamek, M. E., & Dunkle, R. E. (1993). Research on older families when more than one member responds: Producing and interpreting findings. *Journal of Aging Studies, 7,* 215-228.

May, L. (1998). *Masculinity and morality.* Ithaca, NY: Cornell University Press.

McAdams, D. P. (1984). Human motives and interpersonal relationships. In V. J. Derlega (Ed.), *Communication, intimacy, and close relationships* (pp. 41-70). San Diego: Academic Press.

McAdams, D. P., Healy, S., & Krause, S. (1984). Social motives and patterns of friendship. *Journal of Personality and Social Psychology, 47,* 828-838.

McAdams, D. P., & Powers, J. (1981). Themes of intimacy in behavior and thought. *Journal of Personality and Social Psychology, 40,* 573-587.

McCall, G. J., & Simmons, J. L. (1978). *Identities and interactions: An examination of human associations in everyday life* (Rev. ed.). New York: Free Press.

McCormick, N. B. (1994). *Sexual salvation: Affirming women's sexual rights and pleasures.* New York: Praeger.

McCrae, R. R., & Costa, P. T. (1988). Psychological resilience among widowed men and women: A 10-year follow-up of a national sample. *Journal of Social Issues, 44*(3), 129-144.

McDonald, H. B., & Steinhorn, A. I. (1990). *Homosexuality: A practical guide to counseling lesbians, gay men, and their families.* New York: Continuum.

McFall, R. (1982). A review and reformulation of the concept of social skills. *Behavioral Assessment, 4,* 1-33.

McKenry, P. C., McKelvey, M. W., Leigh, D., & Wark, L. (1996). Nonresidential father involvement: A comparison of divorced, separated, never married, and remarried fathers. *Journal of Divorce and Remarriage, 25,* 1-12.

McLanahan, S. S., & Sandefur, G. (1994). *Growing up with a single parent.* Cambridge, MA: Harvard University Press.

McLaren, P. (1997). *Revolutionary multiculturalism: Pedagogies of dissent for the new millennium.* Boulder, CO: Westview.

McWhirter, D. P., & Mattison, A. M. (1984). *The male couple.* Englewood Cliffs, NJ: Prentice Hall.

Mead, M. (1968). *Sex and temperament in three primitive societies.* New York: Dell. (Original work published 1934)

Mead, M. (1977). Jealousy: Primitive and civilized. In G. Clanton & L. G. Smith (Eds.), *Jealousy* (pp. 115-127). Englewood Cliffs, NJ: Prentice Hall.

Mederer, H. J. (1993). Division of labor in two-earner homes: Task accomplishment versus household management as critical variables in perceptions about family work. *Journal of Marriage and the Family, 55,* 133-145.

Meeks, B. S., Hendrick, S. S., & Hendrick, C. (1998). Communication, love, and relationship satisfaction. *Journal of Social and Personal Relationships, 15,* 755-773.

Melamed, T. (1991). Individual differences in romantic jealousy: The moderating effect of relationship characteristics. *European Journal of Social Psychology, 21,* 455-461.

Mellen, S. L. W. (1981). *The evolution of love.* San Francisco: Freeman.

Menaghan, E. G., Kowalski-Jones, L., & Mott, F. L. (1997). The intergenerational costs of parental social stressors: Academic and social difficulties in early adolescence for children of young mothers. *Journal of Health and Social Behavior, 38,* 72-86.

Messman, S. J., & Canary, D. J. (1998). Patterns of conflict in personal relationships. In B. H. Spitzberg & W. R. Cupach (Eds.), *The dark side of personal relationships* (pp. 121-152). Mahwah, NJ: Lawrence Erlbaum.

Metts, S. (1992). The language of disengagement: A face-management perspective. In T. L. Orbuch (Ed.), *Close relationship losses: Theoretical approaches* (pp. 111-127). New York: Springer-Verlag.

Metts, S. (1994). Relational transgressions. In W. R. Cupach & B. H. Spitzberg (Eds.), *The dark side of interpersonal communication* (pp. 217-239). Hillsdale, NJ: Lawrence Erlbaum.

Metts, S. (1997). Face and facework: Implications for the study of personal relationships. In S. Duck (Ed.), *Handbook of personal relationships: Theory, research, and interventions* (2nd ed., pp. 373-390). Chichester, UK: Wiley.

Metts, S., & Bowers, J. W. (1994). Emotion in interpersonal communication. In M. L. Knapp & G. R. Miller (Eds.), *Handbook of interpersonal communication* (2nd ed., pp. 508-541). Thousand Oaks, CA: Sage.

Metz, M. E., Rosser, B. R. S., & Strapko, N. (1994). Differences in conflict resolution styles among heterosexual, gay, and lesbian couples. *Journal of Sex Research, 31,* 1-16.

Meyer, M. H., & Bellas, M. L. (1995). U.S. old-age policy and the family. In R. Blieszner & V. H. Bedford (Eds.), *Handbook of aging and the family* (pp. 263-283). Westport, CT: Greenwood.

Meyering, R. A., & Epling-McWerther, E. A. (1986). Decision-making in extramarital relationships. *Lifestyles: A Journal of Changing Patterns, 8,* 115-129.

Mickelson, K. D., Kessler, R. C., & Shaver, P. R. (1997). Adult attachment in a nationally representative sample. *Journal of Personality and Social Psychology, 73,* 1092-1106.

Miell, D., & Duck, S. (1986). Strategies in developing friendships. In V. J. Derlega & B. A. Winstead (Eds.), *Friendship and social interaction* (pp. 129-143). New York: Springer-Verlag.

Mikulincer, M. (1995). Attachment style and the mental representation of the self. *Journal of Personality and Social Psychology, 69,* 1203-1215.

Mikulincer, M. (1998). Adult attachment style and individual differences in functional versus dysfunctional experiences of anger. *Journal of Personality and Social Psychology, 74,* 513-524.

Mikulincer, M., & Florian, V. (1998). The relationship between adult attachment styles and emotional and cognitive reactions to stressful events. In J. A. Simpson & W. S. Rholes (Eds.), *Attachment theory and close relationships* (pp. 143-165). New York: Guilford.

Mikulincer, M., Florian, V., & Weller, A. (1993). Attachment styles, coping strategies, and posttraumatic psychological distress: The impact of the Gulf War in Israel. *Journal of Personality and Social Psychology, 64,* 817-826.

Mikulincer, M., & Nachshon, O. (1991). Attachment styles and patterns of self-disclosure. *Journal of Personality and Social Psychology, 61,* 321-331.

Mikulincer, M., & Orbach, I. (1995). Attachment styles and repressive defensiveness: The accessibility and architecture of affective memories. *Journal of Personality and Social Psychology, 68,* 917-925.

Milardo, R. M. (1982). Friendship networks in developing relationships: Converging and diverging social environments. *Social Psychology Quarterly, 45,* 162-172.

Milardo, R. M. (1986). Personal choice and social constraint in close relationships: Applications of network analysis. In V. J. Derlega & B. Winstead (Eds.), *Friendship and social interaction* (pp. 145-165). New York: Springer.

Milardo, R. M. (1987). Changes in social networks of men and women following divorce. *Journal of Family Issues, 8,* 78-96.

Milardo, R. M. (1992). Comparative methods for delineating social networks. *Journal of Social and Personal Relationships, 9,* 447-461.

Milardo, R. M., & Allan, G. (1997). Social networks and marital relationships. In S. Duck (Ed.), *Handbook of personal relationships: Theory, research, and interventions* (2nd ed., pp. 505-522). Chichester, UK: Wiley.

Milardo, R. M., & Wellman, B. (1992). The personal is social. *Journal of Social and Personal Relationships, 9,* 339-342.

Miller, B., & Marshall, J. C. (1987). Coercive sex on the university campus. *Journal of College Student Personnel, 47,* 38-47.

Miller, G. A., Galanter, E., & Pribram, K. H. (1960). *Plans and the structure of behavior.* New York: Holt.

Miller, J. (1986). *Toward a new psychology of women* (2nd ed.). Boston: Beacon.

Miller, L. C. (1990). Intimacy and liking: Mutual influence and the role of unique relationships. *Journal of Personality and Social Psychology, 59,* 50-60.

Miller, L. C., & Berg, J. (1984). Selectivity and urgency in interpersonal exchange. In V. J. Derlega (Ed.), *Communication, intimacy, and close relationships* (pp. 161-206). San Diego: Academic Press.

Miller, L. C., & Fishkin, S. A. (1997). On the dynamics of human bonding and reproductive success: Seeking windows on the adapted-for-human-environment interface. In J. Simpson & D. Kenrick (Eds.), *Evolutionary social psychology* (pp. 197-235). Mahwah, NJ: Lawrence Erlbaum.

Miller, L. C., & Kenny, D. A. (1986). Reciprocity of self-disclosure at the individual and dyadic levels: A social relations analysis. *Journal of Personality and Social Psychology, 50,* 713-719.

Miller, R. B., Hemesath, K., & Nelson, B. (1997). Marriage in middle and later life. In T. D. Hargrave & S. M. Hanna (Eds.), *The aging family: New visions in theory, practice, and reality* (pp. 178-198). New York: Brunner/Mazel.

Miller, R. S. (1995). Embarrassment and social behavior. In J. P. Tangney & K. W. Fischer (Eds.), *Self-conscious emotions: The psychology of shame, guilt, embarrassment, and pride* (pp. 322-339). New York: Guilford.

Miller, R. S., & Leary, M. R. (1992). Social sources and interactive functions of emotion: The case of embarrassment. In M. S. Clark (Ed.), *Emotions and social behavior* (pp. 202-221). Newbury Park, CA: Sage.

Milliones, J. (1980). Construction of a black consciousness measure: Psychotherapeutic implications. *Psychotherapy: Theory, Research, and Practice, 17,* 175-182.

Mintz, S., & Kellogg, S. (1988). *Domestic revolutions: A social history of American family life.* New York: Free Press.

Minuchin, P. (1992). Conflict and child maltreatment. In C. U. Shantz & W. W. Hartup (Eds.), *Conflict in child and adolescent development* (pp. 380-401). New York: Cambridge University Press.

Mischel, W. (1966). A social learning view of sex differences in behavior. In E. Maccoby (Ed.), *The development of sex differences in behavior* (pp. 93-106). Stanford, CA: Stanford University Press.

Moller, L. C., Hymel, S., & Rubin, K. H. (1992). Sex typing in play and popularity in middle childhood. *Sex Roles, 26,* 331-353.

Mongeau, P. A., Hale, J. L., & Alles, M. (1994). An experimental investigation of accounts and attributions following sexual infidelity. *Communication Monographs, 61,* 326-344.

Monsour, M. (1992). Meanings of intimacy in cross- and same-sex friendships. *Journal of Social and Personal Relationships, 9,* 277-295.

Monsour, M. (1997). Communication and cross-sex friendships across the life cycle: A review of the literature. In B. R. Burleson (Ed.), *Communication yearbook 20* (pp. 375-414). Thousand Oaks, CA: Sage.

Montemayor, R. (1983). Parents and adolescents in conflict: All forms some of the time and some forms most of the time. *Journal of Early Adolescence, 3,* 83-103.

Montemayor, R., & Brownlee, J. (1987). Fathers, mothers, and adolescents: Gender-based differences in parental roles during adolescence. *Journal of Youth and Adolescence, 16,* 281-291.

Montgomery, B. M. (1993). Relationship maintenance versus relationship change: Dialectical dilemma. *Journal of Social and Personal Relationships, 10,* 205-224.

Montgomery, B. M. (1994). Communication in close relationships. In A. L. Weber & J. H. Harvey (Eds.), *Perspectives on close relationships* (pp. 67-87). Boston: Allyn & Bacon.

Montgomery, M. J., Anderson, E. R., Hetherington, E. M., & Clingempeel, W. G. (1992). Patterns of courtship for remarriage: Implications for child adjustment and parent-child relationships. *Journal of Marriage and the Family, 54,* 686-698.

Montgomery, M. J., & Sorell, G. T. (1997). Differences in love attitudes across family life stages. *Family Relations, 46,* 55-61.

Moore, G. (1990). Structural determinants of men's and women's personal networks. *American Sociological Review, 55,* 726-736.

Moore, R. L. (1998). Love and limerence with Chinese characteristics: Student romance in the PRC. In V. C. de Munck (Ed.), *Romantic love and sexual behavior: Perspectives from the social sciences* (pp. 251-283). Westport, CT: Praeger.

Morrison, D. R., & Cherlin, A. J. (1995). The divorce process and young children's well-being: A prospective analysis. *Journal of Marriage and the Family, 57,* 800-812.

Morrow, G. D., Clark, E. M., & Brock, K. F. (1995). Individual and partner love styles: Implications for the quality of romantic involvements. *Journal of Social and Personal Relationships, 12,* 363-387.

Mosher, D. L. (1988). Sexual path preferences inventory. In C. M. Davis, W. L. Yarber, & S. L. Davis (Eds.), *Sexuality-related measures: A compendium* (pp. 188-192). Lake Mills, IA: Graphic Publications.

Moss, M. S., & Moss, S. Z. (1995). Death and bereavement. In R. Blieszner & V. H. Bedford (Eds.), *Handbook of aging and the family* (pp. 422-439). Westport, CT: Greenwood.

Motley, M. T. (1990). On whether one can(not) not communicate: An examination via traditional communication postulates. *Western Journal of Speech Communication, 54,* 1-20.

Muehlenhard, C. L. (1988). Misinterpreted dating behaviors and the risk of date rape. *Journal of Social and Clinical Psychology, 6,* 20-37.

Muehlenhard, C. L., & Cook, S. W. (1988). Men's self-reports of unwanted sexual activity. *Journal of Sex Research, 24,* 58-72.

Muehlenhard, C. L., & Falcon, P. L. (1990). Men's heterosocial skill and attitudes toward women as predictors of verbal sexual coercion and forceful rape. *Sex Roles, 23,* 241-259.

Muehlenhard, C. L., & Linton, M. A. (1987). Date rape and sexual aggression in dating situations: Incidence and risk factors. *Journal of Counseling Psychology, 34,* 186-196.

Mullen, P. E., & Martin, J. L. (1994). Jealousy: A community study. *British Journal of Psychiatry, 164,* 35-43.

Mundt, C., Fiedler, P., Ernst, S., & Backenstrass, M. (1996). Expressed emotion and marital interaction in endogenous depressives. In C. Mundt, M. J. Goldstein, K. Hahlweg, & P. Fiedler (Eds.), *Interpersonal factors in the origin and course of affective disorders* (pp. 240-256). London: Gaskell Academic.

Murphy, B., & Zorn, T. (1996). Gendered interaction in professional relationships. In J. T. Wood (Ed.), *Gendered relationships* (pp. 213-232). Mountain View, CA: Mayfield.

Murphy, B. C. (1989). Lesbian couples and their parents: The effects of perceived parental attitudes on the couple. *Journal of Counseling and Development, 68,* 46-51.

Murray, S. L., Holmes, J. G., & Griffin, D. W. (1996). The self-fulfilling nature of positive illusions in romantic relationships: Love is not blind but prescient. *Journal of Personality and Social Psychology, 71,* 1155-1180.

Murrell, S. A., Norris, F. H., & Chipley, Q. T. (1992). Functional versus structural social support, desirable events, and positive affect in older adults. *Psychology and Aging, 7,* 562-570.

Murstein, B. I. (1970). Stimulus value role: A theory of marital choice. *Journal of Marriage and the Family, 32,* 465-481.

Murstein, B. I., Merighi, J. R., & Vyse, S. A. (1991). Love styles in the United States and France: A cross-cultural comparison. *Journal of Social and Clinical Psychology, 10,* 37-46.

Myers, J. L. (1979). *Fundamentals of experimental design* (3rd ed.). Boston: Allyn & Bacon.

Nardi, P. M., & Sherrod, D. (1994). Friendship in the lives of gay men and lesbians. *Journal of Social and Personal Relationships, 11,* 185-200.

National Research Council. (1989). *A common destiny: Blacks and American society.* Washington, DC: Author.

National Research Council. (1996). *Understanding violence against women.* Washington, DC: Author.

Neimeyer, R. A., & Neimeyer, G. J. (1983). Structural similarity in the acquaintance process. *Journal of Social and Clinical Psychology, 1,* 146-154.

Nelson, W. L., Hughes, H. M., Handal, P., Katz, B., & Searight, H. R. (1993). The relationship of family structure and family conflict to adjustment in young adult college students. *Adolescence, 28,* 29-40.

Newcomb, A. F., & Bagwell, C. L. (1995). Children's friendship relations: A meta-analytic review. *Psychological Bulletin, 117,* 306-347.

Newcomb, A. F., & Brady, J. E. (1982). Mutuality in boys' friendship relations. *Child Development, 53,* 392-395.

Newcomb, A. F., Bukowski, W. M., & Pattee, L. (1993). Children's peer relations: A meta-analytic review of popular, rejected, neglected, controversial, and average sociometric status. *Psychological Bulletin, 113,* 99-128.

Newsom, J. T., & Schulz, R. (1996). Social support as a mediator in the relation between functional status and quality of life in older adults. *Psychology and Aging, 11,* 34-44.

Nielsen, L. (1999). Stepmothers: Why so much stress? A review of the literature. *Journal of Divorce and Remarriage, 30,* 115-148.

Niemeijer, R. (1973). Some applications of the notion of density. In J. Boissevan & J. C. Mitchell (Eds.), *Network analysis studies in human interaction* (pp. 45-64). The Hague, Netherlands: Mouton.

Nolen-Hoeksema, S. (1987). Sex differences in unipolar depression: Evidence and theory. *Psychological Bulletin, 101,* 259-282.

Nolen-Hoeksema, S., McBride, A., & Larson, J. (1997). Rumination and psychological distress among bereaved partners. *Journal of Personality and Social Psychology, 72,* 855-862.

Noller, P. (1986). Sex differences in nonverbal communication: Advantage lost or supremacy regained? *Australian Journal of Psychology, 38,* 23-32.

Noller, P. (1996). What is this thing called love? Defining the love that supports marriage and family. *Personal Relationships, 3,* 97-115.

Nyquist, L., Slivken, K., Spence, J., & Helmreich, R. L. (1985). Household responsibilities in middle-class couples: The contribution of demographic and personality variables. *Sex Roles, 12,* 15-34.

Oakley, A. (1974). *Women's work: The housewife, past and present.* New York: Pantheon.

Oatley, K., & Johnson-Laird, P. N. (1987). Toward a cognitive theory of emotions. *Cognition and Emotion, 1,* 29-50.

O'Bryant, S. L., & Hansson, R. O. (1995). Widowhood. In R. Blieszner & V. H. Bedford (Eds.), *Handbook of aging and the family* (pp. 440-458). Westport, CT: Greenwood.

O'Connor, P. (1992). *Friendships between women.* New York: Guilford.

O'Connor, T. G., Hetherington, E. M., & Clingempeel, W. G. (1997). Systems and bidirectional influences in families. *Journal of Social and Personal Relationships, 14,* 491-504.

Oden, S., & Asher, S. R. (1977). Coaching children in social skills for friendship making. *Child Development, 48,* 495-500.

Offer, D., Ostrov, E., & Howard, K. (1981). *The adolescent: A psychological self portrait.* New York: Basic Books.

Oggins, J., Leber, D., & Veroff, J. (1993). Race and gender differences in black and white newlyweds' perceptions of sexual and marital relationships. *Journal of Sex Research, 30,* 152-160.

Ognibene, T. C., & Collins, N. L. (1998). Adult attachment styles, perceived social support, and coping strategies. *Journal of Social and Personal Relationships, 15,* 323-345.

Ohbuchi, K., Chiba, S., & Fukushima, O. (1996). Mitigation of interpersonal conflicts: Politeness and time pressure. *Personality and Social Psychology Bulletin, 22,* 1035-1042.

O'Keefe, M. (1997). Predictors of dating violence among high school students. *Journal of Interpersonal Violence, 12,* 546-568.

Oldenburg, C. M., & Kerns, K. A. (1997). Associations between peer relationships and depressive symptoms: Testing moderator effects of gender and age. *Journal of Early Adolescence, 17,* 319-337.

O'Leary, K. D., Barling, J., Arias, I., Rosenbaum, A., Malone, J., & Tyree, A. (1989). Prevalence and stability of physical aggression between spouses: A longitudinal analysis. *Journal of Consulting and Clinical Psychology, 57,* 263-268.

O'Leary, K. D., & Beach, S. R. H. (1990). Marital therapy: A viable treatment for depression and marital discord. *American Journal of Psychiatry, 147,* 183-186.

O'Leary, K. D., Malone, J., & Tyree, A. (1994). Physical aggression in early marriage: Pre-relationship and relationship effects. *Journal of Consulting and Clinical Psychology, 62,* 594-602.

Olien, M. (1978). *The human myth.* New York: Harper & Row.

Oliker, S. J. (1989). *Best friends and marriage.* Berkeley: University of California Press.

Oliver, M. B., & Hyde, J. S. (1993). Gender differences in sexuality: A meta-analysis. *Psychological Bulletin, 114,* 29-51.

Olweus, D. (1978). *Aggression in the schools: Bullies and whipping boys.* Washington, DC: Hemisphere.

Omark, R. R., Omark, M., & Edelman, M. (1975). Formation of dominance hierarchies in young children. In T. R. Williams (Ed.), *Psychological anthropology* (pp. 289-316). The Hague, Netherlands: Mouton.

Ono, K. A. (1998). Communicating prejudice in the media: Upending racial categories in *Doubles.* In M. L. Hecht (Ed.), *Communicating prejudice* (pp. 206-220). Thousand Oaks, CA: Sage.

Orbuch, T. L. (1997). People's accounts count: The sociology of accounts. *Annual Review of Sociology, 23,* 455-478.

Orbuch, T. L., Harvey, J. H., Davis, S. H., & Merbach, N. (1994). Account-making and confiding as acts of meaning in response to sexual assault. *Journal of Family Violence, 9,* 249-264.

Ornish, D. (1998). *Love and survival.* New York: HarperCollins.

Osmond, M. W. (1987). Radical-critical theories. In M. B. Sussman & S. K. Steinmetz (Eds.), *Handbook of marriage and the family* (pp. 103-124). New York: Plenum.

O'Sullivan, L. F., Byers, S., & Finkelman, L. (1998). A comparison of male and female college students' experiences of sexual coercion. *Psychology of Women Quarterly, 22,* 177-195.

Owen, W. F. (1993). Metaphors in accounts of romantic relationship terminations. In P. J. Kalbfleisch (Ed.), *Interpersonal communication: Evolving interpersonal relationships* (pp. 261-278). Hillsdale, NJ: Lawrence Erlbaum.

Owens, G., Crowell, J., Pan, H., Treboux, D., O'Connor, E., & Waters, E. (1995). The prototype hypothesis and the origins of attachment working models: Adult relationships with parents and romantic partners. *Monographs of the Society for Research in Child Development, 60*(2-3, Serial No. 244).

Pagel, M. D., Erdley, W. W., & Becker, J. (1987). Social networks: We get by with (and in spite of) a little help from our friends. *Journal of Personality and Social Psychology, 53,* 793-804.

Paikoff, R. L., & Brooks-Gunn, J. (1991). Do parent-child relationships change during puberty? *Psychological Bulletin, 110,* 47-66.

Pakenham, K. I. (1998). Couple coping and adjustment to multiple sclerosis in care receiver-carer dyads. *Family Relations, 47,* 269-277.

Pan, H., Neidig, P., & O'Leary, K. D. (1994). Predicting mild and severe husband-to-wife physical aggression. *Journal of Consulting and Clinical Psychology, 62,* 63-71.

Papernow, P. (1993). *Becoming a stepfamily: Patterns of development in remarried families.* San Francisco: Jossey-Bass.

Papini, D., Datan, N., & McCluskey-Fawcett, K. (1988). An observational study of affective and assertive family interactions during adolescence. *Journal of Youth and Adolescence, 17,* 477-492.

Park, K. A., & Waters, E. (1988). Traits and relationships in developmental perspective. In S. Duck (Ed.), *Handbook of personal relationships* (pp. 161-176). Chichester, UK: Wiley.

Parke, R. D., & Buriel, R. (1998). Socialization in the family: Ethnic and ecological perspectives. In W. Damon & N. Eisenberg (Eds.), *Handbook of child psychology, Vol. 3: Social, emotional, and personality development* (pp. 463-552). New York: John Wiley.

Parker, J. G., & Asher, S. R. (1993a). Beyond group acceptance: Friendship adjustment and friendship quality as distinct dimensions of children's peer adjustment. In D. Perlman & W. H. Jones (Eds.), *Advances in personal relationships* (Vol. 4, pp. 261-294). London: Jessica Kingsley.

Parker, J. G., & Asher, S. R. (1993b). Friendship and friendship quality in middle childhood: Links with peer group acceptance and feelings of loneliness and social dissatisfaction. *Developmental Psychology, 29,* 611-621.

Parker, J. G., & Gottman, J. M. (1989). Social and emotional development in a relational context: Friendship interaction from early childhood to adolescence. In T. J. Berndt & G. W. Ladd (Eds.), *Peer relationships in child development* (pp. 95-131). New York: John Wiley.

Parker, J. G., Houlihan, K. G., & Casas, S. E. (1997, April). *Assessing children's best friendships: Conceptual issues and the development and evaluation of a new Q-sort instrument.* Paper presented at the biennial meeting of the Society for Research in Child Development, Washington, DC.

Parker, J. G., Saxon, J. L., Asher, S. R., & Kovacs, D. M. (1999). The friendship experience in middle childhood and adolescence: Implications for understanding loneliness. In K. J. Rotenberg & S. Hymel (Eds.), *Loneliness in childhood and adolescence* (pp. 201-221). New York: Cambridge University Press.

Parker, J. G., & Seal, J. (1996) Forming, losing, renewing, and replacing friendships: Applying temporal parameters to the assessment of children's friendship experiences. *Child Development, 67,* 2248-2268.

Parker, S., & de Vries, B. (1993). Patterns of friendship for women and men in same- and cross-sex relationships. *Journal of Social and Personal Relationships, 10,* 617-626.

Parkes, C. M., & Weiss, R. S. (1983). *Recovery from bereavement.* New York: Basic Books.

Parks, M. R. (1997). Communication networks and relationship life-cycles. In S. Duck (Ed.), *Handbook of personal relationships: Theory, research, and interventions* (2nd ed., pp. 351-372). Chichester, UK: Wiley.

Parks, M. R., & Eggert, L. L. (1991). The role of social context in the dynamics of personal relationships. In W. H. Jones & D. Perlman (Eds.), *Advances in personal relationships* (Vol. 2, pp. 1-34). London: Jessica Kingsley.

Parks, M. R., Stan, C., & Eggert, L. (1983). Romantic involvement and social network involvement. *Social Psychology Quarterly, 46,* 116-130.

Parrott, T. M., & Bengtson, V. L. (1999). The effects of earlier intergenerational affection, normative expectations, and family conflict on contemporary exchanges of help and support. *Research on Aging, 21,* 73-105.

Parrott, W. G. (1991). The emotional experiences of envy and jealousy. In P. Salovey (Ed.), *The psychol-ogy of jealousy and envy* (pp. 3-30). New York: Guilford.

Pasley, K., & Ihinger-Tallman, M. (1990). Remarriage in later adulthood: Correlates of perceptions of family adjustment. *Family Perspectives, 24,* 263-274.

Pasley, K., Koch, M. G., & Ihinger-Tallman, M. (1993). Problems in remarriage: An exploratory study of intact and terminated remarriages. *Journal of Divorce and Remarriage, 20,* 63-83.

Patterson, C. J. (1995). Families of the lesbian baby boom: Parents' division of labor and children's adjustment. *Developmental Psychology, 31,* 115-123.

Patterson, D. G., & Schwartz, P. (1994). The social construction of conflict in intimate same-sex couples. In D. D. Cahn (Ed.), *Conflict in personal relationships* (pp. 3-26). Hillsdale, NJ: Lawrence Erlbaum.

Patterson, G. R. (1982). *Coercive family processes.* Eugene, OR: Castalia.

Patterson, G. R., & Bank, L. (1989). Some amplifying mechanisms for pathologic process in families. In M. R. Gunnar & E. Thelen (Eds.), *Minnesota Symposium on Child Psychology* (pp. 167-209). Hillsdale, NJ: Lawrence Erlbaum.

Patterson, M. L. (1995). A parallel process model of nonverbal communication. *Journal of Nonverbal Behavior, 19,* 3-29.

Patzer, G. L. (1985). *The physical attractiveness phenomena.* New York: Plenum.

Paul, E. L. (1997). A longitudinal analysis of midlife interpersonal relationships and well-being. In M. E. Lachman & J. B. James (Eds.), *Multiple paths of midlife development* (pp. 171-206). Chicago: University of Chicago Press.

Paul, L., Foss, M. A., & Galloway, J. (1993). Sexual jealousy in young women and men: Aggressive responses to partner and rival. *Aggressive Behavior, 19,* 401-420.

Paulson, S., Hill, J., & Holmbeck, G. (1991). Distinguishing between perceived closeness and parental warmth in families with seventh-grade boys and girls. *Journal of Early Adolescence, 11,* 276-293.

Penn, M. L., Gaines, S. O., Jr., & Phillips, L. (1993). On the desirability of own-group preference. *Journal of Black Psychology, 19,* 303-321.

Pennebaker, J. (1990). *Opening up.* New York: William Morrow.

Pennebaker, J. W., & Harber, K. D. (1992). Overcoming traumatic memories. In S. A. Christianson (Ed.), *The handbook of emotion and memory: Research and theory* (pp. 359-387). Hillsdale, NJ: Lawrence Erlbaum.

Pennebaker, J. W., Mayne, T. J., & Francis, M. E. (1997). Linguistic predictors of adaptive bereavement. *Journal of Personality and Social Psychology, 72,* 863-871.

Peplau, L. A. (1983). Roles and gender. In H. H. Kelley, E. Berscheid, A. Christensen, J. H. Harvey, T. L. Huston, G. Levinger, E. McClintock, L. A. Peplau,

& D. R. Peterson (Eds.), *Close relationships* (pp. 220-264). New York: Freeman.

Peplau, L. A. (1991). Lesbian and gay relationships. In J. C. Gonsiorek & J. D. Weinrich (Eds.), *Homosexuality: Research findings for public policy* (pp. 177-196). Newbury Park, CA: Sage.

Peplau, L. A., & Amaro, H. (1982). Understanding lesbian relationships. In W. Paul, J. D., Weinrich, J. D. Gonsiorek, & M. E. Hotvedt (Eds.), *Homosexuality: Social, psychological, and biological issues* (pp. 233-248). Beverly Hills, CA: Sage.

Peplau, L. A., & Campbell, S. M. (1989). The balance of power in dating and marriage. In J. Freeman (Ed.), *Women: A feminist perspective* (4th ed., pp. 121-137). Mountain View, CA: Mayfield.

Peplau, L. A., & Cochran, S. D. (1980, September). *Sex differences in values concerning love relationships.* Paper presented at the annual meeting of the American Psychological Association, Montreal.

Peplau, L. A., & Cochran, S. D. (1981). Value orientations in the intimate relationships of gay men. *Journal of Homosexuality, 6*(3), 1-19.

Peplau, L. A., & Cochran, S. D. (1990). A relational perspective on homosexuality. In D. P. McWhirter, S. A. Sanders, & J. M. Reinisch (Eds.), *Homosexuality/heterosexuality: Concepts of sexual orientation* (pp. 321-349). New York: Oxford University Press.

Peplau, L. A., Cochran, S. D., & Mays, V. M. (1997). A national survey of the intimate relationships of African American lesbians and gay men: A look at commitment, satisfaction, sexual behavior, and HIV disease. In B. Greene (Ed.), *Ethnic and cultural diversity among lesbians and gay men* (pp. 11-38). Thousand Oaks, CA: Sage.

Peplau, L. A., Cochran, S. D., Rook, K., & Padesky, C. (1978). Women in love: Attachment and autonomy in lesbian relationships. *Journal of Social Issues, 34*(3), 7-27.

Peplau, L. A., Padesky, C., & Hamilton, M. (1982). Satisfaction in lesbian relationships. *Journal of Homosexuality, 8*(2), 23-35.

Peplau, L. A., Rubin, Z., & Hill, C. T. (1977). Sexual intimacy in dating relationships. *Journal of Social Issues, 33*(2), 86-109.

Peplau, L. A., Spalding, L. R., Conley, T. D., & Veniegas, R. C. (in press). The development of sexual orientation in women. *Annual Review of Sex Research, 10.*

Peretti, P. O., & Pudowski, B. C. (1997). Influence of jealousy on male and female college daters. *Journal of Social Behavior and Personality, 25,* 155-160.

Perlman, D., & Peplau, L. A. (1981). Toward a social psychology of loneliness. In S. Duck & R. Gilmour (Eds.), *Personal relationships in disorder* (pp. 31-56). San Diego: Academic Press.

Perlman, S. D., & Abramson, P. R. (1982). Sexual satisfaction among married and cohabiting individuals.

*Journal of Consulting and Clinical Psychology, 50,* 458-460.

Perry, D. G., Kusel, S. J., & Perry, L. C. (1988). Victims of peer aggression. *Developmental Psychology, 24,* 807-814.

Perry-Jenkins, M., & Crouter, A. C. (1990). Men's provider role attitudes: Implications for household work and marital satisfaction. *Journal of Family Issues, 11,* 136-156.

Perry-Jenkins, M., Seery, B., & Crouter, A. C. (1992). Linkages between women's provider role attitudes, psychological well-being, and family relationships. *Psychology of Women Quarterly, 16,* 311-329.

Peters, A., & Liefbroer, A. C. (1997). Beyond marital status: Partner history and well-being in old age. *Journal of Marriage and the Family, 59,* 687-699.

Petronio, S. (1991). Communication boundary management: A theoretical model of managing disclosure of private information between marital couples. *Communication Theory, 1,* 311-335.

Petronio, S. (1994). Privacy binds in family interactions: The case of parental privacy invasion. In W. R. Cupach & B. H. Spitzberg (Eds.), *The dark side of interpersonal communication* (pp. 241-258). Hillsdale, NJ: Lawrence Erlbaum.

Pettigrew, T. F. (1988). Integration and pluralism. In P. A. Katz & D. A. Taylor (Eds.), *Eliminating racism: Profiles in controversy* (pp. 19-30). New York: Plenum.

Petty, G. M., & Dawson, B. (1989). Sexual aggression in normal men: Incidence, beliefs, and personality characteristics. *Personality and Individual Differences, 10,* 355-362.

Pfeiffer, S. M., & Wong, P. T. P. (1989). Multidimensional jealousy. *Journal of Social and Personal Relationships, 6,* 181-196.

Phillips, L., Penn, M. L., & Gaines, S. O., Jr. (1993). A hermeneutic rejoinder to ourselves and our critics. *Journal of Black Psychology, 19,* 350-357.

Phillipson, C. (1997). Social relationships in later life: A review of the research literature. *International Journal of Geriatric Psychiatry, 12,* 505-512.

Phinney, J. S. (1986). The structure of 5-year-olds' verbal quarrels with peers and siblings. *Journal of Genetic Psychology, 147,* 47-60.

Piaget, J. (1965). *The moral judgment of the child.* New York: Free Press. (Original work published 1932)

Pickett, K. (1995). *Love in the 90s: B. B. and Jo: The story of a lifelong love.* New York: Warner Books.

Pierce, G. R., Lakey, B., Sarason, I., & Sarason, B. (1997). *Sourcebook of social support and personality.* New York: Plenum.

Piercy, K. W. (1998). Theorizing about family caregiving: The role of responsibility. *Journal of Marriage and the Family, 60,* 109-118.

Pietromonaco, P. R., & Barrett, L. F. (1997). Working models of attachment and daily social interactions.

*Journal of Personality and Social Psychology, 73,* 1409-1423.

Pietromonaco, P. R., & Carnelley, K. B. (1994). Gender and working models of attachment: Consequences for perceptions of self and romantic relationships. *Personal Relationships, 1,* 63-82.

Pietropinto, A., & Simenauer, J. (1977). *Beyond the male myth: What women want to know about men's sexuality* [Survey]. New York: Times Book.

Pines, A., & Aronson, E. (1983). Antecedents, correlates, and consequences of sexual jealousy. *Journal of Personality, 51,* 108-136.

Pinney, E. M., Gerrard, M., & Denney, N. W. (1987). The Pinney Sexual Satisfaction Inventory. *Journal of Sex Research, 23,* 233-251.

Pipp, S., Shaver, P., Jennings, S., Lamborn, S., & Fischer, K. W. (1985). Adolescents' theories about the development of their relationships with parents. *Journal of Personality and Social Psychology, 48,* 991-1001.

Pistole, M. C. (1989). Attachment in adult romantic relationships: Style of conflict resolution and relationship satisfaction. *Journal of Social and Personal Relationships, 6,* 505-510.

Planalp, S. (1993). Friends' and acquaintances' conversations II: Coded differences. *Journal of Social and Personal Relationships, 10,* 339-354.

Planalp, S., & Benson, A. (1992). Friends' and acquaintances' conversations I: Perceived differences. *Journal of Social and Personal Relationships, 9,* 483-506.

Pleck, J. H. (1985). *Working wives, working husbands.* Beverly Hills, CA: Sage.

Plutchik, R. (1984). Emotion: A psychoevolutionary theory of emotion. In R. Plutchik & H. Kellerman (Eds.), *Emotion: Theory, research, and experience* (Vol. 2, pp. 221-257). San Diego: Academic Press.

Polanyi, M. (1958). *Personal knowledge: Towards a post-critical philosophy.* Chicago: University of Chicago Press.

Poppen, P. J., & Segal, N. J. (1988). The influence of sex and sex role orientation on sexual coercion. *Sex Roles, 19,* 689-701.

Porter, R. E., & Samovar, L. A. (1998). Cultural influences on emotional expression: Implications for intercultural communication. In P. A. Andersen & L. K Guerrero (Eds.), *Handbook of communication and emotion* (pp. 451-472). San Diego: Academic Press.

Porterfield, E. (1978). *Black and white mixed marriages.* Chicago: Nelson-Hall.

Potuchek, J. (1992). Employed wives' orientations to breadwinning: A gender theory analysis. *Journal of Marriage and the Family, 54,* 548-558.

Prager, K. J. (1995). *The psychology of intimacy.* New York: Guilford.

Prager, K. J. (1999a). The intimacy dilemma: A guide for couples therapists. In J. Carlson & L. Sperry (Eds.), *The intimate couple* (pp. 109-157). New York: Brunner/Mazel.

Prager, K. J. (1999b). The multi-layered context of intimacy. In J. Carlson & L. Sperry (Eds.), *The intimate couple* (pp. 7-32). New York: Brunner/Mazel.

Prager, K. J., & Buhrmester, D. (1998). Intimacy and need fulfillment in couple relationships. *Journal of Social and Personal Relationships, 15,* 435-469.

Prins, K. S., Buunk, B. P., & Van Yperen, N. W. (1992). Equity, normative disapproval, and extramarital relationships. *Journal of Social and Personal Relationships, 10,* 39-53.

Pruchno, R. A., Burant, C. J., & Peters, N. D. (1997). Understanding the well-being of care receivers. *The Gerontologist, 37,* 102-109.

Prusank, D. T., Duran, R. L., & De Lillo, D. A. (1993). Interpersonal relationships in women's magazines: Dating and relating in the 1970s and 1980s. *Journal of Social and Personal Relationships, 10,* 307-320.

Putnam, J., Markovchick, K., Johnson, D. W., & Johnson, R. T. (1996). Cooperative learning and peer acceptance of students with learning disabilities. *Journal of Social Psychology, 136,* 741-752.

Pyke, K., & Coltrane, S. (1996). Entitlement, obligation, and gratitude in family work. *Journal of Family Issues, 17,* 60-82.

Pyke, K. D. (1994). Women's employment as a gift or burden? Marital power across marriage, divorce, and remarriage. *Gender & Society, 8,* 73-91.

Radecki-Bush, C., Bush, J. P., & Jennings, J. (1988). Effects of jealousy threats on relationship perceptions and emotions. *Journal of Social and Personal Relationships, 5,* 285-304.

Radecki-Bush, C., Farrell, A. D., & Bush, J. P. (1993). Predicting jealous responses: The influence of adult attachment and depression on threat appraisal. *Journal of Social and Personal Relationships, 10,* 569-588.

Raffaelli, M. (1992). Sibling conflict in early adolescence. *Journal of Marriage and the Family, 54,* 652-663.

Ragsdale, J. D. (1996). Gender, satisfaction level, and the use of relational maintenance strategies in marriage. *Communication Monographs, 63,* 354-369.

Ramsey, J. L., & Blieszner, R. (1999). *Spiritual resiliency in older women: Models of strength for challenges through the life span.* Thousand Oaks, CA: Sage.

Rando, T. (1993). *Treatment of complicated mourning.* Champaign, IL: Research Press.

Rao, K. V., & De Maris, A. (1995). Coital frequency among married and cohabiting couples in the U.S. *Journal of Biosocial Science, 27,* 135-150.

Raphael, B. (1983). *The anatomy of bereavement.* New York: Basic Books.

Raphael, S. M., & Robinson, M. K. (1980). The older lesbian: Love relationships and friendship patterns. *Alternative Lifestyles, 3,* 207-230.

Rawlins, W. (1983a). Negotiating close friendship: The dialectic of conjunctive freedoms. *Human Communication Research, 9,* 255-266.

Rawlins, W. (1983b). Openness as problematic in ongoing friendships: Two conversational dilemmas. *Communication Monographs, 50,* 1-13.

Rawlins, W. K. (1992). *Friendship matters: Communication, dialectics, and the life course.* New York: Aldine de Gruyter.

Rawlins, W. K. (1994). Being there and growing apart: Sustaining friendships through adulthood. In D. J. Canary & L. Stafford (Eds.), *Communication and relational maintenance* (pp. 275-294). San Diego: Academic Press.

Reason, P. (1994). Three approaches to participative inquiry. In N. K. Denzin & Y. S. Lincoln (Eds.), *Handbook of qualitative research* (pp. 324-339). Thousand Oaks, CA: Sage.

Reedy, M. N., Birren, J. E., & Schaie, K. W. (1981). Age and sex differences in satisfying love relationships across the adult life span. *Human Development, 24,* 52-66.

Regan, P. C. (1996). Sexual outcasts: The perceived impact of body weight on sexuality. *Journal of Applied Social Psychology, 26,* 1803-1815.

Regan, P. C. (1998a). Of lust and love: Beliefs about the role of sexual desire in romantic relationships. *Personal Relationships, 5,* 139-157.

Regan, P. C. (1998b). Romantic love and sexual desire. In V. C. de Munck (Ed.), *Romantic love and sexual behavior: Perspectives from the social sciences* (pp. 91-112). Westport, CT: Praeger.

Regan, P. C. (1998c). What if you can't get what you want? Willingness to compromise ideal mate selection standards as a function of sex, mate value, and relationship context. *Personality and Social Psychology Bulletin, 24,* 1288-1297.

Regan, P. C. (in press). The role of sexual desire and sexual activity in dating relationships. *Social Behavior and Personality.*

Regan, P. C., & Berscheid, E. (1995). Gender differences in beliefs about the causes of male and female sexual desire. *Personal Relationships, 2,* 345-358.

Regan, P. C., & Berscheid, E. (1996). Beliefs about the state, goals, and objects of sexual desire. *Journal of Sex and Marital Therapy, 22,* 110-120.

Regan, P. C., & Berscheid, E. (1997). Gender differences in characteristics desired in a potential sexual and marriage partner. *Journal of Psychology and Human Sexuality, 9,* 25-37.

Regan, P. C., & Berscheid, E. (1999). *Lust: What we know about human sexual desire.* Thousand Oaks, CA: Sage.

Regan, P. C., Kocan, E. R., & Whitlock, T. (1998). Ain't love grand! A prototype analysis of the concept of romantic love. *Journal of Social and Personal Relationships, 15,* 411-420.

Regan, P. C., Levin, L., Sprecher, S., Christopher, S., & Cate, R. (1998). *Partner preferences: What characteristics do men and women desire in their short-term sexual and long-term romantic partners?* Unpublished manuscript, California State University, Los Angeles.

Register, L. M., & Henley, T. B. (1992). The phenomenology of intimacy. *Journal of Social and Personal Relationships, 9,* 467-481.

Reilly, M. E., & Lynch, J. M. (1990). Power-sharing in lesbian partnerships. *Journal of Homosexuality, 19*(1), 1-30.

Reinhardt, J. P. (1996). Importance of friendship and family support in adaptation to chronic vision impairment. *Journal of Gerontology: Psychological Sciences, 51,* P268-P278.

Reis, H. T., & Knee, C. R. (1996). What we know, what we don't know, and what we need to know about relationship knowledge structures. In G. J. O. Fletcher & J. Fitness (Eds.), *Knowledge structures in close relationships: A social psychological approach* (pp. 169-191). Mahwah, NJ: Lawrence Erlbaum.

Reis, H. T., & Shaver, P. (1988). Intimacy as interpersonal process. In S. W. Duck (Ed.), *Handbook of personal relationships: Theory, relationships, and interventions* (pp. 367-389). New York: John Wiley.

Reis, H. T., Wheeler, L., Spiegel, N., Kernis, M. H., Nezlek, J., & Perri, M. (1982). Physical attractiveness in social interaction. II: Why does appearance affect social experience? *Journal of Personality and Social Psychology, 43,* 979-996.

Reis, H. T., Yi-Cheng, L., Bennett, M. E., & Nezlek, J. B. (1993). Change and consistency in social participation during early adulthood. *Developmental Psychology, 29,* 633-645.

Reisman, J. M., & Shorr, S. I. (1978). Friendship claims and expectations among children and adults. *Child Development, 49,* 913-916.

Reiss, I. L. (1964). The scaling of premarital sexual permissiveness. *Journal of Marriage and the Family, 26,* 188-198.

Reiss, I. L. (1967). *The social context of premarital sexual permissiveness.* New York: Holt, Rinehart & Winston.

Reiss, I. L. (1986). A sociological journey into sexuality. *Journal of Marriage and the Family, 48,* 233-242.

Renshaw, P. D., & Brown, P. J. (1993). Loneliness in middle childhood: Concurrent and longitudinal predictors. *Child Development, 64,* 1271-1284.

Renzetti, C. M. (1992). *Violent betrayal: Partner abuse in lesbian relationships.* Newbury Park, CA: Sage.

Rholes, W. S., Simpson, J. A., & Blakely, B. S. (1995). Adult attachment styles and mothers' relationships with their young children. *Personal Relationships, 2,* 35-54.

Rholes, W. S., Simpson, J. A., Blakely, B. S., Lanigan, L., & Allen, E. A. (1997). Adult attachment styles, the desire to have children, and working models of parenthood. *Journal of Personality, 65,* 357-385.

Rholes, W. S., Simpson, J. A., & Grich, S. J. (1998). Attachment orientations, social support, and conflict resolution in close relationships. In J. A. Simpson & W. Steven (Eds.), *Attachment theory and close relationships* (pp. 166-188). New York: Guilford.

Richards, M. H., Crowe, P. A., Larson, R., & Swarr, A. (1998). Developmental patterns and gender differences in the experience of peer companionship during adolescence. *Child Development, 69,* 154-163.

Richardson, L. (1985). *The new other women.* New York: Free Press.

Richardson, L. (1997). *Fields of play: Constructing an academic life.* New Brunswick, NJ: Rutgers University Press.

Ridge, R. D., & Berscheid, E. (1989, May). *On loving and being in love: A necessary distinction.* Paper presented at the annual convention of the Midwestern Psychological Association, Chicago.

Ridley, J. (1996). Couples presenting with jealousy: Alternative explanations. *Journal of Cognitive Psychotherapy, 10,* 63-73.

Riessman, C. (1990). *Divorce talk: Women and men make sense of personal relationships.* New Brunswick, NJ: Rutgers University Press.

Riggio, R. E. (1986). Assessment of basic social skills. *Journal of Personality and Social Psychology, 51,* 649-660.

Riggio, R. E., & Zimmermann, J. (1991). Social skills and interpersonal relationships: Influences on social support and support seeking. In W. H. Jones & D. Perlman (Eds.), *Advances in personal relationships* (Vol. 2, pp. 133-155). London: Jessica Kingsley.

Riggs, D. S., & O'Leary, K. D. (1996). Aggression between heterosexual dating partners: An examination of a causal model of courtship aggression. *Journal of Interpersonal Violence, 11,* 519-540.

Rimé, B., Mesquita, B., Philippot, P., & Boca, S. (1991). Beyond the emotional event: Six studies of the social sharing of emotion. *Cognition and Emotion, 5,* 435-465.

Risman, B. J. (1989). Can men mother? Life as a single father. In B. J. Risman & P. Schwartz (Eds.), *Gender in intimate relationships* (pp. 155-164). Belmont, CA: Wadsworth.

Risman, B. J., Hill, C., Rubin, Z., & Peplau, L. A. (1981). Living together in college: Implications for courtship. *Journal of Marriage and the Family, 43,* 77-83.

Risman, B. J., & Johnson-Sumerford, D. (1998). Doing it fairly: A study of postgender marriages. *Journal of Marriage and the Family, 60,* 23-40.

Roberto, K. A., & Scott, J. P. (1984-1985). Friendship patterns among older women. *International Journal of Aging and Human Development, 19,* 1-10.

Roberts, J. E., Gotlib, I. H., & Kassel, J. D. (1996). Adult attachment security and symptoms of depression: The mediating roles of dysfunctional attitudes and low self-esteem. *Journal of Personality and Social Psychology, 70,* 310-320.

Roberts, L. J., & Linney, K. D. (Under review). Observing intimacy process behavior: Vulnerability and partner responsiveness in marital interactions.

Roberts, L., & Prager, K. J. (1997, July). *Intimacy, diaries, and videotape: Conceptualizing and measuring intimacy.* Roundtable presented at the annual meeting of the International Network on Personal Relationships, Oxford, OH.

Roberts, N., & Noller, P. (1998). The associations between adult attachment and couple violence: The role of communication patterns and relationship satisfaction. In J. A. Simpson & W. S. Rholes (Eds.), *Attachment theory and close relationships* (pp. 317-350). New York: Guilford.

Robin, A. L., & Foster, S. L. (1989). *Negotiating parent-adolescent conflict: A behavioral-family systems approach.* New York: Guilford.

Roese, N. J. (1997). Counterfactual thinking. *Psychological Bulletin, 121,* 133-148.

Rogers, L. E. (1989). Relational communication processes and patterns. In B. Dervin, L. Grossberg, B. J. O'Keefe, & E. Wartella (Eds.), *Rethinking communication, Vol. 2: Paradigm exemplars* (pp. 280-290). Newbury Park, CA: Sage.

Rogers, L. E., Castleton, A., & Lloyd, S. A. (1996). Relational control and physical aggression in satisfying marital relationships. In D. D. Cahn & S. A. Lloyd (Eds.), *Family violence from a communication perspective* (pp. 218-239). Thousand Oaks, CA: Sage.

Rook, K. S. (1984). Promoting social bonding. *American Psychologist, 39,* 1389-1407.

Rook, K. S. (1989). Strains in older adults' friendships. In R. G. Adams & R. Blieszner (Eds.), *Older adult friendship: Structure and process* (pp. 166-194). Newbury Park, CA: Sage.

Rook, K. S., Pietromonaco, P. R., & Lewis, M. A. (1994). When are dysphoric individuals distressing to others and vice versa? Effects of friendship, similarity, and interaction task. *Journal of Personality and Social Psychology, 67,* 548-559.

Root, M. P. P. (Ed.). (1992). *Racially mixed people in America.* Newbury Park, CA: Sage.

Root, M. P. P. (Ed.). (1996). *The multiracial experience: Racial borders as the new frontier.* Thousand Oaks, CA: Sage.

Roper Organization. (1980). *The 1980 Virginia Slims American women's opinion poll: A survey of contemporary attitudes.* New York: Author.

Roschelle, A. R. (1997). *No more kin: Exploring race, class, and gender in family networks.* Thousand Oaks, CA: Sage.

Rose, A. J., & Asher, S. R. (1999a). Children's goals and strategies in response to conflicts within a friendship. *Developmental Psychology, 35,* 69-79.

Rose, A. J., & Asher, S. R. (1999b, April). *Seeking and giving social support within a friendship.* Paper presented at the biennial meeting of the Society for Research in Child Development, Albuquerque, NM.

Rose, S., & Frieze, I. (1989). Young singles' scripts for a first date. *Gender & Society, 3,* 258-268.

Rose, S., Zand, D., & Cini, M. (1993). Lesbian courtship scripts. In E. D. Rothblum & K. A. Brehony (Eds.), *Boston marriages: Romantic but asexual relationships among contemporary lesbians* (pp. 70-85). Amherst: University of Massachusetts Press.

Rose, S. M. (1984). How friendships end: Patterns among young adults. *Journal of Social and Personal Relationships, 1,* 267-277.

Rose, S. M. (1985). Same- and cross-sex friendships and the psychology of homosociality. *Sex Roles, 12,* 63-74.

Rose, S. M., & Serafica, F. C. (1986). Keeping and ending casual, close, and best friendships. *Journal of Social and Personal Relationships, 3,* 275-288.

Rosenblatt, P. C., Karis, T. A., & Powell, R. D. (1995). *Multiracial couples: Black and white voices.* Thousand Oaks, CA: Sage.

Rosenbluth, S. (1997). Is sexual orientation a matter of choice? *Psychology of Women Quarterly, 4,* 595-610.

Rosenbluth, S. C., Steil, J. M., & Whitcomb, J. H. (1998). *Marital equality: What does it mean?* Journal of Family Issues, 19, 227-244.

Rosenzweig, J. M., & Lebow, W. C. (1992). Femme on the streets, butch in the sheets? Lesbian sex roles, dyadic adjustment, and sexual satisfaction. *Journal of Homosexuality, 23*(3), 1-20.

Ross, H. S., Filyer, R. E., Lollis, S. P., Perlman, M., & Martin, J. L. (1994). Administering justice in the family. *Journal of Family Psychology, 8,* 254-273.

Rotenberg, K. J., & Sliz, D. (1988). Children's restrictive disclosure to friends. *Merrill-Palmer Quarterly, 34,* 203-215.

Roter, D. L. (1991). *The Roter Interaction Analysis System (RIAS) coding manual.* Baltimore, MD: Johns Hopkins University Press.

Roth, S., & Cohen, L. J. (1986). Approach, avoidance, and coping with stress. *American Psychologist, 41,* 813-819.

Rubenstein, C. M., & Shaver, P. (1982). *In search of intimacy.* New York: Delacorte.

Rubin, K. H., Bukowski, W., & Parker, J. G. (1998). Peer interactions, relationships, and groups. In W. Damon & N. Eisenberg (Eds.), *Handbook of child psychology,* Vol. 3: *Social, emotional, and personality development* (pp. 619-700). New York: John Wiley.

Rubin, L. B. (1985). *Just friends.* New York: Harper & Row.

Rubin, Z., & Shenker, S. (1978). Friendship, proximity, and self-disclosure. *Journal of Personality, 46,* 1-22.

Ruddick, S. (1989). *Maternal thinking.* Boston: Beacon.

Rueter, M. A., & Conger, R. D. (1995). Antecedents of parent-adolescent disagreements. *Journal of Marriage and the Family, 57,* 435-448.

Rusbult, C. (1987). Responses to dissatisfaction in close relationships: The exit-voice-loyalty-neglect model. In D. Perlman & S. Duck (Eds.), *Intimate relationships: Development, dynamics, and deterioration* (pp. 209-238). London: Sage.

Rusbult, C. E. (1983). A longitudinal test of the investment model: The development (and deterioration) of satisfaction and commitment in heterosexual involvements. *Journal of Personality and Social Psychology, 45,* 101-117.

Rusbult, C. E., & Buunk, B. P. (1993). Commitment processes in close relationships: An interdependence analysis. *Journal of Social and Personal Relationships, 10,* 175-204.

Rusbult, C. E., Drigotas, S. M., & Verette, J. (1994). The investment model: An interdependence analysis of commitment processes and relationship maintenance phenomena. In D. J. Canary & L. Stafford (Eds.), *Communication and relational maintenance* (pp. 115-140). San Diego: Academic Press.

Rusbult, C. E., Verette, J., Whitney, G. A., Slovik, L. F., & Lipkus, I. (1991). Accommodation processes in close relationships: Theory and preliminary empirical evidence. *Journal of Personality and Social Psychology, 60,* 53-78.

Russell, A., & Searcy, E. (1997). The contribution of affective reactions and relationship qualities to adolescents' reported responses to parents. *Journal of Social and Personal Relationships, 14,* 539-548.

Russell, D. E. H. (1982). *Rape in marriage.* Bloomington: Indiana University Press.

Russell, K., Wilson, M., & Hall, R. (1993). *The color complex: The politics of skin color among African Americans.* New York: Anchor Books.

Rust, P. C. (1992). The politics of sexual identity: Sexual attraction and behavior among lesbian and bisexual women. *Social Problems, 39,* 366-386.

Rust, P. C. (1995). *Bisexuality and the challenge to lesbian politics: Sex, loyalty, and revolution.* New York: New York University Press.

Rutter, M., Graham, P., Chadwick, O., & Yule, W. (1976). Adolescent turmoil: Fact or fiction? *Journal of Child Psychology and Psychiatry, 17,* 35-56.

Ryff, C. D., Schmutte, P. S., & Lee, Y. H. (1996). How children turn out: Implications for parental self-evaluation. In C. D. Ryff & M. M. Seltzer (Eds.), *The parental experience in midlife* (pp. 383-422). Chicago: University of Chicago Press.

Sabourin, T. C. (1995). The role of negative reciprocity in spouse abuse: A relational control analysis. *Journal of Applied Communication, 23,* 271-283.

Sacco, W. P., & Dunn, V. K. (1990). Effect of actor depression on observer attributions: Existence and impact of negative attributions toward the depressed.

*Journal of Personality and Social Psychology, 59,* 517-524.

Sagi, A., & Hoffman, M. L. (1976). Empathic distress in newborns. *Developmental Psychology, 12,* 175-176.

Sagrestano, L. M., Christensen, A., & Heavey, C. L. (1998). Social influence techniques during marital conflict. *Personal Relationships, 5,* 75-89.

Sagrestano, L. M., Heavey, C. L., & Christensen, A. (1998). Theoretical approaches to understanding sex differences and similarities in conflict behavior. In D. J. Canary & K. Dindia (Eds.), *Sex differences and similarities in communication: Critical essays and empirical investigation of sex and gender in interaction* (pp. 287-302). Mahwah, NJ: Lawrence Erlbaum.

Salem, D. A., Zimmerman, M. A., & Notaro, P. C. (1998). Effects of family structure, family process, and father involvement on psychosocial outcomes among African-American adolescents. *Family Relations, 47,* 331-341.

Salovey, P., & Rodin, J. (1986). The differentiation of social-comparison jealousy and romantic jealousy. *Journal of Personality and Social Psychology, 50,* 1100-1112.

Samp, J. A., & Solomon, D. (1998). Communicative responses to problematic events in close relationships I: The variety and facets of goals. *Communication Research, 25,* 66-95.

Sanchez, L. (1994). Gender, labor allocations, and the psychology of entitlement within the home. *Social Forces, 73,* 533-553.

Sandefur, G. D., McLanahan, S., & Wojtkiewicz, R. A. (1992). The effects of parental marital status during adolescence on high school graduation. *Social Forces, 71,* 103-121.

Sanders, S. A., & Reinisch, J. M. (1999). Would you say you "had sex" if . . .? *Journal of the American Medical Association, 281,* 275-277.

Sandmaier, M. (1995, July/August). The gift of friendship. *The Family Therapy Networker,* p. 23.

Santrock, J. W., & Sitterle, K. (1987). Parent-child relationships in stepmother families. In K. Pasley & M. Ihinger-Tallman (Eds.), *Remarriage and stepparenting: Current research and theory* (pp. 273-299). New York: Guilford.

Sarason, B. R., Sarason, I. G., Hacker, T. A., & Basham, R. B. (1985). Concomitants of social support: Social skills, physical attractiveness, and gender. *Journal of Personality and Social Psychology, 49,* 469-480.

Sarason, I. G., Sarason, B. R., & Pierce, G. (1994). Social support: Global and relationship-based levels of analysis. *Journal of Social and Personal Relationships, 11,* 295-312.

Sarvis, T., & Prager, K. J. (1999). *Partner's contribution to need fulfillment in couple relationships.* Unpublished honors thesis, University of Texas at Dallas.

Savin-Williams, R. C. (1996). Dating and romantic relationships among gay, lesbian, and bisexual youths. In R. C. Savin-Williams & K. M. Cohen (Eds.), *The*

*lives of lesbians, gays, and bisexuals* (pp. 166-180). Orlando, FL: Harcourt Brace.

Savin-Williams, R. C., & Berndt, T. J. (1990). Friendship and peer relationships. In S. Feldman & G. Elliot (Eds.), *At the threshold: The developing adolescent* (pp. 277-307). Cambridge, MA: Harvard University Press.

Saxon, J. L., & Asher, S. R. (1999). *Distinguishing between the behavioral and affective features of children's friendships: Implications for the understanding of loneliness.* Manuscript in preparation.

Scanzoni, J. (1979). Sex role influences on married women's status attainments. *Journal of Marriage and the Family, 41,* 793-800.

Scanzoni, J., Polonko, K., Teachman, J., & Thompson, L. (1989). *The sexual bond.* Newbury Park, CA: Sage.

Schaefer, M. T., & Olson, D. H. (1981). Assessing intimacy: The PAIR Inventory. *Journal of Marital and Family Therapy, 7,* 47-60.

Scharfe, E., & Bartholomew, K. (1994). Reliability and stability of adult attachment patterns. *Personal Relationships, 1,* 23-43.

Scharfe, E., & Bartholomew, K. (1995). Accommodation and attachment representations in young couples. *Journal of Social and Personal Relationships, 12,* 389-401.

Scherer, K. R. (1994). Affect bursts. In S. H. M. Van Goozen, N. E. Van de Poll, & J. A. Sergeant (Eds.), *Emotions: Essays on emotion theory* (pp. 161-193). Hillsdale, NJ: Lawrence Erlbaum.

Scherer, K. R., & Wallbott, H. G. (1994). Evidence for universality and cultural variation of differential emotion response patterning. *Journal of Personality and Social Psychology, 66,* 310-328.

Scherer, K. R., Wallbott, H. G., Matsumoto, D., & Kudoh, T. (1988). Emotional experience in cultural context: A comparison between Europe, Japan, and the United States. In K. R. Klaus (Ed.), *Facets of emotion: Recent research* (pp. 5-30). Hillsdale, NJ: Lawrence Erlbaum.

Schilit, R., Lie, G., & Montagne, M. (1990). Substance use as a correlate of violence in intimate lesbian relationships. *Journal of Homosexuality, 19*(3), 51-65.

Schless, A. P., Schwartz, L., Goetz, C., & Mendels, J. (1974). How depressives view the significance of life events. *British Journal of Psychiatry, 125,* 406-410.

Schlundt, D. G., & McFall, R. M. (1985). New directions in the assessment of social competence. In L. L'Abate & M. A. Milan (Eds.), *Handbook of social skills training and research* (pp. 22-49). New York: John Wiley.

Schmaling, K. B., & Jacobson, N. S. (1990). Marital interaction and depression. *Journal of Abnormal Psychology, 99,* 229-236.

Schmitt, B. H. (1988). Social comparison in romantic jealousy. *Personality and Social Psychology Bulletin, 14,* 374-387.

Schreurs, K. M. G., & Buunk, B. P. (1996). Closeness, autonomy, equity, and relationship satisfaction in lesbian couples. *Psychology of Women Quarterly, 20*, 577-592.

Schroeder, D. A., Penner, L. A., Dovidio, J. F., & Piliavin, J. A. (1995). *The psychology of helping and altruism: Problems and puzzles.* New York: McGraw-Hill.

Schwartz, D., Dodge, K. A., & Coie, J. D. (1993). The emergence of chronic peer victimization in boys' play groups. *Child Development, 64*, 1755-1772.

Schwartz, J. C., & Shaver, P. (1987). Emotions and emotion knowledge in interpersonal relations. In W. H. Jones & D. Perlman (Eds.), *Advances in personal relationships* (Vol. 1, pp. 197-241). Greenwich, CT: JAI.

Schwartz, P. (1992). Who informs the public about close relationships? *Bulletin for the International Society for the Study of Personal Relationships, 8*, 1-3.

Schwartz, P. (1994). *Peer marriage.* New York: Free Press.

Schwartz, P., & Rutter, V. (1998). *The gender of sexuality.* Thousand Oaks, CA: Pine Forge.

Schwarz, J. (1972). Effects of peer familiarity on the behaviors of preschoolers in a novel situation. *Journal of Personality and Social Psychology, 24*, 276-284.

Seal, D. W., Agostinelli, G., & Hannet, C. A. (1994). Extradyadic romantic involvement: Moderating effects of sociosexuality and gender. *Sex Roles, 31*, 1-22.

Segrin, C. (1998). Interpersonal communication problems associated with depression and loneliness. In P. A. Andersen & L. K. Guerrero (Eds.), *Handbook of communication and emotion: Research, theory, applications, and contexts* (pp. 215-242). San Diego: Academic Press.

Selman, R. L. (1980). *The growth of interpersonal understanding: Developmental and clinical analyses.* San Diego: Academic Press.

Selman, R. L., & Schultz, L. H. (1990). *Making a friend in youth: Developmental theory and pair therapy.* Chicago: University of Chicago Press.

Seltzer, J. (1994). Consequences of marital dissolution for children. *Annual Review of Sociology, 20*, 235-266.

Seltzer, M. M., Krauss, M. W., Choi, S. C., & Hong, J. (1996). Midlife and later-life parenting of adult children with mental retardation. In C. D. Ryff & M. M. Seltzer (Eds.), *The parental experience in midlife* (pp. 459-489). Chicago: University of Chicago Press.

Senchak, M., & Leonard, K. E. (1992). Attachment styles and marital adjustment among newlywed couples. *Journal of Social and Personal Relationships, 9*, 51-64.

Shackelford, T. K., & Buss, D. M. (1996). Betrayal in mateships, friendships, and coalitions. *Personality and Social Psychology Bulletin, 22*, 1151-1164.

Shackelford, T. K., & Buss, D. M. (1997). Cues to infidelity. *Personality and Social Psychology Bulletin, 23*, 1034-1045.

Shannon, J. W., & Woods, W. J. (1991). Affirmative psychotherapy for gay men. *Counseling Psychologist, 19*, 197-215.

Shantz, C. U. (1987). Conflicts between children. *Child Development, 58*, 283-305.

Shantz, C. U., & Hobart, C. J. (1989). Social conflict and development: Peers and siblings. In T. J. Berndt & G. W. Ladd (Eds.), *Peer relationships in child development* (pp. 71-94). New York: John Wiley.

Shapiro, R. S., Simpson, D. E., Lawrence, S. L., Talsky, A. M., Sobocinski, K. A., & Schiedermayer, D. L. (1989). A survey of sued and nonsued physicians and suing patients. *Archives of Internal Medicine, 149*, 2190-2196.

Sharabany, R., Gershoni, R., & Hoffman, J. E. (1981). Girlfriend, boyfriend: Age and sex differences in intimate friendship. *Developmental Psychology, 17*, 800-808.

Sharpsteen, D. J. (1991). The organization of jealousy knowledge: Romantic jealousy as a blended emotion. In P. Salovey (Ed.), *The psychology of jealousy and envy* (pp. 31-52). New York: Guilford.

Sharpsteen, D. J., & Kirkpatrick, L. A. (1997). Romantic jealousy and adult romantic attachment. *Journal of Personality and Social Psychology, 72*, 627-640.

Shaver, P., Furman, W., & Buhrmester, D. (1985). Transition to college: Network changes, social skills, and loneliness. In S. Duck & D. Perlman (Eds.), *Understanding personal relationships* (pp. 193-219). London: Sage.

Shaver, P. R., & Brennan, K. A. (1992). Attachment styles and the "big five" personality traits: Their connections with each other and with romantic relationship outcomes. *Personality and Social Psychology Bulletin, 18*, 536-545.

Shaver, P. R., Collins, N., & Clark, C. L. (1996). Attachment styles and internal working models of self and relationship partners. In G. J. O. Fletcher & J. Fitness (Eds.), *Knowledge structures in close relationships: A social psychological approach* (pp. 25-61). Mahwah, NJ: Lawrence Erlbaum.

Shaver, P. R., & Hazan, C. (1985). Incompatibility, loneliness, and "limerence." In W. Ickes (Eds.), *Compatible and incompatible relationships* (pp. 163-184). New York: Springer-Verlag.

Shaver, P. R., & Hazan, C. (1988). A biased overview of the study of love. *Journal of Social and Personal Relationships, 5*, 473-501.

Shaver, P. R., & Hazan, C. (1993). Adult romantic attachment: Theory and evidence. In D. Perlman & W. H. Jones (Eds.), *Advances in personal relationships* (Vol. 4, pp. 29-70). London: Jessica Kingsley.

Shaver, P. R., Hazan, C., & Bradshaw, D. (1988). Love as attachment: The integration of three behavioral systems. In R. J. Sternberg & M. Barnes (Eds.), *The psychology of love* (pp. 68-99). New Haven, CT: Yale University Press.

Shaver, P. R., Morgan, H. J., & Wu, S. (1996). Is love a "basic" emotion? *Personal Relationships, 3,* 81-96.

Shaver, P. R., Schwartz, J., Kirson, D., & O'Connor, C. (1987). Emotion knowledge: Further explorations of a prototype approach. *Journal of Personality and Social Psychology, 52,* 1061-1086.

Shea, B. C., & Pearson, J. C. (1986). The effects of relationship type, partner intent, and gender on the selection of relationship maintenance strategies. *Communication Monographs, 53,* 354-364.

Shea, L., Thompson, L., & Blieszner, R. (1988). Resources in older adults' old and new friendships. *Journal of Social and Personal Relationships, 5,* 83-96.

Sheppard, V. J., Nelson, E. S., & Andreoli-Mathie, V. (1995). Dating relationships and infidelity: Attitudes and behaviors. *Journal of Sex & Marital Therapy, 21,* 202-212.

Sherrod, D. (1989). The influence of gender on same-sex friendships. In C. Hendrick (Ed.), *Close relationships* (pp. 164-186). Newbury Park, CA: Sage.

Shimanoff, S. (1980). *Communication rules.* Beverly Hills, CA: Sage.

Shucksmith, J., Hendry, L. B., & Glendinning, A. (1995). Models of parenting: Implications for adolescent well-being within different types of family contexts. *Journal of Adolescence, 18,* 253-270.

Shulman, S., Elicker, J., & Sroufe, L. A. (1994). Stages of friendship growth in preadolescence as related to attachment history. *Journal of Social and Personal Relationships, 11,* 341-361.

Siegel, K., & Glassman, M. (1989). Individual and aggregate level change in sexual behavior among gay men at risk for AIDS. *Archives of Sexual Behavior, 18,* 335-348.

Sigman, S. J. (1991). Handling the discontinuous aspects of continuing social relationships: Toward research on the persistence of social forms. *Communication Theory, 1,* 106-127.

Silberstein, L. (1992). *Dual-career marriage: A system in transition.* Hillsdale, NJ: Lawrence Erlbaum.

Sillars, A. L. (1980a). Attributions and communication in roommate conflicts. *Communication Monographs, 47,* 180-200.

Sillars, A. L. (1980b). The sequential and distributional structure of conflict interactions as a function of attributions concerning the locus of responsibility and stability of conflicts. In D. Nimmo (Ed.), *Communication yearbook 4,* (pp. 217-235). New Brunswick, NJ: Transaction Books.

Sillars, A. L., & Weisberg, J. (1987). Conflict as a social skill. In M. E. Roloff & G. R. Miller (Eds.), *Interpersonal processes: New directions in communication research* (pp. 140-171). Newbury Park, CA: Sage.

Sillars, A. L., & Wilmot, W. W. (1994). Communication strategies in conflict and mediation. In J. A. Daly &

J. M. Wiemann (Eds.), *Strategic interpersonal communication* (pp. 163-190). Hillsdale, NJ: Lawrence Erlbaum.

Silver, R. C., & Wortman, C. B. (1980). Coping with undesirable life events. In J. Garber & M. E. P. Seligman (Eds.), *Human helplessness: Theory and applications* (pp. 279-375). San Diego: Academic Press.

Silverberg, S. B., & Steinberg, L. (1990). Psychological well-being of parents with early adolescent children. *Developmental Psychology, 26,* 658-666.

Silverstein, C. (1981). *Man to man: Gay couples in America.* New York: William Morrow.

Silverstein, M., & Bengtson, V. L. (1997). Intergenerational solidarity and the structure of adult parent-child relationships in American families. *American Journal of Sociology, 103,* 429-460.

Silverstein, M., & Long, J. D. (1998). Trajectories of grandparents' perceived solidarity with adult grandchildren: A growth curve analysis over 23 years. *Journal of Marriage and the Family, 60,* 912-923.

Simmons, R. G., Burgeson, R., & Reef, M. J. (1988). Cumulative change at entry to adolescence. In M. Gunnar & W. A. Collins (Eds.), *Development during the transition to adolescence: Minnesota symposia on child psychology* (Vol. 21, pp. 123-150). Hillsdale, NJ: Lawrence Erlbaum.

Simon, R. (Ed.). (1995, July/August). The mystery of friendship [Special feature]. *The Family Therapy Networker.*

Simons, R. L., & Associates. (1996). *Understanding differences between divorced and intact families.* Thousand Oaks, CA: Sage.

Simons, R. L., Lin, K., & Gordon, L. C. (1998). Socialization in the family of origin and male dating violence: A prospective study. *Journal of Marriage and the Family, 60,* 467-478.

Simpson, J. A. (1987). The dissolution of romantic relationships: Factors involved in relationship stability and emotional distress. *Journal of Personality and Social Psychology, 53,* 683-692.

Simpson, J. A. (1990). Influence of attachment styles on romantic relationships. *Journal of Personality and Social Psychology, 59,* 971-980.

Simpson, J. A., Campbell, B., & Berscheid, E. (1986). The association between romantic love and marriage: Kephart (1967) twice revisited. *Personality and Social Psychology Bulletin, 12,* 363-372.

Simpson, J. A., & Gangestead, S. (1991). Individual differences in sociosexuality: Evidence for convergent and discriminant validity. *Journal of Personality and Social Psychology, 59,* 1192-1201.

Simpson, J. A., & Kenrick, D. T. (Eds.). (1997). *Evolutionary social psychology.* Mahwah, NJ: Lawrence Erlbaum.

Simpson, J. A., Rholes, W. S., & Nelligan, J. S. (1992). Support seeking and support giving within couples in an anxiety-provoking situation: The role of attachment styles. *Journal of Personality and Social Psychology, 62*, 434-446.

Simpson, J. A., Rholes, W. S., & Phillips, D. (1996). Conflict in close relationships: An attachment perspective. *Journal of Personality and Social Psychology, 71*, 899-914.

Simpson, S. (1994). *Late love: A celebration of marriage after fifty.* Boston: Houghton Mifflin.

Sinclair, S. L., & Nelson, E. S. (1998). The impact of parental divorce on college students' intimate relationships and relationship beliefs. *Journal of Divorce and Remarriage, 29*, 103-129.

Singer, I. (1984). *The nature of love: Vol. 1. Plato to Luther* (2nd ed.). Chicago: University of Chicago Press.

Singh, D. (1993). Adaptive significance of female physical attractiveness: Role of waist-to-hip ratio. *Journal of Personality and Social Psychology, 65*, 293-307.

Singh, D. (1995). Female judgment of male attractiveness and desirability for relationships: Role of waist-to-hip ratio and financial status. *Journal of Personality and Social Psychology, 69*, 1089-1101.

Singleton, L. C., & Asher, S. R. (1977). Peer preferences and social interaction among third-grade children in an integrated school district. *Journal of Educational Psychology, 69*, 330-336.

Skopin, A. R., Newman, B. M., & McKenry, P. (1993). Influences on the quality of stepfather-adolescent relationships: View of both family members. *Journal of Divorce and Remarriage, 19*, 181-196.

Small, S. A. (1995). Action-oriented research: Models and methods. *Journal of Marriage and the Family, 57*, 941-955.

Smetana, J. (1988). Adolescents' and parents' conceptions of parental authority. *Child Development, 59*, 321-335.

Smetana, J., Yau, J., Restrepo, A., & Braeges, J. L. (1991). Adolescent-parent conflict in married and divorced families. *Developmental Psychology, 27*, 1000-1010.

Smetana, J. G. (1989). Adolescents' and parents' reasoning about actual family conflict. *Child Development, 60*, 1052-1067.

Smith, D. E. (1987). *The everyday world as problematic: A feminist sociology.* Boston: Northeastern University Press.

Smith, R. M., Goslen, M. A., Boyd, A. J., & Reece, L. (1991). Self-other orientation and sex-role orientation of men and women who remarry. *Journal of Divorce and Remarriage, 15*, 3-31.

Snidjers, T., & Kenny, D. A. (1999). The social relations model for family data: A multilevel approach. *Personal Relationships, 6*, 471-486.

Sociaal en cultureel Planbrureau. (1998). *Sociaal en Cultureel Rapport.* Rijswijk, The Netherlands.

Solano, C. H. (1986). People without friends: Loneliness and its alternatives. In V. J. Derlega & B. Winstead (Eds.), *Friendship and social interaction* (pp. 225-246). New York: Springer-Verlag.

Sommers, S. (1984). Reported emotions and conventions of emotionality among college students. *Journal of Personality and Social Psychology, 74*, 385-393.

Spalding, L. R., & Peplau, L. A. (1997). The unfaithful lover: Heterosexuals' stereotypes of bisexuals and their relationships. *Psychology of Women Quarterly, 21*, 611-625.

Spanier, G. B. (1976). Measuring dyadic adjustment. *Journal of Marriage and the Family, 38*, 15-28.

Spanier, G. B., & Margolis, R. L. (1983). Marital separation and extramarital sexual behavior. *Journal of Sex Research, 19*, 23-48.

Spelman, E. (1988). *Inessential woman.* Boston: Beacon.

Spence, J. T., & Helmreich, R. L. (1978). *Masculinity and femininity: Their psychological dimensions, correlates, and antecedents.* Austin: University of Texas Press.

Sperling, M. B., & Lyons, L. S. (1994). Representations of attachment and psychotherapeutic change. In M. B. Sperling & W. H. Berman (Eds.), *Attachment in adults: Clinical and developmental perspectives* (pp. 331-347). New York: Guilford.

Spievak, E. R. (1999). *The effects of writing on symptoms of posttraumatic stress disorder.* Unpublished manuscript, University of Louisville.

Spitzberg, B. H., & Cupach, W. R. (1989). *Handbook of interpersonal competence research.* New York: Springer-Verlag.

Spradley, J. P. (1979). *The ethnographic interview.* New York: Holt, Rinehart & Winston.

Sprecher, S. (1986). The relation between emotion and equity in close relationships. *Social Psychology Quarterly, 49*, 309-321.

Sprecher, S. (1989). Premarital sexual standards for different categories of individuals. *Journal of Sex Research, 26*, 232-248.

Sprecher, S. (1992). Social exchange perspectives on the dissolution of close relationships. In T. L. Orbuch (Ed.), *Close relationship losses: Theoretical approaches* (pp. 47-66). New York: Springer-Verlag.

Sprecher, S. (1994). Two sides to the breakup of dating relationships. *Personal Relationships, 1*, 199-222.

Sprecher, S. (1998a). Insiders' perspectives on reasons for attraction to a close other. *Social Psychology Quarterly, 61*, 287-300.

Sprecher, S. (1998b). Social exchange theories and sexuality. *Journal of Sex Research, 35*, 32-43.

Sprecher, S., Aron, A., Hatfield, E., Cortese, A., Potapova, A., & Levitskaya, A. (1994). Love: American style, Russian style, and Japanese style. *Personal Relationships, 1*, 349-369.

Sprecher, S., Cate, R., & Levin, L. (1998). Parental divorce and young adults' beliefs about love. *Journal of Divorce and Remarriage, 28*, 107-120.

Sprecher, S., Felmlee, D., Metts, S., Fehr, B., & Vanni, D. (1998). Factors associated with distress following the breakup of a close relationship. *Journal of Social and Personal Relationships, 15,* 791-809.

Sprecher, S., & McKinney, K. (1993). *Sexuality.* Newbury Park, CA: Sage.

Sprecher, S., McKinney, K., & Orbuch, T. L. (1991). The effect of current sexual behavior on friendship, dating, and marriage desirability. *Journal of Sex Research, 28,* 387-408.

Sprecher, S., Metts, S., Burleson, B., Hatfield, E., & Thompson, A. (1995). Domains of expressive interaction in intimate relationships: Associations with satisfaction and commitment. *Family Relations, 44,* 203-210.

Sprecher, S., & Regan, P. C. (1998). Passionate and companionate love in courting and young married couples. *Sociological Inquiry, 68,* 163-185.

Sprecher, S., Regan, P. C., McKinney, K., Maxwell, K., & Wazienski, R. (1997). Preferred level of sexual experience in a date or mate: The merger of two methodologies. *Journal of Sex Research, 34,* 327-337.

Sprenkle, D. H., & Weis, D. L. (1978). Extramarital sexuality: Implications for marital therapists. *Journal of Sex and Marital Therapy, 4,* 279-291.

Sroufe, L. A., Carlson, E. A., & Shulman, S. (1993). Individuals in relationships: Development from infancy through adolescence. In D. C. Funder, R. D. Parke, C. Tomlinson-Keasey, & K. Widaman (Eds.), *Studying lives through time: Personality and development* (pp. 315-342). Washington, DC: American Psychological Association.

Sroufe, L. A., Egeland, B., & Carlson, E. A. (1999). One social world: The integrated development of parent-child and peer relationships. In W. A. Collins & B. Laursen (Eds.), *Relationships as developmental contexts: Minnesota Symposia on Child Psychology* (Vol. 29, pp. 241-261). Mahwah, NJ: Lawrence Erlbaum.

Stacey, J. (1988). Can there be a feminist ethnography? *Women's Studies International Forum, 11,* 21-27.

Stacey, J. (1990). *Brave new families: Stories of domestic upheaval in late twentieth century America.* New York: Basic Books.

Stack, C. (1974). *All our kin: Strategies for survival in a black community.* New York: Harper & Row.

Stafford, L., & Canary, D. J. (1991). Maintenance strategies and romantic relationship type, gender, and relational characteristics. *Journal of Social and Personal Relationships, 8,* 217-242.

Stanley, L. (1990). Feminist praxis and the academic mode of production: An editorial introduction. In L. Stanley (Ed.), *Feminist praxis: Research, theory, and epistemology in feminist sociology* (pp. 3-19). London: Routledge.

Staples, R., & Boulin Johnson, L. (1993). *Black families at the crossroads: Challenges and prospects.* San Francisco: Jossey-Bass.

Starrels, M. E., Ingersoll-Dayton, B., & Neal, M. B. (1995). Intergenerational solidarity and the workplace: Employees' caregiving for their parents. *Journal of Marriage and the Family, 57,* 751-762.

Stearns, P. N. (1993). History of emotions: The issue of change. In M. Lewis & J. M. Haviland (Eds.), *Handbook of emotions* (pp. 17-28). New York: Guilford.

Steiger, J. H. (1980). Tests for comparing elements in a correlation matrix. *Psychological Bulletin, 87,* 245-251.

Steil, J., & Weltman, K. (1991). Marital inequality: The importance of resources, personal attributes, and social norms on career valuing and domestic influence. *Sex Roles, 24*(3/4), 161-179.

Steil, J. M. (1994). Equality and entitlement in marriage. In M. Lerner & G. Mikula (Eds.), *Entitlement and the affectional bond* (pp. 229-258). New York: Plenum.

Steil, J. M. (1997). *Marital equality: Its relationship to the well-being of husbands and wives.* Thousand Oaks, CA: Sage.

Steil, J. M., & Whitcomb, J. (1992, July). *Conceptualizations of equality.* Paper presented at the Sixth International Conference on Personal Relationships, Orono, ME.

Stein, C. H., Bush, E. G., Ross, R. R., & Ward, M. (1992). Mine, yours, and ours: A configural analysis of the networks of married couples in relation to marital satisfaction and individual well-being. *Journal of Social and Personal Relationships, 9,* 365-383.

Stein, N., Folkman, S., Trabasso, T., & Richards, T. A. (1997). Appraisal and goal processes as predictors of psychological well-being in bereaved caregivers. *Journal of Personality and Social Psychology, 72,* 872-884.

Steinberg, L. (1981). Transformations in family relations at puberty. *Developmental Psychology, 17,* 833-840.

Steinberg, L. (1988). Reciprocal relation between parent-child distance and pubertal maturation. *Developmental Psychology, 24,* 122-128.

Steinberg, L., Dornbusch, S. M., & Brown, B. B. (1992). Ethnic differences in adolescent achievement: An ecological perspective. *American Psychologist, 47,* 723-729.

Sternberg, R. J. (1986). A triangular theory of love. *Psychological Review, 93,* 119-135.

Sternberg, R. J. (1987). *The triangle of love: Intimacy, passion, commitment.* New York: Basic Books.

Sternberg, R. J. (1988). Triangulating love. In R. J. Sternberg & M. L. Barnes (Eds.), *The psychology of love* (pp. 119-138). New Haven, CT: Yale University Press.

Sternberg, R. J. (1995). Love as a story. *Journal of Social and Personal Relationships, 12,* 541-546.

Sternberg, R. J. (1996). Love stories. *Personal Relationships, 3,* 59-79.

Sternberg, R. J. (1998). *Love is a story.* New York: Oxford University Press.

Sternberg, R. J., & Barnes, M. L. (1985). Real and ideal others in romantic relationships: Is four a crowd? *Journal of Personality and Social Psychology, 49,* 1586-1608.

Sternberg, R. J., & Grajek, S. (1984). The nature of love. *Journal of Personality and Social Psychology, 47,* 312-329.

Stets, J. E., & Henderson, D. A. (1991). Contextual factors surrounding conflict resolution while dating: Results from a national study. *Family Relations, 40,* 29-36.

Stets, J. E., & Pirog-Good, M. A. (1989). Sexual aggression and control in dating relationships. *Journal of Applied Social Psychology, 19,* 1392-1412.

Stets, J. E., & Straus, M. A. (1989). The marriage license as a hitting license: A comparison of assaults in dating, cohabiting, and married couples. In M. A. Pirog-Good & J. E. Stets (Eds.), *Violence in dating relationships: Emerging social issues* (pp. 33-52). New York: Praeger.

Stewart, R. B. (1983). Sibling attachment relationships: Child-infant interactions in the Strange Situation. *Developmental Psychology, 2,* 192-199.

Stinson, L., & Ickes, W. (1992). Empathic accuracy in the interactions of male friends versus male strangers. *Journal of Personality and Social Psychology, 62,* 787-797.

Straus, M. A. (1979). Measuring intrafamily conflict and violence: The Conflict Tactics (CT) Scales. *Journal of Marriage and the Family, 41,* 75-88.

Straus, M. A. (1990). Social stress and marital violence in a national sample of American families. In M. A. Straus & R. J. Gelles (Eds.), *Physical violence in American families* (pp. 181-202). New Brunswick, NJ: Transaction Publishers.

Straus, M. A. (1993). Physical assaults by wives: A major social problem? In R. J. Gelles & M. A. Straus (Eds.), *Current controversies on family violence* (pp. 67-87). Newbury Park, CA: Sage.

Straus, M. A., & Gelles, R. J. (1990a). How violent are American families? Estimates from the national family violence resurvey and other studies. In M. A. Straus & R. J. Gelles (Eds.), *Physical violence in American families* (pp. 95-112). New Brunswick, NJ: Transaction Publishers.

Straus, M., & Gelles, R. (1990b). *Physical violence in American families: Risk factors and adaptations to violence in 8,145 families.* New Brunswick, NJ: Transaction Publishers.

Strauss, A., & Corbin, J. (1990). *Basics of qualitative research: Grounded theory procedures and techniques.* Newbury Park, CA: Sage.

Stroebe, M. S., Gergen, M. M., Gergen, K. J., & Stroebe, W. (1992). Broken hearts or broken bonds: Love and death in historical perspective. *American Psychologist, 47,* 1205-1212.

Stroebe, M. S., & Stroebe, W. (1987). *Bereavement and health: The psychological and physical consequences of partner loss.* London: Cambridge University Press.

Struckman-Johnson, C. (1988). Forced sex on dates: It happens to men, too. *Journal of Sex Research, 24,* 234-241.

Sugarman, D. B., & Hotaling, G. T. (1989). Dating violence: Prevalence, context, and risk markers. In M. A. Pirog-Good & J. E. Stets (Eds.), *Violence in dating relationships: Emerging social issues* (pp. 3-32). New York: Praeger.

Sullivan, H. S. (1953). *The interpersonal theory of psychiatry.* New York: Norton.

Suman, H. C. (1990). The role of physical attractiveness and eye contact in sexual attraction. *Journal of Personality and Clinical Studies, 6,* 109-112.

Summers, P., Forehand, R., Armistead, L., & Tannenbaum, L. (1998). Parental divorce during early adolescence in Caucasian families: The role of family process variables in predicting the long-term consequences for early adult psychosocial adjustment. *Journal of Consulting and Clinical Psychology, 66,* 327-336.

Sunnafrank, M. (1986). Predicted outcome value during initial interactions: A reformulation of uncertainty reduction theory. *Human Communication Research, 13,* 3-33.

Surra, C., & Milardo, R. (1991). The social psychological context of developing relationships: Psychological and interactive networks. In D. Perlman & W. Jones (Eds.), *Advances in personal relationships* (Vol. 3, pp. 1-36). London: Jessica Kingsley.

Surra, C. A., & Bohman, T. (1991). The development of close relationships: A cognitive perspective. In G. J. O. Fletcher & F. D. Fincham (Eds.), *Cognition in close relationships* (pp. 281-305). Hillsdale, NJ: Lawrence Erlbaum.

Susman-Stillman, A., Hyson, D., Williams, F., & Collins, W. A. (1997). Adolescent psychosocial development and adherence to treatment for insulin-dependent diabetes mellitus. In J. A. McNamara, Jr., & C.-A. Trotman (Eds.), *Creating the compliant patient* (pp. 73-102). Ann Arbor, MI: Center for Human Growth and Development.

Swain, S. (1989). Covert intimacy: Closeness in men's friendships. In B. J. Risman & P. Schwartz (Eds.), *Gender in intimate relationships* (pp. 71-86). Belmont, CA: Wadsworth.

Symons, D. (1979). *The evolution of human sexuality.* Oxford, UK: Oxford University Press.

Szinovacz, M. (1996). Couples' employment/retirement patterns and perceptions of marital quality. *Research on Aging, 18,* 243-268.

Szinovacz, M., & Ekerdt, D. J. (1995). Families and retirement. In R. Blieszner & V. H. Bedford (Eds.), *Handbook of aging and the family* (pp. 375-400). Westport, CT: Greenwood.

Szymanski, L. A., Devlin, A. S., Chrisler, J. C., & Vyse, S. A. (1993). Gender role and attitudes toward rape in male and female college students. *Sex Roles, 29*, 37-57.

Tajfel, H., & Turner, J. C. (1979). The social identity theory of intergroup behavior. In S. Worchel & W. Austin (Eds.), *Psychology of intergroup relations* (pp. 33-47). Chicago: Nelson-Hall.

Tangney, J. P. (1995). Shame and guilt in interpersonal relationships. In J. P. Tangney & K. W. Fischer (Eds.), *Self-conscious emotions: The psychology of shame, guilt, embarrassment, and pride* (pp. 114-139). New York: Guilford.

Tannen, D. (1990). *You just don't understand.* New York: William Morrow.

Taraban, C. B., Hendrick, S. S., & Hendrick, C. (1998). Loving and liking. In P. A. Andersen & L. K. Guerrero (Eds.), *Handbook of communication and emotion: Research, theory, applications, and contexts* (pp. 331-351). San Diego: Academic Press.

Tardy, C. H., & Dindia, K. (1997). Self-disclosure. In O. D. Hargie (Ed.), *The handbook of communication skills* (pp. 213-235). London: Routledge.

Tarrier, N., Beckett, R., Harwood, S., & Ahmed, Y. (1989). Comparison of a morbidly jealous and a normal female population on the Eysenck Personality Questionnaire. *Personality and Individual Differences, 10*, 1327-1328.

Tavris, C. (1992). *The mismeasure of woman.* New York: Simon & Schuster.

Taylor, C. J. (1986). Extramarital sex: Good for the goose? Good for the gander? *Women and Theory, 5*, 289-295.

Taylor, R. J., Chatters, L. M., Tucker, M. B., & Lewis, E. (1990). Developments in research on black families: A decade review. *Journal of Marriage and the Family, 52*, 993-1014.

Taylor, S. J., & Bogdan, R. (1984). *Introduction to qualitative research methods: The search for meanings* (2nd ed.). New York: John Wiley.

Teachman, J. D. (2000). Diversity of family structure: Economic and social influences. In D. H. Demo, K. A. Allen, & M. A. Fine (Eds.), *Handbook of family diversity* (pp. 32-58). New York: Oxford University Press.

Teachman, J. D., Paasch, K., & Carver, K. (1996). Social capital and dropping out of school early. *Journal of Marriage and the Family, 58*, 773-783.

Testa, R. J., Kinder, B. N., & Ironson, G. (1987). Heterosexual bias in the perception of loving relationships of gay males and lesbians. *Journal of Sex Research, 23*, 163-172.

Thibaut, J. W., & Kelley, H. H. (1959). *The social psychology of groups.* New York: John Wiley.

Thoits, P. (1992). Identity structures and psychological well-being: Gender and marital status comparisons. *Social Psychology Quarterly, 55*, 236-256.

Thomas, C. (1971). *Boys no more.* Beverly Hills, CA: Glencoe.

Thomas, D. L., & Wilcox, J. E. (1987). The rise of family theory: A historical and critical analysis. In M. B. Sussman & S. K. Steinmetz (Eds.), *Handbook of marriage and the family* (pp. 81-102). New York: Plenum.

Thompson, A. P. (1983). Extramarital sex: A review of the research literature. *Journal of Sex Research, 19*, 1-22.

Thompson, B. (1996). Time traveling and border crossing: Reflections on white identity. In B. Thompson & S. Tyagi (Eds.), *Names we call home: Autobiography on racial identity* (pp. 93-109). New York: Routledge.

Thompson, E. (1991). The maleness of violence in dating relationships: An appraisal of stereotypes. *Sex Roles, 24*, 261-278.

Thompson, L. (1991). Family work: Women's sense of fairness. *Journal of Family Issues, 12*, 181-196.

Thompson, L. (1992). Feminist methodology for family studies. *Journal of Marriage and the Family, 54*, 3-18.

Thompson, L., & Walker, A. J. (1982). The dyad as the unit of analysis: Conceptual and methodological issues. *Journal of Marriage and the Family, 44*, 889-900.

Thompson, L., & Walker, A. J. (1989). Gender in families: Women and men in marriage, work, and parenthood. *Journal of Marriage and the Family, 51*, 845-871.

Thompson, L., & Walker, A. J. (1995). The place of feminism in family studies. *Journal of Marriage and the Family, 57*, 847-865.

Thompson, S. C., & Sobolew-Shubin, A. (1993). Overprotective relationships: A nonsupportive side of social networks. *Basic and Applied Social Psychology, 14*, 363-383.

Thomson, E., Hanson, T. L., & McLanahan, S. S. (1994). Family structure and child well-being: Economic resources vs. parental behaviors. *Social Forces, 73*, 221-242.

Thomson, E., McLanahan, S. S., & Curtin, R. B. (1992). Family structure, gender, and parental socialization. *Journal of Marriage and the Family, 54*, 368-378.

Thorne, B. (1986). Girls and boys together . . . but mostly apart: Gender arrangements in elementary schools. In W. W. Hartup & Z. Rubin (Eds.), *Relationships and development* (pp. 167-184). Hillsdale, NJ: Lawrence Erlbaum.

Tolhuizen, J. H. (1989). Communication strategies for intensifying dating relationships: Identification, use, and structure. *Journal of Social and Personal Relationships, 6*, 413-434.

Tolhuizen, J. H. (1992, November). *The association of relational factors to intensification strategy use.* Paper presented at the annual meeting of the Speech Communication Association, Chicago.

Tomlin, A. M., & Passman, R. H. (1991). Grandmothers' advice about disciplining grandchildren: Is it accepted by mothers, and does its rejection influence grandmothers' subsequent guidance? *Psychology and Aging, 6,* 182-189.

Treboux, D., Crowell, J. A., Owens, G., & Pan, H. S. (1994, February). *Attachment behaviors and working models: Relations to best friendship and romantic relationships.* Paper presented at the annual meeting of the Society for Research on Adolescence, San Diego.

Triandis, H. C. (1994). *Culture and social behavior.* New York: McGraw-Hill.

Trinke, S. J., & Bartholomew, K. (1997). Hierarchies of attachment relationships in young adulthood. *Journal of Social and Personal Relationships, 14,* 603-625.

Tripp, C. A. (1975). *The homosexual matrix.* New York: Signet.

Trivers, R. L. (1971). The evolution of reciprocal altruism. *Quarterly Review of Biology, 46,* 35-57.

Trivers, R. L. (1972). Parental investment and sexual selection. In B. Campbell (Ed.), *Sexual selection and the descent of man* (pp. 136-179). Chicago: Aldine.

Tucker, P., & Aron, A. (1993). Passionate love and marital satisfaction at key transition points in the family life cycle. *Journal of Social and Clinical Psychology, 12,* 135-147.

Uchino, B. N., Cacioppo, J. T., & Kiecolt-Glaser, J. K. (1996). The relationship between social support and physiological processes: A review with emphasis on underlying mechanisms and implications for health. *Psychological Bulletin, 119,* 488-531.

Ulin, M., & Milardo, R. M. (1992, November). *Network interdependence and lesbian relationships.* Paper presented at the National Council on Family Relations, Orlando, FL.

U.S. Bureau of the Census. (1995). *Statistical abstract of the United States: 1995.* Washington, DC: Government Printing Office.

U.S. Bureau of the Census. (1998). *Statistical abstract of the United States: 1998.* Washington, DC: Government Printing Office.

Vandell, D. L., & Hembree, S. E. (1994). Peer social status and friendship: Independent contributors to children's social and academic adjustment. *Merrill-Palmer Quarterly, 40,* 461-477.

van de Vliert, E., & Euwema, M. C. (1994). Agreeableness and activeness as components of conflict behaviors. *Journal of Personality and Social Psychology, 66,* 674-687.

Vandewater, E. A., & Lansford, J. E. (1998). Influences of family structure and parental conflict on children's well-being. *Family Relations, 47,* 323-330.

Vangelisti, A. L. (1994a). Family secrets: Forms, functions, and correlates. *Journal of Social and Personal Relationships, 11,* 113-135.

Vangelisti, A. L. (1994b). Messages that hurt. In W. R. Cupach & B. H. Spitzberg (Eds.), *The dark side of interpersonal communication* (pp. 53-82). Hillsdale, NJ: Lawrence Erlbaum.

Vangelisti, A. L., & Sprague, R. J. (1998). Guilt and hurt: Similarities, distinctions, and conversational strategies. In P. A. Andersen & L. K. Guerrero (Eds.), *Handbook of communication and emotion: Research, theory, applications, and contexts* (pp. 124-149). San Diego: Academic Press.

van IJzendoorn, M. H., & Bakermans-Kranenburg, M. J. (1997). Intergenerational transmission of attachment: A move to the contextual level. In L. Atkinson & K. J. Zucker (Eds.), *Attachment and psychopathology* (pp. 135-170). New York: Guilford.

Veneziano, R. A., & Rohner, R. P. (1998). Perceived paternal acceptance, paternal involvement, and youths' psychological adjustment in a rural, biracial southern community. *Journal of Marriage and the Family, 60,* 335-343.

Van Fossen, B. E. (1981). Sex differences in the mental health effects of spouse support and equity. *Journal of Health and Social Behavior, 22,* 130-143.

Van Yperen, N., & Buunk, B. (1990). A longitudinal study of equity and satisfaction in intimate relationships. *European Journal of Social Psychology, 20,* 287-309.

Van Yperen, N., & Buunk, B. (1991). Sex-role attitudes, social comparison, and relationship satisfaction. *Social Psychology Quarterly, 54,* 169-180.

Van Zessen, G. J., & Sandfort, T. M. (Eds.). (1991). *Seksualiteit in Nederland.* Amsterdam: Swets & Zeitlinger.

Vaughn, B. E., Kopp, C. B., & Krakow, J. B. (1984). The emergence and consolidation of self-control from eighteen to thirty months of age: Normative trends and individual differences. *Child Development, 55,* 990-1004.

Vaughn, C. E., & Leff, J. P. (1976). The influence of family and social factors on the course of psychiatric illness: A comparison of schizophrenic and depressed neurotic patients. *British Journal of Psychiatry, 129,* 125-137.

Veiel, H., Crisand, M., Stroszeck-Somschor, H., & Herrle, J. (1991). Social support networks of chronically strained couples: Similarity and overlap. *Journal of Social and Personal Relationships, 8,* 279-292.

Veroff, J., Douvan, E., & Hatchett, S. J. (1995). *Marital instability: A social and behavioral study of the early years.* New York: Praeger.

Veroff, J., Sutherland, L., Chadiha, L., & Ortega, R. M. (1993). Newlyweds tell their stories: A narrative method for assessing marital experiences. *Journal of Social and Personal Relationships, 10,* 437-457.

Viorst, J. (1986). *Necessary losses.* New York: Fawcett.

Visher, E. B., & Visher, J. S. (1996). *Therapy with stepfamilies.* New York: Brunner/Mazel.

Vitaro, F., Tremblay, R. E., Kerr, M., Pagani, L., & Bukowski, W. M. (1997). Disruptiveness, friends' characteristics, and delinquency in early adolescence: A test of two competing models of development. *Child Development, 68,* 676-689.

Von Dras, D. D., & Siegler, I. C., (1997). Stability in extraversion and aspects of social support at midlife. *Journal of Personality and Social Psychology, 72,* 233-241.

Vuchinich, S. (1984). Sequencing and social structure in family conflict. *Social Psychology Quarterly, 47,* 217-234.

Vuchinich, S. (1987). Starting and stopping spontaneous family conflicts. *Journal of Marriage and the Family, 49,* 591-601.

Vuchinich, S. (1990). The sequential organization of closing in verbal family conflict. In A. D. Grimshaw (Ed.), *Conflict talk: Sociolinguistic investigations of arguments in conversations* (pp. 118-138). New York: Cambridge University Press.

Vuchinich, S., Emery, R. E., & Cassidy, J. (1988). Family members as third parties in dyadic family conflict: Strategies, alliances, and outcomes. *Child Development, 59,* 1293-1302.

Vuchinich, S., Vuchinich, R., & Wood, B. (1993). The interparental relationship and family problem-solving with preadolescent males. *Child Development, 64,* 1389-1400.

Wacker, R. R. (1995). Legal issues and family involvement in later-life families. In R. Blieszner & V. H. Bedford (Eds.), *Handbook of aging and the family* (pp. 284-306). Westport, CT: Greenwood.

Waldner-Haugrud, L. K., Gratch, L. V., & Magruder, B. (1997). Victimization and perpetration rates of violence in gay and lesbian relationships: Gender issues explored. *Violence and Victims, 12,* 173-184.

Walker, A. J., Pratt, C. C., & Eddy, L. (1995). Informal caregiving to aging family members: A critical review. *Family Relations, 44,* 402-411.

Walker, A. J., Pratt, C. C., & Oppy, N. C. (1992). Perceived reciprocity in family caregiving. *Family Relations, 41,* 82-85.

Walker, K. (1994). Men, women, and friendship: What they say, what they do. *Gender & Society, 8,* 246-265.

Walker, K. (1995). "Always there for me": Friendship patterns and expectations among middle- and working-class men and women. *Sociological Forum, 10,* 273-296.

Walker, L., & Taylor, J. (1991). Family interactions and the development of moral reasoning. *Child Development, 62,* 264-283.

Walker, W. D., Rowe, R. C., & Quinsey, V. L. (1993). Authoritarianism and sexual aggression. *Journal of Personality and Social Psychology, 65,* 1036-1045.

Walster, E., & Walster, G. W. (1978). *A new look at love.* Reading, MA: Addison-Wesley.

Walster, E., Walster, G. W., & Berscheid, E. (1978). *Equity: Theory and research.* Boston: Allyn & Bacon.

Walster, E., Walster, G. W., & Traupmann, J. (1978). Equity and premarital sex. *Journal of Personality, 36,* 82-92.

Walters, A. S., & Curran, M. (1996). "Excuse me, sir? May I help you and your boyfriend?": Salespersons' differential treatment of homosexual and straight customers. *Journal of Homosexuality, 31*(1/2), 135-152.

Waters, E., Merrick, S., Albersheim, L., Treboux, D., & Crowell, J. (in press). Attachment from infancy to early adulthood: A 20-year longitudinal study of relations between infant Strange Situation classifications and attachment representations in adulthood. *Child Development.*

Watson, M. A. (1981). Sexually open marriage: Three perspectives. *Alternative Lifestyles, 4,* 3-12.

Watzlawick, P. J., Beavin, J., & Jackson, D. (1967). *Pragmatics of human communication: A study in interactional patterns, pathologies, and paradoxes.* New York: Norton.

Weaver, S., & Coleman, M. (1998, November). *A grounded theory study of women's role construction in stepfamilies.* Paper presented at the annual meeting of the National Council on Family Relations, Milwaukee, WI.

Weaver, S. E., & Coleman, M. (1999, November). *A mothering but not a mother role: A grounded theory study of the nonresidential stepmother role.* Paper presented at the Theory Construction and Research Methodology Workshop at the National Council on Family Relationships Annual Conference, Irvine, CA.

Weber, D. J., & Vangelisti, A. L. (1991). "Because I love you . . .": The tactical use of attributional expressions in conversation. *Human Communication Research, 17,* 606-624.

Weinberg, M. S., & Williams, C. J. (1988). Black sexuality: A test of two theories. *Journal of Sex Research, 25,* 197-218.

Weinberg, M. S., Williams, C. J., & Pryor, D. W. (1994). *Dual attraction: Understanding bisexuality.* New York: Oxford University Press.

Weinfield, N. (in press). Attachment and the representation of relationships from infancy to adulthood: Continuity, discontinuity, and their correlates. *Child Development.*

Weinglass, J., & Steil, J. M. (1981, August). *When is unequal unfair? The role of ideology.* Paper presented at the annual meeting of the American Psychological Association, Los Angeles.

Weinstock, J. S., & Rothblum, E. D. (Eds.). (1996). *Lesbian friendships: For ourselves and each other.* New York: New York University Press.

Weis, D. L., & Felton, J. R. (1987). Marital exclusivity and the potential for future marital conflict. *Social Work, 32,* 45-49.

Weiss, R. L., & Heyman, R. E. (1997). A clinical research overview of couple interactions. In W. K.

Halford & H. J. Markman (Eds.), *Clinical handbook of marriage and couples intervention* (pp. 13-41). London: Wiley.

Weiss, R. S. (1973). *Loneliness: The experience of emotional and social isolation.* Cambridge, MA: MIT Press.

Weiss, R. S. (1975). *Marital separation.* New York: Basic Books.

Weiss, R. S. (1986). Continuities and transformations in social relationships from childhood to adulthood. In W. W. Hartup & Z. Rubin (Eds.), *Relationships and development* (pp. 95-110). Hillsdale, NJ: Lawrence Erlbaum.

Weiss, R. S. (1991). The attachment bond in childhood and adulthood. In C. M. Parkes, J. Stevenson-Hinde, & P. Marris (Eds.), *Attachment across the life cycle* (pp. 66-76). London: Tavistock/Routledge.

Weiss, R. S. (1998). A taxonomy of relationships. *Journal of Social and Personal Relationships, 15,* 671-684.

Weiss, R. S., & Richards, T. A. (1997). A scale for predicting quality of recovery following the death of a partner. *Journal of Personality and Social Psychology, 72,* 885-891.

Weissberg, R. P., & Greenberg, M. T. (1998). School and community competence-enhancement and prevention programs. In W. Damon, I. E. Sigel, & K. A. Renniger (Eds.), *Handbook of child psychology, Vol. 4: Child psychology in practice* (pp. 877-954). New York: John Wiley.

Weissman, M. M. (1987). Advances in psychiatric epidemiology: Rates and risks for major depression. *American Journal of Public Health, 77,* 445-451.

Wellman, B., & Wellman, B. (1992). Domestic affairs and network relations. *Journal of Social and Personal Relationships, 9,* 385-409.

Wellman, B., & Wortley, S. (1989). Brothers' keepers: Situating kinship relations in broader networks of social support. *Sociological Perspectives, 32,* 273-306.

Wells, K. B., Stewart, A., Hays, R. D., Burnam, M. A., Rogers, W., Daniels, M., Berry, S., Greenfield, S., & Ware, J. (1989). The functioning and well-being of depressed patients: Results from the Medical Outcomes Study. *Journal of the American Medical Association, 262,* 914-919.

Welwood, J. (1990). *Journey of the heart: Intimate relationships and the path of love.* New York: HarperCollins.

Wentzel, K. R., & Caldwell, K. (1997). Friendships, peer acceptance, and group membership: Relations to academic achievement in middle school. *Child Development, 68,* 1198-1209.

Werebe, M. J. G. (1987). Friendship and dating relationships among French adolescents. *Journal of Adolescence, 10,* 269-289.

Werking, K. (1997). *We're just good friends: Women and men in nonromantic relationships.* New York: Guilford.

Werner, C., & Parmelee, P. (1979). Similarity of activity preferences among friends: Those who play together stay together. *Social Psychology Quarterly, 42,* 62-66.

Werner, C. M., Altman, I., Brown, B. B., & Ginat, J. (1993). Celebrations in personal relationships. In S. Duck (Ed.), *Social contexts and relationships* (pp. 109-138). Newbury Park, CA: Sage.

Werner, H. (1957). The concept of development from a comparative and organismic point of view. In D. B. Harris (Ed.), *The concept of development: An issue in the study of human behavior* (pp. 125-148). Minneapolis: University of Minnesota Press.

West, C., & Zimmerman, D. (1983). Small insults: A study of interruptions in cross-sex conversations between unacquainted persons. In B. Thorne, C. Kramarae, & N. Henley (Eds.), *Language, gender, and society* (pp. 102-117). Rowley, MA: Newbury House.

West, C., & Zimmerman, H. (1987). Doing gender. *Gender & Society, 1,* 125-151.

West, L., Anderson, J., & Duck, S. (1996). Crossing the barriers to friendships between men and women. In J. T. Wood (Ed.), *Gendered relationships* (pp. 111-127). Mountain View, CA: Mayfield.

Whiffen, V. E., & Johnson, S. M. (1998). An attachment theory framework for the treatment of childbearing depression. *Clinical Psychology: Science and Practice, 5,* 478-493.

Whisman, M. A. (in press). Depression and marital distress: Findings from clinical and community studies. In S. R. H. Beach (Ed.), *Marital and family processes in depression.* Washington, DC: American Psychological Association.

Whitbeck, L. B., Hoyt, D. R., & Huck, S. M. (1994). Early family relationships, intergenerational solidarity, and support provided to parents by their adult children. *Journal of Gerontology: Social Sciences, 49,* S85-S94.

White, G. L. (1981). A model of romantic jealousy. *Motivation and Emotion, 5,* 295-310.

White, G. L. (1984). Comparison of four jealousy scales. *Journal of Research in Personality, 18,* 115-130.

White, G. L., & Mullen, P. E. (1989). *Jealousy: Theory, research, and clinical strategies.* New York: Guilford.

White, L. (1994). Growing up with single parents and stepparents: Long-term effects on family solidarity. *Journal of Marriage and the Family, 56,* 935-948.

White, L., & Keith, B. (1990). The effect of shift work on the quality and stability of marital relations. *Journal of Marriage and the Family, 52,* 453-462.

Whitsett, D., & Land, H. (1992). Role strain, coping, and marital satisfaction of stepparents. *Families in Society, 73,* 79-91.

Wickens, T. D. (1993). Analysis of contingency tables with between-subjects variability. *Psychological Bulletin, 113,* 191-204.

Wiggins, J. D., & Lederer, D. A. (1984). Differential antecedents of infidelity in marriage. *American Mental Health Counselors Association Journal, 6,* 152-161.

Wiggins, J. S. (1991). Agency and communion as conceptual coordinates for the understanding and measurement of interpersonal behavior. In W. M. Grove & D. Cicchetti (Eds.), *Thinking clearly about psychology* (Vol. 2, pp. 89-113). Minneapolis: University of Minnesota Press.

Wilcox, B. L. (1981). Social support in adjusting to marital disruption: A network analysis. In B. H. Gottlieb (Ed.), *Social networks and social support* (pp. 97-117). London: Sage.

Wilkie, J. (1993). Changes in U.S. men's attitudes toward the family provider role, 1972-1989. *Gender & Society, 7,* 261-279.

Wilkie, J. R., Feree, M. M., & Ratcliff, K. S. (1998). Gender and fairness: Marital satisfaction in two-earner couples. *Journal of Marriage and the Family, 60,* 577-594.

Wilkinson, D. (1993). Family ethnicity in America. In H. P. McAdoo (Ed.), *Family ethnicity in America: Strength in diversity* (pp. 15-59). Newbury Park, CA: Sage.

Williams, D. (1985). Gender, masculinity-femininity, and emotional intimacy in same-sex friendships. *Sex Roles, 12,* 587-600.

Williams, E. J. (1959). The comparison of regression variables. *Journal of the Royal Statistical Society B, 21,* 396-399.

Williamson, G. M., & Clark, M. S. (1992). Impact of desired relationship type on affective reactions to choosing and being required to help. *Personality and Social Psychology Bulletin, 18,* 10-18.

Wills, T. A. (1991). Social support and interpersonal relationships. In M. S. Clark (Ed.), *Prosocial behavior: Review of personality and social psychology* (Vol. 12, pp. 265-289). Newbury Park, CA: Sage.

Wilmot, W. W. (1994). Relationship rejuvenation. In D. J. Canary & L. Stafford (Eds.), *Communication and relational maintenance* (pp. 255-273). San Diego: Academic Press.

Wilmot, W. W., Carbaugh, D. A., & Baxter, L. A. (1985). Communicative strategies used to terminate romantic relationships. *Western Journal of Speech Communication, 49,* 204-216.

Wilmot, W. W., & Shellen, W. W. (1990). Language in friendships. In H. Giles & W. P. Robinson (Eds.), *Handbook of language and social psychology* (pp. 413-431). New York: John Wiley.

Wilmot, W. W., & Stevens, D. C. (1994). Relationship rejuvenation: Arresting decline in personal relation-

ships. In D. Conville (Ed.), *Uses of structure in communication studies* (pp. 103-124). New York: Praeger.

Wilson, B. F., & Clarke, S. C. (1992). Remarriages: A demographic profile. *Journal of Family Issues, 13,* 123-141.

Winstead, B. A., Derlega, V. J., Lewis, R. J., Sanchez-Hucles, J., & Clark, E. (1992). Friendship, social interaction, and coping with stress. *Communication Research, 19,* 193-211.

Wise, A. J., & Bowman, S. L. (1997). Comparison of beginning counselors' responses to lesbian vs. heterosexual partner abuse. *Violence and Victims, 12,* 127-135.

Wiseman, J. P. (1986). Friendship: Bonds and binds in a voluntary relationship. *Journal of Social and Personal Relationships, 3,* 191-211.

Wojtkiewicz, R. A. (1992). Diversity in experiences of parental structure during childhood and adolescence. *Demography, 29,* 59-68.

Wood, J. T. (1993). Gender and relationship crises: Contrasting reasons, responses, and relational orientations. In J. Ringer (Ed.), *Queer words, queer images: The (re)construction of homosexuality* (pp. 238-264). New York: New York University Press.

Wood, J. T. (1994). *Who cares? Women, care, and culture.* Carbondale: Southern Illinois University Press.

Wood, J. T. (1997a). Different views of different cultures: Clarifying the issues. *Personal Relationships, 4,* 221-228.

Wood, J. T. (1997b). *Gendered lives: Communication, gender, and culture.* Belmont, CA: Wadsworth.

Wood, J. T. (1998a). *But I thought you meant . . . : Misunderstandings in human communication.* Mountain View, CA: Mayfield.

Wood, J. T. (1998b). Ethics, justice, and the "private sphere." *Women's Studies in Communication, 21,* 127-140.

Wood, J. T. (1999). *Gendered lives: Communication, gender, and culture* (3rd ed.). Belmont, CA: Wadsworth.

Wood, J. T. (2000). *Relational communication: Continuity and change in personal relationships* (2nd ed.). Belmont, CA: Wadsworth.

Wood, J. T., & Inman, C. (1993). In a different mode: Recognizing male modes of closeness. *Journal of Applied Communication Research, 21,* 279-295.

Wortman, C. B., & Silver, R. C. (1989). The myths of coping with loss. *Journal of Consulting and Clinical Psychology, 57,* 349-357.

Wright, P. H. (1988). Interpreting research on gender differences in friendship: A case for moderation and a plea for caution. *Journal of Social and Personal Relationships, 5,* 367-373.

Wright, P. H., & Scanlon, M. B. (1991). Gender role orientations and friendship: Some attenuation, but gender differences abound. *Sex Roles, 24,* 551-566.

Wu, Z. (1994). Remarriage in Canada: A social ex-change perspective. *Journal of Divorce and Remarriage, 21,* 191-224.

Wysocki, T., White, N. H., Bubb, J., Harris, M. A., & Greco, P. (1995). Family adaptation to diabetes: A model for intervention research. In J. L. Wallander & L. J. Siegel (Eds.), *Adolescent health problems: Behavioral perspectives* (pp. 289-304). New York: Guilford.

Yankeelov, P. A., Barbee, A. P., Cunningham, M. R., & Druen, P. B. (1995). The influence of negative medical diagnoses and verbal and nonverbal support activation strategies on the interactive coping process. *Journal of Nonverbal Behavior, 19,* 243-260.

Yates, M. E., Tennstedt, S., & Chang, B. (1999). Contributors to and mediators of psychological well-being for informal caregivers. *Journal of Gerontology: Psychological Sciences, 54,* P12-P22.

Youngblade, L. M., & Belsky, J. (1992). Parent-child antecedents of 5-year-olds' close friendships: A longitudinal analysis. *Developmental Psychology, 28,* 700-713.

Youniss, J. (1980). *Parents and peers in social development.* Chicago: University of Chicago Press.

Youniss, J., & Smollar, J. (1985). *Adolescent relations with mothers, fathers, and friends.* Chicago: University of Chicago Press.

Yovetich, N. A., & Rusbult, C. E. (1994). Accommodative behaviors in close relationships: Exploring transformation of motivation. *Journal of Experimental Social Psychology, 30,* 138-164.

Zajonc, R. B. (1968). Attitudinal effects of mere exposure. *Journal of Personality and Social Psychology, 9*(Monograph Suppl. No. 2, Pt. 2).

Zillmann, D. (1990). The interplay of cognition and excitation in aggravated conflict. In D. D. Cahn (Ed.), *Intimates in conflict: A communication perspective* (pp. 187-208). Hillsdale, NJ: Lawrence Erlbaum.

Zimiles, H., & Lee, V. E. (1991). Adolescent family structure and educational progress. *Developmental Psychology, 27,* 314-320.

Zimmerman, C. C., with Broderick, C. B. (1956). The family as a self-protective system. In C. C. Zimmerman & L. Cervantes (Eds.), *Marriage and the family* (pp. 101-117). Chicago: Henry Regnery.

Zimmerman, M. A., Salem, D. A., & Maton, K. I. (1995). Family structure and psychosocial correlates among urban African-American adolescent males. *Child Development, 66,* 1598-1613.

# Name Index

# Subject Index

medical personnel for, 282
networks, 275-277
old age and, 89-90
origins of behavior, 274-275
perceptions of, 277
relational issues, 279-280
romantic relationships and, 279-280
stepfamilies, 156-157
workplace, 282-284
Sociology, xii
Solace behavior, 279, 283
Solve behavior, 283
Spouses:
 bereavement at loss, 363-364
 friendship experiences, 42
 joint networks, 34
 limitation of term, 34
 relationship processes, 40
 *See also* Marriage
Standard social relations model (SRM), 13-14
 components of, 14
 families, 15-17
 friendship networks, 14-17
 questions addressed with, 14-15
 round-robin data structure, 14
Standpoint theory, 304-305
Stepchildren:
 challenges for, 162-165
 living with stepparents, 165-166
Stepfamilies:
 deviant groups, 157-158
 incomplete institutionalization of, 157
 reconstituted nuclear families, 158
 social support of, 156-157
 *See also* Remarried families
Stepparents:
 challenges for, 162-165
 nonresidential, 156, 165
 stepchildren living with, 156, 165-166
 types of, 156
Stepparent-stepchild relationships, 162-165
Stories, as symbolic codes, 253-254
Strange Situation, 68, 187
Strategic relationship maintenance, 248
Stress:
 attachment, coping and, 192-194
 managing through conflict, 268-269
 social, intimate violence and, 333
Stress generation theory, depression and, 350-351
Subjectivity, 30
Sulking, 278

Support:
 perceived, 349
 social. *See* Social support
Support activation behavior, 278-279, 281
Supportive relationships, 274-275
Suspicious jealousy, 324

Tactics, communication, 246
Tensions, 248
Termination, relationship, 248
Thematic Apperception Test (TAT), 239
Theory of triangles, 40-41
Traditional couples, 262
Tranquil relationships, 182
Transitions, 248
Triangular theory of love, 207-208
Triangulation theory, 40-41

Unprovoked jealousy, 324

Verbal behavior, 233-234
Victimization, children's friendships and, 51-52
Violence:
 attachment and, 200
 intergenerational transmission of, 333
 physical, 331-332
 romantic relationships and, 310-311
 same-sex couples and, 119-120

Warmth, interpersonal, 172
Withdrawal response, 176
Within-dyads independent variables, 6-7, 10-11
Women:
 as providers, 129-130. *See also* Employment, married women
 and
 friendships between, 306-307
 in labor force, 126
 sexually coercive, 342
Workplace:
 exchange relationships and, 282-284
 friendships in, 71-72
 social support in, 282-284

Xenophobia:
 attribution theory on, 99
 multicultural/multiracial relationships and, 105

# About the Editors

CLYDE HENDRICK obtained his Ph.D. from the University of Missouri, Columbia, with a major field in social psychology and secondary interests in sociology and philosophy. He has taught at Humboldt State University, Kent State University, the University of Miami, and Texas Tech University. He currently is Paul Whitfield Horn Professor of Psychology at Texas Tech University. He has conducted research in many areas of social psychology and has served in a variety of editorial functions. He was the first editor of *Personality and Social Psychology Bulletin,* served as acting editor of *Journal of Personality and Social Psychology,* and served as editor of *Review of Personality and Social Psychology.* For many years, he and Susan Hendrick have pursued a collaborative research program on love and sex attitudes. They also have collaborated on three books and as coeditors of the Sage Series on Close Relationships, a book series consisting of nearly 20 volumes.

SUSAN S. HENDRICK obtained her Ph.D. from Kent State University, with a major field in counseling psychology and secondary interests in social psychology and family studies. She was in practice as a psychologist and has taught at the University of Miami and Texas Tech University. She currently is Professor of Psychology and Professor of Human Development and Family Studies at Texas Tech University, where she conducts research on close relationships, emphasizing relationship satisfaction. She has served on the editorial boards of several journals, has served as associate editor of *Journal of Social and Clinical Psychology* and *Journal of Social and Personal Relationships,* and has served as president of the International Network on Personal Relationships. For many years, she and Clyde Hendrick have pursued a collaborative research program on sex and love attitudes. They also have collaborated on three books and as coeditors of the Sage Series on Close Relationships, a book series consisting of nearly 20 volumes.

# List of Contributors

Katherine R. Allen
*Virginia Polytechnic Institute and State
    University*

Peter A. Andersen
*San Diego State University*

Steven R. Asher
*Duke University*

Anita P. Barbee
*University of Louisville*

Steven R. H. Beach
*University of Georgia*

Ellen Berscheid
*University of Minnesota*

Rosemary Blieszner
*Virginia Polytechnic Institute and State
    University*

Brant R. Burleson
*Purdue University*

Bram P. Buunk
*University of Groningen*

Daniel J. Canary
*Arizona State University*

F. Scott Christopher
*Arizona State University*

Marilyn Coleman
*University of Missouri*

W. Andrew Collins
*University of Minnesota*

Michael R. Cunningham
*University of Louisville*

Pieternel Dijkstra
*University of Groningen*

Kathryn Dindia
*University of Wisconsin–Milwaukee*

Judith A. Feeney
*University of Queensland*

Beverley Fehr
*University of Winnipeg*

Mark A. Fine
*University of Missouri*

Stanley O. Gaines, Jr.
*Pomona College*

Lawrence H. Ganong
*University of Missouri*

Laura K. Guerrero
*Arizona State University*

Andrea M. Hansen
*University of Michigan*

John H. Harvey
*University of Iowa*

Heather Helms-Erikson
*Pennsylvania State University*

Deborah A. Kashy
*Texas A&M University*

Michael W. Kirch
*Purdue University*

Brett Laursen
*Florida Atlantic University*

Maurice J. Levesque
*Elon College*

James H. Liu
*Victoria University of Wellington*

Sally A. Lloyd
*Miami University*

Susan J. Messman
*Pennsylvania State University*

Sandra Metts
*Illinois State University*

Robert M. Milardo
*University of Maine*

Patricia Noller
*University of Queensland*

Heather A. O'Mahen
*University of Georgia*

Letitia Anne Peplau
*University of California, Los Angeles*

Karen J. Prager
*University of Texas at Dallas*

Pamela C. Regan
*California State University, Los Angeles*

Nigel Roberts
*University of Queensland*

Amanda J. Rose
*University of Missouri*

Leah R. Spalding
*University of California, Los Angeles*

Susan Sprecher
*Illinois State University*

Janice M. Steil
*Adelphi University*

Alexis J. Walker
*Oregon State University*

Julia T. Wood
*University of North Carolina at Chapel Hill*